AF700064

ANDERSON'S
Law School Publications

Administrative Law Anthology
Thomas O. Sargentich

Administrative Law: Cases and Materials
Daniel J. Gifford

An Admiralty Law Anthology
Robert M. Jarvis

Alternative Dispute Resolution: Strategies for Law and Business
E. Wendy Trachte-Huber and Stephen K. Huber

American Legal Systems: A Resource and Reference Guide
Toni M. Fine

Analytic Jurisprudence Anthology
Anthony D'Amato

An Antitrust Anthology
Andrew I. Gavil

Appellate Advocacy: Principles and Practice, Second Edition
Ursula Bentele and Eve Cary

Basic Accounting Principles for Lawyers: With Present Value and Expected Value
C. Steven Bradford and Gary A. Ames

A Capital Punishment Anthology (and Electronic Caselaw Appendix)
Victor L. Streib

Cases and Problems in Criminal Law, Third Edition
Myron Moskovitz

The Citation Workbook: How to Beat the Citation Blues, Second Edition
Maria L. Ciampi, Rivka Widerman, and Vicki Lutz

Civil Procedure Anthology
David I. Levine, Donald L. Doernberg, and Melissa L. Nelken

Civil Procedure: Cases, Materials, and Questions, Second Edition
Richard D. Freer and Wendy Collins Perdue

Clinical Anthology: Readings for Live-Client Clinics
Alex J. Hurder, Frank S. Bloch, Susan L. Brooks, and Susan L. Kay

Commercial Transactions Series: Problems and Materials
Louis F. Del Duca, Egon Guttman, Alphonse M. Squillante, Fred H. Miller, Linda Rusch, and Peter Winship
- Vol. 1: Secured Transactions Under the UCC
- Vol. 2: Sales Under the UCC and the CISG
- Vol. 3: Negotiable Instruments Under the UCC and the CIBN

Communications Law: Media, Entertainment, and Regulation
Donald E. Lively, Allen S. Hammond, Blake D. Morant, and Russell L. Weaver

A Conflict-of-Laws Anthology
Gene R. Shreve

Constitutional Conflicts, Parts I & II
Derrick A. Bell, Jr.

A Constitutional Law Anthology, Second Edition
Michael J. Glennon, Donald E. Lively, Phoebe A. Haddon, Dorothy E. Roberts, and Russell L. Weaver

Constitutional Law: Cases, History, and Dialogues
Donald E. Lively, Phoebe A. Haddon, Dorothy E. Roberts, and Russell L. Weaver

The Constitutional Law of the European Union
James D. Dinnage and John F. Murphy

The Constitutional Law of the European Union: Documentary Supplement
James D. Dinnage and John F. Murphy

Constitutional Torts
Sheldon H. Nahmod, Michael L. Wells, and Thomas A. Eaton

A Contracts Anthology, Second Edition
Peter Linzer

Contracts: Contemporary Cases, Comments, and Problems
Michael L. Closen, Richard M. Perlmutter, and Jeffrey D. Wittenberg

Contract Law and Practice: Cases and Materials
Gerald E. Berendt, Michael L. Closen, Doris Estelle Long, Marie A. Monahan, Robert J. Nye, and John H. Scheid

A Corporate Law Anthology
Franklin A. Gevurtz

Corporate and White Collar Crime: An Anthology
Leonard Orland

A Criminal Law Anthology
Arnold H. Loewy

Criminal Law: Cases and Materials
Arnold H. Loewy

A Criminal Procedure Anthology
Silas J. Wasserstrom and Christie L. Snyder

Criminal Procedure: Arrest and Investigation
Arnold H. Loewy and Arthur B. LaFrance

Criminal Procedure: Trial and Sentencing
Arthur B. LaFrance and Arnold H. Loewy

Economic Regulation: Cases and Materials
Richard J. Pierce, Jr.

Elements of Law
Eva H. Hanks, Michael E. Herz, and Steven S. Nemerson

Ending It: Dispute Resolution in America
Descriptions, Examples, Cases and Questions
Susan M. Leeson and Bryan M. Johnston

An Environmental Law Anthology
Robert L. Fischman, Maxine I. Lipeles, and Mark S. Squillace

Environmental Law Series
Jackson B. Battle, Robert L. Fischman, Maxine I. Lipeles, and Mark S. Squillace
- Vol. 1: Environmental Decisionmaking: NEPA and the Endangered Species Act, Second Edition
- Vol. 2: Water Pollution, Second Edition
- Vol. 3: Air Pollution, Second Edition
- Vol. 4: Hazardous Waste, Third Edition

Environmental Protection and Justice
Readings and Commentary on Environmental Law and Practice
Kenneth A. Manaster

European Union Law Anthology
Karen V. Kole and Anthony D'Amato

An Evidence Anthology
Edward J. Imwinkelried and Glen Weissenberger

Federal Antitrust Law: Cases and Materials
Daniel J. Gifford and Leo J. Raskind

Federal Evidence Courtroom Manual
Glen Weissenberger

Federal Income Tax Anthology
Paul L. Caron, Karen C. Burke, and Grayson M.P. McCouch

Federal Rules of Evidence Rules, Legislative History, Commentary and Authority 1997-98 Edition
Glen Weissenberger

Federal Rules of Evidence Handbook, 1997-98 Edition
Publisher's Staff

Federal Wealth Transfer Tax Anthology
Paul L. Caron, Grayson M.P. McCouch, Karen C. Burke

First Amendment Anthology
Donald E. Lively, Dorothy E. Roberts, and Russell L. Weaver

International Environmental Law Anthology
Anthony D'Amato and Kirsten Engel

International Human Rights: Law, Policy, and Process, Second Edition
Frank C. Newman and David Weissbrodt

Selected International Human Rights Instruments and Bibliography For Research on International Human Rights Law, Second Edition
Frank C. Newman and David Weissbrodt

International Intellectual Property Anthology
Anthony D'Amato and Doris Estelle Long

International Law Anthology
Anthony D'Amato

International Law Coursebook
Anthony D'Amato

Introduction to the Study of Law: Cases and Materials
John Makdisi

Judicial Externships: The Clinic Inside the Courthouse
Rebecca A. Cochran

Justice and the Legal System: A Coursebook
Anthony D'Amato and Arthur J. Jacobson

A Land Use Anthology
Jon W. Bruce

Law and Economics Anthology
Kenneth G. Dau-Schmidt and Thomas S. Ulen

The Law of Disability Discrimination
Ruth Colker

ADA Handbook: Statutes, Regulations and Related Materials
Publisher's Staff

The Law of Modern Payment Systems and Notes, Second Edition
Fred H. Miller and Alvin C. Harrell

Lawyers and Fundamental Moral Responsibility
Daniel R. Coquillette

Microeconomic Predicates to Law and Economics
Mark Seidenfeld

Patients, Psychiatrists and Lawyers: Law and the Mental Health System, Second Edition
Raymond L. Spring, Roy B. Lacoursiere, and Glen Weissenberger

Preventive Law: Materials on a Non Adversarial Legal Process
Robert M. Hardaway

Principles of Evidence, Third Edition
Irving Younger, Michael Goldsmith, and David A. Sonenshein

Problems and Simulations in Evidence, Second Edition
Thomas F. Guernsey

A Products Liability Anthology
Anita Bernstein

Professional Responsibility Anthology
Thomas B. Metzloff

A Property Anthology, Second Edition
Richard H. Chused

Public Choice and Public Law: Readings and Commentary
Maxwell L. Stearns

The Regulation of Banking
Cases and Materials on Depository Institutions and Their Regulators
Michael P. Malloy

Science in Evidence
D.H. Kaye

A Section 1983 Civil Rights Anthology
Sheldon H. Nahmod

Sports Law: Cases and Materials, Third Edition
Ray L. Yasser, James R. McCurdy, and C. Peter Goplerud

A Torts Anthology
Lawrence C. Levine, Julie A. Davies, and Edward J. Kionka

Trial Practice
Lawrence A. Dubin and Thomas F. Guernsey

Unincorporated Business Entities
Larry E. Ribstein

FORTHCOMING PUBLICATIONS

A Copyright Law Anthology: The Technology Frontier
Richard H. Chused

Environmental Law: Air Pollution, Third Edition
Mark S. Squillace and David R. Wooley

International Civil Procedure Anthology
David S. Clark and Anthony D'Amato

International Taxation: Cases, Materials, and Problems
Philip F. Postlewaite

Natural Resources: Cases and Materials
Barlow Burke, Jr.

Readings in Criminal Law
Russell L. Weaver, John M. Burkoff, Catherine Hancock, Alan Reed, and Peter Seago

European Union Law Anthology

EUROPEAN UNION LAW ANTHOLOGY

KAREN V. KOLE
Visiting Associate Professor of Law
The University of Tulsa College of Law

ANTHONY D'AMATO
Leighton Professor of Law
Northwestern University School of Law

ANDERSON PUBLISHING CO.
CINCINNATI, OHIO

EUROPEAN UNION LAW ANTHOLOGY
KAREN V. KOLE AND ANTHONY D'AMATO

Anderson Publishing Co.
2035 Reading Road / Cincinnati, Ohio 45202
800-582-7295 / e-mail andpubco@aol.com / Fax 513-562-5430
World Wide Web http://www.andersonpublishing.com

ISBN: 0-87084-205-6

Contents

Preface

Europe was devastated by World War II. The Marshall Plan of 1947 planted the seeds for an economic recovery that has never abated since then. In 1951 the major European nations established the European Coal and Steel Community. Six years later it was transformed into the European Economic Community. By 1973, with the addition of Denmark, Ireland, Norway, and the United Kingdom, it was called the European Community. The name changed again (perhaps for the last time) with the signing of the Maastricht Treaty in 1992; now it is the European Union, or "EU." New members include Greece, Portugal, Spain, and in 1990 a unified Germany. In 1995, Austria, Finland, and Sweden joined the EU. A new single unit of currency, the "Euro," is planned to come into existence in 2002. In an astonishingly short period of historical time, the EU has developed from the hostility and fear of war-torn countries in 1945 to a relatively harmonious market without economic frontiers. To the extent that we can think of the EU as a single federalized state, it is today, from an economic standpoint, the most powerful state in the world.

But the EU is even more than that. It is a fascinating microcosm of a new globalized economy. The economic problems that are being worked out in Europe contain lessons for other countries in moving toward a global legal regime of economic development through comparative advantage. And as European economic problems become increasingly resolved, ancient social and political differences are also receding into the background. Europe is thus providing a social and political model for the rest of the world as well.

Professor Eleanor M. Fox has underscored "the brilliant basic concept of lifting the frontiers that stood as border barriers around each of the nation-states," and through gradual centralization of governmental authority, ensuring that "neither governments nor private firms could replace these [frontiers], either directly or indirectly, by border restraints or discriminating measures." But it is too early to tell whether the economic union will further evolve into a political union, or whether the individual states will retain a significant amount of governmental power. Yet it is clear that the EU is here to stay and that its economic power and potential are growing with each passing day.

In this Anthology we have tried to paint a comprehensive picture of the development of the EU to where it is today, and to look toward the future especially with an eye to how the United States will fit into that future. We have relied heavily on articles from European journals, which are sometimes difficult to obtain in the United States. It is important for American law students to see how Europeans think about the legal issues and problems of the EU.

Even as we were finishing this book, the Amsterdam Treaty was drafted and then was finalized in late 1997. Among other improvements, the Treaty will expand human rights and citizenship. By mid 1998 we expect the European Council to decide which countries qualify for membership in the EU under the requirements of the Maastricht Treaty, which sets forth stringent monetary and fiscal criteria for entry into a monetary union with a fixed rate of exchange. Thus, even as we study the EU, we find that the object of our study is undergoing major evolutionary changes. It is a fascinating time to explore this astonishing transformation of what used to be called, but no longer can usefully be called, the "Old World."

Acknowledgment

Professor Kole wishes to acknowledge the significant help of her research assistant at the University of Tulsa School of Law, Robert Lee, and the secretarial support of the school. Professor D'Amato would like to thank his assistant Mary Finn for her usual excellent help in all stages of the production of this Anthology, Northwestern librarian Irene Berkey and her colleagues for their research assistance, and Dean David Van Zandt for his overall support and encouragement of this project.

List of Contributors

Frederick M. Abbott
Thomas E. Abeltshauser
Anthony Arnull
Martin Bangemann
Rene Barents
Gerhard Bebr
Joxerramon Bengoetxea
Karl-Jurgen Bieback
Marko Bros
Adrian Brown
Alec Burnside
Ilona Cheyne
Robert J. Coleman
Alfred F. Cornard
Tamara Ray Crockett
Dierdre Curtin
Anthony D'Amato
Alan Dashwood
A. David Demiray
Bas de Regt
Philippe De Smedt
Chris Docksey
Timothy W. Dowdy
Claus-Dieter Ehlermann
Martin E. Elling
Matthew J. Eshelman
Ian Forrester
Eleanor M. Fox
*Giorgio Gaja
David J. Gerber
Lawrence W. Gormley
Harris
Trevor C. Hartley
Michael D. Hodges
Frederic Yves Jenny
Heike Jung
David T. Keeling
David Kennedy
Heinrich Kirschner
Karen V. Kole
John Temple Lang
Julian Lonbay
*Nicholas MacGowan
Paul D. Marquardt
Philip Mead
Carl Meyntjens
Daniela Napoli
Hans Nelson
Hans-Jorg Niemeyer
Christopher Norall
Steve Peers
Robert Polnman
Mary Quinn
Lynn E. Ramsey
*Hjalte Rasmussen
J. Rinze
Brent D. Rose
Wulf-Henning Roth
Daniel L. Rubinfield
*Philippe Sands
Matthew L. Schemmel
Uwe H. Schneider
Cynthia B. Schultz
David Seymour
Josephine Steiner
Tyson Storch
*Brenda Sufrin
Niels Thygesen
Victor Vandebeek
George Vandersanden
Marc Van Der Woude
Spencer Weber Waller
Philippa Watson
David E. Webb
Joseph H. H. Weiler
Richard Whish
Eric L. White
Robin White
Christopher A. Whytock

Chapter 1

What is EU Law?

I. Introduction

A. Vision of Europe: Lessons for the World[1]

The effort of the European Union ("Union" or "EU") to create a market without frontiers is daunting. Yet I submit that this enterprise, with certain modifications, provides a microcosm for the challenge facing the trading nations of the world in an increasingly globalized economy. The seeds of this global enterprise are likely to be sown in the next round of the General Agreement on Tariffs and Trade, in its new incarnation as the World Trade Organization. For the global community, seeking greater openness, access, and economic opportunity and the attendant benefits of freedom, there are lessons to be learned from Europe.

Europe is grappling with a panoply of questions that will, in one decade or another, present themselves to the world, and while the world may not choose Europe's answers to the questions, it will be the wiser for confronting them.

To stabilize the conditions for peace in an erstwhile warring Europe, and to establish the conditions for a robust economy with markets sufficiently large to support efficient firms, six nations at the center of Western Europe designed and signed the Treaty of Rome in 1957. The brilliant basic concept was to lift the frontiers that stood as border barriers around each of the nation-states, and to assure that neither governments nor private firms could replace them, directly or indirectly, by border restraints or discriminatory measures, or measures of equivalent effect. These first principles are enshrined in Articles 2, 3, and 5 of the Treaty of Rome, in the four freedoms, and in the articles establishing a common competition policy, which apply not only to private actors but also to state-owned enterprises, state-licensed enterprises, and state aids.

The vision of free movement across a Europe without frontiers has a seamless character. National trade laws, such as antidumping and countervailing duty laws, were abolished. Trade law was transmogrified into freedom of movement law, and the right to undistorted competition. In this sense, for the internal market, trade law became "undistorted-competition law," and the "undistorted-competition law" of the internal market caught public and private distortions alike.

---

[1] Eleanor M. Fox, *Vision of Europe: Lessons for the World*, 18 Fordham Int'l L.J. 379-87 (1994). © 1994 Eleanor M. Fox. Reprinted by permission.

The first principles of the EU internal market centrally prohibit "beggar thy neighbor" restraints—restraints by one nation or its citizens designed to profit by imposing costs on another member nation or its citizens. Thus, it was and is absolutely forbidden for Germany to order its producers to combine to exploit the French, or for French producers to cartelize to exploit the Germans. Parochial, nationalistic restraints are utterly forbidden.

It was recognized, however, that some normal and not parochial public or private action may have spillover effects on one's neighbors and it was necessary to devise principles to distinguish legitimate from illegitimate measures. Some of these measures would be legitimate simply because they served a proper national interest, but only if they were propor tional and narrowly tailored to serve that interest. Other such measures would be legitimate because they also served larger objectives of the European Union, such as "lifting up" the least well off regions of the Union and thereby enhancing social and economic cohesion. For all permitted derogations from the one-Europe vision, transparency and proportionality were, and are, necessary conditions.

Moreover, especially after the border barriers were lifted, two phenomena appeared regarding different national regimes regulating a variety of conditions, such as product safety and the environment. First, sometimes the regimes clashed, or the need to comply with several systems imposed unnecessary costs, interfering with inter-Member State trade. Second, firms operating in regimes with a higher level of regulation thought themselves to be at an unfair competitive disadvantage because of the costs of regulation. Third, for some problems, such as environmental spillovers, common solutions would be superior to individual solutions. Accordingly, the Union developed methodologies for bringing bodies of law into harmony; and for goods in transit not subject to common policy, it developed the rule of law that member nations must give mutual recognition to the regulations (e.g., safety certifications) of one another.

The system's effectiveness depends upon acceptance of Union law in the Member States. Accordingly, the Court of Justice of the European Union (the "Court of Justice") has ruled that Union law is supreme, and clear rules of Union law are directly applicable in the Member States; that is, they are a part of the body of the law of each nation.[2]

The paragraphs above concern economic foundations. Omitted, therefore, is the governance process within the Union, including the processes by which legislation is proposed and passed—a realm often described with the epithet, "democracy deficit." Along with the perceived democracy deficit is the perception of bureaucratic excess, and the claim that "bureaucrats in Brussels" extend their tentacles into the lives of the distant country men and women. Can a nation retain an acceptable share of power and responsibility while conferring power on supranational institutions whose word is supreme? The question resonates, and properly so; but yet, as we move rapidly towards the twenty-first century, a Europe with restored frontiers is all but unthinkable.

---

[2] The principles of the EU blueprint for freedom of trade without discrimination have easy application to free trade areas beyond the Union. They have long applied in the European free trade area. As Eastern Europe has spectacularly democratized and moved to freer markets, the European Union has brought the most basic of its first principles eastward.

The shrinking world itself is in search of principles to assure openness, non-parochialism, and methodologies for bringing disparate regulatory regimes into harmony.

I begin with the Court of Justice. From the outset, this distinguished judicial institution took virtually all available opportunities to make Union institutions robust and to endow them with the necessary powers to assure the emergence of a vital, integrated Europe. While the activism has been criticized on grounds of process and interpretation, it has been credited with making possible a meaningful European Union that is a player in the world today.

Fittingly, Advocate General Carl Otto Lenz describes the supremacy of Union law and its reception into the Member States, and the mechanism by which Member State courts may and often must pose questions to the Court of Justice to assure that the Member State courts give the proper interpretation to Union law and that Union law is uniformly applied. The prospect of varying interpretations is viewed by Advocate General Lenz not as an expression of possibility and diversity but as "a potential danger . . . [to] the functioning of the EU legal system as a whole"—as well it might be when states as diverse as France and Great Britain are charged with applying common (external) customs regulations and implementing the common agricultural and social security systems. It is perhaps of some interest that in one of the few cases detailed by Advocate General Lenz to explain the system of reference, the Court's answer to a British court's question directed the British court to do an act (temporarily refusing to apply an Act of Parliament) that the British constitutional system forbade.

A step away from government enterprise with power is the private firm with power, whose acts are regulated by Article 86 of the EU Treaty, as described by John Temple Lang, a Director in the Directorate General for Competition. Mr. Temple Lang thoroughly analyzes the EU law on companies' duties to supply competitors and to grant access to essential facilities. The seamless quality of EU law reappears. Just as governments may not discriminate against non-nationals in the internal market, firms with control over essential facilities may not discriminate (against outsiders), without justification (e.g., no spare capacity). Just as governments may not block access to markets, dominant firms may not deny access. Just as governmental trade-restraining action, if allowed at all, must be proportional, dominant firm acts that block significant economic opportunities are forbidden if not justified, and they cannot be justified if they are not proportional to achieve proper objectives.

A critique may be made, and has been made, regarding substantive law under Article 86. EU law's deficit of economic analysis, and its overbreadth in finding dominance and in imposing duties to deal have been noted. The point I make here runs in the other direction; the point is that the EU, uniquely, has seen and acted on the links between government and private trade-restraining action, especially market-blocking action, even while the trading nations of the world appear to have just discovered the gap between trade law and competition law and are searching for ways to understand the commonalities and to bridge the gap.

Telecommunications, which two decades ago was highly regulated by national and local authorities of nationalistic and often discriminatory bent, is now at center stage in the global economy. Liberalization from intrusive regulation is occurring throughout the world just as world competition is intensifying and telecommunications, linked with other media, is seen as the foundation for fluid trans-world communications; a partner in the global information superhighway. The European Union has worked hard and long on liberalizing telecommunications. EU liberalization includes not only legislation—some standardization, mutual recognition and harmonization—but also competition law enforcement to assure that the firms with power do not take the seductive opportunities to enhance their profits at the expense of consumers and competitors. The telecommunications industry provides a window for observing the integrated and linking economic policies of the Commission.

Centralism versus autonomy remains an overriding and overarching tension. Mr. Paul D. Marquardt[3] explores the roots and modern usage of the word and the doctrine "subsidiarity." He observes the incorporation of subsidiarity into the Treaty on European Union; a concept heralded as the means and method to save the autonomy of the member nations. In the view of Mr. Marquardt (I believe), the rhetoric of subsidiarity is a cynical ploy to keep the critics of the European Union at bay while offering nothing to the con cerned Europeans who wish to preserve the souls of their nations. Indeed, he makes the argument that subsidiarity, which dictates that power be preserved at the lowest possible level for effective formation and implementation of policy, dictates that the most significant power will flow up to the European institutions in the name of technological efficiency, and that most other powers will devolve to a local level, bypassing the nation state. Thus, a cruel hoax.

I am not persuaded of the emptiness and perversity of subsidiarity. To the contrary, I view the concept as one of conceptual beauty, providing a framework for addressing the challenge of the twenty-first century.[4] Particularly is this so for a community of nations whose future depends not only on national uniqueness and choice but also on common cause. Even for those who, like me, are attracted to the seamless economic blueprint for Europe, the observations of Mr. Marquardt are an important call to action. Unless subsidiarity itself becomes a doctrine that is transparent and meaningful in decreeing the devolution of power, it will muddy rather than clarify the waters of Europe.

The Work of Europe is relevant to The Work of the World, but with differences. The major difference is that the trading nations of the world have no need for the depth of integration that galvanized Europe. Yet, like Europe, the world would, in my view, profit from greater openness of markets, less parochialism, higher levels of transparency and market access, and harmonization of regimes of regulation when disparate systems are costly and harmony will facilitate freedoms and opportunities and tend to improve standards of living without trampling upon important values. For its internal market, Europe has grappled with the many facets of these problems. Many answers

---

[3] Paul D. Marquardt, *Subsidiarity and Sovereignty in the European Union*, 18 Fordham Int'l L.J. 616-640 (1994). © 1994 Paul D. Marquardt. Reprinted by permission.

[4] The challenge is to discover what linkages should be forged at higher than national level to avoid narrow nationalism and thereby to unleash opportunities for the peoples of the world, and to determine how the linkages should be forged in view of the objective to preserve maximum national and local autonomy consistent with the linking regime.

for the world trading system are bound to be different.[5] But Europe has posed and is posing the right questions, and for this reason, the world can learn from Europe.

B. Will Europe Become a "Free Trade Area"?[6]

Long gone is the "benign neglect" of those on Wall Street and Pennsylvania Avenue that led the United States press to coin the sinister "Europessimism" concept of the early 1980s. Indeed, during last year, many East Coast analysts have depicted Europe as a five trillion dollar economy, thus granting the EU the economic powerhouse status it deserves. But awe often goes hand in hand with envy, which has resulted in the fashionable East Coast notion of "Fortress Europe."

Before killing this myth, one crucial but often forgotten issue must be clarified: there is indeed nothing more legitimate for the Union than wanting to achieve one single market, abolishing national frontiers, and letting goods, persons, services and capital circulate freely. After all, this is one of the very essential goals set out in the 1950s when the European Union was created. Some people still take the simplistic view that these endeavors will result in the setting up of a "free-trade area" in Europe. The difference between a free-trade area and the Union is fundamental both in philosophical and political terms. The European Union's future reaches far beyond the 1992 Internal Market concept. The latter, however important, is merely a step towards a true political union.

Quite obviously, the Internal Market concept has captured the imagination of the world. Its content and its consequences are at the center of an intensive debate. This is a direct consequence of the dawning conviction that the Internal Market program is now unstoppable and will change the face of both the Union and the world economy.

There is widespread anxiety that the Union might erect a protective wall around its Internal Market and turn its back on the liberal world economic system. The nightmare prospect of a "Fortress Europe" has repeatedly made the headlines. These anxieties are paradoxically accompanied by fears inside the Union that the breaking down of internal barriers might operate above all to the advantage of foreign companies who sell within the Union market, and thus provide our partners with gratuitous benefits. Both fears are without foundation. The achievement of the Internal Market is of economic benefit not only to Union citizens, but also to the world economy as a whole. The related external policy measures also will represent a coherent approach based on a sober analysis of Union interests and respect for those of our partners.

The impact on the world economy of the Internal Market will depend partly on the predictable economic consequences of the replacement of fifteen separate markets by

---

[5] For example, Europe needed a common competition policy to effectuate deep market integration and to prevent a patchwork of disparate and warring national industrial policies from blocking its way. No similar need drives the trading national of the world and a much more minimal system of linking principles and national enforcement is possible and I believe desirable.

[6] Martin Bangemann, *Symposium: 1992: Doing Business In the European Internal Market: Fortress Europe: The Myth*, 9 NW J. Int'l Bus. 480-86 (1989). © 1994 Martin Bangemann. Reprinted by permission.

one, and partly on the content of the accompanying external policy measures. Both Union producers and foreign exporters will benefit directly from operating in an Internal Market with a generally uniform set of regulations, standards, testing and certification procedures. They will no longer have to face divergent sets of requirements, nor intra-Union border controls. All will gain from lower costs and from the exploitation of the economies of scale offered by a market of over 320 million consumers.

The now widely known Cecchini report[7] has estimated the macroeconomic consequences which will follow the completion of the internal market, even in the absence of additional external policy measures. These estimates suggest that intra-Union trade should increase by some 10% in the medium term. The improved competitiveness of Union producers will also stimulate Union exports to the rest of the world by 10%. Imports into the Union, which will accompany its increased growth, will also rise.

In a word, the combination of the increased dynamism, which is inherent in the creation of the Internal Market, and the exploitation of the opportunities it will provide to pursue growth-orientated macroeconomic policies will allow the Union to provide a powerful new stimulus to the world economy, many of whose problems stem precisely from the sluggish growth it has experienced in recent years.

The total impact of the Internal Market on our partners will also be determined in part by the content given to its external policy dimension. This policy is not new. The Treaty of Rome, which provided for the removal of all customs barriers between Member states, also set up a common external policy, in particular with respect to the Common Market it created. This gave the Union an external identity to match its intensifying internal integration. The 1992 program simply extended and deepens this Internal Market philosophy and introduces the mechanisms to achieve it. It is therefore natural that they be accompanied by a corresponding extension and completion of external policy. This means the development of Union rules for access to the market for third country producers in all those areas in which the Internal Market is achieved. In many cases, this will mean the replacement of existing Member States' policy measures by Union action.

The need to extend the scope of Union external policy action in this way has been misunderstood by some as an intention to raise the level of protection. To the contrary, its content will be closely related to the objectives it is intended to achieve. The European Council, during the so-called European Summit, has expressed a general policy line as follows:

> The Internal Market should not close in on itself. In conformity with the provisions of GATT, the Union should be open to third countries, and must negotiate with these countries where necessary to ensure access to their markets of Union exports. It will seek to preserve the balance of advantages accorded, while respecting the identity of the Internal Market of the Union.[8]

---

7 ISBN 92-825-8605-7.

8 Meeting of the European Council, in Hannover, West Germany (June 27-28, 1988).

This important statement underlines the Union's commitment to the liberal multilateral trading system. This commitment reflects the reality that the Union is the world's largest trading partner and that external trade plays a much larger proportional role in its economy than in those of other major trading partners.

The logic of the Internal Market assumes that by lowering the costs and increasing the home market base of European companies, these companies will be in a stronger competitive position *vis-à-vis* third-country producers, both in Europe and in international markets. The full benefits of this increased competitiveness can only be reaped if it can be translated into increased world trade on the basis of comparative advantage. This is an argument for reinforcing the existing liberal, multilateral trade system by seeking the mutually advantageous opening of world markets, not for triggering a protectionist spiral which could only reduce market opportunities for competitive union producers. In other words, "Fortress Europe" does not make sense. The Union's commitment to liberalization is not rhetoric. It is the simple reflection of our interests, which coincide with those of our partners.

Moreover, building such a fortress would be suicidal. With over 20% or more of world trade, the EU is by far the most open trading partner in the world. We have nothing to gain through protections. Three divergent classes of external policy measures in connection with the Internal Market can be distinguished. Some are indispensable if internal barriers are to be removed, many are covered by the existing international obligations of the Union, and others represent virgin territory with respect both to Union policy and to international rules.

The best example of external policy measures which are indispensable are the gaps which still exist in the common commercial policy itself. These gaps are a result of the wide divergences between the import regimes applicable in individual Member States. One area of concern is the quantitative restrictions placed on some imports from Japan and Eastern Europe. Another area of concern is the limits fixed for individual Member States within the Union's quotas under bilateral textile agreements, and for sensitive products in its Generalized System of Preferences for developing countries. Such measures will make no sense when border posts disappear between our Member States, because they will no longer be enforceable. After 1992, the Union's rules on imports from third countries will need to be fully unified. In many cases, the national restrictions will simply be eliminated. This may require Union assistance to restructure certain sensitive sectors.

A second class of measures concerns those many areas in which new external action will be fully subject to the Union's existing obligations, whether these be multilateral—such as GATT and the Organization for Economic Cooperation and Development ("OECD")—or bilateral—such as the European Free Trade Association ("EFTA"), Loma, and the Mediterranean Countries. These agreements are already based largely on procedures directed towards the progressive liberalization of world markets. Thus, the extension of the scope of Union action within them will result, once again, in a worldwide decrease, not an increase, of protection.

Finally, a number of measures will break new ground by extending Union external action to fields not covered by international rules. Here the same logic applies. The same objective of worldwide market opening needs to be pursued.

How can this objective be achieved? GATT experience shows that in multilateral negotiations designed to liberalize access to markets, progress is made by all participants exchanging "concessions" in such a way that a mutually advantageous balance of benefits for all parties emerges from the negotiations. This technique is often described as being based on a concept of "overall reciprocity." In this sense, reciprocity is an accepted and central element of trade policy. As a recent report by the Congressional Research Service on the 1992 program pointed out: "Reciprocity has been a central concept of U.S. trade policy since the adoption on unconditional most-favored-nation (MFN) treatment in 1923."

In passing, it is important to note that overall reciprocity implies neither that all countries make the same concessions, nor that all countries are required to contribute equivalent concessions. The level of contribution possible may depend on the level of development of a country. There is no question of the Union demanding concessions from its developing country partners which they are unable to make.

In many policy areas, the multilateral pursuit of liberalization has been underway for decades. As already noted, the international obligations which the Union has entered into as part of this process (e.g., GATT and OECD) will continue to be fully respected. In those areas not yet covered by existing rules, such as much of the services trade, it will be the Union's aim to achieve a further liberalization through the negotiation of new international agreements. The Uruguay Round negotiations provide a major opportunity to do this. When they are successfully concluded, the commitments to which the Union subscribes will be fully reflected in its external regime.

Until such agreements have entered into force, it would be foolish for the Union to extend the benefits of its own liberalization process to third countries unilaterally. At that time, it would be reasonable to expect comparable liberalization measures from these countries. On the other hand, these benefits will be available to our partners where a mutual balance of advantages, in the spirit of GATT, already exists or can be achieved through negotiations. This, of course, implies the maintenance of conditions on access to the Union market. These conditions will be maintained, however, only where they are not contrary to our obligations, and pending the achievement of a satisfactory degree of overall reciprocity as part of a multilateral or bilateral negotiating process. This approach does not imply that our trading partners should adopt legislation identical to our own; that would be quite unreasonable. Neither are we seeking "sectoral reciprocity" in the sense of balancing trade in each sector between the Union and each of its partners. We have successfully prevented the United States from introducing this sectoral reciprocity into its law.

The Union's message is clear: it is proposing to third countries a partnership designed to ensure that the liberalization, which is inherent to the achievement of the Single Market, echoes around the world. Far from building a fortress, the Union is taking the lead in proposing a new, cooperative effort to revitalize the world economy.

The outside world is right to recognize the importance of this program to complete the Internal Market and to examine its possible impact on third countries. The fact that interest often leads to anxiety and concern highlights the need to explain carefully what is involved. The Union's decision-making process is already exceptionally transparent and unhurried, but as the pace of legislative change quickens in the approach to

1992, there may be a need for more intensified use of existing channels of consultation with third countries when individual proposals could have a direct bearing on international trade. The Union has always been and will remain open to requests for such consultation.

But such a readiness should not be misread: the Single European Act,[9] which updated the EU treaties of the end of the 1950s, defines the ingredients of the Internal Market. This Act is neither a scrap of paper nor a declaration of good intent. The Single European Act has a clear constitutional value. It is Union law endorsed by all Parliaments and Governments of the Member States. The Maastrict Treaty[10] has solidified and focussed the goals of the EU. The European Union is not negotiable and is here to stay.

C. Historical and Current Perspectives

1. Historical Perspectives and Priorities[11]

The idea of European unity is perhaps as old as Europe itself, but ironically no single force impacted so greatly on aspirations for integration as the outcome of World War II. The war's destruction, Europe's decline in importance relative to the emerging superpowers, and the threat posed to Western Europe by the specter of Soviet-backed communism made Europeans dream of a united democratic Europe—strong, prosperous, peaceable.

a. Era of Establishment: The 1950s

Franco-German reconciliation was deemed a prerequisite for both lasting peace and united action. In 1951 Belgium, France, West Germany, Italy, Luxembourg, and the Netherlands (the Six) signed the Paris Treaty and created the European Coal and Steel Community (ECSC). The ECSC marked a milestone because it brought Germany and France together and because, for the first time, national governments ceded part of their sovereignty, albeit on a limited basis, to a supranational authority.

In March 1957, the Six signed the Treaties of Rome, which established the European Atomic Energy Commission (Euratom) and the European Economic Union (EEU). The Paris and Rome Treaties (Treaties) form the "constitution" of the EU. The immediate objective of the EEU was the establishment of a customs union that would guarantee free movement of goods, services, capital, and people (the Four Freedoms) among Member States.

b. Sporadic Progress: The 1960s

In July 1968 eighteen months ahead of schedule, the EEU implemented the customs union and the common external tariff, but significant difficulties in other areas hin-

---

9 Single European Act, 30 O.J. (No. L 169) 1 (1987).

10 Treaty on European Union [Maastricht Treaty].

11 Martin E. Elling, *The Emerging European Community: A Framework for Institutional and Legal Analysis*, 13 Hastings Int'l & Comp. L.R. 511-30 (1990). © 1990 Martin E. Elling. Reprinted by permission.

dered broader progress. Specifically, although Denmark, Ireland, Norway, and the United Kingdom applied for EU membership in 1962, French President Charles de Gaulle's mistrust of British intentions delayed admission of these countries until 1973.

The EU budget created further crisis. In 1965 France rejected a proposal to allocate the levies on imports charged at its external frontiers to the EU. The impasse was only resolved by granting each member country the right to veto any issue it considered of "vital interest." This was a major blow because it delayed the implementation of majority voting that had been scheduled to take effect at that time.

c. *Consolidation: The 1970s*

Though the 1970s remained a time of external shocks and significant stagnation, the EU made a number of advancements. Innovations included the European Political Cooperation (EPC), founded in 1970, whereby members agreed to consult before deciding on major foreign policy issues, and the European monetary "snake" established in 1972 as a system for foreign exchange coordination within Europe. Also, in 1979 the first direct elections to the European Parliament were held in member countries.

d. *Expansion and Reaffirmation of Initial Goals: The 1980s*

The 1981 admission of Greece and the admission of Portugal and Spain in 1986 boosted the EU's population from 260 to 321 million inhabitants. According to recent figures, the EU of Twelve accounts for twenty-two percent of world trade. This expansion along Europe's southern flank has bolstered the EU's claim that it is the nucleus of a future united Europe.

In 1985 the Council of Ministers adopted the White Paper, a detailed plan for completing the internal market. It detailed roughly three hundred actions that had to be agreed upon in order to realize the internal market. The White Paper received broad support from the public, the Member State governments, and the institutions of the EU. The White Paper detailed the creation of a larger, more competitive market, and thus persuaded national politicians to prioritize the goal of a unified Europe.

The implementation of the Single European Act (SEA) in July 1987 has had great institutional and significance. This Act provided the operational changes necessary to implement the White Paper and laid the foundation for more ambitious and rapid progress toward full union. The SEA extended qualified majority voting in four fields: the internal market, research and development, economic and social cohesion, and improvement of working conditions. It also extended the Treaties to cover monetary and environmental policy, increased the Commission's and Parliament's powers of implementation and oversight, and, for the first time, brought foreign policy cooperation officially under the Treaties.

In the 1980s, the EU underwent tremendous revitalization. Economic competition, a perception that the superpowers were too little concerned with the interests of Europe, and United States pressure on Europe to assume responsibility for its own defense have all led to a significant rediscovery of the ideal of European union.

e. *The Treaty of Maastricht*[12]

In December 1991, the leaders of the twelve EU Member States met in the Dutch town of Maastricht to travel further down the track toward economic and monetary union. The Treaty of Maastricht aims to form closer economic, social, and political ties. The Treaty covers a broad range of economic provisions, including a single European currency, coordinated fiscal policies and a central bank. Maastricht expressly recognized EU competence to legislate in social areas such as education, the environment and scientific research and development. The Treaty also outlines provisions for determining a common security policy that might eventually lead to a common European defense.

2. General Priorities

a. *The Customs Union*[13]

Since 1968 the EU has been the world's largest nonnational customs union in trade terms. Neither tariffs nor quotas have been imposed on intra-EU trade and there is one common external tariff. Efforts to achieve an internal market by 1992 center on the elimination of nontariff barriers to intra-EU trade. The customs union has stimulated trade among members. In 1958 trade among EU members was only 34.5 percent of the total foreign trade of these same countries. In 1987 it had risen to 58.7 percent. The EU also maintains a common trade policy and a coordinated, if not always uniform, foreign assistance program. The four Lomé Conventions (1975, 1979. 1985, and 1989), concluded with sixty-six African, Caribbean, and Pacific (ACP) countries, evidence the cooperation in these fields.

b. *The European Political Cooperation (EPC)*

The EPC, sanctioned by the SEA in 1987, serves as the framework in which members coordinate their foreign policies and seek to develop a joint EU foreign policy. Members must consult each other before deciding major foreign policy matters. EU foreign ministers and ambassadors worldwide increasingly formulate joint strategies, and in international fora, the EU often speaks with one voice. The EU often issues joint communiques on world events, but less frequently undertakes joint action. Exceptions include the EU's swift support for the United Kingdom in the Falklands War and the Union's development of a code of conduct for EU firms to follow in South Africa.

The ever closer links between foreign policy bureaucracies, which the EPC mandates, have led to the rise of parallel foreign policy positions between member countries. Still, some experts question whether a dramatic improvement, beyond the gradual overlap of national foreign policies, is possible given the loose framework of the EPC. However, the EU's leadership in coordinating assistance to Hungary and

---

12 Matthew J. Eshelman, *The Maastricht Train: Slowing Down for Sharp Curves*, 11 Dickinson J. Int'l L. 608 (1993). © 1993 Matthew J. Eshelman. Reprinted by permission.

13 Martin E. Elling, *The Emerging European Community: A Framework for Institutional and Legal Analysis*, 13 Hastings Int'l & Comp. L.R. 511 (1990). © 1990 Martin E. Elling. Reprinted by permission.

Poland showed that the EPC will continue to develop in matters where members have largely coincident interest.

c. *The European Monetary System (EMS)*

Since 1979 when the EMS, with its exchange rate controls, replaced the monetary "snake," there has been a degree of foreign exchange stability in Western Europe never known before.

The "snake" exchange rate arrangement set margins of fluctuation for EU currencies vis a vis the United States dollar. The margins maintained fluctuations of the United States dollar which were wider than the margins set for the EU currencies, in accordance with official International Monetary Fund policy. Thus, while the United States dollar might fluctuate within a 4.5 percent range, the "snake" kept fluctuations in EU currencies within a narrow 2.25 percent range.

The stability resulting from the adoption of the EMS exchange rate mechanism and the macroeconomic policy convergence that accompanied it, facilitated the growth of larger EU-wide companies, fostered intra-EU commerce, and furthered the internal market.

There is much speculation about the development of an Economic and Monetary Union (EMU) with a central bank and a single currency.[14] In June 1988 the EU decided to remove all barriers to capital flows by 1992 and assembled a committee of central bank presidents, under the leadership of Jacques Delors, to propose means of erecting the EMU. However, serious obstacles remain. The United Kingdom's unwillingness to support full monetary union as well as Franco-German rivalry over control of monetary policy have traditionally been formidable limiting factors.

Despite these limitations, and over the U.K.'s direct objection, the European Council, at its December 1989 Strasbourg summit, voted to proceed with implementation of the EMU as recommended by the Delors Committee.[15] The first stage should be completed on July 1, 1990. The European Council, noting that the necessary majority existed under article 236 of the EEU Treaty, agreed to convene an Intergovernmental Conference charged with amending the Treaties with a view toward eventual implementation of the complete EMU by the end of 1990.

3. The Structure of the European Union

Understanding the functioning of the EU is important in developing and maintaining legal and business ties with Europe. Legal, economic, and political questions once addressed to national capitals are now handled by the EU in Brussels. The government of the EU has five principal organs: the Commission, the Council of Ministers, the European Council, the Parliament, and the Court of Justice.

---

[14] Harris, Legal Implications of European Monetary Union, 130 New L.J. 1083, 1084 (1989).

[15] 41 European Community News (Washington) 6 (Dec. 11, 1989).

a. *The Institutions and their Development*[16]

The three founding treaties established four main institutions: the European Parliament, the Council, the Commission and the Court of Justice.[17] I will consider the dividing line be tween the responsibilities of the Union and those of the Member States in the legislative, executive and judicial areas. At the same time, the separation of powers between the four main institutions of the EU will become apparent.

In the legislative sphere under the treaties, there are various procedures involving three institutions: the Commission, the European Parliament and the Council. They have different functions and different powers, according to the subject matter to be regulated. It is, however, possible to make some general observations.

The Commission is the High Authority of the first Union, the Coal and Steel Union. In that Union the impressive title reflected a great deal of political power. The High Authority was composed of nine members appointed by the Governments of the six original Member States. According to the treaty, they were to be completely independent in the performance of their duties and were neither to seek nor to take instructions from any government.[18] They had, and still have in the sectors of coal and steel, the right to legislate. The Council participates in the legislative procedures, but the real power is vested in the High Authority.

This supranational approach was diluted when the Member States founded the two later Unions in 1957. The legislative functions of the Commission were reduced considerably. The Commission was given the right to propose legislative measures to the Council and to take part in its deliberations, but, with some exceptions, it lost the right to enact regulations or laws. One exception is that, on the basis of a regulation adopted by the Council, the Commission still can enact subordinate regulations.

Under Article 144 of the EEU Treaty, a motion of censure of the European Parliament against the Commission can lead to the resignation of the Commission. If a motion of censure is approved by a two-thirds majority, the Commission is to resign as a body. In practice, no motion of censure has ever been carried.

The Maastricht Treaty has provided for participation of the European Parliament in the appointment of the Commission. According to Article 158 of the EEU Treaty, the President of the Commission is to be nominated by the governments of the Member States after consultation of the European Parliament. The governments of the Member States are then, in consultation with the nominee for President, to nominate the other persons whom they intend to appoint as members of the Commission. The President and the other members are subject to a vote of approval by the European Parliament before they are appointed by common accord of the governments of the Member States. These new rules clearly augment the authority of the President of the

---

16 Heinrich Kirschner, *The Framework of the European Union under the Treaty of Maastricht*, 13 J. L. & Comm. 235-40 (1994). © 1994 Heinrich Kirschner. Reprinted by permission.

17 Martin E. Elling, *The Emerging European Community: A Framework for Institutional and Legal Analysis,* 13 Hastings Int'l & Comp. L.R. 511 (1990). © 1990 Martin E. Elling. Reprinted by permission.

18 ECSC Treaty Art. 9(1)-(2).

Commission. The influence that the Parliament can exercise in this politically sensitive field will be seen when the rules are first applied in 1994.

The main legislator of the EU is the Council. This institution is not based on the model of the United States Senate. It is composed of the representatives of the Governments of the Member States at a ministerial level. If decisions are made by a qualified majority, their votes have different weightings according to the importance of the respective Member States. Sometimes decisions are made on a simple majority vote or on a unanimous basis. This decision-making procedure reflects the very old European tradition of a congress of ambassadors managing a federal entity. Similar institutions were already in existence before the French Revolution, for instance in the Holy Roman Empire. Today, the ministers of the Member States meet regularly. The Councils are divided into specific policy areas; therefore, the ministers for agriculture comprise the Council for Agriculture, the ministers of finance make up the Council for Budgetary Affairs, the ministers for economic affairs or trade meet for matters concerning the commercial policy, and so forth. Their meetings are prepared by the civil servants of the respective Member States and by members of the Commission's staff.

The legislative power of the Council can be compared with the limited functions of the European Parliament. The Council was originally only a consultative body composed of delegates designated by the national parliaments. Today, its members are directly elected. As to the future, Article 8b of the EEU Treaty confers on citizens of other Member States the right to vote and run as a candidate in elections of the European Parliament in the Member State in which they reside under the same conditions as nationals of that State. Under a proposal unanimously approved by the Commission, in consultation with the European Parliament, this right is subject to the Council's regulations.

The participation of the Parliament in the various legislative procedures of the Union has been considerably reinforced by the Maastricht Treaty. However, even the mechanisms of the Maastricht Treaty do not provide for a true bicameral legislature consisting of two equal Houses. The reason for this system may reflect the unwillingness of some political forces to give up the legislative power that they hold, directly, or indirectly, in the Council, in favor of a supranational parliament that is difficult to influence. The result of the system is often criticized. It is regrettable that this so-called democratic deficit affecting the legislative power of the EU probably will not disappear in the near future.

In the field of executive power, the Member States play a vital role. National authorities implement Union law and perform the tasks of routine administration in the application of Union rules. For instance, the Common Customs Tariff, which is based upon Council regulations, is applied by the national customs authorities of the Member States. There is no Union customs service.

Only in some limited areas do the Commission and the Council themselves perform executive functions. Thus, Articles 85 through 90 of the EEU Treaty and Regulation No.17/62 of the Council, which organize the procedures for the enforcement of the antitrust rules of the EEU Treaty, endow the Commission with necessary executive powers. The Union institutions also manage their own staff. They appoint civil servants, raise taxes from their salaries and impose disciplinary sanctions. Apart from such specific fields, however, the executive power within the Union lies with the Member States.

The legal structures of the first two powers are of course reflected in the field of judicial power. Only insofar as the institutions are vested with genuine legislative or executive power must Union law be enforced by the Court of Justice. In all other fields, national authorities applying Union law remain subject to the jurisdiction of their national courts.

Under the jurisdiction of the Court of Justice, the Judges and the Advocates-General assume all the duties which, in the Member States, are allocated to the various courts and branches of the judicial administration. The issues arising in the Court of Justice range from constitutional issues to administrative, fiscal, labor, social and antitrust matters.

Because of these extensive areas of jurisdiction, heavy workload of the Court became a problem. This problem eventually led the Member States and the Council to establish a Court of First Instance which, in 1989, was attached to the original Court of Justice. For the first four years, the Court of First Instance heard mainly competition and staff cases. However, in 1993 its jurisdiction was considerably extended, and the Maastricht Treaty allows for a further extension of the jurisdiction of the Court of First Instance.

Thus, since 1989 a two-tier system of legal protection has been developing within the Union. The Court of Justice is performing the new task of reviewing the decisions of the Court of First Instance on points of law. In this respect, the Court of Justice can be compared to the Supreme Court of the United States. In addition, the Court of Justice has always performed the second role, which also corresponds to the functions of a Supreme Court, of guaranteeing the uniform application of Union law by the national courts. The national courts, particularly the administrative and tax courts of the Member States, have to supervise the application of Union law by the various national authorities.

If, for instance, the Common Customs Tariff is applied in a harbor or airport of a Member State by the local customs office, the administrative or tax courts of that Member State have jurisdiction over decisions in question. However, this may lead to the danger of divergent rules on the same question in various Member States, which could distort the flow of imports. To avoid this danger, the Court of Justice has jurisdiction, under Article 177 of the EEU Treaty, to give preliminary rulings on the interpretation of the Treaty and on the validity and interpretation of acts of the institutions. Any court or tribunal of a Member State may request the Court of Justice to give such a ruling if it considers the ruling necessary to enable it to give judgment. Where the question is raised before a court against whose decisions there is no judicial remedy under national law, that court is obliged to bring the matter before the Court of Justice. The object of this system of preliminary rulings, which are binding within the framework of the corresponding national proceedings, is to ensure the uniform application of Union law by and within the Member States. Therefore, although an appeal never lies from a national court to the Court of Justice, the traditional role of a Supreme

Court has been conferred upon the Court of Justice to guarantee the uniform application of the law.

My description of the judicial power would not be complete without mentioning the role of the Commission in monitoring compliance with the treaties by the Member States. Under Article 169 of the EEU Treaty, the Commission may deliver a reasoned opinion stating that a Member State failed to fulfill an obligation under the Treaty. If the State concerned does not comply with that opinion within a period designated by the Commission, the Commis sion may bring the matter before the Court of Justice. The Court may then find that the Member State has indeed failed to fulfill the obligation in question.

Under the EEU Treaty, neither the Commission nor the Court were entitled to impose sanctions on the Member States. The Maastricht Treaty has, however, amended Article 171 of the EEU Treaty. Under the new version of that article the Court "may," in the future, impose a lump sum or a penalty payment on the Member State in question. Article 88 of the ECSC Treaty, which already contained a similar power, has never been applied in practice. Since implementation of new Article 171 of the EEU Treaty also appears to be very difficult, it seems rather improbable that penalties will be imposed on the Member States.

i. The Commission: Initiator and Executive[19]

The Commission is, in many ways, akin to the prime minister of a parliamentary system, but it relies on the Council of Ministers to enact its proposals. The Commission consists of one or more representatives from each Member State who are appointed to four-year terms by mutual agreement of member governments. Commissioners, who are subject to parliamentary removal, must act in the interest of the EU and are prohibited from receiving instructions from national governments. Nearly 15,000 officials in twenty directorates-general support the Commission in its work. Over ten percent of these employees are interpreters and translators necessitated by the EU's nine official languages.

The Commission has virtually the exclusive right of legislative initiative. The Council may only create EU law, as opposed to treaty law, when it acts on proposals of the Commission. The Commission receives guidelines and authority from the Council for the implementation of specific acts that the latter has adopted. The Commission, as executive, then has the responsibility to implement them. The Commission is also responsible for guaranteeing compliance with the rules of the common market. It has the power to fine individuals and companies for breaching EU competition rules. Such rulings may be appealed. The Commission has the authority to prosecute violations of EU law. Additionally, it is the Commission that negotiates trade and agricultural agreements with third countries.

[19] Martin E. Elling, *The Emerging European Community: A Framework for Institutional and Legal Analysis*, 13 Hastings Int'l & Comp. L.R. 511 (1990). © 1990 Martin E. Elling. Reprinted by permission.

ii. The Council of Ministers: Decision Maker

The Council consists of ministers from member governments, and its presidency rotates every six months among them. The ministers' titles vary with their duties: transportation ministers decide on liberalizing EU trucking, health ministers enact policies to combat AIDS, and foreign ministers generally coordinate the politically sensitive work of their ministerial colleagues. Decisions are made using a weighted voting system "apparently based in part on population and in part on economic strength"[20] of member countries.

The Council can only act on Commission proposals and it can only alter them by unanimity. If the Council adopts a non-Commission proposal, it becomes a binding intergovernmental agreement rather than EU law. These agreements, however, enjoy almost the same enforcement by Union organs as EU law itself. Though the SEA extended qualified majority voting to new areas, unanimity is still sought to the extent practicable.

iii. The European Council: Coordinator and Facilitator

The European Council is composed of heads of state who meet with the President of the Commission. This body has met at least twice a year since 1975; before then there were only informal summits of the heads of government. The SEA sanctioned the European Council, but withheld any lawmaking powers; these are reserved to the Council of Ministers. However, the decisions of the heads of government are routinely transformed into EU law by their ministerial colleagues.

iv. The European Parliament: Directly Elected Advisor

Since 1979 the Parliament consists of MPs directly elected in member countries. Prior to 1979 Euro-MPs had been selected by and from the national parliaments. This change increased the Parliament's legitimacy, even in areas where its powers are severely limited. The Parliament currently consists of 518 members, elected for five years, who sit in party rather than national groupings.

Because the EU does not have a permanent capital, the Parliament's work is divided between three cities—plenary sessions in Strasbourg, staff headquarters in Luxembourg, and specialized committee meetings in Brussels. Notwithstanding recent efforts by the Parliament to concentrate more of its activity in Brussels, the travails of the Parliament still appear as an extended game of musical chairs.

The Parliament lacks the law-making authority of a national legislative body. Rather, it oversees the legislative processes of the Commission and Council. It must also give its opinion on Commission proposals before they are acted on by the Council. The Commission often revises its work to reflect parliamentary concerns. The SEA established a new "cooperation procedure" whereby Parliament can amend Commission and Council proposals in four areas: the internal market, improvement of work-

---

[20] Smits & Herzog, *Law of the European Economic Community—A Commentary on the E.E.C. Treaty*, Vol 4, 5-118 (1988). NEAA. KJE 4443.319575. A3865, 1976.

ing conditions, technology and research, and regional policy. In these areas, amendments may be overridden only by unanimity in the Council.

The Parliament can also dismiss the Commission by a two-thirds majority, although it has never done so. It must approve the EU budget, and through its unwillingness to do so, may influence overall spending priorities. The SEA gave Parliament the power to veto treaties with third countries, and it must also consent to the admission of new members.

v. The Court of Justice: Union Arbiter

The Court, with its seat in Luxembourg, is comprised of thirteen judges and six advocates-general. The Justices are appointed by consent of the members, but must be independent and impartial. Upon request of an EU organ, a government, or an individual citizen, the Court may nullify any measure adopted by the Commission, the Council, or a national government which is incompatible with EU law. This is a far-ranging mandate that invites the Court to be active in the development of a comprehensive body of EU laws and decisions.

When court action in a member country leads to a disputed point of EU law, a national court may apply to the Court of Justice for a ruling on the applicability of EU law. Judgments of the Court overrule those of national courts and thus create a unique supranational legal regime. On the invitation of the Commission, the Court may also give binding opinions on agreements that the EU proposes to enter with third countries.

The Court is increasingly active in the development of the EU and its legal system. For example, the Court affirmed the direct applicability of such EU treaty-imposed principles, as equal pay for men and women and the right of professionals to practice throughout the Union.

b. Institutions after Maastricht[21]

Article 4 EU gives the Court of Auditors the status of an institution; consequently, there are now five Union institutions: the Commission, the Council, the Parliament, the Court of Justice and the Court of Auditors after Maastricht. For certain purposes the European Central Bank has the same rights and obligations as an institutions, but it does not have official institutional status.

i. The Commission

The most important change regarding the Commission is that the European Parliament must approve the appointment of members of the Commission, whose term of office is extended from four years to five (beginning in 1995). New provisions have been adopted concerning the appointment of the President of the Commission, which reflect the greater importance this office has come to have. It is now provided that the governments of the member States will nominate the President after consulting the European Parliament. The nominee for President will then be consulted by the governments when they nominate the members of the Commission. Article 158(2) (third

[21] Trevor C. Hartley, *Constitutional and Institutional Aspects of the Maastricht Agreement*, 42 I.C.L.Q. 221-26 (1993). © 1993 Trevor C. Hartley. Reprinted by permission.

paragraph) provides: "The President and the other members of the Commission thus nominated shall be subject as a body to a vote of approval by the European Parliament." After approval by the European Parliament, they are appointed, as before, by common accord of the member States.

Since the European Parliament must approve the appointments *en bloc*, it cannot disapprove individual appointments. Presumably, if it objected strongly enough to a particular appointment, it could disapprove all the appointments and indicate that it would be prepared to change its mind only if the offending nominee were replaced. If the Parliament attempted such a maneuver, a trial of strength could result. It is stated in Article 159 EU that, save in the case of compulsory retirement, members of the Commission remain in office until they have been replaced. This means that if the Parliament blocked the appointment of new members of the Commission, the old members could remain in office indefinitely. Whether the member States or the Parliament gave way first would no doubt depend on the circumstances.

ii. The European Parliament

The right of the Parliament to approve appointments to the Commission, together with its power under Article 144 EEU/EU (unchanged) to secure the dismissal of the Commission by passing a motion of censure by a two-thirds majority, goes some way towards making the Commission responsible to the Parliament. However, one cannot say that it is genuinely responsible in the true democratic sense, since, when a motion of censure is passed, the existing Commission continues in office until a new Commission is appointed. This means that if the Parliament passed a motion of censure, the member States could nominate the same persons again for reappointment. If the Parliament refused to accept their appointment, they would nevertheless continue in office. In the last resort, therefore, the Parliament cannot force out the Commission if the latter retains the confidence of the member States.

Probably the most important new power given to the Parliament is that of legislating jointly with the Council. This is discussed below. In addition, the Parliament is given a right to veto legislation in certain cases (for example, measures on immigration under Article 8a(2) EU). Further new powers concern international agreements. These too are considered below.

Article 138b (second paragraph) EU gives the Parliament the right, acting by a majority of its members, to request the Commission to submit any "appropriate proposal" on matters on which it considers that a Union act is required for the purpose of implementing the Treaty. There is of course no obligation on the Commission to comply. Article 138c gives the Parliament a further power, that of setting up a Committee of Enquiry (at the request of a quarter of its members) to investigate alleged contraventions or maladministration in the implementation of Union law (except where the matter is already pending before a court). The detailed provisions covering the exercise of this right are to be determined by common accord of the Parliament, the Council and the Commission. This will presumably cover the powers of committees of enquiry (for example, whether they can force Union officials, Commissioners and ministers of national governments to give evidence).

Article 138e gives the Parliament the power to appoint an Ombudsman, an official who appears to bear a close resemblance to the British Parliamentary Commissioner for Administration. The Ombudsman can receive complaints from any citizen or resident of the Union concerning maladministration in the activities of Union institutions or bodies, with the exception of the Court of Justice and the Court of First Instance acting in their judicial roles. Where the Ombudsman establishes an instance of maladministration, he must refer the matter to the institution concerned, which has three months to inform him of its views. The Ombudsman then forwards a report to the Parliament and the institution concerned. The person lodging the complaint must be informed of the outcome. The Parliament does not, however, have power to provide redress in the event that the complaint is upheld. Perhaps it is hoped that the institution or body concerned will do this.

Article 138e(4) provides that the Parliament may, after seeking an opinion from the Commission and with the approval of the Council acting by a qualified majority, lay down regulations and general conditions governing the performance of the Ombudsman's duties.

iii. Legislative Powers

The most important development in this field is that legislative powers have now been given to the Parliament and Council acting jointly. As a result, there are now three institutions which can adopt regulations, directives or decisions: the Parliament and Council acting jointly, the Council acting alone and the Commission acting alone.

The procedure for joint Parliament-Council legislation is laid down in Article 189b EU. The first step is for the Commission to submit a proposal to the Parliament and the Council. Then the Council, acting by a qualified majority after obtaining the opinion of the Parliament, adopts a common position. It informs the Parliament fully of the reasons which led it to adopt the common position. The Commission also informs the Parliament of its position. The Parliament then has three months in which to act. If it approves the common position, the Council adopts the act in accordance with the common position. If, on the other hand, the Parliament indicates, by an absolute majority of its members, that it intends to reject the common position, it informs the Council. The latter may then convene a meeting of the Conciliation Committee (see below). If this produces no result and the Parliament confirms, by an absolute majority of its members, its rejection of the common position, the proposed act is deemed not to have been adopted.

The Parliament can also propose amendments to the common position. These must be adopted by an absolute majority of members. The amended text is forwarded to the Council and Commission, and the latter delivers an opinion on the amendments. The Council then has three months to act. If, acting by a qualified majority, it approves the amendments, it amends its common position and adopts the act with the amendments. However, if the Commission gave a negative opinion on the amendments, the Council can adopt them only if it is unanimous. If, on the other hand, the Council does not approve the act as amended, a meeting of the Conciliation Committee will be convened by the President of the Council in agreement with the President of the Parliament.

The Conciliation Committee has an equal number of members from the Council and the Parliament. On the Council's side, it may consist of all the members of the Council or their representatives. The two sides of the Committee vote separately and it cannot take a decision unless both sides agree. Consequently, there must be both a qualified majority of the representatives of the Council on the one side and a majority of the representatives of the Parliament on the other. The Commission takes part in the proceedings and attempts to reconcile the positions of the two sides. The Conciliation Committee has six weeks to act. If it approves a joint text, the Parliament, acting by a majority of votes, and the Council, acting by a qualified majority, have a further six weeks in which to adopt the act in accordance with the joint text. If one of the two institutions fails to adopt it, the act is deemed not to have been adopted.

If the Conciliation Committee fails to agree on a joint text, the position is as follows. If the Council takes no action within a further period of six weeks beginning at the end of the period of six weeks given to the Conciliation Committee, the act is deemed not to have been adopted. If, on the other hand, the Council confirms its original common position (that adopted before the conciliation procedure was put into operation) either as it stands or with some of the amendments proposed by the Parliament, the act is deemed to have been adopted unless it its rejected by the Parliament, acting by a majority of members, within six weeks of its adoption by the Council. In exercising its powers, the Council must act by a qualified majority.

It is interesting to analyze the voting majorities needed under the joint legislative procedure. The Council always votes by a qualified majority (except where it wishes to approve an amendment to which the Commission objects). The Parliament normally acts by an absolute majority of its members, but this does not apply where it approves the common position of the Council: in such a case no specified majority is mentioned, which means that it acts by an absolute majority of votes cast. Moreover, no more than an absolute majority of votes is required for approving a joint text agreed by a Conciliation Committee. In other words, a majority of members is required where the Parliament wishes to block the Council's proposals, but a majority of votes is sufficient if it approves the Council proposals.

The joint procedure is reminiscent of the co-operation procedure under the Single European Act and, like it, it applies only where a particular provision of the Treaty so provides. There is, however, provision in Article 189b EU for its application to be extended on the basis of a report to be submitted to the Council by the Commission by 1996. The co-operation procedure laid down in the Single European Act continues to apply where the Treaty so provides.

It is instructive to compare the new procedure with the co-operation procedures. The two procedures have much in common, but one significant difference is that under the joint procedure the Parliament can definitively reject any Council proposal provided it acts by an absolute majority of its members. Under the co-operation procedure, on the other hand, the Council can override a parliamentary rejection if it acts unanimously. It is by virtue of this feature that the joint procedure constitutes a genuine power of co-decision.

Where the Parliament proposes amendments, the position is more complex. Let us assume that the Council wishes to accept the Parliament's amendments. Although the text of Article 149(2) EEU is not as clear as one might have wished, it seems that under the co-operation procedure the Council votes by a qualified majority only if the amendments are positively accepted by the Commission; otherwise, it must act unanimously. In the case of the joint procedure, on the other hand, the position seems to be reversed: the Council can act by a qualified majority unless the Commission positively rejects the amendment. This is a diminution in the powers of the Commission, but it is unlikely to be of practical importance since one assumes that the Commission will always express its opinion.

If the Council wishes to reject the whole measure at this point, the position is similar under the two systems. Under the co-operation procedure, if the Council does nothing for three months, the measure automatically falls. Under the joint procedure, the matter goes to the Conciliation Committee, but assuming no agreement is reached in that Committee, the measure will fall if the Council takes no action within six weeks.

If the Council wishes to reject the Parliament's amendments, it is in a stronger position under the co-operation procedure than under the joint procedure. Under the former, it acts by a qualified majority if it has the support of the Commission; otherwise, it acts unanimously. In either case, it can either confirm its original position or adopt new amendments of its own. This cannot be challenged by the Parliament. Under the joint procedure, on the other hand, though the Council acts by only a qualified majority, it is limited to confirming its original common position (possibly with some of the Parliament's amendments), and this can be vetoed by the Parliament if it acts by an absolute majority of members within six weeks. In other words, if the Parliament can muster an absolute majority of its members, it can prevent the Council from overriding its wishes. This is an important difference.

It is a truism that the Union is not really democratic. Rectifying this, however, is not easy. There are two difficulties, one well known and the other less so. The well-known difficulty is that any increase in the powers of the European Parliament must entail a diminution in the powers of the member States, something which many national governments are unwilling to countenance. The less well-known problem is that any increase in the powers of the Parliament must probably also entail a diminution in the powers of the Commission.

How have the Commission's powers fared under the new procedure? As a general principle, the foundation of the Commission's legislative power is its right to make proposals. It retains this right under the new procedure. However, the right to make proposals is of little value if those proposals can be easily amended. Consequently, the Commission gains considerable bargaining power from the rule that the Council must be unanimous in order to amend the Commission's proposals. It is true that the Council can refuse to adopt a measure unless the Commission agrees to amend it, but if the Commission is determined, it may well be able to force the Council to accept a compromise.

Under the co-operation procedure, the Commission's prerogatives are fully respected: amendments proposed by the Parliament which are not accepted by the Commission can be adopted by the Council only if it is unanimous. Prior to the appointment of a Conciliation Committee, the same it true under the joint legislative procedure. Once a Conciliation Committee has been appointed, however, the position is different: a text agreed by the Conciliation Committee can be adopted by the Council by a qualified majority even if the Commission objects. Once the conciliation procedure comes into operation, therefore, it is possible for the Commission's proposal to be amended by a qualified majority in the Council even in the Commission objects. This is a significant weakening of the Commission's power: the Commission's loss is the Parliament's gain.

A Conciliation Committee is set up whenever the Council does not approve the Parliament's amendments within three months. Consequently, if the Council wishes to approve an amendment of the Parliament which the Commission rejects, but cannot muster a unanimous vote, it merely has to wait for three months and set up a Conciliation Committee, which can adopt the amendment by a qualified majority as far as the Council is concerned. The amendment can then be approved by the Council, acting by a qualified majority. In other words, the only effect of a Commission veto is to delay adoption of the measure. The result is that, while the Council still cannot itself amend the Commission's proposals unless it is unanimous, it can adopt the Parliament's amendments by a qualified majority even if the Commission objects. This is one of the most important differences between the joint procedure and the co-operation procedure: under the latter, the Parliament's power to amend—surely more important in practice than its power to reject—was really no greater then under the procedure existing prior to the Single European Act.

c. *Beyond Maastricht*[22]

i. Origins and Goals of the White Paper

Support for the White Paper emerged across Europe for three principal reasons: changes in the international political economy made action appear imperative; a permissive domestic political climate was in evidence in leading EU countries; and instability in East-West relations gave European leaders renewed cause to cooperate in economic as well as political matters. The Commission and the Council, however, have brought into their deliberations a myriad of ancillary initiatives designed to integrate members more broadly.

By 1985 the "go-it-alone" strategies adopted in Europe to cope with both the oil price shocks and increased competition from Japan and the NICs, had been largely discredited. In 1987 EU unemployment averaged 10.6 percent, and between 1980 and 1987 consumer prices in the Union jumped 68.4 percent, and between 1982 and 1987 annual growth in Union GDP averaged only 2.3 percent. These figures compared with 6.1 percent and 41 percent, and 4.3 percent, respectively, for the United States. Europeans were quick to ascribe the disparity in economic progress to American efforts at deregulation.

These economic imperatives, coupled with a new political climate in principal EU countries, provided fertile ground in which to resow the seeds of integration. Historically, the United Kingdom has been more skeptical of integration than the other Mem-

22 Martin E. Elling, *The Emerging European Community: A Framework for Institutional and Legal Analysis,* 13 Hastings Int'l & Comp. L.R. 511 (1990).

ber States. Nevertheless, Prime Minister Thatcher sought to prevent the United Kingdom from becoming an "outcast at the outskirts" of Europe. The goals of 1992, in their narrowest sense essentially an experiment in market deregulation, fit nicely with the British Conservative Party's economic goals. French President Mitterand, after failed attempts at socialist reflation in 1981 and 1982, was more than ready to embark on cooperative economic management. Renewed integration, he hoped, would offer France a greater leadership role in Europe. West German Chancellor Kohl, who came to power on promises of market liberalization, was also anxious to embrace European proposals parallel to his own. Kohl, like Mitterand, desired the increased clout a more unified Europe might bring Germany.

The heightened Cold War rhetoric of the early 1980s, and the perception by many West Europeans that Europe was akin to a pawn in a complex geostrategic game between reckless superpowers, did much to strengthen their conviction that they must assert greater influence over events on their own continent. The 1986 Reykjavik Summit, in which the Soviet Union and United States seemed close to agreement on issues vital to Europe, only underscored the need for Europe to speak with one voice.

ii. Obstacles to, and Forces in Favor of, the Internal Market

Observers hailed the White Paper as a masterful effort to move the EU toward a united market that embraced 320 million consumers. By focusing on practical ends rather than political means, the White Paper left undone the task of defining the most politically acceptable ways of achieving these goals. It also gave European politicians a finite checklist of concrete goals for which to aim.

Both the "Euro-euphoria" currently in evidence in Europe and the isolated nationalist backlash obfuscate the extent to which there has already been achievement, and the obstacles that lie ahead. Already great progress has been charted. By June 1989 the Commission, Council, and Parliament had fully passed 134 of the 279 necessary measures toward 1992. An additional ninety-seven proposals were awaiting final approval of Parliament. This means that the EU organs have roughly three years in which to enact the remaining half of the necessary measures. While many of these directives have direct effect, others must be translated into law by the national legislative bodies. This latter process has been exceedingly slow in some member countries, but the Court can partially remedy such failings by ruling against Member States who fail to have laws on the books by January 1, 1993. The Council has not acted solely on the politically expedient proposals, leaving to the end those likely to halt or reverse integration. For example, while it has not yet finally acted on the harmonization of the national value added taxes (VATs), a necessary prerequisite to dismantling border checks and one of the most contentious issues, it has already adopted directives that will eliminate all impediments to capital flows within the EU. The latter had been viewed by experts as one of the most vital yet difficult issues to tackle.

The obstacles to full and timely achievement of the goals of the White Paper are still formidable. Important groups oppose integration. Among these are medium-sized industries which have been sheltered by nontariff barriers, some trade unions in wealthier member countries that fear the loss of jobs to poorer regions, and a variety of nationalist elements in various Member States.

According to prevailing European view, eliminating internal border checks will require the harmonization of immigration and asylum policies, a uniform gun control law, harmonization of VAT rates, and copious other harmonizations (far more, in fact, than exist between the American states). For example, for border checks to fall Denmark would have to cancel its longstanding passport union with non-EU Nordic countries. Radical and violent groups such as the Irish Republican Army, Basque separatists, and the Red Army Faction also give EU members pause about eliminating all internal border inspections. In an effort to prepare for the elimination of border checks, the Benelux countries, France, and West Germany agreed on October 30, 1989, to allow their police to pursue and arrest criminals across their common borders.

While the obstacles remain formidable, there exists a broad coalition of powerful elements that favor the White Paper goals. The coalition is comprised of highly competitive major industries, some trade unions, most financial service institutions, economists, free-market politicians, and pro-European intellectuals. Business is pushing both the Council and Commission hard to maintain their prescribed deadline.

Moreover, EU members have used education campaigns to strengthen support for 1992. They hope these will provide momentum to the White Paper project. With few exceptions, the governments that staked their political futures on economic integration have just faced or will face reelection between now and 1992. Barring a major economic downturn, they will find it difficult to renege on their promises of a more united and prosperous Europe.

The directives liberalizing capital flows in the EU may help support efforts at closer union. Once these directives are fully in effect, European banks will be far less regulated than their United States counterparts and thus, will enjoy unrestricted access to 320 million potential clients. This development could release economic forces that will pull the Twelve closer together by compelling harmonization of economic policies and perhaps requiring a European central bank.

Finally, there are concrete economic reasons for believing the push toward economic and political union will continue. Economic competition from Japan and the NICs will likely persist. One very respected report recently highlighted the economic gains attendant the completion of the internal market; 1992 will likely boost EU GDP by at least five percent, reduce prices by six percent, and create two million jobs. The savings could total 170 to 250 billion ECUs for the twelve member states at 1988 prices. With business leaders taking these predictions as fact there is great pressure on politicians to deliver on their promises.

Setbacks will accompany progress, but business interests and European-minded politicians now represent the driving force behind the EU. The most likely obstacle to rapid progress may be the nationalist backlash that could materialize in some countries, or the instability generated by the decay of Soviet hegemony in Easter Europe. The recent progress of the far right in some state and local elections in West Germany, most notably the Republicans, is a troubling example of potential obstacles to integration. As the European "noose" gets tighter, politicians may be tempted to go it alone and reassert their national sovereignty.

iii. Beyond 1992: The Dynamics of Self-Sustained Integration

EU leaders have begun laying the groundwork for self-sustained integration after 1992. They have initiated a range of programs to develop a "People's Europe" in which the benefits of increased union are tangible to all citizens. Efforts to develop an EU identity and to increase cross-border contacts are central to this plan.

iv. Nurturing a European Identity

At the symbolic level, the EU adopted a Union flag (twelve gold stars in a circle on a blue background), an anthem (the Ode to Joy from Beethoven's Ninth Symphony), and replaced national passports with standardized EU passports. Looking to the successor generations, school textbooks are being rewritten to put more emphasis on the EU and to highlight the commonalities among the member cultures. A single European communications market is being established in which all broadcasters will be guaranteed equal access to national markets. As France's European Affairs Minister recently asked, "What would remain of our cultural identity if audiovisual Europe consisted of European consumers sitting in front of Japanese television sets showing American programs?" The elimination of border checks is the cornerstone of the "People's Europe," but this achievement may have to wait until sometime in the future.

v. Bringing Europeans Together

The Commission and Council assume that as contacts between citizens increase, so too will pressure on members to break down barriers to free cultural and social exchange. Education exchanges have been initiated to bring future elites together. The Comett program (Programme of the Union in Education and Training for Technology) initiated in 1987, fosters cooperation between universities and industry at the European level. In its first year it financed 108 university-industry training partnerships and 1,067 transnational placements of students in industry. The Erasmus program (European Union Action Scheme for the Mobility of University Students) encourages and assists students to complete a portion of their studies in another EU country.

The Union has also adopted directives that will make a variety of professional diplomas universally accepted in the EU. These measures, along with recent extensions of the right of professionals to live and practice anywhere in the EU, will greatly increase the mobility of citizens. Additionally, since 1981 in Ireland and Denmark, and since 1983 in the Netherlands, all EU citizens have had the right to vote in local elections. The Council currently has a measure before it that would enact such a provision EU-wide. The development of voting rights for EU residents living outside their country of origin would greatly change the political dynamics of European integration.

In recent years, other forms of intra-EU contact have blossomed. In 1985 for instance, almost two-thirds of all holidays taken by EU residents outside their own country were taken in other EU states. In the long run such widespread contacts will foster European identity. Perhaps of more immediate significance, however, is the surge in intra-EU corporate mergers. In 1984 before the adoption of the White Paper, there were only about sixty cross-border corporate mergers. That figure rose to roughly 160 such mergers in 1987. Such developments spurred labor unions, consumer groups, and other lobbyists to form EU-wide umbrella organizations to lobby in Brussels. This variety of transnational contacts will Europeanize political actors in the Union and their political programs.

vi. Today and Tomorrow[23]

The EC of today may be characterized as a customs union, with additions reminiscent of a common market and an array of cooperative activities that facilitate intercourse and strengthen the bonds among the Member States. The EU exists, however, as a more dynamic and far-reaching institution than this portrayal would admit.

The CAP, established in 1962, stands as the EU's most prominent and problematic accomplishment. The CAP was designed to avoid massive dislocation of farmers in the emerging common agricultural market. It ensures uniform prices throughout the EU on most agricultural goods and guarantees farm workers a standard of living comparable to that of workers in other economic sectors. This has led to a system of preferences for EU produced agricultural goods. At times "wine lakes" and "butter mountains" have vexed the EU because of CAP-sheltered over-production. In 1987, for instance, CAP expenditures totaled 65.9 percent of the EU budget.

On November 1, 1993, the Treaty on European Union, which was signed in Maastricht on February 7, 1992,[24] went into effect following ratification by Germany. This ratification took place after the German Federal Constitutional Court handed down a decision on October 12, 1993, which dismissed several objections directed against the federal law.

The Maastricht Treaty is part of the European Union's Constitution. There is no single document embodying a classic constitution in the European Unions. There is, however, a series of treaties by the Member States that comprise the constitution of a single state. This series consists of the three treaties that establish the three communities and several amendments. Examples of these amendments include provisions concerning the accession of new Member States to the European Union, provisions reinforcing the internal cohesion of the Union, the Single European Act of 1986 and, of course, the Maastricht Treaty.

The constitutional character of the treaties is demonstrated by their rank in the hierarchy of Union law. An EU regulation, a rule of law which is generally and directly applicable in all Member States, may be declared invalid by the Court of Justice if it is deemed inconsistent with the treaty upon which it is based. This procedure results in the parallel phenomenon of unconstitutional laws in a State governed by a single written constitution.

Amending the treaties can only be accomplished if all Member States ratify the provision in conformity with their respective constitutional requirements. Typically, the constitutional rules of each country will allow amendments only in conformity with special and complicated procedures.

The treaties, however, are not the only source of constitutional law in the Unions. In a long line of decisions, the Court of Justice has developed general principles which

---

[23] Supra note 11, 515-16.

[24] Treaty on European Union [Maastricht Treaty].

are common to the laws of the Member States and which today form part of the Constitution. An example is the principle of proportionality; this principle provides that EU measures are not to go beyond what is necessary to achieve the objectives of the Treaty. Another example is the Court of Justice's use of these general principles to guarantee fundamental rights within the Union, as the treaties do not contain a full catalogue of fundamental rights and freedoms. The European Convention for the Protection of Human Rights and Fundamental Freedoms concluded within the framework of the Council of Europe (which is an international organization not to be confused with the EU) has been used for the purpose of finding those general principles. Article F(2) of the Maastricht Treaty now provides an express basis for the protection of fundamental rights "as guaranteed by the European Convention for the Protection of Human Rights and Fundamental Freedoms signed in Rome on November 4, 1950 and as they result from the constitutional traditions common to the Member States, as general principles of Union law." For the time being, Article F(2) may resolve the problem of the absent catalogue of fundamental rights.

d. The Cooperation of the Member States[25]

From the outset, the EEU Treaty did not confine itself to dealing with the institutions and competences of that Union. Under Article 220, the Member States are to enter into negotiations with each other with a view to securing:

- the protection of persons and the enjoyment and protection of rights under the same conditions as those accorded by each State to its own nationals;
- the abolition of double taxation within the Union;
- the mutual recognition of companies . . . [and the] possibility of mergers . . .;
- the simplification of formalities governing the reciprocal recognition and enforcement of judgments of courts or tribunals and of arbitration awards.

The Treaty thus permitted the Member States to conclude international conventions concerning matters which clearly related to the process of economic integration and which could have been regarded as reserved exclusively to the Union.

One such example is the 1968 Brussels Convention on Jurisdiction and the Enforcement of Judgments in Civil and Commercial Matters. This convention is not a part of Union law, as is demonstrated by the separate accessions of new Member States to the Convention. A separate protocol, however, gives the Court of Justice some powers of interpretation similar to those vested in it by Article 177 of the EEU Treaty. However, this does not mean that jurisdiction is "automatically" conferred.

Furthermore, Article 224 of the EEU Treaty allows a Member State to adopt the necessary measures in the event of substantial internal disturbances, of serious international tension or in the event of war. Even though Article 224 provides for a procedure of consultation between the Member States and Article 225 provides for judicial control by the Court of Justice, it may be inferred from these articles that the Member States retain the essence of sovereignty.

---

[25] Heinrich Kirschner, *The Framework of the European Union under the Treaty of Maastricht*, 13 J.L. & Comm. 235 (1994).

The Single European Act underlined the importance of the cooperation of the Member States. The Act contained a provision concerning rules on mutual information and consultation in the sphere of foreign policy known as "Title III." The Member States thereby undertook, under Article 30 of the Act, to consult each other, to develop common objectives, to determine common positions, to refrain from impeding the formation of a consensus and to refrain from impeding the joint action which this could produce. Furthermore, they envisaged a closer cooperation on questions of European security. All this was regulated outside the scope of the three existing Treaties.

The Member States did not therefore transfer the field of foreign policy to the Union by the Single European Act. However, they had to admit that as a result of the economic responsibilities of the Union, a certain external policy of the Union had already been developed. One example was in the field of economic sanctions. The Single European Act had to provide that this common external policy of the Union should be consistent with the policies agreed to in European Political Cooperation. For the rest, however, the Member States did not accept any federal element, and of course no provision was made for majority voting. The Commission was made responsible for ensuring, within its own sphere of competence, that the consistency mentioned above was sought and maintained. Further, the Parliament was to be kept regularly informed. As for the Court of Justice, Article 31 of the Single European Act precluded the application of Title III to the provisions of the founding treaties concerning the powers of the Court of Justice. Foreign policy thus remained the responsibility of the Member States because it would be difficult to implement a common policy concerning issues such as conflicts in Eastern Europe or the Middle East.

The Maastricht Treaty did not change the picture. Article A of the Treaty establishes a European Union. The wording of this article gives the misleading impression that a new legal entity, a Union, is established but the Maastricht Treaty does not do so. According to Article A, the Union is founded on the three existing communities which remain legal entities in their own right and continue to fulfill their different responsibilities. They can therefore be considered as the first pillar of the Union, the other two pillars being situated in the field of cooperation carried out by the Member States.

One Union institution, the European Council, consists of the Heads of States or Government of the Member States and of the President of the Commission. The European Council provides the Union with an impetus for developing and defining its "general political guidelines." The European Council must therefore not be confused with the Council of Ministers as a legislative institution in the three Unions. This is demonstrated by Article 103(2) of the EEU Treaty which obliges the Council to adopt recommendations on economic policies on the basis of guidelines of the European Council (prepared, of course, by the Council itself).

The second pillar of the Union pertains to the cooperation of the Member States in the field of a common foreign and security policy. Title V of the Maastricht Treaty builds on the ideas of the Single European Act by regulating the procedures for a common foreign and security policy to be discussed within the European Council and the Council. The Commission is associated with the work carried out in that field. The European Parliament is consulted and informed, and it may then question the Council and make recommendations to it. However, no jurisdiction is transferred to the

Court of Justice. Article 228a of the EEU Treaty is designed to guarantee consistency between the common positions or joint actions adopted in the field of the common foreign or security policy and the measures of the EU concerning economic relations with third countries.

In the fields of justice and domestic affairs, the provisions are more complex. Article 100c of the EEU Treaty controls decisions of the Council on visa obligations for nationals of third countries after consulting the European Parliament. For other issues, Title VI of the Maastricht Treaty contains new rules for cooperation comparable to those already discussed in the context of Article 220 of the EEU Treaty. Under Title VI, the third pillar of the Union, the Member States are to inform and consult one another via the Council in areas such as:

- asylum policy,
- immigration policy,
- combating drug addiction and international fraud,
- judicial cooperation in civil and in criminal matters,
- customs cooperation,
- police cooperation.

The legal instruments envisaged are, without prejudice to Article 220 of the EEU Treaty, conventions of the Member States rather than regulations of the Union. The conventions may stipulate that the Court of Justice is to have jurisdiction to interpret their provisions and to rule on disputes regarding their application. This is optional, not obligatory. For the rest, the Court of Justice is, again, not given jurisdiction with respect to the cooperation of the Member States as laid down in Title VI. The Commission is associated with the work in the areas in question to the extent that the European Parliament is to be informed and consulted and it may ask questions or make recommendations. Under the Maastricht Treaty, therefore, the matters falling under Title VI are to be dealt with by political cooperation between the Member States, not by Union legislation adopted by the Parliament and the Council. If these issues are to be transferred into the field of true Union legislation, Article K(9) of the Maastricht Treaty consequently requires an amendment to the Treaty.

e. The Legal Nature of the Union

The first pillar of the Union demonstrates that the Union is neither an international organization, such as the United Nations and the Members of the so-called UN family, nor a confederation. In several important sectors the Member States have transferred their competences to the three communities; these communities act as supranational entities comparable to a federal state. They have the power to adopt regulations which have general application and are directly applicable in all Member States. The most important institution, the Council, often acts by a qualified majority of its members like a true federal institution. The machinery of justice in the Unions is akin to a national legal system, like that of the United Kingdom or Ireland, rather than to the International Court of Justice in the Hague.

On the other hand, the two remaining pillars of the Union prove that the Union is not a federal state. Notwithstanding the prefederal elements just mentioned, too many matters remain within the fields of political cooperation between the Member States that are only linked to the Union. Foreign policy, security matters and a considerable part of the internal policy are withheld from the Union.

Because the Union is not considered an international organization, a confederation or a federal state, the question of its legal nature is still undecided. A plausible answer has been given by the German Federal Constitutional Court in its judgment of October 12, 1993, which stated that "the Treaty establishes an association of States for creating an ever-closer union among the peoples organized into states of Europe, not a state based upon a single European nation."

The Member States have decided to create the Union by continuing to use the traditional federal approach within the Unions, while opting for intergovernmental cooperation outside of Union spheres. Both components are covered by the notion of an "association of states." Only the future will show whether they will coexist or one will prevail over the other.

f. Prospects[26]

The European Union is not just a common market but rather a nascent political union. Unless the underlying conditions in the global marketplace fundamentally change, Europeans will continue to see the need to act jointly in the economic and, to an increasing degree, the political spheres; the EU will remain at the heart of the varied pan-European initiatives that are likely to proliferate in the years ahead.

Observers believe the prospects for the EU are promising. The White Paper program is already opening up the European marketplace and contributing to the development of a European identity. Strong support for the EU exists among the peoples of Europe. In 1988 sixty-nine percent of EU residents polled said that the EU was a good thing. Support was highest in Italy (eighty-five percent) and lowest in Great Britain and Denmark (fifty percent). The winds of change and renewal which have swept the countries of Eastern Europe in the past year have given statesmen in the West pause to consider the effects these changes may ultimately have on European integration. Soviet leader Gorbachev has repeatedly proposed the eventual formation of "One European House" under whose roof the European countries of East and West would live in some kind of peaceful cooperation. While it is clear that newly unleashed market forces may ultimately lead to a number of new applications for admission to the EU, it is the German Question which is most troubling to European observers.

The opening of the Berlin Wall may have the greatest long-term impact on European integration. The delicate balance of power nurtured over the years within the EU may become distorted, and may in turn seriously strain the working relationship between Bonn and Paris. German reunification may either tend to split the countries of Western Europe apart or propel them together at an increased rate.

In the immediate future, the West German bureaucracy will be distracted by the myriad tasks attendant to monetary and political union with the territory of East Germany. For the foreseeable future its financial resources will be significantly diverted

---

26 Martin E. Elling, *The Emerging European Community: A Framework for Institutional and Legal Analysis*, 13 Hastings Int'l & Comp. L.R. 511 (1990). © 1990 Martin E. Elling. Reprinted by permission.

to the reconstruction of the eastern half of a united Germany. In fact, if EU development funds flow to the underdeveloped regions of a united Germany, Germany may for the first time become a net financial recipient within the Union.

In the interim period before reunification, East Germany will continue to enjoy virtual membership in the EU's customs union. Pursuant to a protocol note to the Rome Treaties, under EU law goods produced in East Germany must be allowed the same free circulation in the Union as goods produced in West Germany. In the unlikely event that reunification were a protracted matter, West German firms would now relocate to East Germany, in order to circumvent the minimum wage and social benefits which may be enacted under the European Social Charter. Such an occurrence would seriously undermine the quid pro quo which enticed Southern European countries like Greece, Portugal, and Spain to join the Union.

On the other hand it is very likely that fears of "West German drift" will finally give countries like Denmark and Great Britain the needed impetus to become champions of fuller union. The EU itself grew in part our of a realization that European peace and prosperity were predicated on reconciliation with Germany. West German business itself appears to fear a possible pull by the East and is determined to keep Bonn on target with European integration.

Progress in European integration can be halted but the dynamics of the process, especially after the White Paper, will make it very difficult to reverse. This will especially remain the case if the European Union continues to face increased competition in world markets, and if a modicum of stability is maintained on both sides of the European divide in years ahead.

i. Another (Critical View) of the European Union: The fiction of a single institutional framework[27]

The Union does not possess legal personality or standing as such under international law. For external purposes, in particular with regard to the conclusion of Treaties, it must fall back on action by the Union under Article 228 EU or agreements by the 12 Member States. In addition the Council and the Commission are conferred with responsibility for ensuring the consistency of the Union's activities as a whole in the context of *inter alia* the Union's external relations (Article C). For internal purposes the Union "borrows" the institutions and organs of the Unions even in an extra-Union context. There is no separate budget for the extra-Union tasks of the Union, the administrative expenditure being simply charged to the budget of the European Unions.

The putative claim of Article C that the Union shall be served "by a single institutional framework" can, in the light of the substantive provisions of the Treaty, be described, not too unkindly, as mere lip-service to an ideal. It is single only in the sense that the intergovernmental pillars do not have institutions of their own. The only truly Union institution is the European Council. Apart from that some of the EU institutions (Council, Commission, Parliament but, explicitly, not the Court of Justice) have been generously put at the disposal of the Union but in a manner different to their classic

[27] Deirdre Curtin, *The Constitutional Structure of the Union: A Europe of Bits and Pieces,* 30 C.M.L.R. 27-69 (1993).

Treaty functions. This has rightly been described as more "an institutional 'géometrie variable' than a single framework."

The Union as established in the Maastricht Treaty reveals a highly convoluted structure. It does not, as might have been expected, simply take the place of the existing Communities or elevate the latter into the "Union." Nevertheless, to a certain extent the focal point can be said to be the existing three Communities (not merged into one) and the *acquis communautaire* enshrouding them. The three existing communities continue to exist as separate legal persons and embrace themselves a variety of institutional schemes. Some distance away and standing alone and apart (except for a scattering of "passerelles" or one-way bridges) from the three "Community" supports are two distinct "pillars," one on foreign policy and security policy (hereafter: CJHA). The main stuctural attachment which these two pillars have with with the Community structure as such by means of a loose, tarpaulin-like structure (under the heading of an undefined "European Union") suspended artificially and tenuously above both loose pillars and the Community as such. The CFSP pillar already existed and was expanded upon. Significant in this respect is the reliance placed on the Western European Union (WEU) which is categorized as "an integral part of the development of the Union" and which is empowered to elaborate and implement decisions and actions of the Union which have defence implications—despite the fact tht two Member States do not belong to the WEU. The new crutch added to support some of the weight of the tarpaulin is the pillar of CJHA, a hybrid non-vertical pillar which materially intersects with the existing Community EC competences in some important respects.

The CFSP and CJHA pillars largely use the Council as an instrument of intergovernmental cooperation and pass over in silence the role of the Commission (as initiator) and the European Parliament. Provision is made, for example, for the Commission to be "fully associated" (whatever that might mean it does not necessarily embrace its classic Treaty functions) with the intergovernmental tasks in CFSP and CJHA but the Commission's monitoring tasks (Articles 155 and 169 EEU) were explicitly omitted. In any event, the Commission will have to share its (reduced) influence with the "Coordinating Committee" consisting of senior national officials which can also bring matters to the attention of the Council at its own initiative. The European Parliament is "regularly informed" and may "ask questions of the Council or make recommendations to it" and hold a debate on progress made. The general jurisdiction of the Court of Justice is specifically excluded not only with regard to CFSP and CJHA but also with regard to Title I (the "common provisions"). With regard to CJHA, the only possibility is that conventions (on matters relating to asylum, immigration policy and policy regarding nationals of third countries, combating drug addiction or fraud) adopted on the basis of Article 220 EU may stipulate express jurisdiction for the Curt of Justice to interpret their provisions and to rule on any disputes as to their application.

The lie is further given to the aim of "a single institutional framework" when one considers the institutional arrangements pursuant to the Social Policy Agreement (concluded between 11 Member States only). Whatever conclusion is ultimately drawn as to its legal characterization as an annex to the EU Treaty (via a Protocol adopted by the 12 Member States), Union or intergovernmental, it remains an acutely anomalous construction. It contains provisions relating to the Union institutions as such, involving them in the elaboration of the "acts and divisions" of the "group of 11" taken pursuant to the Agreement. Article 3 of the Agreement, for example, confers the Commission with new duties over a variety of fields, especially in the context of the enhanced role assigned to labor and management. This means that the Commission has henceforth a bicephalous (the opposite of single!) existence—and responsibility—with regard to two overlapping sets of provisions.

Finally, it must be noted in the context of an avowed "single" institutional framework, the Council has a distinctly chameleon character with regard to its role in the European Union. In the context of economic and monetary policy, provision is made that the Council of the European Union meets "in the composition of Head of State or Government" and that the "Council" thus constituted takes decisions. This is certainly novel. It follows that some inter-governmental contamination of the Union "pillar" has taken place. One is left with the distinct overall impression that in the mind of the inter-governmental drafters it is permissible to envisage different decision-making procedures and functions for institutions depending on the subject matter under consideration, EMU, social policy, free movement of persons etc. Such fragmentation does nothing to help the overall coherence or transparency of the Union institutional system nor indeed to further the claim of a "single" institutional framework.

ii. Maastricht and Beyond: Introduction[28]

The exact fate of the Maastricht Agreement is not yet clear. For this reason, an examination of its provisions seems worthwhile in order to ascertain their consequences for the Union and the member States. The purpose of this article is to conduct such an examination with regard to the provisions of the Agreement which have major constitutional implications (for either the Union or the member States) or which significantly affect the existing institutions of the Union.

The Conference held in Maastricht in December 1991 resulted in a new treaty, signed in Maastricht on 7 February 1992, called the Treaty on European Union ("TEU"). A large part of this Treaty is taken up with amending the EEU Treaty, though other parts stand in their own right. The EEU Treaty will henceforth be known as the Treaty Establishing the European Union ("EU"), and the EEU is renamed the "European Union."

As its name implies, the Treaty on European Union is intended to establish the European Union, and it is stated to mark a new stage in the creation of "an ever closer Union among the peoples of Europe." The Union is to be founded on the European Unions, as supplemented by the policies and forms of co-operation established by the Treaty on European Union. The new developments brought about in the Treaty on European Union include further extensions of Union competence in the fields of external relations, security and defense (though these are still separated from normal Union activities) as well as certain institutional changes. The most important development, the establishment of a common currency, will not apply to the United Kingdom unless the British government and Parliament so decide.

[28] Trevor C. Hartley, *Constitutional and Institutional Aspects of the Maastricht Agreement*, 42 Int'l & Comp. L.Q. 213 (1993). © 1993 Trevor C. Hartley. Reprinted by permission.

II. General Principles of Law

A. The Foundational Period: The "Constitutionalization" of the Union Legal Structure[29]

Starting in 1963 and continuing into the early 1970's and beyond, the European Court of Justice in a series of landmark decisions established four doctrines that fixed the relationship between Union law and Member State law and rendered that relationship indistinguishable from analogous legal relationships in constitutional federal states.

1. The Doctrine of Direct Effect

The judicial doctrine of direct effect, introduced in 1963 and developed subsequently, provides the following presumption: Union legal norms that are clear, precise, and self-sufficient (not requiring further legislative measures by the authorities of the Union or the Member States) must be regarded as the law of the land in the sphere of application of Union law. Direct effect (a rule of construction in result) applies to all actions producing legal effects in the Union: the Treaty itself and secondary legislation. Moreover, with the exception of one type of Union legislation, direct effect operates not only in creating enforceable legal obligations between the Member States and individuals, but also among individuals inter se. Critically, being part of the law of the land means that Union norms may be invoked by individuals before their state courts, which must provide adequate legal remedies for the E.C. norms just as if they were enacted by the state legislature.

The implications of this doctrine were and are far reaching. The European Court reversed the normal presumption of public international law whereby international legal obligations are result-oriented and addressed to states. Public international law typically allows the internal constitutional order of a state to determine the method and extent to which international obligations may, if at all, produce effects for individuals within the legal order of the state. Under the normal canons of international law, even when the international obligation itself, such as a trade agreement or a human rights convention, is intended to bestow rights (or duties) on individuals within a state, if the state fails to bestow the rights, the individual cannot invoke the international obligation before national courts, unless internal constitutional or statutory law, to which public international law is indifferent, provides for such a remedy. The typical remedy under public international law in such a case would be an inter-state claim. The main import of the Union doctrine of direct effect was not simply the conceptual change it ushered forth. In practice direct effect meant that Member States violating their Union obligations could not shift the locus of dispute to the interstate or Union plane. They would be faced with legal actions before their own courts at the suit of individuals within their own legal order.

---

[29] Joseph H.H. Weiler, *The Transformation of Europe*, 100 Yale L.J. 2413-20 (1991).

Individuals (and their lawyers) noticed this practical implication, and the number of cases brought on the basis of this doctrine grew exponentially. Effectively, individuals in real cases and controversies (usually against state public authorities) became the principal "guardians" of the legal integrity of Union law within Europe similar to the way that individuals in the United States have been the principal actors in ensuring the vindication of the Bill of Rights and other federal law.

2. The Doctrine of Supremacy

The doctrine of direct effect might not strike all observers as that revolutionary, especially those observers coming from a monist constitutional order in which international treaties upon ratification are transposed automatically into the municipal legal order and in which some provisions of international treaties may be recognized as "self-executing." The full impact of direct effect is realized in combination with the second "constitutionalizing" doctrine, supremacy. Unlike some federal constitutions, the Treaty does not include a specific "supremacy clause." However, in a series of cases starting in 1964 the Court has pronounced an uncompromising version of supremacy: in the sphere of application of Union law, any Union norm, be it an article of the Treaty (the Constitutional Charter) or a minuscule administrative regulation enacted by the Commission, "trumps" conflicting national law whether enacted before or after the Union norm. Additionally, although this has never been stated explicitly, the Court has the "Kompetenz-Kompetenz" in the Union legal order, i.e. it is the body that determines which norms come within the sphere of application of Union law.

In light of supremacy the full significance of direct effect becomes transparent. Typically, in monist or quasi-monist states like the United States, although treaty provisions, including self-executing ones, may be received automatically into the municipal legal order, their normative status is equivalent to national legislation. Thus the normal rule of "later in time" (*lex posteriori derogat lex anteriori*) governs the relationship between the treaty provision and conflicting national legislation. A national legislature unhappy with an internalized treaty norm simply enacts a conflicting national measure and the transposition will have vanished for all internal practical effects. By contrast, in the Union, because of the doctrine of supremacy, the E.C. norm, which by virtue of the doctrine of direct effect must be regarded as part of the Law of the Land, will prevail even in these circumstances. The combination of the two doctrines means that Union norms that produce direct effects are not merely the Law of the Land but the "Higher Law" of the Land. Parallels to this kind of constitutional architecture may, with very few exceptions, be found only in the internal constitutional order of federal states.

3. The Doctrine of Implied Powers

One possible rationale underlying the Court's jurisprudence in both direct effect and supremacy has been its attempt to maximize the efficiency by which the Union performs the tasks entrusted to it by the Treaty. As part of this rationale, one must consider the question of specific powers granted the Union to perform these tasks. Direct effect and supremacy will not serve their functions if the Union does not have the necessary instruments at its disposal. The issue in which this consideration came to the fore, in 1970, was the treaty-making power of the Union. The full realization of many E.C. internal policies clearly depended on the ability of the Union to negotiate and conclude international treaties with third parties. As is the case with Member States, the problems facing the Union do not respect its internal territorial and jurisdictional boundaries. The Treaty itself was rather sparing in granting the Union treaty-making power, limiting it to a few specified cases.

In its landmark decision of that period (the period circa 1971) the European Court held that the grant of internal competence must be read as implying an external treaty-making power. The European Court added that Union international agreements would be binding not only on the Union as such, but also, as appropriate, on and within the Member States. The significance of this ruling goes beyond the issue of treaty-making power. With this decision, subsequently replicated in different contexts, the European Court added another rung in its constitutional ladder: powers would be implied in favor of the Union where they were necessary to serve legitimate ends pursued by it. Beyond its enormous practical ramifications, the critical point was the willingness of the Court to sidestep the presumptive rule of interpretation typical in international law, that treaties must be interpreted in a manner that minimizes encroachment on state sovereignty. The Court favored a teleological, purposive rule drawn from the book of constitutional interpretation.

In a parallel, although much less noticed, development, the European Court began to develop its jurisprudence on the relationship between areas of Union and Member State competence. The Treaty itself is silent on this issue. It may have been presumed that all authority granted to the Union was to be shared concurrently with the Member States, subject only to the emerging principle of supremacy. Member States could adopt national policies and laws, provided these did not contradict Union law in the same sphere.

In a bifurcated line of jurisprudence laid in place in the early 1970's and continued thereafter, the European Court developed two complementary doctrines: exclusivity and preemption. In a number of fields, most importantly in common commercial policy, the European Court held that the powers of the Union were exclusive. Member States were precluded from taking any action per se, whether or not their action conflicted with a positive measure of Union law. In other fields the exclusivity was not an a priori notion. Instead, only positive Union legislation in these fields triggered a preemptive effect, barring Member States from any action, whether or not in actual conflict with Union law, according to specific criteria developed by the Court.

Exclusivity and preemption not only constitute an additional constitutional layer on those already mentioned but also have had a profound effect on Union decision-making. Where a field has been preempted or is exclusive and action is needed, the Member States are pushed to act jointly.

4. The Doctrine of Human Rights

The last major constitutional tremor was in the field of human rights. The Treaty contains no Bill of Rights and there is no explicit provision for judicial review of an alleged violation of human rights. In a much discussed line of cases starting in 1969, the Court asserted that it would, nonetheless, review Union measures for any violation of fundamental human rights, adopting for its criteria the constitutional traditions common to the Member States and the international human rights conventions to which the Member States subscribed. This enormously complex jurisprudence will be discussed later in this Article, but its symbolic significance in a "constitution-building" exercise deserves mention here. The principal message was that the arrogation of power to the Union implicit in the other three doctrines would not be left unchecked. Union norms, at times derived only from an implied grant of power, often directly effective, and always supreme, would be subjected to a human rights scrutiny by the Court. This scrutiny is important given the "Democracy Deficit" in Union decisionmaking.

If nothing else, this jurisprudence was as clear an indication as any of the audacious self-perception of the European Court. The measure of creative interpretation of the Treaty was so great as to be consonant with a self-image of a constitutional court in a "constitutional" polity. It should be noted further that the human rights jurisprudence had, paradoxically, the hallmarks of the deepest jurists' prudence. The success of the European Court's bold moves with regard to the doctrines of direct effect, supremacy, implied powers, and human rights ultimately would depend on their reception by the highest constitutional courts in the different Member States.

The most delicate issue in this context was that of supremacy. National courts were likely to accept direct effect and implied powers, but found it difficult to swallow the notion that Union law must prevail even in the face of an explicit later-in-time provision of a national legislature to whom, psychologically, if not in fact constitutionally, Member State courts owed allegiance. Accepting supremacy of Union law without some guarantee that this supreme law would not violate rights fundamental to the legal patrimony of an individual Member State would be virtually impossible. This especially would be true in Member States like Italy and Germany where human rights enjoy constitutional protection. Thus, even if protection of human rights per se need not be indispensable to fashioning a federal-type constitution, it was critical to the acceptance by courts in the Member States of the other elements of constitution-building. One by one, the highest jurisdictions in the Member States accepted the new judicial architecture of Europe.

The skeptic may, however, be justified in challenging the "new legal order" I have described incorporating these doctrines, especially the sharp lines it tries to draw in differentiating the "new" Union order from the "old" public international law order. After all, a cardinal principle of international law is its supremacy over national law. The notion of direct effect, or at least self-execution, is also known to international law, and implied powers jurisprudence has operated in the jurisprudence of the International Court of Justice as well. If international law shares these notions of supremacy, direct effect, and implied powers, the skeptic may be correct in challenging the characterization of Union development in the Foundational Period as something out of the ordinary.

One reply is that the Union phenomenon represents a quantitative change of such a magnitude that it is qualitative in nature. Direct effect may exist in international law but it is operationalized in so few instances that it must be regarded as the exception which proves the general rule of its virtual nonexistence. In the Union order direct effect is presumptive. The question of supremacy, however, brings the key difference between the two systems into sharp relief. International law is as uncompromising as Union law in asserting that its norms are supreme over conflicting national norms. But, international law's horizontal system of enforcement, which is typically actuated through the principles of state responsibility, reciprocity, and counter measures, gives the notion of supremacy an exceptionally rarified quality, making it difficult to grasp and radically different from that found in the constitutional orders of states with centralized enforcement monopolies.

The constitutionalization claim regarding the Treaties establishing the European Union can only be sustained by adding one more layer of analysis: the system of judicial remedies and enforcement. It is this system, as interpreted and operationalized by the European judicial branch, that truly differentiates the Union legal order from the horizontality of classical public international law.

B. General Principles after Maastricht[30]

The Treaty on European Union (Maastricht Agreement) has provisions on three matters of general principles of law and constitutional importance: human rights, subsidiarity and citizenship.

1. Human Rights

For the first time explicit reference is made to human rights in a Union treaty. It is declared, first, that the systems of government of Member States are "founded on the principles of democracy." It is then stated:[31]

> The Union shall respect fundamental rights, as guaranteed by the European Convention for the Protection of Human Rights and Fundamental Freedom signed in Rome on 4 November 1950 and as they result from the constitutional traditions common to the Member States, as general principles of Union law.

This provision does no more than put in treaty form the result achieved by the case law of the European Court; nevertheless, it is still of importance.

2. Subsidiarity

This concept is now established as a general principle in the Union treaties. In the Preamble to the Treaty on European Union, it is declared that, in the process of creating an ever closer union among the peoples of Europe, decisions will be taken "as closely as possible to the citizen in accordance with the principle of subsidiarity." It is also stated, in the final paragraph of Article B of the Treaty, that, in achieving the objectives of the Union, the principle of subsidiarity (as defined in Article 3b EU) will be respected.

---

[30] Trevor C. Hartley, *Constitutional and Institutional Aspects of the Maastricht Agreement*, 42 Int'l & Comp. L.Q. 213 (1993). © 1993 Trevor C. Hartley. Reprinted by permission.

[31] Art. F(2) TEU.

Article 3b EU contains three paragraphs. In the first, it is laid down that the Union "shall act within the limits of the powers conferred upon it by this Treaty and of the objectives assigned to it therein." This appears to be an express foundation of the doctrine of *ultra vires*, but the effect of the phrase "and of the objectives assigned to it therein" is not entirely clear. It probably means that, even when acting within the powers conferred upon it, the Union may use those powers only in order to attain the objectives assigned to it. This is already the law under the doctrine of misuse of powers ("détournement de pouvoir") as laid down in Article 173 EEU, which remains as Article 173 EU. Moreover, under Article 235 EEU, which continues as Article 235 EU, the Union can take the measures necessary to attain its objectives, even if there is no express power to do so. Since this must itself be regarded as a power conferred by the Treaty on the Union in terms of the first paragraph of Article 3b, the restrictions laid down in that paragraph are of only limited effect.

It seems, therefore, that the first paragraph of Article 3b does not bring about any very significant change in the law, though it may be regarded as underlining the importance of the Union's keeping within its powers.

The principle of subsidiarity is defined and established by the second paragraph of Article 3b, where it is stated:

> In areas which do not fall within its exclusive competence, the Union shall take action, in accordance with the principle of subsidiarity, only if and in so far as the objectives of the proposed action cannot be sufficiently achieved by the Member States and can therefore, by reason of the scale or effects of the proposed action, be better achieved by the Union.

This is a good definition as far as it goes, but it should be noted that it adopts the principle of subsidiarity only in areas which do not fall within the exclusive jurisdiction of the Union, and it is far from clear which areas should be so regarded. The Commission takes the view that an area falls within the exclusive jurisdiction of the Union if the Treaties impose on it an obligation to act because it is regarded as having sole responsibility for the performance of a particular task, and it has identified the following areas as satisfying this criterion: the removal of barriers to the free movement of goods, persons, services and capital; the common commercial policy; the general rules on competition; the common organization of agricultural markets (the CAP); the conservation of fisheries resources; and the essential elements of transport policy. This is a large area, but the Commission has made clear that it will expand as integration progresses.

Moreover, if one looks at the decisions of the European Court on the treaty-making powers of the Union, it seems that whenever the EEU Treaty gives the Union a power to take binding measures, and the Union exercises that power by adopting legislation or entering into an international agreement in a given area, that area is thenceforth regarded as falling within the exclusive jurisdiction of the Union. In other words, once the Union has "occupied the field," the Member States are precluded from entering into international agreements in that field. If the European Court were to apply this principle with regard to Article 3b, any given area would be regarded as falling within the exclusive jurisdiction of the Union once the Union had occupied the field;

consequently, subsidiarity would be applicable only when the Union legislated for the first time in a new field.

The third paragraph of Article 3b states: "Any action by the Union shall not go beyond what is necessary to achieve the objectives of this Treaty." At first sight, this might appear to cover more or less the same ground as the first paragraph; however, it seems that it was intended to establish in Treaty form the principle of proportionality, one of the general principles of law applied by the European Court.

The effectiveness of these provisions may be considered from both a political and a legal point of view. From a political point of view, they may make the Commission more restrained in the measures it proposes and the Council more cautious in the measures it accepts. At the Edinburgh Summit in December 1992, the European Council adopted a document intended to ensure that the principle of subsidiarity is observed in the everyday working of the Union institutions. The document attempts to give a more concrete form to the principle and sets out practices and procedures which will require Union institutions to take subsidiarity into account at every stage of the legislative process. An inter-institutional agreement giving fuller effect to this is envisaged.

From a legal point of view, the question to be considered is the extent to which the European Court would be prepared to declare measures invalid for infringement of the principle of subsidiarity. Clearly, the political effectiveness of subsidiarity depends to a considerable extent on its legal effectiveness: the Commission and the Council will not adopt a measure if it is likely to be declared invalid by the Court.

In order to challenge a Union measure on the basis of Article 3b, an applicant would have to establish the objectives of the measure and show that those objectives could be attained as well (if not better) through action by the Member States. Both of these requirements present difficulties. Most measures adopted by the Union have a number of objectives, some general and some specific. If any one of the objectives could be better attained by Union action, the European Court would probably regard that as sufficient to justify the measure (though it might by prepared to strike down clearly severable parts which did not fulfil the requirements of Article 3b).

If uniformity of application is necessary to attain the objectives of the measure, then, almost by definition, Union action will be needed. There are many areas in which this is the case. Measures concerning the environment are an example. It is normally said that such measures must apply uniformly in all Member States; otherwise, States which applied a higher level of protection would be at a competitive disadvantage compared with those applying a lower level, since manufacturers in the latter would have lower costs. Similar arguments can be made regarding most measures in the social and labor fields.

In practice, it will almost always be possible to formulate the objectives of the measure in different ways. In defending the measure, the Commission and the Council will argue for a formulation which requires Union action. One can even expect that the preamble and wording of the measure will be drafted so as to facilitate this.

In such a situation, everything will depend on the European Court. It will decide whether the measure falls within an area in which the Union has exclusive jurisdiction; it will formulate the objectives of the measure, and it will decide whether they can be better achieved by Union action. All these questions involve so many imponderables that it will almost always be possible for the Court, if it wishes, to find grounds for upholding the measure. As a result, the effectiveness of subsidiarity will depend, to a considerable extent, on the attitude and policy of the European Court.

Until now the Court's policy has always been to expand Union power and to restrict that of the Member States. This policy may be illustrated with regard to many issues, not least that of the Court's own jurisdiction. As far as the powers of the Union are concerned, it finds its most striking illustration in the development by the European Court of the doctrine of implied powers, which permits the Commission to legislate, and the Union to sign treaties, without any express authorization in the EEU Treaty. If this policy continues, it is unlikely that any significant measures will be struck down by the Court on the basis of Article 3b.

It is interesting to note that the issues raised under the second paragraph of Article 3b are not greatly dissimilar to those which arise under Article 235 EEU, which empowers the Council to adopt measures if "action by the Union should prove necessary to attain . . . one of the objectives of the Union." Although measures passed under Article 235 have been successfully challenged on other grounds, no one appears ever to have argued that action by the Union (as distinct from that by the Member States) was not necessary to attain the objective in question. This may be significant.

3. Citizenship

Part 2 of the Treaty Establishing the European Union is devoted to citizenship of the Union. It creates a citizenship of the Union, and provides that every person holding the nationality of a Member State will be a citizen of the Union. It then states:

> Every citizen of the Union shall have the right to move and reside freely within the territory of the Member States, subject to the limitations and conditions laid down in this Treaty and by the measures adopted to give it effect.

This provision seems to give a general right of free movement subject to the same conditions as apply, under the EEU Treaty or under Union legislation, to the rights of free movement already in existence. At the present time, there is no general right of free movement; instead, there are rights for specific groups of people, such as workers, self-employed persons and providers of services. If you add all these groups together, however, they cover almost everyone. This follows from Council Directive 90/364/EEU, which grants the right of residence to all nationals of Member States (now, all Union citizens) who do not already enjoy that right under any other provision of Union law, provided they are covered by sickness insurance and have sufficient resources to avoid becoming a burden on the social assistance system of the host Member State. The effect of the Maastricht Agreement is to replace these separate categories by a general right. However, it is subject to the same limitations and conditions as before. These would include the requirement (applicable to persons to whom Directive 90/364 applies) of having sufficient means of support and the proviso (applicable to all categories of immigrants) concerning limitations justified on grounds of public policy, public security or public health. It is doubtful, therefore, whether the new provision adds anything to pre-existing immigration rights for Union citizens.

Article 8c EU provides that every citizen of the Union who is in the territory of a non-Member State in which his own Member State has no diplomatic or consular representation is entitled to protection by the diplomatic or consular authorities of any other Member State on the same conditions as a national of that Member State. Before the end of 1993 the Member States must establish among themselves the rules necessary to bring this provision into operation, and they must commence the necessary international negotiations.

Article 8d EU gives every citizen the right to petition the Parliament and to apply to the Ombudsman (established by Article 138e EU).

Though the establishment of a Union citizenship is of great symbolic importance, it is noteworthy that all the provisions creating significant changes are subject to implementation either by measures to be adopted by the Council acting unanimously or by agreement between the Member States.

4. The Union System of Judicial Review[32]

As mentioned above, the hierarchy of norms within the European Union is typical of a nonunitary system. The Higher Law of the Union is, of course, the Treaty itself. Neither Union organs nor the Member States may violate the Treaty in their legislative and administrative actions. In addition, Member States may not violate Union regulations, directives, and decisions. Not surprisingly, then, the Union features a double-limbed system of judicial review, operating on two levels. Two sets of legislative acts and administrative measures are subject to judicial review: (1) the measures of the Union itself (principally acts of the Council of Ministers, Commission, and European Parliament), which are reviewable for conformity with the Treaties; and (2) the acts of the Member States, which are reviewable for their conformity with Union law and policy, including the above-mentioned secondary legislation.

Needless to say, the effectiveness of review of the second set of measures assumes critical importance. I, therefore, focus only on that aspect of judicial review here.

a. Judicial Review at the Union Level

Either the Commission or an individual Member State may, in accordance with Articles 169-72 of the EEU Treaty, bring an action against a Member State for failure to fulfill its obligations under the Treaty. Generally, this failure takes the form either of inaction in implementing a Union obligation or enactment of a national measure contrary to Union obligations. The existence of a mandatory and exclusive forum for adjudication of these types of disputes sets the Union apart from many international organizations.

The role of the Commission is even more special. As one commentator noted, "[u]nder traditional international law the enforcement of treaty obligations is a matter to be settled amongst the Contracting Parties themselves. Article 169, in contrast, enables an independent Union body, the Commission, to invoke the compulsory jurisdiction of the European Court against a defaulting Member State."

---

32 Joseph H.H. Weiler, *The Transformation of Europe,* 100 Yale L.J. 2403, 2419-2422 (1991).

At the same time, the "intergovernmental" character of this procedure and the consequent limitations on its efficacy are clear. Four weaknesses are particularly glaring:

(1) the procedure is political in nature; the Commission (appropriately) may have nonlegal reasons not to initiate a prosecution;
(2) a centralized agency with limited human resources is unable adequately to identify, process, and monitor all possible Member State violations and infringements;
(3) Article 169 may be inappropriate to apply to small violations; even if small violations are properly identified, dedicating Commission resources to infringements that do not raise an important principle or create a major economic impact is wasteful; and finally, and most importantly,
(4) no real enforcement exists; proceedings conclude with a "declaratory" judgment of the European Court without enforcement sanctions.

b. Judicial Review at the Member State Level

The weaknesses of Articles 169-172 are remedied to an extent by judicial review within the judicial systems of the Member States in collaboration with the European Court of Justice. Article 177 provides, inter alia, that when a question concerning the interpretation of the Treaty is raised before a national court, the court may suspend the national proceedings and request a preliminary ruling from the European Court of Justice in Luxembourg on the correct interpretation of the Treaty. If the national court is the court of last resort, then it must request a European Court ruling. Once this ruling is made, it is remitted back to the national court which gives, on the basis of the ruling, the opinion in the case before it. The national courts and the European Court are thus integrated into a unitary system of judicial review.

The European Court and national courts have made good use of this procedure. On its face the purpose of Article 177 is simply to ensure uniform interpretation of Union law throughout the Member States. That, apparently, is how the framers of the Treaty understood it. However, very often the factual situation in which Article 177 comes into play involves an individual litigant pleading in national court that a rule, measure, or national practice should not be applied because it violates the Union obligations of the Member State. In this manner the attempts of Member States to practice selective Union membership by disregarding their obligations have become regularly adjudicated before their own national courts. On submission of the case, the European Court has rendered its interpretation of Union law within the factual context of the case before it. Theoretically, the European Court may not itself rule on the application of Union law. But, as one scholar notes:

> [I]t is no secret . . . that in practice, when making preliminary rulings the Court has often transgressed the theoretical border line . . . . [I]t provides the national judge with an answer in which questions of law and of fact are sufficiently interwoven as to leave the national

judge with only little discretion and flexibility in making his final decision.[33]

The fact that the national court renders the final judgment is crucial to the procedure. The binding effect and enforcement value of such a decision, coming from a Member State's own court, may be contrasted with a similar decision handed down in declaratory fashion by the European Court under the previously discussed Article 169 procedure. A national court opinion takes care of the most dramatic weakness of the Article 169 procedure: the ability of a Member State, in extremis, to disregard the strictures of the European Court. Under the 177 procedure this disregard is impossible. A state, in our Western democracies, cannot disobey its own courts.

The other weaknesses of the 169 procedure are also remedied to some extent: individual litigants are usually not politically motivated in bringing their actions; small as well as big violations are adjudicated; and, in terms of monitoring, the Union citizen becomes, willy-nilly, a decentralized agent for monitoring compliance by Member States with their Treaty obligations.

The Article 177 system is not complete, however. Not all violations come before national courts; the success of the system depends on the collaboration between national courts and the European Court of Justice; and Member States may, and often have, utilized the delays of the system to defer ruling.

On the other hand, the overall effect of the judicial remedies cannot be denied. The combination of the "constitutionalization" and the system of judicial remedies to a large extent nationalized Union obligations and introduced on the Union level the habit of obedience and the respect for the rule of law which traditionally is less associated with international obligations than national ones.

It is at this juncture that one may speculate about the most profound difference between the Union legal order and international law generally. The combined effect of constitutionalization and the evolution of the system of remedies results, in my view, in the removal from the Union legal order of the most central legal artifact of international law: the notion (and doctrinal apparatus) of exclusive state responsibility with its concomitant principles of reciprocity and countermeasures. The Union legal order, on this view, is a truly self-contained legal regime with no recourse to the mechanism of state responsibility, at least as traditionally understood, and therefore to reciprocity and countermeasures, even in the face of actual or potential failure. Without these features, so central to the classic international legal order, the Union truly becomes something "new."

At the end of the day the debate about the theoretical difference between international law and Union law may have the relevance of some long-lasting theological disputes—i.e., none at all. Whatever the differences in theory, there can be no argument that the Union legal order as it emerged from the Foundational Period appeared in its operation much closer to a working constitutional order, a fact which, as will shortly

---

33 Rasmussen, *Why is Article 173 Interpreted Against Private Plaintiffs?*, 5 Eur. L. Rev. 112, 125 (1980).

emerge, had a fundamental impact on the way in which it was treated by its Member States.

5. International Agreements under Maastricht[34]

It is now made clear by Article 228 EU that the Council must authorize the Commission before it can open negotiations, that the Council can appoint a committee to assist the Commission in the negotiations and that the Council can issue directives to the Commission for the conduct of the negotiations. Previously, these were all standard procedure, but they are now given legal form.

a. Voting by Council

It was not previously specified how the Council would vote on international agreements (except in the case of association agreements under Article 238 EEU, in which unanimity was required). It is now provided that the Council will vote by a qualified majority except in the case of Article 238 and in the case where unanimity would be required for the adoption of an internal rule.

b. Powers of the European Parliament

Previously, only agreements under Article 238 (association agreements) could be vetoed by the Parliament. It is now provided that, in addition, the assent of the Parliament must be obtained in the case of agreements establishing a specific institutional framework by organizing co-operation procedures, agreements having important budgetary implications for the Union and agreements entailing amendment of an act adopted under the joint legislative procedure. The Parliament does not, however, have power to veto an agreement merely because it falls within an area for which internal rules can be adopted only under the co-operation procedure or the joint legislative procedure, unless, in the latter case, an amendment of an existing measure is necessary.

It is further provided that the Council must consult the European Parliament in all other cases except for tariff and trade agreements under Article 113(3) EEU/EU. The Council can, however, lay down a time limit for the Parliament to deliver its opinion and, if no opinion is given by the due date, act without it. The right of the Parliament to be consulted over international agreements was in fact recognized as early as 1983 in the Solemn Declaration on European Union adopted in Stuttgart, and in one respect this procedure could be regarded as a setback for the Parliament since the Solemn Declaration appears to cover all "significant agreements," including—apparently—tariff and trade agreements.

6. Legal Remedies under Maastricht

a. Enforcement Actions

The most important change regarding legal remedies concerns the procedure of enforcement actions under Articles 169-171 EEU/EU. It is now provided that a financial penalty may be imposed on Member States which fail to take the necessary mea-

---

[34] Trevor C. Hartley, *Constitutional and Institutional Aspects of the Maastricht Agreement*, 42 I.C.L.Q. 221 (1993).

sures to comply with the judgment of the European Court. If a Member State does not obey a judgment, the Commission, after giving the member State a hearing, issues a reasoned opinion specifying the ways in which it has failed to comply. If the Member State does not then comply within the time limit laid down by the Commission, the latter may bring the case before the Court. When doing so, the Commission specifies the amount of the "lump sum or penalty payment" to be paid by the Member State. If the Court of Justice finds that the Member State concerned has not complied with its judgment, it may impose a lump sum or penalty payment on it. This could presumably be the same as, greater than, or less than that proposed by the Commission. It is not made clear what the difference is between a lump sum and a penalty payment, but the latter may perhaps be based on the length of time it takes the Member State to comply.

There is no statement in the Treaty as to how such a penalty will be enforced. This contrasts with Article 88 ECSC (never yet applied) which provides that the Commission (with the assent of the Council acting by a two-thirds majority) may suspend payment of sums due to the defaulting Member State or take measures (or authorize other Member States to take measures) "to correct the effects of the infringement".

b. Annulment Actions

There are some interesting amendments to Article 173. First (as one would expect) joint acts of the Parliament and the Council are included among the list of acts against which annulment proceedings may be brought. Acts of the European Central Bank are also included. Measures adopted by the Parliament acting alone are subject to review only to the extent to which they produce legal effects *vis-à-vis* third parties. It is further provided that the Parliament and the European Central Bank may bring proceedings under Article 173 "for the purpose of protecting their prerogatives."

c. Failure to Act

Previously, actions could be brought by the European Parliament under Article 175, but they could not be brought *against* it. This has now been changed to allow actions to be brought against the Parliament. The European Central Bank is also brought into the picture: proceedings may be brought by it under Article 175 in areas falling within its competence; actions may also be brought against it.

d. Preliminary References

Article 177 has been amended to allow the European Courts to rule, on a reference from a national court, on the validity and interpretation of acts of the European Central Bank. Previously it could rule only on the acts of the institutions of the Union. Since the Court of Auditors now enjoys the status of an institution, the Court can also rule on its acts.

e. Indirect Challenge

Article 184 EEU has been amended to cover regulations enacted by the European Central Bank and those enacted jointly by the Parliament and the Council.

f. Tort Actions

Article 215 EEU has been amended to permit an action for non-contractual liability to be brought against the European Central Bank or against its servants acting in the performance of their duty.

7. Inter-Governmental Activities under Maastricht

Certain areas of policy have always been kept outside the system set up by the three basic treaties (ECSC, EEU and Euratom), and objectives in these areas have been pursued by inter-governmental, rather than by supranational, means. At first, there was no specific legal framework for these activities, but this was changed by the Single European Act, which laid down the basic objectives and institutional structures for what was called "European Political Co-operation" ("EPC"). The Treaty on European Union builds on this foundation with provisions outside the ambit of the EU Treaty which concern two areas: foreign and security policy, on the one hand, and justice and home affairs, on the other. In these areas, inter-governmentalism is still the ruling principle: the focus of activities is the Council; unanimity is the normal way of reaching decisions (though, as will be seen below, it is now possible for the Council to agree—unanimously—that certain matters will henceforth be decided by majority voting); the role of the Commission and Parliament is little more than consultative; and the Court is almost entirely excluded. These features stand in stark contrast to the increasingly federalist character of activities under the EEU/EU Treaty.

a. Common Foreign and Security Policy

The Union treaties first obtained a foreign-policy dimension in 1987 when Part III of the Single European Act ("SEA") came into force, though the origin of European Political Co-operation has been traced back as far as 1969. Initially, EPC was rigorously separated from Union matters and the Union institutions were excluded from EPC deliberations. In time, however, this changed, and the Single European Act provided that the Commission would be "fully associated with the proceedings of Political Co-operation" and that the European Parliament would be "closely associated" with it.

Article 30 of the Single European Act created an institutional structure for EPC. It made provision for regular meetings of Ministers of Foreign Affairs to discuss EPC and created a Political Committee, to some extent parallel to COREPER[35], consisting of political directors from the 12 foreign ministries. Provision was also made for a European Correspondents' Group, working groups and a secretariat based in Brussels. The contracting State holding the Presidency of EPC was given responsibility for initiating action and co-ordinating positions.

These provisions are now repealed by the Treaty on European Union and replaced by Title V. This establishes a common foreign and security policy "CFSP," which member States are obliged to support "actively and unreservedly in a spirit of loyalty and mutual solidarity." The CFSP is to be pursued by two means: systematic co-operation and joint action. The former is based on consultation, common positions (to which the

[35] The COREPER is the committee of permanent representatives.

policies of member States must conform) and co-ordinated action. The latter comes into operation if the Council decides (on the basis of guidelines from the European Council) that a matter is to be the subject of joint action. When taking such a decision, it will lay down the scope, objectives and duration of the joint action, together with the means, procedures and conditions for its implementation. When operating within the scope of the CFSP, the Council must always be unanimous, except that, when adopting joint action or at any stage during its development, the Council may decide (unanimously) that certain matters will in future be decided by a qualified majority.

Issues having defense implications are not subject to the provisions regarding joint action. They are covered by Article J.4, which envisages the eventual framing of a common defense policy which "might in time lead to a common defense." The Western European Union "WEU" is declared to be an integral part of the development of the European Union and has the function of implementing decisions of the latter which have defense implications. The defense policy of the European Union must be compatible with the common security and defense policy established within the framework of NATO. Bilateral co-operation between two more Member States is permitted, provided it operates within the framework of the WEU and the Atlantic Alliance and does not run counter to the common defense policy provided for in the Treaty on European Union.

The institutional structure set up under the Single European Act is to a large extent continued. The implementation of common measures is the responsibility of the Member State holding the Presidency (assisted by the previous and next Member States to hold the Presidency). The Commission is fully associated with this task. Member States which are permanent members of the UN Security Council must "ensure the defense of the positions and interests of the Union, without prejudice to their responsibilities under the provisions of the UN Charter." Diplomatic and consular missions of Member States and their representations to international organizations must co-operate in ensuring that common positions and common measures are complied with and implemented.

The Presidency must consult the European Parliament on the main aspects and basic choices of the CFSP and ensure that the views of the Parliament are duly taken into consideration. The Parliament may ask questions of the Council and make recommendations to it.

Overall control of the CFSP rests in the hands of the European Council. It defines the principles and general guidelines, while the EU Council takes the decisions to implement it. The Commission is fully associated with the work carried out in the CFSP field. Administrative expenditure which the CFSP entails for the Union institutions is charged to the budget of the EU. The Council may decide (unanimously) that operational expenditure will also be charged to the EU budget; or it may decide that it will be charged to the Member States.

b. Co-operation in the Fields of Justice and Home Affairs

A similar system has been set up for co-operation in the fields of justice and home affairs, which cover: asylum policy, controls on the Union's external frontiers (i.e. those with non-Member States), immigration from non-Member States, drug addiction, international fraud, judicial co-operation in civil and criminal matters, customs co-operation and police co-operation for combating serious international crime. These are regarded as matters of common interest: the Treaty requires the Member States to consult, collaborate and co-ordinate their action in these fields. The Council may adopt joint positions and joint action. There is also provision for the Council to draw up conventions to be adopted by the Member States. Unless provided to the contrary by such conventions, measures to implement them will be adopted within the Council by a majority of two-thirds of the contracting States. Other aspects of the system parallel those for the common foreign and security policy.

8. Opting Out

One of the most interesting features of the Maastricht Agreement is the way it makes special provision for particular Member States, most notable (but not only) the United Kingdom. This takes various forms: a Member State may be excluded from participation in a particular activity (on the ground that it has not fulfilled the necessary requirements) or it may choose not to participate. Only the latter may be termed "opting out," but both forms could be viewed as the beginning of a Europe *à la carte.*

The mechanism of exclusion is illustrated by Article 109k EU, which comes into operation once a decision has been taken to proceed to the third stage of economic and monetary union ("EMU"). It provides for the Council to decide which Member States fulfil the necessary conditions for the adoption of a single currency. Those that do not qualify are referred to as "Member States with a derogation" and their voting rights in the Council are suspended with regard to decisions on certain matters. Since the requirements for participation in the single currency are unlikely to be met by all member State, it seems inevitable, if EMU goes ahead according to the Treaty provisions, that the Union will be split into a core of single-currency States and a penumbra of "Member States with a derogation." The latter will not participate in decision-making on the management of the European currency.

An example of opting out, also with regard to EMU, is to be found in the Protocol on Certain Provisions Relating to the United Kingdom of Great Britain and Northern Ireland, which provides that the United Kingdom is not obliged to move to the third stage of EMU unless its government and Parliament so decide. Of course, even if the United Kingdom decided that it wished to move to the third stage, the Council might not consider that it met the necessary requirements. In such a case, it would become a Member State with a derogation.

If the United Kingdom decided not to move to the third stage, the relevant Treaty provisions would not apply to it, and it would retain its powers in the field of monetary policy. Its voting rights in the Council would, however, be suspended with regard to those provisions, and it would have no right to participate in the appointment of the President and other members of the Executive Board of the European Central Bank. Moreover, many provisions concerning the European System of Central Banks would not apply to it.

The Protocol on Social Policy may be regarded as an example of immediate opting out. This makes provision for all the Member States except the United Kingdom to implement the 1989 Social Charter by means of an Agreement on Social Policy (often referred to, misleadingly, as the "Social Chapter"). The Protocol (to which the Agreement is annexed) authorizes the 11 Member States to have recourse to the institutions, mechanisms and procedures of the Treaty for the purpose of taking among themselves, and applying as far as they are concerned, the acts and decisions required for giving effect the Agreement. The United Kingdom will not take part in Council deliberations on such measures and the definition of a "qualified majority" under Article 148(2) EU is modified accordingly. Acts adopted by the Council for this purpose, and the financial consequences thereof, will not apply to the United Kingdom.

Although the effect of this is to allow the United Kingdom to opt out of this area of Union action, the position in strict law is that the 11 Member States have decided among themselves to adopt the Agreement on Social Policy, and the United Kingdom has agreed that they may use the mechanisms of the Union to give effect to it. Consequently, if the Social Protocol did not come into force with the rest of the Maastricht Agreement, it would not mean that the United Kingdom would be automatically bound by the Agreement on Social Policy: the only result would be that the 11 contracting States would have to find some other means of giving effect to the Agreement on Social Policy.

9. The Danish Referendum and the Edinburgh Summit

At the Edinburgh meeting of the European Council, held on 12 December 1992, an attempt was made to lay the groundwork for a reversal of the 1992 Danish referendum. Some way had to be found of making the Maastricht Agreement more palatable to the Danish electorate. The difficulty facing the meeting was that this had to be done without formally amending the Agreement, since any amendment would have required the ratification process to begin again in those Member States where it was already completed and would reopen many contentious issues.

To meet the problem, the Edinburgh Summit produced the following: the Decision of the Heads of State and Government, Meeting within the European Council, Concerning Certain Problems Raised by Denmark on the Treaty on European Union; the Declaration of the European Council on Social Policy, Consumers, the Environment and Distribution of Income; the Declaration of the European Council on Defense; two unilateral declarations by Denmark, one on citizenship of the union and one on cooperation in the fields of justice and home affairs; and a Final Declaration. It was expressly stated that these instruments are "fully compatible with the Treaty" and apply exclusively to Denmark, not to any other existing or acceding Member State.

a. The Decision of the Heads of State and Government

The Decision contains five sections. Section A, entitled "Citizenship," states that citizenship of the Union does not in any way take the place of national citizenship and the question whether an individual possesses the nationality of a Member State will be settled solely by the law of that State. Section B (Economic and Monetary Union) declares that, since Denmark has exercised its power to opt out of the third stage of EMU, it will not participate in the single currency. Section C (Defense Policy) states that Denmark will not participate in decisions of the Union having defense implications. Section D (Justice and Home Affairs) declares that Denmark will participate fully in co-operation with regard to justice and home affairs. Section E, headed "Final Provisions," provides that the Decision will take effect on the entry into force of the Treaty on European Union. Denmark may at any time, however, inform the other member States that it no longer wishes to avail itself of all or part of the Decision.

Though adopted at a meeting in the European Council, the Decision is an act of the Member States, not of the Council. It is also clear that the Member States were acting under their inherent sovereign powers, not under powers conferred on them by Union law. It seems that the Member States intended the Decision to be legally binding, and it is probably an international agreement in simplified form. It is likely that the European Court would take it into account in interpreting the Maastricht Agreement. Whether the Court would regard itself as bound by it is a different question, but this is unlikely to arise unless, contrary to the expressly stated belief of the Member States, the Decision conflicts with some provision of Union law.

The Prime Minister is reported to have said that, as the Decision is a legally binding agreement between governments, the International Court of Justice would have jurisdiction to rule on it. However, Article 219 EEU precludes Member States from submitting a dispute "concerning the interpretation or application of this Treaty" to any method of settlement other than those provided for in the Treaty itself. This would exclude recourse to the International Court to the extent that the Decision affects the "interpretation or application" of the EEU Treaty. Section A (Citizenship) and Section B (Economic and Monetary Union) both concern amendments to the EEU Treaty. Consequently, Article 219 EEU would preclude member States from submitting to the International Court any dispute concerning the effect of those sections on the interpretation or application of the EEU Treaty. Section C (Defense Policy), on the other hand, concerns a part of the Treaty on European Union (Article J) which stands in its own right and is not an amendment to the EEU Treaty; moreover, the European Court of Justice has no power to interpret Article J. Consequently, there seems to be nothing in Union law that would preclude an application to the International Court with regard to Section C.

b. *The Declarations by the European Council*

The Declaration on Social Policy, Consumers, the Environment and Distribution of Income states that the Treaty on European Union does not prevent any member State from adopting more stringent protection measures compatible with the EU Treaty with regard to social policy, consumer protection and the environment. It also declares that the provisions of the Treaty on European Union, including those on EMU, permit each member State to pursue its own policy regarding the distribution of income and the maintenance and improvement of social welfare benefits.

In the Declaration on Defense, the Council notes that Denmark will renounce its right to exercise the Presidency of the Union in every case involving matters with defense implications. On these occasions, the Danish President will be replaced according to the normal rules applicable where the President is indisposed.

Unlike the Decision, the Declarations are acts of the European Council. It is uncertain what legal effect they have, since it is doubtful whether Union law gives the Council power to adopt binding acts in circumstances such as these; nevertheless, the

European Court would probably take them into account (without being bound by them) in interpreting Union law.

c. *Unilateral Declarations by Denmark*

These Declarations consist mainly of statements regarding existing Union law and provisions in the Maastricht Agreement, no doubt set out in an attempt to reassure Danish voters. In the Declaration on Citizenship it is emphasized that Union citizenship is a different concept from citizenship of a Member State and does not give the right to obtain Danish citizenship.

Paragraph 4 of the Declaration on Citizenship puts other Member States on notice that any provision adopted under Article 8e EU to add to the rights associated with citizenship of the Union will require another referendum in Denmark (or a five-sixths majority in the Danish Parliament). The Declaration on Co-operation in the Fields of Justice and Home Affairs makes clear that the same applies to any decision under Article K.9 of the Treaty on European Union. Under the Maastricht Agreement, decisions under both these provisions have to be adopted by each Member State in accordance with its constitutional requirements; consequently, Denmark is perfectly entitled to make its ratification conditional on a referendum.

d. *Conclusions*

By and large, these instruments are taken up with restating existing law or giving notice of action that Denmark intends to take (or has taken). It seems, therefore, that the Member States were generally, if not wholly, correct in stating that they do not conflict with the Maastricht Agreement or with the existing provisions of Union law. In any event, it is unlikely that the question will ever arise for decision before a court of law. Whether these instruments will have the desired effect in Denmark, on the other hand, remains to be seen.

10. Future

a. *The Ethos of European Integration: Europe as Unity and Europe as Union*[36]

As indicated above, 1992 also brought to the fore questions, choices, and contradictions in the very ethos of European integration. I shall explore these questions, choices, and contradictions by construing two competing visions of the Promised Land to which the Union is being led. The two visions are synthetic constructs, distilled from the discourse and praxis of European integration.

Unitarian and communitarian visions share a similar departure point. If we go back in time to the 1950 Schuman Declaration and the consequent 1951 Treaty of Paris establishing the European Coal and Steel Union, these events, despite their economic content, are best seen as a long-term and transformative strategy for peace among the states of Western Europe, principally France and Germany. This strategy tried to

[36] Joseph H.H. Weiler, *The Transformation of Europe,* 100 Yale L.J. 2413 (1991). © 1991 Joseph H.H. Weiler. Reprinted by permission.

address the "mischief" embodied in the excesses of the modern nation-state and the traditional model of statal intercourse among them that was premised on full "sovereignty," "autonomy," "independence," and a relentless defense and maximization of the national interest. This model was opposed not simply because, at the time, it displayed a propensity to degenerate into violent clashes, but also because it was viewed as unattractive for the task of reconstruction in times of peace. The European Union was to be an antidote to the negative features of the state and statal intercourse; its establishment in 1951 was seen as the beginning of a process that would bring about their elimination.

At this point, the two visions depart.

According to the first-unity-vision, the process that started in 1951 was to move progressively through the steps of establishing a common market and approximating economic policies through ever tighter economic integration (economic and monetary union), resulting, finally, in full political union, in some version of a federal United States of Europe. If we link this vision to governance process and constitutional structure, the ultimate model of the Union and the constitutionalized treaties stands as the equivalent, in the European localized context, of the utopian model of "world government" in classical international law. Tomorrow's Europe in this form would indeed constitute the final demise of Member State nationalism and, thus, the ultimate realization of the original objectives through political union in the form of a federalist system of governance.

The alternative-union-vision also rejects the classical model of international law which celebrates statal sovereignty, independence, and autonomy and sees international legal regulation providing a "neutral" arena for states to prosecute their own ("national") goals premised on power and self-interest. The union vision is, instead, premised on limiting, or sharing, sovereignty in a select albeit growing number of fields, on recognizing, and even celebrating, the reality of interdependence, and on counterpoising to the exclusivist ethos of statal autonomy a notion of a union of states and peoples sharing values and aspirations.

Most recently, it has been shown convincingly, not for the first time, how the classical model of international law is a replication at the international level of the liberal theory of the state. The state is implicitly treated as the analogue, on the international level, to the individual within a domestic situation. In this conception, international legal notions such as self-determination, sovereignty, independence, and consent have their obvious analogy in theories of the individual within the state. The idea of union is thus posited in juxtaposition to the international version of pure liberalism and substitutes a modified communitarian vision.

Since the idea of "union" is currently in vogue and has become many things to many people, I would like to explain the meaning I attach to it in this transnational European context. The importance of the EEU inter-statal notion of union rests on the very fact that it does not involve a negation of the state. It is neither state nor union. The idea of union seeks to dictate a different type of intercourse among the actors belonging to it, a type of self-limitation in their self-perception, a redefined self-interest, and, hence, redefined policy goals. To the interest of the state must be added the interest of the union. But crucially, it does not extinguish the separate actors who are fated to live in an uneasy tension with two competing senses of the polity's self, the autonomous self and the self as part of a larger union, and committed to an elusive search for an optimal balance of goals and behavior between the union and its actors. I say it is crucial because the unique contribution of the European Union to the civilization of international relations—indeed its civilizing effect on intra-European statal intercourse—derives from that very tension among the state actors and between each state actor and the Union. It also derives from each state actor's need to reconcile the reflexes and ethos of the "sovereign" national state with new modes of discourse and a new discipline of solidarity. Civilization is thus perceived not in the conquering of Eros but in its taming.

Moreover, the idea of Europe as union not only conditions discourse among states, but it also spills over to the peoples of the states, influencing relations among individuals. For example, the Treaty provisions prohibiting discrimination on grounds of nationality, allowing the free movement of workers and their families, and generally supporting a rich network of transnational social transactions may be viewed not simply as creating the optimal conditions for the free movement of factors of production in the common market. They also serve to remove nationality and state affiliation of the individual, so divisive in the past, as the principal referent for transnational human intercourse.

The unity vision of the Promised Land sees then as its "ideal type" a European polity, finally and decisively replacing its hitherto warring Member States with a political union of federal governance. The union vision sees as its "ideal type" a political union in which Union and Member State continue their uneasy co-existence, although with an ever-increasing embrace. It is important also to understand that the voice of, say, Thatcher is not an expression of this union vision. Thatcherism is one pole of the first vision, whereby Union membership continues to be assessed and re-evaluated in terms of its costs and benefits to a Member State, in this case Great Britain, which remains the ultimate referent for its desirability. The Union is conceived in this way of thinking not as a redefinition of the national self but as an arrangement, elaborate and sophisticated, of achieving long-term maximization of the national interest in an interdependent world. Its value is measured ultimately and exclusively with the coin of national utility and not union solidarity.

I do not think that 1992 can be seen as representing a clear preference and choice for one vision over the other. But there are manifestations, both explicit and implicit, suggesting an unprecedented and triumphal resurgence and ascendancy of the unity vision of Europe over the competing vision of union: part and parcel of the 1992 momentum. If indeed the road to European union is to be paved on this unity vision, at the very moment of ascendancy the Union endangers something noble at its very core and, like other great empires, with the arrival of success may sow the seeds of self-destruction.

Why such foreboding? Whence the peril in the unity vision?

At an abstract logical level it is easy to challenge the unity vision which sets up a fully united Europe as the pinnacle of the process of European integration. It would be more than ironic if a polity with its political process set up to counter the excesses of statism ended up coming round full circle and transforming itself into a (super) state. It would be equally ironic that an ethos that rejected the nationalism of the Member States gave birth to a new European nation and European nationalism. The problem with the unity vision is that its very realization entails its negation.

But the life of the Union (like some other things) is not logic, but experience. And experience suggests that with all the lofty talk of political union and federalism we are not about to see the demise of the Member States, at least not for a long time. The reports leaking out of the intergovernmental conference suggest fairly modest steps on this road.

That being the case, the unease with the unity vision nonetheless remains. For if the unity ethos becomes the principal mobilizing force of the polity, it may, combined with the praxis and rhetoric of the 1992 single market, compromise the deeper values inherent in the union vision, even if the Union's basic structure does not change for years to come.

I suggested above that these values operated both at the interstate level by conditioning a new type of statal discourse and self-perception and at the societal and individual level by diminishing the importance of nationality in transnational human intercourse. How then would the unity vision and the 1992 praxis and rhetoric corrode these values?

The successful elimination of internal frontiers will, of course, accentuate in a symbolic and real sense the external frontiers of the Union. The privileges of Union membership for states and of Union citizenship for individuals are becoming increasingly pronounced. This is manifest in such phenomena as the diffidence of the Union towards further enlargement (packaged in the notion of the concentric circles), in the inevitable harmonization of external border controls, immigration, and asylum policies, and in policies such as local European content of television broadcasting regulation. It assumes picaresque character with the enhanced visibility of the statal symbols already adopted by the Union: flag, anthem, Union passport. The potential corrosive effect on the values of the union vision of European integration are self-evident. Nationality as referent for interpersonal relations, and the human alienating effect of Us and Them are brought back again, simply transferred from their previous intra-Union context to the new inter-Union one. We have made little progress if the Us becomes European (instead of German or French or British) and the Them becomes those outside the Union or those inside who do not enjoy the privileges of citizenship.

There is a second, slightly more subtle, potentially negative influence in this realm. A centerpiece of the agenda for further integration is the need of Europe to develop the appropriate structures for a common foreign and defense policy. It has indeed been anomalous that despite the repeated calls since the early 1970's for a Europe that will speak with one voice, the Union has never successfully translated its internal economic might to commensurate outside influence. There could be much positive in Europe taking such a step to an enhanced common foreign and security policy. The potential corrosive element of this inevitable development rests in the suspicion that some of the harkening for a common foreign policy is the appeal of strength and the vision of Europe as a new global superpower. Europe is a political and economic superpower and often fails to see this and discharge its responsibilities appropriately. But the ethos of strength and power, even if transferred from the Member State to the European level, is closer to the unity rather than union notion of Europe and, as such, partakes of the inherent contradiction of that vision.

All these images and the previous question marks are not intended as an indictment of 1992 and the future road of European integration. Both in its structure and process, and, in part, its ethos, the Union has been more than a simple successful venture in transnational cooperation and economic integration. It has been a unique model for reshaping transnational discourse among states, peoples, and individuals who barely a generation ago emerged from the nadir of Western civilization. It is a model with acute relevance for other regions of the world with bleak histories or an even bleaker present.

Today's Union is impelled forward by the dysfunctioning of its current architecture. The transformation that is taking place has immense, widely discussed promise. If I have given some emphasis to the dangers, it is not simply to redress a lacuna in the literature. It is also in the hope that as this transformation takes place, that part, limited as it may be, of the Union that can be characterized as the modern contribution of Europe to the civilization of interstatal and intrastatal intercourse shall not be laid by the wayside.

Chapter 2

Constitutional Structure

I. Supremacy of European Union Law[1]

> "The European Economic Community is a Community based on the rule of law, inasmuch as neither its Member States nor its institutions can avoid a review of the question whether the measures adopted by them are in conformity with the basic constitutional charter, the Treaty." Case 294/83, *Parti écologiste 'Les Vertes' vs. European Parliament* [1986] E.C.R. 1339, 1365.

Thirty-five years ago, a group of European statesmen set out to do something that nobody had ever done before. They wrote a treaty which in due course would convert itself into a constitution. How far this change has gone and what kind of constitution is emerging is the question before us.

Anyone who tells you that it is easy to change the way large numbers of people do things is either a liar or a management consultant. The European Founding Fathers knew that what they wanted had to be done gradually. Jean Monnet wrote that economic integration and setting up a Union institution with binding legal powers over States would be "the first practical foundations of a European federation indispensable for the preservation of peace." The European Founding Fathers were frank about what they were doing. They said they were "determined to lay the foundations of an ever closer union among the peoples of Europe." They gave the Court of Justice the power of judicial review of Union acts. They visualized direct elections though not at first to the European Parliament that they were setting up. But they had no blueprint for the ultimate objective. If they had openly drafted a constitution, it would not have been adopted. They drafted only a foundation, a framework, a "*traité-cadre*." Europe has no Federalist Papers.

All previous federations have either been set up progressively, or have been formed by a group of States not really independent of one another, or have been set up by force. So the European Union has good reasons for not being quite like any other federation. In fact, it is one of the only genuinely new political inventions in this cen-

[1] John Temple Lang, *The Development of European Community Constitutional Law,* 13 Dublin U. L.J. 36 (1991). © 1991 John Temple Lang. Reprinted by permission.

tury. In law there is no greater scope for creativity than in helping to build a whole new legal system.

The European Union Treaty said that some rules of Union law would be "directly applicable," without national implementing measures, in the laws of the Member States. The controversy about this at the time shows how strong the political limits were then, and why the Founding Fathers had to proceed slowly.

Because they were writing a treaty, which would only become a constitution later, they did not even say that Union law would prevail over national laws in the courts of the Member States. That principle, essential in the constitutional law of any federation but not a rule which is found in the texts of treaties, was declared by the Court of Justice five years after the Treaty came into force.

Because they wanted their treaty to grow into a constitution, the draftsmen wrote no clause defining Union jurisdiction or State powers. But they knew what they were doing: Hallstein said, "We are not in business, we are in politics."

There is a risk that if you don't know where you want to go, you may end up somewhere else. The fact that the European Union has avoided that risk is largely due to guidance from the Court. A treaty, even a brilliantly conceived treaty, does not grow into a constitution without a lot of effort. Advocate General Mancini has said that "The Court has sought to 'constitutionalize' the Treaty, that is, to fashion a constitutional framework for a federal-type structure in Europe." The constitutional law principles of the Union are mostly found in the judgments of the Court, and not in the Treaty. As a result of the Court's case law, the Union is more integrated legally than it is politically. (The Court repeatedly uses the phrase "in the present state of Union law" to indicate that new legislation is needed). So, like Molière's Monsieur Jourdain, who was surprised to find that he had been talking prose all his life, European lawyers have suddenly seen something which the court has always remembered: in John Marshall's words, "it is a constitution that we are expounding."

Any human society in which some powers are exercised by the constituent bodies and some by the center, on the basis of a basic legal framework, will have the essential characteristics of a federation. It is useful, especially for lawyers accustomed to a federal constitution, to analyze the Union accordingly. But the Union is not a federal State. Today, at least, it is not a State at all, it is *sui generis*. A federation is only a paradigm for the Union.

If you do not admit that you are writing a constitution, you fail to say certain things which you would otherwise certainly include. This means that the courts have to decide whether the things you have omitted are there or not. In the Union, the Court has filled many of the gaps left in the Treaties. The Court has built up the constitutional law of the Union by defining the elements of the Union's legal system. In doing so, it has had to reconcile two objectives: the need to make the Union effective, and the need to impose safeguards on the exercise of Union powers, to protect minority interests within the European Union. The Court has done this not by protecting State powers, but by making effective safeguards directly available under Union law.

A. The Primacy of Union Law: The Basis for Fundamental Rights

One of the main foundations on which the Court has built extensively is the principle of the supremacy of Union law. The Court has used this principle, which it had itself established, to hold: (1) that rules of Union law which are directly applicable in national courts prevail over the national law of Member States. They prevail not only in the case of direct conflict, but also when the national law would interfere with the operation of Union law. "Every national judge is also a Union law judge." (2) that rules of Union law which are not directly applicable in national courts can nevertheless be relied on by private citizens and companies in litigation against national authorities.

To these basic safeguards for the effectiveness of the Union legal system, the Court has in effect added a Bill of Rights, by a remarkable series of judgments.

During the 1960s, German constitutional lawyers argued that the Union Treaties contained no fundamental rights provisions, and that the Federal Republic of Germany could not confer powers on the Union which were not subject to review by the German courts for compatibility with the German Constitution. The Court rightly saw these arguments as threats to the primacy of Union law over national law. In answer, it held that principles of fundamental human rights were part of the law which the Court must apply when it exercises its powers of judicial review of Union acts. The Court said that these principles of fundamental rights were to be drawn from the European Convention on Human Rights, and from the constitutions of Member States of the Union. In effect, in this respect at least there is a common law of the Union.

Seldom in the history of law has so serious a difficulty been solved so as to benefit a legal system so profoundly. According to Advocate General Mancini: "Reading an unwritten bill of rights into Union law is . . . the most striking contribution the Court has made to the development of a constitution for Europe."

This impressive piece of judicial legislation was not prompted by some flagrant violation of human rights, but by the need to uphold the principle of the primacy of Union law. The driving force of the Union is no longer limited to avoiding another European war and setting up a single market: it now has a moral element.

The Single European Act, and other Union documents, now contain explicit references to the European Convention on Fundamental Rights.

Fundamental rights, as the Court sees them, include rights under a number of general legal principles which are in some ways closer to administrative law than to constitutional law. These include the principle of proportionality, which says that no official measure may impose cost or inconvenience on private citizens which is clearly unnecessary or out of proportion to the aim to be achieved—clearly an important safeguard for citizens' rights.

Another principle is that of legal certainty—the principle that the law should at any time be ascertainable—which prohibits retroactive measures except in limited circumstances, invalidates excessively vague legislation, and creates an administrative law rule similar to estoppel. These general principles of law are both substantive rules which, on occasion, invalidate Union measures, both legislative and executive, and also rules for the interpretation of Union legislation. Unlike the fundamental rights rules, there was no single European document anywhere setting out these principles: the Court imported them from the national laws of Member States to aid the exercise of its powers of judicial review.

It seems clear that both these general principles of Union law and the Union rules on fundamental rights apply not only to Union measures but also to measures adopted by Member States in the sphere of Union law. This is important because Union law is decentralized: most of Union law is implemented and applied by Member State authorities. The Union institutions are far too small to carry out Union policies by themselves. They rely on national authorities to do so. The Union legal system is a symbiosis, not a structure parallel to national authorities, so both must be subject to all the same safeguards for private rights. In this respect also Union law principles prevail over national laws, even national laws implementing Union policies. Because Union fundamental rights rules are directly applicable they prevail over national law even in the courts of Member States. So Union law has limited the powers of Member States over their own citizens.

The Union list of fundamental rights and of general principles of administrative law is open-ended: the Court may add to them if necessary.

Another consequence of the supremacy of Union law is equally logical, but perhaps less obvious. Unlike most federations, the Union's fundamental law contains no list of exclusive Union or national powers. There is no residue of powers reserved to Member States. Reading the Treaties one gets the impression that all the Union's powers are concurrent. The Court, on the basis of the EEC Treaty, has decided that the Union has exclusive powers over external trade and other aspects of "commercial policy," and over sea fisheries, mergers in the coal and steel industry, and certain nuclear matters, and where national powers are preempted by exhaustive Union legislation. Recently, the Union also has got exclusive powers over large corporate mergers.

Since Union legislation always prevails over national law, Union legislation, once adopted, can be amended only by the Union.

So every piece of Union legislation creates *pro tanto* an area of exclusive Union legislative power. This is much more important than in any federation known to me, because the Treaties gave the Union such wide (non-exclusive) legislative powers. In effect, there is a moving boundary between Union and State powers, and the boundary moves only in one direction. Union constitutional law is dynamic, not static: it was never intended to be changeless. The original intent was for development.

I do not need to stress the essentially constitutional nature of all these principles. The primacy of federal law, its expanding scope and its direct application to private citizens, are normal in a federation.

B. Separation of Powers, European Union Style

Within the original six Member States of the Union, the separation of legislative, executive and judicial powers advocated by Montesquieu is well respected. In the Union it was cast aside: the Commission, in many respects the Union executive, is the only body with power to propose legislation. The power to adopt legislation is separated from the power to initiate it.

The legislature, the Council, is composed of representatives of the executives, not the legislatures, of Member States. The power to negotiate treaties is separated from the power to ratify them, and it is the Union legislature which ratifies them. The only directly elected body, the Parliament has, with some very important exceptions, only advisory powers. In each case the explanation lies in the reluctance of Member States in 1956 to confer wide powers on the Union institutions.

C. The Union Legislative Process

Its legislative process was one of the Union's political inventions. It is a compromise between the intergovernmental agreements of classical international organizations and a fully federal legislature. The primary Union law making body is the Council which is an intergovernmental body. But the Council can legislate only on the basis of a proposal from the Commission, and the Commission's independence is guaranteed by the Treaty so that it can make neutral, objective proposals in the interests of the Union as a whole. This responsibility, and its duties as enforcer of the Treaties, places great demands on the integrity, courage, and intelligence of the members of the Commission. The interests of Member States which are in a minority are protected by the rule that although the Commission's proposal can be adopted by a qualified majority, it can be amended only by a unanimous vote of the Council, or by the Commission itself. There is weighted voting for qualified majorities: Member States have not got equal votes, but the smaller States have votes out of proportion to their size.

The Commission's obligation to make its proposals in the interests of the whole Union is a political duty, not directly enforceable by legal rules. But another series of legal principles provide protection for the interests of Member States, of companies, and of individuals. The Union legislature is not sovereign: there is judicial review of the compatibility of legislation with the Treaty and with the rules on fundamental rights. Every Union measure must also be based on a specific legal power, which not only determines whether the measure can be adopted by qualified majority or not, but also determines the nature of the reasons which must be given for the measure, in the preamble of the measure itself. If sufficient reasons are not given, or if the reasons are inappropriate to the legal basis claimed, the measure can be annulled on that ground alone. The duty to state the reasons for each measure, in the measure itself, is a valuable assurance of open government, and the duty not to discriminate obliges the legislature to explain why one situation is not being treated in the same way as other, apparently similar, situations.

These rules apply to all legal measures adopted by the Union, to decisions in individual cases, as well as to general legislative measures.

D. The Means of Protection of Private Rights

Union law creates rights for individuals and companies. If a Union measure is a decision addressed to an individual or company (e.g., an antitrust or antidumping decision), its validity can be challenged directly in the Union courts in Luxembourg. Rights under directly applicable rules can be relied on in national courts against anyone. Rights under rules which need implementation ("directives") can be relied on against the authorities of a State which should have implemented them, whether or not it has done so, though they can be relied on against private parties only to the extent that they have been implemented. The fact that so many rules of Union law can be relied on against State authorities in national courts makes Union law extremely effective especially because of the rule that Union law prevails over inconsistent Member State law.

Curiously, the Court has not yet clearly decided in what circumstances an individual or company has a right under Union law to recover damages from a State for injury caused by breach of a directly applicable rule. I believe that there is a right to damages in all such cases. If I am proved right, Union law will be equipped with an enforcement weapon of great power: many protectionist or discriminatory State measures are prohibited by directly applicable rules, and it would be very salutary indeed if States had to pay damages for every infringement.

Individuals and companies may not sue national authorities in the Union Court, nor may they bring proceedings there against the Commission if they are in substance proceedings against a Member State. But they may achieve a similar result, if they are determined enough, by proceedings in national courts, in which the relevant questions of Union law can be referred by the national court to Luxembourg. Union law is fully enforceable in all courts.

E. The Legal Duties of the Member States to Cooperate with Union Institutions

Another great foundation on which the Court has built Union constitutional law is Article 5 of the EEC Treaty. This is a general provision obliging Member States to ensure fulfillment of the obligations arising out of the Treaty or resulting from action taken by the institutions of the Union, to facilitate the achievement of the Union's tasks, and to abstain from any measure which could jeopardize the attainment of the objectives of the Treaty.

The Court knew that it was a constitution which it was interpreting and, as civil law lawyers do, deduced concrete precise results from general words. Indeed, it went further. It said that Article 5 "is the expression of the more general rule imposing on Member States and the Union institutions *mutual* duties of genuine cooperation and assistance" (emphasis supplied). Once again, the court has deduced a constitutional principle significantly broader than the words of the Treaty themselves. This principle is essential in the Union, especially because there is no fixed frontier between Union and State powers.

The area of concurrent Union and State powers is so wide that strict duties of cooperation are essential (*Physical Protection of Nuclear Materials Ruling*, 1978).

Because Union policies and legislation are implemented and applied largely by national authorities, and not through separate federal agencies, the need for cooperation, (and the scope for observation of Union policy) is much greater than it is in the United States.

The duties of Member States which the Court has deduced from the general words of Article 5 are already far reaching and various. They include:

- the duty to give full effect to Union law, and to clarify the national position under Union law.
- the duty to enforce Union law, and not to encourage breaches of it.
- the duty to comply with fundamental rights rules and the "general principles of law" (proportionality, legal certainty, etc.).
- the duty to implement Union objectives.
- the duty to provide information to the Commission and to consult it.
- the duty to act jointly with other Member States.

The court is establishing another new Union contribution to federal theory: legal duties of cooperation in a sphere of concurrent powers, rather than theoretically fixed frontiers between Union and State powers.

F. The Foreign Relations Law of the Union

The division of powers between the Union and its Member States in the sphere of foreign relations has also a number of features which are quite different from those of normal federations:

- the Union has, so far, no legal powers in the spheres of foreign policy or defense.
- the powers of the Union over "commercial policy" (i.e., trade policy and a wide but so far imprecisely defined area of other external economic relations) were declared to be exclusive by the Court, not by the Treaty itself. The Court has always stressed the need for unity in the Union's external relations.
- the Court has ruled that the Union has implied concurrent treaty-making power in all areas in which it has power to adopt Union measures, even when no internal measures have yet been adopted. As a result, the treaty-making procedure in many areas involves all the same steps as in the case of internal Union legislation (consultation with the Parliament and the Economic and Social Committee) which is lengthy and inconvenient.
- treaties are negotiated by the Commission, acting in its basic role as the body responsible for the interests of the Union as a whole, but ratified by the Council.
- treaties can be self-executing within the Union ("have direct effects"). If not drafted in this way, they can be implemented either by a Union measure (a regulation or a directive) or by the Member States. Member States are bound by the Treaty to give effect to any international agreement to which the Union is a

party, even if the Union has not implemented it, and even if the State in question is not a party itself.

Since breach of a treaty to which the Union is a party is a breach of Union law, the Court has compulsory jurisdiction over the State in such a case.

Perhaps the most unusual, and certainly the most inconvenient, feature of the Union's external relations law is that both the Union and the Member States have, and regularly exercise, treaty making powers in the same spheres. I know of no other federation in which treaty making powers are regularly exercised concurrently. All federations are diverse internally, but most are unified externally. This odd situation results from the wide range of concurrent powers of the Union and the States. This means that sometimes both the Union and its Member States are parties to the same treaty, as in the case of the Vienna Convention on the Protection of the Ozone Layer. This can necessitate special provisions dealing with the responsibility for implementing the treaty in question, and to negotiating difficulties, both for the Union side and for other States dealing with it. I have already said that the division of powers between the Union and its Member States is not fixed, but changing. The Court, always anxious to reinforce Union solidarity, has said that other parties to a treaty need not determine which obligations will be carried out by which. "Mixed" agreements, with both the Union and its Member States as parties, are wholly new international law problems, caused because the Union's unique constitution falls short of a traditional federation with unified treaty-making powers.

Under Union constitutional law there seems to be a traditional hierarchy of legal rules. Subject to them, public international law, treaties to which the Union is a party, and Union legislation take precedence over State laws, in that order. Since a treaty entered into by the Union or one of its Member States might, in theory, be contrary to the Union constitution, diplomats negotiating with the Union need to know something of Union law. Under the Vienna Convention on the Law of Treaties, they would certainly be treated as being aware of, for example, the well known rule that only the Union, and not is Member States, has power to enter treaties on trade and other commercial policy matters.

The Union has not got unlimited treaty making powers: the Court in an Advisory Opinion has ruled that there are strict limits on the extent to which the Union could confer powers on an international body set up with non-Member States, and there are still some areas in which the Member States have exclusive powers. However, the Advisory Opinions of the Court can ensure that in practice the Union never exceeds its powers.

G. Union-Member State Relations

Compared with a conventional federation, there are several curious features of the Union-State division of powers:

- the Treaty contains no list of Union or State powers.
- although States have great concurrent powers, there is no State action doctrine: States have no power to create exceptions to Union law.

- States' powers are not derived from the Union constitution: the Treaty is the basis of the Union's constitutional law, but not that of the States' constitutions. There are thirteen *grundnorms* in the Union. But insofar as Union rules now form part of the States' constitutional laws, the States can alter them only by amending the Treaty.

H. Decentralization and Delegation of Union Power to Member State Authorities

Apart from the Member States' own powers, the Union's powers are exercised through State authorities in a variety of ways. The most important, in economic terms, are the day-to-day administration of much of the Union's agricultural policy and its customs regime. All directives are implemented by measures at State or regional level. Another example is the State legislation providing criminal penalties for breach of Union rules on, for example, fisheries: in some States it is not thought appropriate for the Union to exercise powers in the sphere of criminal law. In addition, even where the Union has exclusive powers (as in trade, fisheries, or where the Union has adopted comprehensive legislation), Member States may have powers delegated to them, and may even take measures as trustees on behalf of the Union in order to protect its interests. The Member States must then act only with the consent of the Commission. Because the action is taken on behalf of the Union, the Commission's role in the legislative process must be maintained as far as possible.

One version of the principle of "subsidiarity" is that governmental action should as far as possible be taken at the lowest level (Union, national, regional or local) at which it can be effective. This is of course a justification both for decentralizing of Union powers and for refraining from Union action in areas where national or regional action can be as satisfactory. The more the principle of subsidiarity is acted on, the more important it will be for national and regional authorities to comply with, and enforce, Union law.

I. Non-Participation by Some Member States in Union Arrangements Associated with the Union—A "Two Speed Europe"

Another odd feature of Union constitutional practice, which results from incomplete integration, is the fact that some Member States are not participants in some regimes associated with the Union, in which you would expect them all to participate. The best known example of this is the United Kingdom's long refusal to join the Exchange Rate Mechanism of the Union's monetary system. Another is the long delay in Denmark and Ireland becoming parties to the Union Patent Convention. The possibility that some Member States may not be parties is also allowed for by the Union Copyright Convention. This flexibility and pragmatism contrasts with the very clear statement in the

Single European Act that acceptance of the foreign policy provisions of that Act are a *sine qua non* for Union membership: Member States cannot join the Union for economic purposes and not for political purposes.

J. Regional Authorities within Member States

Several Member States of the Union either are themselves federations or have delegated extensive governmental powers to regional authorities. These situations give rise to various issues under Union Constitutional law:

- regional authorities are bound, within their powers, by all the rules of Union law prohibiting discrimination and protectionism, and by all the duties of cooperation resulting from Article 5. However, if a regional authority fails to fulfill one of these obligations, it is the national government, not the regional authority, which is brought before the Court. This is important: the widespread failure to implement directives, especially environmental directives, is due to regional authorities taking their duties under Union law less seriously than national governments.
- regional authorities may have standing to challenge decisions of the Union institutions of special interest to them, such as a Union decision prohibiting the granting of a subsidy.

K. The Features of the Present Constitution of the Union

The Union constitution, viewed simply as a constitution, is still clearly incomplete, and has a number of striking features.

Apart from those already mentioned, the most obvious is the great power of Member States:

- the budgets of the States are very large in comparison to the Union budget.
- State government representatives form the Union's principal legislative body.
- there are wide areas of State powers which are exclusive in practice.
- much Union law is enforced by the States' authorities.

Another obvious feature is the great power of the Council when it acts unanimously: it acts in many respects as both legislature and executive.

Apart from the legal constraints already outlined, its powers are reduced in practice by the reluctance of States to act jointly unless necessary, and by their difficulty in agreeing.

You will see that the Union's constitution is unlikely to produce strong leadership.

The third striking feature is the limited powers—essentially advisory, except in budgetary matters—of the directly elected Parliament, the "democratic deficit." The Parliament has no power to initiate legislation. These limited powers are constantly exercised, with a view to maximizing them, and they were substantially increased by the Single European Act, which itself was the result of an initiative of the Parliament.

A fourth unusual feature is that some rules of purely economic law, for example antitrust rules, have constitutional status and cannot be changed.

Napoleon said that a constitution should be "short and obscure" presumably because that made it flexible. The Union constitution, the Treaties, are certainly not short, but because they are framework treaties rather than normative Treaties they are surprisingly flexible.

So the constitution of the Union is taxonomically an odd animal indeed.

The Union, unlike the United States in 1787, so far shows no signs of giving itself a whole, new, coherent, codified constitution, on conventional federal lines. It is planning another round of specific amendments to the basic Treaties. The key to changing the Union into a normal federation, making the Council into a Senate representing States instead of a body representing State governments, has not yet been mentioned. The journey's ultimate destination is still unknown. But unfortunately an operation which can only be accomplished by many small steps runs the risk of being frustrated by many small minds. As J.M. Keynes said, "the difficulty is not to get acquainted with new ideas, it is to get rid of the old ones." Much of the controversy about Union and State power has been conducted unintelligently, either in terms of "sovereignty" (never defined and so never understood as a divisible bundle of powers), on the basis of suspicions that the Union is either a "Socialist" or a "Capitalist" ogre, or otherwise in shrill caricature. The Union is seen as a threat to States' powers, not yet as a debate about the allocation of limited powers of government.

L. The Future

Soia Mentschikoff, in *Federalism and the New Nations of Africa*, said that in a federation the central government should control "foreign affairs, matters of currency, communications, transport, banking, international and interstate trade, and bankruptcy." We are not there yet, but we are getting there. Union law already covers some of these areas: there are, or soon will be, proposals dealing at least partly with all the others. There is still no general power to tax, and no power to raise armed forces.

But while recognizing that the Union constitution is still incomplete, we should recognize what it has already achieved. War between the Member States of the Union is not now merely impossible. It is inconceivable. That is a gigantic achievement. Struggles over power that used to call out troops now call out lawyers. They are almost as expensive, but not so destructive.

The European Union has a constitution a little like that of the US before 1787, and Europe as a whole is creating new constitutions from scratch, rather as it was in 1815. But now governments can be legitimate only if they are based on democracy. Democracy, if it is to last, must be based on prosperity. Prosperity must, in European circumstances, be based on economic integration of national free markets. The challenge is to reconcile economic integration with legitimate nationalism. The main problems for Europe today are to restore and consolidate democracy and prosperity in Eastern Europe and to restore the identities of suppressed minorities (President Wilson's problem). The Union can show how to solve both problems. Both the "deepening" and "widening" of the European Union are possible and necessary. The Court, within its judicial role, has both "deepened" the constitution of the Union by strengthening and adding to the obligations expressly listed in the Treaties and "widened" it by importing the European Convention on Human Rights which is shared by a wider Europe than the Union.

Americans are impatient people, and frequently ask why the Union cannot become, in one step, a United States of Europe. Be patient, Jacques Delors has said, "History is speeding up." Remember, the homogeneity of the US in 1787 was apparent, and not real. The US Constitution would have been much harder to agree on if slaves and native Americans had been represented in the discussions. We, in Europe, are trying to do something similar entirely democratically, and we are not trying to do it when everyone knows that new ideas are needed. In times of great change, people are willing to change greatly; it is much harder to persuade them to change on their own initiative.

Any strategy begins with a vision. Europe has gotten this far because of two brilliant legal insights which followed Monnet's perception that economic integration would progressively lead to political integration. The two legal insights were that fundamental rights could be ruled judicially to be part of Union law, and that unity in external relations would progressively lead to internal integration as well. Both these legal insights seem to be due largely to one great lawyer, Pierre Pescatore, the European John Marshall. He probably contributed more than any other single person to the fact that the Court has always had a strategic vision which was both dynamic and statesmanlike, and has made such good use of the available materials and the opportunities which presented themselves. The Court has provided an entirely new Union legal system with the foundations it needed in the Member States' laws. It now has continuity, sources of new ideas, legitimacy, integration, and acceptability. In other words, the European Union has already a constitution.

Questions and Comments for Your Consideration

1. The United States Constitution is, of course, a written, self-contained document. In radical contrast, the British "Constitution" is an unwritten constitution. The British Parliament may enact any law whatsoever without fear of it being overturned on the grounds of unconstitutionality by any court. The "constitution" is thus a sense of restraint on the part of Parliamentarians, a sense that laws ought not to be proposed or enacted which depart too radically from centuries of British tradition.

2. Is the European Union's "constitution" closer in form to the American or the British model? In substance?

3. Do you agree with John Temple Lang, the author of the essay you have just read, that the Founding Fathers of the American Constitution had a comparatively easy job in 1787 because they did not give enslaved Americans a voice in drafting or ratifying the Constitution?

4. Do you agree with the implicit premise in John Temple Lang's essay that it is important for European countries to have a constitution? In considering this question, imagine that all the countries of North and South American were to get together and attempt to have a Western Hemispheric Union modeled on the European Union. Suppose a treaty were drafted that would have the same content as all the treaties to date that comprise the "constitution" of the European Union. Finally, suppose that you are asked to state your position whether or not the United States should join this new Western Hemispheric Union. Would you be in favor? Or against? Why? Now suppose you are a citizen of one of the countries of Western Europe. How many, if any, of the reasons you just gave—regarding the United States joining or not joining the Western Hemispheric Union—seem to apply to the country of Western Europe that you are now "representing"?

II. Judicial Interpretation

A. On Court Ideology[2]

The thrust of the social task of courts is to render essentially predictable judgments. According to most accumulated scholarship, predictability flows from the availability of the main characteristics of judges' adjudicative work. It is that from some "applicable," basically pre-existing and ideally neutral and principled norm, and following an adversary process, the independent judge, by utilizing a reasoning dictated by pre-established thought-techniques amongst which logic is of pre-eminence, arrives as a normally inescapable "winner-take-all" verdict which except for a possible appeal definitively settles the case and conflict brought before this court.

This portrait is not solely descriptive. Instead, it is loaded with ideology. The ideal is that judicial authority and legitimacy flows from courts' simultaneous realization of all the above-mentioned five core elements of the judicial task. In this perception, the more completely the ideal is translated into judicial reality, the richer is judicial authority and legitimacy believed to be. Inversely, without authority and legitimacy there will be no "court" in the ordinary sense of this word. Therefore, judges ought to live up to the ideal. The portrait has ceased to be solely factual and has entered the realm of deontology and metaphysics.

The underlying sociological rationale of the need for an ideal-type performance is, in Professor Dawson's words, that it meets society's "deeply felt and constant need for trustworthy neutrals." From an ideal-type performance, Dawson says, follows courts "peculiar power to enlist obedience and impose control." And he continues: "Neutrality and trust were not necessarily forfeited when judges made up the rules as they went along, as in medieval England." On the other hand the experience of France reveals that:

---

2 Hjalte Rasmussen, *Between Self-Restraint and Activism: A Judicial Policy for the European Court*, 13 E. L. Rev. 28-38 (1988). © 1988 by Hjalte Rasmussen. Reprinted by permission.

> there are limits to the allegiance that judges can inspire. The judges of pre-revolutionary France became partisans in political strife for a reason that seemed to them persuasive—that other political agencies had failed as restraints on royal absolutism. In their attempt to fill a great gap in French political institutions they brought disaster on themselves and caused a lasting impairment of their own function whose effects in France are not yet spent.[3]

1. Four Fundamental Premises of Judicial Research

Four fundamental premises underlie any judicial-activism research. The first is, as Professor Schemers has rightly emphasized, that "The Court's constitutional role is enormous."[4] The second is intimately interconnected—that the Court's constitutional role is, nonetheless, not boundary-free. The European Court's judges should not be considered "a unique body of impervious legal technicians above and beyond the political struggle."[5] Yet, if a boundary does exist, there resides an interest in locating it. At the very least, its approximate location must be determined or understood by those involved in making judicial decisions or in commenting on their role in political integration. Judicial research has as yet only paid a limited attention to this problem.

A comparative perspective constitutes the third premise. Indeed, as is well known, during the formative years of the American Union, the United States Supreme Court's constant *leitmotif* in adjudication of the nation's federalism conflicts was the Constitution's "more-perfect-union" declaration. The parallel between the American Court's endeavors then, and the centralizing tendencies of the European Court's "ever-closer-union" inspired case law some 150 years later, is self-evident. This is of considerable interest, because experience informs us that early Supreme Court's activism triggered widespread and often violent accusations that the Court was violating the Constitution's presumed balance of powers between the central and the local governments by steadily carving out State powers, thereby infringing on the States' rights. In so doing, the Supreme Court was believed to usurp constitution-making powers.

American constitutional history also informs us that several other confrontations between the Supreme Court and the political arms of government occurred at later points of time, following the Court's promotion of values that powerful segments of the body politic did not fully share. At stake in each of these confrontations was the United States Supreme Court's authority and legitimacy. The fourth premise may be thus formulated: With hindsight we know that the American Court has survived all attacks. Today its prestige in American society is enormous and its authority is largely unchallenged.

In the European Union, no similar hindsight provides us with a similarly comfortable assurance that the European Court will emerge unweakened from similar con-

---

[3] The quotes are from J.P. Dawson, *Oracles of the Law*, Thomas Cooley Lectures, University of Michigan, Ann Arbor, 1968.

[4] Henry G. Schermers in preface to Hjalte Rasmussen, *On Law and Policy in the European Court of Justice: A Comparative Study in Judicial Policymaking* (Martinus Nijhoff, 1986).

[5] Martin Shapiro, *On Law and Politics in the Supreme Court* (Free Press of Glencoe, 1964).

frontations with its countervailing powers, be they Union institutions or State-associated agencies or interests. No regime is likely to accept important political powers wielded by an isolated judicial corps free of political restraints. Indeed, if the European Court were to be seen to overstep the boundaries of its functions and if court-curbing or court-destroying initiatives were launched accordingly, the European Court might well come out ruined in its authority and legitimacy. A day-to-day erosion of the European Court's authority and legitimacy would be ruinous too. Such outcomes would not be catastrophic solely for the European Court but for the entire Union experience, precisely because the European Court has been in the past an important source of Union regulatory legitimacy—a source which the Union could not afford to witness drying out under the weight of an uncontrolled pro-Union activism. It is likely that the Union also in the future will remain uniquely dependent on the Court for much of its integrational progress.

2. The Thrust of the EC Activism Discussion

The entire activism discussion thus, in a manner, deals with the protection-destruction issue in relation to the European Court's original and accumulated authority and legitimacy. The paradox is probably unavoidable. At stake in any powerful promotion of political integration by judicial decision is always the court's unfettered ability to continue to promote precisely political integration. This is inevitably so because the European Court has to invent legal constructions to the political problems under adjudication with which enforcement agencies on Union and national levels will comply; and because noncompliance and defiance is likely to flow from a perception of the European court as a usurper of political power.

Using the method-of-interpretation language we may now rephrase that question in the following manner: how liberally may the Union judge, following his perception of the (correct) policy-orientation, which ought to prevail in judicial decision, give preference to teleology over text: to some nebulous *effect necessaire* over Treaty provisions which do not ordain such effect; or give preference to systematic construction in order to incorporate visions of the Founders into operational constitutional law; or give preference to society's apparently changing taste for more integration, at least if it is judicially decreed at high speed?

There should, despite the observations which have been made in the preceding paragraphs, exist no doubt that the preamble *self-evidently* offers interpretative guidance to the European judges. And as the Union experience went on, some evidence is also supportive of the proposition that the judges' frequent use of the "ever-closer-union" *leitmotif* was tolerated as warranted; in some quarters it even drew applause. This is merely one side of the coin, however.

Indeed, students of courts in general and of the European Court in particular, will not be strangers to the proposition that any court has to calculate its activism nicely because miscalculation is likely to provoke clashes with other organs of government. Careful calculation becomes a complicated matter, however, only because activism feeds on itself. Once begun, the activist course often must not only continue, it must also intensify. If it does not, litigants' deceived expectations are ultimately at a risk of turning other future client-litigants away from the court-rooms where the particular offered, respectively demanded, value-promotion used to be available. Yet, our experience seems to confirm that late arriving litigants will become increasingly demanding. They will arrive in court with high hopes that new (pro-Union) terrain is likely to be taken under the judicial plough, merely for the asking. Whence: not only continuation but intensification.

Be this as it may, the question about how calculation is technically made remains unanswered. If a normative theory of Union Law interpretation were available the answer could be given. Indeed, activism would be excessive (miscalculated) above or beyond these interpretative results warranted by the theory. "Above and beyond that limit" clashes with the other organs of government would develop. Yet a normative theory does not exist.

3. No Normative Theory of Interpretation of Union Law

Is the formulation of a normative theory of interpretation of Union law feasible? I submit that at the present stage of development of the Union and of its law this question should be answered in the negative. I shall here explain why, but, first, outline the circumstances of which a normative theory would have to take full account.

The peculiarities of Union law interpretation, include:

(1) that the Union was created by a covenant between fully sovereign States;
(2) that, neither at the moment of creation nor at any subsequent point of time, have the political circumstances normally believed to condition a successful federalization of independent states been present;
(3) that the *travaux préparatoires* have remained and probably will remain inaccessible for the purpose of interpretation of Union law;
(4) that the Treaty-draftsmen's legacy, the Treaties, are documents frequently displaying widely incompatible declarations of intent (incompatibility most notably emerges between the Preamble [plus the opening Articles] and many of the operational Articles) and
(5) that since the inception of the Union merely 30 years ago, the number of component parts has risen at a quick pace from six via nine and 10, to 12.

The claimed impossibility of construction of a normative theory, pretending to represent anything but an academic interest, follows if one considers the necessity for such a theory to be grounded upon some sort of a consensus in relation to the integration/co-operation experiment's fundamental values. Indeed, if a genuine consensus about the basic supra-nationalism/integration-value ever existed, intervening changes in the value-priorities of the Union's body politic may have triggered changes in the substantive ingredients of that consensus and in the conjecture in which it operates. This is the stumbling block. Indeed, as long as nothing remotely resembling a consensus in that respect is not at hand—and I submit that it is not and that it will hardly develop in any foreseeable future—any attempt to formulate a normative interpretative theory is doomed to failure.

This conclusion is compelling since the necessary balancing of the relative weight of the five core elements of any normative theory enumerated above must—and can only—be accomplished if the sixth ingredient, the consensus element, is a known variable. As long as that consensus is still, at best, in the making, to construe a theory about judicial decisions' possible contribution to political integration/co-operation—or its future potentiality for relieving society of the freezing effects of political inertia—remains a nonsensical enterprise—or—perhaps more precisely put, an enterprise of almost exclusive academic interest. Be this even as it may, no-one else has as yet (to my knowledge) successfully tried out his inventive skills in establishing such a theory.

Finally, needless to say, it is not possible to turn to the European Court for an authoritative answer to our question about a normative theory. This follows because it is precisely the European Court's interpretative handling of its business that has led to our present activism investigations. To turn to the European Court would, indeed, amount to little more than to entrust the guardianship of cabbage to goats.

In the real world, not one ideology but a *multitude* of ideologies and theories of interpretation of Union law are in current circulation, simply because many lawyers and some laymen alike do have some yardstick of that sort of their own making. These yardsticks will usually be on a fairly unsophisticated level, but, most importantly, they will bear the inevitable imprint of the characteristics of the legal-cultural background of the many persons in question. One of the real problems in connection with the activism discussion in the Union context is precisely that, without using a common standard or test, and often only by intuition, most of us believe that we will recognize an "excessive" activism when we see it in operation. It may be regrettable but it is inescapable that for reasons set out above, no single one of this multitude of activism tests, or a suitable mix of elements of some of them, may at the present stage of development of Union law, be fused or elevated to normative prominence.

4. An Alternative, Sociological Yardstick

If the construction of a normative theory is not a viable tool for our activism analysis, another measuring rod may be made available. Indeed, beyond the subjective I-know-it-when-I-see-it tests, a second *more* objective level of activism analysis may be identified. The proposed second-level test must be legal-sociological in nature. It operates by way of a careful and comprehensive collection of the known reactions to the European Court's jurisprudence given by society's countervailing powers. Such case law data represents the positive and the negative policy-signals or policy-inputs relevant to the role of judicial decision in European political integration.

The countervailing powers range from the co-ordinate arms of the Union's own government to courts, parliaments, administrations, legal commentators, press, etc. of the various Member States. Hence, indirectly this test builds on the myriad of level-one evaluations of the European court's case law. The quintessence and merits of the proposed policy-input study is that it avails the members of the European Court as well as commentators of its case law with the same basic data to be used as a measuring rod for identifying the limits to activism. Methodologically and factually synchronized, a meaningful if not agreeable, discussion of the existence or not of the conflict-laden phenomenon of judicial activism may take off on the basis of those data.

As it has already appeared the proposed test is only more objective. It is not ideal objectivity. It is therefore still quite possible that two or more evaluations arrive at different conclusions. However regrettable, this circumstance does not, I submit, ruin the test's validity or viability which resides in that an interpersonal control has been made possible. If misunderstood the proposed acceptability-of-activism test might be taken to suggest that the judge's registration of the surrounding society's favorable or critical reception of his case law aims at making him subservient to the fluctuating whims and policy preferences of the power elites of the moment. This is not so, although it is true that he should collect the policy-inputs in order to decide whether his case law is acceptable or unacceptable and whether it, if unacceptable ought to be modified or not. Far from urging the judge to seek to please the bastions of political power, I want to emphasize that it is one of the most important virtues of the judge's function generally, and especially of judicial review (in the Union and elsewhere), not to be strictly bound to the environment's powers and pressures.

The European judges are merely bound to ensure "that in the interpretation and application of the Treaty the law is observed." EEC Article 164. Article 164 does not, however, help the judge whose case law triggers protest, evasion or/and defiance. Article 164 does not inform him where that Article's solemn obligation must give in to another, as fundamental prerequisite of supreme constitutional umpiring and judicial policy-involvement. This is that in the long run, "given adamant public demand, a constitutional court ultimately must defer to the people's choice." In other words, the judge will have to conform his decisional output to election-day results. This criterion implies that, although a judge should never act as the red-robed puppet of the powerful, it is equally indisputable that judicial authority and legitimacy will erode if, for lengthy periods of time, the judge pursues policies which fly in the face of some prevailing value-consensus in society. The critical hours of confrontation between the Hughes Court and American Society led by President Roosevelt in 1936, a confrontation which ended with judicial submission, illustrates well this point.

There are in fact indications that some members of the European Court may also feel that the Court has gone too far. To illustrate this point, I shall quote from a recent article written by Judge T. Koopmans:

> Maybe we ought to go back to the second role (of judicial function): a *minimal* role. It seems that American case law is heading for that result. It is, more than formerly, based on the essential peace-making function of the law and is being stripped of its more daring and activist sidelines. A similar evolution may be taking shape in the European Communities, especially in the case law of the European Court. If this trend exists, and if it continues, it will make life more difficult for the Union's political institutions especially the Commission. In the past, the Commission often thought it could rely on the Court's help when its case was likely to strengthen European integration. In the future, perhaps it will only be able to do so when it can show a solid legal basis, as the Court's willingness to construct such a basis on its own initiative may diminish.[6]

[6] T. Koopmans, *The Role of Law in the Next Stage of European Integration,* 35 I.C.L.Q. 925 (1986).

Questions and Comments for Your Consideration

1. Hjalte Rasmussen, the author of the essay you have just read, reminds us of the nineteenth century history of constitutional interpretation by the United States Supreme Court. In those years, the Court, lead by Chief Justice John Marshall, adopted a nationalistic view of the powers of the national government, especially in economic matters. The Court consistently ruled in favor of parties who took an expansive view of the Commerce Clause and the Necessary and Proper Clause. Would you say that Justice Marshall was adopting a political perspective in his interpretation of the Constitution? Was he siding politically with the nationalists as opposed to the states-righters?

2. Let us assume that your answer to Question 1 is "Yes." The more difficult question is: can any judge (whether it be John Marshall or anyone else) set aside such "political" perspectives and decide each case "neutrally"? What would it mean to decide a case (such as the landmark case whether Congress had the power to create a national banking system) "neutrally"? Is it psychologically possible for a judge to be "neutral" in such cases? And even if it is, wouldn't "neutrality" also be a "political" position?

3. Suppose the following question were asked of a prospective candidate for appointment to the European Court: "Do you believe in the importance of the European Union?" Suppose she answers, "Yes I do." Would her answer signal to you that she might become too activist a judge in the sense that Mr. Rasmussen talks about in his essay? In any given case that she is called upon to decide, might she not—consistently with her answer to the question—decide either that the claimed additional step should be taken to help strengthen and tighten the European Union, or that the claimed additional step should not be taken because it jumps a little too much and is likely to meet resistance on the part of the public and hence set back the cause of European unity? If she could consistently take either position, aren't Mr. Rasmussen's fears misplaced?

4. Mr. Rasmussen argues that there can be no normative theory of interpretation unless it is grounded upon a consensus in relation to the integration/co-operation experiment's fundamental values. Do you agree? Is it impossible to have a normative theory of interpretation that is opposed by a majority of persons in a community? Why must there be a consensus before you are entitled to have a normative theory?

B. Development of European Law[7]

No doubt the European Court of Justice ("ECJ") has added significantly to many areas of EC law. It has also been regarded as authoritative by the other EC institutions and

[7] Giorgio Gaja, *Beyond the Reasons Stated in Judgments*, 92 Mich. L. Rev. 1966-1976 (1994).

has successfully imposed its views on Member States' courts, which in most cases are entrusted with the application of EC law and the solution of conflicts between EC law and Member States' legislation. Although Article 177 of the EC Treaty established the ECJ as the ultimate interpreter of EC law, this Treaty mandate did not necessarily provide a guarantee that the ECJ's rulings would generally be accepted in practice. It seems fair to state that widespread acceptance has in fact occurred, despite the ECJ's strong profederalist line on issues such as (i) the competence of EC institutions over areas like the protection of the environment about which the Treaty was originally silent; (ii) the supremacy of EC law over Member States' legislation; and (iii) the ability of private parties to invoke Treaty provisions and acts by EC institutions that apparently require implementing legislation.

How did the ECJ achieve all this? Joseph Weiler provided one ingenious explanation about ten years ago[8] when he linked the judicial development of EC law with the EC decisional framework: the fact that EC institutions had been unable, for political reasons, to adopt major legislative measures without the consent of the governments of all the Member States made it possible for the latter to accept the supremacy of EC law and other innovations that the ECJ masterminded. In other words, had EC legislation progressed by majority decisions as the Treaty provided, the Court's case law would have come under political challenge. This explanation would now require some adjustment if one intended to confirm it with regard to the present circumstances, because significant developments have taken place in the normative process, mostly through the Single European Act (SEA) and the Treaty on the European Union treaties which have come into force after their unanimous acceptance on the part of all the Member States. A series of important decisions have been adopted by the EC Council by majority vote.

The absence of individual opinions and the collective drafting of judgments partially explain the fact that "discovery"[9] often yields little with regard to the decisions of the ECJ. While judges publish articles that refer to decisions given by the ECJ, they generally do not critically analyze their own decisions, and on the whole they faithfully comply with their obligation under Article 2 of the ECJ statute "to preserve the secrecy of the deliberations of the Court."[10] The Commission and Member States often intervene in proceedings before the Court and may bring economic and social consequences of prospective rulings to the Court's attention. However, the written briefs are

---

[8] Joseph H.H. Weiler, *The Community System: The Dual Character of Supernationalism,* 1 Y.B. Eur. L. 267 (1981).

[9] "[F]actors that, put together, actually led to the decision as it was reached at a given point in space and time and to the real process whereby the decision was reached . . . . These factors can be of a psychological nature (hence the expression "psychological process"), of a sociological nature (factors relevant to the explanation of social action), or they can be idiosyncratic factors: related to the situation and context, or special characteristics of the institution such as resources, time, working conditions, etc." Joxerramon Bengoetxea, *The Legal Reasoning of the European Court of Justice: Towards a European Jurisprudence.* Oxford: Clarendon Press, p. 114 (1993).

[10] Court of Justice of the European Communities, Selected Instruments relating to the Organization, Jurisdiction and Procedure of the Court 61 (1963).

not usually available to scholars, who must rely upon the short summaries included in the judges' reports for the hearings, the Advocate Generals' opinions, and the judgments. Confidential information, moreover, serves only to provide background knowledge for the Court, as it may not be published.

A variety of factors that are not stated in the ECJ's decisions often influence the answers to even apparently technical questions. The much-discussed question of the horizontal direct effect of EC directives provides a pertinent example.

Under Article 189 of the EC Treaty, a directive "shall be binding, as to the result to be achieved, upon each Member State to which it is addressed, but shall leave to the national authorities the choice of form and methods."[11] This article was originally understood to imply that implementing legislation by Member States was required before a rule stated in a directive could be invoked in courts. However, in a series of decisions in the 1970s, the ECJ held that some provisions included in directives because they were unconditional, complete, and precise would have direct effect, that is, they could be invoked in courts against Member State authorities. This part of the ECJ's case law caused the most criticism by some of the Member States' higher courts—the French Conseil d'Etat in *Cohn-Bendit*[12] and the German Bundesfinanzhof in *Re Value Added Tax Directives*[13]—which determined that the ECJ's view was incompatible with the wording of Article 189 of the EC Treaty and thus refused to accept the idea that directives could have direct effect. This refusal came at a time of vehement media criticism of the ECJ's activism, especially in France.

It hardly seems a coincidence that, after such intense criticism, the ECJ limited the direct effect of directives by specifying that directives, unlike provisions in the EC Treaty, could not be invoked by an individual against another individual, or, in other words, could not have horizontal direct effect. The Court first achieved this goal by stating in *Ratti*[14] that the direct effect of a directive was a sanction for Member State noncompliance with their obligations under the directive. This statement appeared to imply that directives could not be invoked against individuals, a point that was made shortly after *Ratti* in an influential article written by Judge Pescatore in a leading French periodical.[15] The ECJ emphatically asserted that directives could only have vertical effects in *Marshall*.[16]

---

11 Treaty Establishing the European Economic Community [EEC Treaty], Art. 189.

12 *Minister of the Interior v. Cohn-Bendit*, 1 C.M.L.R. 543 (1980).

13 1 C.M.L.R. 527 (1982).

14 Case 148/78, *Pubblico Ministero v. Ratti*, 1979 E.C.R. 1629. The ECJ held that "a Member State which has not adopted the implementing measures required by the directive in the prescribed periods may not rely, as against individuals, on its own failure to perform the obligations which the directive entails." 1979 E.C.R. at 1642.

15 Pierre Pescatore, *L'Effet des Directives Communitaires: Une Tentative de Démythification*, Recueil Dalloz Sirey 171, 176 (1980).

16 Case 152/84, *Marshall v. Southampton and S.-W. Hampshire Area Health Auth.*, 1986 E.C.R. 723, 749.

The ECJ asserted the existence of direct effect "by saying that it must go beyond the letter of the provision and have regard to the useful effect of EC law," whereas it rejected the idea of a horizontal direct effect "by claiming, in a rhetorical appeal to authority, that it was strictly adhering to the wording of Article 189. This contradiction must be criticized from the point of view of rational practical discourse."

To reinforce what seems to be the more plausible reconstruction of the ECJ's case law on the horizontal direct effect issue, it is also significant to note that, once the resistance of Member States' courts to the direct effect of directives subsided, the ECJ to some extent proceeded toward recognizing their horizontal direct effect. The Court stated in its 1990 decision in *Marleasing*[17] that Member States' legislation, even if enacted before a directive, had to be interpreted in cases between individuals "in the light of the wording and the purpose" of the directive even, as was no doubt the case in *Marleasing*, at the cost of distorting national legislation.[18] Thus, directives, although they are still denied horizontal direct effect, may impinge in practice on the relations between individuals.

In systematizing the ECJ's decisions, a distinction can be drawn between clear cases and hard cases, the latter category encompassing those cases in which an interpretation in the narrow sense of the word is required. The ECJ's practice runs as follows: "Justification in clear cases is rather straightforward and follows roughly a deductive scheme. Justification in hard cases follows deductive schemes only as a general outline: the final decision is presented deductively, but the intermediate, enthymematic steps cannot be deductively justified, although they can be rationally justified in the law."[19]

Both types of cases contain a major premise in a syllogism. In clear cases, the major premise may represent the contents of an earlier ruling by the ECJ on the same or a similar question. "The main rationale of *acte clair* in this type of ECJ decision is authority."[20] In other instances, clarity of the norm may be "a felicitous, sincere statement" or else "a device to disguise interpretation."[21]

In so-called hard cases of the type that "usually involves a doubt regarding the formulation of the premises that will lead to a decision in the law"[22] justification is seen as an attempt to persuade the legal audience that the adopted interpretation does no violence to the legal order and that its consequences are at least not undesirable. Several arguments (reasons) will be offered by the interpreter in support of the proposed interpretation. These arguments mutually support each other in order to persuade an audience that the proposed interpretation is more coherent and fits better with exist-

---

[17] Case C-106/89, *Marleasing SA v. La Comercial Internacional de Alimentación SA*, 1990 E.C.R. I-4135.

[18] 1990 E.C.R. at I-4158-59.

[19] Joxerramon Bengoetxea, *The Legal Reasoning of the European Court of Justice: Towards a European Jurisprudence*, Oxford: Clarendon Press, p. 193 (1993).

[20] *Id.* at 205.

[21] *Id.* at 206.

[22] *Id.* at 221.

ing law and leads to better results than other rival interpretations (coherence and consequences are relative).[23]

This passage rightly points to the ECJ's traditional practice of giving more than one argument to justify a certain result. However, it should also be noted that, especially in recent years, the Court states its reasons very briefly. In many preliminary rulings on the interpretation of EC law, one of the few paragraphs giving the reasons fully corresponds to the operative part of the judgment. While the use of this technique does not imply that there is no justification, it provides an indication of the ECJ's reluctance to develop arguments. Scantily reasoned judgments may have the advantages of offering fewer opportunities for the reader's criticism and of leaving the ECJ freer when making further decisions; however, such judgments hardly persuade. This new way of stating the reasons has yet to affect the overall authoritativeness of the ECJ's decisions. One possible explanation is that, while it is expected that a judicial decision should not read like an oracle, political actors and Member State courts do not consider the reasons for the decision to be that important.

In *CILFIT*,[24] the ECJ stated some general guidelines on the interpretation of EC law. The first of these guidelines requires an attempt to reconcile the different language versions of Union provisions, although the ECJ often tends to play down the inevitable differences in the meaning of texts written in the ten official languages. The second guideline is more significant: it states that "legal concepts do not necessarily have the same meaning in Union law and in the law of the various Member States."[25] The idea that concepts of EC law are autonomous must be read in conjunction with the third and last guideline: "Finally, every provision of Union law must be placed in its context and interpreted in the light of the provisions of Union law as a whole, regard being had to the objectives thereof and to its state of evolution at the date on which the provision in question is to be applied."[26]

The ECJ's criteria for interpretation in fact go further than those criteria that were outlined in *CILFIT*. Bengoetxea groups them into different categories: "semiotic criteria," "systemic and contextual criteria," and "dynamic criteria." He provides the following summary of the various categories:

> Semiotic criteria look at the linguistic features of the lanuage which legal norms use. Contextual criteria lay the emphasis on the static perspective; they place the text under interpretation in a spatial context (*sedes*). Systemic criteria are used with a view to drawing inferences from different norms which are interrelated. They give a static picture of EC law. I have classified under the general term "dynamic criteria" three types of arguments: functional, teleological, and consequentialist arguments. These arguments are related to the dynamic context in

---

23 *Id.* at 225.

24 Case 283/81, *Srl CILFIT and Lanificio di Gavardo SpA v. Ministry of Health*, 1982 E.C.R. 3415.

25 1982 E.C.R. at 3430.

26 *Id.*

> which norms operate. Arguments are drawn from the value-laden conception that norms are to be interpreted in such a way that they function effectively (functional arguments), or from the objectives which some norms of the legal order either formulate explicitly or are seen as pursuing (teleological arguments), and finally from the consequences to which the proposed interpretation for those norms leads (consequentialist arguments). These criteria give something like a moving picture of EC law: each figure in the picture is understood in its relations to the other figures and in its development in the picture through time.[27]

However, the ECJ has stated:

> Although the practical consequences of any judicial decision must be carefully taken into account, it would be impossible to go so far as to diminish the objectivity of the law and compromise its future application on the ground of the possible repercussions which might result, as regards the past, from such a judicial decision.[28]

Bengoetxea notes that:

> the most interesting substantive reasons are those which originate in principles which did not originally appear in the Treaties, *e.g.*, human rights (in their liberal, social, and cultural versions), the protection of the environment, consumer protection, etc. The acceptability approach is most relevant in such cases; it could be argued that some of these values have made their way into EC law (through judicial decision-making and through legislation) when there has been an "adequate" (rational?) consensus concerning their urgency within the different audiences to which decisions are addressed.[29]

This observation may appear to be a quibble, but it shows how difficult it is to write a general overview of the ECJ's reasoning without a thorough knowledge of the various areas of EC law on which the Court's judgments were rendered. Also, in an analysis of justification it may well be necessary to go beyond an examination of the wording of the judgments in order to identify the proper category in which a case should be included and to explore why certain criteria were not relied upon in a particular judgment. The latter type of analysis, however, is clearly beyond the reach of a general survey, which may still provide a useful framework for more specific inquiries.

A general study focuses some questions regarding the use of "dynamic criteria" of interpretation. I shall frame them as questions, although some replies are implicit. First,

---

27 *Supra* note 19 at pp. 251-52.

28 1976 E.C.R. at 480.

29 *Supra* note 19 at p. 273.

it may be useful to recall that in the passage of the decision in *CILFIT* quoted above[30] the ECJ mentioned the need to refer to the "state of evolution" of EC law when interpreting a legal rule. The use of dynamic criteria implies that Treaty provisions and, likewise, acts adopted by EC institutions may acquire a meaning other than that originally intended. Is this consistent with the ECJ's idea in *Salumi*[31] that the Court's interpretation of a rule of EC law "clarifies and defines where necessary the meaning and scope of that rule as it must be or ought to have been understood and applied from the time of its coming into force"?[32] Should not the retrospective effect of interpretation be limited when a rule is interpreted on the basis of a dynamic criterion? Moreover, as the use of dynamic criteria implies that a provision may acquire a new meaning in the future, how can one assume, as the Court suggested in *Salumi* and other decisions,[33] that, once the ECJ has interpreted a provision of EC law, this provision has become clear? Could not the future use of dynamic criteria induce the ECJ to give a different meaning to the same provision?

C. Precedent and the Court of Justice[34]

Lawyers educated in the common law tradition often ask whether the Court of Justice of the European Communities applies a doctrine of precedent in reaching its decisions. In the common law world, the doctrine of precedent embodies more than the elementary principle that courts should try to be consistent. In certain circumstances, the doctrine has the effect of requiring a judge to follow a decision given in a previous case, even though, given a free hand, he might prefer not to do so. The potentially binding nature of judicial decisions is one of the characteristic features of the common law and it has a profound effect on the way in which judgments are reasoned.

It is important to examine the general approach of the Court of Justice to its previous decisions and, more specifically, to consider the way in which the Court deals with those decisions in its judgments. The early practice of the Court of First Instance in this context must also be addressed.

1. The General Position

The general position may be stated very simply: the Court is not bound by its previous decisions but in practice it does not often depart from them. A doctrine of binding precedent on common law lines would have been entirely inappropriate in what was originally a court of first and last resort, many of whose decisions could only be

---

30 *Supra* note 24.

31 Joined Cases 66, 127, and 128/79, *Amministrazione delle Finanze v. S.r.l. Meridionale Industria Salumi*, [1980] E.C.R. 1237.

32 1980 E.C.R. at 1264 (operative part).

33 *See in particular* the decision in *CILFIT*. Case 283/81, *Srl CILFIT and Lanificio di Gavardo SpA v. Ministry of Health*, [1982] E.C.R. 3415.

34 Anthony Arnull, *Owning up to Fallibility: Precedent and the Court of Justice*, 30 C.M.L.R. 247-66 (1993).

changed by amending the Treaties, a cumbersome process requiring the agreement of all the Member States and ratification by each of them in accordance with their respective constitutional requirements. It was therefore imperative that the Court should have the power to change the direction of its case law and to depart from its previous decisions, particularly in cases with important constitutional implications.

The general position is exemplified by the extent of the freedom enjoyed by the national courts of the Member States to request preliminary rulings from the Court of Justice under Article 177 EEC. Since the Court of Justice is not bound by its own previous decisions, the national courts are not precluded from taking this step merely because the point of Union law at issue has been dealt with by the Court. Indeed, in *Molkerei-Zentrale Westfalen v. Hauptzollamt Paderborn*,[35] the court was expressly asked by a German court whether it wished to maintain the judgment it had given in a previous case. The Court proceeded to reconsider whether that judgment was well-founded and concluded that there was no reason for giving a fresh interpretation to the provision of the Treaty at issue.

A national court may even make more than one reference in the same proceedings, although in practice this happens only exceptionally. However, the Court of Justice acknowledged in *Pretore di Salò v. Persons Unknown*[36] that a second reference "may be justified when the national court encounters difficulties in understanding or applying the judgment, when it refers a fresh question of law to the Court, or again when it submits new considerations which might lead the Court to give a different answer to a question submitted earlier." Nonetheless, national courts should not use the right to refer further questions "as a means of contesting the validity of the judgment delivered previously."

A corollary of the absence of a doctrine of binding precedent in Union law is that the distinction between the *ration decidendi* of a judgment of the Court and *obiter dicta* loses much of its significance. The distinction is important in the common law because it is only the *ratio* of a case which is capable of binding other courts in the future. As Advocate General Roemer explained in *Netherlands v. High Authority*,[37] however, "the question where, in judgments [of the Court of Justice], the decisive grounds of judgment end and any *obiter dicta* begin seems to me in any case to be of secondary importance. In each case everything that is said in the text of the judgment expresses the will of the Court."

2. Dealing with the Case Law

Of course, like all courts, the Court of Justice tries to be consistent in the decisions it reaches. Thus, in proceedings under Article 177 EEC in which the Court is asked to rule on a point it has already dealt with, it will, in the absence of any suggestion that

---

[35] Case 28/67, [1968] E.C.R. 143. *Cf.* Case C-269-90, *Technische Universität München v. Hauptzollamt München-Mitte*, judgment of 21 Nov. 1991.

[36] Case 14/86, [1987] E.C.R. 2545.

[37] Case 9/61, [1962] E.C.R. 213 at p. 242. *Cf.* the Opinion of A.G. Warner in Case 112/76, *Monzoni v. FNROM*, [1977] E.C.R. 1647 at pp. 1661-63.

the previous case was wrongly decided, simply repeat its earlier ruling. Indeed, where a question referred to the Court for a preliminary ruling is "manifestly identical to a question on which the Court has already ruled," the Court is empowered by Article 104(3) of its Rules of Procedure to give its decision by reasoned order in which reference is made to its previous judgment.

The main difference between the Court of Justice and common law courts in this respect lies, it is submitted, not in the absence of a doctrine of binding precedent, but in the way in which the Court deals with its previous decisions in its judgments. For many years, the Court rarely referred in its judgments to its previous decisions. Even when repeating a passage verbatim, it did not acknowledge the source. As two commentators have observed, "It was as if by some remarkable coincidence a group of judges chose to express a proposition relevant to the case in hand in exactly the same words as they, or perhaps a different group, had chosen to use on another occasion."[38]

Nowadays, the Court frequently cites previous decisions in its judgments and even gives the references so that the reader can look them up. According to one commentary, "it is harder to say whether this is because there is more previous case law to refer to or because since 1973 some of the Court's judges come from a legal system in which the binding force of previous cases is accepted."[39]

Whatever the reason for the change in the Court's practice, the reader of its judgments will be struck by the fact that previous decisions are normally only cited by the Court in support of its argument: authorities which point the other way are rarely mentioned. Indeed, they are sometimes presented by the Court as if they support the line it has chosen to take. This practice is liable to cause serious confusion among those who have the task of giving effect to the Court's judgments and may as a result jeopardize the proper application of Union law.

Unfortunately, in some cases the Court refers to previous decisions but then departs, often without explanation, from the outcome those decisions seem to suggest, with the result that their status is frequently left unclear.

3. Precedent in the Court of First Instance

The establishment of the Court of First Instance has raised further questions about the binding force of judicial precedent in Union law. In particular, it is necessary to consider whether the Court of First Instance is bound by its own previous decisions (where they have not been overturned) and whether it is bound by the decisions of the Court of Justice.

There can be little doubt that the Court of First Instance is not bound by its previous decisions, even where they have been upheld by the Court of Justice. There is no written rule stating that it is so bound and it would be surprising for a tribunal, the vast majority of whose Members come from a civil law background, to treat itself as

---

[38] Mackenzie, Stuart and Warner, "Judicial Decision as a Source of Community Law" in Grewe, Rupp and Schneider (Eds.), *Europäische Gerichtsbarkeit und Nationale Verfassungsgerichtsbarkeit: Festschrift zum 70. Geburtstag von Hans Kutscher* (1981), 273-81 at p. 277.

[39] Schermers and Waelbroeck, *Judicial Protection in the European Communities,* 4th ed., para. 171 (1987).

obliged to follow decisions which it did not believe led to the right result in the instant case. It goes without saying that the Court of First Instance tries to be consistent in the decisions it takes and that it is likely to depart from its own previous decisions only rarely.

As far as the decisions of the Court of Justice are concerned, there are two situations in which the Court of First Instance is expressly bound by them. The first is laid down in Article 54 of the Statute of the Court of Justice, which provides that, where the Court of Justice upholds an appeal against a decision of the Court of First Instance but decides to refer the case back to the Court of First Instance for judgment, the latter is bound by the decision of the Court of Justice on points of law. Secondly, where the Court of Justice finds that an action brought before it falls within the jurisdiction of the Court of First Instance, it is required by the second paragraph of Article 47 of the Statute to refer the action to the Court of First Instance, which is not entitled to decline jurisdiction. In other words, the Court of First Instance is bound by the decision of the Court of Justice that the case falls within the jurisdiction of the former.

It is submitted that, outside these two situations, the Court of First Instance is not bound by the decisions of the Court of Justice. In other words, where, on appeal to the Court of Justice, it is argued that the Court of First Instance has failed to follow the case law of the Court of Justice, it will always be open to one of the parties (or to an intervener) to argue that, even if this is the case, the Court of First Instance nonetheless came to the right decision in the circumstances. Such an argument is, of course, likely to fail unless good reasons are advanced for departing from the case law of the Court of Justice. Since the Court of Justice is not bound by its own previous decisions, however, it can always be invited to dismiss an appeal against a decision of the Court of First Instance, even if that decision cannot be reconciled with the case law of the Court of Justice.

The early practice of the Court of First Instance suggests that it regards the case law of the Court of Justice as highly persuasive. It is therefore likely to be followed in all but the most exceptional circumstances. However, the Court of First Instance has shown itself willing to distinguish decisions of the Court of Justice. In *BASF and Others v. Commission*,[40] the applicants sought the annulment of a Commission decision relating to a proceeding under Article 85 of the Treaty in the PVC sector. One of the grounds put forward by the applicants was that the Commission had infringed its own Rules of Procedure, the first paragraph of Article 12 of which provides that: "Acts adopted by the Commission, at a meeting or by written procedure, shall be authenticated in the language or languages in which they are binding by the signatures of the President and the Executive Secretary."[41]

The Commission sought to rely on the judgment in *Nakajima All Precision v. Council*,[42] where the Court of Justice said the purpose of the internal rules of a Union institution was to ensure the proper functioning of its services in the interests of effi-

---

40 Joined Cases T-79/89 etc., judgment of 27 Feb. 1992.

41 O.J., English Special Edition, Second Series VII—Institutional Questions, p. 9, as amended by Commission Decision 75/461, O.J. 1975, L199/43.

42 Case C-69/89, [1991] E.C.R. I-2069, paras. 49 and 50.

cient administration. According to the Court of Justice, it followed that natural and legal persons could not rely on an alleged breach of those rules, since they were not intended to ensure the protection of individuals.

Notwithstanding the apparently general terms of the ruling in the *Nakajima* case, the Court of First Instance took the view that it was limited in scope:

> The Court [of First Instance] considers that the judgment must be interpreted as meaning that it is necessary to distinguish between those provisions of an institution's Rules of Procedure whose infringement may not be relied upon by natural and legal persons because they are concerned solely with the internal working arrangements of the institution and cannot affect their legal situation and those whose infringement may be relied upon because, as is the case with Article 12 of the Commission's Rules of Procedure, they create rights and are a factor contributing to legal certainty for such persons.[43]

This passage shows that the Court of First Instance will not blindly follow the case law of the Court of Justice. Rather it will seek to find a solution which is compatible with that case law and appropriate in the circumstances of the case, leaving it to the Court of Justice to intervene should it be thought to have gone too far.

4. Conclusion

The apparent reluctance of the Court of Justice to confront inconsistencies in the case law may be due in part to the collegiate nature of its decisions, which often embody a number of compromises. Although the Court's decision can in theory be taken by majority vote, the absence of any provision for the publication of dissenting judgments may make those in the majority reluctant to simply disregard the views of those in the minority. This process is not conducive to the rigorous analysis of previous decisions such as that which may often be found in the Opinions of the Advocate General.

These difficulties seem intractable: it is inevitable that the Court's decisions will be the product of collaboration among the Judges involved. Moreover, while the terms of office of Judges are limited to the relatively short, but renewable, period of six years, dissenting judgments cannot realistically be envisaged since they would expose Judges to political pressure.

It is possible, however, that the Court's diffidence in dealing with its previous decisions is also due to another factor, the influence of which may be starting to wane. That factor is an unwillingness to accept that judicial decisions may constitute a source of law outside the confines of the dispute in which the decision was reached. Although this suggestion causes little surprise to the common law lawyer, civil lawyers do not strictly speaking regard the decisions of courts as a source of legal rules. On this view, the task of the judge is to apply the relevant provisions correctly and the way in which this may have been done in other cases merely offers him guidance. Thus, it is not uncommon for the highest court in some civil law jurisdictions to depart from previous case law without acknowledging that they are doing so.

---

43 *Supra* note 40.

Questions and Comments for Your Consideration

1. The ECJ is a hybrid court in that it uses a mixture of civil law and common law doctrines and procedures. The doctrine of precedent comes from the common law world and basically starts from the premise that courts should try to be consistent in their decisions. Does the ECJ follow the common law approach whereby it is bound by previous decisions? If not, why not?
2. Assuming that the ECJ is not bound by precedent, is the ECJ consistent in its decisions? What is the main difference between the common law doctrine of precedent and that of the way the ECJ is consistent in its decisions? Does the difference stem from the freedom the ECJ is allowed in citing previous cases and then departing from their outcome?
3. The Court of First Instance is a relatively new court. Does this explain fully the willingness of the Court of First Instance to find the case law of the Court of Justice highly persuasive?
4. Anthony Arnull, the author of the above article, concludes that the apparent reluctance of the ECJ to confront inconsistencies in its case law may be due in some part to the compromises embedded in the decisions. Also, that the absence of any provision for the publication of dissenting views allows the majority to simply disregard the views of the minority. The author concludes that this process is not conducive to the rigorous analysis of previous decisions such as that which may often be found in the Advocate General's Opinions. What do you think of the decision making process of the ECJ? Why do courts in the United States publish dissenting opinions?

D. The ECJ and Interpretation of International Agreements[44]

The Court of Justice has so far had little opportunity to develop a detailed or coherent approach to the question of how it may use and incorporate international law as it affects the Union. However, as the Union has extended its competence over areas in which Member States no longer possess exclusive, or any, right to make international agreements, so the case law on the relationship between international law and Union law has gradually extended to follow suit. Recent decisions, such as the *FEDIOL* cases[45] and *Sevince*,[46] and the Union's ratification of environmental treaties, such as the

[44] Ilona Cheyne, *International Agreements and the European Community Legal System,* 19 E. L. Rev. 581-98 (1994). © 1994 Ilona Cheyne. Reprinted by permission.

[45] Case 70/87, *EEC Seed Crushers' and Oil Processors' Federation (FEDIOL) v. EC Commission,* [1989] E.C.R. 1781; [1991] 2 C.M.L.R. 489; Case 187/85 *EEC Seed Crushers' and Oil Processors' Federation (FEDIOL) v. Commission of the European Communities and Another,* [1988] E.C.R. 4155; Case 188/85, *EEC Seed Crushers' and Oil Processors' Federation (FEDIOL) v. EC Commission of the European Communities,* [1988] E.C.R. 4193.

[46] Case C-192/89, *Sevince,* [1992] 2 C.M.L.R. 57.

Montreal Protocol[47] and Basel Convention,[48] offer a convenient opportunity to examine the status of international law in the legal system of the Union. The questions they raise about the constitutional powers of the Court to apply, and of individuals to rely upon, international law are likely to become critical as the Union undertakes more varied international obligations.

The case law on commercial policy in relation to the GATT has, naturally, been the most fruitful in illuminating the relationship between international and Union law. However, the permissive and broadly worded characteristics of the GATT have allowed the Court to develop some of its interpretative techniques relatively gradually while allowing some fundamental issues to remain unanswered. The limited nature of the questions so far considered by the Court has avoided outright judicial conflict with the executive institutions over the implementation of international agreements.

Challenges have tended to fall into two groups. First applicants have argued that the Union has violated international provisions whose wording permits considerable latitude of interpretation by the executive institutions. In *FEDIOL* (Case 187/85), for example, one of the relevant questions concerned the accuracy of the Commission's interpretation of the term "subsidy." The Court accepted its interpretation on the grounds that the term was not defined in the GATT or associated Subsidies Code[49] and that it fell within a range of reasonable interpretations of the term. Secondly, applicants have tried to show that a decision not to employ one of several responses permitted to the Union was wrongly made. An example is whether the Commission has acted in a way that is "necessary in the interests of the Community" under the wording of the antidumping regulation, Regulation 2176/84.[50] This is a legislative formula which reflects the international law right of parties to the GATT to take action in response to subsidies conferred on trade competitors. In this sort of case, the GATT and the Subsidies Code allow, but do not require, a protective response. As an available right, rather than an unavoidable duty, the Commission is clearly allowed considerable discretion in its choice and the Court's right to exercise judicial review over its decision is correspondingly limited. It is likely, however, that increasing clarification and elaboration of such obligations through new agreements and dispute settlements, as well as the undertaking of more precise prescriptive obligations under environmental agreements, will result in the Court having to take a more restrictive view of the Union's freedom of action in its external affairs.

1. Legal and Theoretical Perspectives

The European Union is a product of international law, created by the political will of its founding States expressed in an international treaty. The Treaty has created an inter-

---

47 Montreal Protocol on Substances that Deplete the Ozone Layer 1987, 26 ILM 154 (1987).

48 Basel Convention on the Control of Transboundary Movements of Hazardous Wastes 1989, 28 ILM 649 (1989).

49 Agreement on Interpretation and Application of Arts. VI, XVI and XXIII of the General Agreement on Tariffs and Trade, GATT, BISD (1980) 26 Supp. 56.

50 [1984] O.J. L201/1.

national organization which operates as a separate entity from its members, its organs possessing the capacity to take legally effective decisions in their own right. The recognition of its international legal personality by non-Member States and other international organizations allows it to operate upon the international plane as a subject of international law.[51] As such, it is subject to relevant international customary law and may acquire legal rights and obligations under agreements with other subjects.

In its internal aspect, however, the Union legal system has, through the agency of its Court of Justice, taken on a unique character. The Court has identified the Union as being a separate and independent entity, constituting "a new legal order of international law."[52] This uniqueness can be explained by reference to three important and well-known developments within the Court's jurisprudence. First, the so-called "direct effect" doctrine, under which some provisions of Union law can be relied upon by individuals, has allowed them to participate in the judicial process to a degree which is unique under an international treaty. Secondly, the establishment of the supremacy of Union law over national law[53] in *Van Gend en Loos* was expressly derived by the Court, *inter alia*, from the intention of the parties to the Treaty to create a legal regime which was outside the automatic application of international law rules. Thirdly, the Court established the doctrine of "parallelism" which has allowed Union competence in external affairs to expand beyond those expressed in the Treaty in order to match its increasing competence over internal affairs.[54]

The Union has therefore made its legal system separate from, though remaining bound by, international law. Questions that fall outside the scope of the Treaty remain to be dealt with under the international law between the Member States or between the Member States and non-Member States. The Union legal system may indeed be separate and different from international law proper, but the distinction is neither clear cut nor static and the Court may, from time to time, be required to define the boundaries. The founding rules on which the Court of Justice may exercise jurisdiction and review the acts of the other institutions have been broadly stated and broadly interpreted. Since the Treaty is silent as to the exact power of the Court to control the executive institutions' exercises of external affairs, the Court will eventually have to define its own powers in this regard. Its reluctance to be any more specific than necessary in its current case law is a reflection of the many pitfalls, both legal and political, that attend these questions. As we have seen above, the Court functions in a legal system which incorporates institutions, Member States and individuals and is increasingly being required to deal with alleged failure to comply with or correctly interpret international law. The Court is also in a position to ensure, indirectly, that the international legal rights of non-Member States are protected in their dealings with the Union. The concepts of coordination or harmonization, developed as a more sophisticated and prac-

[51] *See Reparations* Opinion, 1949 ICJ Reports; Case 22/70, *Commission v. Council (AETR)*, [1971] E.C.R. 263; [1971] C.M.L.R. 335.

[52] Case 26/62, *Van Gend & Loos*, [1963] E.C.R. 1; [1963] C.M.L.R. 105.

[53] *See* Case 6/64, *Costa v. ENEL*, [1964] E.C.R. 585; [1964] C.M.L.R. 425.

[54] Case 22/70, *Commission v. Council (AETR)*, [1971] E.C.R. 263; [1971] C.M.L.R. 335.

tical response to the difficulties of the theoretical debate between monism and dualism, seem particularly appropriate and helpful in the analysis of the Court's role in reconciling conflicts between international and Union law.

2. Direct Applicability, Hierarchy and Direct Effect

The issue here is the extent to which responsibility for, and power over, the observance of international law falls upon the Court. This question may be divided into three aspects. First, what position does international law have within Union law and, in particular, in relation to its hierarchy of primary sources and secondary legislation? Secondly, bearing in mind the important practical effect of individual actions in bringing such questions into the judicial arena, to what extent can individuals rely upon international law as having direct effect? How is this affected by the method by which it is incorporated into Union law? Thirdly, to what extent may the Court of Justice use international law to curtail the discretion of the other institutions in the creation and interpretation of international and Union law?

There is, of course, considerable legislative implementation of international agreements within Union law by regulations and decisions. Our first inquiry, however, must be whether international law has any direct applicability within the Union legal system with or without internal implementing acts.[55] To put it another way, may a challenge be made to the validity of actions by Union institutions or national governments on the grounds of violation of an international obligation binding on the Union? May such a challenge be made to the validity of the implementing legislation itself? This issue is often confused with the more narrow, though important, question of direct effect, concerning whether an international provision can be invoked by an individual. A related question is whether different methods of external adoption and internal implementation alter either the direct applicability or the direct effect of an international agreement.

Within the context of Union law, it is possible to say that the terms direct applicability and direct effect have essentially the same meaning. The test is to all intents and purposes the same and, as Hartley states, the differences between regulations and other instruments for this purpose "are neither clear cut nor important enough to warrant a special term to describe them." In addition, the Court of Justice itself does not appear to make a distinction between the two terms. The tests for each must overlap, since there cannot be direct effect without there also being direct applicability. There are, however, significant differences between the two concepts as they relate to international agreements.

a. *Direct Applicability*

For the purposes of direct applicability, a provision must generally be unconditional, sufficiently clear and precise to be judicially applied, and require no further implementation by an institution with discretionary power in the matter. The court of Justice has said that an international agreement will be directly applicable "when, regard being had to its wording and the purpose and nature of the agreement itself, the pro-

55 Sometimes referred to as self-executing.

vision contains a clear and precise obligation which is not subject, in its implementation or effects, to the adoption of any subsequent measure."[56]

The Court of Justice has asserted its jurisdiction over international obligations binding upon the Union by stating that they "must be determined by reference to the relevant provisions in the Union legal system and not to those which gave them their previous force under national legal systems."[57] Thus, where the Union has competence over the subject-matter, the constitutional right to determine and apply international law obligations within the legal systems of the Member States has been established as belonging to the Court of Justice as the arbiter of Union law. This is justified by the need for uniform application of all obligations binding within the Union legal system.

The effect of direct applicability within the Union legal system is that international agreements take priority over secondary legislation and other Union acts and can be used to challenge their validity, though not the provisions of the Treaty itself.[58] The former may be challenged under Articles 169, 170 or 173 by the Commission or Member States and by individuals under Article 173 and sometimes under Article 177. The Court may therefore use international law in exercising its judicial review function over both secondary legislation and discretionary administrative acts of the other institutions, although it must be subordinate to the Union's founding treaties within the Union legal system.

Although the principle is clearly established, there has been disagreement as to how it works in practice, primarily concerning the operation of Article 228, and Articles 173 and 177. The Court has recently clarified its approach to these questions and, by doing so, has acknowledged that a certain degree of pre-emption belongs to the executive institutions.

The Court has referred to agreements adopted "by the Community," in the wording of Article 228 EEC, as "an integral part of Community law,"[59] and the mere act of adoption is apparently sufficient without further internal implementation. Equally, international agreements originally ratified by the Member States and which subsequently fall within the shared or exclusive competence of the Union, such as the GATT, are accepted as being equally binding on the institutions and Member States despite the fact that they do not fall strictly under Article 228. Some writers are content to explain this by analogy with Article 228, others argue that it occurs by transfer of sovereignty from the Member States to the Union with the consent of the third parties. The Court has variously referred to itself as having "replaced" or substituted for the Member States in the GATT.

The Court of Justice has therefore grouped together all international agreements binding on the Union for the purposes of direct applicability of international obligations. It has made no distinction for purposes of jurisdiction between the GATT, which the Union has adopted informally, and the Antidumping Code to which the

---

56 Trevor C. Hartley, *The Foundations of European Community Law* (2nd ed., 1988).

57 Case 38/75, *Nederlandse Spoorwegen,* [1975] E.C.R. 1439; [1976] 1 C.M.L.R. 167.

58 Art. 189 EEC; Cases 21-24/72, *International Fruit,* [1972] E.C.R. 1219; [1975] 2 C.M.L.R. 1.

59 Case 181/73, *Haegerman,* [1974] E.C.R. 449.

Union is a signatory. In *SPI*, it explained its right to interpret the Tariff Protocols on the basis of Article 228 and the GATT on the basis of ensuring uniform application and interpretation throughout the Union respectively.[60]

International agreements may be implemented directly, by incorporating the wording of the agreement or its provisions into the secondary legislation, or indirectly, by indicating (typically in the preamble) that it is the purpose of the legislation to put the agreement or its provisions into effect. Two regulations considered in the most recent *FEDIOL* cases[61] are good examples. For instance, Regulation No. 2176/84[62] (the "Antidumping Regulation") dealing with foreign dumping and subsidies, was intended, according to its Preamble, to put the relevant rules of the GATT and associated codes into effect within the Union legal system. In contrast, Regulation 2641/84[63] ("the New Commercial Policy Instrument"), allows individuals to seek protection against "any illicit commercial practices,"[64] defined in the regulation as being "incompatible with international law or generally accepted rules."[65] In principle, the superiority of an international agreement over secondary Union law and acts must mean that its provisions cannot be affected by the wording of its internal implementation since the implementing act itself can be challenged as being incorrect.

b. Direct Effect

It follows from the above discussion that the strict question of whether an international agreement is directly applicable is relevant only where there is a question as to whether further internal implementation is required. In many cases, the facts do not give rise to any difficulty. The issue of direct effect, however, is rather more problematic. While it may be argued that direct effect can be assumed for any Treaty Article or Union legislation which satisfies the test of direct applicability, a more cautious approach is called for with regard to international agreements. The intentions of the parties and the implications of finding direct effect require separate and careful consideration. It must be both a finding of direct applicability and the satisfying of a more narrow test of whether individuals are entitled to rely upon its provisions.

The practical consequences of finding direct effect for international agreements are clearly important. The direct effect doctrine in Union law has had the result of allowing private individuals, untrammeled by the political and economic hesitations of the Member States and institutions, to raise issues with which the Court could promote the integration of the Union. One commentator has argued that, if the Court had not taken its position allowing individual reliance on the Treaty, "Community law would have remained an abstract skeleton and a great variety and number of Treaty violations

---

60 Cases 367-9/81, *SPI and SAMI*, [1983] E.C.R. 801.

61 *Supra* n. 45.

62 Now Regulation 2423/88, [1988] O.J. L209/1, though the wording at issue remains the same.

63 [1984] O.J. L252/1.

64 Preamble and Art. 1.

65 Art. 2(1).

would have remained undisclosed and unredressed."[66] The same argument can be made with respect to international agreements and the reluctance of institutions to enforce them. Ehlermann, for example, suggests that one reason that the Union does not use Article 169 is because "it dislikes the idea of using specifically Union provisions to do non-member countries' business for them."[67] In the light of repeated accusations of Union trade protectionism in particular, and in the absence of Member State legal actions in this field, the issue of whether concerned individuals can bring actions reliant upon the provisions of the GATT has become of considerable importance. In practice, greater direct effect would mean that increased judicial attention would be paid to the protection of those individuals who would particularly benefit from the implementation of GATT freedoms, such as consumers. At present, only domestic producers are likely to be in a position to take advantage of the GATT. They may, for example, initiate antidumping investigations of foreign importers under Union legislation. The possibility of GATT-derived provisions being used for protectionist purposes by producers would be somewhat balanced by permitting consumers to rely directly upon the GATT. It would allow the latter to argue against protectionism in the Union in a way that Union legislation, by its very nature, is unlikely to allow. In a more general sense, therefore, direct effect would lead the Court to play a greater harmonizing role by giving more emphasis to the objectives of the GATT within the Union.

Both the Commission and the Court of Justice itself have been reluctant to allow direct effect for international agreements such as the GATT for practical reasons. However, there are also legal difficulties in allowing individual reliance upon, and judicial interpretation of, broadly worded provisions. Fundamentally, it may be asked whether it is desirable for the Court of Justice to become frequently involved in adjudicating upon the Union's actions under an agreement such as the GATT. First, it makes it more likely that the Court of Justice will be called upon to make a binding decision which interferes with the freedom of the other Union institutions to act in external affairs. Secondly, the Court of Justice would be in danger of making a decision, albeit within Union law, that was at variance with findings of other domestic tribunals or the Contracting Parties of the GATT. These problems would apply less forcefully to actions brought by Member States who, it can be argued, would have a greater appreciation of the international implications involved.

The question of whether an individual can rely upon an international agreement is likely to arise either under Article 173 or through a referral by a national court under Article 177. The Court of Justice has made it clear, in *International Fruit* for example, that international agreements fall within the wording of Article 173 for the purposes of individual actions. Any remaining uncertainties as to the direct effect of international agreements are therefore limited to referrals from national courts under Article 177 where questions concerning the application of international agreements in Union law may be raised in private litigation.

---

[66] Stein, *Lawyers, Judges, and the Making of a Transnational Constitution* (1981) 75 AJIL 1 at p. 6.

[67] Ehlermann, *Application of GATT Rules in the European Community*, in Hilf, Jacobs and Petersmann (1986) pp. 138-139.

The Court has established in *SPI and SAMI* that it has jurisdiction to examine such international agreements under Article 177 on the grounds of ensuring uniform application and interpretation throughout the Union. However, the fact that the Court has jurisdiction to consider an act of one of the institutions or national legislation in the light of an international agreement, whether formally or informally adopted, does not necessarily mean that an individual may rely upon it. This has become particularly clear in the case of the GATT, which has not yet been found to have direct effect. In early jurisprudence concerning Article 177, the Court of Justice appeared to be prepared to review the legality of Union acts regardless of whether individual complainants could show direct effect.[68] However, it later gave clear indications that direct effect is crucial to the question of whether or not it will review the validity of Union acts under Article 177.[69] This is arguably an over-restrictive interpretation of Article 177 which simply provides for the jurisdiction of the Court on questions concerning "the validity and interpretation of acts of the institutions" and to furnish a mechanism for a national court to ask for a preliminary ruling that it considers "necessary to enable it to give judgment." Where an individual cannot directly rely upon an international agreement to challenge national or Union acts or legislation, the national court may still discover that it cannot make a finding without having that aspect of Union law clarified by the Court of Justice. The present position of the Court is to curtail its own jurisdiction unnecessarily by reference to the separate issue of direct effect.

c. *Test Used to Find Direct Effect*

What test does the Court apply to discover whether an international agreement should have direct effect? At first, it said merely that a provision could only be relied upon if it was "capable of creating rights of which interested parties may avail themselves in a court of law."[70] The Court has applied this test by examining two aspects, sometimes, but not always, together. First, it has examined "the spirit, general scheme and terms" or the objective and nature of the agreement as a whole.[71] Secondly, it has considered whether the specific provision relied upon is clear and unconditional.[72] For example, in *Pabst*,[73] the Court applied both tests and was able to find that the Association Agreement with Greece had direct effect. It has not applied the same reasoning to find direct effect for decision of a body set up under a treaty. In *Sevince*,[74] the Court found that, where an agreement is by itself too general and conditional to be relied upon by individuals, further elucidation of its provisions by an authoritative body may cure that

---

68 Case 40/72, *Schroeder*, [1973] E.C.R. 125; [1973] C.M.L.R. 824.

69 *See SIOT, SPI and SPAM*.

70 *International Fruit, supra* n. 58.

71 *Id.*

72 *Bresciani*, [1974] E.C.R. 129.

73 *Pabst*, [1982] E.C.R. 1331; [1983] 3 C.M.L.R. 11.

74 Case C-192/89, *Sevince*, [1992] 2 C.M.L.R. 57.

defect and give rise to direct effect. It must be assumed, however, that the agreement as a whole would still need to satisfy the general test with regard to its nature and objective, general spirit and terms.

The Court's refusal to grant direct effect to the GATT so far has been based on its flexibility of interpretation, the opportunity for derogation from its obligations and the existence of an institutional dispute settlement procedure. It should be noted, however, that the mere existence of powers to derogate will not always prevent direct effect. Nor has the existence of consultation or dispute settlement procedures under an agreement always prevented the Court from allowing individuals to rely upon it. This is inevitable since potentially all international agreements have dispute settlement procedures available to them, such as negotiation or reference to the International Court of Justice or other forms of international tribunal. The important point is that these procedures are available for, and only appropriate in, disputes between governments. The mere existence of international machinery should therefore be treated as an irrelevance in the case of challenge to the validity of a Union act under which private interests are affected and where there is clearly a private legal rather than international policy argument.

Some clues as to when direct effect of international agreements may be considered appropriate can be found in the way in which the Court, in its admittedly sparse case law, has tended to emphasize the closeness of the purpose of the international argument to that of the Treaty of Rome. Thus, in *Bresciani* and *Pabst*, the relevant provisions of association agreements were held to have similar purposes to those of the Treaty of Rome and could therefore be allowed direct effect. Similarity of wording is not in itself sufficient. One judge of the Court has suggested, with regard to direct effect, that international agreements be viewed as a series of concentric circles around the Union. The closer the agreement to the purpose of the Union, the more likely direct effect will be found. This would presumably occur for two reasons. First, there is more likelihood that the parties to the agreement intended to permit, or at least not exclude, direct effect and thus the appropriate rules of interpretation of international law according to the intentions of the parties may be followed. Secondly, the need for uniform application within the Union legal system will be proportionately greater if the essential principles and purposes of the Union are not to be subverted or weakened by the operation of such international agreements.

In this analysis, the need for clear and unconditional provisions is primarily a requirement for direct applicability, and direct effect only follows if the test of "the spirit, general scheme and terms" is also satisfied. This is supported indirectly by the Court of Justice's judgment in *FEDIOL* (Case 70/87) which, although concerned with an action under Article 173, may be broad enough on this point to cover questions which reach the Court under Article 177. The Court acknowledged that it had in the past held that various GATT provisions were not sufficiently precise to confer rights upon individuals capable of being invoked by them before the national courts despite the existence of Union legislation intended indirectly to put them into effect. But the Court offered a sharp rebuff to the Commission by stating that those previous judgments could not be used to prevent individuals from relying on GATT provisions in order to obtain a ruling on whether conduct complained of under Regulation No.

2641/84 constitutes an illicit commercial practice. Under Article 2(1) of that regulation, "illicit commercial practices" are to be defined according to international law, including the provisions of the GATT. The Court seems here to be suggesting that individuals can rely on GATT rules when they have been directly imported by the enacting regulation. Where a legislative provision of this type is at issue in a national court, and gives rise to a referral under Article 177, it should therefore be possible for an individual to rely upon the international law rules in question, whether or not direct effect would otherwise be allowed.

This is significant because earlier cases have tended to suggest that the crucial characteristic of direct effect in an international agreement is that the provision is sufficiently clear and unconditional, although this has the effect of combining and sometimes confusing the separate issue of direct applicability and direct effect. However, the *FEDIOL* case suggests that this emphasis on precision can be misleading. Direct effect can also occur when an international provision is imported into Union law by virtue of legislation, even though the fact that it has been imported into Union law does not necessarily make it any more precise. The overriding reason for giving direct effect in such a case then becomes the intention that it should have direct effect, on the part of the Union legislature if not the other parties to the agreement.

However, if direct effect can be found through direct legislative implementation when not otherwise available, the decision of whether individuals should be able to challenge institutional acts on the basis of many of the Union's international obligations lies firmly in the hands of the legislative institutions. It appears to raise, in other words, the same issues on which the Court has already been judicially active in developing its concept of direct effect in Union law. However, the Court has clearly been more reluctant to grant direct effect for international agreements other than those imported through legislation, despite apparent similarities between international and Union law for these purposes. It may be argued, for example, that the original parties to the EEC Treaty did not intend to allow individual reliance upon it and that the Court has thus already ignored the apparent intentions of the parties to an international agreement. Equally, the Court has used an argument justifying the supremacy of internal Union law, namely the need to ensure that its interpretation be as uniform as possible, to justify its role of interpreting international agreements as part of Union law.

However, it has been pointed out by a number of commentators that there are good reasons for distinguishing between international law provisions and Union laws for the purposes of direct effect.[75] As Bebr points out,[76] the concept of direct effect was developed in relation to the inner workings of the Union legal order, both as a legal system in its own right and as a creation of its constitutional treaties or its institutions, as a "primary instrument of integration."[77] In particular, the nature and purpose of an external international agreement may be significantly different to that of the EC Treaty. Thus the specific purposes of developing the doctrine of direct effect may be neither easily nor appropriately transferred to a creation outside the Union legal system.

---

[75] Bebr, *Agreements Concluded by the Community and Their Possible Direct Effect* (1983) 20 C.M.L.R. 36-38.

[76] *Id.*

The Court has so far expressed its functions in terms of Union law, including the obligation to comply with international obligations binding on the Union. However, the result is very similar to what might be expected from a tribunal applying international law. In fact, some commentators argue strongly that the decisive rule on whether individuals should be able to rely upon international agreements within Union law is one of international law since the domestic interpretation or application of the international agreement may affect the rights of the other states parties.

A fundamental principle of international law is that interpretation of international agreements must be based on the intentions of the other parties to the agreement. Although the Court has not expressly described it as such, its test of examining the general scheme, nature and objective of the agreement and whether the provision relied upon is clear and unconditional is consistent with saying that those provisions were intended by the parties to be relied upon by individuals. The argument that the provisions of an agreement are too vague and may be derogated from by governmental action is a powerful one against finding direct effect because it is difficult to imply any intention on the part of the governments signing such an agreement to confer or allow individual reliance on it. Thus the Court's approach to direct effect is seen to be founded primarily on the intention of the parties to the international agreement and of the Union itself. It can be explained as the Court fulfilling the judicial function of harmonization, as well as a matter of policy in avoiding conflict with, and potential embarrassment for, the other Union institutions that have competence in external affairs.

3. Conclusion

It is clear that a decision by the Court that an international agreement should be applied so as to restrain the Union's freedom of action in external affairs would lead to considerable consequences of a political and constitutional nature. Although international agreements have been found to have direct effect and have been applied by the Court of Justice, their implications in this respect have been quite limited. Some aspects of the Court's own jurisprudence and the acceptance of prescriptive international obligations, most notably in the field of environmental protection, may well lead to these issues being put squarely in its path.

There are, as noted above, two characteristics of the GATT provisions so far considered by the Court of Justice which have allowed it to avoid direct conflict with the executive institutions. The first is the breadth of interpretation they allow. The second is the permissive nature of many of those provisions which allow more than one course of action. The executive act or legislation implementing those provisions has therefore fallen into a discretionary area, either in interpreting broadly worded provisions or in deciding what action should be taken on behalf of the Union. The GATT provisions considered by the Court have turned out to be sufficiently precise for the Court to implement in terms of direct applicability, but sufficiently open-ended in their wording to allow the executive institutions a degree of interpretation of law and fact and to deny direct effect. A GATT panel decision, however, may well have the effect of defining obligations more precisely, or specifically prohibiting a particular practice. A recent example is the *Tuna-Dolphin* panel report,[78] which clarifies the prohibition of certain trade practices under the GATT including import restrictions based on methods of production. It is now clear that certain Union measures are probably illegal under the GATT, such as the Union's Leghold Trap Regulation[79] and Seal Pup Directive[80] prohibiting the import of furs and other products from listed animals caught using particular methods. Under the reasoning of the *Sevince* case, such panel decisions could both allow direct effect and reduce the scope of executive interpretation of the clarified provisions.

Such a development would have the benefit of leading to greater reliance upon, and therefore greater effectiveness for, the GATT within the Union. At the same time, it could promote more uniform interpretation of the GATT amongst its parties. However, it would also give rise to potential problems. What would be an authoritative body for these purposes? A GATT panel presumably would suffice but the adoption procedure is problematic, particularly if the EC were the defendant party to the dispute, since it is dependent upon the agreement of all the disputing parties.[81] The agreement of the defendant state would mean that the illegality would be unlikely to continue and, in any case, the Court of Justice might consider an adopted agreement to be negotiated settlement, more akin to a political compromise than a judicial decision. If, on the other hand, the decision were not adopted, the chances of the Court relying upon it as an authoritative decision would be even less, thus in practice falling into line with the executive institutions' view of the matter. To go further, would the Court be prepared to accept as authoritative bodies other international panels applying obligations consistent with the GATT, such as in the United States-Canada Free Trade Agreement[82] or the North American Free Trade Agreement?[83] Though the panels of these bodies would not be authoritative in the same sense as a GATT dispute panel, or a finding by the GATT Contracting Parties, their power to make binding decisions would, ironically, increase the legal weight of their findings because of their relative independence from the consent of the disputing parties. However, the Court is likely to be reluctant to depend upon the findings of other bodies not directly connected to the Union or under its control, although it is to be hoped that the Court would be prepared to look upon their findings as persuasive.

Even if the Court avoids relying upon clarification offered by GATT or other panels, it is increasingly likely that the Union will, in any case, become bound by precise

---

77 *Id.* at p. 66.

78 *United States—Restrictions on Imports of Tuna*, GATT BISD 39S/155, 30 ILM 1594 (1991).

79 Council Regulation (EEC) No. 3254/91, [1991] O.J. L308/1.

80 Council Directive 83/129/EEC, [1983] O.J. L91/30.

81 This will change under the new World Trade Organization regime agreed to in the Uruguay Round, although panel or appellate findings will be subject to rejection by consensus in the Dispute Settlement Body.

82 27 ILM 281 (1988).

83 32 ILM 289, 605 (1993).

obligations. There is, after all, an increasing tendency to codify and tighten GATT obligations through agreements. In addition, environmental treaties may have significantly different characteristics from the GATT on which much of the case law of the Court has so far been based. The GATT's charter of principles leaves considerable scope for interpretation, negotiation, granting of waivers and unilateral defensive measures. Environmental agreements, such as the Montreal Protocol, tend to be more precise and more prescriptive. It is likely, in the latter case, that executive discretion in determining fact and interpreting law will be diminished and that the finding of direct effect will occur more often. After the Single European Act and Treaty of European Union, it would be hard to argue that the nature and objectives of such agreements were not in accord with those of the Treaty. There would be less political risk attached to judicial intervention, and a lower degree of discretion retained by the institutions. The issues skirted around by the Court in the commercial arena may well require closer attention in the environmental field.

As a result, the likelihood of the Court of Justice coming into conflict with the other Union institutions is increasing, even though the area of external affairs is jurisdictionally weighted in the latter's favor. The Court may be faced directly with the question of whether it could or should prevent the Union from acting in a way which was clearly in violation of international law. The Court has not yet definitively outlined its powers with regard to controlling the executive institutions' discretion in external affairs. It would be possible for it to assume a self-limited role by controlling only the exercise of external powers which directly affected private and state interests within the Union, and leaving all other aspects to the discretion of the institutions. Such an approach could go so far as to hold that the executive institutions had the ultimate discretion as to whether to comply with international law at all. In other words, it could be open to the Court to accept that a decision not to follow a clear international legal obligation could only be reviewed by the Court where there was a direct internal Union consequence. Such an approach could still be compatible with the principle that observance of international law is a matter of Union law, since it leaves open the question of whether observance of international law *qua* international law is a matter of Union law.

It is submitted, however, that such a view would be an unfortunate and unnecessarily restrictive interpretation of its powers. The institutions are required to comply with the Treaty under which they derive their powers, including those in relation to external affairs, and it is clear that the Court has the power and duty to ensure that the Treaty is complied with. The Member States have the right to require compliance with international obligations since the Union acts in their name and it must act within the constraints of the Treaty, including "any rule of law relating to its application."[84] The question of direct effect would not affect the legal reasoning of the case. The Court of Justice therefore has the power to prevent outright violations, even of legal obligations that are external to the Union legal system, and it should not necessarily be assumed that the executive institutions' right to conduct external affairs is entirely discretionary

[84] Art. 173 EC.

where not limited expressly by the EC Treaty. Logically, the Court's jurisprudence so far points to the need to ensure that the institutions act within the Treaty and that should extend to observance of international law. Unless the Court is prepared to give way to the jurisdiction of the executive institutions in this area, the inevitable conclusion must be annulment of their acts or legislation on the grounds of international law.

The essential underlying issue is that the balance of powers and control within the Union, the tension between the discretion of the Commission to act in external affairs and the role of the Court in the field of judicial review between the institutions, Member States and individuals, including its responsibility for ensuring that the international law obligations of the institutions and Member States, are observed. As Ehlermann points out, giving direct applicability to international rules "entails a decisive shift of responsibility from the executive to the judiciary. The judiciary takes over functions normally reserved for the executive. And in the Union this shift of powers, as we have seen, cannot be reversed by the legislator; it is final."[85]

Questions and Comments for Your Consideration

1. Ilona Cheyne, the author of above article, asks whether a challenge may be made to the validity of actions by union institutions or national governments on the grounds of violation of an international obligation binding on the Union. How do the concepts of direct applicability and direct effect bear on the answer to this question?
2. How has the ECJ asserted its jurisdiction over international obligations?
3. The ECJ makes no distinction for the purposes of jurisdiction between international agreements which the Union has adopted informally and those which it has formally adopted. What is the ECJ's reasoning in not distinguishing between the two?
4. Why has the ECJ refused to grant direct effect to the GATT? What test does the ECJ use to determine whether direct effect should be granted? Is this test satisfactory?

[85] Ehlermann, *Application of GATT Rules in the European Community*, in Hilf, Jacobs and Petersmann, *The European Community and GATT* (1986) p.127 at 137.

Chapter 3

The Internal Market

I. Freedom of Movement of Goods

A. The Internal Market and the Common Market[1]

The literature on Community Law is divided about the meaning of the concept of "internal market." Each of the three possible interpretations of this concept in relation to that of the "common market" is defended. Some authors take the position that internal market means less than common market. Another point of view is that the two concepts coincide, while the view is also defended that internal market comprises more than "common market." Although numerous provisions of the Treaty refer to "a" or "the" common market, this concept is nowhere defined.

First it is possible to define this concept in terms of what, according to the Treaty, had to be realized at the end of the transitional period. The objective of the Community "is the attainment of a single market," as the Court recognized already in an early stage of European integration. Seen from this perspective, the common market requires the merging of national markets into a single market for the whole of the Community territory, through the elimination of all obstacles by which these markets are separated. In the Court's case law this single market is conceived of as a situation which corresponds to that of a national market. "The Treaty seeks to create a single market reproducing as closely as possible the conditions of a domestic market," as the Court put it in 1982,[2] while in the same year the common market was described as involving the "elimination of all obstacles to intra-Community trade in order to merge the national markets to those of a genuine internal market."[3]

Ano.ther approach is to define the common market in terms of individual economic freedom. According to an almost classical definition, a common market means a market on which the actors are free to invest, to lend money, to produce, to work, to offer or to buy goods and services at any place in the Community where the economic

---

1 Rene Barents, *The Internal Market Unlimited: Some Observations on the Legal Basis of Community Legislation*, 30 C.M.L.R. 85-109 (1993) at p. 102. © 1993 Kluwer Academic Publishers. Reprinted with permission.

2 Case 15/81, *Schul v. Inspecteur der Doune*, [1982] ECR 1409, ground 31.

3 *See* Case 240/83, *Procureur de la Republique v. ADBHU*, [1985] ECR 531, ground 9.

conditions are the most favorable. The function of the common market is then to guarantee the operator the right to economic liberty, i.e. to contract, to exploit his property and to choose his profession anywhere in the Community market and subject to restrictions which the Community legislature by virtue of its powers under the Treaty may impose.

These approaches indicate that, in any case, the common market concerns the full implementation of the four freedoms and a regime of undistorted competition, as has also been acknowledged by the Court. What may seem relevant in this discussion is the distinction between the establishment of the common market and its functioning. The establishment of the common market relates to the four freedoms, its functioning to the regime of undistorted competition (Article 3f). From Article 8a it would result that "internal market" only relates to the establishment of the common market. However, in the Court's case law this distinction has never been considered as relevant. On the contrary, according to established case law, Articles 30 and 59 also relate to trade obstacles resulting from disparities between national legislations, which are prohibited if they are not covered by an escape clause in the Treaty or by an imperative requirement. Consequently the scope of these freedoms relates to undistorted competition as well.

The attainment of the internal market thus concerns the establishment as well as the functioning of the common market, which in practical terms means that both concepts are identical.

1. Basic Principles[4]

The cornerstone of the European Community is the principle of the free movement of goods. That principle requires that goods placed on the market in any Member State may be traded freely throughout the Community. No customs duties or charges having equivalent effect may be levied on trade between Member States; nor may such trade be subject to quantitative restrictions—meaning quotas and prohibitions—or to measures having equivalent effect. The principle of free movement applies not only to goods produced in a Member State, but also to goods originating in nonmember countries once they have been duly imported into a Member State and any customs duties payable under the Common Customs Tariff have been accounted for.

2. Articles 30-36

The relevant provisions are contained in Articles 30 to 36 of the EEC Treaty. Article 30 prohibits "[q]uantitative restrictions on imports and all measures having equivalent effect . . . between Member States." Article 34 makes similar provision in relation to exports. Article 36 qualifies that basic principle of free movement by expressly authorizing prohibitions and restrictions justified on a number of grounds, notably public morality, public health, and the protection of industrial and commercial property.

---

[4] David T. Keeling, *The Free Movement of Goods in EEC Law: Basic Principles and Recent Developments in the Case Law of the Court of Justice of the European Communities*. 26 Int'l Lawyer 467-83 (1992). ©1992 David T. Keeling. Reprinted with permission.

The case law on these provisions is voluminous. Since 1963 the Court has delivered over 460 preliminary rulings related to the free movement of goods. In addition, it has given judgment in over 102 actions brought by the European Commission under Article 169 of the EEC Treaty for a declaration that a Member State has failed to fulfill its Treaty obligations in connection with the free movement of goods.

One brief point should be made before embarking on a review of that case law. Although the language of Articles 30 and 34 is virtually identical, the Court has always taken a less rigorous attitude towards restrictions on exports than towards restrictions on imports, presumably on the ground that Member States are far less likely to impede exports. The Court considers that Article 34 applies only to measures that have as their specific object or effect the restriction of exports and thus establish a difference in treatment between a Member State's domestic trade and its export trade. In *Groenveld v. Produktschap voor Vee en Vlees*[5] the Court held that Article 34 was not infringed by a Dutch law that prohibited sausage manufacturers in the Netherlands from stocking or processing horsemeat. Obviously the law affected exports in a sense, since it prevented Dutch sausage makers from manufacturing horsemeat sausages for export to other Member States. However, the nondiscriminatory nature of the law meant that it was not contrary to Article 34.

In relation to measures restricting imports, the Court has been far more stringent. It has opted for an extremely wide definition of the concept of measures having equivalent effect to a quantitative restriction on imports. The leading case is *Procureur du Roi v. Dassonville*,[6] in which the Court held that: "All trading rules enacted by Member States which are capable of hindering, directly or indirectly, actually or potentially, intra-Community trade are to be considered as measures having an effect equivalent to quantitative restrictions."[7]

The breadth of that definition of measures having equivalent effect has been amplified by a ruling in *Van de Haar and Kaveka de Meern*[8] to the effect that even a slight hindrance to imports is sufficient to bring Article 30 into play. Thus, at least in theory, even a measure that causes a slight, indirect, potential hindrance to trade between Member States offends against Article 30.

3. The *Cassis de Dijon* Principle

The greatest obstacles to trade between Member States are due to disparities between national legislation regarding, for example, technical standards, the composition of foodstuffs, sizes, packaging, labeling, and so forth. Obviously the best solution to such obstacles to trade is to strike at the root of the problem by eliminating the disparities in national legislation. To that end, Article 100 of the EEC Treaty (now supplemented

---

5 Case 15/79, *Groenveld v. Produktschap voor Vee en Vlees*, 1979 E.C.R. 3409, [1979-1981 Transfer Binder] Common Mkt.Rep. (CCH) P 8617 (1979).

6 Case 8/74, *Procureur du Roi v. Dassonville*, 1974 E.C.R. 837, 14 C.M.L.R. 436 (1974).

7 *Id.*, 14 C.M.L.R. at 453-54.

8 Joined Cases 177 and 178/82, *Public Prosecutor v. Jan van de Haar and Kaveka de Meern*, 1984 E.C.R. 1797, [1983-1985 Transfer Binder] Common Mkt.Rep. (CCH) P 14,094 (1984).

by Article 100a) empowers the Council of Ministers to adopt directives harmonizing legislation that directly affects the establishment or functioning of the common market. Many such directives have been issued.

But harmonization is a slow process and may not even be perceived as desirable by everyone. It follows that obstacles resulting from disparities in national legislation will continue to hamper trade between Member States for a long time to come. Initially, it was thought by many that, provided a Member State applied its legislation without distinction to domestic goods and to goods produced in other Member States, there was no breach of Article 30. In other words, it was believed that Article 30 only prohibited discriminatory measures. That myth was shattered in 1979 by the Court's judgment in *Rewe-Zentral v. Bundesmonopolverwaltung fur Branntwein*.[9] In that case the German authorities refused to authorize the marketing in Germany of a French liqueur known as Cassis de Dijon on the ground that the liqueur did not comply with a German provision under which such beverages must have a minimum alcohol content of 25 percent. The German authorities argued that since the German provision applied without distinction to domestic and imported products it was not caught by the prohibition laid down in Article 30. The Court rejected that argument and held that obstacles to trade caused by disparities in national laws were permitted only in so far as the provisions in question were necessary to satisfy mandatory requirements relating in particular to the effectiveness of fiscal supervision, the protection of public health, fair trading, and consumer protection.

Cassis de Dijon—as the case became known—was indeed a landmark judgment. As a result of the decision, many of the obstacles to trade resulting from disparities in national legislation were swept aside, whereas it had previously been thought that such obstacles could only be removed by harmonization of national laws. But in another sense the judgment was a backward step because the Court recognized a new catalogue of exceptions to the principle of free movement, additional to those expressly listed in Article 36 of the Treaty. The exact relationship between the Article 36 exceptions and the mandatory requirements recognized in *Cassis de Dijon* and in subsequent judgments has been the subject of considerable debate—more debate perhaps than the issue is worth. Three points should be noted:

First, the mandatory requirements recognized in *Cassis de Dijon* can only save measures that apply without distinction to domestic and imported goods, whereas Article 36 may save measures that do not satisfy that test, provided that they do not constitute arbitrary discrimination or a disguised restriction on trade.

Secondly, the Court has consistently held that, since Article 36 derogates from a fundamental principle of the Treaty, it must be construed narrowly. Thus the grounds listed in Article 36 justifying restrictions on free movement are exhaustive. On the other hand, the list of mandatory requirements recognized in *Cassis de Dijon* is not a closed category, as is proved by the fact that the Court has occasionally added to it.

---

[9] Case 120/78, *Rewe-Zentral v. Bundesmonopolverwaltung fur Branntwein*, 1979 E.C.R. 649, [1978-1979 Transfer Binder] Common Mkt.Rep. (CCH) P 8543 (1979).

Thirdly, whatever ground is invoked as justification for a measure restricting free movement, whether it be an interest mentioned in Article 36 or a mandatory requirement under *Cassis de Dijon*, the measure in question will be tested against the principle of proportionality. The measure will only be upheld if (a) it is an appropriate means of attaining the objective in question (for example, the protection of public health or fair trading) and (b) the objective could not be attained by other means less restrictive of trade between Member States.

Since 1979 the Court has delivered many judgments confirming the principle that goods manufactured and marketed in a Member State in accordance with the local legislation may be imported into any other Member State unless some mandatory requirement justifies their exclusion. The Court has for instance condemned a Belgian law requiring margarine to be sold only in cube-shaped packets,[10] a German law prohibiting the use of additives in beer,[11] and an Italian law permitting only durum wheat to be used for the manufacture of pasta.[12] On the other hand, the court has upheld a Danish law prohibiting the use of nonreturnable bottles, thus recognizing the protection of the environment as an additional mandatory requirement.[13]

It is sometimes suggested that goods originating in nonmember countries cannot benefit from the *Cassis de Dijon* principle.[14] That view does not accord with the wording of Article 9(2) of the Treaty or with the case law of the Court of Justice, which holds that, once such goods have been duly imported into a Member State and any customs duties payable have been accounted for, they must be treated in the same way as goods originating in the Community.[15] If the goods comply with one Member State's legislation and have been placed on the market there bona fide, their admission to other Member States may be restricted only on the grounds mentioned in Article 36 or in order to satisfy some other mandatory requirement.

4. Legislation Governing the Circumstances in which Goods May Be Marketed

a. The Nature of the Problem

All the cases referred to in the previous section had one thing in common: the Member State concerned prohibited the sale of goods not manufactured in accordance with certain rules governing the physical characteristics of goods. The obstacles to trade resulting from such legislation are manifest. Laws regulating the composition and pre-

---

10 Case 261/81, *Rau Lebensmittelwerke v. De Smedt,* 1982 E.C.R. 3961, [1981-1983 Transfer Binder] Common Mkt.Rep. (CCH) P 8979 (1982).

11 Case 178/84, *Commission v. Germany*, 1987 E.C.R. 1227.

12 Case 407/85, *3 Glocken GmbH v. USL Centro-Sud*, 1988 E.C.R. 4233.

13 Case 302/86, *Commission v. Denmark*, 1988 E.C.R. 4607.

14 Eric L. White, *In Search of the Limits to Article 30 of the EEC Treaty,* 20 C.M.L.R. 235, 259-80 (1989).

15 Case 41/76, *Donckerwolke v. Procureur de la Republique*, 1976 E.C.R. 1921, 20 C.M.L.R. 535 (1976) (paras 17-18).

sentation of goods, or prescribing technical standards for goods, have an obvious capacity to impede trade between Member States if applied to imported goods. They would rapidly lead to what is sometimes called the "balkanization" of the economy.

In recent years the Court has been faced with a number of cases in which Article 30 and the *Cassis de Dijon* principle have been invoked, not in relation to legislation governing the physical characteristics of goods, but in relation to legislation governing the circumstances in which goods may be marketed—rules as to where, when, by whom, how, or at what price goods may be sold, or rules on the advertising of goods.

Such legislation may impede trade between Member States, but the obstacles are much less obvious than in the case of legislation of the type in issue in *Cassis de Dijon*. For example, a law restricting the sale of alcohol to certain types of establishments impedes trade less than a law prohibiting the sale of alcohol altogether. As a result the Court has had great difficulty when confronted with rules governing marketing circumstances, and it has not always been consistent in its approach to the concept of measures having equivalent effect. Two conflicting strains are evident in the case law: the *Oebel* strain and the *Oosthoek* strain.

In cases belonging to the *Oebel* strain the Court adopts a narrow construction of the concept of measures having equivalent effect and excludes a particular measure from the scope of Article 30, even though the measure has an undeniable capacity to affect trade between Member States. In cases belonging to the *Oosthoek* strain the Court adopts a broad construction of the concept of measures having equivalent effect, assumes that a particular measure may in principle be caught by Article 30, and then proceeds to examine whether it is justified. In the course of that examination the Court sometimes gives the impression that it is laboring to avoid undue interference in areas for which the Member States are primarily competent.

b. The Oebel *Strain*

In *Oebel*[16] the Court ruled that German legislation prohibiting the transport and delivery of bakers' wares to consumers and retailers between 10:00 P.M. and 5:45 A.M., the object of which was to ensure compliance with a prohibition on night work in bakeries, could not have the effect of restricting imports or exports between Member States. That statement cannot be taken at face value. Since transport and delivery to wholesalers was excluded from the prohibition, the effect on intra-Community trade was admittedly slight. But some effect must have existed, especially in frontier zones. The *Oebel* ruling must be read in light of the facts of the case. Mr. Oebel, the manager of a bakery in Wiesbaden, Germany, was prosecuted for allowing his staff to work at night. Such a prosecution was unlikely to affect imports from other Member States. It would have

---

[16] Case 155/80, *Oebel*, 1981 E.C.R. 1993, [1979-1981 Transfer Binder] Common Mkt.Rep. (CCH) P 8767 (1981).

[*Editor's Note*: The author's statement of the *Oebel* Case may be ambiguous. In that case, the Court ruled that the German legislation in question affected all traders without distinction as to nationality, and hence was permissible under the EEC—even if in fact the legislation had the practical effect of impacting more severly upon imports than upon locally produced baker goods.]

been a different matter if a baker from Strasbourg had been apprehended at 5:00 A.M. while on his way to deliver bread to shops in Karlsruhe.

In *Blesgen v. Belgium*[17] a Belgian restaurant owner was prosecuted for stocking and selling spirits of an alcoholic strength exceeding twenty-two degrees. In Belgium, although such goods could be sold in shops, their sale for consumption on the premises in bars and restaurants was prohibited at that time by a law designed to combat alcoholism.[18] Mr. Blesgen argued that the law was contrary to Article 30 of the Treaty inasmuch as it affected the importation and sale of spirits imported from other Member States. The Belgian Court of Cassation asked the Court of Justice whether such legislation amounted to a measure having equivalent effect under Article 30 and, if so, whether it was justified on grounds of the protection of health under Article 36.

In a much-criticized judgment the Court held that legislation of the type described was not caught by Article 30. The Court observed, somewhat implausibly, that the legislation "has no connection with the importation of products and for that reason is not of such a nature as to impede trade between Member States."[19] That statement was highly tendentious because Belgium, although the home of a substantial brewing industry, is not a noted producer of strong liquor; obviously the spirits that people would have drunk in Belgian bars and restaurants, if the law had allowed them to, would to a large extent have been imported from other Member States. Moreover, many customers of bars and restaurants in Belgium who were denied the chance to drink Scotch whisky or French cognac doubtless ended up consuming Belgian beer. Hence, whatever the object of the law might be, it was discriminatory and protectionist in effect.

It is of course arguable that, if the Belgian law had been found to be contrary to Article 30, it would have been saved by Article 36 as being justified on grounds of the protection of health. A curious feature of some of the Court's case law on the free movement of goods is that, though most of the judgments are defensible as to the result, the reasoning by which the result is reached is sometimes defective. The measure at issue in *Oebel* might have been defended on the ground that it was an appropriate means of protecting the health of workers in the baking industry.

For some years *Oebel* and *Blesgen* were regarded as something of an anomaly. It was thought that they were isolated examples of a narrow interpretation of Article 30. *Oebel* and *Blesgen* have recently made something of a comeback in a series of judgments concerned with a British Act of Parliament restricting the operation of sex shops. Under the British Act such establishments may in certain circumstances be subjected to a licensing requirement. *Quietlynn v. Southend Borough Council*[20] concerned a prosecution for operating an unlicensed sex shop. The defendants argued that the licens-

---

17 Case 75/81, *Blesgen v. Belgium*, 1982 E.C.R. 1211, [1981-1983 Transfer Binder] Common Mkt.Rep. (CCH) P 8823 (1982).

18 The law in question has since been repealed.

19 *Blesgen,* Common Mkt.Rep. P 8823 at 7745.

20 Case C-23/89, *Quietlynn v. Southend Borough Council*, 1990 E.C.R. I-3059.

ing requirement, which resulted in their being excluded from the main shopping areas, was contrary to Article 30 since much of their merchandise was imported from other Member States and the effect of the Act was to reduce their sales of such goods. The English court found that the legislation indirectly reduced in absolute terms the volume of imports from other Member States. The Court of Justice nonetheless refused to entertain the suggestion that such legislation might be a measure having equivalent effect within the meaning of Article 30. The Court observed that the Act applied without distinction to domestic and imported products. It cited *Oebel* and *Blesgen*, stated that such legislation had no connection with intra-Community trade, since the products in question could be marketed through licensed sex shops and other channels, and concluded that the Act was not intended to regulate trade in goods within the Community and was not therefore of such a nature as to impede trade between Member States.

Once again the Court's judgment is defensible in the result since the public morality exception in Article 36 would almost certainly have saved the British legislation, but the reasoning is questionable. The fact that national legislation is not intended to regulate trade in goods within the Community does not necessarily mean that it cannot impede trade between Member States. Exactly the same could have been said of the German law prohibiting the sale of *Cassis de Dijon* with less than 25 percent alcohol. Nor should the nondiscriminatory nature of the legislation necessarily remove it from the scope of Article 30. It has been axiomatic since the *Cassis de Dijon* judgment that nondiscriminatory measures do not automatically escape the prohibition laid down by Article 30.

c. *The* **Oosthoek** *Strain*

Oebel, *Blesgen*, and *Quietlynn* are all the more surprising if compared with the judgments representing the *Oosthoek* strain. The first example of that strain is *Oosthoek's Uitgeversmaatschappij*.[21] A Dutch law prohibited the practice of promoting sales by means of offering gifts. Oosthoek marketed in the Netherlands, Belgium, and part of France Dutch-language encyclopedias printed partly in the Netherlands and partly in Belgium. The company was prosecuted by the Dutch authorities for offering gifts such as an atlas or a dictionary to promote sales of its encyclopedias. Oosthoek raised a defence based on Article 30 and the matter was referred to the Court of Justice. On the face of it, the interference with interstate trade was minimal, but the Court nevertheless held, perhaps a little surprisingly in view of what it had said in *Blesgen* a few months earlier, that legislation that forced a trader to abandon a particular marketing method might be contrary to Article 30. The Court then proceeded to enquire whether the Dutch legislation was justified on grounds of consumer protection and held that it was.

In a sense of course, the result was the same as in *Oebel, Blesgen*, and *Quietlynn*, because the restrictive measure adopted by a Member State was found to be compat-

[21] Case 286/81, *Oesthoek's Uitgeversmaatschappij*, 1982 E.C.R. 4575, [1981-1983 Transfer Binder] Common Mkt.Rep. (CCH) P 8895 (1982).

ible with Community law, but the means by which that result was reached were very different. In *Oebel*, *Blesgen*, and *Quietlynn* the Court maintained, rather unconvincingly, that trade between Member States could not be affected by the national measure and therefore excluded all possibility of a breach of Article 30. In *Oosthoek* the Court recognized that the national measure might infringe Article 30, even though arguably the effect on trade between Member States was less significant than in the other cases, and then found that the measure was justified.

In *Buet*[22] the Court had to consider a French law that prohibited the door-to-door selling of educational material. Mr. Buet managed a company that used such methods to sell English-language teaching material manufactured in Belgium. He was prosecuted and sentenced to a term of imprisonment. In his appeal he argued that the French law was contrary to Article 30, and the case was referred to the Court of Justice.

Citing *Oosthoek,* the Court ruled that to deprive a trader of a method of marketing whereby he realized almost all his sales might constitute an obstacle to imports even though the legislation in question applied to domestic and imported products without distinction. Adopting a classical *Cassis de Dijon* approach, the Court then enquired whether that obstacle to free movement was necessary to satisfy mandatory requirements such as consumer protection or fair trading. The Court observed that measures restricting free movement must be proportionate to the aim pursued, and that if a Member State had at its disposal less restrictive means of attaining the same aims it must use them. Observing that the consumer could normally be adequately protected by means of a statutory right to cancel a contract concluded at home, the Court went on to state that the risk of an ill-considered purchase increased when the product in question was educational material since the potential customers, who were often behind with their education and anxious to catch up, were particularly vulnerable. On that basis the Court held that it was permissible for a national legislature to prohibit canvassing at private residences.

Two judgments appear to confirm that the *Oosthoek* strain is dominant and that the *Oebel* strain is on the wane, notwithstanding *Quietlynn*. In *GB-INNO-BM v. Confederation du Commerce Luxembourgeois*[23] the Court was asked to give a preliminary ruling in proceedings that arose out of an attempt by an organization representing Luxembourg shopkeepers to prevent the owners of a supermarket situated in Arlon, just across the Belgian border, from distributing advertising matter to households in Luxembourg. The advertising did not comply with the Luxembourg law on unfair competition, according to which sales offers involving a temporary price reduction may not state the duration of the offer or refer to previous prices. The advertising did, however, comply with Belgian law.

The Court found that the application of the Luxembourg legislation to the Belgian supermarket's advertising was capable of breaching Article 30. Observing that the obstacle to trade was due to disparities between national laws, the Court proceeded to examine—under the *Cassis de Dijon* approach—whether the restriction on trade was

---

22 Case 382/87, *Buet v. Ministere Public*, 1989 E.C.R. 1235.

23 Case C-362/88, *GB-INNO-BM v. Confederation du Commerce Luxembourgeois*, 1990 E.C.R. I-667.

justified as being necessary in order to satisfy mandatory requirements relating to consumer protection. The Court held that there was no such justification, essentially on the ground that Community policy, as laid down in a program adopted by the Council of Ministers, requires that consumers should have access to information so that they can make their purchasing decisions in full knowledge of the facts; a regulation that denies consumers access to a particular type of information, even though the information is perfectly accurate, cannot be justified in the name of consumer protection.

The judgment in *Aragonesa de Publicidad Exterior v. Departamento de Sanidad y Seguridad Social de la Generalitat de Cataluna*[24] also dealt with a restriction on certain forms of advertising. The parliament of Catalonia, one of the autonomous regions of Spain, passed a law prohibiting the advertising of beverages containing more than twenty-three degrees of alcohol in cinemas, on public transport, and along streets and roads. Two advertising agencies were charged with infringing that law. They contended that the law was contrary to Article 30, since it restricted the advertising of products originating in other Member States. The Court of Justice was asked to give a preliminary ruling.

The Court stated unequivocally that such legislation must in principle be regarded as a measure having equivalent effect under Article 30. However, it went on to hold that the restriction on trade was justified, under Article 36, on grounds of the protection of public health. The case provides a good illustration of how an Article 36 analysis works in practice. In order for the Catalan legislation to enjoy the benefit of Article 36 it was necessary to establish: (a) that the legislation contributed to its stated goal of protecting public health; (b) that the restriction on trade caused by the legislation was not disproportionate in relation to that goal; and (c) that the legislation did not constitute arbitrary discrimination or a disguised restriction on trade, within the meaning of the second sentence of Article 36. As regards the first two points, the acceptability of the legislation was never in much doubt. On the third point it was argued that the legislation was discriminatory because it permitted the advertising of the typical products of Catalonia (still and sparkling wine) and prohibited the advertising of typical imported products (whiskey and cognac). The Court rejected that argument, observing that Catalonia is in fact a substantial producer of alcoholic drinks that exceed the threshold of twenty-three degrees. The Court might also have noted that the threshold is based on an objective criterion, since strong liquor is in principle more harmful to health than less alcoholic beverages. On that basis the case could have been distinguished from an earlier case, *Commission v. France*,[25] in which the Court condemned a French provision that banned the advertising of spirits made from grain but permitted the advertising of spirits made from wine. The legislation at issue in *Blesgen* could have been upheld on the same basis if the Court had found it contrary to Article 30 and proceeded to enquire whether it could be saved by Article 36.

---

[24] *See* Joined Cases C-1/90 and C-179/90 *Aragonesa de Publicidad Exterior v. Departamento de Sanidad y Seguridad Social de la Generalitat de Cataluna*, para. 13 (Judgment of July 25, 1991).

[25] Case 152/78, *Commission v. France*, 1980 E.C.R. 2299, [1979-1981 Transfer Binder] Common Mkt.Rep. (CCH) P 8691 (1980).

d. The Sunday Trading Cases

Against this background of conflict between cases belonging to the *Oebel* strain and cases belonging to the *Oosthoek* strain we must examine the Court's case law on Sunday trading.

In many European countries the law restricts or prohibits the opening of shops on Sundays. On the face of it, nothing in the EEC Treaty suggests that the regulation of shop opening hours is anything other than a matter for the national legislatures. Nor is it immediately obvious that laws requiring shops to close on Sundays are an obstacle to trade between Member States. However, some years ago a chain of do-it-yourself stores called "B & Q" started opening on Sundays in England in defiance of the British Shops Act 1950. When prosecuted, it contended that the British statute was contrary to Article 30, arguing that its total sales would decline if it were forced to close on Sundays and that, since some of the goods it sold were manufactured in other Member States, the effect was to reduce the volume of imports. Magistrates' Court sought a preliminary ruling from the Court of Justice.

But the Court seems to have been reluctant to state openly that a ban on Sunday trading might be a measure having equivalent effect within the meaning of Article 30. Instead it began by citing the *Cinetheque* judgment,[26] in which the Court had held that a French ban on the sale or hire of videocassettes during the first twelve months after a motion picture's release was not compatible with the principle of free movement unless any obstacle to Community trade thereby created did not exceed what was necessary to ensure the attainment of the objective in view and unless that objective was justified with regard to Community law.

The Court had no difficulty in holding that the second criterion was satisfied in the case of legislation restricting Sunday trading: Rules regarding the opening hours of retail premises "reflect certain political and economic choices in so far as their purpose is to ensure that working and non-working hours are so arranged as to accord with national or regional sociocultural characteristics, and that, in the present state of Community law, is a matter for the Member States."[27]

So far the Court's judgment is unobjectionable. In relation to the other criterion—namely, whether the obstacle to trade exceeded what was necessary to attain the aim in question—the Court's performance is less satisfactory. For some reason it resurrected a rather obscure legislative provision adopted in 1969, namely Article 3 of Commission Directive 70/50.[28]

That directive was based on Article 33(7) of the Treaty, which empowered the Commission to issue directives establishing the procedure and timetable for abolishing measures having equivalent effect. In 1969 the Commission took the view that nondiscriminatory measures relating to the marketing of goods did not normally constitute measures having equivalent effect. The directive therefore required, by Article 2,

---

[26] Joined Cases 60/84 and 61/84, *Cinetheque S.A. v. Federation Nationale des Cinemas Francais*, 1985 E.C.R. 2605, [1985-1986 Transfer Binder] Common Mkt.Rep. (CCH) P 14,220 (1985).

[27] Case 145/88, Torfaen Borough Council n. B & Q, 1989 E.C.R. 3851, 59 C.M.C.R. 455 (1989).

[28] 1970 O.J.SPEC.ED. I 17.

the abolition of all discriminatory measures that hinder imports and, by Article 3, the abolition of:

> [M]easures governing the marketing of products which deal, in particular, with shape, size, weight, composition, presentation, identification or putting up and which are equally applicable to domestic and imported products, where the restrictive effect of such measures on the free movement of goods exceeds the effects intrinsic to trade rules.

Since that approach had long since been rejected by the Court in *Cassis de Dijon*, it is a little surprising that the Court should have placed such reliance on it in the *B & Q* case and held that the test for assessing the compatibility with the Treaty of the Sunday trading law was whether "the restrictive effect of such measures on the free movement of goods exceeds the effects intrinsic to trade rules."[29] What is even more surprising is that the Court then held that the question whether specific national rules in fact remain within that limit was a question of fact to be determined by the national court. The result was a preliminary ruling of almost Delphic obscurity that gave the national court little guidance as to the compatibility of the national legislation with the Treaty. The matter has inevitably been the subject of much further litigation in the English courts, culminating in another reference to the Court of Justice.

In the meantime the Court has given a second judgment on the issue of Sunday trading, pursuant to references for a preliminary ruling from French and Belgian courts.[30] In France and Belgium the employment of workers on Sundays is prohibited, subject to certain exceptions. A number of large stores decided to open on Sundays and employed staff for that purpose in defiance of the national laws. When proceedings were taken against them, the cases were referred to the Court of Justice.

The resulting judgments are interesting to compare and contrast with the *B & Q* judgment delivered only fifteen months earlier. In *Conforama* and *Marchandise* the Court expressly recognized that the legislation in question might have a negative effect on imports and recalled that in *B & Q* it had held that a ban on Sunday trading was not compatible with the principle of the free movement of goods unless the resulting obstacle to Community trade did not exceed what was necessary to attain the objective in question and unless that objective was justified with regard to Community law. As in *B & Q*, the Court held that the objective pursued by the legislation was justified. But the *Conforama* and *Marchandise* judgments differed from *B & Q* when it came to assessing whether the obstacles to Community trade exceeded what was necessary to attain the objective in question. No reference was made to Directive 70/50, and the judgments gave no suggestion that the matter was a question of fact to be determined by the national court. Instead the Court simply observed that the restrictive effects on trade resulting from the legislation in question did not appear excessive with regard to the objective pursued. Accordingly, the Court ruled that the prohibition laid down in

---

29 *B & Q*, 1989 E.C.R. at 3889.

30 *See* Case C-312/89, *Conforama* (Judgment of Feb. 28, 1991); Case C-332/89, *Ministere Public v. Marchandise* (Judgment of Feb. 28, 1991).

Article 30 did not apply to national legislation prohibiting the employment of workers on Sundays.

The apparent conflict between *B & Q* and the later rulings has not escaped the attention of the English courts. The House of Lords has recently referred questions to the Court of Justice, asking in substance whether the clear determination of compatibility with Article 30 made in *Conforama* and *Marchandise* also applies to the English provisions on Sunday trading.[31]

e. Conclusions

If the object of this article were to defend the Court of Justice against a charge of inconsistency, it would be easy to point out that the measures at issue in *Oosthoek, Buet, GB-INNO-BM* and *Aragonesa de Publicidad Exterior* were all caught by the principle—first formulated in paragraph 15 of the *Oosthoek* judgment—that "Legislation which restricts or prohibits certain forms of advertising and certain means of sales promotion may, although it does not directly affect imports, be such as to restrict their volume because it affects marketing opportunities for the imported products."[32] A similar statement occurs in the other three judgments belonging to the *Oosthoek* strain. The measures at issue in *Oebel, Blesgen, Quietlynn*, and the Sunday trading cases, on the other hand, do not fall so squarely within that formula.

It is submitted, however, that an attempt to distinguish the two groups of cases on that basis would be futile. In the first place, the measures at issue in *Blesgen* and *Quietlynn* did in fact restrict "certain means of sales promotion" inasmuch as they prevented goods from being marketed through certain channels. But the overwhelming objection to such a distinction is that it would be entirely devoid of logic. To pretend that a law prohibiting the advertising of strong alcoholic drinks in certain places may affect intra-Community trade, whereas a law prohibiting the sale of strong alcoholic drinks in certain establishments can have no such effect, is simply ludicrous. If any distinction at all is to be made between the two types of measure, it is the prohibition on sale—rather than the prohibition on advertising—that should be treated more sternly by the Court, since it inevitably affects trade to a greater degree. Similarly, it would make no sense to argue that a law prohibiting the door-to-door selling of certain products is in principle caught by Article 30 but that a law prohibiting the sale of certain products in bars and restaurants lies entirely outside the scope of Article 30.

It is submitted therefore that the Court should in future attempt to be more consistent in its approach to measures governing the circumstances in which goods may be marketed. Two avenues are open to it: Either it may in all cases adopt the broad approach of *Oosthoek* and apply the *Dassonville* formula more or less literally; or it may look for a modified version of that formula that would catch all measures that genuinely interfere with trade between Member States, to the exclusion of measures

---

[31] *See* Case C-169/91, *Stoke-on-Trent Council v. B & Q* (referred to the Court of Justice by order of 19 June 1991).

[32] Case 286/81, *Oosthoek's Uitgeversmaatschappij*, 1982 E.C.R. 4575, [1981-1983 Transfer Binder] Common Mkt.Rep. (CCH) P 8895, at 8546 (1982).

whose effect on such trade is remote and contingent. But the search for such a formula is perilously difficult and for that reason it may be preferable for the Court to construe the concept of measures having equivalent effect broadly, as in the *Oosthoek* strain of case law, and to be correspondingly generous in examining whether a particular measure is justified either under Article 36 or by reference to "mandatory requirements."

On the question of justification, a striking feature of the Sunday trading judgments and of the earlier *Cinetheque* judgment is that they do not use the expression "mandatory requirements." Instead they simply require that the measure restricting trade should be "justified with regard to Community law." That seems to imply a lower standard of justification. The objectives pursued by the measures in question do not have to be mandatory (that is, imperative or overriding); they merely have to be consistent with Community policy or at least not repugnant to it. The application of a lower standard of justification in such cases is not without logic, since the measures in question are less restrictive of intra-Community trade than the type of measure at issue in *Cassis de Dijon* and similar cases. However, if the Court is applying a lower standard of justification it should say so openly and explain why. It should also apply the same standard in all cases relating to measures that regulate the circumstances in which goods may be marketed, as opposed to measures governing the physical characteristics of goods, for which the criteria laid down in *Cassis de Dijon* remain valid.

B. The Judgment in *HAG II*

No survey of recent case law on the free movement of goods would be complete without mentioning the judgment in *CNL Sucal v. HAG AG* (known as *HAG II*).[33] The case was concerned with one of the grounds expressly mentioned in Article 36 as justifying exceptions to the principle of free movement, namely the protection of industrial and commercial property. The judgment is important for two reasons: first, because the Court reappraised the misguided negative attitude towards trademarks displayed in some of its earlier judgments, and secondly, because the Court expressly overruled, for the first time in its history,[34] one of its previous judgments.

At the beginning of the century a German company (HAG Bremen) began producing decaffeinated coffee under the trademark "HAG," which it registered in Germany. Later it also registered the mark in Belgium and Luxembourg and transferred those registrations to a Belgian subsidiary that it had established. After the Second World War the assets of the Belgian subsidiary, including the trademark "HAG," were confiscated as enemy property. In 1947 they were sold to the Van Oevelen family, which subsequently assigned the mark to a firm called Van Zuylen. The result was

---

[33] Case C-10/89, *SA CNL Sucal NV v. HAG GF AG*, 1990 E.C.R. I-3711, 59 C.M.L.R. 571 (1990) [hereinafter *HAG II*].

[34] It is true that in Case C-70/88, *European Parliament v. Council*, 1990 E.C.R. I-2041, the Court effectively overruled its earlier decision in Case 302/87, *European Parliament v. Council*, 1988 E.C.R. 5615. However, the Court did not on that occasion expressly recognize that it was overruling one of its previous decisions.

that in Belgium and Luxembourg the mark was owned by Van Zuylen, whereas in Germany and other countries the mark was still owned by HAG Bremen. In 1971 HAG Bremen started to sell coffee in Luxembourg under the HAG mark. Van Zuylen's attempt to obtain an injunction restraining HAG Bremen's infringement of its trademark failed after the Court of Justice had stated in a preliminary ruling that:

> To prohibit the marketing in one Member State of a product legally bearing a trademark in another Member State for the sole reason that an identical trademark, having the same origin, exists in the first State, is incompatible with the provisions for the free movement of goods within the Common Market.[35]

The principle thus enunciated became known as the doctrine of common origin. From the outset it was ferociously attacked by a host of critics and had few defenders. Its implications were disturbing. The doctrine appeared to mean, for example, that, where an undertaking had disposed of a trademark by assignment in one country—even years before the EEC was created—but retained an identical mark in another country, the assignor and assignee could each use the mark in the other's territory, notwithstanding the confusion thus engendered for the consumer. The doctrine of common origin would also mean, if the 1974 ruling were construed literally, that the owner of the mark in Belgium and Luxembourg could use it in Germany, where the registration still belonged to the original owner, HAG Bremen. That is exactly what came to pass.

In 1979 the firm Van Zuylen fell into the hands of the Swiss company Jacobs Suchard AG (of which CNL Sucal was a wholly owned subsidiary). Jacobs Suchard AG was the market leader for coffee products in Germany, except for decaffeinated coffee; that sector was dominated by HAG Bremen. The mark "HAG" is in fact almost a synonym for decaffeinated coffee in Germany. Jacobs Suchard AG thus had an obvious interest in acquiring the Belgian and Luxembourg registrations of the HAG trademark and supplying decaffeinated coffee under that mark to the German market. That is precisely what it began doing in 1985. When HAG Bremen applied to the German courts for an injunction to restrain the infringement of its trademark, the matter was eventually referred to the Court of Justice.

The Court was faced with three choices. It could: (1) extend the scope of the doctrine of common origin and allow the acquirer of the expropriated mark to use it in the territory of the original owner; (2) distinguish the two cases on the ground that the acquirer of the expropriated mark, like a party to an assignment, voluntarily participates in the fragmentation of the mark or at least knows that he is acquiring a fragmented mark, whereas the victim of the expropriation does not consent to the fragmentation of the mark; or (3) abandon the doctrine of common origin completely and recognize that following the subdivision of a trademark, at least a subdivision that took place before the EEC had even been conceived of, each proprietor is entitled to the exclusive use of the mark in its own territory.

---

[35] Case 192/73, *Van Zuylen v. HAG*, 1974 E.C.R. 731, [1974 Transfer Binder] Common Mkt.Rep. (CCH) P 8230 (1974) [hereinafter *HAG I*].

The first option, which was of course the one favored by CNL Sucal, was most unlikely to be accepted because it would have given extraterritorial effect to the expropriation that took place in Belgium and would have deprived HAG Bremen of the exclusive use of the mark in Germany even though it had never consented to the fragmentation. That would hardly have been consistent with the Court's case law as it had developed subsequent to *HAG I*.[36]

The second option was based on the assumption that, where a trademark comes into divided ownership as a result of an assignment, the assignor who retains the mark in one Member State and the assignee who acquires it in another Member State may use the mark in each other's territory. The Court's judgment in *Sirena v. Eda*[37] supports that assumption. If the assumption were correct, it would be logical to treat the purchaser of the expropriated mark in the same way as an assignee, but it would not be logical to treat the victim of the expropriation in the same way as the assignor, since it did not consent to the operation.

The Court chose the third option—rightly, it is submitted—and expressly overruled *HAG I*. It did so after a radical reappraisal of the importance of trademarks, which in some earlier judgments had been treated rather contemptuously by the Court. The negative attitude had been initiated by Advocate General Dutheillet de Lamothe who, in his Opinion in *Sirena v. Eda*, made a far-fetched comparison between a brand of shaving cream and penicillin in an attempt to prove that patents are more worthy of protection than trademarks.

In *HAG II*, by way of contrast, the Court recognized that trademarks constitute "an essential element of the system of undistorted competition which the Treaty seeks to establish and maintain." A trademark could only perform its essential function of guaranteeing to the consumer that all goods on which it is placed have the same commercial origin if the proprietor retained the exclusive right to use it. That conclusion was not affected by the fact that the mark in question having originally belonged to a single person in two Member States and that person having been deprived of it in one of those States as a result of an expropriation before the creation of the EEC. After the expropriation the mark continued to fulfill its function, independently in each of the territories concerned, of guaranteeing that all goods bearing the mark came from the same source.

Although it was not strictly necessary for the Court to overrule *HAG I*, it is submitted that it was right to do so because of the unacceptable confusion that would ensue for consumers if entirely separate persons, between whom there is no legal or economic link, were allowed to use the same trademark in the same territory. A

---

36 *See* Case 19/84, *Pharmon v. Hoechst*, 1985 E.C.R. 2281, [1985-1986 Transfer Binder] Common Mkt.Rep. (CCH) P 14,206 (1985), in which the Court held that the proprietor of a patent may oppose imports of products manufactured with the patented process in another Member State by a person who has obtained a compulsory license under a parallel patent held by the same proprietor. It would not be logical to treat a person whose trademark was expropriated without compensation less favorably than a patent-holder against whom a compulsory license was issued.

37 Case 40/70, *Sirena v. Eda*, 1971 E.C.R. 69, [1971-1973 Transfer Binder] Common Mkt.Rep. (CCH) P 8101 (1971).

degree of confusion is of course inevitable when a trademark belongs to different persons in different countries, especially in an age of international travel. Such confusion is regrettable—the more so in a common market—but it cannot be eliminated by allowing each proprietor of the mark to use it in the territory of the other. It must also be remembered that the Van Oevelen family gave valuable consideration for the purchase of the Belgian and Luxembourg marks in 1947 and were entitled to assume that, as the law stood then, the transaction was valid and they were obtaining an exclusive right. They could not have known that the EEC Treaty would come into existence twelve years later. The judgment in *HAG II* thus corrected an injustice perpetrated by the Court in *HAG I*.

HAG II is also important, in a more general sense, because it demonstrates an enlightened attitude towards the relative value of precedent. The Court of Justice, following the tradition of civil law countries, had never before expressly overruled one of its previous decisions. It had occasionally ignored a precedent that it apparently wished to depart from, but it had never expressly indicated that it considered a previous decision wrong. From that point of view also, *HAG II* is a welcome development.

C. The Application of Article 30 to Private Parties[38]

It is suggested that if Article 30 applies to the actions of private parties, then such an application will be more extensive and strict in nature than the application of the said Article to the actions of Member States (and public authorities), as private parties will not be able to derogate from the provisions of Article 30 to the same extent as Member States, having recourse to *all* the provisions for derogation in Article 36 of the Treaty. Article 36 provides:

> The provisions of Articles 30 to 34 shall not preclude prohibitions or restrictions on imports, exports or goods in transit justified on grounds of public morality, public policy or public security; the protection of health and life of humans, animals or plants; the protection of national treasures possessing artistic, historic or archaeological value; or the protection of industrial and commercial property. Such prohibitions or restrictions shall not, however, constitute a means of arbitrary discrimination by or a disguised restriction on trade between Member States.

It is suggested that the above exceptions of public morality, public policy and public security could not be used by private parties as these matters are of general and national interest and therefore properly the sole concern of the Member States. Private parties could avail themselves of the exception concerning the protection of industrial and commercial property, at least for the purpose of safeguarding rights that constitute

[38] Mary Quinn and Nicholas MacGowan, *Could Article 30 Impose Obligations on Individuals?*, 12 E.L. Rev. 163-178 (1987).

the specific subject matter of such property. Private parties may possibly avail of the remaining grounds of exceptions.

There is a further way in which the application of Article 30 to private parties will be more extensive than its application to Member States. This relates to the mandatory requirements exceptions found in *Cassis de Dijon*. In that case, the European Court stated:

> Obstacles to movement within the Community resulting from disparities between the national laws relating to the marketing of the products in question must be accepted insofar as those provisions may be recognized as being necessary in order to satisfy mandatory requirements relating in particular to the effectiveness of fiscal supervision, the protection of public health, the fairness of commercial transactions, and the defense of the consumer.

Although the list of mandatory requirements found in that case is not exhaustive, of those specified, it would seem that probably private parties could only ever satisfy the mandatory requirements relating to the fairness of commercial transactions and the defense of the consumer (and then, only where the private party concerned has attempted to avail himself of the disparity in the appropriate national laws).

There is nothing in the text of Article 30 to prevent the imposition of obligations under this Article, even where a private party is acting unilaterally, or even in a non-legally binding way. However, such an interpretation of the Article would have serious consequences. It is suggested, therefore, that in applying Article 30 to the "measures" taken by private parties, the European Court should adopt the approach it has taken in the cases where it was decided that articles of the Treaty which are addressed to Member States may impose obligations on private parties. In one of these cases, *Walrave,* the European Court emphasized that the obligations imposed by the Community law in issue, could only be imposed with regard to *legal relationships* that were located within the Community and where the party on whom the obligation was being imposed engaged in an *economic activity*.

Besides restricting the application of Article 30 to situations where there is a legal relationship and where an economic activity is being pursued, there is a further possible restriction on the application of Article 30 to private parties in the absence of implementing measures at Community or national level. This would be to restrict the application to measures which amount to a "direct and overt discrimination," by adopting the approach taken by the European Court in the *Second Defrenne* case. However, it is suggested that this possible restriction has been ruled out by the judgment of the European Court in the *Cassis de Dijon* case, which held that Article 30 applied to indistinctly applicable measures without the need for any implementing legislation. However, *Cassis de Dijon* drew a distinction between distinctly applicable measures and indistinctly applicable measures in that it established a less severe regime for the latter by means of the mandatory requirements. This distinction need not be maintained were the European Court to interpret Article 30 so as to impose obligations on private parties. It would be open to the European Court not to follow the *Cassis de Dijon* case in conjunction with its judgment in the *Irish Souvenirs* case, since those cases, in common with all the other cases on Article 30, only concerned "measures" taken by Member States and not by private parties. Therefore, the European Court could hold that recourse could be had to the mandatory requirements in relation to distinctly applicable measures taken by private parties and not by Member States. It is suggested, however, that it is unlikely that the European Court would ever extend the principle of mandatory requirements to distinctly applicable measures merely to restrict the application of Article 30 to private parties, as there are other means of restricting such an application without undermining the prohibitions of Article 30 and the principles laid down in the European Court's case law to date in relation thereto.

It is suggested that as Article 30's application to private parties is potentially wider in scope than its application to Member States the said Article should only impose obligations on a private party *vis`a vis* another party where:

(a) a legal relationship exists between the parties;
(b) the "measures" of the party intended to be bound by the provisions of Article 30, are legally binding acts,
(c) the "measures" of the party intended to be bound by Article 30 are taken in pursuance of an economic activity.

This would mean that Article 30 would only apply to the following types of measures:

(a) legally binding acts of Member States/public authorities,
(b) non-legally binding acts of Member States/public authorities,
(c) legally binding acts of private parties.

Non-legally binding measures taken by private parties would not constitute measures within the meaning of Article 30.

In addition, a further limitation on the application of Article 30 to measures taken by private parties is suggested. Article 30 should only be applied where no other Treaty provision is applicable. There should be no parallel application of Article 30 and other Treaty provisions to the actions of private parties. It is submitted that this limitation would preserve the scheme, purpose and balance of the Treaty, without leaving a lacuna in Community law.

In conclusion, it is suggested that there are compelling policy considerations which should make the European Court extremely reluctant to interpret Article 30 as imposing obligations on private parties. Even if the European Court does so interpret Article 30, the Court would be likely to do so in a most restrictive way. The European Court is likely to take a cautious rather than a teleological approach to the interpretation of Article 30 given the present day political realities facing the Communities, and despite the fact that the result is likely to be less *communautaire* than otherwise might be hoped for.

D. Limits Arising out of the Notions Used in Article 30 Itself—"Quantitative Restriction on Imports," "Measures of Equivalent Effect" and "Between Member States"[39]

1. The Meaning of "Quantitative Restriction on Imports"

a. The GATT

The authors of the Treaty were clearly aware of the provisions of the General Agreement on Tariffs and Trade of 1947 ("the GATT") when they drafted Articles 30 to 36.

Article XI, paragraph 1 of the GATT which is entitled "General Elimination of Quantitative Restrictions" reads as follows:

> No prohibitions or restriction other than duties, taxes or other charges, whether made effective through quotas, import or export licenses or other measures, shall be instituted or maintained by any contracting party on the importation of any product of the territory of any other contracting party or on the exportation or on the sale for export of any product destined for the territory of any other contracting party.

Paragraph 2 provides for certain exceptions which are listed in Article XX. This latter provision contains remarkable similarities to Article 36.

It should be noted that, insofar as it relates to imports, Article XI of the GATT only concerns prohibitions and restrictions applying to products *originating* in the territory of another party ("product of the territory"). Article 30, on the other hand, is less explicit and merely refers to quantitative restrictions and measures of equivalent effect "between Member States." Another feature of this provision which is worthy of note is that this provision only applies to measures taking effect at the border ("on the importation"). Internal measures which *discriminate* against products *originating* in other territories are dealt with in Article III of the GATT which entitled "National Treatment on Internal Taxation and Regulation." Paragraph 1 of this provision states:

> The contracting parties recognize that . . . [certain internal measures] . . . should not be applied to imported or domestic products so as to afford protection to domestic production.

More specifically, paragraph 4 provides:

> The products of the territory of any contracting party imported into the territory of any other contracting party shall be accorded treatment no less favorable than that accorded to like products of national origin in respect of all laws, regulations and requirements affecting their internal sale, offering for sale, purchase, transportation, distribution or use.

---

[39] Eric L. White, *In Search of the Limits to Article 30 of the EEC Treaty,* 26 CML Rev. 235-80 (1989). ©1989 Kluwer Academic Publishers. Reprinted by permission of the publisher.

Again, Article 30 is more simply expressed. It makes no distinction between internal measures and those taking effect at the border.

i. The position taken by the Court of Justice

The Court of Justice has not often drawn a distinction between quantitative restrictions on imports and measures of equivalent effect. Recent cases often do not refer to either notion but rather to the previous case law of the Court. In an early case, Case 2/73, *Geddo v. Ente Nationale Risi,*[40] the Court of Justice defined a quantitative restriction on imports as covering measures which amount to a total or partial "restraint" (in French "prohibition") of imports whereas a measure of equivalent effect was considered to also include any "encumbrance" (in French "entrave") having the same effect. (As sometimes happens, the French text is much clearer than the English translation.)

In Case 34/79, *R v. Henn and Darby,*[41] the Court held the import prohibition on pornographic materials (which reflected similar international measures prohibiting pornography) to be a quantitative restriction on imports (justified under Article 36) even though the national court had asked whether it constituted a measure of equivalent effect.

Finally, in a recent case, *Commission v. Ireland,*[42] the Court of Justice stated the requirement for an import license to be a quantitative restriction on imports.

ii. Conclusion

Although the case-law contains very little guidance, it appears that the Court treats all total or partial prohibitions on imports as quantitative restrictions on imports, even if they also apply to national production and treats all other obstacles or barriers as measures of equivalent effect. The case-law of the Court does not make any distinction between measures taking effect at the border and internal measures. It is submitted therefore, that a quantitative restriction on imports within the meaning of Article 30 may be defined as any measure which is capable of limiting imports to a finite quantity, including the quantity zero.

b. Which Measures May Be Considered as Having Equivalent Effect to Quantitative Restrictions on Imports

This article proposes a definition for the notion of measure of equivalent effect to a quantitative restriction on imports which encompasses all those measures which hinder the establishment of the Common Market but does not also cover those measures in respect of which Member States can safely be allowed to take divergent paths without endangering this objective. This definition will first be developed from teleological considerations in the light of the *Cassis de Dijon* case-law and then applied to a

40 Case 2/73, *Geddo v. Ente Nationale Risi,* [1973] E.C.R. 865 at Recital 7.

41 [1979] E.C.R. 3795.

42 Case 288/83, *Commission v. Ireland* (Cypress Potatoes), [1985] E.C.R. 1761.

series of inoffensive State measures to which Article 30 would apply according to the *Dassonville* formula. It will be demonstrated how this definition explains the judgments of the Court which cannot be reconciled with the *Dassonville* formula.

c. The Proposed Definition

Although, leaving aside the Court's case-law, the meaning of "quantitative restriction on imports" may appear relatively clear, the notion of "measure of equivalent effect" to a quantitative restriction on imports is much more difficult to define. The effects of a quantitative restriction on imports are of course to limit or reduce imports. The objective and consequence are normally to advantage and protect domestic production. To say that a measure of equivalent effect must limit imports to a defined quantity would make it indistinguishable from a quantitative restriction on imports. To require that it need only reduce imports immediately raises the question of whether this effect need be direct or whether an indirect effect would suffice. Quantitative restrictions on imports, of course, have a *direct* effect on imports. But if the notion of measures of equivalent effect were to be limited to measures directly affecting imports, all purely internal measures (e.g., restrictions on marketing) would escape the prohibition. In other words, the term "measures of equivalent effect" would do no more than cover the "similar measures" referred to in Article XI of the GATT and not the protective internal measures referred to in Article III of the GATT.

Having established that the notion of measures of equivalent effect in Article 30 must include measures indirectly limiting imports, the next question which arises is whether a reduction of imports must be demonstrated (statistically?) or whether the mere possibility of such a reduction suffices. Clearly, the compatibility of a national measure with a directly applicable provision of Union law cannot be allowed to depend on purely factual considerations which may indeed vary from day to day. Its legality must be capable of confirmation in the abstract. In other words, only a potential effect on trade is required. It is no doubt considerations of this kind that led the Court of Justice to its famous definition of measure of equivalent effect in *Dassonville*. The problem with this definition however is, as will be demonstrated more fully below, that it is far too wide. It has often appeared necessary therefore, to conclude that a measure of equivalent effect must also have the other effect of a quantitative restriction on imports—to advantage or protect domestic production. This is the origin of the discrimination theories of Article 30 (but does not form the basis of the approach advocated in this article). It is clear that measures which discriminate against imports are contrary to Article 30. This is true both of formal discrimination (unjustified difference in treatment) and material discrimination (unjustified equal treatment), indeed, all measures which give an advantage to domestic production which is unavailable to imports fall under this definition. Marenco has attempted to explain the whole of the Court's case-law up to 1984 on this basis. He explained the *Cassis de Dijon* line of cases by considering as discriminatory or protectionist the attitude of the legislator who regulated a market on the basis of the rules and traditions applying to production on the national territory without taking account of the rules and traditions of other Member States, thus advantaging national production. Most commentators, however, find this view untenable both for reasons of principle and on the basis of the case-law of the Court. Even Marenco had to admit that considerations of protective effect or discrimination formed no part of the Court's reasoning in most of its judgments.

There are some judgments of the Court of Justice which clearly show that Member State measures may be contrary to Article 30 even though no advantage is given to domestic production. Significantly, these are all cases of prohibitions. For example, in Cases 60-61/84, *Cinéthèque*, the Court of Justice expressly stated that the effect of the French measure (prohibition of the distribution of video cassettes for a period of two years following release of the film in cinemas) was "not to favor national production as against the production of other Member States, but to encourage cinematographic production as such." It went further to hold that the measure fell under Article 30 (and was justified by a mandatory requirement). There was also no discernible advantage for national production in Case 216/84, *Commission v. France* (milk substitutes), as national production of milk substitutes was prohibited in the same way as imports. The only protective effect was for milk production and genuine milk products but the contested measures in no way disadvantaged the genuine milk products of other Member States in their possibilities of access to the French market. Since these two cases concerned *prohibitions* rather than mere restrictions, they represent "quantitative restrictions on imports" according to the definition given above rather than merely "measures of equivalent effect." (The Court did not use either term in its judgments but rather referred to the "principle of the free movement of goods" in *Cinéthèque* and generally to its previous case-law in the milk substitutes case).

However, it is logically rather unsatisfactory to consider that a "quantitative restriction on imports" need not have any protective effect for national production but that a measure of equivalent effect to a quantitative restriction should have such an effect. A protective effect for national production cannot therefore be an element of our definition of "measure of equivalent effect."

The Court of Justice often describes as being a measure of equivalent effect to a quantitative restriction on imports the "obstacles to trade to movement in the Union resulting from *disparities between the national laws* relating to the marketing of the products in question"[43] and the application to products *legally produced and marketed* in other Member States of national legal provisions.[44] The philosophy of the Court appears to be that Article 30 be interpreted in the light of its objective which is the creation of a unified market. This is apparent for the first time in the judgment of the Court in Case 78/70, *Deutsche Grammophon,*[45] and most recently in Case 207/83, *Commission v. United Kingdom* (origin marking),[46] where the Court said:

---

[43] Recital 8 of *Cassis de Dijon*, [1979] E.C.R. 649.

[44] *See*, in particular, Recital 14 of *Cassis de Dijon*, also Recital 7 of the judgment of 23 Feb. 1988 in Case 216/84, *Commission v. France* (milk substitutes) (not yet reported).

[45] [1971] E.C.R. 487 at Recital 12.

[46] [1985] E.C.R. 1201.

> As the Court has had occasion to emphasis in various contexts, the Treaty, by establishing a common market and progressively approximating the economic policies of the Member States seeks to unite national markets in a single market having the characteristics of a domestic market.[47]

Accordingly, goods should be manufactured wherever the conditions are most favorable. These conditions need not only relate to the economic environment, they should also include the legal environment. If the legal situation in one Member State is particularly favorable for the manufacture of a particular product, then production should be centered there, in the same way as producers should be free to seek out the most favorable economic climate.

National rules are inconsistent with this principle if they hinder the free circulation of such goods for reasons relating to or arising out of the different legal and economic environment in which they were produced. This, it is submitted, is the explanation for the Court's reference to "disparities between national rules."

The different legal and economic environment of the Member State of origin finds its expression in the different *characteristics* of an imported product compared with the national product. Consequently, as the judgment of the Court in *Cassis de Dijon* clearly shows, Member States are not entitled to require that imported products have the same *characteristics* as are required of, or are traditional in, domestic products unless this is strictly necessary for the protection of some legitimate interest. There is not, however, the same need to require the rules relating to the *circumstances* in which certain goods may be *sold or used* in the importing Member State to be overridden for this purpose as long as imported products enjoy *equal access* to the market of the importing Member State compared with national goods. In such a case the imported product is not deprived of any advantage it derives from the different legal and economic environment prevailing in the place of production. In fact, any reduction of total sales (and therefore imports) which may result from restrictions on the circumstances in which they may be sold does not arise out of *disparities* between national rules but rather out of the *existence* of the rules in the importing Member State.

It will be shown *infra* that this distinction between the *characteristics* required of imported products and the *circumstances* in which they may be sold is implicit in the case- law of the Court of Justice. The *Cassis de Dijon* line of cases all relate to barriers to trade arising out of disparities between national rules on the *characteristics* required of products. The cases in which the Court has not followed the wide definition of the notion of measure of equivalent effect to a quantitative restriction on imports are those relating to the *circumstances* in which a product may be sold or used; i.e., to where, by whom, or how it may be sold or used or at what price it may be sold. The proposed definition of a measure of equivalent effect to a quantitative restriction on imports for indistinctly applicable measures based on the *Cassis de Dijon* case-law is therefore *the application by a Member State to products legally produced and marketed in another Member State of its national rules relating to the characteristics*

---

47 [Id. a]t Recital 17

required of such products on its territory (which therefore prevents this product from benefitting in the importing Member State from the advantages arising out of its production in the different legal and economic environment prevailing in the other Member State). The *Cassis de Dijon* case-law shows that the term "characteristics" includes the composition, size, shape, and weight of goods as well as their presentation, denomination and labeling. State measures which are entirely neutral in their effect on goods legally produced and marketed in other Member States, because they only regulate the circumstances in which all goods of the same kind may be sold or used, should not be regarded as falling under Article 30.

Member States often regulate which persons may sell certain goods for a variety of motives. For example it is not uncommon to find rules which provide that medicines may only be sold by pharmacists, spectacles by opticians, sex articles by licensed sex shops, cigarettes by tobacconists, fish by fishmongers and, believe it or not, coffins by undertakers. These are trading rules and they affect imports (by channeling them) in much the same way as the Belgian rules in *Dassonville*. They may also keep prices high and reduce total sales (including imports). True, they apply to domestic products in the same way as imports but that, according to the *Cassis de Dijon* case-law, is not relevant. Rules relating to *where* goods may be sold will often have the same effect (for example, drugs must be sold in a pharmacy rather than by a pharmacist). Another example of rules relating to where goods may be sold are planning restrictions; if a man is not allowed to establish a motor car dealership in the middle of a residential area, he will no doubt sell fewer imported cars than if this were allowed. Similarly, restrictions on trading hours may reduce total sales of products to an extent that varies according to the nature of the product involved and thus reduce imports of certain products. For example, restrictions on the opening hours of British pubs and continental cafés reduce, as they are probably intended to, total consumption of alcoholic drinks and thus imports of such products. Of course many of these restrictions may qualify for an exception from Article 30, but others may not—exceptions to fundamental Treaty provisions must be strictly construed. Some restrictions of this kind are no doubt motivated by economic considerations. It may be that some Member States restrict the outlets for certain products so as to preserve small corner shops (e.g., tobacconists) from competition by supermarkets. Others may give pharmacists a monopoly in the sale of pharmaceutical products so as to compensate them for having to stock expensive and rarely-used medicines. The Court of Justice has consistently rejected attempts to justify an exception from the fundamental principle of the free movement of goods for economic motives of this kind. Other restrictions may have become so outdated, anomalous and even arbitrary over time that they can no longer be justified. For example, in the United Kingdom you may purchase a pornographic magazine on a Sunday but not a Bible and motor car accessories but not household accessories. Such restrictions do not however prevent imports from gaining access to the national market and benefitting there from the advantages accruing to them out of the different legal and economic environment of the Member State of production. They do not stand in the way of uniting national markets into a single market having the characteristics of a domestic market. Even politically centralized States tolerate local variations in the rules relating to who may sell certain goods and when and where they may be sold.

There is even less reason for the Union, whose cultural and social diversity is greater than that of any of its Member States, to restrict the freedom of its composite parts to regulate such matters in a neutral and general manner. How has the Court of Justice dealt with cases involving restrictions of this kind?

In Case 155/80, *Oebel*,[48] the Court considered the applicability of Articles 30 and 34 of the Treaty to rules regulating the times at which ordinary and fine bakers' wares could be transported and delivered. Restrictions on the times at which these products could be delivered affected their availability for sale to final consumers and thus reduced, potentially, the quantities, including the quantities of imported products, which would be sold to consumers. Such restrictions are analogous in their effects to restrictions on the times at which products can be sold. The Court held that "[i]f such rules are confined to transport for delivery to individual consumers and retail outlets only, without affecting transport and delivery to ware-houses or intermediaries, they cannot have the effect of restricting imports or exports between Member States. In this case, indeed, trade within the Union remains possible at all times, subject to the single exception that delivery to consumers and retailers is restricted to the same extent for all producers, wherever they are established. Under these circumstances such rules are not contrary to Article 30 and 34 of the Treaty."[49]

In Case 75/81, *Blesgen*,[50] the Court held that Article 30 did not apply to a Belgian law which prohibited the sale and consumption of spirits in public places since the restrictive effect of this measure on imports did not exceed that intrinsic to trade rules and no distinction was made based on nature or origin. The Court concluded that the measure had "in fact no connection with the importation of the products and for that reason is not of such a nature as to impede trade between Member States."[51] The Belgian ban on the sale of spirits in cafés undoubtedly led to a reduction of consumption and therefore restricted imports of spirits and certainly came under the *Dassonville* formula. It may also be noted here that the barrier to trade in *Blesgen* in no way depended upon any disparities between the Belgian rules and those in any other Member State.

d. Rules Relating to how Goods May Be Sold

Related to the question of where, when and by whom goods may be sold, are rules relating to *how* they may be sold. For example, it may be prohibited to sell spirits from automatic vending machines, cigarettes in a self-service store or encyclopedias on the doorstep; these selling methods may be particularly effective and their prohibition consequently reduce overall sales and thus imports. The same applies to restrictions on advertising. A ban on television advertising of a particular category of product, the consumption of which the government thinks should not be encouraged, will surely reduce its overall sales. A similar argument could be made for restrictions on the times

48 [1981] E.C.R. 1993.

49 [Id. at] Recital 20.

50 [1982] E.C.R. 1211.

51 [Id. at] Recitals 8 and 9.

at which "clearance sales" may be held or the types of "special offers" which can be made. Although they may reduce imports and thus come within the *Dassonville* formula as extended by *Cassis de Dijon*, general and neutral restrictions of this kind do not restrict access of imported goods to the market for reasons connected with the different economic and legal environments in the Member State of origin and thus do not, according to the definition proposed in this article, fall under the prohibition of Article 30. The limited case-law of the Court which deals with restrictions of this kind tends to support this conclusion.

In a judgment,[52] delivered some months after *Cassis de Dijon*, the Court of Justice held that France failed to comply with its obligations under Article 30 of the EEU Treaty by "subjecting advertising in respect of alcoholic beverages to discriminatory rules." As the operative part of the judgment indicates, this case turned on whether the French rules were discriminatory. France maintained that they were based on perfectly objective criteria; the Court of Justice found otherwise. However, if Article 30 applies to restrictions on *how* goods may be sold in the same way as it applies to the characteristics which goods must have in order to be able to be sold on the national market, this debate would have been unnecessary. It would have sufficed to show that the French rules reduced sales and therefore imports (which they surely did) and that they were unjustified or disproportionate. This conclusion is confirmed by the judgment of the Court in Cases 314-316/81 and 83/82, *Waterkeyn*,[53] a sequel to Case 152/78, *Commission v. France*, referred to *supra*, in which a French court asked for guidance on the consequences to be drawn from the judgment in that case. The Court of Justice stated that:

> The only inference which must be drawn from the judgment to which the preliminary question refers is therefore that, as far as advertising is concerned, the French Republic must treat alcoholic beverages originating in other Member States in the same way as competing national products [54]

There is however one judgment of the Court which may appear at first sight to contradict the view propounded above.

Case 286/81, *Oosthoek*,[55] involved a Dutch prohibition on the offering of free gifts as a promotional technique which was subject to certain exceptions in particular where the free gift is usually used or consumed at the same time as the main product. Oosthoek sold encyclopedias both in Belgium and the Netherlands and offered a dictionary or atlas as a free gift to purchasers. It was allowed to do this in Belgium and complained that the Dutch rules forced it to adopt different sales promotion schemes in the two territories which increased its costs.

---

[52] Case 152/78, *Commission v. France*, [1980] E.C.R. 2299.

[53] [1982] E.C.R. 4337.

[54] [Id. at] Recital 12.

[55] [1982] E.C.R. 4575.

The Court of Justice, recalling its *Cassis de Dijon* case-law, considered that:

> Legislation which restricts or prohibits certain forms of advertising and certain means of sales promotion may, although it does not directly affect imports, be such as to restrict their volume because it affects marketing opportunities for the imported products. The possibility cannot be ruled out that to compel a producer either to adopt advertising or sales promotion schemes which differ from one Member State to another or to discontinue a scheme which he considers to be particularly effective may constitute an obstacle to imports even if the legislation in question applies to domestic products and imported products without distinction.

The Court proceeded to consider whether the prohibition was justified by requirements relating to consumer protection and fair trading.

It will be noted that in this case the disparity between the national rules on sales promotion did create a barrier to trade because they related to the *presentation* of products, i.e., prevented the sale of two separate products packaged as one. The presentation of products forms part of their characteristics as demonstrated for example by the facts of Case 227/82, *van Bennekom* (vitamins presented in medicinal form),[56] and by the judgments of the Court in cases involving the *shape* of goods. However, restrictions on how goods may be sold which do not affect their presentation do not have the same effect and are directly comparable to restrictions on where and by whom goods may be sold. They do not therefore come under Article 30 if they are neutral in their effects on imports.

e. *Use Restrictions*

Another category of measures which can hinder trade are use restrictions imposed by Member States on certain goods, including all the rules concerning the way in which products may be manufactured. A good example of a use requirement is the rule that beer in Germany must be brewed from malted barley (the famous *Reinheitsgebot*). This prevents German brewers from importing quantities of maize or rice which they would use for brewing beer as is done in other Member States. The Court of Justice has already held[57] that Germany was in breach of Article 30 preventing imports of such beer. No-one has yet initiated a case which would allow German brewers to escape the *Reinheitsgebot* because it restricts imports of rice or maize, but such a case would seem possible on the basis of the *Dassonville* and *Cassis de Dijon* case-law.

Another interesting question is whether the laws against murder and violence and the carrying of offensive weapons are compatible with the Treaty only to the extent that they are justified under Article 30 (and it can be proved that there are no less restrictive means of protecting the interests involved). These laws undeniably restrict the demand for, and therefore the sales of and also ultimately imports of, guns and knives.

---

56 [1983] E.C.R. 3383.

57 Case 178/84, *Commission v. Germany,* [1987] E.C.R.

Again, the definition of measures of equivalent effect in respect to indistinctly applicable measures proposed in this article gives what surely must be the correct result in such cases. Measures which restrict the use of products in a general and neutral manner do not prevent imported products from benefitting on the national market from the advantages accruing to them from the different legal and economic environment prevailing in the Member State of origin and thus should not be considered as falling under Article 30.

The Court of Justice appears to share this opinion. First it should be recalled that the Court has stated in many of its judgments that, in the absence of common rules, it is for Member States to regulate the production of certain products within their territory but that they must not apply the derived marketing rules to products coming from other Member States except to the extent that this is justified. Any other conclusion would, as noted *supra*, mean that Germany would not be able to maintain the *Reinheitsgebot* even on its own territory, since the fact that brewers cannot use rice and maize to brew beer in Germany reduces the potential for imports of those products.

Then there are two cases which deal directly with use restrictions.

Case 148/85, *Forest*,[58] raised the question concerning the applicability of Article 30 to national legislation establishing quotas for the milling of wheat for human consumption. There was no restriction on the import of flour nor any direct restriction on the import of cereals for milling. The defendant in *Forest* pointed out, however, that the quota system indirectly restricted imports of wheat since it limited the quantity of wheat which could be milled and thus the demand (or potential demand) for imported wheat. Nevertheless, the Court concluded that "such a system of quotas at the level of flour production in fact has no effect on wheat imports and is not likely to impede trade between Member States."

The second case involving a use restriction is Case 118/87, *Openbaar Ministerie v. Nertsvoederfabriek Nederland*, where the Court of Justice held that a Dutch law which required the processing of poultry offal into useful products but only by licensed persons, did not fall under Article 30 so long as it did not prohibit imports. A prohibition on using a product for any purpose except to sell it to a limited number of buyers, is undoubtedly capable of discouraging imports but is not, according to the Court of Justice, contrary to Article 30.

f. Price Controls and Other State Measures Restrictive of Competition

Price controls of any kind will also potentially have the effect of reducing imports. If a minimum price is set, an importer will be able to complain that he would be able to sell more if only he were free to have a more competitive price. If a maximum price is set, another importer will perhaps complain that he is being forced to sell at such a low price that he will reduce his sales efforts or withdraw from the market altogether. If a single fixed price is set, both complaints could be heard. In all cases the *Dassonville* formula is satisfied. The same applies in fact to all interference by the State with free competition. Applying the approach to measures of equivalent effect

[58] [1986] E.C.R. 3449.

proposed in this article, it is clear that price regulatory measures can prevent imports from benefitting from the advantages (whether lower price or higher quality or simply different characteristics) arising for them out of the legal and economic environment of the Member State of origin but that this will depend on the circumstances. It will depend in particular on the level at which the price is set or limited and how it is calculated.

The case-law of the Court of Justice in this field shows that this is precisely the approach followed by the Court in the cases which have come before it. Indeed, this case-law is striking for its failure to apply the *Dassonville* formula literally. The Court of Justice has consistently required some further element than a possible effect on imports to determine whether such a measure falls under Article 30. Thus, where minimum prices are fixed, as in Case 231/83, *Cullet v. Leclerc* (petrol prices),[59] the Court looks to see if prices are fixed according to criteria appropriate to national production (depriving imported products of the possibility of undercutting national products by virtue of their different cost structure). Where maximum prices are involved, which is more frequently the case, the Court of Justice looks to see whether the prices are fixed at a level that "makes the marketing of imported products either impossible or more difficult than that of national products to the detriment of imported products."[60] Where fixed prices are involved, both sets of criteria can be used. Also, in Case 229/83, *Leclerc v. Au Blé Vert* (book prices),[61] the Court of Justice relied on the fact that imported books were treated differently from national books in that in the latter case the publisher fixed the price and in the former the distributor fixed the price (and therefore secured an advantage over his competitors). Similarly, in cases where Member States fix profit margins, the Court of Justice looks to see whether imported products are disadvantaged by the rules.

A recent case decided by the Court on national price controls is particularly instructive. In Joined Cases 80 and 159/85, *Nederlandse Bankkerij Stichting v. Edah*,[62] the Court was confronted with a complex price control system which was probably to the advantage of imports in most cases but, according to the defendant, disadvantaged them in some cases. Domestic bread was subject to a minimum price of Dfl. 1.86 whereas the minimum price for imported bread was equal to cost plus a fixed distribution margin of Dfl. 0.17 (the same margin used to calculate the minimum domestic price) except where this would give a higher minimum price than the Dfl. 1.86 fixed for domestic bread, in which case the latter price applied.

The Court of Justice reasoned as follows:

> Where the same margin, corresponding to the distribution costs of well-organized and efficiently operated distributors, is imposed on the sale of imported bread and taken into account in fixing the minimum

---

[59] [1985] E.C.R. 315. *See also* Case 82/77, *van Tiggele*, [1978] E.C.R. 25.

[60] Quoted from Cases 16-20/79, *Danis*, [1979] E.C.R. 3327 (operative part of the judgment).

[61] [1985] E.C.R. 1.

[62] [1986] E.C.R. 3359.

> price of domestically produced bread, national and imported products are placed on the same footing as regards retailers' ability to pass on a competitive advantage due to their organization and efficient operation, while any competitive advantage derived from the lower cost price of an imported product can be passed on and is not cancelled out. The sale of the imported product is not therefore made in any way more difficult.[63]

The defendant attempted to argue that this system could nonetheless disadvantage imports by preventing them from taking advantage of their competitive advantage, since imported bread with a cost price of Dfl. 1.69 had to be sold at Dfl. 1.86 whereas domestic bread with a cost price of, say, Dfl. 1.72 could also be sold at Dfl. 1.86. The Court of Justice rejected this argument by pointing out that the retailer might prefer the higher profit margin offered by the imported bread in this example and purchase it in preference to the domestic bread. Thus the Court of Justice appears to have effectively adopted in this case the approach advocated in this article by requiring that imported goods benefit from the advantages arising for them out of the legal and economic environment of their place of production (in this case lower cost) and be "placed on the same footing" as national goods.

Another case of State interference in the conditions of competition on its domestic market occurred in Case 238/82, *Duphar*.[64] In this case, the Court of Justice considered that there was an indirect influence on the possibilities of importation but held that if the criteria for the selection of products were objective (made no reference to the origin of the products and were verifiable by any importer), then they would not be contrary to Article 30.

Thus, in these cases, the Court of Justice always looked to see whether imported products are disadvantaged as compared with domestic products and considers them to be compatible with Article 30 if they are not disadvantaged.

2. The Problems of Restrictions on Use or Sale which Depend on the Characteristics of the Product and of Quasi-Prohibitions

When restrictions on the circumstances in which goods may be sold or used depend on their characteristics, they should be, it is submitted, judged according to the *Cassis de Dijon* formula since their effect on imports is analogous (for example, a prohibition on the sale of liqueurs with less than a certain alcohol content in supermarkets or on Sundays while liqueurs satisfying the national rules or traditions may be sold). Such measures are no longer neutral but deprive imported products of the possibility of enjoying the same access to the national market as national products while retaining the benefits arising for them out of legal and economic environment of their country of origin in the same way as in *Cassis de Dijon*.

A more difficult problem arises in the use of restrictions which amount to quasi-prohibitions. The prohibition of a product (whether imported or domestically pro-

63 [Id. at] Recital 15.

64 [1984] E.C.R. 523.

duced) inevitably creates a barrier to trade if the product is allowed in another Member State and the Court of Justice has had occasion to condemn them in several cases; it does not matter whether the prohibition is direct or arises out of the existence of conditions relating to the *characteristics* of the product which are impossible to fulfill or out of restrictions on the *circumstances* in which it may be sold which make sales impossible; in all cases the product is denied any access at all to the national market. Thus, if restrictions on the circumstances in which goods may be used are so severe that they amount to a virtual prohibition of the product (e.g., cigarettes may only be sold on Christmas day), then, it is submitted, they must be assimilated to prohibitions. To judge from the decision of the Court of Justice, in Case 118/87, *Openbaar Ministerie v. Nertsvoederfabriek Nederland*, the restriction on use will have to be very severe before it can be assimilated to a prohibition. The difference of treatment which the Court affords to prohibitions compared with mere restrictions may perhaps be explained by the fact that they are considered to be quantitative restrictions on imports rather than mere measures of equivalent effect.

The conclusion to be drawn is that indistinctly applicable national measures which merely regulate in a general and neutral manner the circumstances in which (i.e., by whom, where, when, or how goods may be sold or used or at what price they may be sold) are not incompatible with the objective of creating a unified market comparable to a domestic market and do not fall under Article 30. If the sale or use of goods is made conditional on their having certain characteristics then Article 30 applies according to the *Cassis de Dijon* principle. If the conditions attached to the sale or use of goods are such as to render such sale or use virtually impossible, then they are to be assimilated to a prohibition and considered to fall under Article 30 (possibly as a quantitative restriction on imports rather than a measure of equivalent effect).

3. The Requirement that the Effect on Trade Must Be Between Member States

The prohibition in Article 30 is of quantitative restrictions on imports and measures of equivalent effect *between Member States*. It thus excludes restrictions on direct imports from third countries (covered by Article 113). How does it apply to imports of third country goods which have already been imported into another Member State?

Article 9(2) of the Treaty provides that:

> [t]he provisions of Chapter 1, Section 1 [elimination of customs duties] and Chapter 2 [free movement of goods] of this Title shall apply to products originating in the Member States and to products coming from third countries in free circulation in Member States.

It may be noted that this provision only provides that Article 30 applies to third country goods in free circulation, and not that it should *apply in the same way* to such goods as it does to Union goods. However, in Case 41/76, *Doncherwolcke,*[65] the Court of Justice interpreted Article 9(2) as meaning that:

---

[65] [1976] E.C.R. 1921.

> as regards the free movement of goods within the Union, products which are entitled to free circulation are definitely and wholly assimilated to products originating in Member States.
>
> The result of this assimilation is that the provisions of Article 30 concerning the elimination of quantitative restrictions and all measures having equivalent effect are applicable without distinction to products originating in the Union and to those which were put into free circulation in any one of the Member States, irrespective of the actual origin of these products.[66]

The Court applied the same reasoning more recently in Case 59/84, *Tezi v. Commission*.[67] In Case 193/87, *Co-Frutta*, the Court of Justice applied the same principle to fiscal discrimination against third-country goods even though Article 95 only refers to products of other Member States and Article 9(2) does not, according to its terms, apply to the Chapter on tax provisions!

The difficulty with the Court's approach to third country goods can be deduced from the judgment in *Donckerwolcke* itself (repeated in *Tezi*) where the Court went on to say:

> However it results from the system of the Treaty that the application of the principles referred to above is conditional upon the establishment of a common commercial policy.
>
> The assimilation to products originating within the Member States of goods in 'free circulation' may only take full effect if these goods are subject to the same conditions of importation both with regard to customs and commercial considerations, irrespective of the State in which they were put in free circulation.[68]

Indistinctly applicable internal rules of the *Cassis de Dijon* kind do not form any part of Union "commercial policy." It is not realistic to suppose that they will ever be uniform throughout the Union. The limit to the application of the principle the Court laid down in *Donckerwolcke* would thus seem to be permanent as regards indistinctly applicable rules of the *Cassis de Dijon* kind. (The measures before the Court in *Donckerwolcke, Tezi* and *Co-Frutta* all applied to imports only).

The case-law of the Court concerning *Cassis de Dijon* type restrictions involving goods originating in third countries is of no assistance to us since the questions of the national courts (they are all Article 177 references) did not attach any importance to the third country origin of the goods.

The main purpose of Article 9(2) may be supposed to have been to render the EEU Treaty acceptable to the other Contracting Parties to the GATT, particularly in light of

66 [Id. at] Recitals 17 and 18.

67 [1986] E.C.R. 887.

68 [1976] E.C.R. 1921 at Recitals 24 and 25.

Art. III and XI and Article I (General Most-Favored-Nation Treatment) which provides, so far as relevant for our purposes, that:

> with respect to all rules and formalities in connection with importation and exportation, and with respect to all matters referred to in paragraphs 2 and 4 of Article III, any advantage, favor, privilege or immunity granted by any contracting party to any product originating in or destined for any other *country* shall be accorded immediately and unconditionally to the like product originating in or destined for the territories of all other contracting parties.

But, as explained in above, the provisions of the GATT relating to these matters do not have the same scope as Article 30. In particular they do not prohibit indistinctly applicable measures of the *Cassis de Dijon* kind. In any case, Article XXIV allows an exception to the Most-Favored-Nation principle in particular for customs unions such as the Union. Article XXIV 8(a) sets out the definition of a customs union (and thus some of the conditions it must fulfill to qualify for the exceptions). It provides:

> A customs union shall be understood to mean the substitution of a single customs territory for two or more customs territories, so that
>
> (I) duties and other restrictive regulations of commerce (except, where necessary, those permitted under Articles XI, XII, XIII, XIV, XV and XX) are eliminated with respect to substantially all the trade between the constituent territories of the union or at least with respect to substantially all the trade in products originating in such territories, and,
>
> (II) subject to the provisions of paragraph 9, substantially the same duties and other regulations of commerce are applied by each of the members of the union to the trade of territories not included in the union.

First of all, it is of interest to note that subparagraph (I) only requires the elimination of restrictions within the union of goods *originating* in such territories. Second, the "regulations of commerce" which must be substantially eliminated within the customs union and uniform towards the outside world can surely only mean measures specifically relating to imports, (i.e., measures of commercial policy) and not include internal measures. There is, after all, no reference in this provision to Article III of the GATT. Accordingly, these provisions would not prevent the Member States from applying indistinctly applicable measures of the *Cassis de Dijon* kind to goods originating in third countries even if they do not apply them to goods legally produced and marketed (i.e., originating) in other Member States.

Why, therefore, should Article 30, in conjunction with Article 9(2), prohibit the application of indistinctly applicable measures of the *Cassis de Dijon* kind to products imported from third countries via another Member State? Such an interpretation would allow third country goods to enter the Union via the Member State with the least restrictive rules and then be entitled to be imported into any other Member State without the goods of those Member States being given reciprocal treatment by the third country involved. It is also contrary to the philosophy behind the prohibition of indistinctly applicable measures of the *Cassis de Dijon* kind as explained above (that producers should be free to take advantage of the legal and economic environment prevailing in a Member State without the access of their products to the market of another Member State being hindered as a result). The decision of the Court of Justice in the *Cassis de Dijon* case itself entirely supports the view that third country goods do not benefit from the principle laid down since it requires the goods to be "lawfully *produced* and marketed in one of the Member States." If third country goods in free circulation really are assimilated to Union goods for *all* purposes by the Treaty, then surely it would have been enough for the Court to state that the goods must have been *lawfully marketed* in a Member State? If they have been lawfully marketed they will necessarily be in free circulation.

E. A Contrary View?

1. Is There a Need for a New Definition?[69]

White has recently attempted to seek the limits to Article 30. He argues cogently that the basic principle in *Dassonville* is far too wide, although he rightly does not attempt to plead for a discrimination criterion in any shape or form. Likewise correctly, he does not propose that regard should be had to protective effect as a part of the definition. White proposes a distinction between national rules relating to the characteristics of products and national rules relating to the circumstances in which goods are sold or used, finding that in the latter case the application of national rules to imported products does not need to be overridden as long as imported products enjoy equal access to the market of the importing Member State with national goods. He then proposes a new definition of a measure having equivalent effect to a quantitative restriction on imports in so far as concerns measures applicable without distinction as to the origin of the goods. This definition in the following terms:

> the application by a Member State to products legally produced and marketed in another Member State of its national rules relating to the characteristics required of such products on its territory (which therefore prevents this product from benefiting in the importing Member State from the advantages arising out of its production in the different legal and economic environment prevailing in the other Member State).

Opponents of the wide view of Article 30 have long argued that a literal application of the basic principle in *Dassonville* would strike down every piece of socio-economic legislation in a Member State. They point to planning rules, sex shop licensing, pub licensing hours, and other examples of national rules essentially dealing with local regulation of economic life and argue that these cannot be affected by Article 30 of the

---

[69] Laurence W. Gormley, *"Actually or Potentially, Directly or Indirectly"? Obstacles to the Free Movement of Goods*, 9 Y.E.L. 197-208 (1989). ©1989 Lawrence W. Gormley. Reprinted by permission.

EEU Treaty. The Court has not been terribly sympathetic to attempts to invoke Union law freedoms in what are wholly national situations—this has already been seen above and is a standpoint which the Court has also taken outside the areas of the free movement of goods. Proponents of the application of the basic principle in *Dassonville* would answer that the wide definition is essential in order that the Court should have the opportunity to review national rules for compatibility with Union law. If certain types of rules are to be held to be outside the scope of Article 30 *per se* then even the abusive application of those rules cannot be the subject of effective review. In the absence of Union action occupying the field the Court was careful not to deny in principle the competence of the Member States to regulate prices; in the health and consumer protection fields the Court has spoken about the Member States having the power to take legitimate measures. In all instances, though, the Court has reserved the power to review the measures in so far as they are capable of affecting inter-State commerce.

The Court tempers the local consequences of the basic principle in *Dassonville* by the application of a rule of reason and by the application of Article 36 EEU. The rule of reason is applied only to equally applicable measures in the absence of Union action and only to the extent to which they are proportionate to legitimate objectives and do not act as a means of arbitrary discrimination or a disguised restriction on trade between Member States. Rule of reason analysis saves planning measures, licensing, and so on to the extent to which they are used for legitimate purposes but will not, of course, save abuses. It accepts that a literal application of the basic principle subjects such measures to Article 30 review and concentrates on evaluating whether the measures are justified. In the instances cited by critics of the basic principle in *Dassonville* the answer lies in the Court's acceptance of socio-economic (as opposed to economic) justifications and its determination not to uphold essentially artificial challenges to national legislation.

It is in this light that White's proposed definition should be viewed. If anything his proposal states not so much the starting point of analysis but the conclusion of what is actually prohibited in global terms. It is respectfully submitted that there is no need for a new definition of measures having equivalent effect for equally applicable measures; rather White's proposal should be viewed as usefully, illustratively restating the application of the principle of mutual acceptance. The mutual acceptance of goods is, though, only one facet of free movement of goods case-law and it is preferable to see the mutual acceptance doctrine as effectively stating a presumption in favor of goods. This is particularly clear when mutual acceptance of health inspections is considered. Here the Court is essentially requiring a presumption in favor of goods which have been tested in another Member State and an acceptance of the health guarantees afforded by the administrative machinery of that Member State. It is submitted that it is undesirable to hive off equally applicable measures and create a separation of what constitutes a measure having equivalent effect to a quantitative restriction in the case of such measures. Indeed, enough damage was done when the Court refused to follow the logical and intellectually coherent analysis of Advocate-General Capotorti in relation to measures applicable irrespective of the destination of the product.[70]

---

[70] In Case 15/79, *P.B. Groenveld BV v. Producktschap voor Vee en Vlees,* [1975] E.C.R. 47 at 63 *et seq.* (Art. 34 EEU).

Yet another departure from *Dassonville* would appear to create an "off limits" zone in relation to Article 30 which would appear to constitute a set of reserved powers for the Member States. Although the Court has acknowledged the powers of the Member States in the absence of Union action it has not left the Member States with unfettered powers and it would be dangerous for any proposed definition to appear to do so. White feels that the danger of applying the basic principle in *Dassonville* literally is that there will be a flood of disappointment litigants who find that they are led on but ultimately disappointed by the principle. Yet even in *Dassonville* itself the Court gave a clear signal that it was prepared to uphold reasonable national measures. In fairness, though, it cannot be said that the Court has helped litigants by the reasoning in many of its judgments. Too often the conclusion (which is invariably correct as to the merits) is less than wholly supported by the reasoning on which it claims to be based. Sticking to a clear application of the basic principle in *Dassonville* and applying the rule of reason or Article 36 EEU as appropriate is, it is respectfully submitted, a better approach from the point of view of guaranteeing the ability of the Court to supervise the actions of Member States. Accordingly, it is felt that there is no need for a separate definition for measures applicable irrespective of the origin of the product. The application of the *Dassonville* approach should not give rise to fears of undue judicial interference in socio-economic life. On the contrary, the Court has shown itself willing to take account of genuine global issues, such as environmental protection, consumer protection, and working conditions. It has at the same time given short shrift to bogus arguments, both on the part of governments and on the part of litigants trying to abuse Union principles. Particularly in the latter case, the Court should either state clearly that this is what litigants are seeking to do or apply the basic principle with the rule of reason or Article 36 to reach a genuine evaluation of the reasonableness or otherwise of the measures. What the Court should not do, it is respectfully submitted, is seek to deny that a measure is capable, actually or potentially, directly or indirectly of hindering intra-Union trade when it patently is.

2. Conclusions

Initial fears that judgments such as *Blesgen* represented a narrowing of the concept of what constituted a measure having equivalent effect to a quantitative restriction on imports have now disappeared and it is clear that the Court is remaining faithful to the basic principle in *Dassonville*. The fact remains, though, that Court's reasoning still leaves much to be desired in relation to the evaluation of socio-economic policy measures. What is at stake is not so much the competence of a Member State to legislate but an assessment of whether the purpose is acceptable and if, in principle, so, whether the measures are proportionate or not. The judgment in *Torfaen* shows that the Court will look at the circumstances in which goods are sold if it is apparent that there is a genuine intra-Union trade argument raised. Perhaps the only way to get the Court to make a concrete evaluation of the United Kingdom's Sunday trading laws would be for the Commission to commence Article 169 EEU proceedings. That, though, is a matter for its discretion. A faithful application of the basic principle in *Dassonville* and use of the rule of reason and Article 36 remains the best way of ensuring that the Member States apply correctly the principle of the free movement of goods so essential for the proper functioning of the common market. The use of clear reasoning by the Court might help discourage the Member States from defending the indefensible with spurious arguments based on cheap political considerations. The free movement of goods does not require consumers to change their ways but offers them the opportunity of broadening their choice and widening their horizons. They remain able to vote with their feet but that choice should properly be left to them and should not be made for them by nanny regulation which ossifies markets and habits.

II. Prohibition of Discriminatory Taxation

A. Introduction[71]

When the European Economic Community (Community) was created in 1957, the six countries (Member States) that signed the Treaty of Rome (Treaty) were seeking to create "a single integrated market free of restrictions on the movement of goods, . . . persons, services, and capital." The Member States recognized that their wide ranging systems of taxation presented a significant obstacle to this goal. Therefore, they requested that the Commission of the European Communities (Commission) determine how their tax systems could be "harmonized" and submit proposals to the Council of Ministers (Council).

The Council was required to act unanimously on the Commission's proposals in issuing directives seeking to "approximate" the Member States' laws and regulations that would "directly affect the establishment or functioning of the common market." Such laws and regulations include indirect and direct tax systems because both systems distort competition by restricting (or encouraging) the movement of goods, services, capital, and persons within the Community.

Although some directives coordinating the structure of indirect taxes were issued during the late 1960s and early 1970s, very little progress was made in coordinating indirect tax rates. The Commission also made many proposals seeking to approximate the Member States' direct tax systems, but no proposals were adopted as directives. Because the Council failed to obtain the required majority on most of the Commission's proposals, the Member States passed the Single European Act (SEA) in 1987.

The SEA amended the Treaty's provisions and shifted the burden to the Council; to act on the Commission's proposals in order "to ensure the establishment and [proper] functioning of the [common] market" by the end of 1992. The SEA has had little to no impact, however, as none of the Commission's significant tax proposals since 1987 have obtained the required unanimity of the Council to be adopted as a directive. One reason is that the Commission has not adequately addressed the economic, political, and social policy objections of the Member States to changes in their tax systems.

---

[71] Brent D. Rose, *Coordinating Taxes in the European Economic Community: What Can be Done by 1992?*, B.Y.U. L. Rev. 1800 (1990). © Brent D. Rose. Reprinted with permission.

Some Member States argue that no tax directives are needed because market forces will coordinate their tax systems once the Community's fiscal border controls are removed at the end of 1992. Other Member States, however, argue that much diversity can exist in their tax systems "without interfering with the establishment" and proper functioning of the "common market."

A selective market forces approach would allow market forces to coordinate the Member State's tax rates, while using directives to coordinate their tax systems and eliminate discriminatory tax provisions. The Commission should allow the Member States and the market to determine the appropriate range and combination of rates that should exist in their countries after 1992, and concentrate its efforts on drafting and obtaining approval on directives coordinating the Member States' tax structures. This selective market forces approach would ensure equal opportunity for all Community citizens and businesses to freely work, locate, and but or sell goods or services in every Member State without fear of discrimination.

B. Existing and Proposed Taxes in the European Community[72]

Many groups and individuals have studied the problems related to taxes in the Community. The most notable studies are (1) the 1963 Neumark Committee Report, (2) the Commission's 1980 "Report on the Scope for Convergence of Tax Systems in the Community" and (3) the Commission's 1985 White Paper (the White Paper) on "Completing the Internal Market."

According to the Commission, the White Paper "remains a valuable yardstick for assessing the progress made towards a [fiscally] frontier-free Europe." The White Paper contained many proposals seeking the approximation and harmonization of indirect taxes. However, the Commission has made many changes in its original proposals and none have obtained the required unanimity of the Council to be adopted as a directive. The 1985 White Paper contained no proposals seeking the coordination of direct taxes. These proposals were to be addressed in a later White Paper. However, no White Paper addressing direct taxes has been issued and the proposals on direct taxes have never been finalized.

Although some coordination of indirect tax structures in the Community has been accomplished, the structures for direct taxes are still in the proposal stage and none of the Commission's tax rate proposals have been adopted as a directive. Therefore, all of the tax rates and most tax structures of the Member States vary considerably. Just how much they vary and how much coordination has been accomplished is discussed below.

It is naive to expect that income tax harmonization in the European Union will be accomplished in the near future, however worthy that goal may be. A complex pattern

[72] Karen V. Kole, *Income Tax Harmonization in the European Union* (Dissertation - Unpublished Draft) (1995). © 1995 Karen V. Kole. Reprinted by permission.

formed by the interaction of different national systems, rates, tax bases and implementation practices, modified by dozens of bilateral double taxation treaties, is the product of many years of legislation which has had national concerns, not the European Union, as its main preoccupation. The resulting system, in so far as it impacts on international business, is thus more a product of historical accident and political expedience that it is the application of the arguments of logic or economics.

Additionally, it is unrealistic to suppose that such a diverse group of systems could be transformed quickly into an ideal model, supposing that such an ideal model could be fashioned. However, as the end of the century approaches, it is timely and appropriate to examine income taxation as potentially one of the most significant areas in which barriers to the European Union internal market remain. The achievement of fair competition is arguably the decisive factor for tax harmonization. The removal of distortions of competition is certainly the most important, if not the only real, criterion to give reasons for harmonizing rates, base or systems. Somewhat less important criteria might be, e.g., the desire for simplification or to achieve higher efficiency within the European Union.

Harmonization is also important as a potential revenue raiser for the money-starved Community. Unfortunately, the political sensitivity of the sovereignty of taxation of a Member State and the fact that market conditions themselves may force Member States to harmonize direct taxation within the Community to stay competitive, may result in a hands-off approach by a Community that has other more pressing concerns to which to turn its attention.

This dissertation is divided into four parts; it considers a range of options available to the European income tax system over the medium and long term. First, the dissertation will consider whether corporate income tax harmonization is consistent with the goals of the European Union, by examining the treaty and the tax provisions contained therein. Second, assuming that harmonization is a goal of the European Union, it will examine the impact of the present income tax systems of the various countries, identify areas in which they present an obstacle to economic activity across borders or distort competition between individuals and organizations of different nationalities. Third, the paper will discuss the possible approaches to harmonization that are potentially available to the European Union. Fourth, in conclusion, the paper recommends feasible reforms which would create a system more attuned to the needs of internationally orientated European businesses, while at the same time reflecting an appropriate balance between national and supranational jurisdiction and sovereignty in fiscal affairs.

1. Criteria for Evaluation of Present and Proposed Systems

There are many ways of assessing the adequacy of tax systems. The criteria are:

1) the tax system should promote economic efficiency, in the usual sense of encouraging the production of output at the lowest cost;

2) the tax system should provide a "level playing field"—equality of treatment, for example, between firms of different nationalities, or between financial investments in different forms;

3) the tax system should be administratively efficient, in the sense that it should not encourage the proliferation of tax avoidance and counteravoidance measures, which tie up considerable resources in both the private and public sectors, and that it should avoid administrative and bureaucratic inefficiency and delays, for example in the processing of refunds;

4) relating to points one and two above, the system should not distort the restructuring of economic activity, either by arbitrarily impeding mergers and acquisitions, or by placing firms of certain nationalities at a disadvantage to others with respect to the takeover activity.[73]

2. Inadequacy of the Present Systems

How well does the current system, i.e., a total of now 15 national income tax systems, perform under the four proposed criteria? Not well, according to many sources, scholarly and practitioner oriented as well. Perhaps the analysis should start with the goal being a Europe-wide business and the obstacles, from a tax standpoint, it is currently faced with. Corporate tax harmonization promotes tax neutral business decisions. Tax neutral business decisions are desirable, because they foster more efficient resource allocation, and this in turn tends to increase the wealth and the standard of living of those within the economy. For this reason, corporate tax harmonization within the EU appears to represent a legitimate community goal from an economic standpoint. Differences in the basis on which tax is applied, i.e., source or residence, in the legal treatment of economic groups, definition of tax base, tax systems and arrangements for relief from double taxation, special rules for controlled companies in other jurisdictions, tax rates and payment arrangements, all have an impact on the effective tax rate facing firms or shareholders with cross-border investments. This Europe-wide business currently faces a system that results in a post tax rate of return that differs according to the country in which it operates, or in which its head office is resident, but it may be less able to compete in a third country with businesses from other EU member states.

Administrative difficulties abound. The tax liability of companies incorporated or resident in different countries can be reduced through foreign holding companies, coordination centers, tax groups, and the like. The inefficiency is compounded by the efforts of the various tax administrations to maintain existing inequalities, such as the use of the controlled foreign company (CFC) provisions. The CFC provisions in the US and UK tax laws place severe burdens on firms from these countries in comparison with their competitors. In a fully harmonized system the problem of intra-group structuring stimulated by EU internal tax distortions would basically disappear but in the interim it is important that changes to the systems should reduce rather that

[73] These are basically the criteria used by the Rudding report although the Rudding Report states them in the following manner: (a) Do the differences in taxation among Member States cause major distortions in the internal market, particularly with respect to investment decisions and competition? Special attention is focused on those distortions considered to be discriminatory. (b) In so far as such distortions arise, are they likely to be eliminated simply through the interplay of market forces and tax competition between Member States, or is action at the Community level required? and (c) What specific measures are required at the Community level to remove or mitigate these distortions?

increase these distortions. In the longer term, there will also be a need to ensure that the competitiveness of EU firms as a whole is not impaired due, for example, to excessive anti-avoidance, for example the CFC, provisions at the EU level.

Mergers and acquisitions are also important. Discrimination arises here in that while most countries provide exemption from, or deferral for, tax on capital gains in the case of purely domestic mergers, there is no general extension of this exemption to cross-border situations. The EC mergers directive, implemented in January 1992, has helped to alleviate this problem but anomalies will still remain due to the current differences in company law in the various member states. Specifically, a distortion will arise because there will be tax advantages to a company with an exemption system in its home country acquiring a company in a country with a foreign tax credit system. These advantages can arise in several ways the most significant of which is due to the fact that a business in a credit system with cross-border operations necessarily suffers the higher rates of tax in the country of operation and the country of the head office, whereas the business in an exemption system will normally only suffer tax in the country of operation. Thus, acquisition of a business in a credit system by a business in an exemption system can reduce that total tax payable.

3. Economic Distortions

It will be taken, as a given, that the goal is overall production taking place at its lowest cost. Two types of distortion arising from the current corporate systems are likely to prevent production taking place at its lowest cost. The first of these distortions is a distortion of where firms or shareholders from a particular country invest. This creates a distortion in the form of a violation of capital export neutrality (CEN). The second type of distortion is a distortion of which firm or shareholder will undertake inward investment to a particular country. If the EU does not have capital import neutrality, investments will not necessarily be made by the most efficient firm. It is literally impossible to estimate empirically the loss of potential output involved, but it will be shown that the current tax systems give rise to both types of distortions.

4. Possibilities for Reform

There are various approaches to reforming the present system. Each approach will necessarily carry with it a certain extent of change necessary to the present arrangements and the priority of which should be given to each area. Some of these possible approaches include EU Directives, bilateral treaties or unilateral decisions of national governments, spurred on by the forces of competition. Unfortunately for the latter approach, competition has not seemed to result in a convergence in the corporate tax rates during the 1980's, although some has been achieved. As a result, there has not been an elimination of the distortions to cross-border investment. It is particularly important to note that any convergence in rates seen in the 1980's may not continue in the 1990's due to the difficult financial times in the 1990's. The use of these directives could certainly lead to a common, though separate, income tax system in all EU countries.

Two other possibilities remain for the harmonization of systems other than common income tax systems focusing on the introduction of some type of a federal system: either a single corporate tax system covering the whole EU or a true federal system. This could incorporate a standard tax base on which national and an EU federal tax were levied. Regardless of the system chosen, following the principle of subsidiarity, taxing rights would remain primarily with the member states. Taxes would be collected from a single company by the Member State of which it was a national, with redistribution between members through a clearing house mechanism. Alternatively, the sourcing principles could be left in place, with the use of an apportionment formula as in the United States.

5. Summary

What is the ultimate goal? The goal, assuming corporate income tax harmonization is a community goal, is to secure the greatest benefit to the community with the minimum amount of disruption. Once an approach is adopted, i.e., common system, single corporate system, or Federal system, where conflicts arise, the decision should usually, but not necessarily, be in favor of doing the easiest and least disruptive changes first. This plan leads naturally to the possibility of a timetable to implement the measures proposed.

C. Tax Provisions in the EU Treaty: General Discussion

In drafting the original framework for the European Union, it is clear that the harmonization of taxes, particularly income taxes, were not a priority to the draftsmen.[74] The 'Tax Provisions', consisting of Articles 95-9, form Chapter 2 of the Common Rules of Part 3 of the EEC Treaty, which is devoted to the 'Policy of the Community.' What this means is that **tax** policy was not considered by the authors of the Treaty to be one of the 'Foundations of the Community'[75] but rather as a part of the Common Rules which are ancillary to the Treaty's main objectives.[76]

---

[74] The 'European Community' has in fact been the commonly used designation for a political entity, composed of a number of distinct legal entities generally identified as a single unit. These are the three Communities, of which two are confined in their application to particular sectors of the economy: the European Coal and Steel Community (ECSC), formed by the Treaty of Paris concluded in 1951 which came into force on July 25, 1952, and the European Atomic Energy Community (Euratom), formed by the Treaty of Rome concluded in 1957 which came into force on January 1, 1958. Also, created in 1958 by a second Treaty of Rome 1957 was the European Economic Community (EEC), the 'everything else' Community, which has acquired a hegemonic position within the political and legal framework of the Community. The EEC Treaty was significantly amended in 1986 by the Single European Act, which sought to give the institutions the powers they needed to achieve the goal of completing the internal market by December 31, 1992. The Treaty of Maastricht, or the "Treaty on European Union," links the three Communities even closer together within the common structure of a European Union, a new entity built around the framework offered by the existing Communities.

[75] The "Foundations" comprise the 'four freedoms', free movement of goods, of workers, of services and establishment and or capital, plus Agriculture and Transport.

[76] The first and third Chapters of the Common Rules deal, respectively, with Competition and Approximation of Laws.

Co-ordination of tax policy is not one of the fundamental freedoms although, as will be shown, it impacts indirectly on all of them. Thus, harmonization of at least direct taxation,[77] rather than indirect taxation, is seen as a means to an end, rather than as an end in itself.

It should, however, be noted, that harmonization measures at the EC level are not the sole and probably not the most important factor in the process of harmonizing actual taxation. In the first place, there is "negative integration," i.e., integration which ensues from mere membership in the EC. One fundamental principle laid down in the EC Treaty is the prohibition on discrimination against goods, services, workers, enterprises and capital from other Member States. This and other fundamental Treaty principles have tax consequences too, limiting Member States' freedom to arrange their national tax systems as they might deem expedient. Sometimes these are consequences the Member States probably did not realize when they signed the Treaty. Secondly, a more important harmonizing factor than EC policy may be the so-called "tax competition" between Member States, leading to "spontaneous" harmonization: neighboring States having a comparable level of infrastructure, social security and public services, cannot afford to diverge greatly in tax burdens, less so as the (other) obstacles within the EC to individual or corporate emigration or cross-border economic activities are gradually removed.

Arguably, economic or social necessity is usually the most powerful incentive for changing national policies. Furthermore, even if tax legislation is harmonized at the Community level, the general tax paying public in one Member State may well consider the actual compliance with statutory tax obligations a matter to be taken more lightly than may be the case in another Member State. Moreover, national administrative practices and national (lack of) lenience on the part of the Tax Collector are not automatically aligned by approximation of tax rates and assessment bases. Harmonization of legislation is not the same as harmonization of national attitudes and *couleur locale*.

Also, it should be stressed that harmonization of taxes, especially of direct taxes, is a highly sensitive area politically. Tax sovereignty is a fundamental part of national sovereignty. One of the most basic rights of national parliaments is the right to vote on taxes. The European Parliament cannot, as yet, be considered to be a sufficient substitute for national parliamentary democratic control. Moreover, taxation is the most important instrument for national economic and social policy. It may be used to redistribute income, to invite investment or to discourage consumption of certain goods, etc. The more harmonization and, therefore, the loss of national freedom of policy in the field of *indirect* taxation progresses, the more the Member States will feel the need to defend their remaining tax sovereignty in the field of *direct* taxation. Finally, a genuine *European* tax hardly exists as such. There is no tax levied at Community level by a Community tax authority (except the payroll tax on the salaries of the EC civil servants, the "Eurocrats"). The Community has its "own resources," for the most part con-

---

[77] Direct taxation is generally considered to be income tax levied directly on income from the entity. Indirect taxation is generally thought of as a tax on goods or services, e.g., the VAT.

sisting of the revenue from customs duties at the outside borders of the EC and a percentage of the national basis of Value Added Tax assessment, but these are levied and collected at national level and the revenue transmitted to the EC is relatively small compared to the part of gross domestic products that national tax burdens account for. At Community level, taxes play a very limited role as a policy instrument. Consequently, the Community hardly has a tax policy of its own. Its policy is one of aligning, in so far as is necessary for a single market, national taxes and tax policies.

The rules on taxation are considerably less detailed than those on such matters as the customs union and agriculture. As Walter Hallstein remarked, "in terms of the common market, the chapter on fiscal provisions is formulated in the most limiting kind of language" and the Treaty "contains only the most timid of starting points."[78] One can speculate that perhaps this approach was used because of the tenuous nature of the beginnings of the Community, but nevertheless the Treaty is the underlying guiding document and without further modification is the guiding instrument.

The tax provisions can be separated into two distinct parts for purposes of this discussion. Articles 95-8 prohibit the imposition of taxation to the extent that it discriminates against goods imported from other Member States and the subsidization by means of taxation, of products exported to other Member States; as such Articles 95-8 correspond to the provisions of the GATT and implicitly authorize the use of the destination principle and of border tax adjustments in intra-Community trade. Article 99 provides a juridical basis for the harmonization of turnover taxes, excise duties and other indirect taxes. Taken together, the provisions derive from the fundamental principles of the Community, as set out in Articles 2 and 3, and especially from the activities listed in paragraphs (A), (f) and (h) or Article 3. These are:

> (A) the elimination, as between Member States, of custom duties and of quantitative restrictions on the import and export of goods, and of all other measures having equivalent effect; . . .
>
> (f) the institution of a system ensuring that competition in the common market is not distorted; . . .
>
> (h) the approximation of the laws of Member States to the extent required for the proper functioning of the common market.

In particular, as the Court of Justice has emphasized on numerous occasions, the tax provisions operate to fill in any loophole which tax procedures might find in the prohibition of customs duties and charges having equivalent effect, and their essential purpose is to contribute to the establishment of a common market which will ensure free trade in goods and equality of competition between goods of different Member States.

Article 95 provides two bases for assessing the discriminatory element in systems of taxation. It provides:

> No Member States shall impose, directly or indirectly, on the products of other Member States any internal taxation of any kind in excess of that imposed directly or indirectly on similar domestic products.

---

[78] W. Hallstein, *Europe in the Making* (London 1972): 156-7.

> Furthermore, no Member State shall impose on the products of other Member States any internal taxation of such a nature as to afford indirect protection to other products.
>
> Member States shall, not later than at the beginning of the second stage, repeal or amend any provisions existing when this Treaty enters into force which conflict with the preceding rules. [79]

However, the essential purpose of Article 95 is not to engender a principle of equivalence in national taxation regimes. This would be impossible at this point of the Community's development given the diversity of national regimes which continue to exist since the Member States retain fiscal autonomy as regards the raising of revenue and the use of taxation as an instrument of redistributive policy. Taxation must, however, be neutral and the Treaty restricts the prohibition to measures which are discriminatory in form or in effect, provided normally in the latter case that there is a protectionist effect in addition. As the Court of Justice put it in the Case 127/75 *Bobie v. HZA Aachen-Nord*, [80] Article 95

> seeks to ensure, by means of the prohibition which it lays down, that an importing Member State does not, by means of internal taxation of imported products and similar domestic products give domestic traders preferential treatment as compared with their competitors from other Member States who sell similar products on the market of that State.[81]

As Article 95(3) indicates, the prohibitions in Articles 95(1) and (2) are unconditional and capable of judicial enforcement in national courts. In addition, both paragraphs have been held by the Court of Justice to be directly effective.[82]

Systems of domestic taxation which do protect domestic products are, *a fortiori*, liable to strict scrutiny under Article 95. For example, in Case 112/84 *Humbolt v. Directeur des Services Fiscaux*,[83] a French car tax which imposed much higher levels of taxation on cars over 16 CV was condemned by the Court of Justice. There are no French cars over 16 CV. The Court pointed out that the effect of the tax was to reduce the competition faced by French cars and could not therefore be regarded as neutral, even though it was not imposed using a criterion overtly based on nationality. On the other hand, in Case C-132/88, *Commission v. Greece*,[84] the Court upheld a taxation system which imposed much heavier burdens on cars with engines above 1800 cc even

---

[79] The effect of paragraph 3 was to require Member States to repeal or modify, not later than January 1, 1962, any taxes that offended against either of the first two paragraphs. Thus, Article 95 became fully effective as from that date.

[80] ECR 1079 at p. 1086.

[81] *Id.*

[82] Case 57/65 *Lutticke v. HZA Saarlouis*-Article 95(1); Case 27/67 *Firma Fink-Frucht Gmbh v. HZA Munchen Landbergerstrasse* (1968) ECR 223-Article 95(2).

[83] 1985 ECR 1367.

[84] 1991, 3 CMLR 1.

though no cars produced in Greece had engines above 1600 cc, because it found that the tax did not have a protectionist effect.

Tax regimes which are, however, effectively protectionist in some circumstances escaped condemnation under Article 95, provided they are operated in a nondiscriminatory way. For example, in Case 21/79, *Commission v. Italy (Regenerated Oil)*,[85] it was held that tax concessions must be extended to non-domestic products even though this may make controls upon their operation more difficult. In Case 148/77, *Hansen v. HZA Flensburg*,[86] which concerned a German regime of tax relief available in respect of spirits made from fruit by small businesses and collective farms, the Court addressed the reasons why certain types of tax regime which implicitly benefit national products may be compatible with Article 95. The Court held:

> At the present stage of its development and in the absence of any unification or harmonization of the relevant provisions, Community law does not prohibit Member States from granting tax advantages, in the form of exemption from or reduction of duties, to certain types of spirits or to certain classes of producers.
>
> Indeed, tax advantages of this kind may serve legitimate economic or social purposes, such as the use of certain raw materials by the distilling industry, the continued production of particular spirits of high quality, or the continuance of certain classes of industry such as agricultural distilleries.[87]

The only requirement is that the preferential system must be extended without discrimination to spirits of the same class coming from other Member States. Regional policy objectives cannot be pursued through measures which differentiate explicitly between products according to whether they originate in a particular region.[88] Also, in the indirect area, it is possible for a Member State to have a taxation policy that is clearly discriminatory in that it taxes similar products differently, and also protectionist in the sense that no domestic products fell into the higher tax band, if "the system of taxation pursued an objective of legitimate industrial policy" compatible with Community principles, namely that of ensuring a reasonable level of employment in certain areas, and of ensuring the survival of agricultural distilleries.[89]

One particularly noticeable feature of these provisions is that, with the exception of Article 98, they relate only to indirect taxes.[90] Direct taxation is not expressly men-

---

85 1980 ECR 1.

86 1978 ECR 1787.

87 *Id.* at 1806.

88 In fact, such a measure may not be classed as part of a system of internal dues at all, but as a CEE prohibited by Article 13(2) (Case C-163/90, *Administration des douanes v. Legros*).

89 *See* Case 46/80, *Vinal v. Orbat*, [1981] ECR 77.

90 Article 98, which with Article 96 permits the refunding, on exported goods, of internal taxation imposed on those goods, prohibits remission of taxes other than indirect taxes.

tioned anywhere in the Treaty; indeed, taxation is referred to in only two other provisions. Article 220 contemplates the adoption of Conventions dealing with a number of subjects, including "the abolition of double taxation within the Community," and the new Article 130F, added in 1986 by the Single European Act, requires the removal of fiscal barriers to co-operation between undertakings and establishments in the field of research and technological development. Both provisions clearly apply to direct as well as to indirect taxation.

The impact of the EEC Treaty upon national fiscal systems is not, however, restricted to those provisions that expressly deal with taxation. Of significant importance is Article 100, which authorizes the Council to issue directives "for the approximation of such provisions laid down by law, regulation or administrative action in Member States as directly affect the establishment or functioning of the common market." A basis is thus provided for the harmonization of direct taxes. However, Article 100A inserted by the Single European Act, expressly excludes "fiscal provisions" from those that may be harmonized by the Council when acting by a qualified majority. Also, Article 17 of the Single European Act amended the wording of Article 99 which now provides for harmonization to the extent "necessary to ensure the establishment and the functioning of the internal market." Various other Treaty provisions may also affect national tax laws relating to either direct or indirect taxation. There are circumstances in which a national tax, charge or other form of levy, might be held to be contrary to the provisions on the free movement of goods,[91] or on state aids.[92] Additionally, provisions which prohibit obstacles to the free movement of workers[93] the freedom of establishment,[94] the freedom to provide services,[95] and the free movement of capital,[96] may all impose restraints upon national fiscal autonomy.

Additionally, it is also true that provisions such as those contracted under the GATT, may impose constraints upon national fiscal laws and policies. A crucial difference, however, between international and Community obligations is that the latter, by virtue of the direct effect and the supremacy of Community law, not only bind the Member States but give rise to rights which may be relied upon by individual taxpayers within the Community. Thus, the obligations not to impose customs duties or taxes that discriminate against products of other Member states, which derive from the provisions of the Treaty, effectively form a part of the fiscal laws of each Member State.[97] One can truly state that "la fiscalite des etats membres est devenue 'communautaire.'"[98]

---

91 Notably Articles 9, 12, 13, 30 and 37.

92 Article 52.

93 Article 48.

94 Article 52.

95 Article 59.

96 Articles 67, 69.

97 Case 26/62, *Van Gend en Loos*; Case 57/65, *Lutticke*.

98 D. Berlin, *Droit Fiscal Communautaire* (Paris 1988): 13.

As was noted, the Treaty provisions that relate to taxation, expressly or otherwise, fall into two categories: those rules that impose restrictions upon the fiscal autonomy of the Member States, for example by prohibiting taxes that discriminate against the products of other Member States, and those that provide a basis or authorization for action by the Community, notably by adopting Directives for the harmonization of the national laws. An essential difference between the two types of provision is that the former constitute fundamental rules of the Community, binding upon the Member States and upon the Community institutions themselves.

By contrast, tax harmonization, whether under Article 99 or 100, requires the unanimous action of the Council. Each Member State consequently has a veto over any proposal to harmonize taxation.

In Article 99, the authors of the Treaty clearly recognized that obstacles to the free movement of goods may result not only from discriminatory national tax measures but also from differences between national tax provisions. They thus established a basis for harmonization of indirect taxes "in the interest of the common market." In particular, the experiences of operating the European Coal and Steel Community had demonstrated that the existing national systems of turnover taxes were incompatible with the objectives of the Community since, due to their cumulative nature, it was almost impossible to ensure the equal treatment of domestic and imported products. Consequently, it was on those taxes that attention was first focused, resulting in the adoption, in 1967, of the common system of value added tax. Further, substantial changes were made in the VAT system in 1977, in order to achieve a greater degree of harmonization of the tax bases necessitated by the adoption of the VAT as an "own resource" in the Community budget and another important set of changes were adopted at the end of 1991 in connection with the elimination of fiscal frontiers and border tax adjustments.

Article 99 also provides for the harmonization of excise duties and other forms or indirect taxation. Progress here has been far more difficult to achieve. There are significant differences in the ways in which Member States tax alcohol and tobacco, reflecting different social attitudes and consumption patterns, and to date there has only been a limited degree of harmonization of the systems of taxing tobacco. A degree of harmonization has also been achieved with respect to tax and duty-free admission of goods privately imported by individuals. Those measures, however, have largely become redundant as of the end of 1992, when all restrictions upon non-commercial importation within the Community should have been abolished.

Progress in the field of direct taxation has proved even more difficult. Apart from a number of measures dealing with duties on the formation of companies' capital, and one providing for the mutual co-operation of national tax authorities, nothing of significance was accomplished until 1990, when two Directives and a Convention were adopted, concerning the tax treatment of cross-border mergers and of corporations with branches or affiliates in other Member States.

Undoubtedly, the requirement that the Council must act unanimously in order to adopt Directives for the harmonization of taxes has made progress difficult and slow; of all their powers, Member States are perhaps most reluctant to surrender any degree of control over their fiscal sovereignty. Nevertheless, the twenty or so substantive measures of tax harmonization that have been adopted over the past quarter of a century add up to a substantial body of Community tax law. And, as with the provisions of the EEC Treaty, this law is reinforced by the principal of direct effect which ensures that Community Directives take effect within the national orders.

D. Indirect Taxes

As mentioned previously, the key provisions of the EEC Treaty concerning taxation are contained in Articles 95 and 96. In addition to those significant provisions, Articles 97 and 98 serve a supplementary purpose and seem to be of little significance currently.

Article 95 provides as follows:

> No Member State shall impose, directly or indirectly, on the products of other Member States any internal taxation of any kind in excess of that imposed directly or indirectly on similar domestic products.
>
> Furthermore, no Member State shall impose on the products of other Member States any internal taxation of such a nature as to afford indirect protection to other products.
>
> Member States shall, not later than at the beginning of the second stage, repeal or amend any provisions existing when this Treaty enters into force which conflict with the preceding rules.

Article 96 provides as follows:

> Where products are exported to the territory of any Member State, any repayment of internal taxation shall not exceed the internal taxation imposed on them, whether directly or indirectly.

What these two provisions accomplish, with reference to the Treaty provisions dealing with customs duties on imports and exports, and charges having an equivalent effect, is to ensure that imported products are not to be taxed more heavily than comparable domestic products, and exported products are not to be subsidized by refunding domestic tax in excess of that which is actually imposed on them.

[B]riefly stated the combination of the two Articles permit the application of the destination principle in intra-Community trade by implicitly allowing the refunding of internal taxes on exports and the imposition of countervailing taxes on imports. Article 95 furthers as the notion of non-discrimination which may be a specific example of the general rule of non-discrimination provided by Article 7 of the EEC.

Indirect taxation consists of value-added and excise taxes.[99] Taxation rates have been very inconsistent from one Member State to another and the Commission is attempting to remedy this. These inconsistent taxes have caused goods moving between community states to receive nearly identical treatment to that of imports enter-

[99] Michael D. Hodges, *Activities in the European Community towards Unifying Taxation and the Elimination of Quantitive Restrictions*, 3 J. Int'l L. & Proc. 185-93 (1994).

ing the EU from foreign nations. The delay and paperwork adds approximately 1.5% to the cost of goods moving within internal borders. A series of EU Commission proposals attempted to establish a rate band which called for standard rates for most goods and services to fall within 14% to 20%, but instead established a standard rate of 4% to 9% for certain basic goods and services. After much debate, a more flexible transitional system was implemented January 1, 1993, and will remain in effect until January, 1997.

1. Value-Added Tax (VAT)

In 1992, there was an agreement to enact a minimum standard value-added tax (VAT). This political agreement included eight directives.[100] The first directive made a minimum standard rate of not less than 15%, with optional reduced rates of no less than 5% on basic goods and services. Basic goods and services include: foodstuffs, water, pharmaceutical products, medical and dental equipment, and transportation services. Included within these directives are many individualized exceptions to meet the needs of individual Member States. This agreement will be in effect from January 1, 1993 to December 31, 1996; continuation beyond 1996 would again require unanimous agreement. At the end of 1992, all Member States took action to insure compliance.

Interestingly, these VAT directives provide for a minimum, not a maximum tax. Establishing a minimum VAT forces some countries to actually increase their tax rates. These increased taxes raise production costs which in turn raise the selling price of exports. This will allow some countries to compete in markets in which they were traditionally at a cost disadvantage. More importantly, these excise duties will prevent dumping which could eliminate all competition. Greece, for example, if allowed to sell olive oil (one of its main exports) without any excise taxes, would close out competition from other Member States. Greece might obtain sole control of the market, and this would effectively circumvent the forces of supply and demand. Thus these minimum excise taxes are regulations aimed at protecting the market where the Commission feels the ordinary forces of supply and demand do not.

2. Excise Duties

The remaining seven of the eight directives relate to excise duties on tobacco, mineral oils, and alcoholic beverages. With respect to tobacco, an agreement was reached in 1992 which set a minimum excise duty on the most popular cigarettes at 57%. The three directives on tobacco also set minimum excise duties on other tobacco products based upon either a percentage of retail selling price or an amount per kilogram.

---

[100] The eight directives were: 92/77, Art. 1, 1992 O.J. (L 316) 1, supplementing 77/388 on general VAT rates; 92/78, 1992 O.J. (L 316) 5, relates to the consumption of manufactured tobacco; 92/79, 1992 O.J. (L 316) 8, is in regard to cigarettes; 92/80, 1992 O.J. (L 316) 10, relates to manufactured tobacco other than cigarettes; 92/81, 1992 O.J. (L 316) 12, defines the mineral oils as they relate to 92/82, 1992 O.J. (L 316) 19; 92/82 establishes the excise rates on mineral oils; 92/83, 1992 O.J. (L 316) 21, relates to excise taxes on alcohol and alcoholic beverages; and 92/84, 1992 O.J. (L 316) 29, sets out rates and exceptions to alcohol and alcoholic beverages.

There has also been some agreement on excise duties with respect to mineral oils. These mineral oils include gasoline, home heating oil, natural gas and kerosene. The two directives on mineral oils set out minimum excise rates but was riddled with exceptions and varied from State to State.

The two directives aimed at alcohol include beer, wine, other fermented beverages, intermediate product, and ethyl alcohol. The directives attempted to set out minimum excise rates on such products, but many problems were encountered due to varying Member State considerations.

The European Commission considers unification of excise duties necessary in particular because VAT is imposed on the prices of goods inclusive of excise duty.[101] As a result of the multiplicator effect of VAT and excise duties, even relatively minor excise-rate differentials already pose a threat to fiscal neutrality and increase the risk of fraud. This multiplicator effect is, however, not the sole nor even the main reason why excise-rate unification is undoubtedly a preliminary condition for the removal of tax barriers. Because excise duties are collected only once, and because of the level of the rates and the size of rate differentials between Member States, these differentials can easily cause shifts in regular trade (and location) patterns. Theoretically it should be possible to allow a spread in excise rates. In order not to exceed transport costs, however, such a spread should be small enough in relation to both existing rates and the rate differentials between Member States that allowing it would not really solve anything and could only raise false expectations.

A case in point is diesel fuel, the transport cost of which is only a few ECUs per 1000 liters, whereas the difference between the lowest and the highest excise rate in the EC is now 179 ECUs per 1000 liters.[102] One must also consider the effect of what are in themselves minor exchange-rate fluctuations within the EC on the specific excise rates as unified at a given moment. Assuming that the specific excise rates as converted to national currencies will not be adjusted all the time to small movements in exchange rates (say within the EMS band), some spread in such rates will arise. If the currency of Member State A rises 1 percent as against the currency of Member State B, the excise duty on diesel will be about 1.8 ECUs higher in A than in B, as long as the national excise rates have not been brought into line with the new exchange rates. The exchange rate effect on the petrol duty (proposed rate: 340 ECUs per 1000 liters) is nearly twice that on the diesel duty, whereas the effect on the alcohol duty (1271 ECUs per 1000 liters) is more than seven times as high.

Agreement on uniform rates of excise duty is, therefore, essential. A rating variant on the European Commission's proposals on excise duties, which would allow additional national levies at the retail-trade level, could at least in theory provide the means to respect the fiscal sovereignty of the Member States to some extent. This vari-

---

[101] Marko Bos and Hans Nelson, *Indirect Taxation and the Completion of the Internal Market of the EC*, Vol XXVII, No.1, J. of Common Market Studies, 27 (1988) © 1988 Marko Bos and Hans Nelson. Reprinted with permission.

[102] With an arithmetic EC average of 153 ECUs per 1000 liters and a consumption-weighted average of 177 ECUs per 1000 liters. The European Commission has opted for the weighted average for its rate proposal.

ant, however, involves major problems of implementation, increases the administrative burden on retailers, and creates the risk of distorting competition by deflections of consumer purchases. It would mean involving the retail trade in the collection of excise duties and its control system, which may necessitate a reduction in the number of distributing channels for some excisable goods. For these reasons it looks unlikely that a rating variant could be recommended in general, but it might be helpful for a country like Denmark where the sale of alcoholic beverages is already subject to strict licensing requirements.

For governments, changes in rates have not only budgetary consequences but also repercussions for policies in the field of, for example, public health, environmental protection, energy conservation or income distribution. For specific industries, the level of taxation determines the retail price and, in this way, the level of final demand. Moreover, in the event of intermediary use of excisable goods (such as fuels), unification of excise duties affects the competitiveness of the firms concerned. In principle, unification of excise duties would contribute to the equalization of the tax components of the cost structure of individual firms. But in practice, unification of only one of the cost components in given industries (for example, the diesel excise duty payable by road hauliers) may lead to undesirable distortions of existing patterns of competitiveness. This could be a reason for proceeding to the harmonization of other tax-determined or collectively fixed cost components (see Commission of the European Communities, 1988).

The Commission's concrete rate proposals are largely based on the current situation in the Member States and not on notions of a target situation. Policy considerations crop up only in the choices between the arithmetic and consumption-weighted averages and in the rate fixing for unleaded petrol, wines and beer. This predominantly pragmatic approach may make it easier to reach political agreement on certain principles and subsidiary policy goals of taxation, and then fix Community rates on this basis. This approach should include a conscious choice between specific and *ad-valorem* duties. For alcoholic beverages and tobacco products the principles of taxing commodities at the same rate can best be given shape by levying, in addition to VAT (the *ad-valorem* element), only a specific excise duty based on quantities of relevant characteristics of excisable goods. Indeed, application of an *ad-valorem* rate increases differences between the prices of different qualities of the same product, thus promoting degradation of quality.

The short-term disadvantages of unification for a given industry or government should not in itself be a reason for abandoning the goal. Market shifts are inherent in the completion of the Internal Market. Moreover, conceding certain objections to unification could frustrate the completion of the Internal Market. For instance, if inadequate harmonization of excise duties were to induce countries to maintain border controls on one product, this would in principle open the door to keeping up customs on all goods.

If excise duties were unified, the tax-exempt transport system between interlinked bonded warehouses, as proposed by the European Commission, is desirable but not strictly necessary to the completion of the Internal Market. Another positive side effect of rate unification is that no mechanism is needed to attribute to Member States excise duties on exported goods, in accordance with the destination principle. When excise rates are uniform, traders will as a rule prefer to pay over excise duties to the taxman at the latest possible moment and, consequently, in the country of destination.

3. Company Taxation[103]

Although some convergence of corporate tax regimes has occurred, it was unlikely that these differences would be reduced without action at the Union level. Thus, the Committee set out three priorities:

1. Removing those discriminatory and distortionary features of countries' tax arrangements that impede cross-border business investment and shareholding;
2. Setting a minimum level for the statutory corporation tax rate and common rules for minimum tax base, so as to limit excessive tax competition between member states intended to attract mobile investment or taxable profits of multinational firms, either of which tends to erode the tax base in the Union as a whole; and
3. Encouraging the maximum transparency of any tax incentives granted by member states to promote investment.

During 1992, little progress was made with regard to company taxation. A change was proposed that would reduce or eliminate double taxation in the case of companies operating within more than one Member State. The elimination of this double taxation would benefit all companies operating within more than one Member State, which includes companies and subsidiaries of the United States.

The EU will likely go further in eliminating double taxation without too much opposition from Member States. The short term tax revenues of double taxation are less beneficial than the long term gains of a single standard tax base that would increase investment throughout Europe. These increased investments would come from not only EU Member States but globally, if countries believed they would be fairly treated in the EU markets. The market forces of supply and demand dictate that, all else being equal, the less expensive company is the better company; double taxation is, ultimately, an expense to be absorbed by the company and then passed on to consumers.

E. Direct Taxation[104]

Interestingly, Article 220, which requires Member States to enter into negotiations with each other with a view to securing for the benefit of their nations the abolition of double taxation within the Community, is intended primarily to apply to direct taxation as

---

[103] Michael D. Hodges, *Activities in the European Community towards Unifying Taxation and the Elimination of Quantitive Restictions*, 3 J. Int'l L. & Proc. 185-93 (1994). © 1994 Michael D. Hodges. Reprinted with permission.

[104] Karen V. Kole, *Income Tax Harmonization in the European Union* (Dissertation—Unpublished) (1995). © Karen V. Kole. Reprinted by permission.

is Article 130 F which was added in 1986 and advocates the removal of legal and fiscal barriers to co-operation between undertakings, research centers and universities.

Why is the notion of harmonization of direct taxes so troublesome to the Community? Several reasons may explain it:

First, from a political standpoint, fiscal control is of ultimate importance to Member States. The fear may be that in a fully harmonized system Member States would see their tax systems, the product of years of cultural, historical accident and political expedience, dissolved and replaced with a national system over which they have little control and garner little return in exchange for relinquishing control. However, following the principle of subsidiarity, taxing rights would remain primarily with the member states and the federal system would be small in comparison with state taxes. Unfortunately, the problem of a single European currency may be forced to be solved before any movement can be expected in this area.

Second, direct taxation is a mystery of sorts to even the most sophisticated tax solicitor. Is it not naive to expect Eurocrats, expert in dealing with bureaucracy and not taxation, to want or be able to tackle such a complicated and sensitive subject? Many scholars and practitioners are having difficulty grappling with such an enormous problem.

Why is harmonization of direct taxes so important to the Community? The mission or goal of the European Union, in the words of one scholar in the area, is:

> therefore a free market ideal that, as far as possible, the territory of the twelve (now fifteen) Member States should resemble a single national market, where there is a level competitive playing field for all economic actors and where distortions of competition based on artificial legal barriers such as differences in consumer protection or environmental regulation will be eliminated.[105]

Steiner goes on to add, with respect to the substantive contribution of the Treaty of Maastricht, that its greatest contribution to "the attainment of European integration lies in its provisions on economic and monetary union, and its introduction of the aim of creating a single currency." [106] In fact, Article B TEU states, in pertinent part:

> To promote economic and social progress which is balanced and sustainable, in particular through the creation of an area without internal frontiers, through the strengthening of economic and social cohesion and through the establishment of economic and monetary union, ultimately including a single currency in accordance with the provisions of this Treaty . . . .[107]

In addition, capital import and export neutrality is desirable to ensure that investment from a commercial perspective is not based merely on favorable tax climates as

---

[105] J. Steiner, *European Community Law*, Macmillan, 1993, at p. 9.

[106] *Id.*

[107] Article B TEU.

opposed to more productive and efficient investment climates. Moreover, the fundamental freedoms (free movement of goods, persons, etc.) will be reinforced and not indirectly affected by the internal tax systems of Member nations. Finally, and perhaps most importantly, budgetary and financial considerations of how to support the rising costs of the Community may force a harmonization and possibly a federal system to come into being.

1. Brief History of Direct Tax Harmonization in the EU

While some commentators have suggested that the contrast between the specific provisions of the EEC Treaty dealing with indirect taxation, and the absence of provisions expressly dealing with direct taxation probably reflects the relative importance that the authors of the Treaty attached to the two forms of taxation, the real reason has been a reluctance on the part of the original founders to tackle an area of such political sensitivity due to the fragile and tenuous nature of the original formation. This evaluation was reflected in the levels of activity, or inactivity, devoted to those subjects and, even now, it is apparent that the highest priority is still attached to the elimination of those fiscal frontiers that take a physical form and whose existence is due to VAT and excise duties. However, once the immediate objective of removing border controls has been achieved, it is probable that the harmonization of direct taxation will assume greater importance. It is instructive, therefore, to trace briefly the evolution of Community policy towards direct taxation and to examine the reasons for the relative lack of progress.

2. The Neumark and Segre Reports

A working group established by the Commission reporting in late 1959, concluded that harmonization of turnover taxation was urgently needed and, in 1960, the Commission responded by establishing three further study groups to examine different aspects of the problem and various alternative solutions and also appointed a Fiscal and Financial Committee, chaired by Professor Fritz Neumark, to study the extent to which the tax systems of the Member States prejudiced the establishment and functioning of the Common Market. The Neumark Report, and the separate reports of Sub-groups A, B, and C were adopted in 1962. Among other things, the Neumark Committee recommended that the first phase of tax harmonization should deal not only with indirect taxation but also with the taxation of dividends and interest and with the problem of double taxation, and that the second phase should include the reform of systems of company taxation. The Neumark report, which was concerned primarily with the impact of direct taxation on conditions of competition, was followed in 1966 by that of the Segre Committee, on the establishment of an integrated capital market within the Community. The Segre Committee did not limit itself to the establishment of an integrated capital market. Rather, it considered a wide range of topics including company law, stock exchange regulation and exchange controls, and focused extensively on fiscal obstacles to the free movement of capital. It concluded that the realization and proper functioning of a European capital market require that fiscal systems do not obstruct the creation of conditions similar to those of an Internal Market. Tax considerations should not influence the choice of location of investments or transactions, nor the choice of an investor between direct investment and investment through an intermediary. The chief fiscal obstacle to an effective capital market were identified as the international double taxation of investment income, and the existence of tax advantages or disadvantages affecting investment in certain countries, and the different attitudes of Member States with regard to the treatment of investment income payable to non-residents and to corporate investors. Among other things, the Segre Report proposed the following:

- the replacement of existing bilateral double taxation agreements by a multilateral Community convention;
- the extension of tax credits, for tax paid by corporations, to non-resident shareholders;
- the abolition of withholding tax on interest payments, or the adoption of a common rate of withholding tax;
- the harmonization of rules governing institutional investors;
- the removal of discrimination against the use of financial intermediaries;
- the harmonization of taxes on the formation of capital.

F. The Arbitration Convention

In addition to the 1990 direct tax package, the Arbitration Convention, 90/436, was introduced. The Arbitration Convention was unique in the sense that it took the form of a Convention rather than a Directive. While this may not seem significant at first glance, it is important. In 1976, the Commission had proposed a Directive [108] which would have allowed the Court of Justice to interpret its provisions and to develop a consistent body of case law throughout the Community; however, the proposed Directive was objected to by several Member States and, ultimately, the measure took the form of a Convention, concluded by the Member States, for the purpose of eliminating double taxation in connection with the adjustment of profits of associated enterprises. The Convention is executed on behalf of the Member States alone, requiring their ratification and makes no provision for referring disputes or questions of interpretation to the Court of Justice.

The focus and purpose of the Convention is to eliminate one particular cause of double taxation that affects multinational enterprises with branches or affiliates in other Member States. The Convention is aimed at the practice of "transfer-pricing" between affiliated members of the same group Transactions between these affiliated members are often not carried out on an arm's length basis to, among other reasons, maximize profits in the country with lower taxes and to minimize them in higher tax jurisdictions. There is also an incentive to manipulate losses in one country versus another if there are profits from affiliated group members that could soak up the losses. Needless to

[108] Proposal of 25 November 1976; OJ 1976, C 301/4. *See also* Van Waardenburg, *Eur. Tax.* 18 (1978): 144.

say, national tax authorities do not like this practice and domestic taxing authorities are given the authority to substitute a "fair" or "arm's-length" price for the price that was actually charged between the affiliated members. While this is certainly proper from the domestic standpoint, the tax authorities of the other country concerned, where there may now have been a corresponding overpayment of tax, have no reason to make a compensating adjustment. If a compensating adjustment is not made, the result is double taxation. While this may not be an improper result if the affiliated group members are guilty of fraud but often an adjustment is made merely because the tax authorities take a different view of what constitutes a proper price than do the parties to the transaction.

Many of the bilateral tax treaties among Member States contain provisions which provide that the competent authorities of the states concerned shall attempt to resolve problems of double taxation by mutual agreement. Unfortunately, the procedure is not automatic and comprehensive and there is no requirement that an agreement between the Member States be reached. The provisions in the bilateral tax treaties are modeled after the provisions contained in Article 25 of the OECD Model Convention of 1977. The Arbitration Convention is more restrictive in scope than the OECD provisions because it relates only to double taxation resulting from adjustment of profits of associated enterprises, i.e., transfer pricing, and does not seem to eliminate the problem of double taxation generally. However, the procedures provided, as discussed below, do seem provide a better procedure for requiring dispute resolution between the Member States.

The Arbitration Convention, pursuant to Article 1, applies where, for purposes of taxation, profits of an enterprise in one contracting state are also included, or are likely to be included, in the profits of an enterprise in another contracting state as a result of an adjustment made by the competent authorities of one of those states, pursuant to Article 4 of the Convention. The Convention also applies where the profits of a permanent establishment of an enterprise in one contracting state are included in the profits of the enterprise in another contracting state, i.e., it applies to the potential double taxation of a branch and its head office, of a subsidiary and its parent, or of two associated enterprises.[109]

In situations where the authorities of a contracting state intend to make such an adjustment, they are required to notify the enterprise in due time and to give it the opportunity to inform the other party to the transaction, so that it may have the opportunity to inform, in turn, the authorities of the other state as provided in Article 5. If, after notification, the two enterprises and the authorities of the other state agree to the adjustment, the matter is ended. Otherwise, two alternatives are available to the complainant. It can appeal against the assessment under the normal procedure provided by domestic law, or it can take advantage of the procedures provided by the Convention. This the entity does by presenting its case to the competent authorities of the state of which it is an enterprise or in which its permanent establishment is based. This

[109] By a joint declaration of the contracting parties, the scope of the convention has been extended to cases involving independent enterprises.

process must be begun within three years of the original notification. The competent authorities of the other state concerned must also be notified pursuant to Article 6 of the Convention.

If the competent authorities of the two Member States concerned fail to reach an agreement within two years to eliminate the double taxation, the Convention requires, under Article 7, that an Advisory Commission be appointed to deliver an opinion on the elimination of the double taxation in issue. The complainant may represent itself in these proceedings. The Commission is required to deliver an opinion within six months. After the Commission renders its opinion, the competent authorities of the two Member States have a further six months to take a decision which will eliminate the double taxation in issue, pursuant to Article 12. In rendering their decision, the competent authorities are not required to accept the solution proposed by the Advisory Committee.

In two cases there is an exception to the duty imposed on the contracting states. Under the laws of some states the competent authorities are not permitted to settle a case by mutual agreement where such a settlement would derogate from a court decision. The United Kingdom is an example of this case. In such a case, Article 7(3) of the Convention provides that no Advisory Commission shall be established unless the time allowed for judicial appeal has passed or the enterprise has withdrawn such an appeal. In effect, the result is that the enterprise must choose whether to appeal or go to arbitration under the Convention. The other situation where there can be an exception is provided under Article 8. Article 8 provides that the contracting states may stay the mutual agreement procedure pending the resolution of judicial or administrative proceedings against one of the enterprises if those proceedings may result in the imposition on the enterprise of a "serious penalty," or to deny the initiation of the Convention procedure where such a penalty has been imposed. The intention would seem to be to deny the facility of arbitration procedure to enterprises found guilty of tax evasion or fraud. However, some of the contracting states have taken a very broad view of what constitutes a serious penalty. For example, in the United Kingdom, a serious penalty comprises any sanction, criminal or administrative, in respect of the fraudulent or negligent delivery of incorrect accounts, claims or returns, and in Ireland it extends even to penalties for failure to file a tax return.

The Convention must be ratified by the contracting states and will enter into force on the first day of the third month following that in which the last instrument of ratification is deposited.

G. The Rudding Report

The Rudding Report[110] compares tax harmonization in five advanced federations focusing in detail on the situations existing in Canada, Switzerland and the United States. According to the report, Canada manifests one of the highest degrees of tax har-

[110] Commission of the European Communities, "Report of the Committee of Independent Experts on Company Taxation," 185-192 (1992) (Rudding Report).

monization at the sub-national level, even though its provinces are more important fiscally than the corresponding governmental subdivisions in the other states examined. The experience of Switzerland is relevant because of its strong reliance on cantonal sovereignty and the diversity of its corporate and personal income taxes. Finally, the situation in the United States is relevant because of the size of its economy.

Because taxation is more consistent within these states, interjurisdictional tax considerations have less impact on business decisions. Assuming other factors remain equal, this should promote more efficient resource allocation within the economy, and, indeed, a tax-neutral allocation of resources appears to be the primary benefit of harmonization.

The restricted nature of EU federalism limits the extent to which comparison between the experiences in these other states and the situation existing in the EU is relevant. Each of these other states has a strong central government and the constituent states have less sovereignty than exists within the EU. In addition, among other things, the structure of the federal and state governments, the size of the states and local economies and of the nature of the state and federal tax systems in each of these states differ substantially among themselves. For these reasons, the comparison in the report is not intended to establish a model for the EU to follow. Nevertheless, it does yield valuable insights regarding the common features of harmonization exhibited in each of these states and factors contributed to achieving harmonization.

As noted in the report, an internal market existed in each of these states prior to harmonization, or evolved in conjunction therewith. In effect, it appears that corporate tax harmonization in other states occurred as a consequence of the existence of an internal market and the confluence of other factors. The implicit causal relationship in the EU, however, is reversed: corporate tax harmonization is pursued as a means to achieve an internal market.

Nothing suggests *a priori* that pursuing corporate tax harmonization would not facilitate achieving a single internal market, and the empirical evidence should not be interpreted as dictating a necessary causal relationship. Of course, the experience of these other states does suggest that harmonization will be more difficult to achieve in the absence of a uniform internal market and many of the other factors that were present in these other states.

1. Factors Facilitating Harmonization

Numerous factors facilitated corporate tax harmonization in the states examined in the Rudding Report. The existence of a federal corporate income tax, common accounting principles and practices, a common commercial code and legal system, and a single currency in each of these states created an environment in which harmonization more readily could occur. The absence of these factors within the EU makes the process more difficult and limits the degree to which harmonization is attainable.

On the other hand, introducing one or more of these factors into the community should aid the harmonization process, and it would appear worthwhile for the Member States to explore opportunities that may be available for this purpose.

As suggested above, non-binding measures should be given preference in the harmonization process. In this context, the experience of the United States may provide some useful insights. As the Rudding Report points out, the existence of a common commercial code in the United States, however, is a relatively recent phenomenon and resulted from private initiative rather than governmental coercion.

Perhaps corporate tax harmonization in the EC could be expedited if similar non-governmental institutions within the EU would take the initiative to assist Member States in introducing some of the factors that have facilitated harmonization in other states. European enterprises, scholars and practitioners (particularly tax counsels to multinational enterprises doing business within and without the EU) could cooperate, for example, in drafting a model European corporate tax code that could then be adopted, with any necessary modifications, by the Member States.

This process has numerous advantages over an approach legislated by the EU, two of which bear emphasizing. First, the model would be proposed by an independent forum and could be evaluated and modified by the individual Member States to accommodate their specific needs, much like the OECD Model treaty forms a basis for tax treaty negotiations in most states. Second, because the model would be developed in the private sector, it could reflect more accurately the needs and concerns of EU enterprises.

With the foregoing in mind, an examination of the more important concerns to deal with in trying to harmonize the systems is required. [T]here are four main areas for consideration: 1) local factors which per se can render a jurisdiction more or less attractive for a particular project in comparison with another member state; 2) local factors which can render a jurisdiction more or less attractive to a particular inward investor; 3) domestic factors affecting outward investment from a jurisdiction; and 4) factors affecting the return to the individual or portfolio investor by his choice of domicile of the corporate vehicle. With this in mind, the focus should be on the fundamental areas of dissimilarity among Member State's tax systems and how these dissimilarities undermine the fundamental goals of the Community with respect to the four freedoms.

2. The Jurisdiction with the Right To Tax

Most of the Member States, in addition to other countries throughout the world, base their taxing jurisdiction on two main criteria, source and residence. Thus, a state will exercise its jurisdiction to levy tax where the income or gain derives from a source within the state or when it is derived by a taxpayer resident in the state. In a cross-border situation the application of these two principles can give rise to double taxation. The situation is exacerbated by the use of different definitions to determine whether the situs of an asset or source of income is in a particular jurisdiction or whether a particular company is resident in a particular state. Most states regard a company incorporated under the company law of a country as resident in that jurisdiction. Some states also regard a company as resident where it maintains its head office, or its seat of management, whilst others use only one of the latter tests and disregard the test based on the place of incorporation. In the case of companies exposed in more than one state to taxation on the ground of residence, the "tie-breaker" provision in most double tax treaties gives the prior right to tax to the state where the place of effective management is located.

Companies are most likely to benefit from the single market if they can manage their business which serves that market as if it were a single market as if it were a single business. However, this implies a large degree of centralized management. Unfortunately, most multinational corporations are organized as groups, often with a separate subsidiary serving each national market. Centralizing management in these circumstances can give rise to problems and additional taxation based on the location of management.

Where the parent of a multinational group is based in one member state and has an operating subsidiary in another, the establishment of centralized management could cause the subsidiary to be regarded as resident in the country of the parent for the purposes of that country's tax and thus liable to full taxation there. Although in these circumstances it is unlikely that the effect of the relevant treaty will be that the country of the subsidiary will recognize that the company is resident in the country of the parent, tax will still be levied there as the country of source of the income. Unless an exemption system applies to the income in question, the net effect will be exposure to the higher charges to tax and additional withholding taxes. Where the degree of management in the country of the parent is not of itself sufficient to cause the subsidiary to be regarded as resident there, it may yet be enough to cause the subsidiary to have a "permanent establishment" there and either under its domestic law or a double tax treaty give that country the right to tax the profits attributable to the permanent establishment. The standard double tax agreement includes "place of management" within the definition of a permanent establishment.

One possible alternative to the risks attendant on operating through dually resident companies would be for a group to convert from operating as a group with a subsidiary in each state to operating as a company with a branch in each state. Currently, however, there are often significant tax costs on converting from a subsidiary to a branch structure and on continuing in that form. In addition to the tax on gains and other items arising on the conversion of a subsidiary to a branch, a number of countries levy a higher rate of tax on the profits of branches than on those of subsidiaries. The European Commission has not proposed a directive to eliminate or reduce such extra taxes on branches similar to the directive to eliminate withholding taxes on dividends from subsidiary to parent.

3. The Taxpayer

In all Member States, the primary taxpayer liable to corporate taxes is the individual corporation. In a number of the Member States, however, it is possible for a group of companies to elect, revocably or irrevocably, for some type of group taxation or fiscal consolidation. "Fiscal consolidation" is the generic term for the ability to set off the losses of one company against the profits of another company within the same group, so that tax is paid on the net profits only. Fiscal consolidation of profits and losses of companies within a Member State can take various forms. In the UK and Ireland, there is no consolidation for tax purposes but members of a domestic group may surrender trading losses and certain other items of unrelieved expenditure to each other. In France, the tax position of all domestic members of the group is calculated separately and then netted off. In Denmark, The Netherlands, Portugal and Spain, a parent and its domestic subsidiaries may present a consolidated balance sheet for tax purposes, under which they are treated as a single taxpayer. The same position may also be attained in Germany and Luxembourg, but only if there is genuine organizational and commercial integration in the group. The concept of fiscal consolidation is only generally available cross-border in Denmark and then only where the parent is a Danish company. France recognizes the concept but in practice permission is hardly ever given for such consolidation. There is a limited cross-border consolidation in Germany in that the German branch of a foreign parent may file a fiscal consolidation with its German subsidiaries.

This absence of consolidations across borders tends to distort the behavior of companies which have a choice of location for a proposed investment. If it is assumed that the investment is expected to incur losses during the first few years after it has been formed, for example, because in the early years it incurs heavy capital expenditure in a country in which the company already has existing activities which generate profits, with which the losses of the new project can be consolidated. This location may not be the one which would have been the most efficient if tax reasons for choosing it had not existed.

4. The Tax Base

At first glance, it would seem that the concept of "tax base" would be one area that countries could easily agree. Unfortunately, at least with regard to the concept of "profits" there is no consensus. Although, uniformly, each Member State seeks to tax the "profits" accruing to, or made by, the company in a particular period, either calendar or accrual method. In the UK and France, for example, a differentiation between income profits and capital gains is made and each category subjected to different rates of tax. On the other hand, The Netherlands does not have a separate capital gains tax. In Luxembourg, the use of a comparative balance sheet rather than an adjusted profit method of calculating the base on which the tax is calculated avoids the problem of having to identify capital gains.

5. The System of Corporate Tax

The major structural difference between the corporate tax systems is the interaction of the tax on corporate income and dividend flows to domestic shareholders. Currently, some Member States employ an imputation system, some the classical system, and one, Greece, the dividend deduction system.

Classical systems do not recognize any identity between the taxed profits of a corporation and the dividends declared out of them. In consequence, the profits are taxed twice: once in the hands of the corporation and again in the hands of the recipient of the dividend. This system is followed, subject to special rules for holding companies, in Luxembourg and The Netherlands. Denmark has recently decided to revert to this system.

Imputation systems give some form of credit for the underlying tax on the company profits out of which the dividend was paid. The mechanics of this vary considerably from Member State to Member State. The UK and Ireland operate an advance corporation tax (ACT) system, under which the tax paid on the payment of the dividend acts both as an advance payment of corporation tax and a partial satisfaction of the liability of the recipient of the dividend. Belgium, France and Portugal give a tax credit to the portfolio shareholders: Germany, Italy and Spain give it to all resident shareholders (parent companies being effectively exempt). If the profits out of which the dividend is paid have not suffered tax at the normal corporate rate, France, Germany and Italy will charge an equalization tax. It is noteworthy that France differentiates between the *avoir fical*, which is the tax credit, and the *precompte*, which is the equalization tax, and gives quite different rights to repayment of the two. UK ACT in a sense does duty as an equalization tax, since it is charged whether or not corporation tax is finally due and is an equalization tax to the extent that it cannot be set against the corporation tax. The right of the company to repayment or offset is linked not only to the final corporate tax liability of the company but also to the receipt by the company during the period of investment income which itself carries a tax credit.

The position is further complicated by the existence of other rules for dividends received by holding companies, themselves variously defined in Member States, and by the operation of tax treaties.

H. What Form of Community Tax System?

1. The Potentials of Tax Harmonization

We have seen that there is no agreed upon EU-concept of what direct tax harmonization might actually include. While the harmonization of indirect taxes might be a starting point, it is rather limited in its usefulness because of the scope and complexity of direct taxation as opposed to indirect taxation. To date, the package of directives and convention is suggestive since it illustrates two approaches which complement each other but which are both limited in their ambitions. These two approaches are 1) reciprocity of treatment without approximation of systems, as exemplified by the mergers directive (partly) and transfer pricing convention and 2) removal of distortions in cross-border transactions, again without significant approximation of systems as exemplified by the parent/subsidiary taxation directive and some parts of the mergers directive. These can best be described as a timid pursuit of both capital-export and capital-import neutrality.

The adoption of a common system, a single system or a federal system of corporate taxation in the EU would all have advantages and disadvantages. The adoption of a common market would provide tax neutrality for the corporate sector without presupposing any ambitious political commitments to deeper political integration. The move to a single system or a federal system would not be essential to the single market programme but it would probably be a further reinforcement of it. Such developments are really inconceivable without prior or at least parallel progress towards real political union in Europe. It remains to be seen whether the current inter-governmental conference on political union and other high level EC decision making bodies will be prepared to contemplate such a significant leap forward.

2. Tax Systems in General

What is a tax system? Details are important in implementation but it is wise not to miss the forest for the trees. The temptation in many discussions of harmonization is to concentrate on the points of detail and to neglect the larger picture. This is unwise. A tax system is more than a combination of base and rates. It has been justly observed that harmonization of rates alone would not reduce the current differences and in fact, considering the intimate relationships of rates and base, could actually exacerbate differences between the systems. The argument can be extended. In the context of the deficiencies of the present system, consideration of the corporate tax system, i.e., the taxation of companies, must include such matters as the interaction between that system and the income tax system, the taxation of individuals and withholding rates, the social security system, local taxation systems, the rate of inflation, the balance of payments and the economic situation generally, and the government's funding needs. There is an inescapable political dimension, therefore, to discussions on harmonization, arising from the substance of possible developments as well as their form.

3. Harmonization as a Means or an End

If harmonization is a means to an end, then it may develop according to the changing ends of the legislators. At present, the avowed end is the completion of the internal market at the end of 1992. To ensure that different tax systems do not raise internal barriers to trade is a limited ambition.

If, on the other hand, harmonization is an end in itself, that suggests a view about the ultimate political shape of the EU which goes far beyond the creation of a single market. On this assumption, that mere approximation and reciprocity of systems will not suffice for the purposes of the ultimate political and economic development of the EU, there appear to be two main possibilities for "full" as opposed to partial harmonization: a single tax system for the whole of the EU, or a federal tax system under which the separate state systems would continue to exist in some form. These imply different views as to the political organization which would have to exist to validate the fiscal structure, though this would be a difference of degree rather than of kind.

The possible forms a totally new system could take are almost infinite in points of detail. Judging from previous EU draft directives and pronouncements, it could be an imputation system. The imputation system has significant benefits in reducing distortion of investment decisions due to the efficient tax results according to the type of funding or legal form, although a classical system would be likely to achieve a greater degree of fiscal neutrality for cross-border investments. In addition, an exemption system would be more neutral than a foreign tax credit system. As far as harmonization of the base is concerned, tax depreciation might well be more closely linked to accounts depreciation but this in itself implies a closer approximation of accounting standards throughout the EU.

The creation of a new system would necessitate making value judgments in specific areas in which the countries with different systems would again no doubt see themselves as being in competition. It therefore contains much the same opportunities for political deadlock as the adoption of an existing system although the choice facing member states would be presented as less stark.

4. A Common System

Adoption of a common system of corporate taxation assumes that the agreement on a common system would be limited to agreement on the system itself, i.e., in effect (a) a double tax relief system, and (b) the taxation of corporate profits and dividend flows which could be adopted by each Member State. This approach is regard by many to be the one which implies the fewest changes to the current and historical political concepts of the EU. This alternative aims for the maximum corporate tax neutrality regarding investment decisions throughout the EU whilst at the same time permitting the Member States to retain their taxing rights and the existing infrastructures to apply the tax system. This alternative would also mean the smallest number of changes to the administration and would fit in with existing structure of multinational groups without preventing changes which a common market might make desirable. A common system could, as at present, encompass quite different tax bases in different Member States, permit a system of grants and incentives to help depressed or other specific areas and complement existing income tax and social security systems although to the extent that these and tax rates were not also harmonized, neutrality would not have been achieved from a commercial viewpoint. One major disadvantage from the retention of national tax administrations would be the tendency for different interpretations of words, rules and concepts by the administration of each of the Member States. The adoption of a common system offers considerable scope for the inertia of any tax administration to cause new rules and systems to be applied along the lines of the previous system with which it was familiar. The divergence of language, concepts and culture within the Member States will give rise to differences even where identical legislation is intended, and in the absence of a common language truly identical legislation is not possible, although this could be remedied by ensuring that there was only one EU tax court to decide matters of law, i.e., interpretation.

Of the main possibilities, it should be noted that the introduction of a common corporate tax system makes the least number of political demands. It does not automatically imply a single or federated system, political union or federation but nor does it rule out any of these or indeed any other possibilities. The introduction of a common system does no more than provide neutrality of corporate tax implications for investors making investment decisions, i.e., it removes one more barrier to the free movement of capital, etc. throughout the EU.

5. The Main Issues with a Common Corporate System

There are two main questions to be addressed when considering which system might be recommended as the common system to be adopted by each of the Member States as the common system for the EU. These are first, which method should be used to avoid the double taxation of foreign income, and second, whether an imputation or a classical system of corporation tax is to be preferred.

6. A Single Corporate Tax System

A single corporate tax system is at once the simplest and also the most radical scheme: a single direct corporate tax system covering the whole of the EU. The advantages are clear. There would be total neutrality regarding investment decisions throughout the EU at least as far as the corporate tax consequences were concerned. In this sense, there would be no borders or barriers at all. The solution would imply a single taxing authority and probably a single tax return for an EU resident business, no matter how many nation-states it was operating in. This would clearly be a huge administrative advantage for companies which at present must produce tax computations in a number of states. Such a system could co-exist with a system of grants and incentives designed to attract business to specific areas. It could potentially co-exist with the survival of national, or perhaps regional, income tax and social security provisions, although this would import an element of inequality into operating costs.

The question then arises under this proposal, is whether the system to be adopted should be an entirely new system or an existing system. If an existing system were to be used there would be three possible approaches. The first would be to agree on an existing system which was generally regarded as the most appropriate and adopt it in its entirety. This is most likely to be impracticable. It is most likely politically unacceptable for any state to admit that the system applied by another state is "better" than its own and from the technical point of view the system developed over a long period by a particular state will be based on and inextricable from the non-tax legal system of the state, as well as having a number of quirks and peculiarities based on special circumstances and special pleading over the years. The second would be to adopt, almost certainly with modifications, the tax system in use by the most powerful economy in the EU, presently Germany, on the grounds that this would cause the least economic dislocation overall. This is unlikely to be politically acceptable. The third would be to work out a kind of lowest common denominator of EU tax systems and then choose the system closest to it. This would mean that the least number of fundamental changes would have to be made to any particular system. The system chosen could then be modified to remove anything which was agreed to be a particular local peculiarity.

If a single corporate tax system came into being in the EU, there would be considerable adjustments required to the position of non-EU resident companies operating within the EU. Where structures were in place there would probably either have to be a grandfathering provision to protect the investor, or at least a transitional period during which any necessary restructuring could take place. Without full scale renegotiation of tax treaties, inequalities in withholding tax rates would remain. An EU norm for withholding rates would have to be established and all treaties approximated to this. Alternatively, no doubt a single treaty network could be put in place, but this would probably take a significant period of time.

Politically, it would seem clear, whichever approach is adopted to the introduction of a single corporate tax system in Europe, this would have to be part of a complete reform of the EU which produced a single political entity. This would imply either that the member states agreed to pool their sovereignty completely in this area, on the pattern of the ECSC or the CAP, or that a new European political entity had been created in which the member states had ceased to have any meaningful power. A single European corporate tax system would not produce complete tax neutrality for companies if all the other factors for disequilibrium, e.g., public expenditure, income tax and social security contributions, remained within the competence of member states.

7. A Federal Corporate Tax System

The alternative of a Federal corporate tax system is not an obviously simple and efficient option as a single system, but it would be considerably more flexible. It would allow for the possibility of a period of transition during which the relationship between the federal and national systems could be adjusted to match the development of the EU institutions.

Clearly this solution would only produce harmonization in so far as the federal system applied in preference to the national systems or the national systems aligned on the federal system. It would still be compatible with a large measure of fiscal autonomy for the member states which would leave in place a number of tax inequalities between the various national systems.

The form which a federal system might take is even more difficult to foresee than a single system. The interaction between the federal and national systems would be the crucial question.

A complementary federal system might simply act as an agency by which tax burdens upon individual companies were evened out across the EU. Alternatively, it would supplant the national systems to a greater or lesser extent. The main issues to be resolved would be whether the federal and national systems would share any taxation principles, including the tax base, or whether there would be some sort of division of taxation rights instead. The latter would seem very difficult to achieve, unless all Member States agreed (say) to tax only those entities with a permanent establishment in the relevant territory on the operations of that permanent establishment, as is now the case in France. In theory, this would leave the federal system free to tax all non-EU operations of an EU resident company plus all non-operating income not sourced in the territory of residence. It is doubtful whether this would be administratively viable and it would do nothing to advance the cause of tax harmonization.

How could this alternative be achieved? It is, of course, useful to review other countries with a federal system of corporate taxation. The United States, with a comparable population to the EU, operates a federal system of corporate taxation. Canada, with a much smaller population but a similar ethnic and historical diversity, also has a federal system. Unfortunately, however, neither the US or Canada really provides a suitable model for the EU in the future. In the United States, the federal system did not have to cope with pre-existing national tax systems of the maturity and sophistication of those in the EU Member States. In Canada, the provincial tax system was actually developed from the federal tax system. In the United States many states have simply adopted the federal standard for their corporation tax, so they have only nominal independence, in practice. In Canada, the federal version is the norm and the provinces have to take a positive decision to derogate from it. In both cases there is a high degree of compatibility between the federal and state tax systems caused by convergence in one case and lack of divergence in the other. The United States and Canada also share the characteristic that it is the federal tax which is the most significant. Even though the states and provinces can impose further fiscal burdens on companies, these are generally seen as secondary in their impact.

In Switzerland, on the other hand, it is the web of cantonal and sub-cantonal taxes which imposes the main burden on companies. Federal corporate taxation, although significant as a proportion of the total tax burden upon companies, is generally regarded as of secondary importance. The cantonal and municipal taxes are normally the most significant proportion of a local company's tax charge and are usually calculated by applying a factor to the federal tax thus using the same base as the federal tax.

Experience from other countries does, however, suggest that a federal standard would be essential. While it is possible to imagine a floating federal levy designed to produce the same overall tax rate in each Member State, there would be a number of serious objections:

1) the harmonization apparently achieved would be largely cosmetic, since national tax bases would remain widely different;

2) it would be open to abuse if Member States raised tax rates in order to spend the revenue within their own jurisdictions;

3) it would be almost impossible to ensure equity at the level of individual corporations;

4) it could lead to double taxation on group profits and further divergence between the credit and exemption systems if relief were given on national principles;

5) it would probably spawn a series of tax avoidance structures using non-EU companies which would in turn force the passage of Controlled Foreign Corporation ("CFC") type legislation either at national or at federal level to combat it with all the increased compliance costs which this would entail.

The adoption of a federal standard would bring us back to the possibilities discussed for a single EU corporate tax system. The transition might be easier to manage, but it would require sustained political will over a long period to achieve it. A staged approach might take the following form:

1) A federal standard would be adopted. Member States would be free to converge on it, but would not be obliged to do so. Federal tax would be set at a rate which was significant but not overwhelming in comparison with national taxes, say at 10 percent (the Swiss rate is 9.8 percent maximum). It would remain for negotiation whether the figure adopted should represent a partial lifting of specific burdens in the Member States as well as a replacement of the present National Insurance systems.

2) At this stage taxing rights would remain primarily with the Member States. Federal tax would be collected by them (and could be deductible for national tax purposes if the national rate were not reduced accordingly). This would preserve at least the appearance of national sovereignty in this area.

3) The main disadvantage at this stage for corporation taxpayers would be the extra layer of tax bureaucracy without any corresponding simplification. The obvious *quid pro quo* would be for all Member States to tax EU operations on the basis of residence only. Thus no company would have to submit more than two sets of computations and would have only one tax authority to deal with. This instep would lead to a significant redistribution of corporate tax revenues within the EU, probably at the expense of Spain, Portugal, Greece and possibly Italy. If the process stopped at this point, any redistribution of income from the center would have to be done through some sort of clearing house mechanism. If this process continued, the problem could become politically less acute. An alternative would be to leave the source principle in place, but to adopt some form of apportionment, such as is widely used in the United States

where the state corporation taxes are computed according to a formula based upon the proportions of sales, assets and payroll coming from each state.

4) It would be possible to stop at this stage. The result would be a partial integration of corporate taxes, but there would still be a considerable element of inequality. The argument might then be that having given an impetus to harmonization without having swept away national fiscal sovereignty in this area, further progress would occur as the result of market forces (i.e., competition between national tax authorities). The existence of a federal standard would in any case create a powerful impulse towards greater tax uniformity.

5) If the political development of the EC were such that swifter progress towards something approaching the American model was possible, then the next step would be for the federal element in corporate taxation to be increased in a phased manner until it became the most significant. During this period, the Member States might be obliged to approximate to the federal standard or to adopt formula apportionment. This would become more necessary the higher the maximum national element was allowed to be.

Having achieved something close to full harmonization, it would be necessary to consider how the revenue would be shared. It can be assumed that in this scenario there would be a need to distribute funds back to the Member States, although the extent to which this was done would differ according to the degree of political sovereignty ceded to the center.

I. Conclusion

The adoption of a common system, a single system or a federal system of corporate taxation in Europe would all have advantages and disadvantages. The adoption of a common system would provide tax neutrality for the corporate sector without presupposing any ambitious political commitments to deeper political integration. The move to a single system or a federal system would not be essential to the single market programme, but it would probably be a further reinforcement of it. Such developments are really inconceivable without prior, or at least parallel, progress towards real political union in Europe. It remains to be seen whether high level EU decision-making bodies will be prepared to contemplate such a significant leap forward.

One very important aspect of moves towards harmonization must therefore be the EU- wide adoption of standards of acceptability in tax planning and a consensus approach on the distinction between avoidance (legal) and evasion (illegal). On present evidence, this may well turn out to be a rather contentious area. The different official language versions of the directive on mergers contain different wording in the section of the directive on tax avoidance indicating deep seated differences in attitude and conceptual context in the different tax authorities.

III. State Aids

A. Introduction[111]

When one considers competition law in the European Community ("Community" or "EC"), it is useful to keep in mind the wording of Articles 2 and 3 of the Treaty Establishing the European Community ("EC Treaty" or "Treaty").

Article 2 states:

> The Community shall have as its task, by establishing a common market . . . and by implementing the common policies or activities referred to in Article 3 . . . to promote throughout the Community a harmonious and balanced development of economic activities, sustainable and non-inflationary growth respecting the environment, a high degree of convergence of economic performance, a high level of employment and of social protection, the raising of the standard of living and quality of life, and economic and social cohesion and solidarity among Member States.

Article 3 states that "[f]or the purpose set out in Article 2, the activities of the Community shall include . . . a system ensuring that competition in the internal market is not distorted." The first Chapter of Title V of the Treaty establishes "rules on competition" applying to undertakings and to "aids granted by States." The provisions on competition of the Treaty should also be read in the context of its preamble, in which the Founding Fathers recognized that "the removal of existing obstacles calls for concerted action in order to guarantee steady expansion, balanced trade and fair competition."

As Helmuth R.B. Schroter stated a few years ago:

> [T]he much broader scope of and plurality of aims pursued by EC competition policy result in making antitrust analysis under Community law a more complicated process than under the antitrust law of the United States which considers "allocative efficiency/consumer welfare" as the sole valid standard.[112]

These considerations have three consequences that are of particular importance in understanding the way the EU competition law is designed or enforced, and in understanding in particular the enforcement of the provisions on state aids. The first element to bear in mind has to do with the concept of competition, which underlies the EU Treaty. Among other things, competition must be fair. As early as the 1960s, the Court of Justice stated that "the elimination of barriers" and "fair competition" were both necessary to bring about a single market.

---

[111] Frederic Yves Jenny, *Competition and State Aid Policy in the European Community*, 18 Fordham Int'l L.J. 525 (1994). © 1994 Frederic Yves Jenny. Reprinted by permission of the publisher.

[112] Helmut R.B. Schroter, *Antitrust Analysis Under Article 85(1) and Article 85(3)*, in 1987 Fordham Corp. L. Inst. 693, 702 (Barry E. Hawk ed., 1988).

As Schroter noted:

> According to the Commission, "the principle of fairness in the market" place not only requires that equality of opportunity must be preserved for all commercial operators in the Common Market. It also highlights the need to take into account the great variety of situations in which firms carry on business and to pay special regard to small and medium firms. Finally, it demands that competition policy take account of the legitimate interests of workers, users and consumers. In that sense the EC competition law not only protects the process of competition, but also the competitors.

The second element to bear in mind is that the primary goal of the EU competition policy is to unify the common market and to prevent private or public market intervention that is or could be incompatible with such a common market. For example, in the *Metro* case,[113] the Court of Justice emphasized that the objective of the Treaty regarding competition policy was to ensure "the creation of a single market achieving conditions similar to those of a domestic market." Schoter goes even further when he states that "in the EU competition policy in general and antitrust policy in particular is primarily 'integration policy' aimed at bringing about a maximum of economic interpenetration and thus merging the separate national markets into a single market of the Community."

This means that interventions in the market mechanism, whether private or public, that establish directly a separation between national markets, such as an export cartel or a price discrimination across national borders, are prohibited. This also means that interventions, which establish differences in the economic circumstances faced by potential competitors, are viewed with extreme suspicion to the extent that the competitors affected are located in different countries or that the intervention could apply to competitors located in different Member States because they could directly or indirectly limit the extent of economic inter-penetration between national markets. As Barry Hawk noted:[114]

> The EC market integration goal results in both stricter rules and a different method of substantive analysis than under US law. . . . [T]he market integration goal is not necessarily consistent with other competition policy objectives, notably promotion of efficiency. At the minimum there is tension (and possible trade-offs) between strict legal rules based on market integration goal and efficiencies, at least in the short term. In this case, the integration goal supersedes the efficiency goal as is suggested by the 1991 report of the Commission on

---

[113] *Metro-SB-Grossmarkte GmbH & Co. KG v Commission*, Case 26/76, [1977] E.C.R. 1875, [1978] 2 C.M.L.R. 1.

[114] Barry Hawk, *Un Tour d'Horizon du Droit et de la Politique de Concurrencem Semaine Juridique*, Oct. 15, 1992, at 1.

> competition policy, which states: [C]ompetition policy has been an important Community instrument used both to promote economic integration and to ensure an efficient allocation of resources. Effective competition is the main stimulus to innovation and higher productivity which underpins policies designed to increase economic growth and welfare. Not only does competition lead to higher output but it also enables consumers to obtain a fair share of this growth. Living standards therefore depend on the maintenance of effective competition. The third important feature of the EC competition law lies in the fact that if the goal of EC competition law is to facilitate the emergence of the common market, then the common market is not an end in itself. Rather, according to Article 2, the common market is a means to promote throughout the Community a harmonious and balanced development of economic activities, sustainable and non-inflationary growth respecting the environment, a high degree of convergence of economic performance, a high level of employment and of social protection, the raising of the standard of living and quality of life, and economic and social cohesion and solidarity among Member States. To achieve these broad goals, Article 3 of the Treaty states, among other things, that the activities of the Community shall include a common policy in the sphere of agriculture and fisheries, in the sphere of transport, in the sphere of the environment, in the strengthening of economic and social cohesion, in the strengthening of the competitiveness of Community industry, and in the promotion of research and technological development.

Two types of trade-offs may thus surface in the application of EU competition law. First, a trade-off between competition in the static sense and dynamic competition, and second, a trade-off between competition and some of the other objectives of the Treaty. Two principles laid out in the provisions of the Treaty related to competition among undertakings allow partial considerations of these trade-offs. First, there is an exemption mechanism that gives a certain amount of flexibility in the enforcement of competition law by allowing some anti-competitive practices that have redeeming values either from the point of view of competition in the long run or from the point of view of the other objectives of the Treaty. Second, such exemptions can only be granted in cases where competition is not eliminated for a substantial part of the products in question. There is no exemption in the case of Article 86, because, by definition, the anti-competitive abuse by a firm holding a dominant position within the common market restricts competition in a substantial part of the European market. However, practices of undertakings which fall under Article 85(1) may be exempted through Article 85(3) if they "contribute[ ] to improving the production or distribution of goods or to promoting technical or economic progress, while allowing consumers a fair share of the resulting benefit"; if they do not impose on the undertakings restrictions that are not indispensable; and if they do not "afford such undertakings the possibility of eliminating competition in respect of a substantial part of the products in question."

Typical examples of such exemptions would include specialization agreements, research cooperation, or joint ventures through which two or more undertakings combine their capacities and knowledge, when the aim of such arrangements is to improve the efficiency of the firms involved. Additionally, agreements that ensure the existence of a new product or service would be exempt. Discussing the question of the relationship between competition law and industrial policy in the European Community, Manfred Caspari concluded:

> [W]hile the competition rules laid down in the EEC Treaty are applied within the framework of an overall and active competition policy, considerations which in a broad sense may be described as industrial policy considerations enter into a number of decisions. The aim is to create efficient undertakings on markets that fulfill this function, undertakings which are willing and able to engage in fair and active competition.

While the three specific features of European competition law outlined above are well known and have been discussed frequently in the analysis of Article 85 and Article 86 decisions, they are also useful for understanding both the provisions of Article 92, which establish the substantive rules for aids granted by Member States, and the case law. In the Chapter devoted to Rules on Competition, the first paragraph of Section 3 of Article 92, entitled "Aids Granted by States," provides: Save as otherwise provided in this Treaty, any aid granted by a Member State or through State resources in any form whatsoever which distorts or threatens to distort competition by favoring certain undertakings or the production of certain goods shall, in so far as it affects trade between Member States, be incompatible with the common market.

The second and third paragraphs of Article 92 detail the exemptions to this rule. Some state aids, including those having a social character, those that compensate for damages caused by natural disasters, and those granted to the economy of certain areas of the Federal Republic of Germany, shall be compatible with the common market. Others may be considered compatible with the common market.

Of particular interest is paragraph 3 of Article 92, which states:

> The following may be considered to be compatible with the common market:
>
> (a) aid to promote the economic development of areas where the standard of living is abnormally low or where there is serious underemployment;
>
> (b) aid to promote the execution of an important project of common European interest or to remedy a serious disturbance in the economy of a Member State;
>
> (c) aid to facilitate the development of certain economic activities or of certain economic areas, where such aid does not adversely affect trading conditions to an extent contrary to the common interest . . . ;

(d) aid to promote culture and heritage conservation where such aid does not affect trading conditions and competition in the Community to an extent that is contrary to the common interest; [and]

(e) such other categories of aid as may be specified by decision of the Council acting by a qualified majority on a proposal from the Commission.

B. The Concept of Aid Within Article 92(1) of the EEC Treaty[115]

1. The Broad Concept of Aid

The first thing an investor must determine when considering a Member State's offer of aid is whether that offer constitutes "State aid" as defined by the EEC Treaty. Article 92(1) of the EEC Treaty defines State aid as "any aid granted by a Member State or through State resources in any form whatsoever." This broad definition encompasses a wide variety of possible aids. It is generally agreed that it includes all forms of positive benefits to a recipient, including actual cash subsidies, as well as any measure that relieves an undertaking of costs it would otherwise have to bear.

Where a company receives a benefit from the State, and the State receives no consideration in return, it is clear that a State aid has been granted. In addition, given that the concept of State aid has been interpreted broadly, a State aid exists when the value of the services or goods provided by the investor is less than the consideration given for them by the State, or, conversely, when the State demands less payment than the value of the goods or services that the State provides to a company. When considering sales agreements, particularly with regard to the sale of building sites by the State to an investor, State aid has been granted if the terms and conditions of the sale depart from normal commercial practice. Examples of State aids are non-repayable subsidies; loans from State-owned financial institutions at reduced rates; reductions in income or corporation tax; capital injection by a public authority; payment of below-market prices for energy; or the sale of real estate at a price below the market value.

Despite the broad concept of aid, not all State measures that benefit a company or groups of companies can be considered State aid within the meaning of Article 92(1). Rather, the purpose of the State measure must aim at conferring a financial advantage on the undertakings concerned, which would result in the State assuming an additional burden. Therefore, a State measure whose purpose is not to confer a cost advantage to certain undertakings, but merely has consequential financial effects, is not considered a State aid.[116]

---

[115] Dr. Hans-Jorg Niemeyer, *State Aids and European Community Law*, 15 Mich. J. Int'l L. 189 (1993). © 1993 University of Michigan Law School. Reprinted with permission.

[116] German law provides the possibility for German shipping lines to employ nationals of third countries under less advantageous working and social conditions than seamen protected by German labor law. Although this German legislation gives German employers a cost advantage which results in lower social security contributions and lower taxes for the State, these consequential financial effects are not a State aid within the meaning of Article 92(1).

2. The Market Economy Investor Principle

In recent years, it has become common for Member States to assist companies, especially those involved in public undertakings, through capital injections. In these cases, the Commission applies the so-called "market economy investor principle." In order to determine whether any aid is involved, the Commission examines whether a private investor, considering the expected return—but ignoring all social, regional, policy, and sectoral considerations—would have been willing to make those contributions in a similar situation. If a private investor would not have been able to expect an acceptable rate of profitability on the capital invested, the capital injection is considered an aid. The Court of Justice accepted this principle as an appropriate method for determining whether a capital injection is considered an aid.

3. Sources of Aid

To be considered State aid, the aid must be granted by a Member State or through State resources. The term "through State resources" includes not only public bodies, but also private companies that are under the control of the State and established or appointed to administer the aid.

Nevertheless, aid granted by a Member State, but financed from EU funds, falls outside the scope of article 92 since the aid must come from the financial resources of a Member State. It should be noted that in recent years, the Commission has become one of the largest financial backers in Europe. Almost 64 billion ECU are available in the budget of the EU for Community subsidies.

4. State Aid Favoring Certain Undertakings

Only those State aids that are granted to certain undertakings or to all undertakings within a particular industry fall within Article 92. Thus, public funds paid out to all undertakings in a Member State are not considered to be State aids. While this distinction is simple enough, the favoring of certain undertakings or sectors is not always obvious. For example, an Italian measure reduced the health insurance costs of all female workers. Upon closer examination, the Commission determined that this measure constituted State aid since it disproportionately benefited textile companies, which employed an above average number of women.

5. The Effect on Competition and on Trade Between Member States

Finally, for a State aid to fall within Article 92, it must distort or threaten to distort competition by favoring certain undertakings and must affect trade between Member States. In order to determine whether competition and trade between Member States is affected, the Commission has to examine the relevant market, the position of the recipient of the aid, the volume of inter-State trade, and the exports of the company concerned. The standard of evidence for distortion is low. The Court of Justice has adopted a broad approach in determining whether State aid distorts or threatens to distort competition. The Court argues that where competition between companies in various Member States exist, any financial aid is capable of distorting competition. The aid artificially strengthens the position of the recipient company, and this hinders the ability of other producers to increase their market shares and exports. This principle applies even if the recipient of the State aid is not engaged in exports. It is sufficient that the aid enables undertakings to maintain or increase their production, thereby reducing the opportunities of competitors from other Member States to export their goods into the recipient's country. Even a relatively small amount of State aid may affect trade between the Member States if there is vigorous competition in that sector, or if the profit margins are small, such as in the textile industry.

Additionally, unlike other competition cases, a *de minimis* threshold applies in State aid cases. Consequently, the relatively small size of the recipient of a State aid does not exclude *a priori* the effect on inter-State trade. As a consequence, the Commission does not have to provide evidence that trade between the Member States is actually affected. It is sufficient that the aid may affect inter-State trade. Nevertheless, it is also clear that not all aids have a perceptible impact on trade and competition between Member States. This is true especially of aid provided in very small amounts, mainly though not exclusively, to small and medium-sized companies, and often under schemes run by local or regional authorities. Based on past experience, the Commission has set a *de minimis* figure at payments of ECU 50,000 to one undertaking for a particular type of expenditure—such as investment or training—over a three-year period. This rule applies to all companies, notwithstanding their size. State aids below this *de minimis* figure do not fall under Article 92(1).

C. Exemptions

The main question in State aids decisions, therefore, is whether the aid qualifies for an exemption or, in other words, whether the State aid fulfills some other goal of the Treaty. There are two types of automatic exemptions: Article 92(2) exemptions and various types of discretionary, Article 92(3) exemptions. The two types of automatic exemptions are: first, State aids that have a social character, are granted to individual consumers, and are granted without discrimination regarding the origin of the product; and second, State aids that are due to exceptional circumstances requiring solidarity, i.e., aids to compensate for the damage caused by national disasters or exceptional occurrences.

Other aids may be exempted. Among these are aids to promote the economic development of severely depressed areas, i.e., areas where the standard of living is abnormally low or where there is serious unemployment. Also included are aids to promote the execution of important projects of common European interest.

Article 92(3)(a) is designed to exempt State aids that compensate for handicaps that would normally deter firms from investing in more backward regions, in which the per capita gross domestic product does not exceed seventy-five percent of the Community average in purchasing power parities. The granting of an exemption on the basis of Article 92(3)(a) is, however, subject to two conditions. First, the aid must concern one of the regions from a Commission list, which includes the whole of Greece, Ireland, Portugal, the Italian Mezzogiorno, Northern Ireland, various provinces of

Spain, and the overseas departments of France. Second, the aid must not lead to the creation of competition-distorting excess capacity in capital intensive industries.

State aids to other regions may be exempted, however, under the provisions of Article 92(3)(c). As far as Article 92(3)(b) is concerned, there are very few cases of "important project[s] of common European interest" justifying an exemption. Those projects are usually associated with programs such as ESPRIT,[117] RACE,[118] or BRITE[119] or with situations in which the Community is confronted by a general threat such as the destruction of the environment. The Commission stated in its 1991 annual report that Article 92(3)(b) could also apply to projects that were important both quantitatively and qualitatively, transnational, and related to the definition of international standards, thus allowing European industry to benefit from the full advantages of a single market. For example, the Commission considered that State aids granted by the governments of France, the Netherlands, and Italy designed to encourage research and development for the definition of a European standard for High Definition Television could be exempted. If the aid examined relates to an important project of common European interest, the Commission also verifies that it does not exceed what is tolerable from a competition policy point of view.

One reason for the Commission's narrow interpretation of Articles 92(3)(a) and 92(3)(b) is that the these provisions do not explicitly condition the granting of the exemption on whether the aid will not significantly affect intra-European trade. In the vast majority of cases, the discussion about the possibility of an exemption is based upon Article 92(3)(c), which concerns aids that "facilitate the development of certain economic activities or of certain economic areas, where such aid does not adversely affect trading conditions to an extent contrary to the common interest."

It is not easy to summarize the principles underlying the Commission's reasoning when it applies Article 92(3)(c). Concurrently, one must consider: the wording of Article 92(3)(c); general principles imbedded in other articles of the Treaty; a variety of specific rules established by the Commission in guidelines or frameworks on State aids that are either horizontal, such as the guidelines dealing with regional aids, aids for research and development, aids for the restructuring of firms, aids for small and medium-sized enterprises, and aids for the environment, or sectoral, such as aids for textile and clothing, synthetic fibers, motor vehicles, shipbuilding, coal and steel, agriculture, and food processing; and the case law.

The Commission has enjoyed considerable discretion in interpreting Article 92(3)(c). This situation, however, may change in the future.

A necessary, but not sufficient, condition for a State aid to be granted an exemption under Article 92(3)(c) is that it be in the common interest of the Community. This concept is not defined in Article 92. Furthermore, the goals of the Community listed in Article 2 of the Treaty are couched in terms so general that the Commission has a

---

117 ESPRIT is an acronym for European Strategy Program for Research in Information Technologies.

118 RACE is an acronym for Research and Development in Advanced Communication Technologies for Europe.

119 BRITE is an acronym for Basic Research in Industrial Technologies for Europe.

sufficient flexibility to decide what interferences in market mechanisms should be legitimized through State aids and to set Community industrial policy agenda.

Before analyzing the criteria used by the Commission to determine what is in the common interest, it should be stressed that the compatibility with the Treaty must be determined in the context of the Community as a whole and not in the context of a single Member State. This has several implications. The first one is to legitimize the fact that Member States are not competent to apply directly the provisions of the Treaty relating to State aids. Second, it means that Member States cannot justify the granting of State aids solely on the basis of the benefits they expect from such aids. For example, a State aid designed to foster economic development in a depressed region in one Member State may not be in the interest of the Community if the region cannot be considered to be economically depressed when compared to all regions in the Community. Thus, in its Tenth Report on Competition Policy, the Commission stated:

> State aids are in principle incompatible with the common market. The discretionary powers of the Commission should only be exercised when the aids proposed by Member States contribute to the achievement of the Community objectives and interest set out in Article 92(3). The national interest of a Member State or the benefits obtained by the recipient of the aid in contributing to the national interest do not by themselves justify the positive exercise of the Commission's discretionary powers. Third, it also means that the Commission has reservations about state aids granted to multinational firms. Indeed, because multinational firms often operate on a global level, state aids designed to help them restructure are not necessarily consistent with what would be in the interest of the Community.

At the most general level, one can say that the Commission views four types of aids favorably: aids for small and medium-sized enterprises, aids for regional development, aids for research and development, and aids for the environment.

Regarding aids for small and medium-sized enterprises, the Community Guidelines on State Aid for Small and Medium-Sized Enterprises states that: "there can be no doubt that state aids for [small and medium-sized enterprises] 'facilitate the development of certain economic activities or of certain economic areas.'" At the same time, the Commission considers that aids to small and medium-sized enterprises are less disruptive of competition than aids to larger firms.

State aids for research and development may also be viewed positively to the extent that they relate to the aim stated in Article 130f(1) of the Treaty, which strengthens "the scientific and technological bases of Community industry and [which encourages] it to become more competitive at the international level." As the guidelines on research and development make clear, the Commission views favorably State aids for basic industrial research, but limits the State aid to fifty percent of the gross cost of the project or program. The Commission feels, however, that if the research and development is more thoroughly applied so that its output more easily and rapidly influences a product market, then there is a greater risk that the State aid will distort competition. Therefore, the ceiling on the admissible State aid decreases as the research is increasingly applied. The Commission also considers that simple improvement of existing facilities does not qualify for an exemption under Article 92(3)(c). To qualify for an exemption under Article 92(3)(c), the investment benefiting from the State aid must lead to the development of new products or the adoption of new processes. State aids for regional development, when applied to regions that suffer from serious socio-economic disparities with the rest of the Community, are viewed favorably and monitored by the Commission to achieve the goals of promoting a "harmonious and balanced development of economic activities" and "convergence of economic performance" as set out in Article 2 of the Treaty. Thus, for example, State aids to investments in central, industrialized regions, cannot exceed 20% of the total investment, whereas in peripheral, lowly industrialized regions, they can represent a larger proportion of the investment.

Finally, environmental aids, which also relate to the goal of achieving "growth respecting the environment," set out in Article 2 of the Treaty, are viewed favorably if they are necessary to help undertakings adapt to laws or regulations, which impose major new burdens relating to environmental protection. In this instance, an undertaking can get an Article 92(3)(b) exemption. If the aid is intended to promote additional efforts going beyond national standards, then the undertaking may qualify for an Article 92(3)(c) exemption.

In sectors facing serious economic difficulties due to international competition, such as motor vehicles, textiles, shipbuilding, coal and steel, and where Member States may have a natural and growing inclination to grant State aids, the Commission has been concerned with limiting such aids. The aid is limited to projects that improve the efficiency of the industry, allow the conversion of firms to activities outside the industry, or allow existing firms to diversify their production towards products that will place them in a better position on the international markets. Such aids are allowed, however, only to the extent that they will not worsen the difficulties of similar industries in other European countries.

In other sectors, State aids may be allowed if they appear necessary to the development or maintenance of existing strategic industries. Thus, for example, the Commission allowed a State aid by the United Kingdom for the restructuring of the last tin mine in Europe. It also allowed a State aid by the United Kingdom for the purchase of industrial equipment for off-shore exploration when this sector was in an early stage of development in Europe. In 1979, however, the Commission withheld approval of the State aid because by then the sector had developed, and the promotion of this sector no longer had strategic importance. Similarly, the Commission may allow State aids to shipyards for the construction of ships so that they can successfully compete against non-European shipyards. However, in such cases the State aid must not exceed the amount necessary to prevent the order from going to a non-European shipyard.

To qualify for the exemptions of Article 92(3)(c), aids that fit the abovementioned general criteria must also meet at least six conditions: they must be transparent; they must be justified by a market failure or an externality; they must not provide continuous artificial support to non-viable undertakings; they must not create over-capacities; they must be proportionate to the goal they seek to achieve; and the restrictions to competition and trade that they entail must not outweigh the expected benefits at the Community level. The transparency requirement is the easiest to understand. To grant an exemption, the Commission must be in a position to know precisely, both quantitatively and qualitatively, what the aid is all about. In particular, the Commission needs to know who the beneficiaries are, what the mechanism of the aid is, what the goal of the aid is, and what the importance of the aid is, both in absolute terms and in proportion to the total investment.

The second condition is more substantive. Exemptions may be invoked only when the Commission is satisfied that without the aid, market forces alone would be insufficient to guide the recipients towards the behavior that the State aid is supposed to encourage and that must be consistent with the other conditions. Thus, on the one hand, the Commission may grant an Article 92(3)(c) exemption for regional aids in certain lagging areas, such as those in which the GDP per inhabitant is in the long run at least fifteen percent lower than the national average, or where the unemployment rate is at least ten percent greater than the national unemployment rate. The Commission must be convinced that without such aids, these areas would not be able to attract sufficient private investment to reduce their deficit. Alternatively, the Commission will refuse to grant an exemption for a State aid to a firm if it is convinced that the proposed investment would be profitable without the aid. The Commission will deny the exemption even if the investment can be considered to have a Community interest, i.e., if it contributes to the development of the firm's region or sector.

State aids designed simply to facilitate the modernization of existing capacities of an unprofitable firm in a sector characterized by existing or potential excess capacity will not be granted an exemption on the basis of Article 92(3)(c) for various reasons. First, the modernization of a firm is, in itself, considered by the Commission to be part of what profit maximizing private investors would normally do, and therefore unrelated to a market failure or an externality. Second, the expansion of capacities or the modernization of a firm in a structurally depressed sector is not likely to alleviate the disequilibrium between supply and demand at the Community level, as would a decrease in capacity or a restructuring of the firm allowing it to redirect some or all of its resources to another sector or to a different market. The profitability of the beneficiary would likely improve from such aids. The burden between supply and demand associated with the structural disequilibrium at the Community level, however, would shift to competing firms of other Member States. Thus, allowing a Member State to grant such aids would eventually give an incentive to other Member States to retaliate by granting aids for the modernization of their firms. Consequently, this succession of aid would not restore the profitability of the sector. The third condition is that State aids must not provide artificial support to unprofitable undertakings. The Commission has repeatedly stated that State aids should not be used to prevent the disappearance of non-viable firms. For example, the Commission, in its decision concerning financing for Sitas,[120] stated:

[120] Commission Decision No. 94/374/EC, O.J. L 170/36, 38 - 39 (1994) [hereinafter *Sitas*].

> With regard to the exceptions provided for in Article 92(3)(c) in respect of aid to facilitate the development of certain economic activities where such aid does not adversely affect trading conditions to an extent contrary to the common interest, the aid is not tied to any restructuring plan ensuring restoration of the firm's viability. It is therefore an operating aid which preserves the status quo by preventing normal market forces from taking effect. The aid cannot, therefore, be considered compatible with the common market.

Fourth, the Commission considers that State aids in sectors characterized by existing or potential excess capacities can be tolerated if, and only if, they contribute to a restructuring of the beneficiaries and a decrease of existing capacities, over and beyond the reductions that would be spontaneously forced on the beneficiaries by the normal working of the market. It must be clear that the restructuring will enable the firm to become profitable without further injection of State aid.

This principle is embedded in various sectoral guidelines or codes. For example, investment aids in the steel sector, characterized by severe excess capacity, cannot, in general, qualify for an exemption under Article 92(3)(c). There is a temporary exemption for Greece, Portugal, and the German landers located in the former German Democratic Republic. To qualify for this exemption, capacity reductions must accompany the aids. Similarly, in the synthetic fiber industry, aids for investments relating to the production and texturization of polyester, polyamide, acrylic, and polypropylene fibers can qualify for an exemption only if they are combined with a capacity reduction of the beneficiary. In the automobile sector State aids for unprofitable manufacturers of passenger vehicles must, among other requirements, include a restructuring plan and a reduction in capacity for the beneficiary. Beyond the requirements set in certain sectoral regulations on State aids, other regulations on aids, for rescue aids, or for environmental investments, specify that such aids must be accompanied by reductions of capacity of the beneficiary.

The general concern of the Commission with overcapacity raises several questions. If interpreted strictly, it implies that a new entrant in the sectors or in the markets considered to be having overcapacity cannot benefit from a State aid, because by definition it cannot reduce its existing capacity, whereas established firms could benefit from such an aid in certain circumstances, i.e., if they met the other conditions set by the Commission.

The concept of overcapacity, as used by the Commission, is not always economically relevant. Capacity utilization is calculated by the ratio of actual sales by the European manufacturers to their total capacity. Overcapacity is calculated by the ratio of total European demand for a product at a competitive price, whether this demand was met by domestic producers or importers, to total capacity by European manufacturers. Except under strong assumptions, for example, no imports and perfect competition among the European manufacturers, these two ratios are unrelated. Indeed the value of capacity utilization ratios, as opposed to excess capacity ratios, is heavily dependent on the market strategy of the manufacturers.

Reliance on the rate of capacity utilization, to assess the propriety of a State aid, can be extremely misleading from the point of view of what an outside observer could consider to be sound economic reasoning. If total capacity is equal to total demand, in which case there is no excess capacity, but forty percent of the demand is satisfied by more efficient non-European importers, who have developed a new technology not present in Europe, then capacity utilization in the industry will be only sixty percent. It is likely that price competition from the efficient non-European competitors will force the market price below the cost of the non-efficient domestic producers, so that they will incur losses. The requirement that a State aid for an investment, such as one designed to introduce a technological innovation in the production process, to improve the efficiency of the sector, be accompanied by a reduction in the production capacity of the beneficiary clearly favors the importers because it reduces the scope of competition from the new efficient European manufacturer.

Even in cases where there are no significant non-European imports, the concern of the Commission with excess capacity can lead to questionable results from the point of view of competition. If, for example, the excess capacity, as measured by the Commission, is due to weak competition, the requirement that the State aid, designed to encourage the introduction of a technological innovation, be accompanied by a reduction in the capacity of the beneficiary may unnecessarily slow down the adjustment of the sector and stifle competition.

In the decisions of the Commission on State aids, competition in the relevant sector is always, implicitly, assumed to be working satisfactorily, or to be excessive, even though there is practically no analysis of the actual intensity of competition. Therefore, the creation of excess capacity through State aids to investments is never considered by the Commission to enhance competition; it is only considered to distort fair competition. However, there is a growing body of economic literature on the impact of excess capacity and the distribution of such excess capacity among firms, as well as competition in oligopolies. This literature suggests, among other things, that an asymmetrical distribution of excess capacity may, in certain cases, enhance competition. Thus, it is possible that some State aids to investment may have the dual effect of distorting fair competition and contributing to the creation of excess capacity, thereby increasing competition in the marketplace.

The final condition set by the Commission for granting an exemption to a State aid is that it must be proportionate to the problem that it is designed to resolve. This will keep distortion to competition at a minimum and will not affect trading to an extent contrary to the common market. Whenever the Commission considers State aid for which one of the sectoral or horizontal Codes applies, it verifies that the aid falls within the limit set in the relevant Code. For example, in the case of State aids for research and development, State aids cannot cover more than fifty percent of the gross cost of a project for basic industrial research or twenty-five percent of the cost of a project for applied research and development. Similarly, to benefit from an exemption under Article 92(3)(c), regional aids designed to facilitate the development of certain economic areas cannot amount to more than thirty percent of the investment. Under the Code for State aids to shipbuilding, operating aids for the production of large vessels must be below nine percent of the cost of the vessel, whereas for vessels costing less than ten million ECU, the maximum level of state aid is 4.5%. The maximum levels of state aids for small and medium-sized firms are usually larger than the maximum for larger firms.

In order to benefit from the exemption of Article 92(3)(c), however, the State aid must also be strictly necessary to correct the problem that justifies the exemption. An example is the Commission's decision concerning aid to be provided by the Irish government for the restructuring of the Aer Lingus group, which was facing a serious financial crisis.[121] The Commission first stated that "the genuine restructuring of Aer Lingus contributes to the development of the air transport sector from a Community standpoint." It then asked itself whether the amount of the aid was "adequate and proportionate to the aim of financing the transition and restore the airline's commercial viability." In assessing that the aid was indeed adequate and proportionate, the Commission took into account the fact that "the equity injected into Aer Lingus will not [lead] to an overcapitalization of the airline but will simply bring its financial ratios into more prudent limits, and, therefore, restore the financial balance." "The strategy pursued by Aer Lingus in its restructuring plan is not over-expansionist" because it will not expand its operating fleet or change the general pattern of its operations, and consequently, does not aim at increasing its market share.

Finally, the State aid must not adversely "affect trading conditions to an extent contrary to the common interest." The Commission does not always make its reasoning explicit, but rather uses its discretionary power to decide whether or not this condition is met or to impose constraints on the granting of the aid so that the condition is met. To establish the extent to which the State aid will affect trading conditions, the Commission takes into consideration a variety of factors, such as whether: the amount of the aid is small when compared to the size of the investment, the market shares of the firms involved are minimal or will decrease, the market is rapidly expanding, there is little intra-Community trade for the product involved, or that the investment will be devoted to the production of goods that will be sold outside the Community.

In its decision on the aid granted by the United Kingdom to SCA Aylesford, a manufacturer of newsprint, the Commission concluded that the investment aid did not adversely affect "trading conditions . . . to an extent contrary to the common interest." The Commission considered that the investment aid would result in an increase in the capacity of production of the firm and that part of the increased production, 100,000 tons or about a third of the increase in capacity, would be sold in other Member States. Nonetheless, the Commission determined that the aid was limited and that although the United Kingdom imported seventy-five percent of its consumption of newsprint, ninety percent of these imports came from non-Community countries. The Commission decisions, however, do not provide clear criteria to assess the extent beyond which the effect of trading conditions due to the State aid will be held to be contrary to the common interest.

[121] *Aer Lingus*, O. J. L54/30 (1994).

D. Should State Aid Control Be Entrusted to an Independent European Competition Office?[122]

The recent controversies about spectacular State aid decisions have produced one new idea. State aid control should be entrusted to an independent European Competition Office. The source of inspiration is obvious. It is the traditional German request to establish an independent European Cartel Office to decide on antitrust matters. The model for such a European Cartel Office is the highly successful and respected Bundeskartellamt in Berlin.

The proposal to entrust State aid control to an independent European Competition Office, though at first sight similar, is of a totally different nature. It is also totally unrealistic, and thus not worth serious consideration.

What are the reasons for this negative assessment? Antitrust rules are addressed to enterprises. Since the Second World War they have spread to many parts of the world. Since the end of the Cold War, they have expanded with extraordinary speed in Central and Eastern Europe, Asia, and Latin America. Their implementation is, almost without exception, entrusted to administrative agencies more or less independent of governments or courts. The EU is one of the few exceptions, which might disappear over time.

As we have seen in the beginning, the situation of State aid control is totally different. State aid rules are not addressed to enterprises, but to States. They limit the freedom of governments, even of parliaments, to grant financial advantages to certain sectors of their economy, irrespective of the technique that may be used, including tax and social security rebates. State aid control is therefore a serious and highly sensitive interference with national sovereignty. It is, as we have explained, unique to the EU.

It is not realistic to assume that this control will be entrusted to a non-political expert panel, such as a Cartel or Competition Office. Because of its very nature, it will remain the responsibility of an essentially political body, such as the Commission.

E. Shrinking Margins of Political Discretion

This statement implies that State aid control requires a wider margin of political discretion than decisions in antitrust matters. It should be noted, however, that this margin is not without limits, as it is exercised under the vigilant eyes of the judges in Luxembourg. Even more important is the fact that the originally wide margin of discretion is constantly shrinking. Two factors work to limit discretion. The first factor is the Commission's own decision making, whether in the form of general statements, such as guidelines, frameworks, notices, etc., or of individual decisions. The second is the jurisprudence of the European Courts. Since 1993, the Court of First Instance has jurisdiction over many State aid cases, and will examine even more thor-

[122] Claus-Dieter Ehlermann, *State Aid Control in the European Union: Success or Failure?*, 18 Fordham Int'l L.J. 1212 (1995).

oughly than the Court of Justice the underlying facts and their economic appreciation by the Commission. It has already been mentioned that applications against State aid decisions are rapidly increasing in number and in sophistication. Judicial review is one of the fastest-growing sectors, if not the fastest-growing, of the Courts' activities in Luxembourg.

F. Increasing Transparency

As in the case of the European Cartel Office, the plea for an independent State Aid Control Agency is motivated at least in part by a perceived lack of transparency. The situation in the Union, however, is more transparent than in any other part of the world, as it is the only place in which all State aid projects are subject to a procedure of prior and systematic scrutiny. In addition, transparency within the EU will increase further over the coming years. The reasons are both political and legal. There is growing demand by Member States for information and explanation of the Commission's decision making practice with respect to State aids granted by other Member States; this demand is reinforced by the overall debate on transparency following the Maastricht Treaty negotiations. Another political factor is the Commission's determination to pursue its policy of issuing more guidelines, frameworks, notices, etc. These documents explain in advance how the Commission will react to certain categories of State aid projects such as regional aid, aid in favor of research and development, the protection of the environment, small and medium sized enterprises, employment, etc.

Legal requirements for increased transparency will be generated by the Courts in Luxembourg, in particular by the Court of First Instance. Observers of the Courts will confirm that the recent jurisprudence shows a tendency to align the procedural rights of private parties in the State aid sector on those which they enjoy in antitrust matters. This tendency is the procedural expression of a fundamental shift that has occurred almost imperceptibly over the last years. Aid granted by a Member State is no longer controlled exclusively or principally in the interest of other Member States, but also, and perhaps even more so, in the interest of the competitors of the intended beneficiaries of the aid. The original macroeconomic approach of the authors of the EEC Treaty is being supplanted progressively by a microeconomic perspective, similar to that which has always dominated substantive and procedural antitrust law.

G. The EU's Interest in Exporting State Aid Control

Because of the high degree of transparency of State aid control in the EU, which will continue to increase in the future, the EU has every interest in advancing the scrutiny of subsidies at the international level. This is true of both substance and procedure, i.e. monitoring. If such rules do not exist or if they are not effectively implemented, non-member countries will benefit gratuitously from the EU's internal control mechanism. Such a situation is clearly not desirable. It might in the end even jeopardize the correct functioning of the EU's own State aid control. Contrary to commonly held views about the risks of subjecting oneself to international rules, the EU has nothing to lose and can only win in exporting its own State aid discipline to other parts of the world.

The EU has successfully done so, through the agreement on the European Economic Area ("EEA"), the so-called Europe Agreements with Central and Eastern European Countries ("CEECs"), and the new Subsidy Code agreed during the Uruguay Round and the most recent Organisation for Economic Co-operation and Development ("OECD") Shipbuilding Agreement.

The most ambitious exercise has been the establishment of the EEA through which all the EU's State aid rules and procedures have been exported en bloc to those EFTA countries which have joined the EEA. Identical EEA State aid control rules are implemented by the EFTA Surveillance Authority ("ESA"), the so-called Second Pillar. At the beginning of this year, ESA had a stock of some 400 State aid cases, most of which were transferred to the Commission when Austria, Finland, and Sweden joined the EU and when simultaneously the non-EU part of the EEA and ESA's central shrunk to Norway, Iceland, and Liechtenstein.

A hardly less ambitious operation has been adopted in the Europe Agreements. The CEECs will respect substantive State aid rules that correspond in principle to those applicable within the EU in similar situations. They will not, however, set up among themselves a plurinational control mechanism like ESA. They will have to ensure the respect of their international obligations towards the EU through strictly national control mechanisms. Whether such a mechanism can be implemented effectively remains to be seen. In the light of the EU's own internal experience, its seems almost impossible. The CEECs, however, have one powerful incentive to succeed. In implementing correctly the State aid disciplines of the Europe Agreements, they can avoid protective measures that the EU might otherwise apply to their exports to the EU. The Europe Agreements place thus a high premium on self-discipline.

In the new multilateral agreement on subsidies and countervailing measures negotiated during the Uruguay Round and to be monitored by the World Trade Organisation, the EU definition of subsidy was adopted. European Union State aid rules and procedures have largely gained admittance with respect to both actionable and non-actionable subsidies, in particular those regarding regional aid.

The recent agreement negotiated in the framework of the OECD on normal competitive conditions in the commercial shipbuilding and repair industry is another example of the convergence of internal State aid policy with external trade policy. Lack of an effective commercial defense instrument against unfair competition on the world market in that sector has obliged the EU for several decades to pursue a very costly sectoral State aid policy, allowing production aid for shipbuilding. By sacrificing this policy, which in any case ran contrary to its general aversion to sectoral aid, the EU obtained, inter alia, the institution in the same agreement of a code protecting it against injurious pricing by shipbuilders in the signatory countries.

H. Strengthening DG IV's Overall Responsibility for State Aid Control

While there is no realistic prospect of entrusting State aid control in the EU to an independent European Competition Office, strong arguments plead in favor of a reorganization of responsibilities within the Commission. Contrary to antitrust matters, which are all attributed to the Directorate General for Competition ("DG IV"), State aid control is traditionally divided among of series of Commission departments. State aids fall within the responsibility of DG IV, with the exception of agricultural aids examined by the Directorate General for Agriculture ("DG VI"), transport aids by the Directorate General for Transport ("DG VII"), fisheries aids by the Directorate General for Fisheries ("DG XIV"), and coal aids by the Directorate General for Energy ("DG XVII"). The explanation for this division of tasks is probably more historical than logical.

An argument may be made for combining State aid monitoring with the overall responsibilities for a given common policy, like agriculture, fisheries, and transport. This argument, however, is only convincing with respect to State aid disciplines that are sector-specific and therefore intimately linked to the particularities of a common policy. It does not carry weight if and in so far as horizontal rules are to be applied, such as aid in favor of disadvantaged regions, research and development, the environment, small and medium-sized enterprises and, most of all, rescue and restructuring aid. In particular, rescue and restructuring operations should in the future be attributed exclusively to DG IV, rather than divided among Commission departments.

Concentration in DG IV would guarantee coherence and consistency. It would also diminish the influence of sectoral considerations. It would strengthen DG IV's position among Commission departments, a consideration that is worth bearing in mind if one thinks of the medium-term perspective of its weakening through the establishment of an independent European Cartel Office for antitrust matters.

IV. Rescue and Restructuring Aids

The recent upsurge of critical comments are not directed against the day-to-day monitoring of State aids by the Commission. The criticism focuses almost exclusively on a few spectacular decisions approving large sums of money injected into certain steel companies, airlines, and the French group Bull. While attitudes of governments are relatively moderate, protests from competitors, particularly from the private sectors, are aggressive. Competitors criticize vociferously the levels of aid, the conditions attached and the recidivist character of some of the restructuring operations.

A. The Traditional Conditions for Restructuring Aids

The Commission's traditional practice with respect to rescue and restructuring aid is many years old, even if it has only recently been clarified in guidelines. In July 1994, the Commission adopted general guidelines for rescuing and restructuring firms in difficulty. In November 1994, it supplemented these guidelines with a communication that applies them specifically to the aviation sector.

Rescue aids are allowed as a short-term, transitional device preceding a restructuring operation. They do not merit closer examination in the context of this Article.

Restructuring aid is subject to a series of conditions which have been expressly approved in principle in a recent decision of the Court of Justice. The most important of these conditions are:

> 1) A restructuring plan which restores the long term viability of the enterprise within a reasonable time scale and on the basis of realistic assumptions as to its future operating conditions.
>
> 2) Aid should not be higher than strictly necessary to enable restructuring. Aid beneficiaries will be expected to make a significant contribution to the restructuring plan. Aid should not provide the enterprise with cash which can be used for aggressive market distorting activities. Aid should not go to finance new investment (like acquisitions) not required to the restructuring. Aid for financial restructuring should not unduly reduce the enterprise's financial charges.
>
> 3) In case of a structural excess of production capacity in a relevant market in the European Community served by the recipient, the restructuring plan must make a contribution, proportionate to the amount of aid received, to the restructuring of the industry . . . by irreversibly reducing or closing capacity.

A similar counterpart will normally not be required if there is no structural excess capacity. The aid will be conditioned only by the obligation not to expand capacity during the implementation of the restructuring plan, except where essential for restoring viability. Capacity reductions in case of structural excess of production capacity will be less important if the restructured enterprise is situated in assisted regions or is a SME.

While the first and second conditions are obvious, the third is not. It has given rise to acrimonious debates among governments and industrialists in the different restructuring rounds, for steel and shipbuilding. Though already accepted in principle by the Court of Justice in earlier judgments and in particular in a recent decision, the amount of capacity reduction will certainly be one of the most vigorously argued issues before the Judges in Luxembourg. The reason is simple. The discussion about the so-called counterpart goes to the very essence, the *raison d'etre*, of State aid control in the EU. Does State aid control protect only or mainly the interests of Member States? Or does it protect also and perhaps even primarily the interest of competitors? Over the years, the emphasis has changed. Originally concerned almost exclusively with Member States, today State aid control is more and more understood as protecting competitors against distortions of competition. It is obvious that the counterpart of a restructuring aid grows in significance and in importance if it is seen as a contribution not only to the improvement of the overall structure of the market, but also to the acceptability of the grant to the competitors. In this perspective, a counterpart is not only required in case of a "structural excess of production capacity in a relevant market in the European Community," but also in the absence of such a situation. There remains of course the question what the counterpart should be in such a case.

The answer should be a reduction of market share. A cut in production capacity might not necessarily be the most appropriate means to achieve this end.

B. Privatization as a Condition?

It is remarkable that the Commission's July 1994 guidelines do not mention one condition that has become very important in the most recent restructuring operations, i.e., privatization. Privatization as a condition for the approval of restructuring aid is obviously a delicate issue. The Commission can take note of the commitment of a Member State to privatize the enterprise to be restructured. Through the viability condition, such a commitment can even become a binding element of the Commission's decision.

Can the Commission require privatization without a prior undertaking by the Member State? At first sight, the principle of neutrality seems to oppose this idea. The viability criterion, however, may again justify it.

Whatever one may think of the reality of the neutrality principle, special circumstances will be necessary to insist on such a condition. The most obvious candidates for privatization requests are recidivists, i.e. public enterprises that have already benefitted from restructuring aid, but that have to be supported again by further grants of State aid. In such a case, the Member State concerned has demonstrated that it is not able to assure viability without the strong presence of a private partner.

It is obvious that privatization can diminish the amount of aid necessary for restructuring. A lower level of aid leads logically to a smaller counterpart, like a smaller reduction of capacity. Such a smaller reduction of capacity can be vital for the survival of the enterprise to be restructured, if bigger cuts would jeopardize its future viability. This is another possible contribution of privatization to the success of rescue and restructuring operations.

C. The "One Time, Last Time" Principle

Another condition which has attracted considerable attention during the last months is only mentioned *en passant* in the July 1994 general guidelines: "Like rescue aid, aid for restructuring should normally only need to be granted once." It is, however, discussed in detail in the November 1994 communication on state aids in the aviation sector. After referring to the Wise Men's (Comite des Sages) Report of February 1994 which had recommended a clear and genuine "one time, last time" condition, the Commission declared:

> Some ideas of the Comite, however, cannot be accepted by the Commission. It is not possible for the Commission to change or disregard the EU Treaty. This means, in particular, that the condition that the aid is the last one has, of course, to be interpreted in conformity

> with Community law. This implies that such a condition does not prevent a Member State from notifying a further aid to a company which has already been granted aid. According to the Court of Justice case law, in such a case the Commission will take all the relevant elements into account. An important element in the Commission's assessment will be the fact that the company has already been granted State aid.
>
> Therefore, the Commission will not allow further aid unless under exceptional circumstances unforeseeable and external to the company.

The practical importance of this statement is obvious. It has been demonstrated by the prospect of a new rescue and restructuring operation for the Spanish airline Iberia and by the public controversies between the Commissioner for Transport in 1993-94, Marcelino Oreja, and the Commissioner for Competition, Karel Van Miert.

It is not our intention to analyze the precise meaning and the legal merit of the different elements of the Commission's statement. Only one aspect should be highlighted in the context of this Article. The "one time, last time" principle is relatively new. It has found its most solid expression in the December 1993 conclusions of the Council giving its assent to the recent restructuring aids in the steel industry. At the request of the Council, all Commission decisions authorizing restructuring aid to certain steel companies are subject to the condition that the Member State concerned "shall not request any further derogation under Article 95 . . . should a return to viability not be achieved by [the end of the restructuring period]." The principle is also to be found by the new multilateral agreement on subsidies and countervailing measures negotiated during the Uruguay Round. Article 5 of the agreement enjoins members not to cause "serious prejudice to the interests of another member." Article 6 specifies that serious prejudice shall be deemed to exist in the case of subsidies to cover operating losses sustained by an enterprise "other than one-time measures which are non-recurrent and cannot be repeated for that enterprise."

Compared with these texts, the Commission's statement in the November Communication on State aids in the aviation sector seems weaker, as it opens the door for second-time aid in case of exceptional circumstances unforeseeable and external to the company. Much depends, however, on the interpretation and practical implementation of this proviso. It would express a common sense principle if it were applied only to real *cas de force majeure* situations, like the Gulf War. It would, however, go much further if the deterioration of the value of a currency were qualified as unforeseeable. Currency fluctuations are normal and have to be taken into account by economic operators. The Commission should allow only real *cas de force majeure* exceptions. If it acted otherwise, it would de facto destroy the "one time, last time" principle in the aviation sector.

D. Must There Always Be a "One Time"?

The "one time, last time" principle leads to a more fundamental consideration. Why should there be a "one time"? Could the Commission simply refuse the authorization of restructuring aid, even if all normal conditions for such an authorization, namely restructuring plan leading to viability, counterpart, aid limited to the strict minimum needed for restructuring, etc., are met?

In order to be perfectly clear, it must be emphasized that the question does not address the situation in which an enterprise cannot be made viable (taking into account the counterpart that is required to compensate the amount of aid necessary for restructuring). In such a situation, the Commission will not authorize the aid.

Our question is based on another hypothesis. The ailing enterprise can be made viable; the necessary counterpart can be provided. Might the Commission nevertheless say no?

From a strictly legal point of view, the answer is affirmative. The Commission is entitled to refuse the authorization. Article 92 does not declare that restructuring aids "shall be compatible with the common market." Restructuring aids have to be justified under Article 92(3) according to which certain aids "may be considered to be compatible with the common market." The vast majority of these aids can only be approved under Article 92(3)(c), which provides for authorization of "aid to facilitate the development of certain economic activities . . . where such aid does not adversely affect trading conditions to an extent contrary to the common interest." The Commission could declare that restructuring aid in a certain sector does affect trading conditions to an extent contrary to the common interest, in view of the particular economic situation in the sector.

It is remarkable that the Commission has never done so. The explanation is clearly political. The declaration that restructuring aids in a certain sector are per se against the common interest would clearly mean an industrial policy for that sector. The Commission is, however, opposed to sectoral industrial policy. It is committed to establishing horizontal rules in order to promote the competitiveness of European industry. The existing practice with respect to restructuring aids is part of that horizontal framework. It is therefore useful to maintain it.

But does this reasoning also apply to those sectors in which the EU has adopted sectoral policies and in which even the Council has been active as a legislator? If the existing State aid discipline for Steel (the so-called Steel Aid Code) does not allow a certain type of restructuring operation, why has the Commission asked the Council for its assent, under Article 95 of the ECSC Treaty, to derogate from the Code and to authorize these operations nevertheless? Again, the explanation is not legal, but political. Every Member State has the right to notify aid, even incompatible with the Code, and ask for a derogation. The Commission, however, has no legal obligation to follow this request. It has done so in part because of its general attitude to restructuring aid under the EU Treaty. It could, however, perfectly well change its mind in view of the particularities of the steel sector and the ECSC Treaty, in particular its fundamental prohibition of State aids in Article 4c. To do so, the Commission would need to avoid the argument that, having asked for derogations for a certain number of enterprises, it would discriminate against the remaining companies which are in difficulties but have not yet had a chance to benefit from a restructuring operation. The new policy would therefore have to be announced sufficiently in advance, allowing for a transitional period during which restructuring operations eligible for a derogation under the existing practice would still be entitled to a derogation from the steel aid code.

V. Fiscal Policy

A. Introduction[123]

Many American—and some European—observers of the changing fortunes of the efforts to achieve an advanced degree of integration in the European Community (EC) are puzzled by the ambition to create an Economic and Monetary Union (EMU) in the EC, extending all the way to the introduction of a common currency and a European Central Bank (ECB) to run a joint monetary policy. Some focus on what they regard as questionable economic benefits of such a move, while others, e.g., Feldstein (1992), suggest that EMU can only be justified in political terms. But, in the latter case, the strategy is seen as very risky because monetary unification would then run well ahead of political union, reversing the order of integration in existing large federal states. Recently this type of criticism has become more widespread in Europe as well. The Maastricht Treaty, signed in February 1992, with EMU as its central and most elaborately stated objective, ran into major difficulties at the ratification stage. Danish voters narrowly rejected the Treaty in a referendum in June 1992, though this result was reversed in a second referendum in May 1993. French voters only passed the Treaty very narrowly in September 1992, while ratification in the United Kingdom nearly brought down the government before it was finally completed in late July 1993. Germany, the largest EU country and traditionally a motor of integration, had visible misgivings about Maastricht, including the requirement to give up the deutsche mark (DM), a source and a symptom of Germany's strength. Though voter misgivings about Maastricht were probably motivated more by other aspects of the Treaty than by EMU and the common currency, many Europeans clearly had grave doubts about the feasibility of achieving the objectives in this area within the tight time schedule foreseen in the Treaty.

The political uncertainty spilled over into the financial markets. The European Monetary System (EMS), which had been seen as an essential stepping stone to EMU, was affected by unprecedented capital flows in September 1992, causing the exit of two major currencies, the lira and sterling. Turbulence continued throughout the winter of 1992/93 with the devaluation of three of the remaining EMS currencies and attacks on several others for which no misalignment had been identified. The Spanish and Portuguese currencies were devalued again in May. Finally, tensions reemerged in July, and interventions once more took on unsustainable proportions. The Council of Finance Ministers in early August widened the EMS margins drastically—from ±2 1/4% to 15%—while maintaining the central rates. This move was designed to make life more difficult for speculators by greatly increasing foreign exchange risk and to give countries more scope for conducting differentiated interest rate policies than in the old EMS. Member States have so far used the additional freedom with caution.

[123] Niels Thygesen, *Why is Economic and Monetary Union An Important Objective For Europe?*, 14 Int'l Rev. L. & Econ. 133 (1994). © 1994 Niels Thygesen. Reprinted by permission.

To some the two interacting destabilizing processes—the difficulties of ratifying Maastricht and the currency turmoil leading to a major relaxation of the EMS—have put off the realization of the objective of EMU and a single currency into a more distant future.[124] Yet it is broadly recognized that it was the very possibility that central rates could still be realigned that spelled the political dissolution of the EMS. Credible EMU with a single currency would have proved more robust in handling the kind of temporary divergence in economic performance and in nonmonetary policies with which the EU has been confronted since the German unification in 1990.

B. Costs and Benefits of a Common Currency

It had not been a central element in the earlier effort to build EMU; in the Werner Report (1970) the single currency was mentioned more as an afterthought. It is clear, for example, in a major EU Commission study on "One Market One Money" in 1990, that there was a perception of the balance of the benefits and costs of a common currency having shifted decisively in favor of the former. This is in sharp contrast to the earlier economics literature of the 1960s and 1970s on so-called optimum currency areas, which is largely agnostic in its analysis of the various criteria that may be applied in deciding upon the size of a monetary union. [There is a] tendency for the benefits of joining a common currency area to rise with the degree of openness of an economy (measured by the share of foreign trade in GDP), while the costs of giving up one's own national currency in favor of a common currency tend to decline as the degree of openness increases. Both costs and benefits may be thought of as measured in percent of GDP. Benefits increase as trade becomes more important, because full exchange-rate stability between trading partners takes on increasing importance as an economy becomes more open. Conversely, costs decline with openness as the exchange-rate instrument inherent in the continued existence of a national currency becomes less usable the more open is the economy; the impact on the price level becomes too important relative to the impact on output and employment. When an economy reaches a certain degree of openness, the benefits of participating in a common currency area will therefore tend to exceed the costs. The perception that this balance has shifted in the course of the 1970s and 1980s for several Member States in the EU is not necessarily related to an increasing degree of openness in the EU economies, although intra-EU trade has tended to become more important over the past decade. The change in perception is rather related to the idea that, for any given level of openness, the costs of participation seem to have shifted downward while the benefits may at the same time have become more visible. More countries would, therefore, today find it advantageous to participate in a common currency area than was the case 10 or 20 years ago, even if their degree of openness is unchanged.

These arguments are admittedly vague, and it is impossible to quantify in any exact way how the balance of benefits and costs comes out for each individual participant.

---

[124] *Editor's note*: the deadline for the European Monetary Union is set on January 1, 1999. On that day the Common European Currency—the Euro—will become a full-fledged currency.

Part of the difficulty lies in the fact that whereas most of the benefits accrue to individual firms and consumers, the costs of participating in a common currency area impinge on the government and on the central bank, who lose some of their policy instruments as they join a common currency area. The benefits are largely microeconomic—improving the efficiency of the economy—while the costs are of a macroeconomic policy nature. Assessing whether benefits exceed costs, therefore, implies complicated weightings of the preferences of different groups in society, touching upon the degree to which governments reflect the balance of preferences in the electorate.

Most analysis of EMU and the common currency has been based on a stable EMS as a standard of comparison. In the final years of the 1980s, for example, exchange rate variability among the currencies participating in the EMS's narrow margins had been reduced to about one-fourth of what it was prior to the formation of the EMS in 1979. Exchange rates within this group of countries had become about as stable as in the 1960s, generally regarded as a heyday of stable exchange rates. This made the additional benefits of moving to a common currency look modest relative to what had already been achieved by stabilizing currencies amongst themselves through the EMS.

Progressing from the stable EMS of the late 1980s to a single currency would, on the basis of an extrapolation of past experience, only yield marginally more trade inside Europe. Surely, it was argued by critics of going all the way to a common currency, the growing sophistication of financial markets could be expected to provide hedging opportunities for the residual risk at moderate cost. Furthermore, the elimination of transaction costs of currency exchange, the other important benefit seen by business enterprises, seemed to many economists to be of almost trivial significance. Yet the business view may be closer to the truth than that of the economists.

The potential savings in transaction costs were estimated to be small but not trivial; the major empirical study of the EU Commission (1990) suggested them to be in the order of 0.3-0.4% of Community GDP, assuming—as seems realistic—that an efficient EU-wide payments and clearing system is developed. Considerable efforts in this direction are currently deployed by a subcommittee of the Committee of EU Central Bank Governors. If bid-ask spreads in currency exchange go up significantly, as the early experience with the higher potential flexibility suggests, the savings become much larger. But this is only the tip of the iceberg. The continuing existence of national currencies would entail substantial indirect microeconomic costs. Firms can more easily engage in price discrimination between national markets when separate currencies allow them to charge higher prices in markets where demand is relatively insensitive. For consumers, used to evaluating prices in their own national currency, it is inconvenient to compare prices in different currencies, even if exchange rates are fixed. Transparency in the Internal Market, and hence competition, would be greatly increased with the more uniform price structure inherent in the transition to a common currency. This is presumably why the latter has won favor also with the consumer organizations in the EU—though not as yet with the consumers they represent. The potential for indirect benefits from a single currency are very much larger than the studies of the most visible gains—larger trade flows from reduced exchange rate volatility and elimination of transaction costs—would suggest. Only a common currency can assure that all the benefits expected from goods market integration will be attained. It is not easy to put a figure to these benefits, but it would appear that some of the very substantial expected gains from creating the Internal Market estimated in the late 1980s could only materialize within a common currency area.

Even these indirect gains are likely to underestimate the total benefits, because they look only at once-and-for-all, or so-called static, effects. The common currency should bring efficiency gains also by raising the rate of growth of output, i.e., in a dynamic sense. The marginal productivity of capital can be expected to increase as a result of a more efficient financial environment; this will raise investment. The higher capital stock means more output with the same labor force; hence the output effects of the initial increase in efficiency may be approximately doubled according to one major study by Baldwin (1991). The welfare effects will be smaller, since the increase in the capital stock has to be paid for by a reduction in consumption. Finally, one may argue that the dynamic benefits of a common currency are still understated to the extent that the risk premium attached to investment is reduced in a more predictable environment for exchange rates and monetary policy. This effect may well be small, as is the impact of reduced exchange-rate volatility on trade flows, but even a very modest increase in the growth rate has a cumulatively significant, exponentially increasing effect on the level of income over time. Even a minute increase in the growth rate would be more important than the direct gains in terms of saved transactions costs. The rather dismissive attitude by many economists, notably in the United States, to the potential microeconomic benefits of a single currency is open to serious criticism. Without overstating the case, it is therefore possible to share the perception of business enterprises that a common currency is a highly desirable complement to the Internal Market. This becomes more obvious if it is kept in mind that the benchmark to which comparisons are made is no longer the stable EMS, as it existed up to September 1992, but rather a system with more exchange-rate flexibility and uncertainty. The potential microeconomic benefits of a common currency stand out more clearly now than in the heyday of confidence in a stable EMS in which many of these benefits could be claimed to have been already largely achieved.

The benefits of the single currency could be overshadowed by two types of macroeconomic costs, both stressed by critics of EMU: the loss of the exchange rate as an instrument of macroeconomic adjustment and the risk of a worsening of macroeconomic performance and policy conflicts resulting from hazardous provisions in the Maastricht Treaty for the European Central Bank and the joint monetary policy to be followed by it.

The importance of the loss of the exchange rate as an instrument or as a safety valve hinges on two empirical issues: (1) What is the likely size of nation-specific shocks to the economies of the participating Member States? (2) Can other instruments of adjustment be assumed to perform adequately?

C. A Comparison of the EU and the United States as Currency Area

Subsequent work by US and European economists has yielded relatively reassuring conclusions from the viewpoint of the feasibility of a common currency area if one looks at data for the eight or nine countries best qualified on economic grounds to go to the final stage. Is the EU further from being an optimum currency area than is the US? [The] conclusion is clearly that it is not, at least not for a "core" group of EU countries: The shocks that hit the original six EU Member States in the 1963-89 period followed a pattern much more similar across countries than was the case for shocks that hit the major US regions. The impression that at least the "core" EU countries are less exposed to nation-specific shocks is confirmed by comparisons of productive structures of EU and US regions. Differences are more striking in the United States. There is no equivalent in Europe of the concentration of energy production in Texas and Alaska, nor is agriculture as dominant in any European country as it is in the US Midwest. The implications of this analysis would appear to be, if the United States, despite its greater regional diversity, raises no doubt as to its capacity to form one currency area, what should prevent (a large part of) the EU from forming one? However, this way of putting the question is too optimistic.

First, one may see the persistence of a common currency throughout the US territory as determined largely by inertia, notably the fact that the United States has constituted a single political unit for a very long period. The dollar has more than two centuries of history behind it, and there would be substantial costs in economic and political terms from breaking up an existing unified currency area. The US experience is less than fully relevant to the evaluation of the desirability of introducing a common EU currency to replace 12 (or fewer) existing national currencies. One might suggest, however, that the likely result of introducing separate currencies for the US regions that experience only a relatively weak correlation with the US economy as a whole would be to impose important net economic costs for the regions in question, despite the capacity of regional currency movements to provide some cushion against unfavorable movements in employment, property prices, and bank failures.

Second, even if one accepts the argument that the United States is indeed further from meeting the criterion of dominance of fairly uniform shocks to the component regions than is the Community, this reassuring fact for Europe may prove temporary. Krugman (1992), in particular, has argued that close national integration and a common currency drive an economy into deeper regional specialization, as can be observed in the United States. Nation-specific shocks would then tend to become more important over time in Europe, provided specialization broadly observes existing national boundaries. Given the already advanced state of specialization within industries rather than of whole industries among EU Member States, it is not obvious whether a continuation and intensification of this process would strengthen rather than weaken the case for maintaining national currencies. Economic regions in Europe do not in general coincide with countries. The logic of regional specialization points, if anything, to a potential need for more currencies than the present 12. Replacing the lira and the

DM with a single European currency would not worsen the mismatch between currencies and economic regions. Only changes in relative prices between sectors can bring real adjustment; they cannot be replaced by manipulating exchange rates between national currencies.

Third, and potentially most important, the United States compensates for its deficiencies with respect to the traditional optimum currency area criterion of dominance of symmetric shocks across its major regions by strongly developed adjustment mechanisms, which jointly provide an alternative to changes in the exchange rate. Labor mobility is higher than within the EU, and fiscal transfer mechanisms are more significant.

Despite the aim of the Rome Treaty to facilitate the mobility of persons, the labor force in the EU remains, for reasons of persistent cultural and linguistic diversity in Europe, fairly immobile. European policymakers would see little purpose in facilitating mobility to the extent that it could become a major mechanism of adjustment. The large EU countries have not even been very efficient at developing labor mobility inside their own frontiers. Labor mobility would not be considered an acceptable response to nation-specific shocks within a future common currency area. In this perspective it is a potentially important defect of EMU that the planned union almost totally lacks the type of fiscal transfer mechanism that operates so as to partly insure US regions against the consequences of region-specific shocks. Yet EMU would become more stable and politically more acceptable to an important part of the EU membership if it were to comprise a mechanism to protect against transitory shocks to unemployment. The philosophy in the Maastricht Treaty that this problem could still be taken care of within a common currency area by differentiated national budgetary policies and the associated changes in borrowing in financial markets, supplemented on rare occasions by ad hoc budgetary measures at the EU level, may not be necessarily unworkable or naive, but it is optimistic.

Ideas along these lines were first advanced in the so-called McDougall Report (1977). They won no political support then or later, probably because the initial budgetary estimates of what would be required were alarming. Recent work to reexamine the issue suggests that if an insurance mechanism is carefully designed to soften the financing of only changes in unemployment relative to the Community average, such a transfer mechanism would put very limited strain on the EU budget, on the order of 0.2% of Community GDP. Points in favor of the proposed mechanism are that it would entail no net costs in the long term and only very limited net transfers to particular Member States.

Implementation of a mechanism along these lines would make a common currency area more robust, but whether it would be strictly necessary to prevent a crisis in EMU after its start remains an open question. If Member States have regained, by meeting somewhat more closely than today the convergence criteria for entry contained in the Maastricht Treaty, some measure of autonomy in their budgetary policy, the task of offsetting unfavorable nation-specific shocks could alternatively be performed by national budgetary actions, allowing automatic stabilizers to operate and possibly adding to them some discretionary measures. To the extent that the shocks are temporary, these national actions would not bring Member States in conflict with the Maastricht requirement of avoiding more permanently "excessive deficits." A Community mechanism would, however, have the advantage over national budgetary actions of uniformity and automaticity in its principle.

The two types of benefits, i.e., that (1) the alternative to EMU could be a relapse into a degree of intra-EU exchange-rate flexibility difficult to reconcile with the integration of markets for goods and services aimed for, and (2) there are significant microeconomic benefits from the common currency, even though the most visible ones—saved transaction costs—are modest. Both of these types of benefits appear to have been either neglected or only very inadequately taken into account by critics of EMU. Governments and central banks have had an interest in pretending the EMS would assure stability and the microeconomic benefits have not been taken sufficiently seriously. With the risk of increasing instability inherent in the recently much relaxed EMS, both will come to the fore.

If the benefits now appear more visible, the costs of a single currency, and of the consequent loss of ability to realign the exchange rate and to conduct a more autonomous monetary policy, do not appear to have increased correspondingly. This paper has refrained from using the most common reason advanced for not considering the abolition of the national currencies a cost, i.e., that exchange-rate changes would not in practice be reserved for the rare and well-timed occasions, when nearly all economists would tend to believe they could facilitate or at least speed up adjustment. Even in such an optimistic scenario the case for retaining exchange-rate changes as an instrument of macroeconomic adjustment is not convincing. If the external shocks hitting the EU economies were symmetrical (or industry specific), modifications of parities would only serve to shift the effects among them. National policy shocks that could upset EMU will be collectively monitored and they would, in principle, be checked. Slow-moving and more permanent sources of divergence, say, a slower trend of productivity increase in one Member State, would have to be offset by a slower rise in wages in the country concerned rather than by continuous depreciation of the currency. Only sizable, temporary, and nationally differentiated (or asymmetric) shocks provide an acceptable rationale for realignments. It is an empirical judgment, very difficult to make with any confidence, to conclude that they are sufficiently important to outweigh the microeconomic benefits of giving up the national currency and the possibility of modifying its value against other currencies. Hence, on purely economic grounds, the case for the common currency remains.

D. Would the Common Currency Assure Stable and Low Inflation?

There is one line of reasoning that was not taken up in the previous section. If it could be convincingly argued that the particular way EMU has been designed might tend to worsen inflationary performance for some, maybe even for the average Member State, and to generate regular conflicts between the new joint monetary authority, on the one hand, and the political authorities in individual Member States or the ECOFIN/Council, that could swing the balance against the common currency.

The European Central Bank will be a remarkable institution in two important respects: (1) the new monetary authority has been given a clearer mandate to pursue the classical central banking function of assuring a stable nominal framework for the EU economy than is the case in national central banking legislation, including that of Germany; and (2) great attention has been given to making the ECB as independent of the national and EU political authorities as possible.

The mandate to maintain price stability as the primary objective of monetary policy in EMU (Art. 105) has come under attack from two sides. German policymakers and academic economists have been critical on the grounds that the framework will still be exposed to greater inflationary risks for Germany and other low-inflation countries than the past EMS, which allowed for occasional realignments and relied on leadership by the Bundesbank. Hence they insist, supported by the latter and recently by the German Constitutional Court, on the toughest possible application of the convergence criteria before the final stage of EMU is started, to minimize the risk that persistent budgetary deficits in practice may make it impossible for the ECB to maintain a clear noninflationary stance. They fear that prudent views may find themselves in a minority in the ECB Council. On the other hand, economists in most other EC countries are concerned that the ECB might put the European economy into a monetary straitjacket, preventing it from developing according to its growth potential and keeping the level of unemployment at an undesirable high level. Governments in Europe are now, mainly individually, groping for measures that could firm up the prospects for recovery. Some have found a remedy in the very substantial devaluations of their currencies since September 1992—notably Italy, Spain, and the United Kingdom—but at the expense of other EU Member States, including Germany.

The EU Commission is trying to find support for a package of stimulatory expenditure measures, mainly in the shape of an acceleration of public investments in European infrastructure. So far, the results have been meager; the so-called growth initiative agreed at the Edinburgh European Council of December 1992 was mainly a catalog of decisions already taken in individual Member States. But the efforts have continued at the Brussels European Council in December 1993. Inflation is rarely mentioned recently as a constraint, except in Germany. Most remarkably, inflation has remained steady and moderate, even in countries that have experienced a substantial weakening of their currencies. The purpose of introducing a common currency and designing a new institutional framework to manage it is not to deal with short-term problems in economic management in a particular conjunctural context, but to facilitate constructive policy responses on the average. Monetary policy would then have been somewhat easier in most countries than it is today. The risk premium on financial assets denominated in currencies of EU countries other than Germany and the Benelux would have disappeared. Since monetary policy in EMU would have had to be guided by a price objective for the area as a whole, which is different from price stability in Germany, and since average inflation in the countries that observed the narrow margins is currently lower than in Germany, interest rates could also have been slightly lower than the benchmark German rates, which have continued to set the floor under European short-term interest rates. Other central banks and governments in the participating countries would then have been able to add their influence to that of the Bundesbank in pushing earlier for a modification of the policy mix in Germany in the direction of tighter budgetary policies. This would anyway be required for Germany to observe the Maastricht criteria. More radical and constructive solutions, including an EMU loan to Germany to finance part of the reunification expenditures, might also have been addressed in the framework of EMU. The consequences for German employment of maintaining a relatively rapid increase in nominal wages would then have become more transparent earlier. But some changes in relative price levels could and should continue to occur as part of the adjustment mechanism within the Union, as they do in existing federal states. In this scenario even the United Kingdom might have found that it could maintain interest rates as low as those currently prevailing. It would be naive to suggest that policies would have become radically different from what has been observed until now. To the extent they would be different, however, the modifications could have been expected to go in the right direction while leaving policy conflicts no worse than today—most likely less painful than what has been observed in 1992-93. In short, it is the contention of this author that it was not a lack of convergence among the participating countries that required the scrapping of the earlier EMS. Looking at convergence in terms of inflation rates and long-term interest rates—the two main nominal criteria in the Maastricht Treaty—the present record is quite satisfactory, both in terms of the average level of these variables and the dispersion around them. Budget deficits are much in excess of the Maastricht criteria—6 1/2 on average as against the reference value of 3%—but the dispersion around this average is smaller than for many years, due to a large common cyclical worsening of all national budget deficits. The situation does not suggest that countries are on such a divergent path from each other that this in itself justifies the breakup of the EMS that occurred in the summer of 1993. These events can only be understood with reference to market perceptions of an increasing risk of divergent policies in the future, as political impatience with high short-term interest rates was expected to snap in one "weak" currency country after the other. Despite relatively good convergence, national governments were unable to dispel these market perceptions; indeed, they began to foster them by their own actions and through collective statements that more flexibility in the EMS in the form of more frequent realignments was now required. In these circumstances it is not surprising that market forces ultimately overwhelmed the authorities and forced a major relaxation of the EMS, though fortunately in the form of wider fluctuation margins around unchanged central rates rather than realignments of the latter.

Full monetary union would have provided a framework more nearly optimal in view of the situation than the relaxed EMS. It is possible, however, that the move to the latter was preferable to sticking with the EMS, as it was in view of the increasingly conflicting attitudes adopted nationally and the decay of the defensive mechanisms to which they had led.

Turning to the independence of the ECB, there is a dichotomy in the criticism parallel to that observable in the discussion of price stability as a primary objective. The two dimensions are, in fact, linked. It would not have been acceptable to give a high degree of independence to the ECB while entrusting it with the task of constantly reinterpreting the objective of monetary policy. Changing the relative weights of macroeconomic objectives is a prerogative of the political authorities; sharing that task with an independent central bank would have led to conflicts between the ECB and ECOFIN. The only way of delegating authority over monetary policy to an independent central bank is on the basis of a fairly simple, preferably unidimensional, objective. Conflicts cannot be avoided between these two bodies, any more than they have been excluded within individual countries where the central bank has considerable independence. Few economists would say, in retrospect, that the performance of the US economy would have been improved by reducing the Fed's independence, used most clearly in a conflictual way in the period of tight money in 1979-82. Nor would they say that obliging the Bundesbank to support the policies of the German government at times of rising inflation, e.g., 1981 or following unification, would have produced a better macroeconomic outcome in a longer term perspective. Firm resistance by the central bank to accommodation is at times essential and constructive. This will remain true in the future EU common currency area as well, and it would have been undermined by giving the political authorities the opportunity to override at times the decision of an otherwise independent ECB.

In summary, EMU with a common currency remains desirable and worth a considerable effort. During the long period of convergence and negotiations of EMU between 1988 and 1992, it could be argued that Member States had borne most of the costs of full monetary unification by converging in a promising way on inflation, but that they had not yet reaped all of the benefits of this process. Admittedly by 1991-92 these benefits had in part been achieved as interest rates finally converged increasingly towards the German (and Dutch) level. The implications of the recent currency crisis of 1992-93 is that the benefits of a common currency relative to the present, potentially much looser, system have gone up drastically, but that the costs of giving up national currencies, and hence the possibilities of modifying their value, will also appear to have risen, at least in the perception of many national policymakers. My own view is that the balance remains in favor of the common currency.

E. Conclusions and Political Considerations

The recent turmoil in exchange markets has strengthened rather than weakened this case, because the crisis demonstrated that the tight EMS as a compromise between flexible rates and fully fixed rates was unstable in a world of increasing capital mobility. It was necessary to move towards one of the "pure" forms of exchange-rate regime. With the preparation for monetary union still inadequate, it appeared desirable for policymakers to opt, temporarily, for more flexibility in the form of a major widening of the fluctuation margins. This should not be taken, however, as a rejection of the concept of monetary union, even in the time perspective of the late 1990s foreseen in the Maastricht Treaty.

The difficulties of ratifying the Treaty, including the continuing reticence of many Germans to accept the implications of the Treaty that some degree of automaticity in progress towards monetary union is a responsibility for those Member States that meet the economic requirements, have made even the longer run realization of monetary union seem more doubtful than two years ago, when the negotiations were completed. At the same time, the crisis in the EMS has shown that the temptation for individual countries to pursue perceived short-term gains through more differentiated national policies—despite the risks of endangering a stable framework, built upon 14 years of experience—is not far beneath the surface. This has strengthened the position of those in Europe who have maintained throughout that it was hazardous to let monetary unification run well ahead of political union. The setup of a European Central Bank of a federal nature to run the EU's joint monetary policy offers one promising challenge for tackling this agenda. A test case for more political union would be to evaluate whether political agreement could be reached on a modest fiscal stabilization scheme along the lines discussed above. Insuring Member States against some of the impact of the residual and modest unfavorable external shocks that affect them temporarily in a differentiated way would be a clear sign of the type of political solidarity among the participants that could make EMU and the single currency more robust.

Chapter 4

Competition Policy

PART I - PERSPECTIVE

I. The Transformation of European Community Competition Law[1]

A. Integration and the Goals of Competition Law

The goal of a unified market dominated this process of construction because it was the central impetus for the "new Europe." To begin to appreciate the centrality and force of this idea, one need only recall that economic cooperation was the last remaining hope for a cooperative Europe that would banish the specter of that continent's nationalist past. Attempts to move toward political union had been rejected, and the plans for a European Defense Community had been defeated. If there was to be a new Europe, it would have to be built on economic cooperation and integration.

In addition to this political goal of replacing conflict with cooperation, the Common Market was seen as serving a variety of economic goals. The Member States were still recovering from the ravages of the Second World War, and economic integration was widely viewed as necessary for rapid economic growth. An integrated market would allow firms to acquire sufficient size to compete effectively on world markets, and consumers would benefit from a larger market with its concomitant economies of scale.

Many Europeans also saw economic integration as the only means of dealing with the combined economic and political power of the United States. Integration represented a means of regaining independence, power, and status vis-a-vis the country that had assumed world leadership in the wake of two world wars.

From its inception, Community competition law has served as a means of achieving this economic integration. Articles 85 and 86 were included in the Treaty of Rome in order to combat restraints on competition that could interfere with the creation of the Common Market. Moreover, the focus in constructing the competition law system during the 1960s was not on protecting competition for the sake of its generic benefits, but on creating a unified market. Consequently, this goal structured competition law thought and institutions.

---

1 David J. Gerber, *The Transformation of European Community Competition Law?*, 35 Harv. Int'l L.J. 97, 101-147. © David J. Gerber. Reprinted by permission.

This does not mean that there was no interest in obtaining the generic benefits of competition. Both the Commission and the Court referred at times to the potential benefits—lower prices, more rapid technological progress, etc.—anticipated as a result of improved competition. These references were imbedded, however, in a discourse and practice that focused on economic integration.[2]

Furthermore, there was little reason to distinguish between these two goals; they were related and mutually reinforcing. To the extent that competition law eliminated obstacles to the flow of goods, services, and capital across European borders, for example, it served the cause of unifying the market while simultaneously benefiting consumers by increasing the number of actual and potential competitors in European markets.

B. Characteristics of the System

Those entrusted with constructing the Community's competition law system were faced with two fundamental questions about its role. The first was how large a role competition law should play: could—and should—it be seriously enforced? Except in Germany, competition law played a minimal role, if any, in government policy and in business decision-making in Europe. As a result, it was widely assumed that Community competition law provisions would not be seriously enforced. That competition law came to play such a significant role may be explained, at least partially, by the recognition that it represented a potentially valuable tool for achieving the Community's central mission of economic integration.

The second issue concerned the nature of the system—was it law or was it politics? Here two quite different images of competition law drawn from fundamentally different national experiences confronted each other. The German participants tended to view the competition law system as fundamentally juridical; legal analysis should be the primary guide to decision-making. Objectivity and neutrality of the juridical process were necessary for achieving any effective progress toward integration and for establishing the legitimacy of Community institutions. Moreover, "ordoliberal" thought, which emphasized the need for a constitutional framework for economic policy, strongly influenced their opinions. In addition, they had recently worked through these issues in a decade-long controversy over the introduction of their own competition law.

The competition law systems of the other Member States, if any, usually were based on an "administrative control" or "industrial policy" model in which political rather than juridical processes were dominant. The French, for example, tended to see

---

[2] The following quote from the Commission reflects how deeply the idea was imbedded:

> Although it is evident that the competition policy of the Community must be directed towards the creation and proper operation of the common market, its effectiveness would, nevertheless, be considerably improved if it were carried out in conjunction with more active competition policies at the national level and with the removal of certain obstacles to the free play of the market in various sectors, such as the fixing of prices and the placing of orders by public authorities.

Commission of the european communities, first report on competition policy 12 (1972).

competition law in political terms, preferring to base decisions on the evaluation by Community officials of the needs of the Community and its Member States at a given time. They were steeped in the values and methods of dirigisme and planification and conceived competition law in that light.[3]

The conflict between these two conceptions of competition law was most intense in the early 1960s. By the late 1960s, however, governmental changes in France and the example of the "German miracle" of economic development had weakened resistance to a juridical conception of competition law. Nevertheless, the conflict has never been fully resolved, and its recent reactivation may make it more portentous now than ever before.

C. Sculpting the System: The Political Process

Given the dearth of experience with competition law in the Member States and the assumption that competition law would play as marginal a role in the Community as in the Member States, it is not surprising that the Council had little interest in becoming directly involved in the structuring of the system.[4] The Council was willing to allow the Commission to play the major role in shaping the competition law system, and the Commission seized the opportunity.

1. Regulation 17 and the Power of the Commission

The preparation of an institutional framework for implementing articles 85 and 86 dominated the agenda of the Commission's competition law officials for approximately half a decade. The process involved extensive and sometimes difficult negotiations among the Council, the Commission, the European Parliament, and Member State governments, culminating in the 1962 enactment of Regulation 17, the blueprint for the institutional structure of the competition law system.[5]

Regulation 17 created a competition law system in which the enforcement and policy-making prerogatives were centered in the Commission and the role of national

---

[3] "Dirigisme" refers to the French tradition of allowing governmental agencies to play a major role in directing private economic activity. "Planification" refers to the practice established after World War II whereby a governmental agency, the "Commissariat General du Plan," created general, non-binding plans for major sectors of the French economy. Henri Guillaume, *Implications of the New Indicative Planning*, in French Industrial Policy (William J. Adams & Christian Stoffaes eds., 1986). For a detailed explanation of French values and methods in industrial policy, see generally Henri Aujac, *An Introduction to French Industrial Policy*, in French Industrial Policy (William J. Adams & Christian Stoffaes eds., 1986).

[4] The Council has the final legislative authority within the Community. It is an explicitly political body in which the Member States are directly represented and pursue their own national interests. The Council may not, however, initiate legislation. This must be done by the Commission, which is the bureaucracy of the Community and represents the interests of the Community as a whole. For further details on this structure, see, e.g., P.J.G. Kapteyn & P. Verloren Van Themaat, Introduction to the Law of the European Communities (Lawrence W. Gormley ed., 2d ed. 1989).

[5] Council Regulation 17/62, 1962 O.J. (204), amended by Council Regulation 59/62, 1962 O.J. (1655), Council Regulation 118/63, 1963 O.J. (2696), and Council Regulation 2822/71, 1971 O.J. (L 285) 49.

legal systems was marginalized.[6] The Treaty of Rome did not dictate such centralization, and prior to the enactment of Regulation 17, national authorities had applied the competition law provisions, sometimes actively. Their marginalization was thus a critical step in constructing the system.

One component of this centralization project was Article 9(3), which required that when the Commission began an investigation under the competition law sections of the treaty, national authorities had to cease their own enforcement activity under the treaty with regard to that conduct. This provision thus discouraged the Member States from initiating their own investigations because such actions would become futile if the Commission began its own inquiry.

A second element was Article 9(1), which provided that only the Commission could issue exemptions under Article 85(3). This eliminated incentives to bring suit in national courts, because such courts could only rule on one of the two issues relevant to the application of Article 85. The combined effect of these provisions was to eliminate any significant role for national legal systems in the enforcement of Community competition law.

The introduction of the notification procedure, which became a pivotal feature of the Community system, enhanced the centrality of the Commission's role. According to Article 4(1) of Regulation 17, the Commission is to be notified of agreements that might violate Article 85, and exemption from Article 85(1) is contingent on the filing of such notification. This procedure gave significant power to the Commission because it meant that the most important practical issue was what the Commission would do about notified agreements. Businesses and their representatives had to turn to the Commission for guidance, and it was there that they could attempt to influence decisions.

In addition to greatly expanding the Commission's role, Regulation 17 also secured for the competition directorate (General Directorate IV or DG IV) a high degree of autonomy in decision-making. France had sought to require that DG IV obtain the approval of a majority of the members of a newly established advisory committee on competition law before sending its recommendations to the full Commission for final decision. Representatives from each Member State would sit on this advisory committee, and thus the need for its approval would have subjected the Commission to a high degree of political influence. Competition law would have developed primarily as a reflection of political decisions by the Member States rather than through juridical processes. This requirement was, however, rejected in Article 10(3). An advisory committee was established, but DG IV was merely required to consult with it before sending decisions to the Commission.

---

6 The Commission's preoccupation (with centralizing enforcement in its own hands) was understandable. The principles embodied in the competition rules were novel and almost revolutionary. They required fundamental changes in deeply ingrained habits of thought and patterns of economic conduct. The officials of the new competition Directorate-General did not trust businessmen, lawyers and judges to apply the rules correctly (or even, as the case might be, in good faith).

Ian Forrester & Christopher Norall, *The Laicization of Community Law: Self-Help and the Rule of Reason: How Competition Law Is and Could Be Applied*, 21 C.M. L. Rev. 11, 13 (1984).

Finally, Regulation 17 gave the Commission extensive investigatory and enforcement powers. For example, Article 14 vested the Commission with authority to enter into any premises relevant to a competition law investigation to examine the books and records of the firms involved, to make relevant copies, and to interview personnel. These powers made the Commission a formidable enforcement agency.

2. The Commission's "Special" Prerogatives in Competition Law

In 1965, the Council further buttressed the autonomy of the Commission in competition law matters by granting it broad powers to "legislate" without approval of the Council. Regulation 17's notification procedure had caused a flood of notifications to the Commission and had placed an enormous burden on a small office. In response, the Council granted the Commission the authority to issue group or "block" exemptions under Article 85(3) in certain situations without the Council's approval. Moreover, the Council included language in Regulation 19/65 indicating that it favored such delegation, and the Commission later began to issue additional block exemptions.

DG IV is the only directorate to have such power, and some consider it unlikely that the Council would initiate such a practice today. Nevertheless, what began as a response to a specific and temporary need (to respond to the flood of notifications) now plays an important role in the system because it further shields DG IV's decision-making authority from political intervention.

The Community's political institutions thus created an institutional framework for competition law which centralized authority in the Commission and minimized the roles of national competition officials and national courts. Moreover, at the Community level it reduced Member State political influence by protecting DG IV from undue political interference.

D. The Court Defines Its Role

The one institution in the system whose role was not subject to definition by the political process was the Court of Justice. The Court had to mold its own role, and, not surprisingly, it chose to put itself in a leadership position. Viewing itself as the principal "motor of integration," the Court took advantage of the special circumstances offered by competition law and made that system an important "vehicle" of integration whose strength would, in turn, further amplify the Court's own power.

The Court's definition of its role in the competition law system was part of the broader process of defining its role within the Community, and here timing was a critical factor. The first significant competition law cases came to the Court in the mid-1960s, just as General De Gaulle's resistance to Europeanization threatened to impede integration and destroy the Community.[7] DeGaulle changed the "constitution" of the Community by demanding a unanimity requirement for virtually all Council decisions, thus hobbling the Community's political organs.[8] As a consequence, the Court was the

---

[7] *See, e.g.*, Joined Cases 56 & 58/64, *Etablissements Consten, S.A.R.L. v. Commission*, 1966 E.C.R. 299.

[8] This refers to the so-called "Luxemburg Accord."

only institution capable of maintaining the momentum of integration. Moreover, the crisis of confidence resulting from these events encouraged the Court to assert a bold leadership role.

The Court thus structured the competition law system to serve as a central tool for promoting integration.[9] It articulated a broad conception of competition law as central to the process of integration, and its decisions in this area sought to make that conception viable and convincing.

The role the Court sculpted for itself in this competition law system centered on intellectual leadership.[10] Rather than limiting itself to ruling on the facts of individual cases, the Court frequently enunciated broad principles and values. It looked to the future and aimed at guiding the Commission in its development of competition policy. As one commentator has suggested, the Court began to provide the Commission with "windows of opportunity" in which the Court indicated its willingness to support particular lines of development of competition law doctrine.[11]

Reflecting the centrality of the goal of integration, the Court made teleology the cornerstone of its interpretative strategy. As in its constitutional case law, the Court interpreted the treaty's competition law provisions in light of its own conception of what was necessary to achieve the integrationist goals of the treaty. It conveyed a clear message that this goal-driven methodology was not merely to be one of many principles to be used in interpreting the treaty, but rather the dominant interpretative method.

The Court's teleological discourse carried centralist values. The Court saw a strong Commission as necessary for achieving integration, and thus it molded competition law doctrine so as to increase the power of the Commission in relation to national authorities. For example, it consistently expanded the geographical scope of Article 85, thereby increasing the jurisdictional prerogatives of the Commission and reducing those of the Member States, and it relied on integrationist goals in justifying this expansion.

E. The Commission and the Birth Pangs of Competition Policy

The centrality of the Court's role was also tied to the enormity of the task faced by the Commission. In effect, DG IV had to create an entire substantive and procedural system and explain it to governmental and business leaders who frequently were either

---

9 According to Ulrich Everling, a former judge of the European Court of Justice, "(i)n evaluating the case law of the Court it is necessary to recognize that the competition rules of the Community serve the central objective of the Community, namely the opening of the markets of the Member States. . . ." Ulrich Everling, *Zur Wettbewerbskonzeption in der neueren Rechtsprechung des Gerichtshofs der Europaischen Gemeinschaften*, 40 WUW 995, 1000 (1990). All translations are by the author, except as otherwise noted.

10 This role had no precedent in European national competition law systems. To the extent that there had been judicial involvement at all in European competition law systems, the courts had functioned primarily as administrative courts, whose primary role was to develop and apply a principled set of controls on the discretionary action of administrative bodies.

11 D.G. Goyder, EEC COMPETITION LAW, Pt. III & *passim,* (1988), at 413.

unfamiliar with such norms or doubted their legitimacy. Moreover, due to the lack of experience with competition law in most Member States, decisionmakers in DG IV did not have a broad base of knowledge on which to draw in determining what those norms should be. Finally, the unanimity requirement in the Council meant that the Commission could not depend for political support on a majority of the Council and thus had to avoid taking action that might unduly offend individual Member States.

As a consequence, the Commission moved very carefully during the foundational period. It had to establish a base of experience to guide its judgments and a political foundation for confidence in its procedures that would support effective enforcement in the future. For much of the period it focused its efforts on procedural issues, most notably the creation of Regulation 17. Enforcement was approached delicately, as shown, for example, by the Commission's unwillingness to levy fines until late in the period.

Under these circumstances, the Commission had little choice but to seek a cooperative relationship with the Court. Both needed cooperation, because neither could achieve its goals independently. Except where national courts request specific interpretations from it, the Court can only pursue its own goals when the Commission takes enforcement action. Similarly, the Commission cannot accomplish its mission without the Court's support of its interpretations and applications of the Treaty.

In the cooperative relationship that evolved, the Commission tended to follow the lead of the Court, thereby taking advantage of the Court's symbolic status and its relative immunity from political pressure. The Court's decisions were understood as applications by a neutral, non-political body of juridically determined principles and therefore were largely shielded from such pressure. The Commission could thus achieve a degree of political security by operating in the Court's "tow."

In this interplay between Court and Commission, the integration imperative was pivotal because it represented a common goal for the two institutions. Each saw an expansive reading of the competition provisions as critical to its own role in moving the Community toward integration. As a consequence, they developed the Community's substantive law in the service of this goal.

F. Substantive Principles of Competition Law

The overriding importance of economic integration as a goal for both the Court and the Commission configured not only the institutional arrangements of competition law, but its substantive content as well. In contrast to national competition law systems, whose primary objective typically is to secure generic benefits associated with competition, Community competition law was shaped to eliminate private restraints on trade across national borders.

The emphasis in Community competition law on vertical relationships (e.g., manufacturer-retailer) between firms is the most important example of this objective. While national legal systems generally focus on horizontal agreements (i.e., those among competitors) because they represent the most obvious distortions of the market, Community competition law has focused on vertical restraints, largely because these represent the most obvious obstacles to transborder trade.

This concern led the Commission to attack a variety of agreements that manufacturers and distributors were using to protect national markets.[12] Where manufacturers could use exclusive distributorships to isolate national markets and protect them from parallel imports, they could effectively use such agreements to re-erect through private means the barriers to trade that the Community had been created to eliminate. The Commission aggressively attacked such agreements, and the Court supported its attacks in broad language signaling that the Court would strike down any agreements used for these general purposes.[13]

A related problem involved the use of industrial property rights to achieve market separation. The Commission and the Court both attacked the use of industrial property rights by manufacturers to prohibit the importation of goods from other Member States and thus to separate markets. Both patents and trademarks were being used for such purposes, and they received priority attention.[14]

Together, the cases from the foundational period established the basic incompatibility with the Treaty of Rome of vertical agreements used to restrict or distort the flow of goods across national borders. The Commission's enforcement efforts were directed primarily at such agreements, and the Court frequently articulated broad principles designed to support those efforts.

There was noticeably less concern with horizontal agreements. In part this was because such agreements were less obviously and directly related to the paramount goal of integration. In addition, enforcement action that might inhibit cooperation risked conflict with other policy goals. The Commission was concerned, for example, with ensuring that European firms be able to compete with their United States rivals. It thus sought to promote cooperative arrangements among such firms, particularly the small and medium-sized enterprises (SMEs) whose survival appeared to be threatened by international competition.

The result was very cautious enforcement of Article 85(1) against horizontal agreements. There was no question that cartels were generally forbidden by that article, and thus the Court and the Commission concentrated on balancing the competition-distorting effects of competitor agreements against other Community interests such as economic progress. They focused, for example, on distinguishing between "hard" agreements, which were basically anticompetitive, and "soft" agreements, which were basically designed to improve competitiveness. Moreover, the Commission tended to allow cooperative agreements between small and medium-sized firms and to concentrate enforcement efforts on agreements involving larger firms.

---

[12] Case 19/77, *Miller Int'l v. Commission*, [1978] ECR 131 (prohibiting an export/import ban) and Case 30/78, *Distillers v. Commission*, [1980] ECR 2229 (prohibiting a pricing scheme establishing different prices for domestic and export sales).

[13] Case 56/65, *Societe Techinique Miniere v. Mashinenbau Ulm GmbH*, [1966] ECR 235.

[14] For patents, see, e.g., Case 24/67, *Parke, Davis v. Probel*, [1968] ECR 55. For trademarks, see, e.g., Case 40/70, *Sirena v Eda*, [1971] ECR 69.

During this initial period, the Commission made little use of the abuse of dominant position provisions contained in Article 86.[15] Although it began in the mid-1960s to make statements about how it might use that provision, the Commission paid relatively little attention to Article 86 until the early 1970s. This was partly out of fear of hampering the growth of Member State firms. In addition, the lack of any well-accepted sense of how the provision should be applied made enforcement by a politically weak Commission highly risky. Article 86 is applicable to market-dominating firms, and the Member States were very concerned about any attempts to interfere with "national champions."

Throughout this period, the Commission was wary of taking action against Member States relating to their own interference with the competitive process. It recognized the potential threat to competition posed by governmental interference, but—presumably, again, because of political concerns—it generally avoided developing and enforcing treaty provisions relating to State aids, governmental monopolies, or government facilitation of private anticompetitive conduct.

G. The Role of National Legal Systems

As we have seen, Regulation 17 sharply curtailed incentives to use national legal systems to vindicate rights provided by Community competition law. Yet an important issue regarding the role of national legal systems remained: the relationship between Community competition law and national competition laws. How much authority did Member States retain in this area? Here the Court developed the basic principle that national competition authorities could apply their own laws independently of the Commission, provided that their activities did not interfere with Community law. Although not without ambiguity, this principle served as an effective coordinating tool by delineating the respective spheres of operation of national and Community authorities. Moreover, given that most national competition laws were still weak during this period, the issue remained of secondary importance in most Member States.

H. The System Takes Shape

As the institutions of the Community shaped the competition law system, their primary concern, as we have seen, was the agenda of economic integration; competition law was politically acceptable precisely because it was critical to achieving this goal. Yet

---

[15] The concept of abuse is not defined in Article 86, but the following examples are provided:

a) the direct or indirect imposition of any inequitable purchase or selling prices or of any other inequitable trading conditions;

b) the limitation of production, markets or technical development to the prejudice of consumers;

c) the application to parties to transactions of unequal terms in respect of equivalent supplies, thereby placing them at a competitive disadvantage; or

d) the subjecting of the conclusion of a contract to the acceptance by a party of additional supplies which, either by their nature or according to commercial usage, have no connection with the subject of such contract.

the Community was new and politically weak. Recognizing this fragility, its institutions sought to construct a competition law system that avoided both excessive political influence of Member States on competition law development and threats to the economic interests of those States. This structuring of the competition law system corresponded to the political exigencies of the period, as the integration imperative both defined the competition law system and provided it with legitimacy.

The system that emerged from these circumstances had three dominant traits. First, enforcement was centralized in Community institutions, and the role of the national legal systems was minimized. Second, the system was conceived primarily in juridical terms. Decisions that were understood as based on generally applicable principles emanating from the Treaty of Rome were thought to be more unifying and stabilizing than political decisions. Finally, the system's substantive focus was on those practices that were most likely to be harmful to the integration process (e.g., vertical restrictions), whereas potential anti-competitive harms that were likely to engender political resistance from Member States generally were avoided.

II. 1973 to the Mid-1980s: From Oil Shocks to "Eurosclerosis"

The "oil shock" that rolled over Europe in the mid-1970s profoundly changed the economic and political context of competition law. The formation of the OPEC oil cartel and the concomitant quadrupling of the price of oil shifted massive economic resources from Europe and the United States to the Middle East, jarring European economies into a recession that was followed by periods of stagflation that would persist for more than a decade.

This new economic situation had important political consequences for the Community. The economic pie that had been steadily growing suddenly threatened to shrink. As unemployment increased, the democratic mechanisms that during the 1960s had dispensed the fruits of economic advancement throughout society now demanded that governments act to protect their nationals (firms as well as individuals) from economic harm. Member States that were supposed to cooperate to achieve common goals now found it more attractive to take from each other in what increasingly looked like a zero-sum game. Governments became hesitant to support Community initiatives that might be seen as sacrificing their own national interests on the Community "altar."

This external jolt to intra-Community relations occurred just as the first expansion of the Community further increased internal obstacles to cooperation. The United Kingdom, Ireland, and Denmark joined the Community in 1973, bringing with them new cultural, political, and legal traditions. Moreover, particularly in the case of the United Kingdom, they also brought with them ingrained attitudes of suspicion, and sometimes hostility, toward the Community.

By the 1980s the Community was suffering from "Eurosclerosis." In most substantive areas there was little apparent movement toward Community goals. Moreover, confidence in the future of the Community ebbed as failures to achieve significant progress led to repeated disappointments.

A. The Court as "Savior"

These economic and political stresses placed new demands on the competition law system that would eventually alter it in fundamental ways. In the short-run, however, they appeared to reinforce existing arrangements, particularly with regard to the role of the Court. Despite serious threats to the Community's future and perhaps to its very existence, both the Council and the Commission remained hobbled by political conflict and the "shadow of the veto," thus increasing pressure on the Court to maintain the momentum of integration. As a consequence, the Court remained the principal "motor of integration" throughout the 1970s and into the 1980s.

In playing this role, the Court relied heavily on the competition law system that had been constructed during the foundational period. That system was perceived as critical to the integration effort and thus enjoyed a large measure of political support. This enabled the Court to use competition law in developing a symbolic discourse of Community progress, even as political events hindered more tangible forms of progress.

1. The Limits of Teleology

The Court continued to provide intellectual leadership by enunciating broad, future-oriented principles in several areas of competition law. Moreover, it continued to expand the scope and enhance the intensity of competition law, relying on the integration imperative for both guidance and political support.

The force of the integration imperative and the widespread political support for the Court's use of competition policy in pursuing integration led, however, to decisions that would later undermine the Court's role in the competition law system. By the early 1970s the Court was paying less attention to the constraints of traditional legal methodology in reaching its decisions, and in so doing it began to erode the "juridical" conception of Community competition law that had supported that role.

The famous *Continental Can* decision revealed how far the Court was prepared to go in this direction.[16] For the first time in a litigated case the Commission sought to use Article 86 to attack an acquisition. The Commission contended that the acquisition represented a change in the structure of the market that increased the dominance of the acquiring firm and thus constituted an abuse of that firm's dominant position within the meaning of Article 86. The Court agreed, and thus sanctioned the apotheosis of the teleological method.

Traditional legal analysis provided little support for this use of Article 86. The text of the treaty did not indicate that Article 86 was applicable to acquisitions. On the contrary, it seemed to indicate that the article was not applicable to such cases. Article 86

[16] Case 6/72, *Europemballage Corp. v. Commission (Continental Can)*, [1973] ECR 215.

referred to the "abuse" of economic dominance, and power could not be "abused" unless it was "used." Yet in *Continental Can* there was merely a change of share ownership. At most, one could say that power was being "acquired." Historical analysis also revealed a clear legislative intent not to provide the Commission with authority to control mergers. Such a provision had been included in the Treaty of Paris (creating the ECSC) on which the framers of the Treaty of Rome relied for many of their ideas in this area, and yet they omitted any such reference.[17] Thus, both textual and historical analyses opposed the application of Article 86 to mergers.

Nevertheless, the Court disregarded these modes of analysis and held that Article 86 could be applied to mergers. Its justification was teleological. It held that the Commission could not accomplish its pro-integration goals without a tool to combat excessive economic concentration and that Article 86 would, therefore, have to be interpreted to provide such a tool. In effect, the Court held that the teleological method could provide the basis for a decision even when the text of the Treaty and the clear intention of the drafters dictated the opposite result. The Court's message seemed to be that its own judgment of the needs of economic integration would dominate its decision-making, regardless of the dictates of more traditional "juridical" methodology.

2. Relations with the Commission

In some respects the Court's relations with the Commission remained as they had been during the foundational period. The Court continued generally to guide and support the Commission, providing "windows of opportunity" for the Commission to pursue and sustaining the Commission's attempts to expand the impact and substantive scope of the competition law provisions.

Particularly after the mid-1970s, however, a subtle change occurred in the relationship between the Court and the Commission. The Court began to demand more from the Commission, requiring that it present increasingly detailed evidence of the actual economic impact of alleged competition law violations rather than relying on formalistic criteria of anti-competitiveness. The Court began regularly to annul Commission actions under Articles 85 and 86 on the grounds that the Commission had provided insufficient evidence to support its claim that a particular restriction on a firm's freedom of action actually would have the effects which were attributed to it.

One reason for the Court's increased rigor may have been a concern that the Commission might enforce Community competition law too aggressively, thus provoking resistance to competition law enforcement and impairing the effectiveness of what had become a critically important tool of integration. The Commission's enforcement efforts had intensified during the early 1970s, and the Court may have perceived the risk of a political "backlash."

The Court's move also reflected a new dynamic within the competition law system that was a response to the political and economic situations of the 1970s. The internal politics of the Community demanded at least the appearance of progress toward integration. Yet, the economic situation increased resistance to Community action that

---

17 Treaty Establishing the European Coal and Steel Community (ECSC Treaty), Apr. 18, 1951, 261 U.N.T.S. 142 (hereinafter ECSC Treaty).

might impair the capacity of European firms to compete both internationally and against each other. The Court's response to these pressures was to supply political "progress" on a conceptual and symbolic level. While strengthening competition law doctrine, it also minimized the economic consequences of these substantive law measures by imposing more stringent evidentiary and procedural requirements on the Commission.

B. The Commission's Balancing Act

The evolution of the Commission's role in the competition law system reflects a similar dynamic. While political circumstances reduced the Commission's role in many areas to that of a "secretariat," competition law was an exception. The Commission had more autonomy here than elsewhere, allowing it to pursue its goals with less political interference. Moreover, because competition law was viewed as essential to the process of integration, the Commission could also count on a degree of political support for its pro-integration activities in this area. Nevertheless, the Commission did not enjoy a political position that would allow it to enforce vigorously competition law norms.

1. The Policy Challenge

The new political and economic climate made the development of competition policy more complicated than it had been during the foundational period. During the earlier period, the goals of economic integration and economic growth generally called for the same basic policy measures because integration was seen as the primary path to prosperity. If the Commission succeeded in creating and administering the "neutral" rules needed to achieve integration, growth would automatically follow.

That image was shattered in the 1970s. The economic reversal undermined confidence in the steady improvement of economic conditions and ignited the fear of even more serious disintegration in the future. Under the new economic circumstances, progress toward integration no longer seemed an adequate goal. While integration remained an important part of Community economic policy, it was recast as a "long-run" answer rather than the answer. There was political pressure on the Commission to take active measures in the short-run to protect European national economies and to strengthen the competitiveness of European firms.

Thus, while competition law remained an important, even necessary, tool for achieving integration, DG IV officials increasingly were impelled to take into account the immediate economic situation of both the Community as a whole and the individual Member States. The result was a shift in the focus of policymaking away from "general" and "neutral" principles and toward immediate and specific policy objectives such as job creation.

2. Enforcement

The new situation presented DG IV with a dilemma. There was pressure on the Commission to enforce competition laws more aggressively than it had in the past in order to maintain the (faltering) momentum of integration. Whereas during the foundational period the Commission's primary role had been to participate with the Court in "making law" (i.e., establishing competition law principles), by the 1970s the Commission had to pay greater attention to securing compliance with the norms that had been established. There was little point in having a sophisticated competition law if its dictates could be ignored with impunity. Moreover, the new economic pressures increased the incentives for firms to do just that—engage in anticompetitive conduct. As a result, the Commission became more vigorous in seeking compliance. For example, it began to levy significant fines for violations of Articles 85 and 86.[18]

Yet these concerns for greater enforcement arose at a time when the obstacles to effective enforcement were increasing. The expansion of the Community meant a major increase in the numbers of firms, markets, and transactions subject to the application of the competition laws, thus requiring a major "educational" effort to assure awareness and understanding of Community norms. Moreover, there was little experience with competition law in the new Member States, and thus firms had to be convinced of the need to change practices such as cartel arrangements that had long been considered not only acceptable, but also normal.

In addition, DG IV was not in a position to increase significantly its enforcement activities. Its resources, for example, were augmented only marginally to respond to this situation. Equally important was the lack of political support for this aspect of DG IV's responsibility. The new economic pressures on the Member States made it difficult for the Commission to take regulatory action that might harm the competitiveness of European firms, and the Commission's unwillingness to increase funding for DG IV may have reflected concern that the directorate might become too aggressive in enforcing competition law norms.

DG IV's enforcement practices were shaped by this dilemma. The introduction of significant fines in a limited number of cases increased incentives for firms to take Community competition law seriously and sent the necessary "community-building" message that the laws were being used to integrate the market. Relatively few firms, however, were harmed by these fines. The Commission's response thus reflected a common theme: the effort to establish community-building norms at low economic cost and with minimum political risk.

C. Substantive Directions

During this second phase of competition law development, vertical restraints remained DG IV's substantive focus, reflecting the continuing perception that the system's central goal was integration and that such restraints were the chief obstacles to integration. Both the Court and the Commission continued to "extend" the application of Article 85 in the area of vertical restraints, although they increasingly operated within the discourse established by previous Court decisions.

---

[18] The first fine was levied in the Quinine cartels cases (Case 41/69, *ACF Chemiefarma NV v. Commission*, [1970] ECR 661; Case 44/69, *Buchler v. Commission*, [1970] ECR 733; and Case 45/69, *Boehringer Mannheim v. Commission*, [1980] ECR 769). For a complete list of fines levied by the Commission in competition law cases, see Lennart Ritter, W. David Braun & Francis Rawlinson, EEC COMPETITION LAW: A PRACTITIONER'S GUIDE 721-34 (1991).

The most dramatic development during this period, however, was the activation of Article 86 and the concept of abuse of a market-dominating position. Seldom used during the foundational period, Article 86 now became a focus of conceptual development and an active area of enforcement. The Court's expansive, teleological reading of Article 86 in Continental Can signaled its willingness to support such a development, and throughout this period the Commission and the Court together broadened the application of the abuse concept.

The new political and economic circumstances of the 1970s encouraged the development of Article 86. The concern during the foundational period that article 86 might interfere with the objective of creating enterprises large enough to combat United States multinationals diminished, as technology, rather than mere size, became the key to international competitiveness. Moreover, Article 86 attracted political support as a response to the new inflationary pressures that arose during the 1970s. While inflation was only a minor threat in the late 1950s and the 1960s, the oil crisis created powerful inflationary pressures, and the Commission used Article 86 to discourage dominant firms from adding to these pressures. Finally, the integration imperative supported this development, because Article 86 cases typically involved vertical relationships that were not subject to Article 85.

The activation of Article 86 provided opportunities for both the Court and the Commission. Since that provision had been used sparingly during the foundational period, the Court could utilize it to maintain the intellectual momentum that had become such an important part of its role in the system. This allowed the Court, for example, to continue to rely on teleology in its decision-making. The development of Article 86 also allowed the Commission to maintain the symbolic momentum of integration without subjecting itself to the political risks of significantly increasing enforcement under Article 85.

While the Commission's enforcement emphasis continued to be on vertical restraints, it increasingly turned its attention to horizontal restraints during the 1970s. By levying fines in several major and well-publicized cartel cases involving large (and often non-Member State) firms, it sent a message that it was not afraid to apply Article 85 to horizontal restraints. At the same time, however, the Commission was also emphasizing the need for cooperation among European firms, particularly small- and medium-sized firms, as a means of competing effectively with United States corporations. Accordingly, it had to be careful not to allow competition law to become an obstacle to such cooperation.

D. The Role of National Legal Systems

The Community competition law system remained firmly in the hands of the Court and the Commission throughout this period. Community institutions made the important decisions, while national courts and competition officials continued to play a decidedly marginal role. Nevertheless, new factors entered the picture that eventually would alter the relationship between national and Community institutions.

The critical conceptual move was the Court's declaration in *BRT v. Sabam* that the competition law provisions of the Treaty were directly applicable in national courts.[19] This decision allowed private firms to seek redress for harms caused by violations of Community competition law by bringing private suits in national courts. The decision opened the way for a shift in the locus of power within the competition law system from Community institutions to national courts, but the impact of the decision would not be felt for more than a decade.

Another development with long-run implications was the growing tendency of Member States to create new competition law regimes or to revise existing ones along the model of the Community system. When Greece entered the Community in 1981, for example, it adopted a competition law modelled on Community competition law. As other countries moved in that direction, a European "model" of competition law became discernible. In the 1980s, this increasing congruence among competition law systems would generate systemic forces that would have been barely imaginable without it.

E. Tremors of Change

From the early 1970s through the mid-1980s, the competition law system did not appear to change significantly. Creation of a unified market remained the overriding objective that continued to structure the relationships between the Council and the Commission and shape the substantive contours of competition law. The urgency of utilizing competition law in the integration process may have even increased because progress seemed so elusive in other areas and because the risk of failure of that process may have seemed even more ominous.

Below the surface, however, new pressures and forces were forming. The respective roles of the Court, the Commission, and the Member States within the competition law system were beginning to change, but the full implications of these mutations remained concealed by the critical need to use competition law to maintain psychological momentum toward integration. All institutions had the same vital interest in achieving this goal, and thus the force of the integration imperative tended to support the system's structures and processes.

With the impending elimination of this imperative and the advent of new political and economic circumstances, these subterranean changes would "erupt" and shake the foundations of the competition law system.

III. Mid-1980s to Early 1990s: The Kaleidoscope Turns

Beginning in the mid-1980s, the system that had been constructed during the preceding three decades began to show signs of fundamental change. Since then, changes in its operational context, as well as in its institutional framework, have altered compe-

[19] Case 127/73, *Belgische Radio en Televise v. SV Sabam*, [1974] ECR 51.

tition law's roles and challenged its identity. As with the transformation of the Community's constitutional system described by Professor Weiler, these changes often have been kaleidoscopic, i.e., numerous small shifts in intra-systemic relationships over many years cumulate to create what appear as abrupt mutations of the system.

A. The Scene Changes

The most prominent change in the context of competition law has been the near unification of the Community's internal market symbolized by the talismanic "1992." Although the goal of achieving a single market by January 1, 1993 has not been fully achieved, most law-based obstacles to trade among the Member States have been eliminated.

The process of eliminating these obstacles had been gradual and halting over three decades, failing to ignite major structural changes in the European economy. The 1992 program engendered widespread confidence, however, that the single market actually would be achieved on or about January 1, 1993, and this confidence translated into rapid economic restructuring during the late 1980s and early 1990s.

A wave of mergers, acquisitions, joint ventures, and "strategic alliances" has significantly increased industrial concentration, in both national and European markets. This, in turn, has brought with it the development of "Euro" law firms, and the Europeanization of financial, insurance, and other services. According to a 1991 commentary, "1992 has already become a reality through the implementation of company strategies (e.g., alliances, mergers, buy-outs, agreements to define 'Community-wide norms', etc.)."

As the 1992 program was set in motion, the Single European Act of 1986 simultaneously introduced changes in the institutional framework of the Community's competition law.[20] That enactment broke the bottleneck of the unanimous voting requirement in the Council that had dominated Community institutional life since the 1960s. While not eliminating the unanimous voting requirement, it significantly increased the range of issues for which qualified majority voting could be used. This meant that, as Professor Weiler asserts, all decision-making was to be made "under the shadow of the vote."[21] It also increased the power and scope of authority of the Commission in several respects, and addressed the problem of the "democratic deficit" in Community institutions by increasing the (still marginal) role of the European Parliament in the Community's legislative process.

Buoyed by the psychological success of the 1992 program, Community leaders reached agreement on further unification proposals at the Maastricht Summit in December, 1991.[22] That agreement focused on achieving a common currency by the

---

20 Single European Act (SEA), Feb. 28, 1986, 1986 O.J. (L 169) 30, reprinted in 25 I.L.M. 506 (1986) (hereinafter SEA).

21 Joseph H.H. Weiler, *The Transformation of Europe*, 100 Yale L.J. 2403 (1991), at 2461.

22 The treaty negotiated at Maastricht, known as the Treaty on the European Union.

end of the decade and expanding the scope of Community prerogatives. Although the luke-warm popular political response to Maastricht has slowed progress toward these ambitious goals, stronger political and monetary integration is still the Community's near-term goal.

The impact of these changes in the context of competition law has been magnified by the actual and probable increases in the size of the Community and in the scope of application of Community law. Actual increases have been twofold. Spain and Portugal became members in 1986, increasing the population of the Community itself by almost 50 million. In addition, the signing in 1992 of the European Economic Area agreement with the members of the European Free Trade Association (EFTA) calls for extension of the application of much of Community law (including competition law) to those countries.

Probable future increases in the size of the Community are also significant because Community officials, governments, and businesses are forced to consider such increases in their long-range planning. Several EFTA members have filed applications for membership, and negotiations concerning membership were initiated with three of them (Austria, Sweden, and Finland) in February, 1993. In addition, there has been pressure on the Community to consider the future membership of post-socialist countries such as Hungary. These actual and probable extensions of the scope of Community law take on an additional dimension in the case of competition law because, with the exception of Sweden, competition law either has been non-existent or has played a decidedly marginal role in the states to which Community law has been or soon may be extended.

Finally, the Single European Act also changed the context of competition law by formally adding new policy goals and values that compete, at least potentially, with those of competition law. For example, it explicitly recognized industrial policy as a Community goal, and it extended the Commission's authority in environmental and social areas.

Taken together, these changes in institutional structures and constitutional relationships fundamentally alter the context in which the competition law system operates. Not surprisingly, they are also generating fundamental changes within that system.

B. The Changing Role of Adjudication

The central mutation in the competition law system involves the Court's intellectual leadership. Beginning in the mid-1980s, judges and former judges of the Court began articulating the notion that the Court should or would become less "activist." They have suggested that the Court may no longer need to play as aggressive a role as it played in the past and that other institutions are now in a position to carry more of the burden of integrating the Community. Although the depth and ultimate impact of these views remain unclear, any such changes in the Court's self-perception necessarily influence its capacity for intellectual leadership.

Some observers have noted changes in the decisions of the Court that tend to reflect the Court's evolving conception of its role. In competition law, as in other areas of Community law, "(t)he Court, which in the first decades issued future-oriented judgments with generalized significance, today endeavors to limit itself to the statements required for the decision of the concrete legal controversy."[23] The Court's opinions tend to focus more narrowly on resolving the issues in the case under litigation through the use of existing concepts, preferably at relatively low levels of abstraction. To this extent, therefore, the Court's intellectual leadership role has diminished, for such opinions cannot "set the agenda" in competition law matters.

The Court's methodology has also evolved in accordance with this change in its leadership role. The teleological reasoning that the Court relied on so heavily during earlier periods has become less evident, as the Court turns increasingly to the manipulation of narrower principles drawn largely from its own previous decisions. Teleology is an appropriate tool for an aggressive court, while reasoning that relies primarily on the authority of existing concepts and decisions comports more easily with a more cautious role.

Reduced reliance on teleology, in turn, undermines the supportive link that the Court had established between teleology and pragmatic style. The predominance of the teleological method allowed the Court to avoid the need to create a well-defined conceptual grammar to support its reasoning. Its style could remain relatively imprecise and pragmatic because the primary criterion for interpreting and applying norms was their utility in achieving the single-market goal, and this goal did not require, or even easily permit, conceptual rigor.

One component of this methodological change has been a shift from the use of relatively formal criteria for evaluating conduct to increasingly "effects-based" criteria. Whereas during earlier periods the Court often was willing to assess the legal characteristics of conduct by reference to the terms of the relevant agreements, it has increasingly demanded that such assessments be based on economic analysis of the likely consequences of such conduct under the specific circumstances of the case.

This shift in analysis has important and largely unrecognized implications for the competition law system. Formal criteria are well-suited to application by the Court, because they allow decisions to be made on the basis of documentary analysis. They require neither detailed investigation of economic circumstances nor sophistication in economic analysis. It is a task for which lawyers are trained and with which judges are comfortable.

In contrast, courts are not well-adapted to evaluating the market effects of conduct. Judges typically have neither the training nor the experience to undertake such evaluations with confidence and expertise. In the case of the European Court, the problem is exacerbated by the diverse national origins of the judges, for each has different economic experiences and different vocabularies for interpreting such conduct.[24] In addi-

---

[23] Ulrich Everling, *Rechtsvereinheitlichung durch Richterrecht in der Europaischen Gemeinschaft*, 50 RABELS ZEITSCHRIFT FUR AUSLANDISCHES UND INTERNATIONALES PRIVATRECHT 193, 208 (1986).

[24] The judges come from twelve different Member States with different histories, cultures, economic and social orders, and, above all, legal systems. They bring their varying traditions, methods and values to adjudication. . . . This situation is important for understanding their decisions. The differing historical, economic and legal backgrounds of the individual judges are particularly influential in competition law matters that require economic evaluation. Ulrich Everling, *Zur Wettbewerbskonzeption in der neueren Rechtsprechung des Gerichtshofs der Europaischen Gemeinschaften*, 40 WUW 995, 1000 (1990), at 996.

tion, the Court's procedures make detailed factual analysis of economic circumstances particularly difficult and inefficient due to the cumbersome fact-taking process and the need for translations.

As a result, the shift in methodology toward requiring additional economic analysis necessarily pushes the Court toward a more marginal role in the system. Because the Court is not in a position generally to carry out such analysis itself, it increasingly must rely on the Commission for the evaluation of economic facts and limit itself to assessing the adequacy of the Commission's procedures in making such evaluations.

The cumulative impact of these mutually reinforcing changes impels the Court to adopt a role in the competition law system akin to that of an administrative court. According to this conception of its role, the Court's basic function is that of assuring that the Commission, as the executive organ of the Community, performs its functions correctly and operates within the rules and principles established for it by the Community's political organs.

The Court increasingly has articulated its own understanding of its role in such terms. For example, in the *Remia* case, it said,

> Although as a general rule the Court undertakes a comprehensive review of the question whether or not the conditions for the application of Article 85(1) are met, it is clear that in determining the permissible duration of a non-competition clause incorporated in an agreement for the transfer of an undertaking the Commission has to appraise complex economic matters. The Court must therefore limit its review of such an appraisal to verifying whether the relevant procedural rules have been complied with, whether the statement of the reasons for the decision is adequate, whether the facts have been accurately stated and whether there has been any manifest error of appraisal or a misuse of powers.[25]

This statement reveals a new conception of the Court's role in competition law matters that does not easily support the Court's intellectual leadership.

A narrowing of the Court's role in the competition law system is fueled not only by changes in the Court's general methodology and self-definition, but also by the impending evaporation of the single-market goal as the keystone of competition law. As we have seen, the Court structured its role in the competition law system around that goal, which was frequently a source of political support for the Court's role. As that goal recedes in importance, political support for bold steps in competition law is likely to weaken as well, and the intellectual force of competition law may be called into question. These increases in both political and intellectual uncertainty do not comport easily with a leadership role.

The creation of the Court of First Instance in 1989 added to this uncertainty. The Court of First Instance now generally hears all cases involving competition law decisions of the Commission, reducing the role of the Court of Justice in the competition

[25] Case 42/84, *Remia v. Commission*, [1985] ECR 2566, 2575.

law system to deciding appeals from the Court of First Instance and responding to questions from Member State courts. As a result, competition law cases have become a less prominent part of the Court's workload, reducing the amount of time the judges spend on such cases and thus diminishing their expertise in, and familiarity with, competition law issues. Moreover, the Court of First Instance necessarily reduces the Court's control over developments within the system. Instead of one judicial voice, there are now two.

Finally, the sheer growth of case law may tend to reduce the opportunities for the Court to exercise intellectual leadership. The notion here is that once the "big" issues have been resolved and the basic conceptual framework has been established, a court has less room to play an aggressive role. There is simply more law, and this tends to restrict the Court's role. The importance of this issue is difficult to assess, however, because there is no *a priori* basis for assessing the degree to which existing conceptual structures constrain the development of legal doctrine. The rapid changes in economic and political circumstances in recent years might well have justified a continued high level of aggressiveness by the Court, but the Court has tended to prefer a more conservative course.

This change in the Court's role has ramifications for the entire competition law system. As the Court's role narrows, its methods and its discourse also become less influential. As the Court plays a lesser role in setting the agenda of competition law and shaping its central decisions, the Commission has less reason to structure its decision-making by reference to the Court's methods. Moreover, there is less reason for others, both inside and outside the system, to utilize the language and the methods associated with the Court.

C. The Commission's Changing Roles

These changes in the role of the Court are intertwined with changes in the role of the Commission. Growth in the Commission's power, authority, and confidence have both reflected and contributed to the erosion of the Court's leadership role.

1. Formulating Policy

The evolution of the Commission's role can be seen in the changing influences on its policy-formulation function. When making policy, DG IV looks to a variety of sources for guidance and responds to many forms of influence, and the relative strength of these sources and influences is changing.

The Commission is, for example, less dependent on the Court than it was during earlier periods. As long as the Court was articulating broad pro-integration goals and competition law principles and enjoyed solid political support for that function, the Commission had to pay careful attention to the Court's agenda. Due to its own relatively insecure political position, the Commission was constrained to follow the Court's lead. Moreover, the Commission could rely on the Court to approve its policy choices as long as they were pro-integration (which they generally were). Furthermore, the Court's high status protected the Commission's initiatives from political attack.

With the impending loss of the integration imperative and the Court's growing reluctance to articulate broad legal principles, there is less reason for the Commission to look to the Court for guidance, and the Court has less guidance to provide.

Similarly, there is less reason for the Commission to construct policy within the constraints of the Court's methodology and discourse. When the Commission depended on the Court's support for the success of its own initiatives, it was important to look to these sources in order to predict the Court's responses. Moreover, by using the Court's own discourse and methods the Commission increased the likelihood of influencing the Court's responses. As the Court's role narrows, these influences are correspondingly diminished, and thus its methods lose some of their force within the competition law system.

The expansion of the Community also contributes to this weakening of the influence of juridical methods. The newer Member States and those states likely soon to enter the Community typically either do not have competition law systems or have competition law systems that are (or until recently were) based on administrative control models. As a consequence, decision-makers from these states often have little or no experience with a juridical conception of competition law and they tend to see competition law in political, rather than juridical, terms.

This reduction in the force of juridical discourse has occurred as the need to accommodate other goals in the formulation of competition policy has grown. For example, there has been increased pressure to consider industrial policy and trade factors in making competition policy decisions. Furthermore, the SEA's sanctioning of social, environmental, and other goals requires the accommodation of these goals in applying Community competition law. The need to integrate these goals provides opportunities for intellectual leadership within the competition law system, but thus far the Court has contributed little to this accommodation. Instead, to the extent that such integration is occuring at all, it is being driven primarily by the Commission and primarily on the basis of political considerations.

2. The Enforcement Challenge

The Commission's enforcement role is also changing in ways that affect the entire system. Since DG IV is responsible for both policy formulation and enforcement, developments that affect one of these functions generally also influence the other. In particular, the institutional and economic changes of recent years have further taxed the Commission's capacity to induce compliance with competition law norms, and the minimal increase in the resources of DG IV has forced the Commission to adopt strategies to compensate for its lack of resources.

One new burden was the expansion of the Community to include Spain and Portugal, which significantly increased the population and area over which compliance must be induced. The inexperience with competition law in these countries added to the burden by increasing the difficulty of adequately informing firms of competition law norms and securing their willingness to respect those norms.

The cross-boundary business consolidations of the late 1980s and early 1990s have also "upped the ante" in the compliance game. As firms have increased in size, the fines imposed by the Commission have become less significant in relation to their financial resources and to the stakes involved in particular policies or transactions. This increases both the willingness and the capacity of such firms to resist or evade Commission enforcement efforts. Furthermore, the elimination of obstacles to the flow of goods and services across national borders provides additional incentives for firms to seek private contractual arrangements that would shield them from increased transborder competition.

Finally, not only have the obstacles to effective enforcement increased, but support for competition law enforcement has also been compromised. Effective enforcement in the Community context presupposes general acceptance of competition law goals. Yet the imminent loss of the integration imperative and the perceived conflict of competition goals with industrial policy, trade, and other goals diminish the moral force behind competition law.

3. From Adjudication to Legislation

As enforcement obstacles and policy uncertainty have increased, the Commission has turned increasingly to legislation to accomplish its objectives. Until the 1980s, the Commission established competition law norms primarily through the process of adjudication. Relying heavily on notifications for its information, the Commission evaluated individual fact situations in relation to the norms developed by the Court and to the Commission's own policy objectives. The Court was at the center of this process, because if the Court failed to support the Commission, it could effectively prevent the Commission from establishing the norms it sought to establish. During the 1980s, however, DG IV turned increasingly away from this procedure and toward legislation as a means of establishing competition law norms. Rather than depending on the Court to articulate norms of conduct in individual cases, it increasingly began to prescribe such norms itself. From formal and binding group exemptions to relatively informal and non-binding general notices, prescription has become the dominant means of establishing conduct norms.

This strategy has many attractions for DG IV. Prescription is generally quicker and less costly than adjudication, which helps to offset the growth of DG IV's workload in relation to its resources. It also addresses the increasing demands made by political and business groups for more "security" in competition law, by providing companies with clearer information about the types of conduct that will probably lead to Commission action. In addition, while adjudication relies on general principles, legislation allows for differentiation according to geographic regions and economic sectors, and this facilitates the development of industrial policy. Finally, legislation tends to increase DG IV's power within the system; legislation is an independent act of the Commission in which the Court has no direct role.

The shift of power from the Court to the Commission has significant consequences for the operation of the system. When the Commission legislates, governments, firms, and lawyers look to the Commission rather than the Court for guidance and opportunities to influence the content of competition law norms. The process of legislative prescription by the Commission replaces the process of adjudication by the Court as the focal point of the system.

The characteristics of the Commission's legislation amplify this impact. For example, an important form of legislation, the block exemption, is highly formalistic. Block exemptions typically provide lists of acceptable, possibly acceptable, and unacceptable clauses. This induces firms to structure their agreements to conform to these checklists, leading to a relatively inflexible legal regime. Moreover, the exemptions often become virtually mandatory. According to one study, "Member States and their business communities tend to regard them not as waivers of the law but as compulsory codes of conduct."[26]

The case of block exemptions illustrates that legislation tends to broaden the existing prohibitions beyond levels established by the Court. In these exemptions, according to one expert, the Commission

> goes exceptionally far beyond that which the European Court wanted to approve, and, on the other hand, regulates in a hair-splitting way the very last details. . . . The result is in the end a very broad prohibition . . ., but some ninety-five percent of the contracts affected are nevertheless allowed under block exemptions created by the Commission.[27]

This further alters the relationship between the Court and the Commission. It permits the Commission to augment its own power and position within the system and undermines the adjudicative role of the Court.

4. The Impact of Merger Control

Another factor that has altered the role of the Commission within the competition law system is the Merger Regulation,[28] which was introduced in 1989 and represents the single most important addition to Community competition law since its inception. The Commission began to call for merger legislation in the early 1970s, but political opposition prevented enactment of such legislation for almost twenty years until the SEA's pro-integration impulses prevailed. While the immediate problems associated with implementation of this new legislation have generated extensive commentary, relatively little attention has been paid to its impact on the system as a whole.

The Merger Regulation provides, in essence, that "concentrations" (including both mergers and certain joint ventures) that have a "community dimension" are subject to Community regulation and removed from the jurisdiction of the national competition law authorities. The Commission must be notified of such mergers prior to implementation, and the Commission may prohibit the merger where it would "create or strengthen a dominant position as a result of which effective competition would be significantly impeded in the common market or in a substantial part of it."[29]

---

[26] Forrester & Norall, *The Laicization of Community Law: Self-Help and the Rule of Reason: How Competition Law Is and Could Be Applied*, 21 C.M.L.R. 11, 15 (1984).

[27] Ernst Niederleithinger, *Schwerpunkte der Diskussion*, 201 SCHRIFTEN DES VEREINS FUR SOCIAL POLITIK 56, 58 (1990).

[28] Council Regulation 4064/89, 1990 O.J. (L 257) 14 [*corrected version of* 1989 O.J. (L 395) 1].

[29] *Id.* at 17.

The introduction of this system has fundamentally altered competition policy in Europe. By centralizing authority to deal with large mergers, it has focused attention on the Commission and greatly enhanced its potential for influencing major business decisions. Whereas prior to the Merger Regulation this authority was scattered among the competition authorities of the Member States (many of which did not, in practice, make significant use of it), efforts to influence decision-making in this area now focus on DG IV. Moreover, because of its enormous political and economic importance, the Merger Regulation immediately became a focus of DG IV's own attention, occupying an exceptionally large part of DG IV's time, resources, and interest and shifting attention away from the conventional areas of DG IV's activity.

The Merger Regulation also represents a shift of influence from the juridical components of the Commission's activity to its political elements. The Court plays virtually no role in the merger area, which is almost exclusively the province of the Commission. This allows political issues to dominate decision-making.

Experience with the Merger Regulation substantiates this claim. By late 1991, the Merger Regulation had been in effect for almost two years, and some sixty-five mergers had been noticed under its provisions without Commission disapproval. This lack of action had led to widespread speculation that the Commission did not have the political courage actually to use the Regulation to prohibit a merger. In October of 1991, however, the Court issued an order prohibiting a merger involving a Canadian corporation, De Havilland, and a French/Italian consortium.[30] The result was a storm of protest from the French and Italian governments alleging that the Commission had been overly legalistic in applying the statute and should have paid greater heed to industrial policy factors. This campaign was taken so seriously that the French government was rumored to be considering an effort to oust the entire Commission. Not surprisingly, the Commission has not prohibited any mergers since then.

The Merger Regulation has significantly affected perceptions of competition law and of the forces at play within it. Its enactment underscored the perception that the interesting and important aspects of competition law were moving to Brussels and away from the national competition authorities. Merger control tends to be the most visible as well as the most economically and politically significant part of competition law, and its migration toward Brussels seemed to presage a time when important issues would be handled primarily at the Community rather than the Member State level.

Yet this very expectation has tended to undermine confidence in Community competition law. The *De Havilland* case demonstrated the degree to which political forces can influence Commission decision-making and the difficulty of enforcing competition law provisions that might have significant adverse consequences on important Member States. The image of power moving to Brussels, combined with the apparent political vulnerability of the Commission's enforcement efforts, suggests a future in

---

[30] Case IV/M.053, *Aerospatiale-Alenia/de Havilland v. Commission*, 1991 O.J. (L 334) 42. See generally Andrew Wachtman, *The European Community Commission* de Havilland *Decision: Potential Problems in Community Merger Control are Realized*, 21 CAP.U.L.REV. 685 (1992); Michael J. Reynolds, *The* de Havilland *Case: A Watershed for EC Merger Control*, 10 Int'l Fin.L.Rev. 21 (1991).

which competition law may play a minor and politicized role rather than its traditional major and juridical role.

5. The Commission and the System

During the last few years the Commission has strengthened and expanded its role in the competition law system. With a new confidence generated by the SEA and the approach of the internal market, it has moved to set the agenda for competition law and provide new momentum for the system. In doing so, the Commission has moved toward the center of the system while the Court has inched toward the margins. This expansion of the Commission's role is likely to have a fundamental impact on the system; it means that, in essence, a political institution has replaced a judicial institution as the driving force within the competition law system.

D. Substantive Law: The "Public Turn"

The changes within the competition law system have been accompanied by a dramatic shift in the system's substantive focus. The Commission has shifted the emphasis in competition law away from its traditional concerns with private conduct and toward the problem of government interference with the competitive process, and the Court has supported this change in focus. As the Commission stated in its 1990 report, "(w)hilst many barriers to intra-Community trade and competition are created by companies themselves . . . it is felt that at the present stage of economic integration in the Community the barriers are greatest in markets currently subject to state regulation."[31]

This heightened concern for the role of governments has taken several forms. It includes, for example, the activation and development of Article 90, which applies the competition law provisions of the treaty to "public" enterprises and enterprises enjoying "special or exclusive rights," except to the extent that such application would obstruct the performance of the public function entrusted to such enterprises.[32] This provision was seldom used until the mid-1980s, but recently it has become an important part of Community competition law.[33]

The Commission has taken several important legislative steps to enhance the application of the competition provisions to State monopolies. In 1988, it issued a directive under Article 90 which required the elimination of the monopoly rights of State-owned enterprises where they had specified negative impacts on competition.[34]

---

[31] COMMISSION OF THE EUROPEAN COMMUNITIES, TWENTIETH REPORT ON COMPETITION POLICY 50 (1990).

[32] Treaty Establishing the European Economic Community [Treaty of Rome] at Art. 90.

[33] Up until the entry into force of the Single European Act, Article 90 was rarely applied, but has recently become a key Treaty provision in connection with the deregulation of certain sectors and in terms of the equal treatment of private and public undertakings.

Claus-Dieter Ehlermann, *The Contribution of EC Competition Policy to the Single Market*, 29 C.M. L. Rev. 257, 264 (1992).

[34] Commission Directive 88/301, 1988 O.J. (L 131) 73.

The new directive extended and intensified the impact of prior directives, which required greater "transparency" for state-owned enterprises (i.e., disclosure of information regarding the state's financial involvement in such enterprises).[35]

The Commission also has intensified the enforcement of Article 90. For example, in the 1991 *Telecommunications Terminals* case[36] the Court held that British Telecommunications, a state monopoly, was not protected from the application of Article 86 to certain activities that appeared to serve a public purpose. The Court distinguished between functions that were inherently governmental and those that were essentially commercial. This decision signaled that the Court would construe exemptions from the competition provisions for public monopolies very narrowly.

The Commission's intensified application of existing rules regarding state aids also reflects its new concern with the impact of governments on competition. The potential political cost of vigorous attacks on state aids had constrained enforcement of these principles until the 1980s, but, supported by the impetus of the SEA, the Commission has made state aids a prominent feature of its recent enforcement activities. Moreover, there has been increasing recognition that this area of law should be integrated with competition law rather than remain separate and distinct from it.

The Court and the Commission also have developed new legal doctrines to address state interference with competition. Of primary importance is the line of cases prohibiting governments from interfering with the effective operation ("effet utile") of Articles 85 and 86. This obligation to refrain from interference began to take shape in the *INNO v. ATAB* case in 1977,[37] but it has only become important since the Court's 1985 decision in *Leclerc v. Au Ble Vert*.[38] The Court has held, for example, that governments may not require compliance with anticompetitive agreements. In the Flemish Travel Agents case, the Court ruled that the Belgian government could not prosecute a travel agent for violating a royal decree requiring compliance with trade association rules that prohibited price competition among travel agents.[39] This doctrine of *effet utile* has also been applied in cases in which the government has encouraged or otherwise supported anticompetitive private activity.[40]

---

35 Commission Directive 80/723, 1980 O.J. (L 195) 35, amended by Commission Directive 85/413, 1985 O.J. (L 229) 20.

36 Case C-202/88, *France v. Commission (Telecommunications Terminals)*, [1991] ECR 1223.

37 Case 13/77, *NV GB-INNO-BM v. Vereniging van de Kleinhandelaars in Tabak*, [1977] ECR 2115.

38 Case 229/83, *Association des Centres distributeurs Edouard Leclerc v. S.A.R.L.*, [1985] ECR 1. ("Member States are . . . obliged under the second paragraph of Article 5 of the Treaty not to detract, by means of national legislation, from the full and uniform application of Community law or from the effectiveness of its implementing measures; nor may they introduce or maintain in force measures, even of a legislative nature, which may render ineffective the competition rules applicable to undertakings.")

39 Case 311/85, *VZW Vereniging van Vlaamse Reisbureaus v. VZW Sociale Dienst van de Plaatselijke en Gewestelijke Overheidsdiensten*, [1987] ECR 3801. See also Case 136/86, *Bureau National Interprofessionel* du Cognac v. Aubert, [1987] ECR 4789 (holding that Community law precluded prosecution on the basis of a regulation establishing, inter alia, quotas for the sale of spirits).

40 Case 66/86, *Ahmed Saeed Flugreisen v. Zentrale zur Bekampfung Unlauteren Wettbewerbs e.V.*, [1989] ECR 803 (holding that government approval of collusive airline tariffs conflicts with the EEC treaty).

This shift toward public rather than private influences on the competitive process has been evident even within traditional areas of competition law. Under Article 86, in particular, the Commission has centered its enforcement efforts on abuses of power by firms either owned or controlled by governments, or by those whose governmental protection has recently been eliminated as part of the privatization process. For example, in the British Telecom case, the Court held that a British telecommunications monopoly had abused its economic power by refusing to sell advertising time to a potential competitor.[41]

These influences have been less marked in the context of Article 85, although some have noted a shift in emphasis from vertical restraints to horizontal restraints. The Commissioner for competition law recently labelled such a shift as "inevitable" in the wake of the 1992 Program. Even here, however, "public" and "political" issues have become increasingly important, particularly in regard to the evaluation under Article 85(3) of so-called "crisis cartels," which often implicate the industrial policy concerns of the Member States.

Finally, as mentioned above, the new and central role of merger control in Community competition law is highly political. Decisions regarding mergers are often a matter of great political concern, because they often involve issues of jobs, taxes, and economic power. As a result, governments demand to be heard, and political factors influence competition law decisions.

This brief review suggests the degree to which the substantive focus of competition law has shifted since the mid-1980s. For almost three decades the predominant, almost exclusive, focus of enforcement and intellectual development within Community competition law was private conduct, particularly vertical restraints on competition. During the last few years, however, concern about governmental activities has shaped the development of Community competition law.

This change may have many implications. The conceptual shift seems likely to be related, for example, to the enhanced role of the Commission in the system. Courts are appropriate agents for dealing with the application of general norms to private conduct, but they tend to be less effective where political issues are central. As the Commission's political position has been improved by the SEA, its willingness to accept the political risks associated with these issues has increased. Moreover, the prospect of enhancing its power within the system has provided an incentive for the Commission to move in that direction.

E. National Systems: The Dilemma of Decentralization

The role of national institutions within the Community competition law system has also begun to change. By the mid-1980s, the European Court had virtually eliminated conceptual limits on the scope of Community competition law. It had expanded the Treaty of Rome's concept of "effect on trade" between the Member States to a point

---

[41] Case 41/83, *Italy v. Commission*, [1985] ECR 873; see also Case 311/84, *Centre belge d'etudes de marche—Telemarketing SA v. Compagnie luxembourgeoise de telediffusion SA*, [1985] ECR 3261.

where few major business transactions fell outside the reach of the Treaty's competition law provisions. Ironically, at about this time calls for decentralizing responsibility for competition law enforcement began to increase. These calls have become part of a broader move toward decentralization associated with the Maastricht negotiations.

Decentralization creates a dilemma. To the extent that it is effective, it reduces the strain on Commission resources, limits or reverses the concentration of political power, and improves compliance. Yet it also reduces the capacity of Community institutions to influence the development of competition law and to use the system in pursuit of their own objectives. Decentralization also amplifies the risk of inconsistencies within the system. As a result, Community institutions have moved slowly and cautiously in this area.

In the competition law context, decentralization has two main components. The first relates to the role of national courts in applying Community law. Recently, the Commission has encouraged complainants to file actions in national courts rather than rely on DG IV to secure compliance with competition law norms. The dramatic increase in the use of group exemptions facilitates such a development, because national courts can rule on whether conduct meets the standards of group exemptions. Despite this development and the judicial establishment of the direct effect of the competition law provisions, the Commission's pleas for the use of national courts have largely gone unheeded.

The second set of decentralization issues relates to the role of national competition authorities within the system. During the foundational period, Member States typically had either no competition law or one that was unimportant. Today, all Member States have competition law regimes, and these have increased in power and significance. Furthermore, they have come to resemble more closely the Community competition law system, as confidence in the future of the Community has encouraged Member States to enact competition law regimes or modify existing regimes to correspond more closely to Community law. Spain and Italy, for example, have recently introduced competition law systems for the first time, and France significantly reformed its loose set of competition-related norms and institutions in 1986, shaping a system akin to that of the Community.

This evolution reduces the need, perceived since the construction of the competition law system, to centralize competition law authority in the Commission. If national competition law authorities are enforcing similar substantive rules in similar ways, there is less reason to place primary responsibility on an already under-staffed Community institution. Resistance to such centralization also draws support from the growing group of competent and influential national competition law officials, who often believe that they can protect competition as well or better than the authorities in Brussels and who generally are disinclined to reduce their power.

The Community's competition law system thus has undergone major changes since the mid-1980s. The goals, methods, and roles of its institutions look very different today than they did less than a decade ago. Although many of these changes began to emerge before the mid-1980s, the new political and economic circumstances brought about by the Single European Act enhanced the scope and impact of these changes and made them "visible."

IV. Transformation and the Search For Identity

Has Community competition law been transformed? It has not in the sense that doctrines or institutions themselves have radically changed. It is the system that has mutated—both its goals and its processes. The image of a self-confident Commission enforcing an increasingly clear set of well-accepted legal principles under the forward-looking and bold guidance of a Court confident of its objectives and methods is not persuasive. The system is more convincingly portrayed as featuring an under-staffed and somewhat uncertain Commission facing new problems, pressures, and demands with diminishing guidance from the Court and increasingly tentative support for its mission. The competition law system thus faces what can aptly be described as an "identity crisis."

A. The Changing Roles of Competition Law

Driven and defined throughout its history by the goal of creating a single market for Europe, the competition law system increasingly must operate without its lodestar. Competition law conceived as a means of achieving economic integration loses its way where such integration already has been achieved. A system constructed and maintained to achieve one primary goal now faces fundamental questions about what it is doing and why. Shorn of its special role in achieving economic integration, the competition law system must redefine its mission, and this process is likely to further destabilize the conceptual framework that has informed competition law.

The resulting uncertainty is exacerbated by increasing demands for accommodation between competition law goals and other goals of the Community. Trade policy, social concerns, and environmental claims, inter alia, must be reconciled with the objectives of competition law. Moreover, these demands have grown more insistent with the approach of the single market and the concomitant elimination of competition law's special status as a "motor of integration." Consequently, just as the keystone of the existing goal structure is being removed (and in part because of the imminence of that removal), lateral pressure from other values and policies is increasing, generating even further uncertainty about the roles of competition law.

One response to this situation would be to turn toward more "generic" competition law goals—i.e., generic benefits associated with protecting the process of competition. Such goals have lived in the shadow of the integration imperative since the foundational period, but they rarely have been explored in their own right, primarily because integrationist and generic goals have been intermingled, and there has been little reason to distinguish between them. This has led to the assumption that "unbundling" these goals will change little and to a lack of concern about the potential impact of eliminating integrationist goals. The assumption, however, remains unexamined, shielded from examination by the natural resistance to changing one's conceptual framework and the political risks of doing so.

Yet removal of the integration imperative necessarily alters competition law goal structures and the associated discourse. Without it, there will be increased pressure on

DG IV's decision-makers to articulate other goals with far more care than in the past. Should market efficiency be the sole goal? If not, which other values should be served and how should such other goals relate to each other, i.e., what should be the new goal structure? These questions are likely to take on increasing urgency as the integration imperative fades.

This process of redefining the system's goals will also require a new language to relate specific decisions to the redefined structure. This will give new contours to some competition law issues and focus attention on other issues that have thus far played little or no role in competition law thinking. For example, the Court may need to define more carefully the concept of competition it employs. The Court generally has been able to skirt this issue, because its primary concern was to reduce barriers to the flow of goods across national borders. This relatively straightforward and "physical" criterion often did not invite deeper analysis. However, a goal structure consisting of generic competition law objectives demands a different concept of "competition" that is likely to be more difficult to define. National competition law systems have wrestled with these issues for decades, but the dominance of integrationist goals has obscured such concerns within Community competition law.

Changes in goals and discourse have also begun to redirect policy initiatives and enforcement energies. The predominant concern with vertical agreements that has been associated with the integration imperative has diminished, for example, as concerns associated with the generic benefits of competition turn attention toward horizontal restraints.

A second possible response to the uncertainties facing European competition law is to avoid them and turn to a different set of problems. This may help to explain the "public turn" of competition law. By turning away from the traditional private areas of competition law and focusing attention on the anticompetitive impact of governments, Community decision-makers avoid, at least temporarily, some of the difficulties involved in changing goals and concepts and "retooling" the system to achieve a new set of objectives. Moreover, by casting the activities of governments as the primary threat to competition, the Court and the Commission can use this relatively "clean slate" to maintain the symbolic momentum critical to the goal of political integration.

Removal of economic integration as the central goal of the competition law system does not mean that issues associated with economic integration will not arise in the future. They will, because the de jure integration of the Community's market does not automatically create de facto integration. Moreover, the existence of national cultures and governments will continue to create incentives for firms and groups of firms to evade the full implications of economic integration. The critical point is that the creation of a unified market removes such issues from their dominant, identity-defining position within the system.

B. Methods: Less Law, More Politics

Another process of erosion is also undermining the system's identity. Not only are the system's goals changing, but the means used to achieve those goals also have been quietly mutating. The "juridical component" that has been the core of the system since its earliest days has been losing influence relative to its political components. At least in some respects, the competition law system is becoming less juridical and more political.

At one level, this politicizing is a natural concomitant of change and uncertainty as to goals. As goals change and become less well-defined, concepts and practices developed to achieve such goals may appear less appropriate and reliable. The resulting lack of confidence in generalized principles may militate, therefore, in favor of increasingly ad hoc, political decision-making.

A more fundamental and pervasive factor relates to changes in the roles played by the Court and the Commission. As the Commission's role becomes more central and the Court's role becomes less dominant, the relative importance of the methods associated with these institutions changes accordingly.

The Court's dominant position in the system assured the centrality of juridical processes. As long as the Court was supplying intellectual leadership for the system, structuring its thought and guiding its development, the dominant discourse of the system was juridical. The principal decisions within the system were viewed as the result of applying juridical methodology to authoritative texts. Until very recently, the political situation within the Community assigned a high value to such "neutral" discourse.

In contrast, the Commission is an explicitly political institution. The more central its role in the system, the more influential political elements are likely to become. Its decisions reflect a variety of pressures resulting from the perceived interests of Member States, interest groups, and other Community institutions. As the Commission becomes less dependent on the Court for intellectual leadership and political "protection," its methods and discourse are likely to become more influential, and the influence of juridical discourse is likely to wane.

The reemergence of the conflict between the juridical model of competition law and an industrial policy model reflects this changed dynamic. That conflict was critically important during the early years of the system, and it was resolved in favor of the juridical model only when the Court stepped forward during the mid-1960s and assumed a bold leadership role within the competition law system. It is perhaps more than coincidence that this conflict has reemerged with new and sharper contours just as the Court has begun to pull back from such a role.

C. A "Transformation" Perspective

The image of Community competition law presented here contrasts sharply with conventional descriptions because it is created by using different lenses and asking different questions. A perspective that focuses on systemic relationships among decision-makers and on the interactions of those decision-makers with sources of decisional authority detects forces that remain undetected from more traditional perspectives, and it is these forces that are driving change.

Viewed from this perspective, the competition law system appears far less stable than many observers assume. The integration of the Community's market has undermined its goal structures as institutional changes have weakened support for its methods, and together these forces are transforming the system. Recognizing these forces thus becomes a matter of some urgency, because the sooner they are recognized, the better will be the opportunities for timely analysis of their implications and for effective responses to them.

Competition law has been central to the economic and political successes that have created a "new" Europe. As the Community moves toward further integration, much may depend on how the competition law system adapts to the political and economic dynamics of a single market. That system has long symbolized the constructive, "community-building" role of law in Europe, and if Community decision-makers adequately appreciate the dimensions and the impact of that system, it may continue to be able to play such a role in the future.

Part II - The Details

I. Company Law[42]

The law concerning the constitution of the firm and development of an EEC corporate law have been important issues at both the national and Community levels during the last twenty years. Due to the approval of the Single European Act and the intention of the European legislator to complete harmonization of the European internal market at the end of 1992, the harmonization projects concerning the constitution of the firm and a statute concerning the European Corporation (Societas "Europea" or "SE") are gaining new attention.

Since the EEC Commission published the so-called, "Green Paper," which contains a comparative analysis of national legal systems' requirements for the structure of corporations and provisions for co-determination rights for employees at the board level, the new proposals concerning the constitution of the firm are taking different "structural options" into account. Accordingly, the fifth directive, the SE regulation and the special SE co-determination directive provide the national legislatures with a choice between several approximately equal options, thus fulfilling the principle of functional equivalence.

Even though this new approach was rather astonishing under a system of legal harmonization, it was necessary due to the very different legal economic historical and even ideological structures in the Member States which created difficulties for the harmonization of corporate law. For example, these problems appeared during the negotiations of the fourth and seventh directives which concerned the law regulating the financial statements of single as well as groups of corporations. The European legislator solved these problems by offering a variety of options to the Member States. Without these options, the directives would not have passed. Of course, it is questionable whether such an approach leads to real harmonization of national legal structures, or whether the European legislator instead freezes these structures only on a European level without any harmonizing effect in the future.

---

[42] Thomas E. Abeltshauser, *Towards a European Constitution of The Firm: Problems and Perspectives*, Mich. J. Int'l L. 1235-1236 (1990).

A. The Statutory Basis[43]

In establishing the European Economic Community, the first Member States created a supranational contractual system which was not only unique concerning its general programs, but also in relation to its legal dimensions. For instance, the EC has law-making authority under the EEC Treaty. Under Article 145, in relation to Articles 2 and 3 of the EEC Treaty, the EC Council has authority not only to coordinate the economic policy of the Member States but also to decide on proposals of the Commission concerning legal harmonization directives and regulations. The Treaty, as well as the law made in accordance with the Treaty, is directly valid and applicable.

The enforcement of the goal mentioned in Articles 2 and 3 of the EEC Treaty requires a broad harmonization of national law. Article 3(h) in particular requires national legal provisions to be harmonized as far as such harmonization is necessary to the functioning of the Common Market. Therefore, legal harmonization is strongly related to the extent of integration already obtained in the EC and therefore has so-called dynamic character which corresponds to the dynamic character of the integration goals of the EC.

The statutory basis for Article 3(h) harmonization is Article 100, as well as Articles 100A, 100B and 189, para. 3 of the EEC Treaty. Article 54(3)(g) of the EEC Treaty in particular regulates the legal harmonization of corporate law. The EC uses the directive, the regulation and agreements under international law to harmonize national law. In doing so the EC not only creates a flexible supranational legal framework, but also considers very different historical, political and ideological traditions in the Member States.

B. The Fifth Directive[44]

By far the most significant area of coordination, and the most contested, is that of governance. Who makes decisions for the corporation, and who chooses the deciders?

The Commission proposed to deal with this subject in a document issued in 1972 and designated "fifth directive." Although a sixth, a seventh, an eighth, an eleventh, and a twelfth directive were proposed and adopted while the fifth was debated and revised, the governance directive continues to be known as the "fifth." Like the directives on capital and on merger, it is directed only to public companies.

The leitmotif of the directive is the control of corporate managers. In one of its aspects, it seeks to reinforce the same interest that has always motivated corporation laws, the interest of shareholders. In another aspect, it gives new recognition to an interest that was previously unmentioned in most corporation laws, the interest of employees. Notably absent is any effort to recognize the interests of the other corporate

---

43 *Id.* at 1245-1246.

44 Alfred F. Cornard, *The European Alternative to Uniformity in Corporation Laws*, Mich. L. Rev. 2182-2187 (1991).

constituencies, such as suppliers, customers, communities, and the national economy, which have emerged as desiderata in U.S. corporation law amendments of the 1980s.

The directive seeks to achieve its objectives through four main devices: (1) requiring independent supervision of management, (2) giving employees a voice in the selection of supervisors, (3) reinforcing the powers of shareholders, and (4) requiring an independent audit of corporate reports.

Although the first draft of the fifth directive was published in 1972, and a second in 1983, a final directive had not been issued by mid-1991, and agreement on it did not seem imminent. The liveliest prospect of implementation of its concepts was the likelihood that the Council would adopt an SE ("European Company") statute that would embody most of the same principles. But the choice of any company to bring itself under the SE statute would be entirely voluntary, and was expected to be embraced by no more than a handful of multinational enterprises.

1. Independent Supervision

The first draft of the fifth directive would have imposed a single formula for the independent supervision of management. Every public company would have a supervisory council (called the "supervisory organ" in the English version of the draft) of which managers could not be members, which would hire and fire the managers. Active management would be carried on by a subordinate manager or board of managers (called the "management organ"). This structure was a virtual reproduction of that prescribed for public companies by German law, which had prevailed in its essentials since 1884. France had authorized a similar structure as an option for public companies in 1967, but it was an innovation that French commentators regarded as a German import.

This assault on national folkways awakened expectable resistance in Member States, which intensified when Great Britain became a Member State in 1973. In 1983, the second draft of the directive offered States a free choice between a "two-tier system" on the German pattern and a "one-tier system" on the pattern that had prevailed in other States, and which is similar to that of the U.S. "board of directors."

The one-tier option differed from the provisions of U.S. corporation laws in requiring that the nonmanagement members of the board must constitute a majority. But this difference was more formal than real, since a majority of U.S. public corporations have adopted nonmanagement majorities in order to validate transactions involving management compensation and other managerial conflicts of interest. In one respect, U.S. case law seems to be even more productive of directorial independence than the directive, since it tends to disqualify from the "disinterested" category directors with family or financial ties to management. The directive, by contrast, seems to require nothing beyond the directors' not holding executive positions.

In placing reliance on the prevalence of nonexecutives in the governing organs, the Community experts were probably inspired by the German experience, in which banks participate actively as shareholders or as shareholders' custodians in the election of supervisory board members. German banks sometimes choose officers of corporate customers or suppliers who would not pass the American test of "disinterest." But the councilors that the banks select are more likely to act independently of management than councilors chosen by the managers themselves.

In other countries, where banks or other financial institutions do not effectively choose the council or management board members, the directive seems to present no obstacle to managers using proxy power to coopt as board members individuals who are bound to the managers by personal relationship or by economic dependence.

2. The Voice of Employees

If the fifth directive was radical in its proposal for supervision of management, it was revolutionary in its proposals for the voice of employees in corporate governance. These proposals applied, however, only to companies that employ five hundred or more individuals.

Under the 1972 draft, corporations would have had to give employees a voice in the selection of members of the supervisory council (which every public company, under this draft, was required to have), in one of two ways. One method, patterned after German law, required the election of at least one third of the council members by employees. The other method, patterned on Netherlands law, called for cooptation of new supervisory council members by the incumbent members, but gave to employee representatives the right to object to any appointment on the ground that the appointment would cause an "imbalance" in regard to the "interests of the company, the shareholders or the workers." These provisions awakened opposition not only from managers and shareholders, but also from labor leaders, especially British labor leaders, who saw the design as a detour around the power of union officers.

The 1983 draft added two new options to the means of representing employees. Under one of the new options, the employees could be given, instead of the right to appoint or to veto appointments of councilors, the right to have a representative body that would be regularly informed about company affairs, and consulted on major changes, plant closings, and substantial cutbacks. Under the other option, employee interests could be protected by any arrangement that was agreed on through collective bargaining and that required informing employee representatives about company affairs, and consulting them on major changes. A parallel set of options was offered for companies with one-tier systems of governance.

3. The Loyalty of Managers and Supervisors

The proposal to place representatives of both shareholders and employees on the governing council or board gave rise to a conceptual puzzle about the nature of the fiduciary duties that would be owed by these representatives of dissimilar constituencies. Were delegates of each class bound to advance the interests of their own class, and to oppose the interests of the other class when interests clashed? Although German law had provided for employees to elect council members since 1950, it had never addressed the possible conflict of the duties of the two classes of members.

The United Kingdom adopted in 1980 an express formulation of a directorial obligation to both shareholders and employees in these terms: "The matters to which the directors of a company are to have regard in the performance of their functions shall include the interests of the company's employees in general as well as the interests of its members." But this provision was directed only to representatives of shareholders, since British law made no provision for representation of employees.

The second draft of the fifth directive proposed answers to the question of conflicting loyalties in these two clauses:

> All members of the management and supervisory organs shall have the same rights and duties . . . .
> All the members of the management and supervisory organs shall carry out their functions in the interest of the company, having regard to the interests of the shareholders and employees.

4. The Powers of Shareholders

The directive's provisions on the powers of shareholders were not very different from those found in U.S. corporations laws. Shareholders must be notified of meetings and of agendas. There were no provisions comparable to those of the U.S. proxy rules requiring the company to inform shareholders about the compensation of officers and directors and the qualifications of directorial candidates. There was no suggestion of a shareholder's right to present proposals at company expense.

One example of a provision that might be regarded as protecting shareholders' voting rights better than U.S. laws do is the prescription that "[t]he shareholder's right to vote shall be proportionate to the fraction of the subscribed capital which the shares represent." This command is subject to an exception for "shares which carry special advantages," which in European parlance usually denote shares that Americans would call "preferred." In practice, the prescription means that common shares have voting rights based on their par values, which generally correspond in Europe to their initial public offering prices. Translated to the United States, it would exclude nonvoting common shares in public corporations.

C. The Constitution of the Firm[45]

1. The Constitution under Industrial Policy Perspectives of the Community

The study of legal harmonization in the field of the company's constitution is particularly interesting, since the Community touches deeply the fundamental values of the Member States. More legalization in the field of corporate structures has occurred. An analysis of this harmonization project thus promises to provide a scale by which to measure success of European integration and the limits of freedom of action within the community.

Today the industrial policy of the Community is part of a general economic policy which contains guidelines for medium-term economic policy through programs drawn up by the Council and by representatives of the governments of the Member States meeting in the Council. The basic principles of this industrial policy aim,

[45] Thomas E. Abeltshauser, *Towards a European Constitution of the Firm: Problems and Perspectives*, Volume Number 11 Mich. J. Int'l L. 1235, 1250-1255 (Summer 1990). Reprinted by permission.

among other objectives, to create a uniform legal, tax and financial order, particularly the restructuring of corporations in order to create a common corporate market. This is to be achieved, apart from the application of European competition law, by specific projects of legal harmonization in fields of law which hitherto produced and partitioned national markets into watertight compartments, supplemented by law widely applied in the Community. Thus, the Commission formulated a political program addressed to corporations, which shifts from the principle of individual adaptation of companies to modified market structures.

The "functions" of legal harmonization of corporate law were altered by this development. Corporate law directives and regulations lost their character as a general framework of rules of law. Instead, they became materially more and more bound within the formulated industrial policy program. The aim was to make it possible for corporations throughout the Community to work together with other such corporations, to make contracts, to establish firms or to merge with other companies, subject to conditions comparable to those with respect to formalities and security of law of individual States. The "policy of the law" revealed itself with the integration of political aims into harmonization programs. Today the program of legal harmonization in the field of corporate law comprises industrial policy functions. A uniform company constitution can considerably facilitate cooperation between companies with different nationalities and very different board structures.

2. The Constitution under Competition and Social Policy Perspectives of the EU

In essence, European competition law and policy constitute an opposite pole to European industrial policy because the latter favors economic concentration in the way explained above while the former controls concentration by avoiding monopolistic European market structures. This polarization increases the importance of efforts to harmonize corporate law and the constitution of the firm. The former neo-liberal approach strongly related harmonization of corporate law to certain economic constitutional structures. Today the national and the European legislator is confronted with a functional change in competition and corporate law. Considering this change, von der Groeben emphasizes that, according to the intention of the EEC Treaty, competition should not be understood as theoretical, complete competition in a transparent market with a polipolistic market structure, a view which in his opinion would be based only on a model theory with no practical value since economic concentration within the Community is increasing. Article 85 of the EEC Treaty protects a so-called "workable competition" model which is based on a functionalist understanding of competition. Accordingly, competition is then bound instrumentally within the objectives of a welfare state system in which economic functions (distribution of income, composition of supply, control of production, technical progress, etc.) are complemented by social policy objectives. The optimum realization of these functions is accomplished with optimum intensity of competition, which, it is claimed, is achieved in the market form of broad oligopoly. In addition, Article 85(3) also shows the relativity of the way in which principles are oriented purely toward competition. The declaration of exemption provided for under this article is subject to exceptions of weak participants in the market in relation to certain goals of industrial, structural and middle class policies of the EEC.

European company constitution rules should therefore be subsumed under competition policy objectives, since harmonization of company constitution rules and legal structures for co-determination rights means similar structural requirements and social cost burdens for companies operating in more than one country within the Community. This can prevent threatened distortions of competition, advance equality of competition and offer protection against a flood of co-determination—a fear created by the German situation.

In addition to the increasing influence of competition policies on European company law, the welfare state and social policies also develop a certain influence on this field of law. Social costs in the context of the discussion concerning Article 117 of the EEC Treaty (rules concerning the social policy of the Community and the harmonization of social welfare provisions of the Member States) were initially regarded as being neutral for competition and company law. Only in exceptional cases did social differences appear relevant to competition and require a harmonization of law. On the other hand, the Social Policy Action Program of the Community, created in 1974, proves that just as much importance was attached to energetic measures in the social sphere as to the achievement of the economic and monetary union. Correspondingly, there also are references to the necessity for co-determination rights in company decisions in the fourth program for the medium-term economic policy of the Community of March 14, 1977.

An essential problem of harmonization of company constitution law is posed by the rapidly increasing internationalization of production structures which caused completely new problems and conflicts for several social groups. There were no legal precautions against this development in the Member States, and today such precautions are evolving only hesitantly.

II. Competition Policy[46]

The basic elements of the Community's competition law system were developed over the first decade and a half of its existence. During this period, the basic goals of the system were formulated and its institutional relationships forged.

The Treaty of Rome includes brief substantive principles relating to restraints on competition but provides little guidance for the construction of a system to apply those principles. Article 85(1) prohibits agreements that restrain competition, giving examples of agreements in this category, and Article 85(3) provides criteria for exemption from this prohibition. Article 86 is similarly general. It prohibits the abuse of a market-dominating position and gives several examples of abuse. These articles apply only to conduct that affects trade between the Member States. Article 90 then adapts the principles contained in these provisions for application to state-owned enterprises. The

[46] David J. Gerber, *The Transformation of European Community Competition Law?*, 35 Harv. Int'l L.J. 97 100-101 (1994). © 1994 David J. Gerber. Reprinted by permission.

treaty framers envisioned (in Articles 87 through 89) that Community institutions would create a system to develop, apply, and enforce these principles.

Not only does the treaty itself provide little guidance for the construction of such a system, but there is little evidence that the framers had any well-developed conceptions of how such a system might look. When the treaty was signed, there had been little experience in Europe with the use of law to protect competition. The only Member State that had paid serious attention to competition law was Germany, but its competition law system was not yet in operation during the drafting of the Treaty of Rome. Moreover, although there were competition law provisions in the laws of the European Coal and Steel Community, relatively little relevant experience had been acquired in applying them.

The treaty thus identified the central problems of competition law and provided general principles of response, but the institutions of the Community were left to construct the competition law system. Gradually, these institutions constructed such a system, guided by changing perceptions of both Community needs and their own interests and reflecting shifting power configurations among the institutions.

A. Article 85

Treaty of Rome, Art. 85 reads as follows:

> (1) The following shall be prohibited as incompatible with the common market: all agreements between undertakings, decisions by associations of undertakings and concerted practices which may affect trade between Member States and which have as their object or effect the prevention, restriction or distortion of competition within the common market, and in particular those which:
> (a) directly or indirectly fix purchase or selling prices or any other trading conditions;
> (b) limit or control production, markets, technical development, or investment;
> (c) share markets or sources of supply;
> (d) apply dissimilar conditions to equivalent transactions with other trading parties, thereby placing them at a competitive disadvantage;
> (e) make the conclusion of contracts subject to acceptance by the other parties of supplementary obligations which, by their nature or according to commercial usage, have no connection with the subject of such contracts.
> (2) Any agreements or decisions prohibited pursuant to this Article shall be automatically void.
> (3) The provisions of paragraph 1 may, however, be declared inapplicable in the case of:
> - any agreement or category of agreements between undertakings;

- any decisions or category of decisions by associations of undertakings;
- any concerted practice or category of concerted practices; which contributes to improving the production or distribution of goods or to promoting technical or economic progress, while allowing consumers a fair share of the resulting benefit, and which does not:

(a) impose on the undertakings concerned restrictions which are not indispensable to the attainment of these objectives;
(b) afford such undertakings the possibility of eliminating competition in respect of a substantial part of the products in question.

1. Prohibition[47]

Article 85(1) prohibits all agreements between undertakings, decisions by associations of undertakings, and concerted practices which may affect trade between Member States, and which have as their object or effect the prevention, restriction, or distortion of competition within the common market. Article 85(1) contains a partial list of specific types of anticompetitive agreements and practices which are prohibited. In this regard, Article 85(1) sets forth a non-exclusive list of prohibited conduct, including agreements or concerted practices which:

(1) directly or indirectly fix purchase prices, selling prices, or other trading conditions;
(2) limit or control production, markets, technical development, or investment;
(3) share markets or sources of supply;
(4) apply dissimilar conditions to equivalent transactions with other trading partners, thereby placing them at a competitive disadvantage; or
(5) make contracts subject to acceptance of supplementary obligations which, by their nature or according to commercial usage, have no connection with the transaction.

The definition of agreements and concerted practices under Article 85 is quite broad. Article 85 applies to both formal and informal agreements. Violations may be proved through direct and circumstantial evidence. Article 85 also reaches concerted practices which may include conduct not rising to the level of a contract, combination, or conspiracy as understood in United States antitrust law.

The requirement of an effect on trade between Member States also is defined expansively. Article 85 requires only a potential effect on trade between Member States. Even agreements between two undertakings in the same Member State will typically fall within Article 85(1) if competition is affected.

---

[47] Spencer Weber Waller, *Understanding and Appreciating EC Competition Law*, 61 Antitrust L.J. 58-67 (1992). © 1992 Spencer Weber Waller. Reprinted by permission.

The European Commission has promulgated a notice setting forth those types of agreements it regards as having only a *de minimis* effect on competition within the Community. The notice states that agreements between undertakings with less than 5 percent of the relevant market and less than 200 million European Currency Units (ECUs) in aggregate annual turnover are regarded as *de minimis* and not likely to affect trade between Member States. However, the Commission notice is merely a general statement of enforcement policy, and is not legally binding. Nonetheless, the notice does represent a formal statement of the enforcement policy of the exclusive Community competition enforcement agency.

The EC has applied a version of the effects doctrine to anticompetitive conduct which takes place outside the Community. Article 85 has been used to attack an international cartel for dyestuffs with members based outside the Community where the undertakings acted through subsidiaries within the Community. Article 85 also has been used against a cartel of wood pulp producers where the anticompetitive agreements are implemented within the Community.

There is a violation of Article 85 if either the purpose or the effect of the agreement is to limit competition in the Community. However, the Commission has refused to apply Article 85 if there is no effect in the Community, even if the conduct took place in Community territory.

All agreements or concerted practices in violation of Article 85(1) are void pursuant to Article 85(2). Because of the direct applicability of Article 85, private persons and undertakings can enforce the provisions of Article 85 in national courts. Article 85 thus is raised frequently both offensively and defensively in connection with national litigation over the enforceability of contractual provisions and intellectual property rights. A litigant also may have a cause of action for damages if national law creates a tort remedy for the violation of the type of duty imposed by the Community competition provisions.

The core of the Community's competition policy is the prevention of cartels and naked restraints of trade between competitors, particularly price agreements and the horizontal division of territories or customers, which work at cross purposes with the goal of the creation of a true European common market. The Commission has brought proceedings against cartels both within and outside the Community where the actions or effects of the cartel fall within the Community and have the requisite potential effect on trade between Member States. There is virtually no possibility of exemption for the classic cartel, and the Commission has used its powers to assess fines to impose tens of millions of dollars in fines on firms that persist with secretive cartel agreements at this late stage in the development of EC competition law.

2. Enforcement through Notification System

Outside of the area of cartel enforcement, Article 85 is enforced primarily through a system of notification of agreements for review by the Commission. This includes a procedure by which parties to an agreement can seek a "negative clearance," which is a formal binding decision of the European Commission that an agreement does not infringe Article 85. The parties may also seek a more informal "comfort letter" from the staff of the Commission which, while not legally binding, has proven to be a useful way to ascertain the intentions of the Commission in a timely fashion. Parties must also notify their agreements in order to be eligible to receive an exemption under Article 85(3) of the EC Treaty, which gives the Commission the power to exempt individual agreements which may restrict competition, but nonetheless serve other important goals of the Community. In addition to the prospect of receiving either a negative clearance, comfort letter, or exemption, notification will toll the imposition of any fines until the Commission reaches a decision on the lawfulness of the agreement or concerted practice.

The parties to an agreement which affects competition within the Community need to identify a positive source of law to avoid the obligation to notify their agreements to the Commission if they wish to avoid the imposition of substantial fines in the event the Commission detects and prohibits the conduct. A person or undertaking must look to sources such as the exemption contained in Article 4(2) of Regulation 17, which is the basic procedural regulation empowering the Commission to act in the field of competition law, the block exemptions issued by the Commission over the years, as well as the notices issued by the Commission.

3. Individual Exemption

In addition to the notification system, the most distinctive feature of EC competition law is the ability of the Commission to issue individual exemptions under Article 85(3) to agreements, decisions by associations, or concerted practices which restrict competition, but nonetheless serve the overall interests of the Community. In order to issue an individual exemption, the Commission must find that the agreement:

(1) contributes to improving production or distribution or promoting technical or economic progress;
(2) allows consumers a fair share of the resulting benefits;
(3) only imposes restrictions that are indispensable in obtaining the benefits outlined above; and
(4) is not capable of eliminating competition in relation to a substantial part of the items in question.

While Article 85(3) is most often applied to exempt anticompetitive agreements that further the goal of Community integration and the transcendence of national markets, there is also more than a hint of industrial policy in its application. Exemptions have been used to achieve the reduction of capacity in certain industrial sectors, maintain employment, preserve oil supplies during the energy crisis, and strengthen the competitiveness of Community producers relative to outside producers.

a. Block Exemption

The problem with Article 85(3) is that it requires the Commission to undertake a lengthy and painstaking consideration of each agreement that is notified. Following enactment of the notification system in 1962 under Regulation 17, the Commission received thousands of notifications of agreements, most of which had little, if any, anticompetitive impact. This deluge of notifications threatened the Commission's limited resources to investigate the truly anticompetitive and more complex agreements, while drowning it in the analysis of routine and benign agreements. Over time, the Commission developed the expertise to standardize its review process and set forth general standards for the exemption of certain types of agreements that were unlikely to restrict competition within the Community. Pursuant to the authorization of the Council of Ministers, the Commission has issued block exemptions, creating an exemption under Article 85(3) for entire categories of agreements and exempting such agreements from notification and individualized review.

The majority of the block exemptions deal either with certain types of vertical restrictions or the cooperation between firms with limited market shares. Each block exemption is lengthy and complex and must be examined in great detail in deciding whether a specific agreement would benefit from the block exemption, and not require notification to the Commission. The principal block exemptions cover agreements related to:

(1) exclusive distribution;
(2) exclusive purchasing;
(3) motor vehicle distribution and service;
(4) patent licensing;
(5) know-how licensing;
(6) franchising;
(7) specialization; and
(8) research and development.

The block exemptions do not represent complete relief from notification of all vertical agreements. They are by no means comprehensive in their coverage. For example, most selective distribution agreements fall between the requirements of the exclusive purchase and exclusive distribution agreements, and are without the benefit of any block exemption under normal circumstances.

While the block exemptions are too lengthy and diverse to neatly summarize, there are some general approaches which the Commission has undertaken throughout the various block exemptions. First, there is no need to notify the Commission if the agreement, decision, or concerted practice falls within a block exemption. However, each undertaking must determine if it and its agreements are eligible for coverage by one of the block exemptions.

Certain of the block exemptions are limited to firms below specified size and market share thresholds. Other block exemptions specify so-called "white lists" of acceptable clauses, conditions, or ancillary restrictions which may benefit under the exemption. Similarly, certain block exemptions contain "black lists" of prohibited clauses, conditions, or ancillary restrictions.

Block exemptions also may contain an "opposition procedure" which requires notification if the agreement contains certain provisions not contained on either the white or black list. Under this procedure, approval is automatic unless the Commission affirmatively opposes the restriction within six months. The Commission has also reserved the power to limit or withdraw the block exemption for particular agreements shown to have an anticompetitive impact within the Community. Finally, regardless of the restrictions imposed by a block exemption, a person or undertaking may still notify the agreement to the Commission and seek an individual exemption under Article 85(3).

b. Vertical Restraints

The Community's principal concern in the area of vertical restraints is the continued division of the common market along national lines. The needs of the Community and the continued process of integration of the common market express themselves in a near total prohibition on vertical restraints which seek to ban parallel imports between Member States. Parallel imports refer to the practice of a purchaser of goods in one Member State of the Community seeking to resell those goods in another Member State to take advantage of price differentials. The Commission has exempted certain vertical territorial divisions which bar active sales within another distributor's territory only where such a restriction is necessary to protect investment, good will, or to prevent free riders.

Any type of vertical restraint establishing a total ban on sales within a particular territory is almost always prohibited, and remains an active area of Commission enforcement including the imposition of substantial fines approaching those imposed for cartel agreements. Bans on accepting or filling orders received from outside a particular territory have been prohibited as amounting to an unlawful prohibition of parallel imports.

B. Article 86

Treaty of Rome, Art. 86 states:

> Any abuse by one or more undertakings of a dominant position within the common market or in a substantial part of it shall be prohibited as incompatible with the common market insofar as it may affect trade between Member States.
>
> Such abuse may, in particular, consist in:
>
> (a) directly or indirectly imposing unfair purchase or selling prices or other unfair trading conditions;
>
> (b) limiting production market or technical development to the prejudice of customers;
>
> (c) applying dissimilar conditions to equivalent transactions with other trading parties, thereby placing them at a competitive disadvantage;
>
> (d) making the conclusion of contracts subject to acceptance by the other parties of supplementary obligations which, by their nature or according to commercial usage, have no connection with the subject of such contracts.

1. Prohibition[48]

Article 86 of the EC Treaty is the Community provision dealing with the unilateral behavior of firms with significant market power. While the jurisprudence of Article 86 is not as well developed as Article 85, the Commission devotes substantial resources to its enforcement.

Article 86 prohibits any abuse by one or more undertakings with a dominant position within the common market, or in a substantial part of it, as unlawful insofar as it may affect trade between Member States. Article 86 is phrased solely in terms of the abuse of a dominant position, since the creation of large firms with substantial market power actually may be conducive to the growth and integration of the common market. Accordingly, the acquisition or creation of a dominant position is not condemned, but the behavior of firms with such a degree of power is strictly scrutinized.

Article 86 also requires only a potential effect on trade with Member States. The potential effect on trade between Member States is defined expansively and the test is virtually identical to that measuring the potential effect on trade between Member States under Article 85.

A dominant position is defined as the ability to act independently of competitive forces. The determination of a dominant position will normally require definition of both a product market and a geographic market. The geographic market can be as small as a part of one Member State and still comply with the language of Article 86 requiring the showing of a dominant position in a substantial part of the Community.

Sixty percent might be, and 30 percent is not sufficient to prove monopoly power. The closest EC equivalent is that 60 percent is nearly always conclusive proof of a dominant position, as little as 45 percent may be sufficient, but below 30 percent rarely will suffice. The concept of shared dominance has been adopted by the Commission and the Court of First Instance, but has not yet been definitively adopted by the Court of Justice.

The ability to pursue exploitive or exclusionary conduct may itself be evidence of a dominant position. The dominant position also may be the effect of the existence of governmental regulation or the conferral of special privileges by the Member States. The Commission and the Court have also relied on other factors such as the extent of vertical integration and the disparity in market shares between the leading firm and its competitors to demonstrate the existence of a dominant position.

Article 86 sets forth a non-exclusive list of abuses, almost identical to that contained in Article 85, including:

(1) directly or indirectly imposing unfair purchase prices, selling prices, or other unfair trading conditions;
(2) limiting production, markets, or technical development to the detriment of the consumer;
(3) applying dissimilar conditions to equivalent transactions with other trading partners, thereby placing them at a comparative disadvantage; and

---

48 Spencer Weber Waller, *Understanding and Appreciating EC Competition Law*, 61 Antitrust L.J. 68-72 (1992).

(4) making contracts subject to acceptance by the other parties of supplementary obligations, which by their nature and commercial usage, have no connection with the subject of the contracts.

All aspects of the behavior of a dominant firm potentially fall within the scope of an abuse within the meaning of Article 86. In particular, Article 86 has been applied extensively to the pricing policies of dominant firms.

2. Application

Article 86 has been applied to prohibit predatory pricing as just one example of an abuse of a dominant position. The Commission has applied both price-cost comparisons as well as a comparison of prices between markets to determine whether the pricing of the dominant firm constitutes an abuse within the meaning of Article 86. Unlike the trend in the United States, the Commission carefully considers evidence of intent and has refused to adopt an exclusively cost-based approach to the question of predation.

The European Court of Justice recently issued its first decision directly dealing with allegations of predatory pricing as an abuse of a dominant position under Article 86. In *Akzo Chemie BV v. European Commission*[49] the Court affirmed the Commission's finding of a violation of Article 86 in connection with an attempt by a dominant producer of industrial chemicals to discipline a smaller rival through predatory pricing across a range of products. The Court found that the respondent had a dominant position by virtue of a 50 percent market share of a relevant market and that its price reductions would constitute an abuse of a dominant position where the price was below average variable cost, or below average total cost where there was also an intent to eliminate a competitor.

Price discrimination between Member States is another pricing policy which is contrary to the aims of the Community and has been condemned under Article 86. Selling at supracompetitive prices can also constitute an abuse of a dominant position.

Article 86 has been applied to a variety of other practices. Highly discretionary year end rebate systems that create disincentives to change suppliers have been held to constitute an abuse of a dominant position. Article 86 also has been applied to refusals to deal by a firm seeking to maintain or reinforce its dominant position. Most recently, the Commission found a violation of Article 86 following the refusal of Aer Lingus to continue an interline agreement with an existing airline which had just begun to compete on certain routes traditionally served by the dominant firm. Tying also has been condemned under Article 86. Although largely superseded by the new Merger Regulation, Article 86 can also be used to attack mergers and acquisitions which constitute an abuse by firms with an existing dominant position.

An abuse of a dominant position can include any abusive conduct which injures consumers or competitors, even if it is the type of conduct which would be lawful if done by a firm without a dominant position. There are no general exemptions available for a firm found to have abused a dominant position, as is the case for anticom-

---

49 *ECS/Akzo II,* 1985 O.J. (L 374) 1, 19-22, aff'd, *AkzoChemie BV v. Commission*, 62/86 (July 3, 1991).

petitive agreements, which can be exempted under Article 85(3). The conduct of a dominant firm can constitute an abuse under Article 86, even if the firm is covered by a block exemption under Article 85(3) for the same conduct. However, the European Court of Justice has shown a sensitivity to the language of Article 86 and has declined to find an abuse in certain trivial or exceptional cases. Abusive conduct also may be excused pursuant to Article 90 of the EC Treaty, which creates an exemption where the application of competition principles would obstruct the performance of specific tasks of undertakings which are assigned to them by Member States.

The Commission may impose fines up to 10 percent of the annual turnover of a party for a violation of Article 86. The Commission may also issue cease and desist orders which can encompass both negative and positive injunctions. Interim relief is also available. The Commission has also reached agreed settlements with respondents, most prominently, IBM's agreement to change its policies regarding product design and disclosure in response to an investigation of its behavior under Article 86.[50] Finally, Article 86 is directly applicable to individuals and undertakings throughout the Community and may be the grounds for a cause of action or defense in the national courts of the Member States.

C. Enforcement of Articles 85 and 86[51]

1. The Characteristics of the EU Market in the Context of EU Competition Policy

a. The Function of Competition

In the case of the EEC, the most important point is that the competition rules must be read in the context of the Treaty as a whole. Teleological interpretation of the Treaty has resulted in some remarkable case-law in the Court of Justice, not least in the area of competition law. The Preamble of the Treaty includes a reference to the need for "balanced trade and fair competition." This term in itself is value-laden. The aims of the Treaty are expressed in Article 2: the promotion of a harmonious development of economic activities, a continuous and balanced expansion, an increase in stability, an accelerated raising of the standard of living and closer relations between the States belonging to the Community. These goals are to be achieved through the establishment of a common market and the approximation of the economic policies of Member States. Article 3(f) provides that the Community shall include in its activities "the institution of a system ensuring that competition in the common market is not distorted." These early provisions of the Treaty are pregnant with meaning, and provide a backdrop against which the competition rules have been, and will continue to be, developed. On a teleological reading, it would be hard to conclude that the competition rules should solely be applied in order to maximize economic efficiency in a narrow, technical, sense.

---

50 European Commission, 14th Report on Competition Policy 77-79.

51 Richard Whish & Brenda Sufrin, *Article 85 and the Rule of Reason*, 7 Y.B. of Eur. L. 12-19 (1987).

In practice, the EEC competition rules have been applied for a variety of purposes—to ensure that markets are kept reasonably open, to protect the consumer, to deal with industries in decline, to protect the process of competition itself, and above all, to assist in the process of integrating the common market. The Commissioner currently responsible for competition has spoken of the need to adopt a positive competition policy, not determined in isolation but integrated with the economic, industrial and social policy of the Community. What other functions Articles 85 and 86 might fulfil remains to be seen. Sometimes the issue of unemployment has arisen in competition cases, and the Commission has referred to it in its Annual Reports. It is not obvious at first that this is an issue that can be considered under Article 85. However, it might be possible to argue that the idea of "economic progress" in Article 85(3) could be interpreted subject to the aim expressed in Article 2 of promoting an "accelerated rising of the standard of living." Regional policy is also an issue of concern to the Commission. We do not mean to suggest that "anything goes" when it comes to applying competition law; however, it is important to emphasize that the Treaty itself envisages an expansive role for the competition rules, and that there is potential for growth in several directions. The Commission will want to hold on to the powers it has under Article 85(3) in order that it can participate fully in the development of competition policy.

b. Market Integration

Following on from the last point, it is particularly important in the case of the EEC to bear in mind that the Treaty states in Article 2 that the means of achieving its aims include the establishment of a common market. After thirty years of the EEC, there is still not a truly common market, and one object of the Single European Act 1986 is to make it more of a reality. It is almost impossible to overstate the importance that is accorded to integration of the market. It has been said, with some justification, that it has been elevated to a goal in itself rather than being the means to an end, as Article 2 clearly states.

One of the reasons that competition law has such a large part to play in the integration of the market is that agreements between undertakings can be very effective in partitioning the market. There are many different ways in which this can occur. Horizontal agreements may involve market-sharing on national lines; a dominant firm may try to prevent inter-state trade in its products; distribution agreements can isolate national markets from one another in numerous ways; agreements involving intellectual property rights are particularly likely to have a geographical dimension, for the rights themselves emanate from purely national systems of law. The integration of the market is promoted through the application of other parts of the Treaty, particularly the provisions of the free movement of goods and services, but the Commission uses the competition rules as an important part of its strategy.

It is necessary to consider what implications this has in institutional and procedural terms. If the sole function of competition law were to be the promotion of economic efficiency, it might be possible to leave the institutions of individual Member States to deal with enforcement, although even this is questionable: different Member States have widely varying experiences of competition law, so that one might expect uneven treatment of economic behavior from one Member State to another. However, EEC law is not solely concerned with economic efficiency, which makes the issue of enforcement more complex. A domestic court is not in a good position, when dealing with Articles 85 and 86, to weigh up different policy considerations, and it is hard to see how the Community interest of market integration would be expressed in domestic litigation. There is no guarantee that all courts throughout the Community would be prepared to give the same weight to the need to bring about an integrated market. It might be possible for the Commission to be represented in some sort of *amicus curiae* role to assist the domestic court, but different courts might give different weight to its views.

Involvement in domestic litigation would lead back to the problem that the Commission is under-resourced: appearances in the courts of twelve Member States could only exacerbate this. It would also require a careful consideration of the procedural law of Member States to ensure that rules of court allowed for appropriate representation. The most appropriate guardian of the Community interest would appear at this stage to be the Commission, acting under the reviewing eye of the Court of Justice. Certainly this is not a issue that could be left in the "magic" of the market in which the Chicago economists place so much faith. It may be the case that the market knows best what level a price should be or whether a firm is being so badly managed that it is ripe for a take-over, although this is contentious but it cannot give expression to the ideal of a common market. That cannot be measured using pricing theory. Furthermore, it would be difficult for the European Court of Justice to protect the Community interest simply in Article 177 references from national courts. This is particularly true since, except in the case of a final court, reference to the European Court of Justice is not obligatory; one need look no further than the enforcement of EEC competition rules in the UK courts to see that the lower courts can go somewhat awry in this area. One of the most effective ways in which the Commission can keep control is through the medium of Article 85(3).

A further complication is the periodic enlargement of the Community. Spain and Portugal are relative newcomers; Norway may join the community in the near future; and there is at least a possibility of further accessions. This being the case, one can expect that the issue of market integration will continue to be a dominant feature in competition law decisions, and that the Commission will remain the most significant watchdog. A related point is that there are particular markets, such as banking and insurance, where the competition rules are applied as one part of the overall strategy of breaking down national barriers to trade.

The pursuit of single-market integration does tend to produce some hard cases, where the injustice to an individual undertaking is the price paid for furthering the Community's goals. The question then is whether there is a convincing way of trading one policy off against the other, or whether this is a clash of competing goals that can only be resolved by unashamedly subordinating one issue to the other.

One famous example of the conundrum is the *Distillers*[52] affair. The company's dual pricing system, underpinned by export disincentives, was condemned by the Com-

---

52 Case 30/78 *Distillers v. Commission* [1980] ECR 2229.

mission, despite the convincing arguments of commercial necessity put forward by the company. The Commission could not tolerate such a strategy of dividing markets, whatever the reasons. Because of the procedural complications of the case, the Court of Justice never gave a judgment on the merits and one can only surmise whether it would have been more sympathetic to Distillers' predicament. In the event, Distillers reacted by withdrawing certain brands from different markets, and so the consumer was deprived of choice while inter-State trade and competition were advanced not one jot. After the hearing in the Court of Justice, Distillers attempted to reach an accommodation with the Commission. In the end, however, the Commission stuck to its original position, that it could not allow division of markets on national lines. This outcome may upset many commentators, but it cannot be described as "wrong" in a legal or economic sense. Instead it means that the Commission has decided, in a hard case, that the broader issue of market integration should prevail over the particular predicament of Distillers.

c. *Institutions*

As far as competition policy is concerned, in the EEC, it was decided at an early stage that the central role should be performed by the Commission. Council Regulation 17/62 gave effect to this decision. The other important body has, of course, been the Court of Justice and, in this area as in many others, it has been responsible for major developments. However, it is not an appropriate body to deal with the mass of complexities involved in competition issues, although it can give important leads, as, for example, in *Pronuptia*[53] and *Nutricia.*[54] There needs to be a body such as the Commission to convert these leads into workable and sufficiently detailed rules. One effect of the rule-of-reason analysis would be that much more responsibility would be given to national courts, and there would be fewer cases in which Article 85(3) would have to be invoked. Whether or not national courts could or should be given this added responsibility has been discussed above.

c. *Time—The Maturity of the Systems*

The EEC system of competition law is not yet mature. It has developed remarkably quickly in many ways, and in recent years, particularly since Peter Sutherland became the Commissioner responsible for competition, the pace of change has accelerated. But the position has not yet been reached, as Forrester and Norall have suggested,[55] at which it would be reasonable to hand over more analysis to the national courts under Article 85(1). The central involvement of the Commission, which is promoted by its current application of Article 85, will remain important for some time. Three points in particular should be made.

---

53 Case 161/84 *Pronuptia de Paris v. Schillgalis* [1986] 1 C.M.L.R. 414.

54 Case 42/84 *Remia BV & Verenidge Bedrijven Nutricia v. Commission* [1987] 1 C.M.L.R. 1.

55 Forrester and Cristopher Norall, *The Laicization of Community Law: Self-help and the Rule of Reason: How Competition Law is and Could Be Applied*, 21 C.M.L.R. 11 (1984).

First, the competition law system would not have developed in the way it has without the Commission's decisive involvement. The Commission has developed its policy on such matters as franchise agreements, specialization and research and development by looking at the agreements notified to it. It is precisely because of the incentive to notify produced by the orthodox analysis under Article 85(1) that the Commission has gained the know-how to be able to publish its block exemptions. The standard pattern is that the Commission grants a few individual exemptions in respect of a particular type of agreement, then distills the principles from them into a draft block exemption. This is as true of the two drafts now being circulated (on know-how and franchising) as it was of the earlier block exemptions.

The second point is that there are important matters that have yet to be sorted out. It is possible that in due course the Commission will want to look into the possibility of producing further block exemptions, for example on trademark and copyright licenses. It is still hoping to produce guidelines on the applicability of Article 85 to joint ventures, although this is a complex issue because of one of the other "immature" aspects of EEC competition law, merger control. The Commission is also directing its attention to parts of the economy which, historically, have enjoyed a kind of de facto immunity from the competition rules.

The third point, already made, is that continuing accessions to the Community retard the process of maturation.

2. Procedures and Enforcement

There is an intimate relationship between the substance of the competition rules and the procedural framework within which they are operated, and much of the criticism of EEC law is really about procedure. However, while considerable attention has been given to the negative aspects of the Commission's procedures, little has been said on the other side of the equation.

The Commission is itself acutely aware of the procedural problems that firms experience in competition law matters. It is a trite but important point that many of these problems would at least recede if the resources of DG IV were to be increased. It is not surprising that it has had some problems in devising and implementing a competition policy for twelve such heterogeneous States as make up the Community. However, it has taken various steps in recent years in order to try to accelerate the decision-making process and to introduce more certainty into the system. It is important to bear in mind that the Commission is subject to the general principles of administrative law when reaching formal decisions and that this means that it must give all interested parties—not just the parties to a particular agreement —a chance to be heard. Speedy decisions and the requirements of procedural fairness are not easily compatible.

The reality of the matter is that many firms are willing to accept a comfort letter as a way of disposing of their case. The Commission's decision not to publish notices prior to a comfort letter, as it suggested it would do in 1983, is unfortunate; it is desirable that decision-making, whether of a formal or informal kind, should be as public as possible, if not from the perspective of the actual parties to an agreement, at any rate in the public interest. It is particularly regrettable that the Commission seems to have decided not to make public the fact that it has changed its policy in this respect.

A further important change has been the introduction into three of the block exemptions of an opposition procedure. Again this procedure does have its legal difficulties, but there are signs already that it is being used, and there must be a reasonable likelihood that it will be more so in the future. Form A/B invites those notifying agreements to consider whether the agreement in question might qualify for the opposition procedure. It may transpire that the opposition procedure will be used more or less according to the block exemption in question.

The Commission is in the process of increasing the numbers of block exemptions. There should shortly be new ones on franchising and know-how licensing, although early comment has suggested that the latter may not be of much assistance, at least to industry in the UK.

One further important change has been the internal reorganization of DG IV, so that specialist teams in particular sectors now see a case through from beginning to end. This should lead to quicker decisions than before. It is certainly the case that, in the last couple of years, the output of DG IV has increased.

It is unfortunate, in the light of the comments just made, that the backlog of cases in the last few years has actually increased. From 1985 to 1986 it increased by 209; 153 of the new notifications came from Spain and Portugal, but the underlying trend is also up. As the Commission remarks, this problem will continue "given the numbers of staff as compared with the volume of work."

A different point on procedure is that the Commission has more power under Article 85 and 86 than it does under other parts of the Treaty. Not surprisingly, this means that it is unenthusiastic about adopting a type of analysis under Article 85(1) which would weaken its influence in competition matters. As pointed out above, the operation of Articles 85 and 86 was delegated by the Council to the Commission at a very early stage; as a result of this, the Commission has both formulated and enforced competition policy, largely independently of the Council and the Member States. Of course, it is subject to political pressures and considerations and to review by the Court of Justice. However, its position is very different in competition matters from the situation in relation to the free movement of goods, for example. In that area, the Commission can cajole national governments, make proposals as to how restrictions on imports and exports might be eliminated, and where necessary, use Article 169 proceedings; however, it is dependent upon the Court of Justice, the Council of Ministers and Member States for real progress. Under the competition rules, it has important powers of its own.

D. Distortions of Competition under Articles 85 and 86[56]

Article 85(1) prohibits agreements whose object or effect is the prevention, restriction or distortion of competition. However, even an agreement which comes within the

---

[56] Richard Whish & Brenda Sufrin, *Article 85 and the Rule of Reason*, 7 Y.B. of Eur. L. 1-4 (1987).

scope of Article 85(1) may be authorized by the Commission where it satisfies the criteria of Article 85(3). To do so, the agreement must contribute to an improvement in the production or distribution of goods or to technical or economic progress, and must yield a fair share of the resulting benefit to consumers; at the same time, it must not contain indispensable restrictions of competition and must not substantially eliminate competition. The tendency of the Commission over many years has been to hold that various types of agreement—for example the exclusive dealing, exclusive purchasing, licenses of intellectual property rights, joint ventures for research and development—infringe Article 85(1), but then to authorize them under the provisions of Article 85(3). Protagonists of the rule of reason would argue that many of these agreements do not in any real sense prevent, restrict or distort competition, so that they ought not to require vindication under Article 85(3). The attractions of this type of analysis are said to be that it would get the Commission off the backs of business people trying to conduct their affairs in the most efficient way possible, and that it would have immense procedural advantages.

Agreements which fall within Article 85(1) are void and unenforceable unless they are exempted under Article 85(3), either individually or under one of the six block exemptions. If one takes the example of two companies anxious to develop jointly a new and technically advanced product, one must ask whether it is reasonable to subject them to the delay involved in seeking an exemption for their agreement, and to the risk that the commercial balance of their relationship will be altered through the intervention of the Commission. It is also arguable that it is inappropriate that an agreement such as this, if unnotified (and not within Regulation 418/85 on research and development agreements), should be void and unenforceable. The parties could theoretically even be fined for entering into an agreement of a type encouraged by the Commission, anxious to foster new technology. The rule-of-reason argument would say that the agreement, far from restricting competition, may introduce a new product on to the market, thus increasing competition overall.

In the case of patent licenses, a licensee may be so uncertain about the risks involved in going into production of a newly patented product that he will only take the license at all if given an exclusive territory. The argument can then unfold perfectly logically: without the exclusivity, the licensee will not enter the market. The licensor may be unable to produce in the licensee's territory (for example, because he lacks the resources—that is why he is looking for a licensee). So, the license with territorial exclusivity creates rather than destroys competition, and should not come within Article 85(1). The same reasoning can be used for exclusive dealing, franchising and other types of agreement.

Advocates of the rule of reason point out that this approach to Article 85(1) would have procedural advantages. Only the Commission has power to grant individual exemptions. Obtaining an individual exemption is a lengthy process, which may involve negotiations whereby the Commission will grant an exemption if certain clauses in the agreement are amended. The Competition Directorate of the Commission (DG IV) is notoriously short-staffed and cannot deal fully with every case notified to it. As a result, the Commission issues each year only a small number of individual decisions granting or refusing exemptions, and some of these are selected for such treatment on policy grounds. Other cases, amounting to over 90 per cent of those notified, are dealt with on an informal basis. This may be by a so-called "comfort letter" to the parties which indicates either that the agreement is not within Article 85(1) at all or that the Commission considers that it qualifies for exemption. The difficulties caused to third parties by this practice have partly been overcome by the Commission's decision to publish in the Official Journal notice of its intention to issue one of these letters. However, comfort letters are problematic for the parties too, as was confirmed in the *Perfumes* cases,[57] for such an administrative letter is not the same as a formal decision and binds neither national courts, third parties nor national competition authorities, but can terminate the provisional validity of an old agreement. The Commission also informally settles some cases after it has commenced proceedings and issues a Statement of Objections if the parties have amended or terminated the agreement or behavior which was allegedly contrary to the competition rules. Again, the legal significance of such a settlement is uncertain.

Faced with these difficulties, the attractions of a mode of reasoning whereby fewer agreements fall within article 85(1) in the first place is obvious. It is questionable, however, whether these procedural problems justify a major reanalysis of Article 85(1): this would rather seem like the tail wagging the dog.

The supporters of the rule of reason would argue that many restrictions *on conduct* are not restrictions *of competition*. They would draw upon US experience in antitrust matters and show that, in applying the Sherman Act of 1890, the Supreme Court has in recent years become much more sensitive about deciding what is meant in that Act by a "restraint of trade." Practices which at one time were consistently condemned under the antitrust laws are now subject to rule-of-reason analysis and upheld. In particular, the "Chicago School" has had a profound impact upon the development of antitrust in the last twenty years and has influenced the partial retreat from antitrust enforcement in the United States. The argument is that, if a US style rule of reason were to be adopted, and particularly if it were based upon the economic thinking of the Chicago School, there would be a radical shift in EEC competition law and practice, and the problems for business caused by the existing rules would, if not evaporate, at any rate diminish. The main emphasis would be on analysis of agreements under Article 85(1), and the main enforcement of the rules could take place in national courts.

[57] Cases 253/78 and 1-3/79 *Procureur de la Republique v. Giry & Guerlain* [1980] ECR 2327 and Case 99/79 *Lancome SA v Etos BV* [1980] ECR 2511.

III. Merger Control Regulation

A. History of the Use of Article 85 and 86 for Merger Control[58]

The *Commission Memorandum on Concentrations of 1966* (1966 Memorandum) represents the first landmark in the history of the application of Articles 85 and 86 to merger control. In the 1966 Memorandum, the Commission defined its position on the application of Articles 85 and 86 to corporate acquisitions. The 1966 Memorandum distinguished between a "concentration" (encompassing mergers and acquisitions) and a mere "agreement" between companies. While the Memorandum stated that it was sometimes difficult to distinguish between an agreement and a concentration, it declared that concentrations were essentially proprietary in nature, but might result from less than total ownership of a company. The 1966 Memorandum concluded that Article 85 did not apply to concentrations, while Article 86, which prohibited the abuse of a dominant position, did apply to concentrations.

In 1972 the Commission confirmed that Article 86 extended to concentrations in the case of *Europemballage & Continental Can Company v. EEC Commission*[59] *(Continental Can)* [appeal before the European Court of Justice (ECJ)]. *Continental Can*, the leading case in Article 86 jurisprudence in the context of concentrations, firmly established that Article 86 applies to a company in a dominant position that acquires a competitor even though Article 86 itself contains no express provision to this effect.

Continental Can Company, Inc., of New York, which had previously acquired control of a German manufacturer of light metal packages, acquired its Dutch license in 1970. In *Continental Can*, the ECJ held that an acquiring company abuses its dominant position when it fetters competition to such an extent that the only undertakings that remain in the market are dependent on the dominant one. However, in subsequent Article 86 cases, the test for "abuse" has become less stringent. An abuse is now defined as an action that hinders the maintenance of the degree of competition in the market. The subsequent Article 86 cases have not involved mergers. However, the Commission has repeatedly stated that it will apply a similar test in merger cases, a policy that presumably will be carried forward in its application of the Regulation.

The classic test of whether an acquiring company enjoys a dominant position *ab initio* was enunciated by the ECJ in the case of *United Brands Company v. EEC Commission.*[60] In *United Brands*, the ECJ defined dominance as "a position of economic strength enjoyed by an undertaking which enabled it to prevent effective competition being maintained in the relevant market by giving it the power to behave to

---

[58] Philippe De Smedt & Georges Vandersanden, *The EC Merger Control Regulation*, 13 Hastings Int'l & Comp. L. Rev. 437 (1990).

[59] *Europemballage Corp. & Continental Can Co. v. EEC Commission*, 1973 E. Comm. Ct. J. Rep. 215, 243-45.

[60] 1978 E. Comm. Ct. J. Rep. 207.

an appreciable extent independently of its competitors, customers and ultimately of its consumers."

The *United Brands* test refers to the "relevant market." The relevant market consists of two components, the relevant product market as well as the relevant geographic market. Prior to the Commission's decision in the case of *Pilkington/BSN-Gervais-Danone* (*Pilkington/BSN*), it was thought that Article 86 did not apply when a company, dominant in a limited geographical sphere, attempted to extend that dominance geographically. However, when the French conglomerate BSN attempted to sell its flat glass division to the United Kingdom glass manufacturer Pilkington, the Commission ruled that the prospective sale violated Article 86 since it strengthened Pilkington's position in the United Kingdom and extended Pilkington's dominance into another geographic area.

British American Tobacco Company and R.J. Reynolds Industries v. EEC Commission[61] (Philip Morris) extended the reach of Article 86. In *Philip Morris,* the cigarette manufacturer Philip Morris agreed to acquire a thirty per cent interest in its competitor, Rothmans, from its South African parent company, Rembrandt. The Commission exempted this proposed acquisition of a competitor and the ECJ upheld the Commission's decision despite a challenge by two other tobacco companies, British American Tobacco and R.J. Reynolds. In the past, the Commission had consistently held that an abuse of a dominant position could only occur if there was a change in control within the target company. In *Philip Morris*, however, the ECJ stated in dicta that Article 86 not only applied to the acquisition of both legal and de facto control, but also applied when the acquisition of a substantial stake gave the acquiring company influence over the commercial policy of the target company. The *Philip Morris* case is better known for being the first case in which the ECJ considered that Article 85 in addition to Article 86 might apply to the acquisition of a minority interest by a competitor if the acquiring company gains substantial influence over the target company.

Applications of Articles 85 and 86 to mergers and acquisitions will not automatically cease with the adoption of the Regulation. The jurisprudence of Articles 85 and 86 will influence the Commission in its application of the Regulation and the ECJ will undoubtedly use such jurisprudence in conjunction with the Regulation in reviewing the Commission's future decisions. Nevertheless, the precise role of Articles 85 and 86 in European mergers remains uncertain now that the Regulation has been adopted.

B. The Mechanism of the Regulation[62]

The following is a summary of the Regulation.

1. In Article 1, the Regulation defines a category of concentrations whose size (measured in terms of worldwide and EEC-wide turnover) and geographical spread

[61] *British American Tobacco Co. and R.J. Reynolds Industries v. EEC Commission*, 1987 E. Comm. Ct. J. Rep. 4487.

[62] Alec Burnside & Carl Meyntjens, *The EEC Merger Regulation and Its Impact on Non-EEC Business*, 1990 B.Y.U. L. Rev. 1383-1393 (1990).

makes them of European-wide concern rather than purely national concern. Such concentrations are referred to as "concentrations with a Community dimension."

2. Since September 21, 1990, undertakings forming such concentrations must give notice to the Commission before they are put into effect. Moreover, implementation of the arrangements must be suspended for three weeks.
3. The Commission must then decide within set time limits whether the proposed concentration would be "compatible with the Common Market." Only compatible concentrations are allowed to proceed. The test of compatibility is whether the concentration would "create or strengthen a dominant position as a result of which effective competition would be significantly impeded in the Common Market or in a substantial part of it."

1. The Purpose of the Regulation

From the outset, the purpose of the Regulation was to establish a clear-cut division between large mergers of a European dimension (concentrations with "Community dimensions") to be scrutinized by the Commission and other mergers which would continue to be reviewed only by the national authorities of the Member States. This division is brought about by the thresholds of Community dimension set out in the Regulation. Above these thresholds, the Commission has jurisdiction; under the thresholds, the authorities of the Member States have jurisdiction. This has become popularly known as the principle of "one-stop" control.

However the Regulation contains the following three exceptions to the principle of one-stop control. First, a Member State can seek to intervene to protect a "distinct market" in its territory and apply its national merger controls to a concentration with Community dimension. This procedure was included at the insistence of West Germany and is therefore sometimes known as the German Clause.

Second, a Member State can intervene on the basis of "legitimate interests" other than those protected by the Regulation, such as public security, plurality of the media, and rules of prudential supervision. Finally, the Commission can intervene below the Community dimension thresholds at the invitation of a Member State.

The first two exceptions to the rule allow Member States to control concentrations despite their Community dimension, whereas the final departure from the rule allows the Commission to intervene in concentrations not having a Community dimension.

The demarcation of powers under the Regulation is further blurred by the ECJ's extended interpretation of Articles 85 and 86 of the Treaty of Rome in *Philip Morris* and *Continental Can*. These cases provided the ultimate catalyst for the adoption of the Merger Regulation, and their importance should not be underestimated. But now that the Regulation has been adopted, the *Philip Morris* and *Continental Can* precedents should have outlived their usefulness. The difficulty is that a regulation cannot modify or restrict the Treaty of Rome. The extended interpretation of Articles 85 and 86 cannot be undone, and some concentrations will therefore continue to be caught by Articles 85 and 86. The problem of the residual effect of Articles 85 and 86 is most acute when applied to concentrations which fall below the Community dimension thresholds of the Regulation and therefore ought to be reviewed by the national authorities of the Member States instead of the Commission. Under such circumstances, there is a risk that the old *Philip Morris* and *Continental Can* precedents will undermine the demarcation of authority intended by the Commission and Council of Ministers. In short, the purpose of the Regulation is the principle of one-stop control. With clear demarcation between the areas of competence of the different regulatory authorities, companies intending to merge should have greater legal security knowing that their merger will only have to pass one hurdle. However, given the three exceptions contained in the regulation itself and the problem of the residual effect of Articles 85 and 86, the objective of one-stop control will often be defeated in practice. Under the Regulation, as before, parties will often find themselves having to submit their arguments simultaneously or successively to the Commission and to one or more Member States, to say nothing, moreover, of any non-EEC authority.

2. The Scope of the Regulation

As observed above, the Regulation defines a category of "concentrations with a Community dimension" as a means of delineating its scope. Any operation which constitutes a "concentration" and which has "Community dimension" falls within the Regulation and is subject to the rule of mandatory notification before it is put into effect. Therefore, in order to know whether the Regulation applies, two questions must be answered: (i) Is there a "concentration"? and (ii) If so, does it have a "Community dimension"?

a. Is There a Concentration?

The term "concentration" is broadly defined to include all operations resulting directly or indirectly in the acquisition of control. The form of the transaction leading to this result is immaterial. For example, concentrations may occur by fusion, by purchase of shares or of assets, under the terms of a contract or through a significant level of board representation. The essential question is one of "control." A concentration occurs where there is a change in the control of a business or "undertaking." Article 3(3) of the Regulation states that "control shall be constituted by rights, contracts or any other means which, either separately or jointly and having regard to the considerations of fact or law involved, confer the possibility of exercising decisive influence on an undertaking." The Regulation specifies two ways in which this possibility of "decisive influence" may arise: (1) through ownership of or the right to use the assets of another undertaking or (2) by virtue of "rights or contracts which confer decisive influence on the composition, voting or decisions of the organs of an undertaking."

Special provision is made in article 3(2) for the application of the Regulation to joint ventures. The Regulation distinguishes between "concentrative" and "co-operative" ventures, with only concentrative joint ventures failing within the Regulation. Because many non-EEC companies have preferred joint ventures to acquisitions as a means of penetrating the European Market, this distinction may be very significant. Article 3(5) creates limited exceptions for temporary shareholders, financial holding companies, and liquidators. No concentration arises where a bank, insurance company, or other financial institution holds securities temporarily for the purpose of reselling them, as long as such a resale takes place within one year of the date of acquisition or the Commission expressly permits a longer resale period. In addition, limitations on use of the voting rights attached to the securities apply during the period the financial institution holds the securities. This temporary shareholders exception is intended to assist financial institutions who acquired shares in the process of underwriting. Acquisitions by certain financial holding companies do not constitute concentrations, provided that the voting rights of the shares held are exercised only to maintain the value of the investment and not to determine the competitive conduct of the undertaking concerned. Finally, no concentration occurs where a liquidator or other comparable officer obtains control of an undertaking.

b. Does the Concentration Have Community Dimension?

Once it has been established that the operation constitutes a concentration in terms of the Regulation, the next question is whether it has Community dimension. The concept of Community dimension sets the dividing line between concentrations to be scrutinized by the Commission and those which remain within the jurisdiction of the national authorities of the Member States. As mentioned above, however, the Commission may obtain jurisdiction over a concentration lacking Community dimension at the invitation of a Member State.

Community dimension is defined in terms of tests based on turnover and geography. The turnover test identifies concentrations exceeding a certain size, while the geographical test achieves a further selection by separating out concentrations whose cross-border implications make them of European rather than national concern. The Community dimension concept is therefore both quantitative and qualitative.

The test of geography is straightforward; a concentration does not have Community dimension if all the undertakings concerned achieve more than two thirds of their Community turnover in the same member state. The effect of this test is to reserve to national merger authorities the right to rule on mergers which are mostly concerned with their national market. The turnover test is more difficult to state; it contains two limbs. The first limb relates to worldwide turnover and the second to turnover within the EEC. The turnover test is satisfied where: (1) the aggregate worldwide turnover of all the undertakings concerned is more than 5,000,000,000 ECUs; and (2) the Community-wide turnover of each of at least two of the undertakings concerned is more than 250,000,000 ECUs.

Worldwide turnover is used to reflect the strength of the merging parties on world markets. The Community-wide turnover test is used as a counter-balance and serves to exclude two types of concentration from the scope of the Regulation. First, it excludes concentrations if the undertakings involved are beneath a certain size. Second, the Community-wide turnover test excludes concentrations which are large enough in terms of size, but which primarily involve turnover outside the EEC.

The thresholds at which a Community dimension exists were fiercely debated in the negotiations on the Regulation. The lower the thresholds, the greater the loss of national sovereignty; thus, it is not surprising that much of the political debate concerned the thresholds. In the Commission's eyes, the present thresholds are no more than an interim stage, and the Regulation provides for them to be reviewed by the end of 1993, at which time the Commission hopes to see them lowered to a worldwide test of 2,000,000,000 ECUs and a Community-wide test of 100,000 ECUs.

3. Procedures of the European Commission

The Regulation requires that all concentrations with Community dimension be reported to the Commission within one week after the event which gives rise to a concentration. This event might be the conclusion of an agreement, the announcement of a public bid, or the acquisition of a controlling interest, whichever is the earliest. Failure to notify, either intentionally or through negligence, may be punished by fines of from 1,000 ECUs to 50,000 ECUs.

The obligation of prior notification is linked with an obligation of suspension; a concentration may not be put into effect for a period of three weeks following notification. During this time, the Commission may decide to extend the suspension. In the absence of such an extension ruling, the concentration may be effected. No doubt, however, most companies will await the outcome of the full procedure because implementation at this stage would be at the risk of the Commission subsequently reaching an adverse decision. The Commission may impose fines of up to ten percent of the aggregate turnover of the undertakings concerned when a concentration is implemented without its permission.

There are two exceptions to the suspension rule. First, the Commission may grant a waiver "in order to prevent serious damage to one or more undertakings concerned by a concentration or to a third party." The second exception is that public takeover bids may be implemented if the Commission has received notice and the acquirer only exercises the voting rights attached to the shares "to maintain the full value" of the securities. The bid may thus proceed, but at the bidder's peril in the event that the Commission later refuses authorization.

The Commission's inquiry into a reported merger proceeds in two main stages. In the first stage, the Commission must make two determinations within a one-month period. The Commission must first verify that a merger notification does indeed disclose a concentration with Community dimension. This first step serves to confirm the Commission's jurisdiction. In principle, the Commission should rule as early as possible on this preliminary jurisdictional question, although it may not officially reach a conclusion until the end of the initial month-long examination period. The Commission must also decide whether the concentration raises any "serious doubts as to its compatibility with the Common Market." Only if these serious doubts are raised will the Commission then open formal proceedings and conduct a full investigation.

As stated above, the Commission has only one month after notification to verify a concentration with Community dimension and to make an initial determination that the concentration raises "serious doubts" concerning compatibility with the common market. This one-month period begins on the day following receipt of the notification and ends with a decision to initiate further proceedings concerning compatibility, to allow the concentration, or that the Commission has no jurisdiction under the Regulation. The one-month period may be extended if the information supplied in the notification is incomplete and is increased to six weeks if the Commission receives a request from a Member State to intervene under the "distinct market" procedure.

If the Commission finds that no serious doubts are raised, it makes a formal decision not to oppose the concentration and declares that the concentration is compatible with the common market, eliminating the need for the second stage of proceedings. However, if the Commission determines that serious doubts are raised, it makes a formal decision to initiate proceedings and then has a further four months to issue a final ruling on whether the concentration is compatible or incompatible with the common market. Generally, the final ruling must be issued within four months of the formal finding of "serious doubt," but the period may be extended in specified circumstances where the undertakings involved have failed to provide the Commission with the necessary information.

In short, a decision from the Commission concerning an uncontroversial concentration may at best be obtained within one month after the notification. In difficult cases, the final decision timetable may run to five months.

4. Powers of the European Commission

The Regulation provides the Commission with both investigatory and enforcement powers, including the power to obtain information when it is not supplied voluntarily, to order "on the spot" investigations to be carried out by the national competition authorities or by the Commission itself, to make its authorization of a transaction conditional, to impose fines and periodic penalty payments for various reasons, to order the divestiture if an "incompatible" concentration has already been implemented, or other corrective action. The powers to obtain information and to investigate may be exercised against any undertaking, whether or not it is involved in the concentration, or against associations of undertakings.

5. The Test of Compatibility

The Commission's appraisal of compatibility with the common market is at the very heart of the Regulation. The Regulation was adopted to give the Commission the power to rule on this issue. The Regulation sets out the test for compatibility, and a series of criteria to be taken into account in applying the test.

The substantive test of compatibility is whether concentrations "create or strengthen a dominant position as a result of which effective competition would be significantly impeded in the Common Market or in a substantial part of it." If such a dominant position is created or strengthened, the concentration is incompatible with the common market and will be blocked. Although at first sight this test resembles the *Continental Can* rule, the test under the Regulation is considerably broader because it does not require a dominant position as a pre-existing condition.

The Regulation lists a series of criteria to be taken into account in assessing the question of compatibility. The combined market share which the merged undertakings would enjoy is probably the most important of these criteria. The Regulation preamble states a presumption that concentrations are compatible with the common market if the joint market share does not exceed twenty-five percent in the common market or in a substantial part of it. In other words, a combined market share of twenty-five percent in a substantial part of the EEC is the point above which further analysis of the effects on competition becomes necessary. Apart from market share, the Commission is required to consider many other factors, including the structure of the markets concerned, the actual and potential competition from other undertakings within or outside the Community, the nature of supply and demand in the relevant market, the market position of the parties, the freedom of choice of third parties, legal or practical barriers to trade, and the advancement of technology and the economy (provided that it is to the advantage of consumers and does not form an obstacle to competition).

Apart from the reference to technical and economic progress, the criteria are all competition related. Some Member States, notably West Germany and the UK, were insistent that European merger control should serve only as an instrument of competition policy and not industrial policy. Other Member States, notably Spain, Portugal and Italy, advocated the inclusion of industrial policy considerations, drawing on the references in the Treaty of Rome to economic and social cohesion and to regional development. Although the Regulation mandates consideration of competition policy in the formal list of criteria, express acknowledgment of industrial policy considerations appears only in Recital 13 to the Regulation; the reference to technical and economic progress gives at best a vague reflection of industrial policy considerations. Thus, the extent to which the Commission may consider industrial policy in determining compatibility with the common market is unclear.

The political tension of the negotiations is therefore left partially unresolved, with the result that the Commission will have an extra degree of discretion in its application of the compatibility test. The borderline of competition policy and industrial policy is in any event an uncertain one, and industrial policy considerations can easily be taken into account behind a veil of competition concerns.

6. Retention of Jurisdiction by Member States[63]

The Regulation allows Member States to apply their own competition laws and procedures to a merger or acquisition in two types of situations. Additionally, in a third type of situation a Member State may intervene on the basis of non-competition grounds.

If a merger or acquisition either does not exceed the relevant sales thresholds, or is so concentrated in one Member State that it constitutes a domestic transaction rather that a transaction with a Community dimension as defined by the Regulation, then that Member State may process the merger or acquisition under its own national laws.

Furthermore, under article 9, the so-called "German Clause," the Commission has the authority to allow a Member State to examine a transaction when the Member State has convinced the Commission that the proposed transaction will have a detrimental effect on competition within a section of the domestic market that represents a distinct market of the given Member State. However, the Regulation also provides that the Commission may refuse to transfer the matter to the Member State in question and to continue to process such a transaction.

Article 21(3) gives the Member States the right to take appropriate measures when necessary to protect legitimate interests not otherwise protected by the Regulation. The legitimate interests that Member States may protect include national security,

---

[63] Philippe De Smedt & Georges Vandersanden, *The EC Merger Control Regulation*, 13 Hastings Int'l & Comp. L. Rev. 444 (1990). © Philippe De Smedt & Georges Vandersanden. Reprinted by permission.

pluralism of the media, and prudential rules applying to financial institutions. A Member State may invoke other legitimate interests, but only with the approval of the Commission.

Member States invoke the principle of media pluralism to prevent undesirable entities from dominating any organ of the media. Similarly, "prudential rules applying to financial institutions" are the national rules of the Member States that prevent undesirable entities from gaining control of financial institutions.

C. Impact of the Merger Control Regulation

1. On EU Law[64]

a. How Does the Test Alter the Substantive EC Law of Merger Control?

The most engaging question raised by the Regulation is how its article 2(3) test will alter the substantive law of EC merger control. There will be no clear answer to this question until the Commission has processed several notifications and the ECJ has reviewed some Commission decisions. The Regulation expressly gives the ECJ the right to review all Commission decisions under Article 21(1). However, an understanding of why the Commission adopted the Regulation reveals clues of how they will likely interpret it.

It is fairly certain that the requirement of an abuse of a pre-existing dominant position under article 86 has been abandoned. The test now includes transactions that create a dominant position. Therefore, the Regulation applies to a situation in which two nondominant companies in the same geographic and product market combine to form a single dominant enterprise. This represents a significant change in EC competition laws and brings it in line with United States antitrust law. Also the test probably applies when a nondominant company acquires a dominant company in the same market, since the acquirer will be transformed from a non-dominant company into a dominant one.

The principal test was more broadly stated in previous drafts of the proposed Regulation and would have given the Commission an even broader scope for blocking potentially anticompetitive mergers. For example, in the draft of November 30, 1988, Article 2 contained the language: "Concentrations which create or strengthen a position as a result of which the maintenance of development of effective competition is impeded in the common market or in a substantial part thereof shall be declared incompatible with the common market."

Thus, the earlier proposal did not require the creation of a dominant position. Commentators characterized this earlier test as involving the strengthening, or creation or, a strong market position as opposed to a dominant one.

The return to the use of the term "dominant position" in Article 2 of the Regulation probably indicates a desire for continuity with Article 86 and merely broadens the

64 *Id.* at 445-449.

scope of prior substantive anti-competition law rather than replaces it. Thus, although the earlier draft of the test was vague, Article 86 may now help define a "dominant position."

b. *Jurisdiction*

The Regulation raises another question: how will the competition authorities of Member States react to the usurpation of their jurisdiction over mergers or acquisitions that have a Community dimension? The Regulation clearly grants the Commission exclusive jurisdiction over mergers or acquisitions having a Community dimension except in the three circumstances outlined below. Article 21(2) states unequivocally: "No Member State shall apply its national legislation on competition to any concentration that has a Community dimension."

Generally, the Regulation applies only to competition questions and does not affect those national laws, rules, and procedures of Member States that pertain to mergers and acquisitions unrelated to competition. However, there are at least two exceptions to the general principle. First, national procedures relating to public bids will probably be amended to address the EC prior clearance procedure introduced by the Regulation. Second, as mentioned before, Article 21(3) of the Regulation permits Member States to veto a proposed merger or acquisition in order to protect legitimate interests.

Besides the stated exceptions, there are at least three situations in which the Commission's attempts to obtain exclusive jurisdiction may be challenged. These three situations test the motivation and desire of Member States to create a truly "one stop shop" administrative hurdle in the completion of a large merger or acquisition.

The first situation, arising under Article 6(1)(b), is one in which the Commission performs its preliminary investigation and determines that, although a concentration may fall within the scope of the Regulation, it does not raise serious anticompetition problems. In such a situation, the Commission will not oppose the proposed transaction and will declare it compatible with the common market. If the Commission truly has exclusive jurisdiction under Article 21(2) of the Regulation, there should be no further competition issues to consider. Unfortunately, at least one national competition authority has expressed the view that the Bundeskartellamt in Germany, the Ministre des Finances in France, and the Office of Fair Trading in the United Kingdom could intervene at this juncture and apply their own national competition rules and possibly veto the transaction. Such intervention would make a mockery of the "one stop shop" concept.

Similarly, if the Commission clears a merger or acquisition after a full three to four month investigation, as per Article 8(2), the Regulation provides that the companies involved are then free to complete the transaction. However, even in this situation, the Office of Fair Trading in the United Kingdom expressed the view that it has the right to intervene, and possibly veto, the acquisition of a United Kingdom company on competition grounds even after the Commission has given its approval.

Finally, a Member State may veto a Commission-approved merger or acquisition on the grounds other than the legitimate interests permitted under Article 21(3). The final paragraph of Article 21(3) states:

> Any other public interest must be communicated to the Commission by the Member State concerned and shall be recognized by the Commission after an assessment of its compatibility with the general principles and other provisions of Community law before the measures referred to above may be taken. The Commission shall inform the Member State concerned of its decision within one month of that communication.

It is not completely clear what would happen if the Commission failed to recognize the alleged public interest of the Member State, and the Member State subsequently chose to ignore the Commission's opinion.

In summary, the success of a "one stop shop" depends on the attitude and goodwill of the relevant authorities of the Member States. Without this cooperation, the Regulation simply will become an additional obstacle to large mergers and acquisitions and will deter major restructuring among large European companies. Thus, the Regulation will hinder, rather than help, the drive toward a single European market.

c. *Problems of Interpretation of the Regulation*

As with any major new piece of legislation, the Regulation contains many ambiguous clauses, which will only be clarified as the Commission processes a number of notifications and a body of ECJ case law develops. This Article merely mentions a few of the possible problem areas. However, it should be noted that the Commission is apparently drafting an implementing regulation that supplements the merger control regulation. This implementing regulation is supposed to deal with *inter alia* notifications, calculation of time limits, and hearings. Therefore, some of the ambiguities mentioned below may be clarified by the implementing regulation.

Article 5 of the Regulation contains the formulas for the calculation of sales to determine whether a proposed transaction possesses a Community dimension. Article 5(4) provides a fairly elaborate description of the parts of a large company's empire that must be included in the calculation of sales. Depending on whether or not they want the Commission to review the proposed transaction, some companies may employ creative accounting. For example, an acquiror may decide that its chances of acquiring a target company are increased if the Commission, rather than the relevant national authorities, reviews the transaction. During the course of the investigation, a great deal of correspondence as well as arguments over accounting principles may be expected between the Commission and the companies.

Another problem for companies is ascertaining the correct time to notify the Commission of the proposed merger or takeover. Article 4(1) states:

> Concentrations with a Community dimension as referred to by this Regulation shall be notified to the Commission not more than one week after the conclusion of the agreement, or the announcement of the public bid, or the acquisition of a controlling interest. That week shall begin when the first of those events occurs.

While the announcement of a public bid is a definite point in time, the other events are not. For example, in a friendly deal it is often difficult to determine exactly when an agreement has been concluded. Does conclusion mean the point when an oral agreement has been reached, when the agreement has been reduced to writing, or when the transaction has been completed? Notification must occur no later than one week after the acquisition of a controlling interest, assuming that the meaning of "controlling interest" under Article 3 is understood.

With legislation as complex as the Regulation, unintentional inconsistencies are inevitable. For example, Article 10(1) states that the Commission's decision whether or not to proceed with a full investigation must be made within one month from the date of the receipt of a complete notification. However, Article 7, which deals with the suspension of mergers, states that a merger may take effect either before its notification, or within the first three weeks following its notification. Therefore, if the Commission is slow to issue a decision following its preliminary investigation, a window of as much as one week exists when the companies involved may proceed with the merger or acquisition before the Commission makes a preliminary decision. Of course, the companies take the risk that the Commission will proceed with a full investigation and ultimately prohibit the merger. The parties would then be faced with the complication and expense of unwinding the entire transaction.

2. On Non-EU Law[65]

a. Non-EEC Mergers Within the Scope of the Regulation

The Community dimension test, discussed in part B(2)(b) above, does not require any physical presence in the EEC. The undertaking concerned need only have turnover in the EEC. Hence, the mere fact that an undertaking is situated completely outside the Community does not imply that its concentrations will always lack Community dimension. The issue is how much turnover it has in the EEC.

Additionally, a concentration does not have to take place within the EEC to be within the scope of the Regulation. Once the test of Community dimension is met, the Regulation applies. Therefore, the Regulation is potentially extra-territorial in effect and applies equally to transactions taking place both inside and outside the EEC when at least two of the parties have a relatively modest level of turnover within the EEC. However, the "two-thirds" geographical test might exclude some foreign mergers otherwise caught by the turnover test if the undertakings' EEC turnover occurs predominantly in the same Member State.

Finally, even if the threshold tests of Community dimension are not satisfied, a Member State may nevertheless invite the Commission to intervene. This procedure could be applied to concentrations occurring outside the EEC, where the turnover within the EEC is too low to satisfy the Community turnover limb of the Community dimension test.

---

[65] Alec Burnside & Carl Meyntjens, *The EEC Merger Regulation and Its Impact on Non-EEC Business*, 1990 B.Y.U. L. Rev. 1395-1400 (1990). © Alec Burnside & Carl Meyntjens. Reprinted by permission.

b. Practical Implications for Non-EEC Mergers

Because the Regulation is capable of extra-territorial application to foreign mergers, the mandatory rules of advance notification and suspension may govern foreign mergers. Violation of these rules could lead to substantial fines. In addition, the time required for the Commission to complete its investigation must now be taken into account when implementing a foreign concentration.

Aside from these procedural issues, the substantive application of the Regulation to such concentrations may be of even greater concern. How will the Commission treat concentrations taking place outside the EEC which nevertheless have Community dimension? Will the Commission seek to apply the Regulation with extra-territorial effect or not? The Commission's view seems to be that regulation of any foreign concentration with Community dimension is justified because it follows from a finding of "Community dimension" that the affair is of real concern to the EEC. The constraints of enforceability may nevertheless limit the Commission in practice to action within the Community (e.g., action against EEC subsidiaries or branches of the merging undertakings). The Commission is also likely to show some restraint when evaluating foreign concentrations in accordance with international principles of comity. Moreover, the Commission's practice may be affected by the law on the extra-territorial application of Articles 85 and 86. Perhaps the European Commission should follow the practice described in the U.S. Department of Justice's "Antitrust Enforcement Guidelines for International Operations" which state as follows:

> The U.S. antitrust laws represent a fundamental and important national policy that generally must be protected when U.S. commerce is significantly affected, even when doing so would require bringing an enforcement action against conduct or transactions that occur outside the United States. Nevertheless, enforcing the U.S. antitrust laws with respect to such conduct or transactions can sometimes conflict with the legitimate interests of other nations. Therefore, as a matter of comity and in the exercise of its prosecutorial discretion, the Department would consider such interests in deciding whether to challenge the transaction. . . .
>
> This does not mean, however, that the Department would never challenge a merger between foreign firms that would have a substantial anticompetitive effect in the United States. [This might be the case, e.g. if either of the companies] . . . had production facilities or substantial distribution assets used to produce or distribute [their product] located in the United States. . . . The Department would likely challenge the merger if it concluded after reviewing such information that the merger would likely result in reduced output and higher prices to U.S. consumers without offsetting efficiency benefits.

Clearly on this basis the Commission should not feel inhibited from intervening in certain non-EEC mergers. Such problems will no doubt be resolved on a case-by-case basis, taking into account political and other relevant factors.

c. *Foreign Acquisitions in the EEC*

i. Reciprocity

Article 24 of the Regulation deals with the problem of reciprocity under the heading "Relations with non-member countries." Paragraph 1 of Article 24 requires that Member States inform the Commission of any general difficulties encountered by their undertakings with concentrations in non-Member countries. Paragraph 2 then requires the Commission to report periodically, together with any recommendations, on the treatment accorded to Community undertakings wanting to enter into concentrations outside the Community.

Moreover, if, on the basis of these reports or other information, it appears to the Commission "that a nonmember country does not grant Community undertakings treatment comparable to that granted by the Community to undertakings from that nonmember country, the Commission may submit [separate] proposals to the Council." The purpose of these proposals is to obtain a mandate for negotiation in order to obtain comparable treatment in that state for EEC undertakings.

The significance of Article 24 should not be exaggerated, as the article only effects international relations and has no impact on undertakings. It was added to the Regulation at the request of the French government, which wanted to make reciprocal treatment a criterion for the appraisal of concentrations involving non-EEC countries. However, reciprocity was never adopted as a substantive criterion. Therefore, Article 24, which is modeled on the reciprocity provisions of the second banking directive, is of political rather than of legal concern.

ii. The Regulation and Joint Ventures

The Regulation makes specific provision for the application of the Regulation to certain joint ventures. These provisions warrant discussion because many non-EEC companies have chosen joint ventures as a means of penetrating the European market. The Regulation creates a distinction between two types of joint ventures: (1) the concentrative joint venture (i.e., one which performs "on a lasting basis all the functions of an autonomous economic entity"), which comes under the Regulation, and (2) the cooperative joint venture (i.e., one "which has as its object or effect the coordination of the competitive behavior of undertakings which remain independent"), which continues to be governed only by Articles 85 and 86 of the Treaty of Rome.

Unfortunately, this distinction remains somewhat vague and uncertain. It may therefore be advisable to give the Commission notice of almost all joint ventures, at least until the proper interpretation of Article 3(2) is established. The Commission has recently published a set of joint venture guidelines as a "notice" in the Official Journal of the European Community which are intended to eliminate some of the existing uncertainties. In the draft version of these guidelines, the Commission lists the two main characteristics of a concentrative joint venture. First, the joint venture must be an independent economic entity, i.e., a complete undertaking established on a long term basis and exercising an independent commercial policy. To be considered a complete undertaking a joint venture must (1) exercise all the functions of a normal undertaking and not just some of them, such as research and development or purchasing or production, and (2) act as an independent supplier and buyer on the market. Whether the requirement of a long term basis is met depends on the time agreed by the parent companies, as well as on the human and material resources of the joint venture; the nature and quantity of the human and material resources must ensure the joint venture's existence and independence in the future. Independent commercial policy means that, within the limits of its corporate objects, the joint venture plans, decides, and acts independently.

The second main characteristic of a concentrative joint venture is the absence of coordination of competitive behavior. This means that the joint venture must not be accompanied by any coordination of the competitive behavior of undertakings that remain independent of each other. There must be an absence of coordination between any of the parent companies as well as between any of the parents and the joint venture.

iii. An EEC/U.S. Treaty on Competition Matters

Speaking to the EEC Chamber of Commerce in New York in March of 1990, Sir Leon Brittan drew attention to the possibility that conflicts of jurisdiction would arise between European merger control under the new Regulation and U.S. merger control. To avoid what he termed "an unseemly and damaging dispute" that might result in cases of sufficient importance, he proposed that consideration be given to the "desirability of a treaty or less formal agreement" between the Community and the U.S. He stated:

> Such an agreement would provide for information gathering and exchange and would lay down a detailed procedure for consultations on cases and issues of common interest. It might even contain an arbitration clause, although the political difficulties of getting that agreed should not be underestimated.

This idea is being pursued actively within the Commission, but at the time of writing no further progress has been reported. Sir Leon may have had in mind a case such as Minorco/Consolidated Gold Fields, one of the Commission's interventions discussed above. That takeover was eventually frustrated in the U.S. courts, even though it had received the Commission's blessing, together with that of the UK's MMC.

d. Potential Protectionist Uses of the Regulation

The Commission's treatment of purely European mergers also has potential to create friction between the EEC and foreign nations. As briefly discussed above, the Regulation states that, when appraising the compatibility of a merger with the common market, the Commission shall take into account—among other things—"the structure of all the markets concerned and the actual or potential competition from undertakings (businesses) located either within or without the Community." Here industrial rather than competition policy reasons could lead the Commission to use the Regulation as a protectionist device, i.e., authorizing and promoting intra-EEC mergers which create strong European companies, and discriminating against non-European would-be purchasers. In other words, when appraising a proposed merger of European competitors, the Commission could have regard to the existence of significant non-EEC companies that compete in the same market and consequently authorize the intra-European merger which would create a single stronger European company, better able to challenge its non-EEC rivals.

IV. Takeovers and Joint Ventures in the EU

A. Takeovers in the EU[66]

1. The Proposed Takeover Code: The EC Turns to the British

On January 19, 1989, the Commission proposed the Thirteenth Council Directive on Company Law, Concerning Takeovers and Other General Bids (Takeover Code). The proposed European Takeover Code is modeled on the British City Code (UK Code) governing takeovers. The UK Code requires an offeror to obtain consent from the Takeover Panel in making a partial bid and also requires that an acquirer of thirty percent of a target company's voting securities make an offer for all the remaining shares, voting or non- voting. The Takeover Code has adopted these provisions.

Once an offer appears imminent under the UK Code, a target board must obtain shareholder approval before it can 1) undertake defensive actions which could frustrate the offer, 2) issue new shares, 3) buy its own shares, 4) sell any material amount of its assets, or 5) enter into contracts other than in the normal course of business. Although the UK Code may make a takeover more expensive than in the U.S., where no mandatory bid for all securities is required, the UK Code ensures equal treatment of all shareholders. Moreover, because the target board must solicit shareholder approval in designing a defense to a takeover bid, the UK Code ensures shareholder participation.

2. Purpose of the European Takeover Code: Creating a Level Corporate Playing Field

The purpose of the Takeover Code, like the UK Code, is to provide for equal treatment of all shareholders during a takeover bid. The Takeover Code is a crucial step towards creating a level playing field for takeovers in the EC because it provides one code for all Member States. Significantly, the shareholders of the offeree company will ultimately decide whether a takeover will take place. The Takeover Code resembles the UK Code where, during the offer period, management cannot undertake any action that could frustrate the bid, without shareholder approval. A critical difference—some argue a crippling one—between the UK Code and the European Takeover Code is that the Takeover Code would be enforced by the courts, with attendant delays and legal costs.

3. Scope of Application

Under Member State law, the Takeover Code would apply to takeovers and other general bids for the securities of a company, where the securities are traded in one of the Member States. Recognized public authorities will regulate and supervise the sale of

[66] Tyson Storch, *Mergers and Acquisitions in the European Community*, 4-Fall Int'l Legal Persp. 124-130 (1992).

securities, and the securities must be accessible to the public. The Takeover Code defines a takeover bid as "an offer made to the holders of the securities of a company to acquire all or part of these securities by payment in cash or in exchange for other securities." This is similar to a tender offer in the United States.

a. Mandatory Bid

The most noteworthy aspect of the Takeover Code is its provision for a mandatory bid for all of a target company's securities. As under the UK Code , a purchaser must make a bid for the all of the company's securities, after he has acquired one-third of the company's voting rights. The mandatory bid avoids partial, speculative bids and protects shareholders who would otherwise be in a minority position and suffer a loss in the value of their shares. After a bid is publicly announced and is thereafter increased, the purchaser must raise the bid to all, even those who have already accepted. The bid must also be in cash or in guaranteed securities.

b. Exemptions to Mandatory Bids

A purchaser is not always obliged to make a full bid once the one-third threshold has been surpassed. He may find refuge either in a specific exemption in Article 4(2c) of the Takeover Code or the supervisory authority may exempt him.

A Member State may adopt any of the 4(2c) specific exemptions to a mandatory bid where the purchaser either acquires the securities without consideration or exceeds the one-third threshold by less than three percent while conforming with the threshold amount within a year. The supervisory authority may also grant an exemption to a mandatory bid but must first consider several principles. First, the supervisory authority must ensure that the target shareholders are offered equal treatment. Second, it must ensure that the target shareholders have adequate time and information to make a decision on the bid and third, the target company's board of directors must refrain from defensive measures to impede the bid. The supervisory authority must also ensure that the target company is not unduly burdened by the bid for an unreasonable period of time. It is responsible for ensuring that the parties to a bid comply with their obligations under the Takeover Code.

4. Notification and Disclosure: How the Takeover Code Works

As soon as the offeror decides to make a bid the offeror must inform the supervisory authority and the target company before making his decision public. The Takeover Code provides several means to publicize a bid, which include publication in a widely-circulated newspaper or direct notice to the shareholders.

The offeror must include information about the bid that will enable shareholders to reach an informed decision. The offeror must also disclose 1) a statement indicating how the purchaser will finance the bid, 2) his objectives in making the bid, 3) his intentions regarding the target company's activities, 4) the intended use of the target company's assets, and 5) his plans regarding the target company's management and employees.

Once a bid is publicly announced any entity holding at least five percent of the voting rights of the target company must immediately disclose any securities acquired and how much they own. An entity must immediately notify the supervisory authority when it acquires one-half of one percent or more of the voting rights of the target company while the bid is still pending. This disclosure is an important means of ensuring that all shareholders of the target company are treated fairly. In addition, in Member States with co-determination laws, the target management must pass along the offer and the management board's opinion to the workers' representatives.

5. Target Board's Opinion

After receiving notice of a takeover bid, the target company's board of directors must issue an opinion to its shareholders. The target board must also state whether the takeover bid is hostile or friendly and must specify whether any of the target directors who are also target shareholders intend to accept the bid. The opinion must be publicized in the same manner the initial bid was.

6. Article 8 Restriction of the Powers of the Board of the Offeree Company

Once the target company is aware that a bid is to be made public, the target board must have shareholder approval to act against it. The target board must specifically have shareholder approval to issue new securities, engage in transactions which would significantly alter the company's net worth, or to have the company acquire its own shares.

B. Joint Ventures in the EU[67]

1. Concentrative or Co-operative?

The distinction between concentrative joint ventures and co-operative ones is critical under European competition law. It forms the basis of the jurisdictional test, determining which substantive and procedural law applies: Merger Regulation 4064/89 or Article 85 of the Treaty of Rome. Put as its simplest, the Merger Regulation deals with 'structural' transactions involving changes in control over an economic entity, whereas Article 85 is concerned with regulating the 'behavioral' relationships between independent entities. However, the dividing line between the two categories of joint venture is far from clear-cut.

a. *If the Joint Venture is Concentrative*

Briefly stated, the following important consequences arise from a joint venture being categorized as concentrative.

> (1) If the joint venture lacks a Community dimension, because the turnover of its parents does not meet the thresholds laid down in the Merger Regulation, neither the Regulation nor Articles

[67] Adrian Brown, *Distinguishing between Concentrative and Co-operative Joint Ventures: Is it Getting any Easier?*, 4 Eur. Comp. L. Rev. 240-246 (1996). © Adrian Brown. Reprinted by permission.

85 and 86 of the Treaty may be applied by the Commission. However, national merger law may still apply.

(2) If the joint venture does have a Community dimension, it must be prenotified to the Commission under the Merger Regulation, normally within one week of the joint venture agreement being concluded. The Commission has the power to fine the parties if the required notification is not made. National competition law cannot apply (the 'one-stop shop' principle).

(3) Following notification, implementation of the transaction is suspended for three weeks and the Commission must take a formal decision within one month. That decision is usually an unconditional clearance. However, if the Commission has serious doubts about the transaction's compatibility with the common market, it will initiate proceedings, leading to a final decision within a further four months.

(4) Article 85 (and Article 86) can only be applied to restrictions of competition which are not directly related to and necessary for the creation of the joint venture transaction and hence are not cleared as ancillary.

b. *If the Joint Venture is Co-operative*

Any joint venture which does not fulfil the Merger Regulation's definition of a concentration will be deemed co-operative and the following consequences will arise:

(1) Article 85 and national competition law may both apply, but not the Merger Regulation.

(2) Article 85 is likely to apply if:

(a) the parents are actual or potential competitors; or

(b) the joint venture forecloses competition in its market or has 'spillover' effects on other markets; or

(c) there are non-ancillary restrictions of competition, such as an unnecessarily long or wide non-compete clause; and

(d) the joint venture has an appreciable effect on trade and on competition and hence is not *de minimus*.

(3) Even if the parties believe that Article 85 applies, they have a discretion as to whether (and when) to notify the joint venture to the Commission for negative clearance or an exemption under Article 85(3). This contrasts with the strict prenotification requirement for concentrative joint ventures under the Merger Regulation.

(4) In dealing with notifications under Article 85, the Commission is under no strict time limit and, assuming it approves, it will usually give a comfort letter rather than a formal decision.

(5) To be eligible for exemption under Article 85(3), a joint venture caught by Article 85(1) must produce certain benefits for con-

sumers and any restrictions on competition must be indispensable to achieving those benefits. This test is stricter than the test under the Merger Regulation, which is that the joint venture does not create or strengthen a dominant position as a result of which effective competition would be significantly impeded.

c. *Moves to Reduce the Differences in Treatment*

It is clear that co-operative joint ventures (unless *de minimis*) endure a much less rapid and more uncertain treatment under Article 85 than concentrative joint ventures under the Merger Regulation. Perhaps the most striking difference is that, while a concentrative joint venture will normally be cleared within one month of notification, the parties to a co-operative joint venture may have to wait for many months before receiving the Commission's approval. In order to reduce this disparity, the Commission has taken steps to speed up the treatment of co-operative joint ventures which are notified under Article 85 and which are 'structural' (although not concentrative) in nature. Having made such a notification, it is open to the parties to request the Commission to apply an accelerated procedure. In such cases, the Commission has indicated that, within two months of receiving a full notification, it will either send a comfort letter or indicate that it has serious concerns. As part of that two-month procedure, the Commission will publish a short notice in the *Official Journal*, calling for third-party comments. While the Commission is under no strict legal obligation to keep to the two-month timetable which it has set itself, it usually manages to do so. This accelerated treatment of joint ventures which are structural but co-operative represents a significant improvement.

As a further step towards reducing the procedural differences in treatment, the Commission has issued new versions of the forms on which concentrative and co-operative joint ventures have to be notified. The new versions of Form CO (for concentrations under the Merger Regulation) and Form A/B (for notification s under Article 85), both issued in December 1994, resemble each other more closely than the former versions. Form CO now includes a new short-form requiring less information to be supplied in relation to certain joint ventures, while the revised Form A/B incorporates new sections calling for more information where accelerated treatment is claimed for a structural (but co-operative) joint venture.

It may also be noticed that in 1993 the Commission amended the block exemption Regulations covering agreements on specialization, research and development, patent licensing and know-how licensing, so that more joint ventures would fall within the scope of those exemptions. Co-operative joint ventures which do fall within one of these four block exemptions do not need to be notified to the Commission for individual exemption, and therefore escape the procedural inconveniences highlighted above.

As a result of the above steps, the differences in treatment between concentrative and co-operative joint ventures have been significantly reduced. Nevertheless, the categorization of a joint venture as either concentrative or co-operative remains a crucial jurisdictional test.

2. The Definition of Concentrative Joint Ventures

Article 3(2) of the Merger Regulation states that:

> the creation of a joint venture *performing on a lasting basis all the functions of an autonomous economic entity, which does not give rise to co-ordination of the competitive behaviour of the parties* among themselves or between them and the joint venture, shall constitute a concentration (emphasis added).

A further precondition for the existence of a concentrative joint venture is that it is subject to joint control by its parents (or at least two of them). All joint ventures which are jointly controlled and satisfy the above definition are concentrative in nature and therefore within the scope of the Regulation (assuming the transaction has a Community dimension). Any other joint venture is deemed co-operative and is outside the scope of the Regulation. The categorization of a joint venture therefore largely depends on the correct interpretation and application of the above definition.

The definition of concentrative joint venture has been developed and refined by numerous Commission decisions under the Regulation. Out of approximately 340 formal decisions taken in the first five years since the Regulation's entry into force in September 1990, almost half have concerned joint ventures. The vast majority have been found to be concentrative, whereas around 20 have been categorized as co-operative and therefore outside the scope of the Regulation. The Commission has summarized and explained its approach in its 1994 Notice on the distinction between concentrative and co-operative joint ventures ('the Joint Venture Notice').

It is apparent from Article 3(2) of the Regulation that concentrative joint ventures are defined in terms of two main characteristics. The positive condition is that the joint venture must perform all the functions of an autonomous economic entity on lasting basis; it is referred to by the Commission as 'full-function.' The negative condition requires that the joint venture does not lead to co-ordination of competitive behavior between the parties.

a. Joint Control

i. Veto rights

When examining a joint venture, the Commission will first verify that there is joint control. The joint venture is jointly controlled if two or more parties have a 'decisive influence' over the joint venture, which usually means the power to veto strategic decisions. Such veto rights are normally set out in the joint venture agreement between the parties and may be enjoyed even by a party which has only a relatively small proportion of the shares or voting rights. This may be the case if there are three or more parties to the joint venture. Joint control has occasionally been found to exist between as many as five (and in one case eight) parties, each with a minority shareholding, because unanimity was required for strategic decisions.

In many decisions, there has been a large imbalance in the size of the shareholdings of the various parties. For example, the majority shareholder may have 80 per cent of the shares in the joint venture, while the minority shareholder only has 20 per cent.

In such cases, for there to be joint control, the veto rights given to the smaller shareholder must go beyond those usually conferred to protect the investment of minority shareholders. For example, rights to prevent the sale or winding up of the joint venture would not, by themselves, be sufficient to confer joint control. Veto rights giving joint control typically relate to the joint venture's business plan, its budget, major investments and the appointment of senior management. The veto rights need not, however, extend to the day to day running of the joint venture.

ii. Strong common interests

Even without veto rights, minority shareholders may exceptionally share in joint control because they are bound to vote together in practice. This might be the case because of a legally binding agreement or because those parties have a strong common interest in acting together. In the absence of such a common interest, the possibility of changing coalitions between the minority shareholders will usually exclude the assumption of joint control.

b. Autonomy

i. The joint venture must have sufficient resources

In order to be full-function and hence concentrative, a joint venture must have sufficient resources, including finance, staff, intellectual property rights and other assets, in order to operate a business activity independently from its parents. Such a joint venture may arise where, for example, two competitors place all of their overlapping or complementary businesses in a particular market into a new corporate entity. Alternatively, two companies may pool their resources in order to enter or strengthen their position on a market in which one or both of them were not previously active. Whatever the circumstances, the essential question is whether the joint venture is given the means to act as an independent operator on its market. This may not be the case if the joint venture merely carries out certain functions for its parents, such as joint research and development or joint selling. In practice, it is sometimes difficult to determine whether the joint venture's on-going ties to its parents are so strong that the venture lacks the necessary independence.

ii. On-going sales from a joint venture to its parents

Where the parent companies of a joint venture remain active in a downstream market, it is common for the joint venture to sell at least some of its production to those parents. This may call into question the status of the joint venture as an autonomous entity on the market.

iii. Joint venture is reliant on purchases from its parents

The converse situation is where the parents remain active in the market up-stream from the joint venture. In such cases, it is common for the joint venture to be reliant on its parents for continuing supplies of raw materials or components. Such reliance may jeopardize the autonomy of the joint venture, unless it operates on a distinct "trade market." If the joint venture adds little value to the product supplied by its parents, it may be seen as little more than a joint sales agency.

iv. Joint venture operates on a trade market

The functions of some joint ventures are limited to sales and distribution rather than production. Where this is the case, some, most or even all of the products sold by the joint venture may be supplied from one or more of its parent companies. Even in this type of situation, the joint venture will be considered autonomous if it performs all the normal functions of a trading company in a distinct 'trade market.' According to the Commission's Joint Venture Notice, such a market is characterized by the presence of companies which specialize in the sale or distribution of products, with or without being vertically integrated with the producers of such products, and where different sources of supply are available. Operators in the trade market are usually required to invest in specific facilities such as outlets, stockholding, warehouses, transport fleets and sales personnel. Examples of such markets include steel stockholding, and the distribution of oil and lubricants, including through petrol stations.

c. Lasting Basis

For a joint venture to be concentrative, its likely duration must be sufficiently long to bring about a lasting structural change. A joint venture will not be concentrative if it is only established for a short finite period, for example where parties come together to construct a power plant but have no interest in its subsequent operation. Periods as short as five years have been held to be sufficiently long, but usually only where there is a possibility that the joint venture will continue for a longer period.

d. Lack of Co-ordination of Competitive Behavior

A joint venture (even if full-function) will not be concentrative if it leads to co-ordination of competitive behavior between independent undertakings, resulting in a restriction of competition. It is the risk of co-ordination between the parent companies which is important. Although Article 3(2) of the Regulation also refers to co-ordination between the parent companies and the joint venture, this type of co-ordination is relevant 'only in so far as it is an instrument for producing or reinforcing the co-ordination between the parent companies.'

The Commission's numerous decisions on the issue indicate that the risk of co-ordination depends to a large degree on the extent to which the parents remain active in the same market as the joint venture.

Chapter 5

Free Movement of Persons

I. The Social Dimension of the European Union[1]

A. Introduction

The nations that make up the European Union plan to complete a single market without trade barriers. To accomplish this unification, the EU legislative bodies must adopt and implement massive legislation. This legislation, which is designed to harmonize national laws and to remove barriers, affects both the economic and the social dimensions of the member nations. If the EU does not properly consider these dimensions, perceived gains from unification may be offset by losses in one or both areas.

The weak impact of EU social legislation affecting workers illustrates the importance of properly considering both the economic and the social consequences of unification. The EU aimed its early social legislation at removing economic barriers and largely ignored the social consequences of its acts, believing that economic growth would automatically bring social progress. When this social progress did not come, the EU members realized they needed to consider social goals independently. However, this realization has not sensitized the EU to the need to balance the social and economic consequences of its legislation. Rather, the EU now often focuses only on social objectives and ignores the economic consequences of its social agenda. This extreme approach has led to opposition to much EU worker legislation by at least one EU member.

B. Historical Developments

1. Treaty of Rome

a. Motivation for the Social Objectives in the EEC Treaty

The EU has little power to legislate social progress. The only legal basis for Union social legislation is the Treaty of Rome (the Treaty). The Treaty, which established the European Economic Union, creates a common market in Europe. The Treaty's provisions are aimed at creating an efficient market by eliminating trade barriers and tariffs and by allowing the free movement of capital and workers.

---

1 Timothy W. Dowdy, *The Emergence of the Social Dimension of the European Economic Community*, 1990 B.Y.U.L. Rev. 1667-86 (1990). © 1990 Timothy W. Dowdy. Reprinted by permission.

In addition, the Treaty contains several social policy provisions. When the EU members signed the Treaty, they believed that social progress would naturally result from economic prosperity and that it was unnecessary to establish social policy in the Treaty. By including social provisions in the Treaty, the EU members did not attempt to create a social policy, but rather to eliminate economic barriers.

During the negotiations of the Treaty, France expressed concern about artificial market distortions facing its companies, such as proportionately greater contributions to the social security system and higher wages for women than those paid in other EU countries. France argued that these additional social costs would make its labor costs artificially high, resulting in distorted production costs that would disadvantage French companies competing with other EU companies. France wanted the Treaty to call for harmonization among EU countries of social security financing and equal pay for women.

Other negotiating countries, led by then-West Germany, disagreed with the French characterization of costs. They argued that these social costs are only a part of the total labor costs to France's economy. They contended that France's market offset the higher social costs through lower wages and taxes, thus equating the total labor costs among EU members. These countries felt that social provisions in the Treaty were not necessary because they would create artificial barriers to trade rather than eliminate them.

The disagreeing countries compromised, and Articles 117, 118, and several other social policy articles ultimately were included in the Treaty. Despite their inclusion, the reason for including these social provisions was to eliminate market distortion, not to provide for the needs of workers.

b. Social Policy

Articles 117 and 118 have been central to the implementation and development of the EU's social dimension. Article 117 sets forth one of the objectives listed in the preamble:

> Member States agree upon the need to promote improved working conditions and an improved standard of living for workers, so as to make possible their harmonization while the improvement is being maintained.
>
> They believe that such a development will ensue not only from the functioning of the common market, which will favor the harmonization of social systems, but also from the procedures provided for in the Treaty and from the approximation of provisions laid down by law, regulation or administrative action.[2]

The provision authorized the Commission of European Communities (Commission), an EU lawmaking body established by the Treaty, to promote improved working conditions and improved living standards and make harmonization possible.

---

2 Treaties Establishing the European Communities 271 (1973) [hereinafter Treaties].

Because members of the Union agreed early that the social programs of the different countries could not be made uniform, their goal was merely to harmonize them.

Article 118 gives the Commission authority to promote close cooperation between EU members in the following fields; labor law and working conditions, basic and advanced vocational training, social security, prevention of occupational accidents and diseases, occupational hygiene, the right of association, and collective bargaining between employers and workers.

Thus, the Treaty gives the EU a minimalist role in legislating social policy. The Treaty allows the Commission to promote certain social objectives, but does not give it direct authority to legislate.

2. The Emergence of the Social Dimension

In the first years of the EU, the Commission attempted to change the focus of the Treaty's social provisions by rejecting economic efficiency as the primary aim and by pursuing harmonization of social policy. This approach caused serious dissension among the members and the employers' associations. In the 1962 European Social Security Conference, which was to bring together representatives from the members, trade unions, employers' associations, and independent experts, the members refused to participate except as observers.

In 1964, communication between the Council of Ministers (the Council) of the Member States and the Commission broke down completely. In December of 1966, the Ministers of Social Affairs of the Member States signed an agreement limiting the Commission's activities and reestablishing cooperation among the members. This compromise signaled a retreat from the Commission's pure social policy approach.

a. Social Action Program

By the beginning of the 1970s, the emerging common market was not automatically generating social progress as had been originally hoped. The Union's minimalist social role was noticeably out of date. In October of 1972, the members asked the Commission to write a social action program to identify and coordinate member efforts in dealing with social problems. In 1974, the Commissions singled out forty priority actions designed to achieve three major objectives: 1) full and better employment, 2) improved living and working conditions, and 3) participation of workers and social partners in decision-making processes.

By adopting a social action program, the Commission changed the role of social policy in the EU from laissez faire to interventionist. Members recognized that they must actively deal with national and supranational social problems created or magnified by the emergence of the EU. They also recognized that many of these problems could be addressed only through greater coordination of national social policies at the EU level.

b. The Social Dimension

The initial social action program was unsuccessful. In attempting to establish the internal market in 1992, the EU had to this point focused mostly on the needs of business and on eliminating obstacles to free trade. Even though the need for coordinated social policy was recognized, there was little progress in this area. High, persistent unemployment, vast regional disparities, and other social problems lead many, including the Commission, to recognize the need to link harmonized social policy with harmonized economic policy among EU members.

The recognition of the social dimension of economic development as an end in itself is now complete. A 1988 Commission report stated that it was time for "new progress" in the area of social policy.[3] The Commission's "new progress" includes purely social objectives which focus on three areas.

First, the Commission will focus on more effective economic and social cohesion. This is to be accomplished primarily by a continued call for the convergence of national economic and social policies. Additionally, the Council has already agreed to spend roughly 50 billion EU units before 1992, mostly on regional projects to deal with the social disruptions caused by the advent of the internal market.

Second, the Commission will focus in promoting improvement in the work environment. Drawing on the authority given to it by the Single European Act, the Commission will promote minimum social requirements, particularly in the area of worker health and safety.[4]

Third, the Commission will focus on a mandate by Article 118B of the Single European Act which requires dialogue between employers and workers at a European level. The Commission has interpreted this provision to mean that "[t]he road to collective European framework convention is . . . open."[5] Out of this dialogue, the idea of a European charter defining fundamental social rights was born.

C. Specific Social Issues and the Social Dimension

The role of social policy in the EU has changed from being a mere by-product of economic objectives to an end in itself. Often the EU's social and economic objectives are so intertwined that it is difficult to tell whether the purpose of the EU is to promote social progress or economic progress. Among the legislation with purely social objectives, some has been supported by the members, while some has created enormous opposition.

1. Sex Discrimination in Employment

A major focus of the Commission's social action program was improving living and working conditions, which included ensuring and promoting equality of treatment between men and women in employment. Sex discrimination in the work place continues in the individual Member States to varying degrees depending on historical and cultural factors. The call by the Commission to eliminate sex discrimination was resisted in the national legislatures of the member nations.

---

3 Commission of the European Communities, The Social Policy of the European Community: Looking Ahead to 1992, 7 (1988) [hereinafter Ahead to 1992].

4 *Id.* at 8.

5 *Id.*

Article 199 of the Treaty calls for equal pay for equal work among men and women. The original purpose of this provision was to eliminate market distortions caused by the disparity among Member States in women's wages, and was included as part of the compromise in the Treaty.

Before the social action program, Article 119 and case law interpreting Article 199 required equal work. Still, most members did not implement these principles into their national laws. Therefore, as a part of the social action program in 1975 and as an impetus to the members, the Council adopted Directive 75/117, which provided for harmonization of national laws on the principle of equal pay. The directive also expanded Article 199's limits by requiring elimination of discrimination based on sex for all aspects and conditions of enumeration. Members were given until February of 1976 to implement the new directive. In 1976, the Commission began infringement proceedings against seven members for non-compliance.

One of the underlying problems of equal pay opportunities for women has been segregation in the work place. Women have generally been relegated to the lower paying jobs in service and tertiary occupations, and have been denied access to higher-paying occupations and positions of responsibility. In response to this problem, the Council passed Directive 76/207, which provided for equal access to employment, vocational training, and working conditions. Members resisted the change, and several refused to implement the Directive.

Another problem was the wide disparity between men and women in social security eligibility requirements and benefits. Two directives were adopted to alleviate this disparity. Directive 79, adopted in 1979, provided for equal treatment between men and women in statutory social security schemes. Directive 86/378, adopted in 1986, provided equal treatment in occupational social security schemes. This directive is unique because it applies international social security standards to social security schemes in the private sector. A third directive has been proposed to tie up any loose ends not covered in the first two directives. The implementation of these directives was also slow.

Although implementation has been slow, the members have supported the equal employment directives and have adopted them. But despite this legislation, sex discrimination in employment still exists in the EU. Women are still much more likely than men to be unemployed or to be in lower paying jobs. "In all the countries of the Union, women face discrimination either in access to vocational training, education, employment prospects, or in the terms and conditions of employment."[6]

Sex discrimination in employment still continues in the EU despite social legislation. One reason may be that the economic downturn of the 1970s and the early 1980s in the EU prevented the members from financing the programs and benefits packages necessary to remove sex discrimination. Also, the downturn may have made women more reluctant to try to enforce their rights under the Treaty and directives for fear of losing their jobs.

---

6 Burrows, *The Promotion of Women's Rights by the European Economic Community*, 17 C.M. L. Rev. 208 (1980).

Probably, however, the continuing disparity is mainly due to traditional social values among the individual members. Until there is a change in social attitudes, sex discrimination will persist. The Treaty, the directives, and other Union legislation have been an impetus for social change, but this change will take time.

2. Worker Participation

Worker participation is another area in which the EU has tried to legislate changes in the social order. Worker participation is an institutional structure which can protect worker's interests by giving them a role in the decision making process. There are varying degrees of worker participation broadly classified in the following ways: 1) collective bargaining; 2) worker representation on advisory or consultive bodies; 3) worker representation on boards of directors; and 4) employee ownership. The proposed directives deal mainly with worker representation or consultive bodies and on boards of directors. Most individual members have had forms of worker participation as part of their national laws for some time.

France passed legislation in 1945 and 1946 creating *comite enterprise* for all undertakings with more than fifty employees. The *comite enterprise* was a consultive board comprised of company officials and employees. The company was required to inform and consult the *comite enterprise* on a variety of business matters such as new production methods, new purchases, general business trends, and planned layoffs or dismissals. Several EU countries have adopted similar worker participation schemes.

The Mitbestimmung, or worker board member in German, traces its legislative roots to the early 1950s. The Worker's Constitution Act of 1952 gave employees of companies with more than 500 employees one-third membership on those companies' supervisory boards. The Codetermination Act of 1976 gave one-half employee membership on supervisory boards for companies with more than 2,000 employees. Other countries, such as Denmark and the Netherlands, have adopted somewhat similar national systems.

The EU's involvement in Union-wide worker participation standards also has a long history. In the late 1960s, the EU was concerned that U.S. multinational corporations were dominating and progressively taking over the Union industrial structure. To compete with the United States, the Europeans needed to create multinational enterprises on the U.S. scale. While transnational mergers were needed to create companies that large, the member's company laws were too diverse to permit such mergers. This situation gave rise to the idea of a "European Company" which is a company incorporated under EU law instead of national laws.

The EU was concerned not to make its company law more favorable for companies than national laws when drafting the European Company law. A more favorable European company law could cause a mass exodus of companies out of national laws into European company law. One consideration was diversity in worker participation. The German Mitbestimmung model was used in the proposed European Company law, because the EU believed that a European law excluding some form of worker participation would be more favorable to companies than national laws.

The European Company law was seen as a temporary solution to the U.S. problem. The Commission decided that the long range solution was to harmonize or converge the company laws of the individual members. The so-called Fifth Company Law Directive attempted to harmonize national laws concerning worker representation on boards of directors.

As first proposed in 1972, the original draft of the Fifth Directive required all large companies in the EU to establish a two-tier board. This two-tier approach is the German Mitbestimmung model, which created a supervisory board to perform the daily operations functions. The model requires that some portion of the seats on the supervisory board be held by workers. It soon became apparent that the Fifth Directive was "unsalable" to the Union, because countries like France and the United Kingdom have "radically different systems and traditions."[7] The Commission later adopted a more flexible approach which provided for one-tier boards and gave companies an option on how to incorporate employee representation on the board.

As the Fifth Directive stalled, the Commission began looking for alternative ways to protect employees. As a part of the social action program of 1977, which called for greater employee involvement in the decision-making process of firms, the Commission proposed a number of directives in an attempt to harmonize national legislation over worker participation.

One of the directives proposed during this time is commonly referred to as the "Vredeling Directive."[8] Some argued that "the place where industrial democracy can be most meaningful is not the boardroom but the shopfloor."[9] If the channels of communication are open between the policy makers and the shopfloor, employees can have more input into decisions that have a direct impact on them. The proposed Vredeling Directive requires multinational companies in the EU, whether the parent company is located in the EU or not, to inform and consult workers' representatives about proposed decisions that might affect working conditions or their livelihood.

Two main criticisms of the initial draft of the proposal were that it allowed employees to by-pass the subsidiary and go directly to the parent for information, and that the company would be required to give out secret information. The Vredeling Directive was amended to deal with these criticisms, but it also stalled.

The Vredeling Directive stalled because of opposition from EU members and because of forceful lobbying by the United States. Some of the members, like Ireland and Luxem-bourg, objected to the proposal because of its potential effect on direct investment. Other countries, particularly the United Kingdom, were concerned about the social implications of changes in their system and traditions.

Both major EU directives in the area of worker participation, the Fifth Directive and the Vredeling Directive, have stalled for basically the same two reasons. First, countries that have developed worker participation schemes different from the model proposed by the Commission feel that the social implications of the proposed changes

---

7 Martin Shanks, EUROPEAN SOCIAL POLICY, TODAY AND TOMORROW 51 (1977).

8 Proposal for a Council Directive on procedures for informing and consulting the employees of undertakings with complex structures, in particular transnational undertakings, 23 O.J. Eur. Comm. (No. C 297) 3 (1980).

9 Martin Shanks, EUROPEAN SOCIAL POLICY, TODAY AND TOMORROW at 52 (1977).

would be too severe. Second, the directives are viewed as placing burdensome restrictions on business. These restrictions reduce the competitiveness of EU businesses and strongly discourage foreign investment.

D. Current and Future Direction of Social Policy in the EU

1. Charter of Fundamental Social Rights

According to several members, the European Commissions, trade unions and others, handling the problem of worker's rights is vital to the EU's success. Mathias Hinterscheid, the Secretary General for the European Trade Union Confederation, stated that unless workers' rights go hand in hand with the establishment of the internal market, the market will fail for lack of the workers' support. The first step the EU has taken to deal with the workers' needs is proposing the Charter.

The Charter is designed to serve two purposes. First, a major political gesture on the part of the Union is needed to win back workers' support for 1992, because the workers have become discontent with their role in the Union and their share of the emerging market's economy prosperity. The EU had previously focused on creating an environment for business prosperity. By providing a broad range of fundamental social protection and guarantees, the Charter assures that the EU is committed to workers' needs.

Second, the main reason articulated for the necessity of the Charter is the problem of social dumping. Social dumping occurs when a company moves its business from a member with high social obligations to a member with lower social obligations to avoid restrictive labor practices or to reduce production costs. Labor's major concern about social dumping is that the level of social obligations in the EU will be driven down to the lowest common denominator by the movement of business to lower obligation states, and that the movement will continue until all of the gains made by unions in countries with higher obligations will be lost. The proposed Charter intends to solve the problem of social dumping by establishing minimum social standards high enough to eliminate the incentive for businesses to move.

2. An Approach to Social Legislation

Just as economic legislation which ignores the social dimension will not be unanimously supported, neither will social legislation which ignores the economic dimension. Social legislation always has both social and economic consequences. The EU should adopt an approach that fosters at least one of the two dimensions, both if possible, but does not adversely affect the other.

Women's rights legislation is an example of this approach. The rationale for equal treatment first began as a means of eliminating market distortion. Then it progressed to a broader view of remuneration, and then to vocational training and access to employment. Finally, it included equal treatment in social security benefits. These are clearly social benefits for women.

Although the focus of the women's rights directives becomes increasingly social, it also enhances the economic dimension. For example, vocational training helps alleviate structural unemployment and improves worker productivity and access to employment, while equal benefits remove possible barriers to free movement of women workers.

The women's rights directives were readily passed with little opposition, although implementation was a little slow. The worker participation directives, on the other hand, were strongly opposed both inside and outside the EU, primarily because of their economic consequences.

Worker participation is an example of promoting only a social position without regard for the economic consequences. The Fifth Directive was proposed to equalize competitive conditions, but the social element of worker involvement soon became its legislative aim, with little consideration for economic consequences. The later Vredeling Directive was simply a continuation of the desire for worker involvement—again without regard for the economic dimension of social legislation. These two directives resulted in opposition and failure.

Like worker participation, the Charter is a purely social document which ignores economic consequences; therefore the EU should not approve it. The EU should seek instead a solution which fosters the same needs of the workers but does not have such negative economic effects. Such an approach would meet the needs of workers and win approval of [skeptical Member States] in its desire to support social progress.

II. The Limited Competence of the EC in the Field of Social Policy[10]

Neither in the political practice of the Union nor in the legal literature of Union law is there any doubt that the competence to regulate social policy rests with the Member States. When drafting the Treaty in the early fifties it was mainly France that wanted to enlarge the competencies of the Union in the field of social policy because it feared that its own high level of social security contributions, which raised French wages and granted a high degree of social protection to French workers, would create a disadvantage in the internal workings of the common market. It was, *inter alia*, the "low wage country" Germany which impeded this initiative. As part of the French initiative Article 119 survived, which deals with the competence of the Union to regulate equal pay for women and men. The Single European Act added only the "working-environment" in Article 118a to those matters which can be regulated by majority vote of the Council, whereas even the regulation of the mobility and the rights and interests of workers have explicitly been excluded from the (qualified) majority rule in Article 100a(2).

[10] Karl-Jurgen Bieback, *Harmonisation of social policy in the European Community,* 32 C. de D. 916-35 (1991). © 1991 Karl-Jurgen Bieback. Reprinted by permission.

The reasons for this "unsocial" character of the Union are manifold:

1. The Union is *only a common market*, it is dominated by economic interests and it can very well function without a common social policy. Therefore the political structure of the Union represents one modern "technocratic" way to regain or stabilize the priority of economic policy and economic development in regard to social policy.
2. The traditional social security *systems of the Member States differ so much* that harmonization is said to be impossible and a waste of political energy. It should however be remembered that most national systems did not acquire their specific structures until after the second world war, only a few years before the Union came into existence. And they are still subject to major changes, Britain giving the best example.
3. The *financial consequences* of a common social policy cannot be calculated and would undermine the financial basis of the EU.
4. In most countries, the UK excepted, social policy is embedded within a network of public and *private, national and regional organisations* which are already too centralised and bureaucratic and do not need another bureaucratic superstructure.
5. Last, but by no means least, social policy is an *indispensable attribute and source of legitimacy* for all modern industrialised states.

A. Competence of EU and Social Policy

1. Free Movement of Labour

Still, the most important competencies in the field of social policy in the EU are Article 48 and following which guarantee the free movement of labour and give the EU the power to regulate it. These articles of the Treaty of Rome grant rights directly to the citizens of the Member States. They form the basis for two major types of EU regulations:

1. The law of non-discrimination which stipulates that no worker or self-employed person, taking residence in another country of the union, is to be discriminated against on grounds of nationality; e.g. that person cannot be excluded from any of the social benefits the Member States provide for their working population.
2. The law of coordination which guarantees that workers moving from one country into another will not be disadvantaged because of their mobility. Therefore social security benefits (except those of a social assistance nature) can be exported and periods of insurance or residence as a worker in one country are aggregated towards relevant periods in the systems of another country. This law is quite similar to the provisions in international social security law which coordinates the different legal systems of sovereign nations or Member States of a confederation.

Only recently the Union has enacted legislation for a general system of mutual recognition of vocational qualifications and the right of residence for students and pensioners. This coordinating law leaves the social security law of the Member States unchanged. However, it will require some substantial adaptations as will be shown later.

2. Special Competencies in the Field of Social Policy

The first major substantial competence of the EU is still the directly binding Article 119 of the Treaty which again grants individual rights to the citizens of the Member States. It guarantees equal pay for men and women and has forced all Member States to change their labour law system in order to realise equal treatment of men and women in all kinds of different remunerations paid by the employer, e.g. occupational benefits and especially occupational pensions.

The Single European Act inserted the second important field of social legislation, *working-environment*, in Article 118a. As this area influences the free movement of means of production (machinery as well as materials), it is not by chance the only matter of social policy which is explicitly subject to majority rule in the legislative body, the Council of Ministers, whereas majority rule has been introduced for most other fields necessary for the completion of the common market (Art. 110a(1)). The EU has developed a program to promote health and safety at work and has already promulgated more than 50 directives which have had considerable impact on the social policy of the Member States. The most recent ones follow the "new" pattern of harmonisation. This acknowledges that all necessary regulations cannot be legislated for by the EU and its institutions, and so it sets only minimum standards through Union law and leaves it to special norm-setting bodies of experts to define them and it does not hinder the Member States from enacting higher standards.

The last major competence is found in the European Social Funds (Art. 123 and following, 130c, 130d) which dispersed in 1988 the quite meager sum of DM14 billion, not even [one-fourth] of what (West) Germany spent in the same year on unemployment benefits and labour market policy. During the last decade the Funds have concentrated their resources on a few innovative programs for less developed regions, especially in supporting retraining efforts and promoting marginalised groups.

All three competencies have wider consequences than might be first imagined.

3. Social Policy by Convergence and the European Charter of Social Rights

As the jurisdiction to harmonise or coordinate is quite narrow, the Treaty of Rome has some instruments to stimulate the voluntary consent and assimilation between the social policy of the Member States (Art. 118) and the social dialogue of the social partners of all Member States (Art. 118b). The 1989 European Charter of Social Rights is part of this policy as it is of legal relevance in a strict sense neither for the Member States nor for their citizens, but rather serves as an instrument to set a frame for the policy of the Commission and for voluntary coordination of the different national policies. The Action Program of the Commission to implement the Social Charter therefore confines itself to the improvement of labour market policy, the free movement of labour, the social protection of some groups of workers, free information of employee representatives and health and safety at work.

B. The Dominance of the "Federal" Competencies

Though not even a "confederation," the Union displays some processes of concentrating competencies and political power which are typical of federal and confederate states. The legal problems connected with this development are more technical, but at least the last one shows that the dominance of the Union means dominance of the market and lower priority for a genuine social policy.

1. Broad Interpretation of the Competence for Social Policy in the "Active Phase" of the Seventies

In analyzing the development of the Union's competence in social policy one has to differentiate between two aspects. One is the very *complicated and restricted procedure* of Union legislation. *Unanimity rule* applies in most matters of social policy. Therefore the representative of one Member State in the Council can hinder every initiative. The matters of (qualified) majority rule in the field of social policy are limited to Article 118a, working environment and health and safety at work.

The second aspect is the *basis and interpretation of the legislative competence of the Union*, which tend to be wide whenever the Council is prepared to use them. The Treaty of Rome and the Single European Act provide for an extensive *competence for all measures necessary to complete the common market* and the free movement of labour and capital (Art. 100, 100a, 235) which is only restricted by unanimity vote (Art. 100 and 235) and in Articles 100 and 100a to the function of merely coordinating the law of the Member States. Although the general competence to regulate through majority rule in Article 100a does not explicitly apply to the free movement of labour and the rights and interests of the workers, its general competence for completing the common market affects many matters of social policy and workers' rights as well. The establishment of a common and free market covers every field of economic and social activity and therefore hardly any domain of politics is outside the ambit of Article 100a as well as 100 and 235. E.g. the European Court of Justice decided that the general competence in Article 100 to legislate for establishing and sustaining the common market may cover social policy as well—just to underline the importance of social security in every market economy. The dominance of the market shows up even in the competencies of the EU. In the late sixties and in the seventies the Council was prepared to use its wide powers in the field of social policy.

In the seventies three directives in the field of *labour law* were based on Articles 100 and 235 which required many changes in most of the Member States: Directive 75/129 concerning collective redundancies; 77/198 concerning transfer of business and safeguarding of employees' acquired rights; 80/987 protecting of employees in the event of insolvency. However, the growth of the union made unanimity more and more difficult which has forestalled further progress. The Commission had proposed directives to set minimum standards for atypical work, parental leave, hours of work and for the disabled. Not one of them has been accepted by the Council of Ministers. The European Parliament proposed to base these directives on a wide interpretation of Article 118a ("working environment") and its majority rule—thus transforming Article

118a into an universal competence for all kinds of protective labour law legislation. Though broad in its wording, Article 118a refers only to the traditional task of protecting health and safety at work.

Although Article 119 gives only jurisdiction to guarantee equal pay for men and women, it served as a basis to enact a complete series of *equality directives* about all aspects of the employment relationship and even social security, all of them explicitly based on Article 235. The last one covers the whole range of social security benefits, with the exception of social assistance. As the concept of equal treatment outlaws not only forms of direct but also of indirect discrimination the ambit of these directives is extremely wide. *Indirect discrimination* is a measure which is apparently neutral, but in fact predominantly affects persons of one sex which cannot be explained by factors other than those related to one sex and which is not justified objectively. The EEU Commission's report about the implementation of Directive 79/7[11] demonstrates many forms of indirect discrimination in the social security law of all Member States. The main fields in occupational benefits as well as social security law are:

- insufficient integration of *part-time workers* in systems of occupational or public insurance benefits and insufficient benefits to part-time workers; this especially puts to question the basic *principle* to grant and calculate benefits in relation to *continuity and seniority of employment and/or contributions*;
- *supplements for dependents* in insurance as well as in social assistance systems within and beyond the exceptions of article 7(d) of the directive;
- *aggregation of family income* in income-tested benefits, which often results in a cut back of the women's benefit;
- *administrative discrimination* where benefits are left to the wide discretion of the adjudicating officer and women do not receive their equal share, e.g. in labour market programmes of unemployment insurance.

As the sexual division of the welfare state is at stake, most areas of labour and social security law have to be changed and harmonised.

However, after the period of extensive implementation of Article 119 in the seventies the subsequent draft directives proposed by the Commission to specify the concept of indirect discrimination and the burden of proof and to complete the legislation in the field of social security have not been accepted by the Council.

The competence in Article 128 allows only the enactment of general principles for a common policy in *vocational training*. In a wide interpretation of this clause the Council however applied it to university education and to specific programmes. Only recently it adopted very specific programmes to promote vocational training, as COMETT I and II for training in new technologies (against were West-Germany and U.K.) and PETRA for the vocational training of youngsters (against was U.K.) which were only based on Article 128 and decided by majority vote, or ERASMUS for university training and cooperation which was based on Article 128 in combination with

[11] COM (88) 768—Council Document Nr. 4110/89.

Article 235 and decided by unanimity. The European Court upheld this wide interpretation of Article 128 in cases concerning PETRA and ERASMUS.

2. Mixed Administration

It is an ambiguous method of financial and administrative cooperation and control for the central state of a federation to influence the process of budgeting and administration of the Member States through offering financial aid for administrative programmes of "common interest" which are established and designed by the federal administration. This method has been well developed by the European Funds. During the past decade they have tried to gain more efficiency by cooperating closely together with the administration of the Member States in programmes instigated by the Funds and financed by them up to only 50%, the other part of the money has to come from the national administrations. Very often the Funds cooperate directly with the local and regional administrations of the Member States by-passing the central and federal government and its coordinating function. Thus, the financial impact of the EU programmes gains considerably and the national administration becomes involved in the social policy of the Union.

3. Wide Competence to Regulate the Free Market for Goods and Services and its "Implied Powers"

However, even on the basis of the competence to regulate the free market of goods and services (Art. 8a, 9, 30 and 59) quite a few issues of social policy can be regulated by the Union and by (qualified) majority in the Council pursuant to Articles 8a and 100a. This development follows the doctrine of "implied powers" inherent in the constitutional law of all federal states allowing for the union or the Union to regulate together with its explicit competencies all necessary, consequential matters ("effet utile" and "effet nécessaire"). As the Union's explicit competencies are mainly those concerning the free market, it is the logic of the market and of market regulation which will dominate and design European social policy.

The free market for goods outlaws all barriers which have the same impact as tariffs and other forms of discrimination ("charge having the equivalent effect" in Article 30 of the Treaty of Rome). One such barrier comprises *safety standards for machines*. Therefore the machine directive was based on Articles 30 and 100a(1) and majority vote, setting cogent standards for all machines traded within the Union. The regulation and control of the safety of machines have traditionally been part of labour and social security law, exercised in most European countries by a public inspectorate and, a German speciality, by the authorities of the public workers compensation insurance *(Berufsgenossenschaften)* run by employers' and union representatives. As this directive is not based on Article 118a it sets an upper limit and its standards cannot be improved by national authorities. Therefore all those national systems of public agencies and standards of safety and health at work will partially lose in importance in favour of the free trade of goods. In addition to this, the German government argued that the machine directive concerned the rights and interest of workers and had needed unanimity in the Council according to Article 100(2).

Up to now the Council could not agree on a concept for a "*European Company*" because the Member States had completely divergent views on many decisive issues, especially the problem of workers' representation on the board. However it is undisputed that the competence of the EU to regulate this matter is based on Article 54(2) and Article 100, now 100a, concerning freedom of establishment, i.e. the free movement of capital and the freedom of investment. As Article 100a excludes matters pertaining to the rights of employees, the newly proposed directive for worker participation and transeuropean companies is based on Article 54(2). A matter of social policy which, in Germany and in the Scandinavian countries is deeply rooted in labour law and which will transform most labour law, systems will thus be dominated by the free movement of capital.

The competence of the Union to regulate the free market of *transport* in Article 75 was the basis for regulating the law of working hours of transnational traffic within the Union.

Most continental Member States have established special social security systems for their agrarian population which receive many state subsidies because of this sector's permanent economic decline. The Commission investigates quite a few of these subsidies on the ground that they are *national subsidies* within the system of the common agricultural market organisation and therefore need the Commission's approval pursuant to Articles 49 and 91. The same applies to subsidies given to enterprises in order to stimulate the employment of marginal workers as part of the national labour market policy.

Even the competence of the EU to regulate the free movement of goods and services seems to dominate some of its other competencies. The EU equality directives allow for "positive actions" (Dir. 76/207, Art. 2(4)), which are measures in favour of women like quotas or *contract compliance programmes*. The latter obliges all those doing business with a state government to develop positive actions to promote women. However, only recently the Commission took action against several German States and their programmes of contract compliance on the ground that this would discriminate against companies of other Member States and impair their equal chances to apply for public contracts in Germany.

C. The Impact of the Common Market on Social Policy

It is, however not only a matter of the dominance of market policy within the competence of the Union but also the establishment of the common market itself that will influence the social policy of the Member States.

1. Social Dumping

As the common market is supposed to increase the economic competition between Member States it is feared that business will invest in those states where enterprises find the highest flexibility in labour management and the lowest labour-costs, i.e. the lowest level of wages, protective legislation and employers' contributions for social security schemes. As a consequence, the most costly systems of social security have to lower their standards to be able to compete on a national, regional and enterprise level. There are many arguments against this opinion and in favour of different developments and consequences.

The future development of the common market and the competition between Member States is quite uncertain. From the history of regional development in the Member States and the debate about regional policy we know that a *market economy does not have a "natural" tendency to equalize economic disparities* between regions but may rather intensify them. The lower level of social protection in the Southern rim of the Union may constitute a necessary condition to survive the competition of the North, and the high level of social protection in the North may be regarded as a sign of economic strength gained in long contest with other industrialised nations on the world market.

The main indicator for competitiveness is not the level of labour costs but the level of *labour costs in relation to productivity*, the unit labour costs. Here Germany or France rank in the lower field while Greece and Ireland score highest.

Competition between locations depends not only on labor costs but also on *other costs and other non-cost factors* like transport and social infrastructure. One can even evaluate a high level of social protection as an economic asset that guarantees productivity and, on the basis of social security systems, a high degree of personal flexibility.

Free movement of capital within the Union already existed in past decades. However (West) German business did not *invest* very much in the low-wage countries of the South in order to take advantage of lower unit-labor costs but to be closer to the regional market and to secure their presence and position there.

Whether social dumping occurs, depends to a large degree on the *common social policy of the EU* and its success in installing a common minimum level of social rights.

2. Mobility of Labor and the Tendency Towards Harmonisation

One of the main, and probably the only effective, social right of employees in the Treaty of Rome is the freedom of movement of workers in Article 48. As already mentioned the law of coordination and the freedom to export acquired social security rights from one country to another have many indirect repercussions on the national social security systems which again exert pressure to move towards more harmonisation.

EC Regulation 1408/71 grants the right to export all "acquired" social security rights regardless of their foundation in social insurance and contributions or in universal national systems and residence/payment of taxes. Only the most basic system, social assistance, is exempted (Art. 4(4)).

In many Member States the economic crisis that started in 1974 and the increase of long-term unemployment have revealed many gaps in the social security net, especially for women and youngsters, which led to the public debate to introduce systems of minimum social income. One common characteristic of all these systems is that they should be distinct from social assistance and its means test. This attribute however moves them within the ambit of Regulation 1408/71 and the freedom of export and principle of aggregation. Therefore such minimum income systems have to be open to all citizens of the union which might raise their costs and might render them incalculable.

Again there are only two harmonising solutions: either the Member States coordinate their reforms in a very intensive way, excluding cumulations as well as deficiencies and harmonising definitions and regulations, or they renounce their plans or try to "nationalise" them.

Exporting rights means that quite a few requirements for benefits like disability and invalidity and their degree have to be checked and decided by the social security administration of another Member State. This matter is dealt with in Regulation 1408/71 Article 40(4) (invalidity) and Article 57(1, 2) (occupational disease) and Regulation 574/72 Article 18 (incapacity for work). The foreign administration's decision has to bind all other administrations because it may affect requirements which are common to different benefits in different countries, it may cost too much to examine the claimant in all countries and the migrant worker may not be capable to undertake the necessary traveling. Therefore it makes much sense that the European Court of Justice has, in a fairly generous interpretation of the Regulations, strengthened the binding power of these decisions. However, such administrative practices demand a basic similarity of legal requirements, expressions and procedures. Otherwise this necessary coordination will not work effectively.

In Germany most invalidity benefits are closely linked to rehabilitation benefits in kind according to the principle of priority of rehabilitation—an internationally accepted and very useful social policy measure. Furthermore, in Germany unemployment insurance is closely linked with employment policy therefore unemployment benefit is subordinate to training and the benefit can be cut when appropriate training is offered. However, only cash benefits, like pensions and unemployment benefit are exported, not benefits in kind, like rehabilitation and retraining. Therefore in export cases the payment of pensions and benefits on the one hand and the delivery of rehabilitation and retraining services on the other hand are split and the priority of rehabilitation training cannot be realised.

All these problems point to one common solution: harmonisation of law and administration either by widening the competence of the Union or voluntary harmonisation of the social policy of the Member States.

III. After Maastricht[12]

The Maastricht Treaty occupies a significant place in the history of the Union. Its ratification has been shrouded in virulent debate: discussion which has not been confined to the provisions of the Treaty itself but has extended to the more fundamental question of the relationship between the Union and its Member States, in particular the division of power between them.

The Treaty is a large and unwieldy document, attended by some 17 Protocols and 31 Declarations, many of which have little to do with the furtherance of Union objec-

[12] Philippa Watson, *Social Policy After Maastricht,* 30 C.M.L.R. 481-513 (1993).

tives but are concerned with the preservation of cherished national values, which it is feared—and to some extent justifiably—may be eroded by the process of European integration.

Social policy appears, at first sight, to have achieved a prominence in the Maastricht Treaty not previously accorded to it in the Union Treaties. Article B, which defined the objectives of the Union, included within these the promotion of "social and economic progress"; Article G, which will become Article 3 of the EU Treaty, states the activities of the Union to include "a policy in the social sphere comprising a European Social Fund" (Article 3(i)). Article F requires the Union to respect " . . . fundamental rights as guaranteed by the European Convention for the Protection of Human Rights and Fundamental Freedoms . . . and as they result from the constitutional traditions common to the Member States, as general principles of Union law."

Does this apparent new emphasis on social policy signify a desire on the part of the Member States to create a true Union policy involving a large scale increase in the existing powers of the Union in this area, an easing of the old tensions which have for so long characterized Union activity in this area? A closer examination of the more specific provisions of the Treaty shows that this may not be so.

In addition to these generally-stated objectives, many sections of the Maastricht Treaty deal more specifically with social policy in the broad sense of that term. Examples include Article 126 (education); Article 127 (vocational training); Article 129 (public health); Article 129a (consumer protection); Article 130a-130p (economic and social cohesion). Three sections in particular deal with social policy as that term is usually understood in Union law: Article G, paragraph 32; the Protocol on Social Policy (Protocol No. 14) and the Protocol concerning Article 119 of the Treaty establishing the European Union (Protocol No. 2). Article G, paragraph 32 introduces a minor amendment into Article 118a to take account of changes introduced by the Treaty to the Union's decision-making procedures. Apart from that change the Maastricht treaty leaves social policy chapter of the EEC Treaty unchanged. However, the Protocol on Social Policy and the Protocol on Article 119 of the Maastricht Treaty have had a significant impact on the general development of social policy within the Union—does that Protocol signify a departure on the part of the vast majority of Member States from their traditional reluctance to acknowledge Union competence with respect to social policy? Is there now a firm commitment on the part of that majority to the development of a Union social policy?

A. The Protocol on Social Policy

To understand the background to the Protocol on Social Policy and its place in the Union legal order it is necessary to remind ourselves of the somewhat checkered history of Union social policy.

1. The Present State of Community Social Policy

The Treaty of Rome makes no specific provision for a Union Social Policy akin, for example, to the Common Agriculture Policy or the Common Commercial Policy. Articles 117-122 are vague and repetitious conferring no real powers upon the Union institutions and little by way of direct rights upon Union citizens. It is plain that the founding Member States are free to regulate in accordance with their national social and economic policies and, more importantly, prevalent values and mores. The Union was regarded as being competent in the social field only to the extent necessary to attain state Union objectives, notably the prevention or distortion of competition arising out of divergences in production costs between Member States due to differences in national social standards, levels of health and safety protection and other similar matters.

Subsequent years have seen a change of attitude on the part of the Member States towards Union competence in the social sphere. For twenty years, since the adoption of the Social Action program, it has been possible to speak of a Union social policy operating in parallel with national social policies, which has been developed as a result of the political will of the Member States to transfer some of their competence in the area to the Union. This has been done voluntarily but not always without hesitation and misgiving.

2. The Social Charter

The adoption of the Social Charter in December 1989, setting out twelve fundamental social rights guaranteed to all Union citizens, marked a firm commitment on the part of its eleven signatory States to the creation of a Union social policy and their apparent willingness, in order to achieve that objective, to cede considerable powers to the Union. The adoption of the Social Charter was accompanied by the Commission's publication of an Action Program, a detailed document of some fifty-four pages containing forty-seven proposals for the adoption of the measures deemed necessary to achieve the objectives of the Charter.

By the end of 1991, the Commission had presented proposals to the Council on virtually all the forty-seven initiatives announced in its Action Program, but in its First Report on the Application of the Charter it expressed " . . . its disappointment at the slow rate at which the Council has been taking decisions on a number of proposals" concluding that " . . . the Commission has presented nearly all the proposals envisaged in its program of work in compliance with the principles of subsidiarity but the Council of Ministers has failed to live up to expectations."

The Charter is not a legally binding document; its provisions must therefore be implemented by reference to the legislative powers set out in the EEC Treaty, or by Member States acting independently and on a national level. This means that the realization of the Charter depends to a much greater extent on the political goodwill of the Member States than many other Union policies. The Charter leaves much of the initiative to the Member States acting on a national level, and with respect to those measures to be adopted on a Union level, in many instances, the only available legal basis requires a unanimous vote in the Council.

In anticipation of the reluctance of some Member States, in particular the United Kingdom, to adopt some of its proposals the Commission has made extensive use of those provisions in the EEC Treaty which require only a qualified majority vote for the adoption of measures in the Council.

Both the Member States and the employer's organizations have severely criticized the use of Articles 100A and 118A as legal bases for social measures which have entailed, on the one hand, a rather broad interpretation by the Commission of the concept of health and safety in Article 118A and, on the other hand, a rather restrictive interpretation of the exclusionary clauses in Article 100A, in order to ensure that proposals are subject to majority voting when they reach the Council for final adoption rather than unanimity, as required by Articles 100 and 235.

3. Failures to Implement the Social Charter

The upshot is that little progress had been made in implementing the Charter when the work of the Intergovernmental Conference on Political Union began. It began to be felt that the crux of problem was the lack of the legal powers essential to fulfil the objectives of the Charter: an increase in those powers would greatly facilitate the realization of these guarantees. In a working document presented by the Commission to the Intergovernmental Conference the Commission attributed the lack of progress in attaining the objectives of the Charter to:

> the wide gap between the powers available under the current legal bases and the ambitions set out in the Charter and the new constraints arising from the completion of the internal market.[13]

To overcome these difficulties the Commission proposed a revision of the social chapter of the Treaty, which, in order to ensure that the Union's economic and social dimension developed in parallel required that "qualified majority of voting should be extended to certain fields, notably some of those, covered by the Charter."[14]

The eleven Member States which were party to the Charter were happy to reiterate their commitment to the objectives set out therein, and to broaden the Union's law-making powers to include, as the Commission suggested, increased qualified majority of voting in many areas of social policy. However, the United Kingdom remained implacably opposed to any expansion of the Union's power in the social sphere. Accordingly, it was agreed among the twelve Member States that the amendments desired by the other eleven Member States should be contained in an agreement signed by those Member States which would form a Protocol annexed to the Maastricht Treaty binding those eleven Member States only.

The refusal of the United Kingdom to accept the proposed amendments to the social policy chapter of the Treaty of Rome, which would have resulted in a considerable transfer of power from the member States to the Union institutions and an increase in the qualified majority voting power of the Council, can be explained by its firmly held belief, expressed forcibly in discussion leading up to the adoption of the Social Charter, and re-iterated in the inter-governmental conference on the draft Treaty, that social policy is a matter for the Member States to regulate: " . . . The Government made it plain to our partners in the period of the Inter-Governmental Con-

---

[13] The Community's Working Document presented to the Intergovernmental Conference on Political Union SEC (91) 500 Final Brussels 30 March 1991 p. 84.

[14] *Id.* p. 86.

ference itself that we saw no case for an extension of the Union powers in these areas or for any increased use of Majority voting."[15]

This attitude can be attributed to a number of factors. Firstly, successive conservative governments in the United Kingdom have espoused a policy of laissez faire. With respect to the labor market, this has meant that terms and conditions of employment should be regulated by market forces within a loose legislative framework. Not illogically, therefore, the United Kingdom government has been and is opposed to increasing the powers of the Union in the social and employment area which they fear would bring about an increase in the regulation of terms and conditions of employment and possibly require the adoption of measures similar to those recently repealed by it.

Secondly, the success of the United Kingdom government in achieving a marked decline in the power of the trade union movement in the 1980s would have led it to view with suspicion any provisions in the draft Treaty which would have threatened to restore the influence of the trade union movement. Proposals to involve trade unions in the legislative process would therefore have been unacceptable as would any attempt to entrust the implementation of Union legislation to management and labor.

4. The Protocol on Social Policy

As a result of the refusal of the United Kingdom to strengthen the competence of the Union in the social sphere, the Protocol on Social Policy came into being.

This approach to a policy to which one Member State feels it cannot subscribe but which is strongly favored by all the other Member States was novel and set an unfortunate precedent for the subsequent agreement of the European Council allowing Denmark to opt out of several sections of the Maastricht Treaty. Union law at all levels provides for derogations from its application, but never before have individual Member States opted out of entire sections of a Union Treaty setting out policies supposedly to be pursued on a Union level.

The end result of the compromise reached between the United Kingdom and its fellow Member States on the place of social policy within the Union is that the Treaty on European Union will provide two possible legal bases for the adoption of social policy measures, namely the provisions in Title VIII entitled "Social Policy, Education, Vocational Training and Youth," Articles 117-122, and the Protocol on Social Policy. In the case of the former the measures will be adopted by, and accordingly be applicable to, the twelve Member States. By contrast, measures based upon the Protocol on Social Policy will only concern the eleven Member States, that is all the Member States except the United Kingdom, which has chosen not to be bound by its provisions.

5. Validity of the Protocol

Is such an arrangement valid? Doubts have been expressed as to the lawfulness of this method of proceeding: it has been suggested the Protocol is not a valid act of Union law, being contrary to the principle of the unity of Union law and potentially distortive

---

15 House of Lords Select Committee on the European Communities: Social Policy after Maastricht. Session 1991-1992 7th Report. Evidence of the Parliamentary Under Secretary for Employment.

of competition. Be that as it may, it is difficult to see how the Protocol on Social Policy could be challenged before the European Court of Justice.

The Protocol is annexed to the Maastricht Treaty. It consists of an agreement between all fifteen States.[16] The Agreement on Social Policy (hereinafter "the Agreement") is annexed to the Protocol and can therefore be taken to form part of it. Assuming that this is correct (arguments have been advanced to the effect that the Agreement is not a community law instrument but rather an intergovernmental agreement, these are discussed below), by virtue of Article 239 of the Maastricht Treaty the Protocols annexed to it "by common accords of the Member States shall form an integral part thereof."

The fact that the Agreement operated only between eleven Member States is of no importance: all fifteen Member States have agreed to this arrangement and, therefore, by virtue of Article 236 of the EEC Treaty, provided all the Member States ratify the Maastricht Treaty, of which the Protocol on Social Policy is an integral part, it is valid. Obviously the situation would be quite otherwise if the United Kingdom had not sanctioned the making of the Agreement.

Being therefore a primary source of Union law, the Protocol is part of the Union constitutions, the Grundnorm of Union law and cannot be challenged.

An analogy may be drawn between the Protocol on Social Policy and Annexes to Acts of Accession of new Member States to the Union which, in general, provide for numerous exceptions to both the applicability of the EEC Treaty itself and Union secondary legislation, but again as they are not acts of either the Council or the Commission they cannot be challenged before the Court. In *Levantina Agricola Industrial SA CPC Espana v. Council*,[17] three Spanish isoglucose producers brought an action under Article 173(2) EEU seeking, *inter alia*, the annulment of certain provisions of Annex 1 to the Act of Accession of the Kingdom of Spain and the Portuguese Republic to the Communities. The Court rejected the action as being inadmissible, holding that it had no jurisdiction to consider the validity of such provisions:

> The adaptations set out in Annex 1 to the Act of Accession . . . are the subject of an agreement between the Member States and the applicant State . . . They do not constitute an act of the Council but provisions of primary law . . . which may not be suspended, amended or repealed otherwise than by means of the procedure laid down for the revision of the original Treaties. . . . It follows . . . that the contested provisions,

---

[16] In its opening paragraph it is stated: THE HIGH CONTRACTING PARTIES NOTING that 11 (Now 15) Member States . . . wish to continue along the path laid down in the 1989 Social Charter; that they have adopted among themselves an Agreement to this end; that this Agreement is annexed to this Protocol . . .

1. Agreement to authorize those 11 Member States to have recourse to the institutions, procedures and mechanisms of the Treaty for the purpose of taking among themselves and applying among themselves as far as they are concerned the acts and decisions required for giving effect to the aforementioned agreement. . . ."

[17] Case 31/86 [1988] ECR 2801.

> which form an integral part of the Act of Accession of the Kingdom of Spain and the Portuguese Republic, do not constitute an act of the Council within the meaning of Article 173 of the EEC Treaty and that consequently the Court has no jurisdiction to consider the admissibility of such provisions.

The Protocol is likewise an act of primary law whose validity is not open to challenge. It can be amended or altered only in accordance with Article N of the Maastricht Treaty.

6. Legal Status of the Protocol

It has been argued[18] that the Agreement of Social Policy is not part of the Protocol on Social Policy but is an independent arrangement made between the eleven signatory States. In this reading, by virtue of Article 239 EEU the Protocol on Social Policy [hereinafter "the Protocol"] is an integral part of the Maastricht Treaty; the Agreement on Social Policy is, by contrast, an inter-governmental agreement. If this analysis is correct, this means that the eleven Member States who are party to the Agreement will act on an inter-governmental level when they are adopting measures pursuant to the Agreement. Such measures will be inter-governmental acts and, therefore, not part of the corpus of Union law. They will not form part of the *acquis communautaire* and will not bind any new Member States.

Is this a valid assessment of the legal status of the Protocol? Can the Agreement on Social Policy be regarded as an independent inter-governmental act which does not form part of the Protocol in spite of the fact that it is annexed to the Protocol, itself a part of the Treaty? Does not the Agreement thereby become part of the Treaty?

Arguments in support of the theory that the Agreement is an inter-governmental act center upon the form and working of the Protocol and the simple fact that a two-fold Union social policy is inconsistent with the traditional concept of the unity of Union law.

Let us examine these arguments. By virtue of Protocol No. 14 the twelve Member States authorized eleven of them to have recourse to the Union institutions, procedures and mechanisms for the purposes of "taking among themselves and applying as far as they are concerned the acts and decisions required for giving effect to the . . . Agreement." The United Kingdom is not to take part in "the deliberations and the adoption by the Council of Commission proposals made on the basis of this Protocol. . . ."

Protocol No. 14 is contrasted with Protocol No. 11 which recognizes that the United Kingdom is not obliged or committed to the third stage of economic or monetary union. Paragraph 5 of Protocol No. 11 enumerated the provisions of the Treaty which will not apply to the United Kingdom. Paragraph 7 further provides that: "The voting rights of the United Kingdom shall be suspended in respect of the acts of the Council referred to in the articles listed in paragraph 5."

[18] Vogel-Polsky, *Evaluation of the Social Provisions of the Treaty on European Union.* Report prepared for the Committee on Social Affairs, Employment and the Working Environment of the European Parliament. DOC EN/CM/202155 at p.3.

The failure to suspend explicitly the voting rights of the United Kingdom with respect to measures adopted in pursuance of the Agreement of Social Policy is taken to be an indication that the intention of the twelve Member States in formulating Protocol No. 14 was only to allow the Union institutions and legislative procedure to be used as a vehicle for operating an inter-governmental agreement.

This reasoning lacks conviction. It presupposes that Protocol No. 14 was adopted with a decree of care and precision which is doubtful, and that the twelve Member States, deliberately, when drafting Protocol No. 14 chose a form of words different from that in Protocol No. 11 in order to indicate that the Agreement on Social Policy was not a Union law act. Given the lack of cohesion in the Treaty as a whole, not to mention the sad fact that its provisions are "deplorably poorly formulated,"[19] it seems likely that the Member States would have intentionally chosen not to express clearly that the Agreement on Social Policy was inter-governmental in nature but to leave the vital question of its status to be deduced from a combination of a few words in the Protocol, and comparison between two very different Protocols. It seems a peculiarly indirect means—in no way guaranteed to succeed—of attempting to attain what could have been achieved by a plain phrase or two.

Moreover from the wording of Protocol No. 14 as a whole, and this includes the Agreement, it is reasonable to conclude that the latter is an inherent part of the Protocol and is therefore, by virtue of Article 239, part of the Treaty. Union institutions, procedures and mechanisms are to be used in the formulation and adoption of measures pursuant to the Agreement; such measures are to be proposed by the Commission; some of the measures are required to be directives and from Article 2(4) of the Agreement it may be inferred that this means Directives within the meaning of Article 189 of the Treaty; reference is made in Articles 3 and 4 of the Agreement to "Union action," and dialogue "at a Union level," and in providing for collective bargaining on a Union level, "[a]greements concluded at a Union level" and "consultation of management and labor at Union level" (Article 3.1) . . . "on the possible direction of Union action" (Article 3.2) and the conclusion of collective bargaining agreements on a Union level (Article 4.1). The wording of Article 3.3, "[i]f . . . the Commission considers Union action advisable it shall consult management and labor . . .," must mean that the twelve Member States did consider that the parties to the Agreement would be acting in a Union capacity when adopting measures under the Agreement. If the Agreement is inter-governmental in nature, phrases such as those cited above have no meaning: they are nonsense and although one may regret the structure and drafting of the Treaty, one must assume that whoever did pen it did not intend to draft in meaningless riddles.

---

[19] Ulrich Everling, *Reflections on the Structure of the European Union*, 29 C.M.L.R. 1053-1077 (1992): "The structure of the Treaty on the Union is peculiar in several respects (1056). [T]he treaty texts are deplorably poorly formulated. . . . Governments should be reminded of what used to be self-evident practice, i.e. using editing committees composed of treaty lawyers, who cast whatever is politically desired into the right legal mold."

7. The Application of the Principle of Subsidarity to Social Policy in the Maastricht Treaty

It remains to discuss the application of the principle of subsidarity to the development of social policy under the Treaty on European Union. Article A(2) and B of the Maastricht Treaty which will become Article 3b(2) of the Treaty on European Union provides that within those areas which do not fall within the exclusive competence of the Union:

> [T]he Community shall take action in accordance with the principle of subsidarity only if and so far as the objectives of the proposed action cannot be sufficiently achieved by the Member States and can, therefore, by reason of the scale or effectiveness of the proposed action be better achieved by the Community.

This provision has assumed an unforeseen magnitude of importance in the year following the adoption of the Maastricht Treaty. The doubts and fears expressed throughout the Union on the increasing power of the Union institutions over the social and economic life of citizens have been assuaged by the promise of a strict application of the principle of subsidarity.

The principle of subsidarity is neither alien to Union law in general nor to social policy in particular, but it is the first time that it has been formally included in any of the Union Treaties as a general principle and its application discussed seriously. In the months following the adoption of the Maastricht Treaty, the Commission detailed its views on how the principle should operate in practice,[20] as did the Ministers of Foreign Affairs of the Member States.

But will the principle of subsidiarity apply to the social policy provisions of the Maastrict Treaty? The principle [of subsidiarity] is said to be applicable only in those areas where the Union does not have exclusive competence. As Toth has pointed out,[21] neither the EEC Treaty nor the Maastricht Treaty make any explicit distinction between exclusive and non-exclusive competence. This makes the application of the principal of subsidarity more difficult. With respect to the provisions in the Social Chapter of the Maastricht Treaty, which are essentially the same as those in the EEC Treaty, it seems that the Union has not got exclusive competence—in fact it has hardly any competence at all. The objectives set out in these provisions can, in general, be attained only if the Union uses its general law-making powers, in particular those contained in Articles 100 and 235. It is unclear how the principle of subsidarity applies to these provisions. Toth concludes that it does not apply,[22] simply because

20 The Principle of Subsidarity: Communication of the Commission to the Council and the European Parliament SEC (92) 1990 Final. Para 2 defines subsidarity as follows: "In the Community context subsidarity means that the functions handed over to the Community are those which the Member States, at the various levels of decision-making, can no longer discharge satisfactorily."

21 A.G. Toth, *The Principle of Subsidarity in the Maastricht Treaty*, 29 C.M.L.R. 1091 (1992).

22 *Id.* at 1095-1096.

measures can only be based upon these provisions when they are necessary for the establishment or functioning of the common market, and this in itself is "an area which undoubtedly is within exclusive Community competence."[23] If one accepts that reasoning, it must be concluded that the social chapter of the Maastricht Treaty, with the possible exception of Article 118A, may not be subject to the principle of subsidarity.

Turning now to the Agreement on Social Policy, the applicability of the principle of subsidarity here will depend on whether one regards that Agreement as being inter-governmental in nature or a Union act. If the former is the case then the principle has no application whatsoever: the eleven signatory Member States can do as they please—within the confines and subject to the principles of the Protocol as a whole—and should a measure be adopted under Article 2(1) of the Agreement by a qualified majority there is nothing that the remaining dissenting Member States can do about it. However if the Agreement on Social Policy is an integral part of Union law it is, by that, subject to the principle of subsidarity: the Union has not got exclusive powers with respect to the matter addressed therein. What will this mean in practice? Will social policy measures, particularly those adopted in pursuance of the objectives of the Social Charter, be adopted at Union or Member State level? Given the lukewarm welcome that many of the Commission's proposals have received within the Council in the two years following the adoption of the Social Charter it is quite legitimate to expect a falling off of legislative acts on a Union level in the social sphere. The Commission as recently indicated unilaterally that it is prepared to withdraw some of its more controversial proposals.[24] In spite of this, the Commission in its review of existing and proposed legislative initiatives in the light of the principle of subsidarity, presented to the European Council in Edinburgh, in which it set out the proposals it intended to withdraw or amend, states, with respect to social policy, that directives based on Article 118A would "not be re-examined but rather will be supplemented . . . by implementing all the provisions of the Charter on Fundamental Social Rights of Workers." By this declaration, the Commission evinces a clear determination to continue with the measures necessary to implement the Charter. At the same time the Member States made it clear in their "Declaration on Social Policy, Consumers, Environment and Distribution of Income," made at the Edinburgh Summit, that the Treaty on European Union enables the Member States to introduce more stringent protection than that provided for in Union measures in the field of working conditions and social policy provided that such measures are compatible with the EU Treaty. Social security receives special mention: here [it] is made quite clear that the Member States are to pursue their own policy with regard to the distribution of income and the maintenance and improvement of social welfare benefits.

8. The Objectives of the Agreement

Article 1 of the Agreement sets out its basic objectives: the promotion of employment, improved living and working conditions, proper social protection, dialogue between management and labor, the development of human resources with a view of lasting

---

23 *Id.* at 1096.

24 Speech of Commissioner for Social Affairs Copenhagen 15 March 1993.

employment and the combating of exclusions. The means whereby these objectives are to be achieved are set out in Articles 2 and 5. The latter reflects Article 118 of the Treaty, requiring, as that provision does, the Commission to " . . . encourage co-operation between Member States and facilitate the coordination of their action in all social fields under this agreement."

Article 5 has no binding legal effects. Like Article 118 of the Treaty it is "more in the nature of a program"[25] but at the same time it can be used as an aid in interpreting the Agreement and secondary legislation made under it. By analogy with Article 118 EEU, it can be presumed that in carrying out its duty under Article 5 the Commission can settle a procedure for consultation which may include requiring Member States to provide information to it, possibly under a binding decision. The information requested and any proposed consultation must concern one of the objects of the Agreement: the Commission is not at liberty to demand information about matters with which it has no competence to deal.

In addition to the objectives set out in Article 1 of the Agreement, Article 6 reiterates the Union's commitment to the principle of equal pay for equal work for men and women. Paragraphs 1 and 2 of Article 6 are identified to Article 119 of the Treaty. Paragraph 3 of Article 6 is new. It permits Member States to maintain or adopt "measures providing for specific advantages in order to make it easier for women to pursue a vocational activity or to prevent or compensate for disadvantages in their professional careers." The objective of this provision, one assumes is to permit—but not oblige—Member States to adopt measures of positive discrimination in order to help women overcome any difficulties they may encounter in combining professional and family responsibilities—difficulties which can, and generally do, prejudice their career development.

Article 6(3) is concerned exclusively with advantages given to women but not to men relating to pay. Examples of measures which might fall within its scope are: payments to cover the cost of child-care; national contributions to an occupational pension scheme; grants to undertake vocational training and possible increased paid holidays to care for children during the seemingly ever lengthening school holidays. The measures must be designed to "prevent or compensate" for disadvantages peculiar to women which make it difficult for them to compete on equal terms with their male counterparts in the workplace by helping them, in a practical way, to overcome such obstacles. Consequently, there can be no question of Article 6(3) being used by Member States to justify maintaining differences in the pensionable ages of men and women.

It is not clear why Article 6 paragraphs 1 and 2 reiterate the provisions of Article 119 of the Treaty of Rome. No legislative power is given in the Agreement to implement the principle of equal pay for equal work. Consequently the eleven signatory states to the Agreement cannot adopt measures in this area. What therefore is the purpose of Article 6 paragraphs 1 and 2? Their presence in the Agreement seems to be meaningless.

---

[25] Case 170/84, *Bilka-Kaufhaus v. Weber Von Hartz*, [1986] ECR 1607.

The heart of the Agreement lies in Article 2: it is there that we find the greatly increased legislative powers which the twelve Member States have agreed that the remaining eleven may use, and the purposes for and the conditions under which they may be used. Article 2 envisages two categories of measures: (i) directives to be adopted by a qualifies majority of votes cast (Article 2(2)) and (ii) other measures (the nature of which is unspecified) which require the unanimous vote of all eleven Member States.

Article 2 does not apply to pay, the right of association, the right to strike or the right to impose lockouts, reflecting the Member States' traditional hostility to the supranational regulation of collective labor rights and pay, many of which are national constitutions.

Article 2(1) provides that with a view to achieving the objectives set out in Article 1 the Union "shall support and complement the activities of the Member States" in the following fields:

- improvement in particular of the working environment to protect workers' health and safety;
- working conditions;
- the information and consultation of workers;
- equality of treatment between men and women with regard to labor market opportunities and treatment at work;
- the integration of persons excluded from the labor market.[26]

These aims are to be attained by means of directives. The Council's power to adopt such directives is subject to five principles set out in the Agreement:

(i) They must be adopted in support of and to complement the activities of Member States.[27] The role of Member States in implementing the Agreement is important. This requirement is similar to that set out in Title 11 of the Social Charter where it is stated: ". . . it is more particularly the responsibility of the Member States in accordance with national practice to guarantee the fundamental social rights in the Charter." However, in contrast to the Social Charter which envisaged that the role of Union legislation, with respect to many of the aims of the Charter, would be confined to setting objectives which will be realized by means of national measures and practices, the Agreement in referring to the complementary role of the Union seems to be looking to the Member States to take the lead;

(ii) directives must "have regard to the conditions and technical rules obtaining in each of the Member States."[28] Again acts made under the Agreement appear to be subject to existing national rules, standards and practices;

(iii) echoing Article 118(a)(2) of the Treaty, the Agreement in Article 2(2) provides that directives may impose " . . . administrative, financial and technical constraints in

---

[26] Art. 2(1) on *Measures to integrate persons excluded from the labor market* is said to be subject to Art. 127 of the Treaty establishing the European Union, which provides for the implementation of a vocational training policy to support and implement the action of Member States.

[27] Agreement Art. 2(1).

[28] Agreement Art. 2(2).

a way which would hold back the creation and development of small and medium sized enterprises";

(iv) directives must consist of "minimum requirements for gradual implementation" and Member States may not be prevented from maintaining or introducing more stringent protective measures compatible with the Treaty.

Article 2(3) sets out another list of areas of social policy in which the Council is competent to act but only on the basis of a unanimous vote and after consulting the European Parliament and the Economic and Social Committee. This list is as follows:

- social security and the social protection of workers;
- protection of workers where the employment contract is terminated;
- representation and collective defense of workers and employers including co-determination, subject to the exceptions set out in paragraph 6 of Article 2;
- conditions of employment for third country nationals legally residing in Union territory;
- financial contributions for the promotion of employment and job creation, without prejudice to the provisions relating to the Social Fund.

In contrast to Article 2(1) and (2) the Council is not required to act by means of any particular instrument: it can adopt whatever instrument it pleases.

9. Modus Operandi

The Protocol and the Agreement are expressed to be "without prejudice to the provisions of the Treaty, particularly those relating to social policy which constitute an integral part of the acquis communautaire." The eleven Member States in their Preamble to the Agreement state that they wish " . . . to implement the 1989 Social Charter on the basis of the acquis communautaire." It is clear, therefore, that the Protocol and the Agreement are grafted on to the Treaty and the acquis communautaire. Measures adopted thereunder must therefore be compatible with both the Treaty and the *acquis communautaire*.

Responsibility for formulating proposals is entrusted to the Commission. The Commission is not unfettered in its exercise of this task: it must consult management and labor before submitting any proposals in the social policy field, to the Council. If, following this consultation, the Commission considers Union action advisable it must further consult management and labor on the content of the envisaged measure. Management and labor must give their opinion to the Commission in the form of an opinion or a recommendation. In the course of such consultations management and labor may inform the Commission of their wish to implement the proposal in question by means of an agreement concluded between them at a Union level in accordance with the procedure set out in Article 4 of the Agreement.

Such an agreement, should be made within nine months, unless management and labor and the Commission decide jointly to extend that period.

Although the Commission must consult management and labor on the content of provisions it intends to propose for adoption on a Union level, there is no obligation on it to accept their views. Furthermore, there appears to be no obligation on the Commission to accede to a request from management and labor to implement a proposal by means of a Union-wide agreement.

Where it is decided that a proposal should be implemented by means of a Union legislative measure as opposed to a Union-wide collective agreement, the following four basic rules apply:

(i) acts and decisions required to give effect to the Agreement are to be adopted in the same way as all other acts or decisions based upon the Treaty provisions;

(ii) the United Kingdom may not take part in any deliberations and the adoption by the Council of Commission proposals made on the basis of the Protocol and the Agreement;

(iii) where measures are to be adopted by a qualified majority they must receive at least 44 votes in their favor as opposed to the minimum of 54 votes required under Article 148(2) of the Treaty;

(iv) finally, and fairly obviously, acts adopted by the Council and any financial costs, other than administrative costs, incurred by the Union institutions are not applicable to the United Kingdom.

It is to be noted that the United Kingdom is only excluded from deliberations within the Council. It can participate in all other stages of the decision-making process leading to the adopting of measures based on the Protocol. It will, therefore, contribute to the content of those measures. At first sight it hardly seems consistent with the scheme of the Protocol to allow United Kingdom representatives to participate in the legislative process up to Council level. If the United Kingdom is not a party to the Protocol, it is difficult to see why it should be permitted to interest itself in the formulation of proposals made under that Protocol.

On reflection, however, it can be argued that the United Kingdom itself is not involved in the earlier phases of the legislative process. Its nationals who are employed within the Union institutions, do not speak for the United Kingdom, although, of course, their opinions may be influenced by the values and culture of that State.

Members of the Commission, although they must be nationals of a Member State are "chosen on grounds of their general competence and [their] independence is beyond doubt."[29] Once appointed, the Members of the Commission must:

> be completely independent in the performance of their duties. In the performance of their duties they shall neither seek nor take instructions from any government or any other body.[30]

An obligation is placed on each Member State "to respect this principle and not to seek to influence the members of the Commission in the performance of their tasks."

The position of the Members of the European Parliament (hereinafter "MEPs") is more questionable. Article 137 of the Treaty provides that the European Parliament is composed of "representatives of the peoples of the States brought together in the Union." On the one hand this phrase may be taken to mean that the position of MEPs is akin to that of the United Kingdom delegation to the Council. On the other hand it

---

[29] Art. 157(1) EEU; Art. 157(1) Maastricht Treaty.

[30] Art. 157(2).

can be argued that the United Kingdom MEPs represent the people of the United Kingdom as opposed to the government of that country and may accordingly participate in the deliberations of the European Parliament in measures proposed on the basis of the Agreement.

On this view it can be concluded that since neither the Commissioners nor the members of the European Parliament represent the United Kingdom it is not unreasonable that they should participate in the making of measures based upon the Agreement.

10. The Increased Role of Management and Labor under the Agreement on Social Policy.

One of the most innovative features of the Protocol is the increased participation it purports to give to management and labor both in the formulation and implementation of Union legislation and the importance the Union attaches to collective bargaining on a Union level. The provision of the Agreements in this respect reflect the Agreement reached on 31 December 1991 between ETUC, UNICE, CEEP on a proposal for the redrafting of Article 118 of the Maastricht Treaty. The Proposal eventually became Articles 3 and 4 of the Agreement on Social Policy.

Three specific roles are envisaged for management and labor the first of which, the consultation of management and labor by the Commission with respect to the desirability and the content of any proposed Union action in the social field, has been described in the preceding section. At the other end of the spectrum, we find that Article 2(4) provides that a Member State may entrust management and labor, at their joint request, with the implementation of directives adopted pursuant to paragraphs 2 and 3 of that Article. That in itself is not new: Member States have always been free to implement directives in any way they please, including by means of legally binding collective agreements, provided always that they constitute a proper implementation of the objectives of the directive, but since each directive is addressed to the Member States it is they who are ultimately responsible for its execution. Article 2(4) emphasizes this latter point, stating that where directives are to be implemented by means of collective agreements, these should be introduced no later than the date on which the directive must be transposed and the Member State concerned is "required to take any necessary measures enabling it at any time to be in a position to guarantee the results imposed by that directive."

Presumably the term "agreement" referred to in Article 2(4) must mean an arrangement which is legally binding and therefore enforceable, and generally applicable. Any collective agreement which does not have binding legal effects or which does not extend to all those sections of the population to which the directive in question is intended to apply will not be considered to be an adequate implementation of it.

In addition to increased involvement in the decision-making process, Article 4 of the Agreement envisages an increased collective bargaining on a Union level. Paragraph 1 of Article 4 states: "Should management and labor so desire, the dialogue between them at Community level may lead to contractual relations, including agreements."

Agreements concluded at Union level may be implemented either in accordance with the procedures or practices specific to management and labor and to the Member

States, or, where they concern matters covered by Article 2 of the Agreement by a Council decision. Such a decision may be taken at the joint request of the signatories or is to be settled by means of collective bargaining carried out in accordance with the rules of each Member State. This arrangement is stated in a Declaration attached to the Agreement to imply ". . . no obligation on the Member States to apply the agreements directly or to work out rules for their transposition nor any obligation to amend national legislation in force to facilitate their implementation." From this Declaration it can be concluded that in the absence of a Council decision incorporating a Union-wide collective agreement into Union law such agreements may not be legally enforceable.[31]

In adopting such a decision the Council shall act by a qualified majority except where the Agreement concerns one or more provisions relating to one of the areas referred to in Article 2(3) in which the Council must act unanimously.

Two points must be noted here: where management and labor wish to implement an agreement made between them, by means of a Council decision, neither the Commission nor the Council can alter the terms of that agreement. The Council may, of course, decline to adopt it, in the terms upon which it was presented to it, but it does not appear to have the power to redraft it. Similarly the Commission, in proposing to the Council the adoption of any collective agreement must forward it to the Council in the terms agreed upon by management and labor. It cannot proceed unilaterally to alter the substance of the collective agreement but it may, of course, propose to the Council that it should be rejected. Whether the Commission can refuse to propose to the Council the adoption of an agreement reached between management and labor is not clear from the Agreement. The answer is probably that it cannot. The procedure set out in Article 4 is designed not so much to seek the Commission's approval of a collective agreement but rather to use the Union's legislative machinery to endow agreements with the legal standing which they might not otherwise have. The objective of lending the Union's legislative apparatus to Union-wide collective bargaining is, one supposes, to encourage management and labor to take the initiative in implementing the Agreement.

It is to be noted, that the participation of management and labor from the United Kingdom is not prohibited in such Union-wide collective bargaining although any agreement which ultimately takes the form of a Council decision, will not be enforceable in the United Kingdom.

Agreements at Union level would include, presumably interconferal agreements, that is agreements between either the ETUC and or UNICE and CEEP, and European sectoral agreements concluded between a European industry committee and the European employers organization for the industry branch or sector in question. Either of the two might well cover a wider geographical area than the European Union.

What exactly is meant by management and labor? Who will be consulted and possibly entrusted with the implementation of Union social policy? Presumably the Commission will deal with Union-wide federations of employers and workers' representatives such as ETUC, CEEP and UNICE, but can it be said that all employ-

---

[31] Foden and Paris, *Nature, implementation and control of Agreements*, in *The European Dimension of Collective Bargaining after Maastricht*, European Trade Union Institute (1992).

ers' and workers' representatives are fairly represented within such federations? If management and labor are to be entrusted with the responsibilities given to them in the Protocol, their membership must be fairly representative. Furthermore, a system of collective bargaining at Union level and the enforcement of agreements resulting from this process will have to be created for the purposes of the Agreement.

The nine month period given to management and labor in Article 3(4) for the conclusion of agreements to implement Union social objectives seems to be rather short compared to the average time period required for the adopted social policy measures by the Union institutions. Admittedly an extension of this limit is possible but it may be vetoed by the Commission.

Article 4 of the Agreement which appears to have as its objective the encouragement of Union-wide collective bargaining indicates a move away from the usual view that collective bargaining is a matter for the Member States to regulate. Article 12 of the Social Charter acknowledges that employers, their organization and workers have ". . . the right to negotiate and conclude agreements under conditions laid down by national law and practice." No mention is made here of the Union having any role in collective bargaining and the Commission's proposed Communication on the role of the social partners in collective bargaining has yet to be adopted.

B. The Protocol on Article 119

Protocol No. 2 to the Maastricht Treaty is entitled "Protocol concerning Article 119 of the Treaty establishing the European Union." It provides that for the purposes of Article 119 of this Treaty, benefits under occupational social security schemes shall not be considered as remuneration if and in so far as they are attributable to periods of employment prior to 17 May 1990, except in the case of workers or those claiming under them who have before that date initiated legal proceedings or introduced an equivalent claim under the applicable national law.

The background to this Protocol can be traced back the judgment of the Court of Justice in *Barber v. Guardian Royal Exchange Assurance Group*[32] in which the Court ruled that a ". . . pension paid out under a contracted out scheme constitutes consideration paid by the employer to the worker in respect of his employment consequently falls within the scope of Article 119 of the Treaty."

The Court, in the interests of legal certainty and in view of the serious difficulties the judgment might create with respect to the financial balance of many contracted out pension schemes, attempted to limit *ratione temporis*, the effects of its judgment. In the now notorious paragraph 45 thereof it ruled that the direct effect of Article 119 of the Treaty may not be relied upon in order to claim entitlement to a pension with effect from a date prior to that of this judgment, except in the case of workers or those claiming under them who have before that date initiated legal proceedings or raised an equivalent claim under the applicable national law. Of all the hundreds of thousands of paragraphs in the Court's judgments none has given rise to such fierce debate as

[32] Case C-262/88, [1990] ECR 1889.

paragraph 45 of the *Barber* judgment, which failed to say clearly how and from when the principle of equality of treatment applied to occupational pensions. Many differing interpretations of it have been advanced. A number of requests for preliminary rulings notably from courts and tribunals in the United Kingdom, Germany and the Netherlands asking for clarification of its meaning are currently pending before the Court.

Prompted by this confusion, the Member States decided to clarify, by way of a Protocol the application of Article 119 in the Maastricht Treaty to occupational pensions: equality of treatment cannot be claimed in respect of benefits under occupational social security schemes which were attributable to periods of employment prior to the date of judgment in the *Barber* case.

This interpretation applied of course only to Article 119 of the Treaty of Rome as amended by the Maastricht Treaty. The effect in time of the *Barber* judgment on occupational pensions in respect of which equality of treatment is claimed on the basis of Article 119 of the EEC Treaty remains to be clarified by the Court of Justice itself. The Court may rule that paragraph 45 of the *Barber* judgment gives the same meaning to Article 119 of the EEC Treaty as the Protocol gives to Article 119 of the Maastricht Treaty. On the other hand it may not, in which case pension administrators will be faced with an unenviable series of complex calculations.

IV. Free Movement of Services[33]

A. Introduction

Freedom to provide services has long taken second place in the Union, but this is about to change. In its White Paper of June 1985 on "Completing the internal market,"[34] the Commission regarded "the establishment of a common market in services as one of the main preconditions for a return to economic prosperity" in Europe. Chapter 3 of the EEC Treaty on "Services" has had a rather "shadowy existence" to date for a variety of reasons.

First, there are reasons associated with the *systematics of the Treaty*:

- The important sector of transport is subject to a special regime in Articles 74-84 EEU. To date there have been no significant moves in this field.
- Under Article 61(2) EEU, the liberalization of banking and insurance services, as far as they are connected with movements of capital, shall be effected in step with the progressive liberalization of movement of capital—and here also little progress has been made.

---

[33] Wulf-Henning Roth, *The European Economic Community's Law on Services: Harmonization*, 25 C.M.L.R. 35-98 (1988). © 1988 Kluwer Academic Publishers. Reprinted by permission.

[34] Commission *Completing the Internal Market*, White Paper from the Commission to the European Council, June 1985, COM (85) 310 final.

- Freedom to provide services is regulated in close association with the freedom of establishment—an association meaningfully expressed not only in Article 60(3) EEU, but, above all, in a reference in Article 66 EEU to Articles 55-58 EEU. This is why, according to widespread opinion, the ban on restrictions in Article 59 of the EEC Treaty amounts to nothing more than a requirement that nationals of Member States shall be treated equally, in conformity with Article 52 EEC Treaty. From this it follows that the harmonization of the different regulations of individual Member States concerning the activities of providers of services appears to be a prerequisite for the development of EEU-wide services from the country of origin.
- In the Council's *harmonization practice*, freedom of establishment and freedom to provide services have always been seen as closely linked, and this connection has been confirmed by the issue of joint directives.

Only in recent times has the close link between the freedom to provide *services* and the free movement of *goods* been stressed, and have questions been raised on the conclusions to be drawn therefrom: both Article 30 EEC *et seq.* and Article 59 EEC *et seq.* regulate—in contrast to Article 52 EEU *et seq.*—the free movement of products in the common market. The inference is that they require similar solutions, at least in principle.

In addition, there are a number of quite practical reasons why the provision of services has been given less attention to date. The "services" chapter is, on the one hand, subsidiary to the "right of establishment" chapter of the Treaty. On the other hand, the chapter on "services" covers a great variety of activities. This may have contributed to the undervaluing of the importance of this freedom.

Those traditional forms of the provision of services which have been at the forefront of harmonization practice to date, i.e., the activities of the self-employed, but also crafts-related and other commercial activities, often only have a local radius. Consequently, it is not the freedom to provide services, but the right of establishment that is at stake: the right of Union citizens to transfer their independent business activities from one Member State to another. In the light of this, it is understandable why the provision of services has been regulated rather as an annex to the establishment provisions in the coordination directives.

Finally, it is probably of some importance that business circles concerned with the provision of interstate services (i.e., banking, insurance, the professions) have shown only a relatively limited interest in an expansion of the domestic markets to form a unified internal market, and that where such an interest in expansion exists, it is considered more advantageous to take the course of establishing branches and/or acquiring subsidiaries in the markets of the Member States concerned.

It can be assumed that not only the complexity of the subject but also this lack of interest on the part of the relevant business circles in an effective amalgamation of national services markets is one reason why it has not always been possible to reach satisfying results within a period of more than 10 to 15 years.

B. The Union's Harmonization Practice: A Changing Concept

Over the years, the Union's harmonization concept has changed substantially. In the early 1960s, on the basis of the "General programme for the abolition of restrictions on freedom to provide services,"[35] a beginning was made with an ambitious target: in the field of the professions in particular, but also in insurance, the aim was to achieve a far-reaching approximation of substantive law. Harmonization of the law on insurance contracts, of training regulations and the law on professional standing and on professional associations of Member States are examples of such high objectives.

An insight into the difficulties associated with the standardization of these matters (by the end of the transitional period only a very small number of the measures prescribed by the Treaty had been completed), the enlargement of the Union by the accession of new members, as well as a decreasing willingness of Member States to compromise, were all reasons for a change in the Commission's harmonization concept in the 1970s: in future, approximation of laws was to be restricted to the absolute minimum necessary. This reorientation has led not only to the removal from the agenda of such fringe areas as correspondence courses, but above all to an increasing reduction in the intensity of regulation considered necessary with regard to qualification requirements for the professions. Finally, we now have the 1985 draft directive "On a general system for the recognition of higher education diplomas,"[36] which abandons any approximation of training courses. Instead of emphasizing the variety of university education in Member States, basic compatibility and the principle of mutual trust between Member States are postulated.

C. The Legal Framework for Harmonization

1. The Function of the Approximation of Laws

Approximation of laws serves as a tool in the EEU: it is neither an objective in itself, nor concerned with the realization of a general legal concept; approximation of laws assists in the purpose-related development of the common market and in safeguarding its function. In the words of Article 3(h) of the EEC Treaty: "The activities of the Community . . . include . . . the approximation of the class of Member States to the extent required for the proper functioning of the common market."

The core of this common market consists of the five freedoms (free movement of goods, persons, services, capital and payments); approximation of laws is intended to dismantle obstacles in the way of these freedoms and to facilitate their practical application. It has, therefore, a supplementary nature, in so far as it comes into action primarily when the Treaty does not already enforce the objectives pursued by it by means of an independent and directly applicable regulation.

---

[35] O.J. 1962, p. 32

[36] COM (85) 355 final, O.J. 1985, C217/3; Bull. of the E.C. suppl. 8/85; statement by the Economic and Social Committee, O.J. 1986, C75/5; amended proposal: COM (86) final, O.J. 1986, C143/7.

A further important aim is to establish a system of undistorted competition (Article 3(f) EEU), to be guaranteed by the approximation of laws (see Articles 100 and 101 EEU).

The approximation of the differing regulations of Member States not only serves to enforce the freedoms and to guarantee fair conditions of competition but also has a necessarily formative nature: approximation of law implies a Union policy in the areas to be approximated.

The common market, as it is to be established in accordance with Article 3 EEU, is a single economic area in which conditions prevail "which come as close as possible to those of a genuine internal market." The aim is "the removal of all obstacles to internal Union trade with the object of amalgamating the national markets into a uniform market."[37]

The establishment of conditions resembling those of an internal market means that the provision of services across borders encounters no greater obstacles than in a purely domestic market: thus, all those specific burdens and obstacles are to be removed which stem from the fact that interstate provision of services is regulated on the level of the Member States and not on the Union level. It is not, therefore, a matter of advancing commercial freedom but merely of Member States.

The Treaty recognizes two instruments by which the conditions resembling a single national market for the provision of services may be realized:

1. The ban directed at Member States on restrictions in the provision of services (Article 59(1) EEU), and
2. The approximation of laws.

The contribution to be made by the approximation of laws to the achievement of the freedom to provide services cannot be determined without looking at the implications of the ban on restrictions contained in Article 59(1) EEU.

If one looks at Article 59(1) EEU as an expression of the principle of non-discrimination, the realization of the unfettered cross frontier provision of services is dependent largely upon a *preceding* coordination of all (non-discriminatory) regulations of Member States which are concerned with services and their application to services furnished from other Member States. The difficulties, delays and inertia in the harmonization process are entirely to the disadvantage of the freedom to provide services.

If one interprets Article 59(1) EEU as going beyond a mere ban on discrimination, to the effect that Member States may restrict the cross-frontier provision of services only to safeguard their general interests and only to the extent necessary for that purpose, both the need for the approximation of laws and its objective appear in a different light.

The function of the approximation of laws now becomes the removal of obstacles to trade only in regard to all regulations that, being in the general interest, can be implemented in the face of the ban in Article 59(1) EEU.

---

[37] Case 15/81, *Schul*, [1982] E.C.R. 1409, at 1431-1432, consideration 33.

As for all regulations not justified by the general interest, the aim is not primarily to remove restrictions on the provision of services but to effect a Union-wide safeguard, and perhaps also to raise the services' quality and ensure fair competitive conditions. A delay in the process of approximation to this end is never to the disadvantage of the freedom to provide services.

The jurisprudence of the European Court of Justice, which can only be mentioned briefly, tends towards an interpretation of Article 59 EEU in this latter sense: In the *van Binsbergen* judgment, which is fundamental to this point, the European Court of Justice interpreted Article 59 EEU as a ban on all restrictions on and obstacles to the international provision of services, in so far as these are not justified by the general interest.[38] This interpretation was later reiterated in essence and more precisely in the *Webb* judgment[39] and in the case concerning German insurance supervision.[40]

This interpretation of Article 59 EEU goes beyond a non-discrimination standard suggesting in particular a common basis with Article 30 EEU, according to which the Court of Justice has developed a far-reaching limitation of national regulatory powers: products that are lawfully produced and marketed in the country of origin can be marketed throughout the Union unless there are compelling exigencies of the general interest (i.e., such as those listed in Article 36 EEU) against such a course of action. In principle, the same should apply to the interstate provision of services.

2. The Legal Bases for Harmonization

a. *Article 56(2) EEU*

Article 56(2) EEC Treaty will only be briefly discussed here. It grants the Union jurisdiction to harmonize those legal and administrative regulations which provide for special treatment for foreign nationals which are "justified on grounds of public policy, public security or public health" under Article 56(1) EEU and are therefore exempted from the ban on restrictions contained in Article 59(1) EEU via Article 66 EEU. The main field of application of this reservation (and at the same time of the harmonization powers under Article 56(2) EEU) lies in the sphere of law on the registration of aliens.

In connection with the provision of services, the most important cases here are those in which those providing the services must go to the country of the recipient. This accords with the fact that the European Court of Justice has so far avoided referring to Article 56(1) EEU in cases where Member States' regulations of (professional) activities have been at stake.

b. *Article 57(1) EEU*

Article 57(1) EEU gives the Union powers to issue directives for the mutual recognition of diplomas, certificates and other evidence of formal qualifications.

---

[38] Case 33/74, *van Bindensberg*, [1974] E.C.R. 1299, at 1309, consideration 12.

[39] Case 279/80, *Webb,* [1981] E.C.R. 3305, at 3325, consideration 17.

[40] Case 205/84, *Commission v. Federal Republic of Germany*, judgment of 4 Dec. 1986, consideration 27.

If Article 59(1) EEU is interpreted as merely a ban on discrimination, Member States retain the capacity to make the provision of cross-frontier services dependent upon the same certificates of professional competence as those required for nationals. Since nationals of other Member States cannot normally provide evidence of such national diplomas, there is an obvious need to revise the law of Member States, removing the impediments to the provision of services resulting from the national character of the vocational training regulations. One way of doing this is to issue directives under Article 57(1) EEU.

If Article 59(1) EEU is interpreted as a ban on all regulations that impede the provision of services without being justified by the general interest, the clear demarcation between the fields of application of Article 59(1) EEU on the one hand and Article 57(1) EEU on the other hand is blurred.

In the sphere of the free movement of goods, the European Court of Justice has held that if a comparable control has been carried out in the exporting country, a simple repetition of a control procedure in the importing country amounts to a contravention of Article 30 EEU despite the fact that such a control is in the interest of the public. If the establishment of conditions resembling an internal market is the prime aim, then unnecessary dual controls have to be avoided. Thus, on the basis of Article 30 EEU, the principle of mutual recognition of equivalent health controls has been realized without the need for an appropriate directive. In accordance with this, an obligation arises for Member States to promote the free movement of goods: where, because of Member States' multiple powers of control, the cross-frontier movement of goods has to endure burdens that cannot arise in a national market, it is the duty of the importing state to consider, in its pursuit of the general interest, whether and to what extent the country of origin has already taken measures to safeguard the general interest claimed.

As regards the provision of services, in principle nothing to the contrary can apply. In the *Webb* judgment, the Court held that regulations restricting the freedom to provide services are compatible with Article 60(3) EEU only in so far as the general interest of the destination state has not already been taken into account by the legal provisions to which those providing the services are subject in the state in which they reside. In another passage the Court also states that a requirement for approval justified by the general interest of the host state may not lead to a mere repetition of administrative controls.

This means that in order to avoid a double burden, the destination state is bound under Articles 59(1) and 60(3) EEU to take into consideration the law of the home country and to investigate the extent to which it contributes to safeguarding the general interest of the destination country. For our purposes, this means that if, in connection with the exercise of an activity, a Member State, as host state, requires a certificate of professional competence based on specific domestic training, this may represent an unnecessary impediment to the provision of services if a diploma, certificate of professional competence, etc., obtained in another Member State, is based on equivalent training.

In conclusion it is no longer possible simply to demarcate the field of application of Article 59 EEU on the one hand and Articles 66 and 57(1) EEU on the other hand according to the aims involved, since the duty to promote freedom in the provision of services established in Articles 59(1) and 60(3) EEC Treaty is aimed at the same target as a directive under Article 57(1) EEU.

According to Article 57(1) EEU, the function of a directive is, then, twofold:

1. A duty to recognize a foreign diploma arises only in cases of demonstrably comparable training schemes. To provide proof of such comparability will be difficult in individual cases, since it is difficult to develop workable criteria for evaluating the quality of training. Here, the directive assumes the function of establishing legal protection for the market sectors concerned, and of relieving both these sectors and the Commission of lengthy legal proceedings. To this extent, the directive contributes to the effectiveness of Article 59 EEU and to its observance by Member States.

2. In all those cases where comparability of training courses cannot be proved Article 57(1) EEU assumes responsibility for facilitating the provision of services over and above the direct ban under Article 59(1) EEU.

Another preliminary question to be decided on the basis of Articles 59 and 60(3) EEU is, however, whether it is even possible for the general interest claimed to warrant that services originating in other EEU countries, and hence the person providing the service, must *comply in full* with the quality requirements of the destination country.

If one considers the basic tenet of the *Cassis de Dijon* judgment,[41] this means that, applied to the provision of services, those providing services can in principle carry on their activities in the entire Union under the quality requirements of their home country. This also means, however, that the destination country can insist only on fulfillment of the requirements of the home country. Within the field of commercial and professional activities it is above all consumer protection and, in individual cases, health protection, that are held to be acceptable general interests justifying the application of national quality requirements. If consumer protection (only) is concerned, it must always be asked whether or not the aim of safeguarding quality control is being pursued to a disproportionate extent. Two aspects in particular should be emphasized here:

1. As for professions, cross-frontier activities are not carried out on a large scale but as individual transactions. Hence national quality standards are not adversely affected.

2. In general, a cross-frontier transaction will be dependent on the requirements of a client, who thus takes a conscious decision in favor of the foreign provider of services and of the standard offered by him. The reference to consumer protection here loses much of its persuasive power, especially where the recipients of the service are commercial undertakings or persons engaged in business.

[41] Case 120/78, *Rewe-Zentral v. Bundesmonopolverwaltung fur Branntwein*, 1979 E.C.R. 649, [1978-1979 Transfer Binder] Common Mkt.Rep. (CCH) P 8543 (1979). See Chapter 3.

[T]here must, therefore, be good reasons in the case of self-employed activities which justify requiring the provider of the service to have undergone training abroad comparable with the national training in order that he may pursue his activities in the destination country. The model regulation in the form of the *home-country principle*, given effect by the lawyers' directive, merely confirms, from this aspect, the model required by Article 59(1) EEU.

The result of this is that an interpretation of Articles 59 and 60(3) EEU as extending beyond a simple ban on discrimination can render almost superfluous, at least for a number of occupations, the issue of directives under Article 57(1) EEU for the purpose of facilitating *freedom in the provision of services*. Issuing a directive may be recommended only in order to assure those concerned of the protection of the law. However, Article 57(1) EEU remains of great importance in facilitating the assertion of the *right of establishment*.

According to its wording, Article 57(1) EEU does not make the mutual recognition of certificates of competence dependent upon previous or simultaneous co-ordination of training regulations. Does this mean that the Union legislature can make mutual recognition binding on Member States when the training regulations are demonstrably of differing quality? Can Member States with a higher level of training for a particular occupation require at least supplementary training as a precondition for the exercise of that activity?

This question is of importance for the provision of services, particularly under the interpretation (rejected here) of the ban on restrictions contained in Article 59(1) EEC Treaty as merely relating to equal treatment of nationals. The question is only of academic interest, however, as long as the principle of unanimous decision-making is retained in the Council. If, on the other hand, the Council were to revert to the majority voting envisaged in the Treaty, the point discussed here could become an important problem.

The systematic construction of Article 57 EEU shows that the authors of the Treaty were indeed aware of the problem. In connection with the aim of co-ordination, Article 57(2) EEU contains a reference to Article 57(1) EEU, but there is no further correlation. This is in noticeable contrast to Article 57(3) EEU, which provides for co-ordination to take priority, with regard to the medical, para-medical and pharmaceutical professions, even over the abolition of discriminatory restrictions during the transitional period. As regards other activities, co-ordination is not given priority in this way. It must be concluded from this that the Treaty wishes to leave it to the Union legislature to decide when and whether co-ordination of vocational training regulations proves necessary. It is not, therefore, possible for Member States to refuse to obey a directive under Article 57(1) EEU, using the argument that the certificate of competence to be recognized is based on training which is not of equivalent value. If there is a need for action in this respect, the Union legislature must act.

In this regard nothing will be changed by the Single European Act; it is true that the addition to the EEC Treaty of Article 100A(4) EEU (given effect in Article 18 of the Single European Act) makes it possible for a Member State to insist, in relation to harmonization measures decided by only a *qualified* majority, that provisions be implemented "which are justified by important requirements in the sense of Article 36 or in reference to the protection of the working environment or the protection of the environment . . . ." However, Article 100A EEU is to come into operation according to its first paragraph "By way of derogation from Article 100 . . .," which is not applicable to our particular problem. This objection also applies, then, to Article 100B EEU.

c. *Article 57(2) EEU*

Under Article 57(2) EEU, the Council can, unanimously (sentence 2) or by qualified majority (sentence 3), issue directives for the co-ordination of (non-discriminatory) legal and administrative provisions of Member States concerning the exercise of independent activities.

3. General Considerations

The status of the ban on restrictions and the approximation of laws is in principle no different here from that in Article 57(1) EEU: If Article 59(1) EEU is to be interpreted only as a ban on discrimination, there is a need for extensive harmonization of at least all the (non-discriminatory) Member State regulations that can permanently impede the international provision of services.

The need for harmonization is somewhat reduced if the ban on restrictions in Article 59 EEU is interpreted as being more extensive; if the *home country principle* applies as regards professional qualifications, approximation of training regulations in order to facilitate the provision of services becomes superfluous. Co-ordination can be limited to regulation of questions relating to vocational supervision.

The question remains whether, under such a broad interpretation of Article 59(1) EEU, the Union still retains powers on the basis of Articles 66 and 57(2) EEU to issue directives for an approximation of vocational training regulations.

Doubts may arise in view of the wording of Article 57(2) in association with 57(1) EEU, which confers competence for co-ordination only for the purpose of "facilitating" the provision of services. The problem is, however, somewhat theoretical: even if, for the purpose of regulating the provision of services, one assumes that there is a loss of Union powers within the framework of Articles 66 and 57(2) EEU, the Union still retains its powers to regulate facilitation in the assertion of the right of establishment. However, even a broad interpretation of Article 59 EEU cannot provide grounds for a loss of powers on the part of the Union; the consequent development of Union law after the *Cassis de Dijon* judgment is to be understood not only as an attempt by the European Court of Justice to make the enforcement of basic freedoms independent of the manifest inertia of the Council, but also as a stimulus for Union legislation. A broad interpretation of Article 30 EEU, and Article 59 EEU as well, cannot, however, lead to the result that it is impossible for either the Member States or the Union to pursue a wholly legitimate regulatory objective.

Despite the reference in the first sentence of Article 57(1) EEU, the co-ordination regulation contained in paragraph 2 is not restricted to circumstances in connection with the mutual recognition of diplomas, certificates, etc., i.e., to the harmonization of training. As is very clear from the second sentence, Article 57(2) EEU is also a basis for the co-ordination of Member State regulations controlling the activities of banks. This also applies to the insurance sector.

To distinguish it from the general clause of Article 100 EEU, the field of application of Article 57(2) EEU can be considered as being restricted to Member State regulations relating to the exercise of independent activities in the sense of Article 60(1); this applies to regulations concerning specific requirements for the person of the provider and to regulations that influence the product provided. However, other regulations affecting the international provision of services—such as the protection of intellectual property—come under Article 100 EEU.

Article 66 in association with Article 57(2) EEU provides the Union with powers of co-ordination for the purpose of facilitating the cross-frontier (interstate) provision of services. One may conclude from this that powers of co-ordination are restricted to situations with interstate application, with the result that Member States alone remain responsible for the regulation of purely interstate provision of services.

However the following point must be made; it is true that the concern of Article 57(2) EEU is not the approximation of laws as an objective in itself, but the facilitation of the international provision of services. This latter aim should lead to solutions that avoid international services being subjected to a stricter standard than purely national activities. Such a solution would run counter to the objective set out in Article 57(2) EEC Treaty; therefore, Union regulatory powers for purely national circumstances are presupposed. The question of whether the Union should exercise its powers in this way (in the spirit of total harmonization) is another story.

4. "Co-ordination"

The directives issued to date to facilitate freedom in the provision of services have aimed only in part at the approximation of legal norms in the sense of comparability of solutions. All the directives contain instead regulations concerned with developing specific solutions aimed at facilitating the provision of services, on the basis of the variety of the legal systems, the territorial application of public law, as well as of the territorial limitations of administrative action:

1. Some regulations contain straightforward and conflict-of-jurisdiction solutions, for example, whether and to what extent, in connection with his activities in the destination country, the provider of the service is to be subject to the vocational law and the law on professional standing there.

2. Special substantive rules and regulations for aliens may deviate from the national standard in order to achieve a solution in line with the objectives of Article 59 EEU. Examples include the replacement of authorization/permission in regard to service activities in the destination country by a mere notification requirement, exemption from the obligation of membership or registration by means of professional association in the form of automatic registration, or *pro forma* membership which may neither delay, nor render more difficult, nor burden with additional costs, activities connected with the interstate provision of services.

3. Finally, there are provisions on the supervision of activities according to which the authorities of the destination country, instead of themselves check-

> ing the vocational qualifications of the provider of services, must rely on a certificate issued by the competent authorities in the home country. There is also a concurrent obligation on the authorities in the home country to issue such a certificate (and withdraw it). This is associated with obligations on the administrative authorities to exchange information, and to give necessary information to the provider of the service.

One may ask whether the Union has the power, under Article 57(2) EEU to make such amendments in the law of the Member States.

There is now unanimous agreement that the Treaty, with its use in various articles of the terms "co-ordination" (Articles 54(3)(g), 56(2) and 57(2) EEU), "approximation" (Articles 3(h) and 100 EEU), "harmonization" (Article 99 EEU) and "adjustment" (Articles 111 and 112 EEU), has created no consciously differentiated system of extensive powers to act for the Union; the terms are used synonymously.

Although there is agreement on this point, there is all the more disagreement concerning the question of what the Treaty means as regards the concepts of approximation, co-ordination, etc. Two basic positions can be distinguished:

"Approximation" of laws can be understood as the equalizing or "levelling" of varying regulations. Approximation of laws is here allotted the function of bringing the relevant national regulations more into line, one with another (without unifying them), so that obstructive effects on trade in the Union no longer arise by reason of continuing variation in the regulations. In this sense, the competence to co-ordinate is limited to overcoming the differences between Member State standards in order to regulate a certain problem; the competence is limited to substantive (public and private) law. Regulations involving conflicts of laws, the development of international substantive rules, and mechanisms for achieving co-operation between the administrations of the Member States in order to overcome territorial restrictions of vocational supervision, must be worked out by other means (i.e., Articles 220 and 235 EEU).

This narrowing-down of the concept involved in the terms "harmonization," "co-ordination" and "approximation" is not, however, convincing. It is true that one might primarily associate with the term "approximation of laws" the idea that "the same facts will be treated in the same way in all Member States,"[42] but the meaning of the term "approximation of laws" also covers any form of approximation of legal *standards*; thus it includes standardization of the law of aliens and all standards with a conflict-of-laws content.

It is true that the term "co-ordination" is used by the Treaty in Article 54(3)(g) EEU in the sense of an equalization of standards generally applicable (with no differentiation between nationals and foreigners), but within the framework of Article 56(2) EEU the important aspect is precisely the standardization and gradual removal of regulations relating specifically to aliens, i.e., those laws discriminating against foreigners.

---

[42] Schwartz, *Zur Konzeptionder Rechtslangleichung in der Europaischen Wirtschaftsgemeinschaft,* in *Festschrift Hallstein* (1966) 474, at 475; Marx, *Funktion und Grenzen der Rechtsangleichung nach Art. 100 EWG-Vertrag* (1976), 96.

The crucial aspects, however, are those of a teleological nature. Alongside mutual recognition of certificates of professional competence under Article 57(1) EEU, co-ordination under Article 57(2) is the very instrument by which the EEC Treaty, over and above the ban in Article 59(1) EEU, seeks to contribute to the removal of all obstacles to the provision of services. Such obstacles do not arise merely because of the varying content of national regulations, but under certain circumstances arise also and precisely because of the mere co-existence of legal systems. The concurrent claims by various Member States to regulate jurisdiction in a given interstate situation lead to obstacles that must be removed by the appropriate limitation of the jurisdiction of the Member States, as well as by the development of rules of international administrative law. This objective can be furthered by the creation of new standards aimed specifically at facilitating the international provision of services.

In its *van Binsbergen* judgment, the Court of Justice has assigned Article 57(2) EEU the task of solving the particular problems which result from the fact that, not having permanently settled there, the provider of services cannot be fully subject to the professional regulations of the country in which the service is provided. In this sense, the term "co-ordination" also includes the development of solutions specifically adapted to the requirements of the interstate provision of services that deviate from the manner in which intrastate transactions are regulated.

Furthermore, a broad concept of co-ordination must be arrived at from the systematic relationship of Article 57(2) and (1) EEU. Article 57(1) EEU provides an instrument the importance of which is not the equalization of the content of legal rights but their adaptation to the problems which of necessity arise from the co-existence of legal systems. Because of the correlation between Article 57(2) and (1) EEU ("for the same purpose"), it must be assumed that the Union has the powers via Article 57(2) EEU not only to provide the necessary preconditions for mutual recognition of diplomas (unification as regards content of vocational training), but also to solve all those problems that may arise in the interstate provision of services because of the territorial limitation of administrative action, in particular of vocational supervision. Article 57(2) EEU therefore also makes it possible for the Union to orientate the administrative law of Member States towards co-operation between the administrative authorities of the states, and in particular to provide for the recognition of attestations, diplomas, certificates, etc., issued by the authorities in the Member States.

5. Article 100 EEU

As regards cross-frontier provision of services, Article 100 EEU comes into play in particular in relation to regulations that do not relate directly to the activities of the provider of the service or to the product supplied by him. Examples include the standardization of trademark law (service trademark), or the law on unfair competition. The Union has, however, been given the power to approximate laws only where regulations "directly affect the setting up or operation of the common market."

Since, under the general clause of Article 100 EEU, the Union was not to be granted comprehensive powers for the harmonization of the entire body of laws in Member States in the economic field, we must interpret the criterion of "directly affect(ing) the establishment or functioning of the common market" as signifying a negative effect on the common market, i.e., in particular on the safeguarding of freedoms and the realization of the system of undistorted competition.[43] In our context, the main question to be answered is whether and to what extent the mere diversity of Member State regulations, for example trademark law, the law on unfair competition, contract and criminal law, results in the lasting impairment of the cross-frontier provision of services. Here, careful judgment is required, and clear distinctions must be made between the individual service branches.

6. Limits on the Power of Approximation of Laws

As regards harmonization, the Union is subject to the limits of the individual jurisdictional norm. Article 66 in association with Article 57(2) EEU takes, above all, as its starting point "the provision of services" in the sense of Article 60 EEU. In this connection, in so far as the main emphasis of the activity regulated, radio, for example, falls within the field of "non-economic" services, over which the Union has no jurisdiction, the principle of proportionality and the need to take Member State regulatory powers into consideration will make it advisable to exercise existing powers with care. It is impossible to consider this in detail here. We shall consider, however, whether and to what extent the Union, in its solutions to the problem of harmonization, is subject to the limits inherent in the EEC Treaty, and in particular, the ban on restrictions contained in Article 59 EEU. Can the Union require, or at least empower, Member States to introduce or retain a regulation which would, as an autonomous act on the part of the Member State, be incompatible with Article 59 EEU?

a. The Problem

Directives frequently contain regulations that may awaken doubts about their compatibility with the EEC Treaty. A few examples will suffice:

- The protective clauses contained in the directives (on the details of the transitional measures) issued in the industrial sector (up to the end of 1969) stipulate that Member States which permit a particular profession to be practiced with no specific proof of qualification can make the exercise of the activity by citizens of other Member States (on the basis of special authorization by the Commission) dependent on requirements other than those applicable to their own citizens, in that they must provide the proof of competence required in their country of origin for the exercise of the activity.

- The co-insurance directive of 1978 stipulates in its Article 2(1)(c) that the leading insurer can be treated by Member States as an insurer who will cover the entire risk. According to one far from unequivocal[44] interpretation, the host state is able, on the basis of Article 2(1)(g), to require the authorization (and establishment) of the leading insurer. The question is whether this interpreta-

[43] Grabitz (-Langeheine), *Kommentar sum EWG-Vertrag*, (1st ed., 1983); Art. 100, margin nos. 32-36.

[44] A.G. Roth, *Internationales Versichercungvertragsrecht*, (1985) 664, at 677 and note 110.

tion can be upheld when the authorization requirement is considered (as the European Court of Justice has held) to infringe Article 59 EEU, at least as regards large-risk insurance contracts.

- In the draft of the second co-ordination directive for non-life insurance (as things stood in 1984), host countries (as defined in Article 3) are also directed to require the insurance company to present to the supervisory authorities a certificate from the home-country authority confirming the fulfilment of solvency regulations (Article 10) in the case of cross-frontier insurance contracts involving large risks. The insurance company may not commence its activities until the authorities of the host country are in receipt of such a certificate (Article 12(1)). Is a restriction of this kind compatible with Article 59 EEU?

b. The Freedoms as Limitations

The prohibitions involved in achieving the freedoms stated by the Treaty are addressed to Member States and not to the Union. A direct commitment by the Union legislature to Articles 30 *et seq.* and 59 *et seq.* EEU is excluded in this respect. But in no way is it to be concluded from this that the freedoms are irrelevant for the Union legislature. The EEC Treaty stipulates that it is the task of the Union to realize the objectives outlined in Article 2 EEU by establishing a "common market." The freedoms of the Treaty form the core of this common market, and subject to any restrictions provided for in the Treaty, they cannot be at the disposal of the Union legislature. Article 3 EEU reads: ". . . the activities of the Union shall include, as provided in this Treaty . . . the abolition, as between Member States, of obstacles to freedom of movement for . . . services . . . ." This amounts to a direct commitment on the part of the legislature: It may act only to remove obstacles, and not to make the cross-frontier provision of services more difficult.

Approximation of laws is the means for promoting the establishment and realization of the common market; this connection results from the wording of both Article 100 and Article 57(2) EEU.

Article 100 EEU grants the Union powers to approximate laws in those cases where Member State regulations "directly affect the establishment, or functioning, of the common market." Whenever the preconditions for direct effect exist, the application of EEU powers is, at the same time, handicapped by the objective of all Union activities in the approximation of laws: approximation of laws must serve to *promote* the common market.

Article 57(2) EEU establishes the aim of harmonization: The coordination of national legal and administrative regulations is effected for the purpose of "facilitating" the adoption and exercise of vocational activities. "Facilitating" means primarily the removal of obstacles and impediments to the cross-frontier provision of services that result from the diversity and territorial nature of the regulations of Member States. Directives under Article 57(2) EEU must be used to facilitate rather than to impede the freedom to provide services.

This also accords in the main with the precedents established by the European Court of Justice. A judgment of 29 February 1982 states that Union bodies must also take into consideration the freedom of internal movement of goods as being a fundamental principle of the common market. This confirms the finding in the *Ramel* judgment, that the Union legislature is prevented from calling into question "what the Union has achieved in relation to the unity of the market."[45] It follows from this that the Union legislature cannot empower or oblige Member States to take measures prohibited under Article 59 EEU.

c. *Article 55(2) EEU*

The only question is whether the principle formulated here may not be subject to an exception with regard to Article 55(2) EEU. Article 55(2) EEU empowers the Council to decide by a qualified majority and at the recommendation of the Commission that Chapter 2 on the right of establishment is not applicable to certain activities. Article 66 EEU also refers to Article 55 EEU, and thus makes it possible to exclude individual activities from the field of application of Article 59 *et seq*.

The rule presents a riddle. Union bodies are given the power to render the freedom of establishment and provision of services ineffective for certain activities, but the nature of these activities is not specified in detail, nor is the decision made dependent upon certain preconditions. Moreover, a qualified majority in the Council is sufficient for this.

The function and scope of Article 55(2) EEU are obscure. Its significance is in practice reduced to zero. It has not as yet been applied in a single instance; this is because a decision of the Council is dependent upon a corresponding proposal from the Commission, and the latter has not as yet submitted such a proposal (nor is it likely to do so in the near future).

The sense of Article 55(2) EEU is perhaps best revealed in its connection with Article 55(1) EEU; according to this paragraph the regulations on the freedoms of establishment and provision of services are not to be applied in relation to an individual Member State to activities connected with the exercise of official authority. Because of the varying forms of individual activities in the Member States that result from this, it is possible that in individual cases inequalities and imbalances may occur which are difficult to accept, and these might justify the application of Article 55(2) EEU.

The wording of Article 55(2) EEU, however, clearly goes beyond the group of cases described here. Moreover, since Article 55(2) in no way implies reference to Article 55(1) EEU, there are no precise limits to the application of Article 55(2) EEU. This rule will, therefore, have to be given a precise meaning perhaps along the lines that, in view of the consequences (running counter to the purposes of integration) of the application of Article 55(2) EEU, only reasons of paramount importance can justify a decision under Article 55(2).

One might wonder whether, on the basis of Article 55(2) EEU, consequences can be drawn in relation to our question concerning the Union legislature's commitment to freedom to provide services. If it is possible for the Council, by only a qualified majority, to remove entirely certain service activities from the field of application of

[45] Case 80, 81/77, *Ramel*, [1978] E.C.R. 972, at 947, considerations 35-36.

Article 59 *et seq*. EEU, must it not then also be possible, as a less radical measure, to establish Union regulations or empower Member States to take measures that weaken the position as regards integration established by Article 59 EEC Treaty and formalized by case law? Such an argument *a majore ad minus* seems unconvincing, however.

To render the chapter concerning the provision of services ineffective, the Council is dependent on a proposal of the Commission. If, in the harmonization process in regard to Article 55(2) EEU, one wished to release the Council from its obligations under Article 59 EEU, there would be a risk that the Commission's monopoly of proposals under Article 55(2) EEU would be undermined. The possibility for the Council, when adopting directives, to depart from the Commission's proposals (Article 149 EEU) imposes a procedural solution according to which the question of Article 55(2) EEU can only be decided by an independent decision.

The consequence of such a decision by the Council not to apply the chapter on the provision of services to a certain activity is that the Union's mandate to harmonize then lapses. The inapplicability of the chapter relating to services also leads, via Article 66 EEU, to the inapplicability of Article 57(2) EEU. But anything that is to be withdrawn from the common services market can then no longer be made the subject of a directive to facilitate the provision of services.

On the whole, therefore, Article 55(2) EEC Treaty cannot justify any weakening of the Union legislature's obligations to the principles of freedom in the provision of services.

d. Article 59 EEU as a Standard of Assessment

The Union legislature's obligation to observe the basic principles of the common market does not necessarily mean that all measures taken unilaterally by Member States which are incompatible with the basic freedoms of the Treaty cannot in general be made the substance of a regulation under Union law.

For the present, no problems are presented by any unilateral Member State regulations which have a disproportionately adverse effect upon the international movement of goods or provision of services, but whose harmonization in fact puts an end to these effects which obstruct international trade. The German Federal regulation concerning minimum alcohol content in liqueurs, complained against in the *Cassis de Dijon* case, would therefore be unobjectionable as a regulation in a directive since its uniform introduction into the law of Member States would not obstruct freedom in the movement of goods.

The position is, however, quite different for all Union regulations that actually impede the interstate movement of goods and provision of services, for example, when, in connection with the movement of goods, the regulations relating to import controls are standardized or when, in connection with cross-frontier provision of services, Member States are empowered or even compelled to make cross-frontier activities dependent upon preceding notification, permission, or the like. Is the Union legislature bound by the limits put on Member States by Article 59 EEU, in the form in which it has been made concrete by case law?

In a ruling in 1977, the European Court of Justice drew attention to a point of continuing relevance: Member States' unilateral regulations naturally reflect their own particular interests. Typically, they seek to protect their own interests, and not that of the Union. Within the framework of Article 30 EEU, and surely under Article 59 EEU, this justifies the exercise of strict control of the regulatory objectives pursued by Member States and of the regulatory instruments they employ for that purpose. It could of course be argued in resolute fashion that any retreat behind the position as to integration achieved by the basic freedoms (as expounded by the European Court of Justice) would be incompatible with the objective of a directive to facilitate the provision of services. Such an argument would, however, be inadequate.

As can be seen in the example of insurance supervision, the facilitation of international provision of services must actually be linked as a whole to *ad hoc* impediments. Progress towards the conditions of an internal market can be achieved here only if the essential functions of the supervision of insurers of other EEU countries are transferred to the supervisory authorities of the relevant countries of origin. This implies, on the one hand, that the authority in the country of origin supervises foreign insurance business (for the protection of the foreign public) and, on the other hand, that this supervisory authority co-operates closely with the authority in the country of activity, which of course also retains complementary supervisory functions. If Article 10(1) of the proposed second co-ordination directive for non-life insurance of 1984 seeks to grant countries of origin the power not to permit the commencement of cross-frontier insurance business (and this also means the conclusion of a single contract) until the insurer has supplied the supervisory authority with declarations and information, this clearly amounts to an obstacle to the international provision of services.

Despite this, such regulation can scarcely be questioned, since it is part of an overall regulatory system for the efficient supervision of insurers, which in general attempts to facilitate international provision of services by shifting the responsibility for supervision from the authorities of the country of activity to the authorities of the country of origin.

Regulations under Union law are issued by a Union body, the Council, "in the Union's general interest." In these regulations, the Union's interest is defined by way of compromise between the different standpoints of Member States. If the European Court of Justice is not to become a substitute European legislature, it will have to exercise some discretion in examining the solutions found by the Council if and in so far as the tendency is for directives issued by the Council, at least in general, to aim at facilitating interstate trade. In its judgment of 29 February 1984, the European Court of Justice takes this into account in its desire to grant the Union legislature, in exercising powers under Articles 43 and 100 EEU and with regard to the peculiarities of the matter to be regulated, discretion in so far as the Council can arrive at its own assessment of the measures necessary to control interstate trade. The European Court of Justice will have to specify more precisely in detail where the boundaries of this discretion lie.

Finally a few more examples may suffice:

The Union regulations that empower Member States to establish stricter requirements for the provision of cross-frontier services by citizens of other EEU countries than for their own nationals are incompatible with the basic principle of Article 59

EEU, which aims precisely at the removal of all discrimination. Corresponding regulations contained in the directives of the 1960s, which were supported by Article 226 EEU during the transitional period, have become null and void since the expiry of the transitional period.

A regulation that makes the granting of public building commissions dependent upon establishment in the home country deprives the freedom to provide services of "any practical effectiveness."[46] Authority embodied in a directive for Member States to require establishment in the case of public building commissions would be diametrically opposed to the basic principle of Article 59 EEU.

The transitional measures contained in the directives relating to industrial and commercial activities permit those Member States which made admission to a profession dependent upon evidence of certain skills and knowledge, to insist, in the case of citizens of other EEU countries, upon several years of practical activity (vocational experience). This enables Member States to adopt measures excluding providers of services from providing cross-frontier services for a certain period. In so far as corresponding regulations, as well as measures taken unilaterally by Member States, are compatible with Article 59 EEU there is no problem. It is a different matter, however, when, for the purposes of Article 59 EEU, providers of services who meet their home country's requirements as to vocational qualifications can in principle be active anywhere in the common market, provided that this is not contrary to the destination country's general interest. Here the Union legislature is acting at the very limits of its discretion.

With regard to Article 2(1)(c) of the directive on co-insurance of 1978, the European Court of Justice, in its judgment of 4 December 1986, has pointed out that in case of ambiguity Union acts have to be interpreted in such a way that they are compatible with the EEC Treaty—such an interpretation should be preferred to an interpretation leading to its voidness. This kind of argument is clearly based on the assumption that Union legislation is bound by Article 59 EEU.

7. A System of Undistorted Competition

The Union legislature is not only committed to the basic principle of freedom to provide services, it is also bound by general principles of law to be derived from the EEC Treaty as the "Constitution" of the Union: proportionality, equal treatment of Member States, uniform validity of Union law, the "common market." Directive practice in the domain of services offers some examples that can be regarded as problematic from one standpoint or another.

We shall examine below the question of whether and to what extent the Union legislature, in the process of co-ordination, must prevent competitive disadvantages that may result from Member State regulations. Competitive disadvantages are to be expected if a directive is itself restricted to minimum standards in order to facilitate participation in the cross-frontier provision of services, but for the rest leaves it to Member States to enforce stricter rules for suppliers established in the home country.

---

46 Case 76/81, *Transporoute*, [1982] E.C.R. 419 at 427-428, consideration 14.

An example of this is the regulation of advertising in the proposed Council directive for the co-ordination of certain legal and administrative provisions on the exercise of broadcasting activities. The proposed directive sets out certain minimum standards as regards separating advertising from the programme (Article 7) and as regards the content of the advertising (Articles 8, 10-12). Transmissions conforming to these requirements may be broadcast in all Member States. Under Article 13(2) of the directive, Member States may employ more detailed or stricter regulations in regard to their national suppliers but not in regard to foreign programmes.

Solutions under Union law that leave it to Member States to establish stricter standards for their national producers deliberately accept competitive disadvantages affecting national suppliers in the domestic market; at the same time, however, they can have a detrimental effect on the interstate provision of services, in so far as suppliers from Member States with stricter standards are competing in the markets of Member States that have tailored their legal standards to the minimum standard only. In establishing its regulations, is the Union legislature justified in leaving so much scope for the distortion of competition?

From the aspect of Union law, those competitive disadvantages that arise in the export of services because of stricter standards in the State of origin present no problems, since these distortions of competition are not created by Union legislation. They arise as a necessary consequence of the authority of the State of origin to establish the basic legal conditions for domestic production of goods and services.

Part of the philosophy of the common market is the toleration, at least to some extent, of differences in basic legal conditions. On this point, the *Spaak Report* reads: "The varying burden on the economy of individual countries arising from, for example, public dues or systems of social security still does not in itself distort the terms of competition, since such differences are generally balanced out by general foreign trade relations, in particular the rate of exchange . . ."[47] And it states later that an approximation of basic conditions is also expected to result at least "in part"—"from the development of the common market itself, and from the interaction of economic forces and the relations between the participants."

The model of a common market is here outlined in which differences in production costs at various EEU locations have to be tolerated. It was meant to leave its development to competition among states and thus to competition among legal systems.

In so far as Article 13(2) of the proposed directive on broadcasting thus allows Member States the opportunity to retain their divergent regulations for radio and television advertising, few objections can be raised to this.

But what is the situation as regards the almost inevitable consequence, that national producers of radio and television programmes may be at a disadvantage not only in foreign markets but also in their relevant domestic market in comparison with suppliers from other EEU countries with less strict advertising standards? This touches on a problem that has been the subject of lively discussion for some considerable time

---

[47] Report of delegation leadres to the Foreign Secretaries, MAE 121 d/56 (corrected) 64.

as concerns the concept of so-called "reverse discrimination," or simply: discrimination against nationals.

In our context, the problems associated with discrimination against nationals are relevant only in so far as the EEC Treaty does not itself already prohibit such discrimination against nationals under Articles 7, 30 and 59 EEU. For, if discrimination against nationals is prohibited under Articles 3, 7, 30 and 59 EEU with direct effect in the legal systems of Member States, the Union legislature could not empower Member States to issue such regulations. Only if the problem of discrimination against nationals does not fall under the EEC Treaty—as can be assumed on the basis of the case law of the European Court of Justice—can there be meaningful discussion of the question of whether the Union legislature, in its directive legislation, must not only ensure the facilitation of the provision of services but also, at the same time, prevent discrimination against nationals under voluntary Member State regulations. Such a thesis cannot, however, be represented as being valid Union law as a matter of course. It is true that the Union legislature is committed to the objective of Article 3(f) EEU: the establishment of a system that protects competition from distortion within the Union. But this objective does not call for a specific method of harmonization only, since the competitive position among suppliers in Member States is determined by a large number of legal, in particular fiscal, factors whose effects on production costs may vary from one Member State to another. Against this background, the objective of Article 3(f) EEU is most certainly satisfied if the Union legislature leaves it to the Member States to take into account the competitive position of national producers in any establishment of stricter standards.

D. Harmonization Policy

Under Articles 57, 100 and 3(h) EEU, the Union is committed to the advancement of the internal market by means of co-ordination. It has fallen considerably behind in this task. We intend to discuss below the difficulties that have impeded co-ordination to date and to indicate considerations that should influence the Union in its work in the immediate future.

1. General Considerations

a. Cost-Benefit Analysis

The Union's co-ordinating measures should be subjected to cost/benefit analysis. The Commission's restricted powers, the almost incalculable cost of the arduous legislative procedures at both Union level and national level, but also the somewhat insignificant effect of the directives because of lax conversion practice in Member States, all indicate that the approximation of laws in the Union should be restricted to essentials. Although it must be assumed that the costs associated with co-ordination are accepted in principle by the Treaty, since long-term benefits will result from the establishment of an internal market, this does not render it unnecessary to question the need for each co-ordinating measure.

From this aspect, mutual recognition of the equivalence of regulations, which is to be made possible by Article 19 of the Single European Act via the new Article 100B(1) EEU, should, for example, be given priority over the harmonization of substantive law via Article 100A EEU. Compared with the approximation of substantive private law, to give another example in the field of consumer protection, solutions by means of harmonized conflict-of-law rules plainly appear to be simpler and cheaper.

b. Harmonization and Diversity

Approximation of laws aiming at "equalizing" or "leveling" the regulations of Member States necessarily means giving up a part of European diversity.

The strongest reservations exist where there will be an intervention in socio-cultural traditions, for example where standardization of vocational training systems in the broadest sense is concerned. In my opinion, there must be good if not compelling reasons to justify a demand for the approximation of standards for purposes of freedom in the provision of services. Preventing competitive disadvantages and protecting consumers will in most cases probably not furnish sufficient reasons for the standardization of vocational training systems in the domain of either industrial activities or the professions.

The actual blocking effect of the power of Member States to act, associated with the harmonization of laws, can erect barriers to reform at Member State level. This not only occasions socio-political tensions but also signifies a degree of *impoverishment*: The competition for more successful solutions possible in a system of decentralized decision making, with individual states acting as laboratories for resolving social problems, is prevented. This calls for reflection on which regulatory problems should be settled at Member State level and which at Union level.

For these reasons, unification of standards of substantive law should always be avoided where solutions in private international law and international administrative law are sufficient to safeguard the freedom in the exchange of services in the common market. This applies—but only as a rule of thumb—to all regulations that concern not the service product itself but the modalities of its "marketing." With regulations of this kind, the application of the law of the country of activity will not usually entail a barrier to the exchange of services.

Consumer protection, contract law, the law of torts, the law on professional standing and the law on professional associations, are all examples of areas which can be left to the jurisdiction of the country of activity (host state). This appears to present no problems provided that providers of services residing in another Member State are not thereby obstructed in the provision of their services. Where this is not the case, the regulation must be eased—perhaps on the model of the provisions for membership in professional organizations in the directives issued to date—by means of special substantive rules. This also applies to impediments arising from conflicting obligations for the individual (as in the law on professional standing in the professions).

The mere fact that the provider of a service must anticipate the application of a legal system differing from that of his home country offers as little justification for co-ordination of the law on professional standing or of the law of torts or contract law as does the fact that a provider of services throughout the EEU is faced in his activities with—potentially—12 different legal systems. In none of the areas where the extent of cross-frontier provision of services is negligible does the need for coordination arise. Here, one can and should wait to see whether the business circles affected themselves feel that the multiplicity of laws is an appreciable obstacle, and only then should action be taken.

As regards the predominantly "product-related" regulations on the provision of services, i.e., the requirements as to the qualifications of the provider or his solvency, the objective of any co-ordination must be to assist enforcement of the home country principle in such a way that the provider of services can also be active across frontiers under the conditions of the home country. Only where the home country principle applies to product-related regulations can it be ensured that providers of services can actually be active across frontiers, in other words that internal market conditions are established. As matters stand, the home country principle is also a conflict-of-laws rule which must of course go hand in hand with the unification of substantive law standards, if and in so far as the difference in "product" standards endangers significant general interests of Member States or may lead to permanent distortions of competition. The actual need for co-ordination cannot, however, be determined here in general terms, but always and only in regard to the individual service.

c. *Administrative Co-operation*

The need for co-operation is imperative in so far as obstacles to the provision of services arising from territorially related administrative action by Member States are concerned. If the objective of realizing internal market conditions is to be achieved without administration at Union level, mechanisms for effective co-operation of Member State administrations must be developed and consolidated. Approximation of laws directed towards co-operation between Member State administrations is indispensable to the realization of freedom in the provision of services if the furnishing of services is subject to Member State supervision.

2. The Various Services

a. *Commercial and Industrial Services*

The long-standing provisional solution of the so-called transitional measures in the field of commercial activities (with the exception of banking and insurance) has obviously occasioned no significant difficulties. This proves that, for the purposes of freedom to provide services, approximation of training systems can in principle be avoided.

It should, however, be considered, as regards the requirements as to vocational training for the purposes of freedom in the provision of services, whether one should perhaps adopt the home country principle in general and simply abolish the "transitional measures": Only in this way would the barriers to cross-frontier activities made possible by the "transitional regulations" be raised for the provider of services, and internal market conditions be achieved.

The need for consumer protection and quality control in the country of activity is not in opposition to such an enforcement of the home country principle: The call for protection of the recipient of the service is not really convincing if the person concerned himself requests this service from abroad and qualitative defects reflect directly on the provider of the service, particularly when the recipient of the service is a trader or an undertaking.

b. *The Professions*

In the domain of the professions, the Commission presented, in its 1985 White Paper, a new concept based upon the mutual recognition of diplomas etc., *without* preceding harmonization of training arrangements, although the Commission's objective was the removal of obstacles to the freedom of establishment. This was put in more concrete terms in the proposal submitted in July 1985 for a directive "On a general system for the recognition of higher education diplomas." With regard to professional activities whose exercise Member States make dependent on possession of one (or several) university diploma(s) or of another diploma whose course of study is conditional upon the conclusion of secondary education, Member States are to be obliged to act in accordance with the home country principle. The university diplomas required for the activity concerned in the country of origin should be regarded as a sufficient qualification. In addition, in the case of non-equivalent training, Member States are granted the competence to require supplementary and adaptive courses, which the country of activity will have to make available.

As regards facilitation of the provision of services, the directive is a step in the right direction.

Only when qualifications acquired in the country of origin are accepted as sufficient are internal market conditions established for the provider of services.

With respect to the professions, the aspect of avoiding impediments to competition is of little consequence. The differences in training among providers of services have only a small impact—if any at all—on the costs of the subsequent activity in providing services. Moreover, better training would tend to raise the quality of the service and thus contribute to the reputation of the provider of the service.

Problems may arise, however, as regards the power granted to Member States to demand compensation for non-equivalent training in the country of origin by requiring either several years of vocational experience or an adaptive course lasting up to three years. These are certainly appropriate—and perhaps also necessary—courses of action for Member States as regards freedom of establishment, but for the purposes of the freedom to provide services they go too far, at least as a general rule. A three-year adaptive course as a prerequisite for providing a service in the host country is in practice equivalent to a total barrier to cross-frontier provision of services. Such a regulation appears to be justified only for the protection of compelling general interests—for example health protection—but not as a general rule. The interest in preserving and safeguarding the quality of professional services is slight where cross-frontier provision of services is not typically conducted on a large scale but where as a general rule recipients of services quite deliberately and in accordance with their individual needs request services from a self-employed person abroad. For this reason the proposed directive does not go far enough. The model regulation in the lawyers' directive—the home country principle—should be the prototype here.

c. *Insurance and Banking*

In the domain of financial services, i.e., insurance and banking, matters are somewhat more complicated. For the purposes of the provision of services, it is not sufficient to declare the law of the home country to be applicable to all product-related regulations. Here, besides conflict-of-law solutions, harmonization of product standards and thus substantive-law solutions are required.

Requirements as to the financial solvency of undertakings (keywords: financial resources, technical reserves) have a direct impact upon the cost of services. Resulting distortion of competition can provide grounds for aligning the relevant standards with one another.

Regulations on financial resources result from specific needs for protection in relation to the provision of financial services. Insurance and banking contracts (in the broadest sense) serve as safeguards against the vicissitudes of life, and are, in the case of long-term contracts, associated to some extent with a permanent transfer of capital to the undertaking. Adequate assessment of the financial situation of the undertaking is virtually impossible for most clients before conclusion of the contract. Over and above this, in the case of long-term contracts they are linked, for better or for worse, to the fate of the undertaking. In some areas at least, such as long-term "Everyman" insurance, this results in imperative needs for protection which must be satisfied by corresponding requirements in regard to the financial resources of the undertaking as well as by supervising the day-to-day business activities.

In the common market, the marketing of financial services will be possible on a mass basis via mail order, agents, the new telecommunication services and via the service centers being established in large department stores. To this extent, matters are different here from, for example, the activities of the self-employed.

Although it can be left to those conducting large-scale business to check the solvency of their contractual partners or to obtain appropriate advice, the need for customer protection is far greater when the customer's decision in favor of a service product of an undertaking is based not upon an informed weighing-up and decision-making by the customer but to a greater or lesser extent upon the undertakings' marketing strategies. From this it follows that unrestricted freedom in the provision of services, at least for contracts with consumers, presupposes that the protective policies of the host state have been sufficiently taken care of through the approximation of the relevant regulations (capital resources, technical reserves) and by effective co-operation between the supervisory authorities of the home country and the country of activity (with the approximation of supervisory criteria).

In the light of the divergent supervisory traditions in Member States, one will be forced to make compromises here. One answer would be to introduce Union-wide minimum standards, and for the rest to leave it to Member States to subject resident undertakings to stricter requirements: competition of legal systems with a "safety net" of minimum standards.

It might be asked whether, on this basis of (partly) standardized supervisory regulations and effective co-operation between supervisory authorities, the law of the home country alone should be applicable to all other aspects of the service *product* or whether also in this respect a further approximation of standards is necessary.

The Commission supports the first alternative. In its White Paper it argues that the basic idea of the *Cassis de Dijon* judgment should be applied to financial services, such as home savings contracts or investment certificates, with the result that negotiable financial products can be on offer anywhere within the common market. Applied to insurance contracts, this means that insurance policies can be offered and sold anywhere under the legal conditions of the insurer's home country. Internal market conditions would thereby be realized for insurers operating in the Union; however, this would be at the expense of important general interests of the respective host states.

Insurance is a *legal product*. The general conditions of an insurer's policy describe the risk accepted by the insurer, define it in various ways (primary, secondary risk limitations), determine the policyholder's obligations and the legal consequences of their contravention, etc. In some Member States, this legal product is the subject of intensive legislation (and case law) oriented towards the protection of policyholders. In the Federal Republic of Germany in particular, administrative control in the form of the General Insurance Conditions licence from the supervisory authorities would be rendered ineffective by realization of the home country principle. To avoid this, as long ago as 1961 the "General programme for the removal of restrictions on freedom in the provision of services" considered co-ordination of national regulations on insurance contracts to be a necessary step on the way to a common insurance market. Since then matters have become more complicated.

In the field of "Everyman" insurance (as also with compulsory insurance), there is a need for consumer protection going beyond the substantive law in the policy-holder's favor: specific "conflicts-justice" considerations apply. There is a call for the application of the law of the country of activity (state of destination) because as a general rule it is asking far too much to expect the policy-holder to ascertain and apply unknown foreign law. The 1984 draft of a second coordinating directive for non-life insurance takes this into consideration: the law of the country of risk applies (at least, in so far as the law of the country of risk does not grant freedom of choice of law). This conflict-of-law solution renders harmonization of the law on insurance contracts superfluous.

In the domain of large-risk insurance—the question of the precise demarcation of this area has been the subject of controversy—the aspects of protection of the policy-holder under private international law and under substantive law lose their significance. Here, freedom of choice of law is possible, associated with a down-grading of imperative protection standards for the policy-holder to dispositive regulations, and thus it is also possible to sell insurance policies under the terms of the legal system of the home country. Thus, co-ordination of the law on insurance contracts for the purpose of facilitating the provision of services seems to be unnecessary as well. Only if, in the future, difficulties arise in large-risk business because of differences in the legal systems of Member States should Reimer Schmidt's proposal be taken up again, the creation of a rulebook containing typical clauses, comparable with INCOTERM, in which the fundamental principles of the law on insurance contracts are established.

V. Free Movement of Workers[48]

It has been recognized that the human resources of the European nations must be unleashed from national boundaries and that, for future prosperity, this objective is perhaps more important than unleashing products. This objective was recognized in the original EEC Treaty which provided for the free movement of persons and for further action to be taken to allow for the recognition of qualifications.

Whilst the EEC Treaty does explicitly provide for the free movement of workers and those who provide services, on the face of it, the new generations of Europeans do not explicitly have rights of movement until they are in fact themselves economically active. Thus there is seemingly no guaranteed right of access to partake of the varied educational offerings available throughout Europe. Nor was there overt provision in the original Treaty to allow the Union to promote mutual awareness and to foster joint educational and research projects. This "Community dimension," important for the success of the single European market, could be imbibed in three main ways. First, through the medium of undertaking non-national educational courses; secondly, by the input of a "Union dimension" into national educational provision; and, thirdly, by direct establishment of Union educational institutions open to all. For all these possibilities question marks arise as to whether the Union has competence to regulate in this area, and how the power to direct policy is to be diverted from national to Union streams.

Within States the growth of *centralized* State power in this area has been through two main channels. First it has grown by the enforcement of over-riding policy principles, often expressed in constitutional terms. For example, in the United States, federal intervention in education, a State power, was enabled by the effects of the 14th Amendment of the Federal Constitution which provided the legal source for federal intervention in matters such as school busing. A second method of growth of central influence has been through the power of the purse (that is, central intervention via funding programs). States overtly use their educational systems for nation-building and attempt to ensure minimum educational standards. These centripetal forces are counteracted by strong regional and cultural pressures to devolve educational control to more local bodies. These pressures include a tendency towards allowing private initiatives in schooling provision (to help ensure a pluralistic society) and even to devolve certain key educational decisions to individuals, at least partially in fulfillment of certain human rights, including those elaborated at a European level.

The Union does have certain key policies that mandate some "legal" action in the educational sphere and is increasingly also using the funding carrot to assert its influence in this realm. It too is subject to strong centrifugal pressures. The section will analyze how the Union is moving in this field and in particular will seek to assess the role of the law in this process. It will first analyze how States have reacted to international intervention in this sphere in the recent past and will then assess Union involvement, looking at the question of jurisdiction and assessing the impact of Union intervention

[48] Julian Lonbay, *Education and Law: The Community Context,* 14 E.L. Rev. 363-87 (1989). © 1989 Julian Lonbay. Reprinted by permission.

and the problems that this intervention has thrown up. As is not uncommon on the Union scene, it is within the steel portals of the European Court that the battle of wills between the Member States, too timid to legislate directly, and the Union interest has been fought.

A. International Law and Education

At the international level, human rights treaties have recognized the role of the State in regulating the right to education in order to "ensure such minimum educational standards as may be laid down or approved by the State."[49] The right is made subject to parental rights to choose non-state schooling and to ensure religious and moral education of their children in conformity with their own convictions, thus forming a limitation on State authority in this field. The rights of minorities in relation to education were left out of the International Bill of Rights, largely at the instigation of the Latin American States who feared that their policies of assimilation of immigrants would be hampered.

At the European level, Article 2 of the First Protocol to the European Convention on Human Rights outlines the rights of children and parents in relation to the provision of education. The *Kjeldsen* case[50] (1976) made it clear that the State had primary responsibility for the educational program subject to conveying controversial topics "in an objective critical and pluralistic manner and respecting the rights of the parents as regards religious and philosophical convictions and the rights of children.

In the European Social Charter there is no direct endorsement of the right to education, but Articles 9 and 10 support the notion of the individual influence over curriculum. In particular they recognize that the development of the abilities of the recipient, and the recipient's rights to seek his/her appropriate career, are for the individual to determine, and for the State to help implement even to the extent of giving "financial assistance."[51]

The power of States to regulate in this field is recognized by International Law subject to the limits mentioned. Education in Western Europe is acknowledged to be a national or sub-national matter there being marked differences in provision, reflecting the European cultural diversity. The educational system of the Republic of Ireland illustrates this autonomy and individualism.

As is well-known, historically English law in Ireland sought to "remove diversity in tongue, language, order and habit"[52] and later on discriminated strongly against Catholics. In reaction and reassertion of independent sovereignty Ireland has sought

[49] International Covenant on Economic, Social and Cultural Rights, 1966 (Article 13(3)). *See* United Nations, *A Compilation of International Instruments* (N.Y., 1988) 7.

[50] *Kjeldsen, Busk Madsen and Pedersen*, Eur. Court H.R. (1976) Ser. A No. 23.

[51] *Cf.* the Community charter of fundamental social rights, COM(89) 248 final (May 30, 1989), revised version in COM(89) 471 final (October 2, 1989).

[52] 1537 28 H. VIII c. 15 (Ir), An Act for the English order, habite, and Language.

to revive the Irish language, and strongly respects the role of the Church in education. As a result the State owns only a handful of primary schools and the school program and ethos is religious. This religious element is also reflected in Irish law and methods of interpretation of the Constitution. The policy of promoting the Irish language, primarily through educational measures, illustrates clearly the cultural aspects of educational provision.

Traditionally education has been reserved by States as a matter falling within their "domestic jurisdiction" and is often the subject of delicate internal political compromises or policies. The Union in entering this arena is treading on thin ice of Member States' sensibilities, though State actions are not entirely independent of restraints from public international law norms in this domain. Western States have strongly resisted 20th century attempts by international organizations to intervene in this area of their jurisdiction.

The League of Nations competence in this field was more or less exclusively Treaty-based and then only in relation to the minorities' treaties. The League's International Committee for Intellectual Co-operation initiated a voluntary mutual inspection of text-books. During the life-time of this initiative only three text-books were complained about, and only one altered. States had the absolute right to retain the text-books without explanation. The efforts of UNESCO to promote international understanding through education have all been on the basis of non-binding norms.

Some of the earliest post World War Two endeavors in the field of European educational co-operation were mounted by the Council of Europe which promoted treaties on equivalence of school certificates; periods of university study; academic recognition of University Qualifications; and also a treaty promoting student exchanges that provided for the continuation of payment of student scholarships to those studying abroad. Of these the first-mentioned has been the most successful, leaving, as it does, less scope for evasion of its terms by the contracting parties.

The recent burst of Union activity in this field has raised anxieties from Western non-Union European States that the purposes of the Council of Europe "to achieve a greater unity between its members" might be threatened by the increasing pace of Union integration.[53] The Union momentum in this field is certainly building up, but causes no threat to the legal regime established by the Council of Europe, and its programs are increasingly being opened to members of the Council of Europe.

Whilst International Law recognizes a pre-existing State role in relation to education, subject to the limits mentioned, the question of Union competence is not so clear. As we have seen a long-established tool of States seeking to reach their inhabitants has been through their schooling and higher educational systems. What are the possibilities for Union action here?

The Union could potentially undertake three types of activities in this sphere. It could seek to establish Union educational institutions open to all nationals of the Member States. If the direct creation of educational institutions is outside the reach of the Union proper, could it not at least allow cross-national access to existing educational

---

[53] J. Hagen, *University Co-operation and Academic Recognition in Europe: The Council of Europe and the Communities*, 22 Euro. J. Ed. 77 (1987).

institutions for nationals of the Member States? A third possibility for the Union would be to "communitize" existing educational institutions thus ensuring to all who attend them a Union dimension in their education.

B. Community Competence and Action in the Field of Education

The history of Union involvement in the educational arena is recounted by Fogg and Jones.[54] The initial resolutions on the matter were inter-governmental later giving way to the familiar "mixed" resolutions. More recently the Union has adopted "educational" decisions in the sense of Article 189.

It is true that the Single European Act (SEA), to some extent, mandates action in the educational sphere by Article 8A, which provides for, *inter alia,* the free movement of persons without frontiers. But it must be noted that the paragraph which includes this phrase also dictates that the internal market is to be "in accordance with the provisions of this treaty" which to some extent diminishes its impact. Political action at the highest level has supported the notion of the development of a "People's Europe," allowing a human dimension to the single internal market. A difficulty for the Union in this respect is that the SEA, unlike the case for the Environmental program and the Research and Development rogram, did not specifically and explicitly increase the competence of the institutions to move into this area. This is not to say that educational policy has been ignored at the Union level, far from it, numerous inter-governmental, quasi-Union resolutions, declarations and decisions have been promulgated. But Union action in the educational sphere has not been "sanitized" by the recent reform of the EEC Treaty.

The small attribution of Union competence in the field of education expresses the realization that in general it is considered a State competence, being linked to national cultural development. The European Court confirmed in *Gravier*[55] that the organization of education and teaching policy are not as such within Union competence. This rules out the direct creation or control of educational institutions.

Article 128 permits the Council of Ministers, by simple majority vote, to "lay down general principles for implementing a common vocational training policy capable of contributing to the harmonious development both of the national economies and of the common market." The extent of competence granted by this article, and the possibility or necessity for utilizing it in conjunction with Article 235 has recently been reviewed in the European Court. In *United Kingdom v. Council*[56] the United Kingdom government challenged the validity of the Action Program for the Vocational Training of Young People. This five year program included detailed implementing measures and

---

54 K. Fogg & H. Jones, *Educating the European Community—Ten Years on,* 20 Eur. J. Ed. 293 (1985).

55 Case 293/83 *Gravier v. City of Liege* [1985] E.C.R. 593 para. 19.

56 Case 56/88 [1989] 2 C.M.L.R. 789.

significant expenditure (40m ECU). Essentially it allowed the Commission to supplement Member State activity that promoted a common vocational training policy (by extending vocational training availability after full-time education), and allowed it to contribute by adding "a Union dimension" to Member State programs. [The Action Program] had been adopted on the basis of Article 128 and Council Decision 63/266. The United Kingdom, together with Denmark and the Federal Republic of Germany, had voted against the decision in the Council of Ministers as they considered that the program should have been based on both Article 128 and Article 235 as it requires significant expenditure and implementing action. The Advocate General Mischo agreed.

The Court however dismissed the application, considering that Article 198 was a sufficient basis for the Decision. It echoed its earlier judgment in the immigration policy cases[57] in stating[58]:

> The fact that the implementation of the common vocational training policy is provided for precludes any interpretation of that provision which would mean denying the Community the means of action needed to carry out that common policy effectively.

The fact that the voting procedure for Article 128 decisions may reflect "a lack of coherence" when compared to procedures as regards other common policies, did not affect the European Court's opinion that the decision in question, which was merely designed to "support and supplement through Union measures the policies and activities of the Member States in the area in question," fell within the scope of Article.

In *Commission* v *Council*[59] the legal basis of the ERASMUS decision, which included both Article 128 and Article 235, was challenged by the Commission. Both the ERASMUS and COMETT decisions had used both Articles 128 and 235 as a legal basis. The Commission had considered it "inopportune" to challenge the COMETT programme but challenged the use of Article 235 in the case of the ERASMUS programme.

Advocate General Mischo found for the Council.[60] The Opinion relied rather heavily on comparing Article 128 with other articles of the EEC Treaty that granted powers to the Community, an approach the European Court did not give great weight to, considering the lack of coherence in "the system for defining fields of competence" and "powers of the institutions and the conditions for their exercise" should not be a critical factor in interpreting the Treaty.

The European Court then found that in principle the Council could adopt the decision on the basis of Article 128 as it mainly dealt with Community information and promotional activity, and imposed obligations on Member States to co-operate. The

---

[57] Cases 281/85, 283-285/85 and 287/85 *Germany and others v. E.C. Commission* [1988] 1 C.M.L.R. 11 (esp. para. 28).

[58] At para. 6 of the judgment.

[59] Case 242/87 *Commission v. Council,* Judgment of May 30 (1989).

[60] Opinion of February 22, 1989.

question that still had to be decided was whether the activities envisioned by ERASMUS fell under the rubic of the common vocational training policy? The European Court examined the scope of vocational training. Readers will be aware that this concept had already been widely interpreted by *Gravier* and subsequent judgments.[61] The European Court affirmed these judgments and ruled that the bulk of ERASMUS activity in universities would be concerned with vocational training, and the few occasions when it would not, could not justify the conclusion that the programme was outside the competence granted by Article 128 in relation to vocational training. Amazingly the European Court is stretching the Community competence to its utmost, contrary to expectations.

The European Court, in fine fettle, went on to declare that the fact that an avowed aim of ERASMUS was to promote a "Citizen's Europe" did not detract from its legality, there being a strong link between the free movement of persons and common vocational training policy, and in any case, it reasoned, why should the general objectives of the Community not be promoted by such a measure?

The European Court also rejected the argument that ERASMUS affected education policy by funding the setting up of a Univerity Network. This would seem to be contrary to its earlier ruling in *Casagrande*[62] which had made it clear that matters of educational policy fell to the Member States. The European Court concluded though that the University Network was actually set up by the universities themselves under their own authority which was not in any way affected by the Community decision. There is here a clear utilisation of the Community of the funding "carrot" method of increasingly centralised influence on education, thus avoiding the pitfalls of direct normative action.

In fact the Commission finally lost the case on the grounds that the research aspects of ERASMUS programme could not be covered by Article 128 alone, thus it was legitimate to call on Article 235 as an additional legal basis for the decision.

The cases have established a generous interpretation of Article 128 and that Article 235 can be used to extend Union competence to the realm of educational policy. No-one has challenged this use of Article 235 to allow the Union competence to promote a People's Europe in the educational sphere.

A further source of jurisdiction is to be found in Article 57 allowing directives on mutual recognition of diplomas and co-ordination of conditions of provisions dealing with the "taking up and pursuit of activities as self-employed persons." There are numerous directives on co-ordination of training and recognition of qualifications, based on Article 57. These obviously have a direct impact on content of courses. Zilioli[63] relates how the entire dentistry curriculum of Italian universities had to be "created" as a result of Directive 78/687.[64] The most far-reaching directive adopted under

---

[61] Notably Case 24/86 *Blaizot* [1989] 1 C.M.L.R. 57 and Case 263/86 *Humbel* [1989] 1 C.M.L.R. 393.

[62] Case 9/74 *Casagrande v. Landeshauptstadt* [1974] E.C.R. 773.

[63] C. Zilioli, *The recognition of Diplomas and its impact on educational policies*, in K. Lenaerts, *ERASMUS: Legal Basis and Implementation*, in Eur. Comm. L. Ed (De Witte ed.) (Nomos, Baden-Baden, 1989), p. 51.

[64] O.J. L. 233/10.

this rubric so far is Directive 89/4857 which deals with the general mutual recognition of qualifications for professional purposes. The Directive follows the direction indicated by the European Court in *Heylens*.[65] The Commission is planning another general directive on mutual recognition of professional qualifications not requiring three years higher education study. The move to general recognition clearly lessens the direct Union impact on national educational courses, which no longer need to be harmonized. The great length of time and mainly unsuccessful efforts of the Commission in the engineering field, for example, indicate how reluctant individuals and organizations within Member States are to abandon national educational traditions and shows a strong resistance to Union attempts in this sphere.

The Commission is however contemplating "securing common agreement on entry qualifications to universities."

It is apparent, from this brief survey, that the very clear attribution of power needed to allow the Union directly to create or control educational institutions is not to be found within the Treaties, though the scope of Article 235 itself may be wide enough to accommodate such an eventuality. It is commonplace however that European schools exist, and there is a European University Institute. These bodies though were established by inter-governmental agreements outside the Union framework. The *ERASMUS* judgment affirmed that the Union would not have had jurisdiction under Article 128 to regulate directly University Networks.

The Commission is aware that attempts by itself to "meddle" so deeply in such a sensitive area would be counter-productive. The European Court could use the *Groener*[66] case to reassure Member States that it too will resist temptation to diminish the cultural diversity of Member States. In this case a Dutch national, Groener, failed an exam in Irish and was consequently refused a full-time teaching post. She argued *inter alia* that teaching was in fact mainly carried out in English and that the requirement of proficiency in Irish (attested by the examination) was therefore unnecessary. Article 3(1) of Regulation 1612/68 disallows indirect discrimination but excepts linguistic discrimination from this rule where knowledge of a language is "required by reason of the nature of the post to be filled." Advocate General Darmon[67] came down in favor of Ireland's regime declaring that "every state has the right to try and ensure the diversity of its cultural heritage."

There has been no attempt to harmonize educational rights. Thus for example whether a particular country permits extensive private schools is, subject to its other international law obligations, entirely a matter for that State, but can still be subject to Union rules. A State may not discriminate against a Union non-national by disallowing him the right to establish such institutions where nationals are permitted to establish them, but could limit everyone's right to establish certain schools, regardless of nationality, again subject to its other international law obligations.

---

65 Case 222/86, *Union Nationale des Éntraineurs et Cadres Techniques Professionels du Football v. Heylens* [1989] 1 C.M.L.R. 901.

66 Case 379/87, *Groener v. Minister for Education* [1989] ECR 3967, [1990] 1 C.M.L.R. 401.

67 Opinion May 16, 1989.

VI. Free Movement of Non-Economic Individuals[68]

Article 3(c) EEU states as a general objective of the Treaty that the Union shall abolish as between Member States obstacles to the "freedom of movement for persons, services and capital." The Articles which specifically implement this treaty goal concern only persons as economic actors, namely workers (Article 48 *et seq.*) and people seeking either to establish themselves or to provide services in another Member State (Articles 52 *et seq.* and 59 *et seq.*). There are no substantive provisions in the Treaty of Rome concerning the wider aspects of the free movement of persons. Payments connected with international tourism are, however, dealt with in Article 106(3) and Annex III of the EEC Treaty. Tourism implies the traveling of individuals who do not have any intention of exercising economic activities during their stay abroad. To what extent can an individual tourist, when crossing a Union border, benefit from rights granted under the EEC Treaty? Does the goal set out in Article 3(c) go wider than the regulation of workers and *providers* of services? Union law has developed in two ways. Firstly, the Court has placed a broad interpretation on the free movement of the individual. Secondly, the European Council has realized the political value of creating a European Union free from internal barriers, thus presenting a favorable image and identity in the eyes of the citizens of the Member States. This is reflected in the changes brought about by the Single European Act.

A. Development of the Right to Free Movement

The first example of secondary legislation extending its scope to cover free movement in a broad sense is Directive 64/220. This Directive (and Directive 73/148 which has replaced it) concerns the abolition of restrictions on movement and residence within the Union for nationals of Member States with regard to establishment and the provision of services. Article l(l)(b) provides that Member States shall abolish restrictions on the movement and residence of nationals of Member States wishing to go to another Member State as recipients of services. Article 1(1) of Directive 64/221 on the application of public policy measures to foreign nationals follows the same path. In this economic approach, one can consider individual tourists to be recipients of services when they travel and spend money abroad.

The political appeal of the concept of the free movement of persons in general caught the imagination of the European Council. The Heads of Government meeting in Paris in 1974 formulated the idea of establishing a passport union and the introduction of a uniform passport. This envisaged, *inter alia*, the abolition of passport controls within the Union. Progress in realizing such lofty objectives has at best been slow. Thus only in 1981 did the representatives of the governments of the Member States meeting in the Council agree to specific details concerning a uniform passport.

---

[68] Marc Van Der Woude and Philip Mead, *Free Movement of the Tourist in Union Law,* 25 C.M.L.R. 117-40 (1988).

Further progress was made at the Fontainebleau Summit of 1984. It was agreed to set up an *ad hoc* committee devoted to promoting and strengthening the image and identity of the Union *vis-à-vis* its citizens, by examining such matters as the abolition of all police and customs formalities concerning intra-Union borders. The conclusions of this committee—the Adonnino Report—and the objectives laid down in the Commission White Paper on Completing the Internal Market, further intensified the pressure for legislative progress. This was indeed recognized at the Milan Summit the following year and was linked to reform of the Treaties culminating in the Single European Act. Apart from the amendments incorporated in the Single European Act, concrete legislation or proposals accepted by the Council to date consist of Resolutions on the uniform passport, controls and the removal of border signs on internal borders. The more controversial legislation concerning the phased abolition of frontier checks and, consequently, the implementation of a regime concerning arms controls, as well as a general right of residence is still before the Council. Further harmonization has also to be agreed regarding the taxation of individuals on personal imports. The Commission has yet to submit proposals for a common regime concerning aliens.

The new Article 8A of the EEC Treaty, as added by the Single European Act, brings together both legal sources of Union competence governing the position of the individual. The second paragraph of Article 8A states:

> The internal market shall comprise an area without internal frontiers in which the movement of goods, *persons*, services and capital is ensured in accordance with the provisions of this Treaty (emphasis added).

The significance of Article 8A is that it appears as the first article of Part Two on the substantive provisions of the EEC Treaty. Thus, Article 8A now provides a sound legal basis upon which the Union may act when legislating for the free movement of the individual.

Apart from these developments in Union law, several Member States have already taken various significant initiatives to facilitate the free circulation of individuals. The most striking example is that taken by the Benelux countries within the framework of the Benelux Union Treaty of 1958. The declaration of the European Council at the Fontainebleau summit also provided the spark for a Franco-German initiative on the reduction of border controls, with a bilateral agreement being concluded on 13 July 1984. Shortly afterwards, the Benelux countries also met and, on 14 June 1985, the Schengen agreement was signed between the five countries, concerning the gradual abolition of checks at common borders. A sixth Member State, Italy, has also indicated a desire to become a party to the Schengen agreement. The Commission in particular has shown no objection to the pursuit of such a(n) (independent) strategy, but has welcomed the possibility of further integration.

B. What Are the Rights of the Union National Abroad?

1. Free Movement

The right to temporarily stay in another Member State is foreseen in Article 60(3), explicitly for providers of services, and implicitly, after the *Luisi and Carbone*[69] ruling, for recipients of services. This essential right derives from the Treaty itself and cannot be made dependent on the previous accomplishment of entry formalities other than those permitted by Union law. Directive 73/148 specifies the nature and scope of these formalities. Persons providing or in receipt of services, who are nationals of a Member State, are entitled to leave and enter a Member State on the mere presentation of an identity card or valid passport. Since 1 January 1985 the form of this passport has been unified. It is to be hoped that the introduction of the European passport will strengthen the idea of European citizenship and will facilitate the circulation of EEU nationals.

The right to stay in another Member State corresponds to the duration of the received service. A residence document (right of abode) has to be issued when the stay lasts longer than three months. In this respect, Directive 73/148 does make a distinction between individuals who establish themselves, who are to be granted the right of permanent residence (Article 4(1)), and individuals who provide (or receive) a service, who are to be granted "a right of abode as proof of the right of residence" (Article 4(2)). When applying for such a document, the applicant has to submit his passport or identity card and proof that he actually falls within the scope *ratione personae* of the Directive (Article 6). In such circumstances the individual may be required to establish proof of actual effective and genuine transactions by submitting concrete evidence, such as hotel reservations, lease or tenancy agreements. As stated above, the economic value of these transactions is not relevant.

Thus, individuals as beneficiaries of services are freely allowed to enter and leave Member States, though the right to stay as a mere potential recipient of services is limited to three months. During the period of stay, the host Member State may also impose the duty to notify one's presence (Article 4(2)).

Exceptions to the right of free movement may be justified only on grounds of public policy, public security and public health. These grounds can be invoked by a Member State within the limits set out by Directive 64/221. This Directive contains some substantive norms and procedural safeguards for the individuals concerned. Interestingly, the Commission did not attempt to argue, in reply to a Parliamentary question concerning the blocking of protesters from West Germany, Luxembourg and Belgium from entering France to demonstrate against nuclear power, that this was justified on public policy grounds. Rather, it was stated that clearly such people were not crossing the border to "carry out an economic activity or to obtain services." Recently, in response to newspaper reports concerning the intention of the government

69 Case 286/82, *Luisi v. Ministero del Tesoro*, [1984] ECR 377.

of the Land of Bavaria to introduce measures restricting the free movement of persons suffering from AIDS, the Commission declared that this would conflict with the Treaty, Directive 64/221 and the Resolution of the Council. The Commission spokesman stated that any measures taken with respect to EU nationals had to be non-discriminatory and in accordance with the Council Resolution proposing coordinated action.

While traveling abroad, individuals who are staying in a Member State may benefit from a special right. They are entitled to emergency medical treatment in all Member States. These individuals have however to fulfill several conditions. Firstly, they should be covered by the social security system of their own Member State. They also have to fill in, before departure, insurance form E 111 which should be handed over to the insurance institution of the Member State where treatment takes place. Reimbursement of medical costs is determined by the rules of this institution.

2. Non-discrimination

All beneficiaries under Union law can avail themselves of the fundamental principle of non-discrimination laid down in Article 7, as elaborated upon in Articles 59 and 60. Article 7 forbids discrimination on grounds of nationality both in law and in fact. Normally, individuals abroad will not need to resort to this protection provided by Union law. In most cases their contact with public authorities of the host Member State will be limited to the border checks carried out by the national authorities. The duration of their stay will often be too short to experience the application of discriminatory rules. Furthermore, states do not have any economic interest in discriminating against foreign nationals, since tourism is an important source of foreign currency.

The State may, however, treat foreigners differently if this is justified by an objective criterion. The obligation to present a valid passport or identity card, for example, can have a discriminatory appearance in Member States where nationals do not have to provide evidence of their identity by means of special identity documents. Nationals of those States, however, automatically possess the right to reside in their country. Special identity checks on foreigners are thus objectively justified to establish their right to reside or to stay there, as distinct from illegal immigrants.

Nevertheless, if an individual does get involved in legal difficulties, due to a car accident for example, he should in principle have access to the same procedures and facilities as are granted to nationals of the host Member State. Free legal aid, however, is at the moment not always available for foreign nationals. After ratification of the Hague Convention of 1980, persons habitually residing in one of the contracting States will be entitled to free legal aid for civil and commercial proceedings under the same conditions as nationals of other States. The Commission has made a proposal for a Council recommendation calling on Member States to ratify this Convention quickly.

Discrimination on grounds of nationality may also occur in relations between private persons. The Court has ruled on several occasions that the fundamental non-discrimination principle, as specified in Articles 45, 52 and 59 of the Treaty, can generate direct effect in these relations. Thus far, however, the Court has only elaborated on such horizontal direct effect with regard to collective private regulation. In any case, even when discrimination by private persons has occurred in individual cases, it would be cumbersome to invoke Union law and the discrimination may be hard to prove.

C. What Are the Remaining Restrictions?

In this section, reference will be made not only to Union proposals to eliminate present obstacles to free movement, but also to any progress made in the context of the Schengen Agreement.

1. Border Controls

Many Union citizens would consider that the difference in treatment between crossing an intra-Union border and any other West European border is small. The Council has in this respect taken a symbolic step. In order to make the Union citizen more aware that internal EEU borders are of a different nature, traffic signs with the words "customs," "Zoll," "douane" etc., are to be replaced by signs indicating the name of the Member State concerned on the background of the Union flag.

Border controls nevertheless remain. Several types of checks may be distinguished. In the first place, with respect to those checks related to the individual's identity, border officials cannot in principle require any other formalities than the presentation of a valid identity document. Travelers are not obliged to answer questions concerning the purpose of the visit, destination, duration etc., the provision of such information not being a prerequisite to the right to cross a border.

In the second place, border officials may seek to check the nature of the goods the individual carries. National legislation concerning the possession of arms and drugs differs considerably from one Member State to another. Diverging tax systems and VAT rates constitute another justification for such controls of goods. These fiscal problems will be discussed further.

Finally, border checks may be necessary to inspect the means of transport of the traveler. Since 1 January 1974 some progress has been made towards abolition of these checks. Directive 72/166 forbids Member States from systematically checking the green cards (the international motor vehicle insurance certificate) of vehicles registered in a Member State. As regards international transport of passengers by coach, some Member States still levy VAT on the transport service provided by a coach company on their territory.

Apart from these tax-related restrictions, the existence of border controls is closely related to the application of diverging national criminal law in general and rules concerning drugs and terrorism in particular. The abolition of these police checks necessitates harmonization of these rules and close cooperation between police authorities.

In its White Book on the completion of the internal market, the Commission envisages various measures to achieve the desired removal of internal border checks. It recommends, firstly, a standstill for all new formalities and the suppression of controls when leaving a Member State. Secondly it has submitted a draft Directive on the approximation of national laws concerning the possession of arms and proposes to do so as regards drugs. Finally, as already mentioned, the removal of internal police checks requires a common entry regime for non-EEU nationals and the general recognition of visas issued by Member States.

A quick adoption by the Council of all these pending and future proposals seems improbable. Terrorism and criminality are delicate matters in which Member States wish to remain sovereign. An effective response to criminality as a growing international problem also requires an international solution. The increasing importance of common external measures was reflected in the discussions at the European Council of London of 5 December 1986, where concern was voiced over terrorism, the misuse of asylum and illegal immigration.

In the meantime, the Council and the representatives of the Member States meeting in the Council have adopted a resolution on the easing of remaining border controls on persons in general. Nevertheless, the implementation of the objective of free passage for Member State nationals at internal borders is only foreseen at a "gradual" pace.

The Commission has submitted a draft Directive to the Council which provides a simplified procedure for Union nationals crossing an intra-Union border who comply with Union law concerning both the free movement of persons and the free movement of goods, in particular as regards the value or quantities of goods admitted free of taxes (draft Article 2; *see* Article 3 Schengen for a similar provision). These nationals will in principle benefit from free passage, whatever the mode of transport used (draft Article 3; preamble Schengen), with the exception of airports, where security checks may still generally apply. Member States are not prevented from carrying out spot checks and controls of a temporary nature in exceptional and specific cases, in particular for security purposes (draft Article 4). Nonetheless, this must not lead to an increase in the number of mobile units which replace the function of the abolished controls.

The principle of free passage would allow persons traveling in private vehicles to cross the border at reduced speed to enable the border authorities to carry out simple visual checks (draft Article 5; Article 2 Schengen). Such persons would be able to affix a special green disc with a letter E on the windscreen as a means of declaring that they comply with the conditions laid down in draft Article 2 (Article 6; *see* Article 3 Schengen). Member States would take the necessary measures to ensure that these visual checks will only be made at one checkpoint for the two adjacent Member States in either direction of traffic (draft Article 8; Article 8 Schengen).

Similar visual checks would be carried out at airports, where the Member States would establish channels designated by green signs for individuals who do not have anything to declare (draft Article 9). Private individuals traveling by train will only be subject to controls when declaring goods on their own initiative (draft Article 11).

Significantly, this draft directive is only regarded as a first stage in the abolition of border controls and formalities. The total abolition of such controls is only envisaged on the achievement of harmonization of legislation with respect to foreigners, further cooperation in the field of security and further fiscal harmonization in the area of value added taxes and excise duties. Of course, this will doubtless take some time.

2. Tax Problems

One of the most important obstacles to the free movement of goods in the Union is the absence of fiscal harmonization. VAT rates and excise duties differ considerably from Member State to Member State. These differences encourage many citizens to engage in cross-border shopping.

At present, Member States may levy indirect taxes on goods bought abroad by their residents. These goods may then be taxed twice: the first time in the Member State where the goods are bought and the second time in the Member State on importation. In order to avoid such generally applied double taxation, Directive 69/169 envisages a system of tax exemptions. Goods bought in the normal course of trade in a Member State cannot be taxed at the moment of importation in another Member State, provided that their quantity or value does not exceed the limits set out by EEU law. The actual tax exemption consists of goods up to a value of 350 ECU and a limited quantity of tobacco, alcoholic beverages, perfumes, coffee and tea. Whilst France and Germany have indicated their desire to raise the level of the exemption, Denmark has decided to reduce the amount of the exemption to 35 ECU for travelers who do not stay abroad for more than 24 hours and Ireland has abolished the exemption for travelers who do not stay more than 48 hours out of the country. The Commission has opened proceedings under Article 169 EEU with respect to these acts.

Problems for the Union traveler arise when he exceeds the limits of the tax exemption. The goods he imports above these limits may be taxed twice, since individuals cannot rely on Union law to obtain a refund of the VAT paid in the Member State of exportation. Individuals as final consumers are normally not to be considered as taxable persons in the sense of Article 4 of the Sixth VAT Directive for whom the Eighth VAT Directive envisages a special refund system.

The Commission has, however, proposed a 16th Directive on the harmonization of rules on VAT to be applied to goods imported by final consumers from one Member State to another Member State. A similar refund system for private individuals is envisaged in this proposal. Unfortunately, this proposal has not yet been adopted.

The Court of Justice has however mitigated this double taxation problem in respect of goods received, against or without payment in another Member State. The Member State of importation has to take into account the amount of VAT levied in the Member State of origin. This amount is still considered to be incorporated in the value of the goods at the moment of importation. The private importer has to prove the facts which justify the taking into account of this amount.

The latest Commission proposals for the internal market concern the removal of fiscal frontiers with respect to value added taxes and excise duties. Briefly, the Commission has proposed to harmonize the levels of VAT rates applied throughout the Union. It is proposed that VAT would be charged on most goods at a rate of between 14% and 20%. Certain goods and transactions—foodstuffs, energy products, water supplies, pharmaceutical products, books, newspapers and periodicals and passenger transport—would have a reduced rate of between 4% and 9% VAT applied to them. With respect to excise duties, the Commission has proposed uniform rates for alcoholic beverages and fuel oils in narrow bands of not more than 2% variation for tobacco goods. A compensatory mechanism is also envisaged to prevent distortions occurring where a Member State is a strong net importer or exporter of goods and services.

3. Currency Export Restrictions

In order to pay for the services he receives in another Member State, the individual will normally have to export currency in cash, checks or otherwise. The Court ruled in *Luisi and Carbone* that Article 106 guarantees the free movement of currency in order to pay for the services to be received. Indeed, if Member States were to restrict the currency exports by individuals, the freedom to receive and indirectly to provide services would be restricted. It should be noted that this liberalization covers only payments made in the currency of the Member State in which the creditor or beneficiary resides. Traveler's checks in US dollars and other means of payment in other currencies are not covered.

Member States are nevertheless still entitled to maintain capital export restrictions in respect of non-liberalized capital movements. They can also restrict already liberalized capital movements in specific circumstances when authorized by the Commission (Articles 73, 108 and 109 EEU). The effectiveness of such Member State restrictions would be limited, however, if each citizen could freely transfer currency under the pretext of being an individual tourist. Thus, the Court also decided in the same ruling that Member States are entitled to verify whether the transfer really does correspond to payments for services in another Member State. The Court stated, however, in this respect, that "the controls introduced for this purpose must be kept within the limits imposed by Union law." The controls may in particular not "limit payments and transfers in connection with the provision of services to a specific amount for each transaction or for a given period." Nor should they be applied in a manner so as to render illusory the freedom recognized by the Treaty or so as to subject the exercise thereof to the discretion of the administrative authorities. Fixing flat rate limits below which no verification is carried out and requiring proof that the amounts transferred have actually been used in connection with the provision of services do not, in principle, exceed the limits of Union law.

These requirements of proof can only be imposed *a posteriori*, after money has been spent by an individual. Indeed, having to prove pre-existing financial obligations would conflict with the capacity of the individual to be a potential recipient of a service.

D. Conclusion

At first glance it might appear doubtful whether the provisions of the EEC Treaty provide any protection for the individual traveling abroad in the Union. However, extensive interpretation of Articles 59 and 60 EEU by the Court of Justice with respect to *recipients* of services has removed any such doubts. This development was mirrored by the political initiatives of the European Council with respect to the establishment of a passport union and a People's Europe. Furthermore, Article 8A of the Single European Act provides an explicit substantive legal basis for the regulation of the position of the individual under Union law. Indeed, the Member States have committed themselves to completing the internal market in 1992, including the removal of internal borders restricting the free movement of goods, services, capital and persons.

Under Union law as it stands, individuals, as beneficiaries of services, can already benefit from the general principles of free movement and non-discrimination. However, many barriers still remain which prevent the full realization of these principles and the establishment of a true internal market.

The existence of comprehensive internal border controls, the lack of a common entry regime at the external borders, diverging national legislation concerning drugs, arms and taxes, and national capital export restrictions all indicate that the achievement of complete free passage for the individual in 1992 does not seem a particularly realistic prospect.

Chapter 6
Human Rights

I. Introduction

Human rights, as defined in the Universal Declaration of 1948, are an essential part of humanity's shared heritage, and where they are not genuinely respected, there can be no question of a lasting peace.[1] This is generally held to be sovereign issue, as it embraces all the economic, social, political and cultural aspects of a country's existence, fields in which states tend to be extremely sensitive and vigilant since they perceive them to be their vital interests.

This creates a knot which unravels in the relationships that develop between states. Initially based entirely on economic interest, it is only at a later stage in such relationships that the recognition of shared values allows countries to establish objectives of such nature which go beyond the merely economic, such as respecting and protecting human rights. The integration process initiated by the European Union has followed this pattern, and the Treaty on European Union (TEU) which entered into force on 1 November 1993 represents a particularly important step forward, as it provides a legal legitimacy for the incorporation of human rights as a key element of the Union's internal and external policies. Article F(2) TEU provides that:

> the Union shall respect fundamental rights, as guaranteed by the European Convention for the Protection of Human Rights and Fundamental Freedoms signed in Rome on 4 November 1950 and as they result from the constitutional traditions common to the Member States, as general principles of Community law.

The original Community Treaties were not concerned with human rights.[2] They were of a relatively narrow (economic) scope and at the time one could still consider it unlikely that the Union could infringe human rights at all. However, this may be, this context has now changed. First of all, because of the evolution of the Union's legal order and the growth of activity of the institutions, people's daily lives are more and more affected by Union law; rights of individuals are increasingly at issue and more

---

1 Daniela Napoli, *The European Union's Foreign Policy and Human Rights, in* THE EUROPEAN UNION AND HUMAN RIGHTS 29 (Nanette A. Neuwahl and Allan Rosas, eds. 1995). © 1995 Kluwer Law International. Reprinted by permission.

2 Nanette A. Neuwahl, *The Treaty on European Union: A Step Forward in the Protection of Human Rights?, in* THE EUROPEAN UNION AND HUMAN RIGHTS 1 (Nanette A. Neuwahl and Allan Rosas, eds. 1995). © 1995 Kluwer Law International. Reprinted by permission.

and more different human rights can become threatened. The creation of the Single Market is only one case in point: the abolition of frontier controls within the Union and the concomitant intensification of controls at its external borders and also within Member States raise questions of human rights, especially in relation to matters such as terrorism and organized crime, drug traffic, AIDS, refugees, racism and xenophobia.

Another reason for the Union to take fundamental rights into account is that the protection of human rights furthers the evolution of a European identity: Even if many people in these Western societies will live their lives without ever experiencing a violation of their fundamental human rights, the knowledge that one's rights are being protected and that one lives in a political society which takes such rights seriously stimulates the emergence of a group consciousness, which may go beyond national frontiers. From the viewpoint of a citizens' Europe of course the protection of human rights can be seen as one of the aspects which make Europe "meaningful."

Furthermore, an adequate protection of human rights also strengthens the Union in the relations with its Member States. The protection of human rights is a primary task which all Member States set themselves. If the Union does not actively protect human rights the Union legal order may come under pressure because the national courts, who regard fundamental human rights as inalienable, might refuse an application of Union law allegedly inconsistent with such principles.

Finally, if the Court of Justice of the European Communities (ECJ) in Luxembourg assumes full responsibility for ensuring the respect for human rights, it is in a position to construe the relevant Union law and its meaning in the light of such fundamental principles, and thus can ensure the uniform application of the law in the same way as it does with European Union law in general. The ECJ's concern with human rights can therefore also have a unifying effect as regards the law which is being applied. The same is true, of course, of an active stand by the Union legislator.

For all those reasons a concern with human rights in the European Union is amply justified.

A. Sex Discrimination[3]

1. Introduction

The principle of equality enjoys a special status under Union law. The Court of Justice has developed the principle of equality into a fundamental right under law, and the Union legislator has made that right available through a wide-ranging legislative code. The consequences of the special status accorded to the principle of equality may be seen mainly through the case law relating to equal treatment in terms and conditions of employment, though some cases on equal pay and social security will be discussed. Other principles and rights have been recognized by the Court which either conflict with, and must be reconciled with, the principle of equality or are compared

---

[3] Chris Docksey, *The Principles of Equality between Women and Men as a Fundamental Right under Community Law,* 20 Indus. L.J. 258-80 (1991). © 1991 Chris Docksey. Reprinted by permission.

and contrasted with it. The result is a constitutional code, which controls both national provisions on equality and even other Union provisions.

2. The Establishment and the Implementation of the Right

The Court announced in 1976 in the second *Defrenne* judgment that Article 119 has a double aim with a particular consequence:

> This double aim, which is at once economic and social, shows that the principle of equal pay forms part of the foundations of the Union.[4]

Two years later, in the third *Defrenne* judgment, the Court expanded the principle of equal pay into a general fundamental right of equality. It declared that "respect for fundamental personal human rights is one of the general principles of Union law. . . . There can be no doubt that the elimination of discrimination based on sex forms part of those fundamental rights."

These judgments recognized that there exists at Union level a general and fundamental right of equality between women and men. The settled view is that this right derives its force from Article 119, because of its status as primary Treaty legislation. However, Article 119, though it undoubtedly enjoys that status, is part of the *implementation* of the principle: it is not the *source*. It has been complemented by an advanced Union legislative code, which presently consists of the five equality directives on pay, employment and vocational training, aspects of statutory and occupational social security, and self-employment. All the legislation on equality, both primary and derived, directly embodies and is sustained by the principle of equality:

> Like Article 119 of the EEU Treaty, those directives [75/117 and 76/207] are of general application, a factor which is inherent in the very nature of the principle which they lay down. New cases of discrimination may not be created by exempting certain groups from the provision intended to guarantee equal treatment for men and women in working life as a whole.[5]

3. The Necessity to Embody a Fundamental Right in EU Legislation

Equality between women and men is a general principle of Union law, a "constitutional" principle which only exists in undiluted form at Union level, at the level of pure principle. It is a particular aspect of the principle of non-discrimination, one of the basic general principles which underpin the whole of Union law. These principles are often applied in direct actions based on Articles 173 and 215 of the Treaty as a protection against arbitrary action by the Union Institutions.

The Court has also recognized that fundamental human rights are "enshrined in the general principles of Union law and protected by the Court."[6] Rights protected have included privacy, property and religion. The Court has acknowledged two main

---

[4] Case 43/76, *Defrenne v. Sabena* [1976] ECR 455 at 472, ground 12.

[5] Case 248/83, *Commissions v. Germany* [1985] ECR 1459 at 1480, ground 16.

[6] Case 29/69, *Stauder v. Ulm* [1969] ECR 419 at 425, ground 7.

sources to which it will look for inspiration: national constitutions and constitutional traditions, and international standards, such as enshrined in the European Convention of Human Rights[7] and Social Charter[8] and ILO Conventions such as Conventions No. 100[9] and 111.[10]

In labor law, however, the only persons protected by such principles directly and without limit are, in effect, the staff of the Union Institutions. Staff cases on equality were cited by the Court itself to justify this premise in the third *Defrenne* case,[11] and have continued to serve to develop the law in this area. In contrast, the Court made it clear in the third *Defrenne* judgment that the principle of equality, albeit a recognized fundamental right, applies at national level only as and when it is embodied in specific Union or national legislation on equality. As only Article 119 was then in force, no remedy existed with regard to matters that fell outside "pay."

This marks the caveat to suggestions that progress may be made by relying on fundamental social rights existing at international level. Commentators have rightly pointed to the legislative block afflicting Union social policy, and have sought to devise ways of circumventing it, whether by way of creative use of the provisions inserted into the Treaty by the Single European Act or by way of creative litigation seeking to enforce other international instruments. Many of these international norms may also be found in the Union Charter, but it also is not Union legislation, just a statement of principles and an invitation to action. These international norms and principles have no direct legal impact; "rather they should be seen as a *source*."[12] Until derived Union legislation is adopted to embody them and put them into effect, one way or another, at national level, the Court will not directly apply them:

> Although it is the duty of the Court to ensure observance of fundamental rights in the field of Union law, it has no power to examine the compatibility with the European Convention of Human Rights of national legislation lying outside the scope of Union law.[13]

4. Other Rights Which Do not Enjoy the Special Status of the Principle of Equality

The recognition of the fundamental right of equality and implementation of the equality legislative code stands in stark contrast to the general labor law rights adopted so far and the treatment of those rights by the Court. Under Union law sex discrimination

[7] Case 30/75, *Prais*; Case 37/75, *Rutili* [1975] ECR 1219; Case 136/79 *National Panasonic.*

[8] Case 24/86, *Blaizot and University of Liège v. Belgium* [1989] 1 CMLR 57.

[9] *See* AG VerLoren van Themaat in Case 61/81, *Commission v. UK* [1982] ECR 2601 at 2621.

[10] Case 149/77, *Defrenne v. Sabena, supra*, at note 4, grounds 27-28.

[11] *Supra* at note 4, ground 29.

[12] Szyszcak, *L'Espace Social Européen: Reality, Dreams or Nightmares?* (1990) 33 German Yearbook of International Law 284, at 306.

[13] Case 12/86, *Demirel* [1987] ECR 3719, at ground 28.

and general labor law legislation are quite separate; indeed the equality legislation is not only autonomous from general labor law but, crucially, is far more developed.

In contrast, the labor law directives do not lay down a code; they are specific rather than general in nature; and they leave a great deal of discretion to Member States. There has only been a partial harmonization of labor law rights, which does not "aim to establish a uniform level of protection for the entire Union by reference to common criteria."[14] As a result, the collective right to information and consultation, though recognized as a fundamental right under various international instruments, notably the Protocol to the European Social Charter, has not yet been accorded the same status as the principle of equality. Individual employment rights have been protected, but they are limited both in their scope and in their potential for further development.

A different type of contrast may be made with the right of non-discrimination on grounds of race or religion. This undoubtedly exists in inchoate form at Union level, but specific primary and derived Union legislation only exists at present with regard to equal treatment on grounds of nationality. This does not directly cover discrimination in employment on grounds of race. Race is thus a good example of a fundamental right which may be recognized by the Court, an aspect of the general principle of equality which has not yet been specifically legislated into Union law. It will not be applicable at national level until it is embodied in appropriate derived Union legislation, possibly similar to that on sexual equality, and thereby brought from Union level into the national arena.

It is interesting to note that a series of apparently unconnected developments are taking place in this area. A political campaign in favor of such legislation has started, led by the Commission for Racial Equality. The Council adopted its Resolution of 29 May 1990 on the fight against racism and xenophobia, which *inter alia* requested the Commission to make a comparative study of laws against racism in the Member States. For its part, the Commission has recommended (again) that the Union itself accede to the European Convention on Human Rights. This development is part of a trend which may, one day, result in legislation embodying a new form of the principle of equality, at least with regard to discrimination in employment on grounds of race.

5. The Impact of the Fundamental Right of Equality

Wyatt has remarked that it is "now well established that when the Union acts as legislator, it is subject to the general principles of Union law, including those safeguarding human rights and fundamental freedoms. Union law may also subject the conduct of Member States to scrutiny according to such standards."[15]

a. On Union Legislation

The core of judgment in Case C-262/88, *Barber*[16] illustrates with regard to the principle of equal pay that the Union legislator may be precluded from validly adopting derogations from such fundamental principles. It confirms that occupational pen-

[14] Case 105/88, *Mikkelsen* (1986) 1 CMLR 310, with regard to Directive 77/187/EEC.

[15] Wyatt, *Enforcing EEC Social Rights in the United Kingdom* (1989) 18 ILJ 197 at 214.

[16] [1990] ICR 616; [1990] ECR 1889.

sions fall within the ambit of "pay" under Article 119 and thereby voids parts of directive 86/378/EEU on occupational social security and the "gap-filling" proposal of statutory and occupational social security. The Commission has considered the legal consequences of the judgment, but the final word in such matters will necessarily be that of the Court.

As both a general principle and a fundamental right, the principle of equality benefits from the rule of interpretation whereby Union legislation must be construed so as not to "produce results which are incompatible with the general principles of Union law and in particular with fundamental rights." This is strikingly reminiscent of the canon of construction developed for use by national courts in construing Union law.

b. On National Law

It is well known that national law, which is inconsistent with any directly effective provisions on equality, is inoperative or cannot be validly adopted, according to the concept of supremacy of Union law laid down in Case 26/62, *van Gend en Loos*. In Case 106/77, *Simmenthal*, the Court has further insisted on the duty of national courts to apply directly effective Union law rather than inconsistent national law. The Court has made clear in a series of cases that provisions of Article 119 and the equality directives have direct effect.

The duty to apply Union law is not limited to directly effective rights. In Case 14/83, *Von Colson*, the Court laid down a canon of construction for national courts, that: "in applying national law and in particular a national law specifically introduced to implement [a directive], national courts are required to interpret their national law in the light of the wording and purpose of the Directive."[17]

This case established what has been called the principle of "indirect effect," which has been most recently affirmed and extended, so as to cover both subsequent and prior national legislation, in Case C-106/89, *Marleasing*.

Nor is the principle limited to provisions of national legislation. In Case C-33/89, *Kowalski*, the Court has subjected collective agreements to the operation of the principle of equality. Rieland has noted that the objective of the equality principle must be achieved by leveling up the provisions concerned, not by simply eliminating them, as would have been the case under the German constitution alone.

The link between the Union and national systems is one that national courts and lawyers find difficult to cope with, as witnesses the need for a second 177 reference out of Ireland in Case-C377/89, *Cotter and McDermott*, or the House of Lords decisions in *Duke v. GEC Reliance*[18] and *Finnegan v. Clowney Youth Training Programme*.[19] There is a fundamental underlying point at issue, which may be understood as "whose law is it, anyhow?" Where matters concerning Union norms on equality in employment, vocational training and social security are concerned, it is the Union's law. Community lawyers must face up to the implications of a clear, entrenched con-

---

17 [1984] ECR 1891, at 1909, ground 26.

18 [1988] ICR 339 (HL).

19 [1990] IRLR 299 (HL).

stitutional right which they must respect, even in the face of an inconsistent Act of Parliament. There is no theoretical conflict: Union law operates through national law, indeed it *is* national law, but it has priority, whether over ministerial certificates, Crown privilege or statute.

6. The Developing Equality Code

The scope of the principle of equality is not fixed. It has developed and will continue to develop with the increasing sophistication of the Court of Justice and changes in the understanding of what constitutes "sex" discrimination. The definition of the principle of equality is open-ended: the equality directives define the principle of equal treatment as being "no discrimination whatsoever on grounds of sex either directly or indirectly." It is now obvious to most people that an employer may not lawfully dismiss a woman or refuse to appoint her to a post or promote her, just because she is a woman, but it was not so at the time of the equality legislation in the mid-70s. Ideas are developing all the time on what behavior is acceptable or at least not lawful, and what constitutes unlawful sex discrimination. Two specific examples exist, which it would have been unrealistic, if not impossible, to discuss even a decade ago.

a. Sexual Harassment

It is increasingly recognized that sexual harassment is a serious problem for women at work. The Report on sexual harassment prepared for the Commission concluded, *inter alia*, that sexual harassment can constitute direct discrimination on grounds of sex. This is because a worker may be treated in a particular way at work which is different to the way a worker of the other sex would be treated. As a result there may be a discrimination based on sex with regard to access to employment, vocational training, working conditions, or dismissal. This is in principle contrary to the Equal Treatment Directive and the national laws implementing it.

As a result of increasing interest in the problem, the then Irish Presidency proposed a Resolution on the Protection of the Dignity of Women and Men at Work, which was adopted by the Council on 29 May 1990. For the first time, there is Union recognition of the problem, a major boost for organizations on the ground such as WASH in the UK and AVFVT in France. The Resolution contains a definition of the unwanted conduct or practices which constitute sexual harassment, which makes it clear that sexual harassment may constitute employment discrimination contrary to the principal of equal treatment, and is designed to serve as an authoritative guide for national courts and tribunals. There is a commitment by Member States to carry out action as employers to address the problem, and encouragement to the Social Partners to include action to address the problem in their collective bargaining. The Resolution includes a request for further action by the Commission, the drawing up of a more detailed Recommendation and Code of Practice which were provisionally adopted on 3 July 1991, pending the Opinion of the Parliament.

b. Pregnancy

Does discrimination on grounds of pregnancy constitute direct discrimination on grounds of sex? The first cases that discussed this point, both in the USA and the UK, held that sex discrimination was not involved, because men cannot be pregnant, and there is therefore no way to compare a pregnant woman with a man. This approach has been overruled in both countries, by legislation in the USA and by case law in the UK. There is similar legislation in Denmark and case law in Ireland. In all these countries, pregnancy discrimination is direct sex discrimination. Pregnancy, or not being pregnant, is incapable of being a sex-neutral criterion.

The Court of Justice settled that pregnancy discrimination constitutes direct sex discrimination under Union law in its judgments of 8 November 1990 in Case 177/88, *Dekker v. VJV-Centrum,* and Case 179/88, *Hertz v. Aldi*. In *Dekker*, a woman was not hired because she was pregnant and because her employer would not be able to receive state funding to pay for a replacement during her maternity leave, due to the rather confused Dutch social security rules on this matter. In *Aldi,* a woman suffered from post-confinement complications, and was dismissed after being ill for more than a hundred days within a year, well outside the maternity protection period. Both cases held that pregnancy discrimination constitutes direct sex discrimination, but in *Aldi* the Court left the maternity protection period to be governed by national law.

In *Dekker*, the Court also held that there is no requirement of fault by the employer or absence of "grounds of exemption provided by national law." This is a welcome decision; it confirms that fault has no role in direct sex discrimination proceedings. It has provoked a debate in Germany[20] and the Netherlands[21] on how to ensure that national law on compensation, which would normally allow an employer to excuse its fault in such circumstances, conforms with the holding. Fresh legislation will probably be required to override existing legislation with regard to compensation for sex discrimination in both jurisdictions.

7. Exceptions from the Principle of Equality

It has been noted that "although the Court accepts that the principle of equality is a fundamental one, it is not absolute and may on occasion have to be reconciled with other principles which the Court regards as equally important." However, the derogations and the exceptions from the principle of equality have been limited to what is expressly permitted by the directive concerned or implicitly permitted following general principles of Union law. The express derogations must be interpreted as strictly as possible to what is required to achieve their legitimate aim.

a. Sex as a Determining Factor

Article 2(2) of Directive 76/207 permits Member States to exclude from the scope of the principle of equality "those occupational activities . . . for which, by reason of their nature or the context in which they are carried out, the sex of the worker constitutes a determining factor." Article 2(2) was intended to allow Member States to exclude activities or occupations which obviously fall outside the scope of sex discrimination,

---

20 Shaw outlines the situation in Germany in *European Judicial Method: Its Application to Sex Discrimination Law* (1990) 19 ILJ 228.

21 *See* Asscher-Vonk (1991) 20 ILJ 152.

such as actors, tenors, models and wet nurses. It is however deliberately open-ended: Article 9(2) of the directive requires Member States to periodically review the scope of the excluded activities and decide whether in the light of social developments they are still justified, and to notify the Commission thereof. There has been an ongoing debate both at national level and between the Commission and Member States as to how far the derogation may legitimately extend at any time.

Many Member States have drawn up a statutory list of permitted exclusions to make it clear what falls within this exception, such as Article 7 of the Sex Discrimination Act. Others, however, had laid down a general exclusion, sometimes modeled on the wording of Article 2(2) itself, which permitted employers to set their own criteria for determining what may be excluded. In Case 248/83, *Commission v. Germany*, the Court held that a legislative catalogue or list of exceptions was not necessary under Article 2(2), but that it was necessary to provide information to the Commission—a "complete and verifiable list, in whatever form, of the occupations and activities excluded"—under Article 9(2) of the directive, to allow the Commission to effectively monitor its application. Germany and the Netherlands duly drew up a national list, inspired *inter alia* by the lists existing in other Member States. But there is a significant difference between the two measures: the German Catalogue is not legally binding on the labor courts in the same way as the list in the Dutch Regulation. It is just a communication to the Commission. The question must remain whether the obligation is simply to provide information on the exceptions to the commission, or whether the exceptions must be delimited in some way, for example, by according a certain status to the list. The Dutch authorities thought it necessary for the list to be legally binding, for example. The potentially ambiguous ruling of the Court may be understood in this light, that Article 2(2) simply "does not have as its object or its effect to require the Member States to exercise that power . . . in a particular manner."

The only complaint successfully raised in that case concerned the scope of the Directive. The Court held that the public sector was covered by the Directive, employing the familiar technique of establishing an important precedent whilst holding that in the circumstances the public sector was adequately covered by the directly enforceable constitutional and public service guarantees of equality enshrined in the Basic Law, in particular Article 3 paragraphs 2 and 3. The holding that the principle of equality is of general application was undoubtedly an important development in the recognition of the special status of the principle of equality. However, the judgment establishes that the Commission must arrive with hard proof of damage arising out of an inconsistency between the Union and national texts, so-called misapplication, of a Directive. This may be compared with the situation concerning non-application, where the Commission simply has to demonstrate an absence of legislation. In effect, the Court has increased the burden of proof on the Commission with regard to alleged misapplication. The judgment is a salutary example of the Court's sensitivity in dealing with provision of national Constitutional provisions.

The Court has made it clear in subsequent judgments that blanket exclusions from the principle of equality are not permitted and must be specifically justified, even when relating to sensitive areas such as prisons and the police. In Case 222/84, *Johnson v. RUC*, the UK unsuccessfully argued that there is a general derogation implicit in the Treaty for all measures covering public safety. The Court held that the various Treaty provisions concerning public safety were of too "limited" and "exceptional" a nature to justify such a proposition. It seems to have implicitly contrasted these limited provisions with the general nature of the right of equality, and preferred the latter. The Court held, however, that public safety may justify a derogation under Article 2(2), if it is proved to be necessary in the specific case, and if it conforms to the principle of proportionality:

> That principle requires that derogations remain within the limits of what is appropriate and necessary for achieving the aim in view and requires the principle of equal treatment to be reconciled as far as possible with the requirements of that [aim].[22]

It may be that Union law has moved on since *Johnston*, and the test of proportionality itself has become stricter, so that it must be shown that there is no other way of achieving the aim which is less restrictive of the principle of equality. One should also note that one is dealing here with a direct derogation from a fundamental principle—"a derogation from a human right as fundamental as that of equal treatment must be appraised in a restrictive manner." As a result, it is difficult to imagine how to argue that public safety in Northern Ireland could only be effectively protected by restricting general policing to men equipped with fire-arms.

b. Protective Legislation for Women

Johnston also concerned the second area of derogation from the principle of equality permitted by the Directive at Article 2(3) concerning in particular the protection of maternity and pregnancy. Once again, the Court adopted a strict approach, and took a narrow view of what national protective legislation for women may be justified:

> Article 2(3) . . . must be interpreted strictly. It is clear from the express reference to pregnancy and maternity that the directive is intended to protect a woman's biological condition and the special relationship which exists between a woman and her child . . . the directive does therefore not allow women to be excluded from a certain type of employment on the ground that public opinion demands that women be given a greater protection than men against risks which affect men and women in the same way . . . .[23]

The Commission discussed the implications of this decision in its 1987 Communication on Protective Legislation for Women. It listed all the national and international protective provisions known to it and subjected them to an analysis of the requirements of the Directive, particularly Articles 3(2)(c) and 5(2)(c), which require Member States to revise protective legislation which is no longer justified. The Commission

[22] [1986] ECR 1651, at ground 38.

[23] [*Id.* at] ground 44.

concluded that many of these national protective laws for women listed were in fact no longer justified and that they should be extended to both sexes or repealed. "Protective legislation should in principle be consistent across sexes and across occupational areas."[24]

The effect of protective legislation on women's employment opportunities is illustrated by the case of *Page v. Freight Hire Tank Haulage*,[25] where a woman heavy goods driver was dismissed on health and safety grounds both against her wishes and in a situation where it was not established that the product being hauled was more dangerous to a woman than to a man. The dismissal was justified under section 51 of the Sex Discrimination Act, which provided for an unacceptably wide exclusion from the scope of the principle of equality, principally with a view to safeguarding health and safety provisions from the effects of the Act.

c. Retirement Age

It used to be thought that Directive 76/207 did not cover discrimination in retirement age, because Article 1(2) thereof, excludes social security matters from its scope, leaving them for subsequent legislation. Directive 79/7 deals with equal treatment in statutory social security schemes, but Article 7 thereof specifically excludes retirement age from its scope. As a result, when Mrs. Marshall wanted to complain of dismissal because she was over retirement age, it was generally thought that she was wasting her time, because of the exclusion. However, she persisted, at her own expense initially, and finally succeeded before the Court of Justice. The Court held that "in view of the fundamental importance of the principle of equality of treatment" the exclusion of social security from the ambit of Directive 76/207 "must be interpreted strictly."[26] As a result, there is a difference between retirement age concerning dismissal, which is covered by Article 5 of Directive 76/207, and retirement age concerning access to a pension, which is excluded from Directive 79/7. The UK has equalized the retirement age with regard to sex discrimination and unfair dismissal protection[27] and subsequently with regard to redundancy protection.[28]

Two more cases on the overlap of these two Directives have now arisen: Cases C-63/91, *Jackson v. Chief Adjudication Officer*, and C-64/91, *Cresswekk v. Chief Adjudication Officer*. In both, the need to apply a strict construction to the exclusion of social security matters from Directive 76/207 will be examined again.

The consequences of this aspect of the *Marshall* judgment show the importance of ensuring that all legislation concerned, and not just that directly implementing the directive concerned, must be brought into line therewith. After *Marshall*, the Employment Protection (Consolidation) Act 1978 had to be changed as well as the Sex Dis-

---

24 COM (87) 105 final, of 20 March 1987, at page 23.

25 [1981] IRLR 13 (EAT).

26 At ground 35.

27 Sex Discrimination Act 1986.

28 Employment Act 1989.

crimination Act 1975. This obligation on Member States to avoid discrimination in legislation was applied to indirect discrimination in pay by Case 171/88, *Rinner-Kühn*. These cases exemplify a more holistic approach to the law, whereby it is not sufficient to monitor specific implementing legislation of the equality directives, but an examination is required of all the diverse pieces of national legislation potentially affected. So far the Court has dealt with retirement age and protective legislation for women. Now the EOC has commenced proceedings for judicial review against the Employment Secretary to challenge the discrimination contained in the thresholds of eligibility for access to certain employment rights in the Employment Protection (Consolidation) Act.

d. Clash of Rights

Some decisions by the Court have been less welcome to the Commission, but can be reconciled none the less with the fundamental rights analysis developed by the Court. The Court is sensitive to other general principles and fundamental rights, and will accord them priority over the principle of equality where necessary. In Case 165/82, *Commission v. UK*, the Court considered various exclusions from the scope of the Sex Discrimination Act.[29] The Court held that, in principle, the exclusion of private households or small employers was contrary to Directive 76/207, since the Directive does not provide such exclusions. However, it does admit the possibility of a derogation under Article 2(2): derogations to the principle of equality may be justified insofar as they are necessary to reconcile its effect with that of another fundamental right, such as respect for private life; and such limitations must be specifically justified. Otherwise they fall outside the scope of Article 2(2) and are unjustified by reason of their generality.

Applying these criteria, the Court held that the UK had shown nothing to justify a general exclusion of private households or small employers. However, the Court accepted that the exclusion of male midwives from the scope of the act was justified "at the present time" in order to protect the woman's right to respect for her "personal sensitivities," subject to the requirement under Article 9(2) to keep this exception under review.

The protection of the mother after confinement and the special relationship of the mother and the young child have been given priority over the rights of fathers and adoptive fathers on a similar basis.

In the event, the Member States concerned have, for the most part, subsequently changed their laws, even though they were not obliged to do so. The UK (and Ireland) included male midwives within the statutory protection against discrimination; Germany changed its *Mutterschutzgesetz* to open up the period outside maternity leave reserved to the mother to both sexes, as parental leave. In Italy, the Constitutional Court has underlined the objective of protecting the interests of the very young child. Where the mother cannot carry out the necessary function because she is dead or severely incapacitated, it has held that the restrictive provision previously protected by the Court of Justice is unconstitutional to the extent that it prevents the father from hav-

---

[29] [1983] ECR 3431.

ing access to "maternity" leave and even+ to rest periods, and so ensure the care and development of the young child.

e. Conflict between Union and International Obligations

A particular problem arises where national legislation is contrary to a Union provision, but is in conformity with and indeed may implement another international obligation. A topical and sensitive example of this conflict is night work for women. France, like four other Member States, has legislation outlawing night work for women in accordance with ILO Convention No. 89 (revised) on Night Work for Women. In Case 345/89, *Ministèere Public v. Stoeckel*, an employer was prosecuted for employing women at night pursuant to a collective agreement. In his defense, he pleaded that Article 5 of the equal treatment Directive had direct effect, rendering the ban on night work for women laid down by Article L213-1 of the Labor Code void or inoperative on this point. He emphasized that France had already been condemned once by the Court for failing to respect the requirements of 76/207 relating to protective legislation.[30]

In its judgment of July 25, 1991 the Court confirmed its holdings in *Marshall* and *Johnston*, that Article 5 is directly effective and that the exceptions to the principle of equality are strictly limited to physiological differences between women and men. The Court was unimpressed by arguments by France and Italy that the greater need to protect women from aggression at night or the need to take account of their heavier family responsibilities justified legislation limiting night work for women. Appropriate measures to take account of the danger of aggression could be devised "without affecting the fundamental principle of equality of treatment between men and women."[31] The Court went on to cite Case 184/83, *Hofmann,* as authority for the fact that it had already held that "the directive did not have the objective of settling problems of family organization or of changing the division of responsibilities within couples."[32]

However, there was a further issue in this case, that France's legislation was not purely national in inspiration but implemented its obligations under Convention No. 89. This raises an interesting issue of Union constitutional law under Article 234 of the Treaty. This states that Member States' international obligations are not affected by those Union obligations. There is, however, a duty to eliminate any such incompatibilities. So it was commonly thought that the Treaty preserves its formal supremacy over Member States' law, even as derived from international obligations, but gives them a breathing space to do something about it. As a result, France's prior international obligations under Convention No. 89 were unaffected by the equal treatment Directive, so that there was only an obligation to eliminate the incompatibility between the two, for example, by denouncing the Convention. Which is what the Commission, albeit rather discreetly, recommended to Member States in 1987.

Neither the Court nor Advocate General Tesauro followed this approach. The Advocate General argued that Article 5 was directly effective, and interpreted the

---

30. Case 312/86, *Commission v. France* [1988] ECR 6315.

31. [*Id.* at] ground 16, unofficial translation.

32. [*Id.* at] ground 17, unofficial translation.

Directive in such a way that carrying out its provisions is not incompatible with the obligations under the Convention. The Directive does not require Member States to allow women to work at night, but simply to treat them in the same way as men. So France could have left in place its restrictions on women's work, as required by the Convention, so long as it did not discriminate in favor of men, for example, by extending the same rules on night work to men. If this caused difficulty, it was always open to France to denounce the Convention.

The Court simply omitted to discuss the issue of Article 234. Its silence on this point may imply that it has accepted the Advocate General's approach, in view of the consequences of its holding on the direct effect of Article 5 of the Directive and its failure to *disagree* with the Advocate General's reasoning. In any event, the result is that French Courts must ensure that there is no discrimination between the sexes with regard to the protective provisions at issue (the Commission has cautiously recommended in the Communication on Protective Legislation that, in effect, the protection for women should not be abolished but rather extended and equalized). Another French Court has now specifically requested the Court to consider the implications of Article 234 and Convention No. 89 for French law (Case C-1168/91, *Levy*).

f. Economic Considerations

One area where the Court has been too willing to limit the operation of the principle of equality is where Member States have stressed the negative economic or financial consequences of a decision in a particular case. As has been noted, the UK and Ireland appeared in the second *Defrenne* case to stress the negative consequences of a holding of direct effect of Article 119 (which did not seem to concern the other Member States, none of which appeared, not even Belgium, the Member State concerned). Similar arguments were advanced in *Barber*. The Court accepted the force of the arguments, as in the *Defrenne* judgment, and thus limited the temporal effect of the judgments in those cases to prospective cases. In effect, it sought to balance the principle of equality and the principle of direct effect on the one hand with (uncosted) economic arguments and the principle of legitimate expectation based on the fact that employers and Member States may have been lulled into a false sense of security.

A similar compromise approach can be seen in the judgments in *Dekker* and *Aldi*. There is no logical difference between discrimination on grounds of pregnancy or discrimination on grounds of post-confinement complications. However, the financial consequences of a broader holding in *Aldi* would have been open-ended, whilst the financial consequences of *Dekker* are necessarily limited to the finite period of pregnancy. The Court therefore left Member States to settle the period of maternity protection, in the absence of a Union norm. *Aldi* was simply an unfortunate test case to bring before the Court of Justice, because, on the facts, the period outside the maternity protection period was just too long. It might well have been differently decided if the complainant had been dismissed a few days or weeks outside the national maternity protection period.

The Court's deference to economic considerations is particularly evident when a Member State pleads the allocation of limited financial resources as objective justification for indirect discrimination in social security, as the Case 30/85, *Teuling Worms,* and Case C-229/89, *Commission v. Belgium*. It is difficult to understand why the Court is prepared to allow Member States such a large margin of discretion, and the latest judgment has been justifiably criticized. However, the judgments are not complete aberrations from principle. They reflect two factors which weaken the impact of the principle of equality, particularly when taken together, with regard to social security. In the second *Defrenne* judgment, the Court held that the objectives of Union policy on equality are both social and economic. This was a step forward, as Article 119 was mainly economic in its inspiration. Thus, the Court is at least prepared to try to reconcile the conflict inherent between the two objectives where it arises as the important factor in the balance. The legislation on equality in social security suffers from an extra disadvantage, namely, that it has a "progressive" nature and thus a partial rather than a general scope. The Court seems to have taken the view that, as Union jurisdiction over policy in this sphere is limited, it should defer to national policy considerations, and has allowed the economic argument full sway. This "tension between the 'economic' and the 'fundamental principle' approaches" is very much one of the "unresolved issues of principle and policy" in this area. Like general labor law rights, it is clear that further Union legislation on statutory social security schemes is required.

8. Direct Effect–Undoing the Damage (Continued)

The holding in the *Marshall* decision, confirming that directives are capable of vertical but not horizontal direct effect, is well known, and the present author has already discussed some of the attempts to undo the damage. In the present context, it is notable that the Court refused to give special treatment to the concept of direct effect, even where the principle of equality was concerned. Only subsequently did the inconsistencies arising from this approach become apparent to the Court, since when there has been a series of decisions limiting the damage of that holding.

Case C-188/89, *Foster v. British Gas*,[33] concerned British Gas before it was privatized, and its then retirement policy which obliged women to retire at 60 whilst men could remain until 65. The women had been dismissed before the 1986 Sex Discrimination Act equalized retirement ages in employment. So the question arose whether they could rely on Article 5 of Directive 76/207 to protect them, as in the case of Mrs. Marshall. The Court offered two criteria for deciding what was an "emanation of the State": where a body is "subject to the authority or control of the State" *or* where it has "special powers beyond those which result from the normal rules applicable to relations between individuals." Thus the Court permitted a wide interpretation of the concept of state employment, so that the function and not the form may equally well be determinative of a body's status. This open-ended approach avoids the danger that individuals may lose their rights when a public service organization with "special powers" is privatized. The Equal Opportunities Review has noted that this "alternative tests" approach would "serve to mitigate to some extent the harsh effects of the Court's decision in *Marshall*." No doubt that was the Court's intention.

The latest and potentially the most significant limitation of the consequences of *Marshall* may be found in the recent decision in Case C-208/90, *Emmott v. Minister*

33 [1990] IRLR 353; [1990] ECR 3313.

for Social Welfare and Attorney General.[34] That case concerned a complainant who received less benefit than a man would have done in equivalent circumstances between the entry into force of Directive 79/9 in December 1984 and the implementation of the necessary Irish equalizing legislation in 1986. The direct effect of the provision concerned was not at issue in this case; it may be regarded as settled law, particularly after the two *Cotter and McDermott* cases.[35] *Emmott* raised a procedural point, whether a woman can be barred from enforcing her rights because she presented her claim out of time. The Rules of the Superior Courts in Ireland require that a claim for judicial review must be brought within three months from the date when the grounds for the application first arose—in this case, the date of entry into force of the Directive in December 1984—unless there are good reasons for extending the time. Mrs. Emmott did not present her claim in time because she only learnt about her rights in 1987, when she heard about the first *McDermott and Cotter* judgment. She then contacted the Irish authorities and was given to believe that her claim would be settled as soon as the doubts raised in the second set of proceedings in Case C-377/89, *Cotter and McDermott,* were resolved. When she did institute proceedings in 1987, the Irish authorities denied her claim and pleaded that, in any event, she was statute barred from presenting it.

The High Court asked whether it is contrary to the general principles of Union law to permit the Irish authorities to rely on the national rules on time limits and delay to defeat Mrs. Emmott's claim. General principles must be applied because there is no harmonized system of Union procedures. Established Union law allows Member States considerable discretion in establishing the procedures for implementing Union-derived rights, subject to two safeguards: the procedures governing recourse to a Union-derived right must not be less favorable than for similar claims regarding purely national rights; and they must not be framed so as to render virtually impossible the exercise of the Union-derived rights.

The European Court adopted a radical approach, and held that time does not start to run until the date when national implementing legislation is correctly adopted. It commenced by restating the "minimum guarantee" of the doctrine of vertical direct effect—that a Member State should not be permitted to benefit from its own failure to implement a Directive—and its consequences with regard to procedural requirements, that a Member State is not justified in "absolving itself from taking in due time implementing measures appropriate to the purpose of each Directive. Until a Directive has been correctly transposed, individuals are unable to ascertain the full extent of their rights." Only from that date is the individual able to react, and as a result the time limits only begin to run from that date.

The Court specifically put aside the logical consequence of the vertical direct effect theory, that individuals may rely on directly effective rights much earlier than such transposition. In the present case, these rights should have become eminently clear, at least to anyone taking proper legal advice, from the date of the first *Cotter and Mac-*

[34] [1991] IRLR 387.

[35] Case 286/85, *McDermott and Cotter v. Minister for Social Welfare and Attorney General* [1987] ECR 1453; Case C-377/89, *Cotter and McDermott v. Minister for Social Welfare and Attorney General* judgment of 13 March 1991, not yet reported.

Dermott judgment. But the Court held that a national limitation period may not begin to run until a Directive has been "properly transposed." Whilst the operative part of the judgment is limited to the case in point, concerning a directly effective right, the approach developed in the body of the judgment is not limited to directly effective provisions of the equality Directives. If so, it may be that anybody may lodge a complaint once the necessary legislation has been passed. In this respect, the judgment may have enormous implications. The existence of a more general judicial objective has been pointed out, that the Court's use of direct effect and leveling up in cases such as *Cotter and MacDermott* has the effect of penalizing Member States for not fulfilling their obligations in due time. *Emmot* would tend to support such an analysis.

9. Perspectives for Legislative Progress

The legal basis of the Maternity Proposal, Article 118A, fulfills Hepple's prediction in 1987 that Article 118A may be capable of justifying initiatives (the other being sexual harassment). His concern at the inadequacy of health and safety as a general legal basis for labor law initiatives remains justified, however. Even if it is successful as a legal base for the Maternity Proposal, neither Article 118A nor the other Treaty provisions inserted by the Single European Act will ever be enough on its own, no matter how broadly the latter may be interpreted. Whilst there is always scope for a purposive interpretation of a Treaty provision when searching for a legal basis, so that it may not be appropriate "to cling too closely to the wording" but rather to give precedence to its "aim and purpose, the *ratio legis*";[36] there are still clear (and deliberate) limits to the scope of the new Treaty bases which make them inadequate for general purposes.

As a result, there can only be significant legislative progress in equal opportunities and labor law when the new democratic procedures (cooperation procedure with the Parliament and Council majority voting) are specifically extended to apply more generally. Otherwise, whilst it will no longer be necessarily impossible to adopt social legislation on a unanimous basis (the decade of the absolute veto is probably over), the compromises necessary to secure unanimity will inevitably result in watered down and unsatisfactory legislation.

The new Union Treaty will probably make it possible for some progress to be made. The greater acceptance of equality policy makes it likely that it will be made easier to enact equality legislation, possibly on the basis of a modified Article 119. With regard to general labor law legislation, there is room for cautious optimism that the unanimity rule will be loosened, whether by way of a list of matters to which the co-operation procedure is applied or the creation of a new strengthened qualified majority procedure for social issues.

10. Conclusions

1. Equality policy is one of the few relatively successful and advanced employment policies at Union level. It enjoys a general measure of acceptance and an autonomy from general labor law which means that developments in one area do not

[36] Per Advocate General Mayras in Case 68/86, *UK v. Council* [1988] ECR 855 at 885.

necessarily affect the other. The major difference between the two areas of policy is not the difficulty in adopting new legislation—unanimity is so far required for legislation in both areas. It is rather that the legislation on employment equality has established a general code, sufficient for the law to be developed by case law in the absence of new legislation. In contrast, further legislation on general labor law—and, exceptionally, on equality in social security—is required before there is a sufficient legislative code which can be purposively interpreted. It is not enough for individual and collective rights to exist at national or international level, or as inchoate fundamental rights. In designing strategy for the future, one should take account of the fact that equality in employment is primarily a legal issue, and may obtain relatively swift results through a litigation strategy, whilst labor law remains primarily a legislative issue, and must be addressed through the political arena.

2. In the legal arena, the principle of equality has generally received sympathetic treatment by the Court. The Court genuinely would like to "do good"; it is justifiably proud of itself and its development of the principle of equality as a fundamental right. It will favor that interest over others in cases that come before it, even to the extent of subordinating competing legal principles. However, unless there is good reason, it will not go further than it has to in order to ensure protection of the right to equality in the circumstances of the case.

3. It is notable that the Court has mainly developed the law in this area by way of preliminary rulings under Article 177. This has made it possible for equality agencies, trade unions and pressure groups to use Union law as a tool in pursuing their domestic legal strategies. It has also made it easier for the Commission itself to influence development of the law than would have been possible under Article 169 alone. It is quicker, and it allows the Commission to act as an advisor to the Court rather than a prosecutor subject to the heavy burden of proof created by the Court itself.

4. The constitutional code laid down by the Directives on equality is an organic code becoming more sophisticated with time. Directive 76/207 specifically incorporates the idea of changing norms with regard to its exceptions. As the meaning and requirements of Union law develop and change, national courts will be required to interpret domestic law in step with those developments, and national legislatures to deal with any inconsistencies or gaps that may remain.

B. Social Security

1. Free movement of workers and social security[37]

a. Minimum Income Benefits

Minimum income benefits are a relatively recent phenomenon in the history of social welfare provision. Traditionally social security systems were based on the insurance principle. A person paid his contributions and received in return the right to certain

---

[37] Philippa Watson, *Minimum Income Benefits: Social Security or Social Assistance?,* 10 E.L. Rev. 334-43 (1985). Reprinted by permission.

benefits. The cost of these benefits was met by the contributions of the insured person, his employer and a subsidy from the State. Social assistance on the other hand, was a discretionary benefit designed to meet the needs of those who were uninsured under the social security system and whose resources were insufficient to cover their needs. Social assistance is financed wholly out of public funds. It is generally regarded as a "safety net" for those who, for whatever reason, are not entitled to social security benefits and who have no other means of income. Social security benefits are usually granted as of right in return for contributions: no inquiry is made into the resources of the claimant. Social assistance, on the other hand, is a discretionary payment awarded as a privilege to those who cannot provide for themselves.

Recent developments in the sphere of social welfare have lead to a change in attitude regarding the role of social welfare provision in the EU society. It is now generally acknowledged that society should guarantee a basic minimum income to all its members as a right regardless of whether they are or ever have been economically active.

This has led to the introduction of minimum income benefits in many of the Member States of the Union. These minimum income benefits may be confined to specified groups of persons, such as the elderly or the handicapped or may be payable to the population as a whole. The level of minimum income benefit is fixed from time to time by law. Persons who satisfy the competent authorities that their income falls below that deemed to be the minimum on which they should be required to live are entitled to claim such benefits as they need to bring their income up to that level. Minimum income benefits therefore have a dual function: they can either supplement other sources of income, such as social security benefits, or they can in themselves form the sole source of income for beneficiaries.

The problem of the entitlement of migrant workers and their dependents to minimum income benefits arises because of the hybrid nature of such benefits. In many cases, it is unclear whether they are social assistance benefits or social security benefits.

The question of entitlement of migrant workers and their families to such minimum income benefits has been the subject of a number of requests for preliminary rulings stretching back over the past 13 years. The first batch of cases came before the Court in the mid-seventies. In the last two years the Court has again been confronted with the problem of whether such benefits can be assimilated to social security benefits and so be deemed to fall within the scope of Regulation 1408/71 or must they be regarded as social assistance?

The Court has held in several cases[38] that the distinction between benefits which are excluded from the scope of Regulation 1408/71 and benefits which come within it rests entirely upon the characteristics of each benefit, in particular its purpose and the conditions for its grant and not on the fact of whether or not the benefit is classi-

[38] Case 139/82, *Paolo Piscitello v. Istituto Nazionale della Previdenza Sociale (INPS)* [1983] ECR 1427, Case 261/83, *Carmela Castelli v. Office national des pensions pur travailleurs salariés (ONPTS)* (not yet reported), Case 249/83, *Vera Hoeckx v. Centre public d'aide sociale de Kalmthout* (not yet reported), Case 12284, *Scrivner and Cole v. Centre public d'aide sociale de Chastre* (not yet reported), Case 157/84, *Frascogna v. Caisse des dépôt et consignations* (not yet reported).

fied under national law as a social security benefit. There is, therefore, no definition in Union law of what constitutes a social security benefit for the purpose of Regulation 1408/71. The scope *ratione materiae* of the Regulation depends upon an objective assessment of each benefit.

In carrying out this assessment the Court has set out two criteria which must be satisfied before a benefit will be considered to fall within the scope of Regulation 1408/71:

1. The legislation under which the benefit is granted must place claimants in a legally defined position as a result of which they have an absolute right to benefit as opposed to a conditional right dependent upon the exercise of discretionary power in their favor.

2. The benefit must cover one of the risks enumerated in Article 4, paragraph 1 of Regulation 1408/71. A benefit which is general in nature, that is which grants as of right a minimum income to all citizens, such as the Belgian Minimex, will not fall within the scope of Regulation 1408/71.

Two other points are worth noting with respect to minimum income benefits and their relationship to Regulation 1408/71:

1. The purpose of the benefit may be twofold. It can guarantee a minimum income to persons who are outside the scope of the social security system and at the same time it can provide a supplementary income to persons who are entitled to social security benefits, the sum total of which falls below the level of the minimum income. There is no requirement to the effect that the benefit must be the sole source of welfare available to the recipient.

2. The *Biason*[39] case appeared to rule that where a minimum income benefit supplemented a social security benefit, it was exportable but otherwise it was not. The Court's ruling in *Piscitello*[40] moved away from its position. It emerges quite clearly from *Piscitello* that whenever a benefit falls within the scope of Regulation 1408/71, it is exportable by virtue of Article 10: there is no question of limiting the right to export minimum income benefits to those payable by way of supplement to social security benefits.

In conclusion, it may be stated that minimum income benefits fall within the scope of Regulation 1408/71 if they relate to one of the branches of social security referred to in Article 4 of the Regulation and if they are awarded as of right to claimants who satisfy all the conditions for entitlement. Should a benefit fail to satisfy this criteria, it may constitute a social advantage within the meaning of Article 7, paragraph 2, of Regulation 1612/68 and therefore be available to the migrant workers or the members of his family who reside in the Member State under whose legislation it is claimed. It will not, however, be exportable.

---

39 Case 24/71, *Caisse régionale d'assurance maladie deParis v. Biason* [1974] ECR 999.

40 Case 139/82, *Paolo Piscitello v. Istituto Nazionale della Previdenza Sociale (INPS)* [1983] ECR 1427.

2. The Right to Welfare: Equality and Equity under Union Law[41]

The rising tide of EEU law in the field of rights for workers and their families has cast up on national shores a number of cases involving the principle of equal treatment. Often EEU law is invoked as a longstop, to remedy possible deficiencies in national law; occasionally it is raised as a measure of last resort, when there is no EEU content at all. The scope of EEU protection in this field is neither clear cut nor fully understood by national courts, whose attitudes swing from the over generous to the downright mean. This uncertainty is hardly surprising, since there is no doubt that the European Court has extended the protection offered by EEU law far beyond its original scope as expressed in the EEU Treaty and secondary legislation. This is particularly true in the sphere of what may loosely be called social welfare.

The term social welfare has been chosen to embrace the many benefits in cash or kind, however financed, which are made available usually, but not necessarily, by a State to its citizens, either in the form of social security provision or "social aid" in the form of supplementary benefits in cash or kind, concessionary rates and rebates, loans, grants, or other benefits. These benefits are costly, and, in times of economic recession and high unemployment, cast an increasingly heavy burden on the working population. States are understandably reluctant to provide such benefits to foreign residents, especially where their residence is temporary. To what extent are EEU citizens or their families resident in a State other than their home State entitled to these benefits? To what extent, and on what basis, is a State, or perhaps a private person, free to deny them?

Article 7[42] EEU lays down the basic principle of non discrimination on the grounds of nationality. This was described in *Uberschar*[43] as merely a "specific enunciation of the general principle of equality. This principle requires that similar situations shall not be treated differently unless the differentiation is objectively justified." A State is free under EEU law to make whatever social provision it pleases, provided it is not discriminatory. The prohibition is on all forms of discrimination, both overt and covert. In the field of social welfare it usually takes the form of a nationality or residence requirement as a precondition for eligibility.

However, the prohibition on discrimination is not universal. It applies only "within the scope of application of the Treaty, and without prejudice to any special provision contained therein."

Article 7 was held in *Walgrave and Koch*[44] to apply only in the context of economic activity, whether in the form of "gainful employment or remunerated services." The principle of equal treatment as expressed in Articles 48(2), 52(2) and 60(3)

---

[41] Josephine Steiner, *The Right to Welfare: Equality and Equity under Community Law*, 10 E. L. Rev. 21, 21-41 (1985). © 1985. Reprinted by permission.

[42] Art. 7 provides: "Within the scope of application of this Treaty, and without prejudice to any special provisions contained therein, any discrimination on the grounds of nationality shall be prohibited."

[43] Case 810/79, [1980] E.C.R. 2747.

[44] Case 36/74, [1975] 1 C.M.L.R. 320.

is designed to guarantee equality of treatment to nationals of EEU countries who seek to work or supply services in a State other than their own. Article 48(2) provides for the "abolition of any discrimination based on nationality between workers of the member states as regards employment, remuneration and other conditions of work and employment." Article 52(2) governing freedom of establishment requires that EEU nationals seeking to pursue activities as self employed persons or to set up and manage undertakings must be allowed to do so "under the conditions laid down for its own nationals by the law of the country where such establishment is effected" . . . Article 60(3) provides that the person providing a service may . . . "pursue his activity in the state where the service is provided under the same conditions as are imposed by that state on its own nationals." In the field of social security Article 51 empowers the Council of Ministers to "adopt such measures in the field of social security as are necessary to provide freedom of movement for workers." Article 51 does not expressly incorporate the principle of equality; but unlike Articles 48, 52 and 60 it expressly extends to workers' dependents.

These broad principles have, as required by the Treaty, been further expanded by secondary legislation. The principle Regulations governing social welfare are Regulation 1408/71 and Regulation 1612/68. The rights to equal treatment for the worker and his family are still rooted in his status as a worker, but they are amplified. Regulation 1408/71, which governs rights to social security, is based on Articles 2[45] and 7 as well as Article 51; its preamble is expressed broadly in terms of "guaranteeing within the union firstly equality of treatment of all nationals of member states under the various national legislations and secondly social security benefits for workers and their dependents regardless of their place of employment or of residence." Regulation 1612/68, which implements the principles of Article 48(2), extends its protection to the worker's family, asserting in its preamble that

> the right of freedom of movement, in order that it may be exercised, by objective standards, in freedom and dignity, requires that equality of treatment shall be ensured in fact and in law in respect of all matters relating to the actual pursuit of activities as employed persons and to eligibility for housing, and also that obstacles to the mobility of workers shall be eliminated, in particular as regards the right to be joined by his family and the conditions for the integration of that family into the host country.

In addition to these two Regulations, Directive 68/360, which implements Article 48(3)(*b*) and (*c*), grants to the worker and his family rights of entry and residence, and Regulation 1251/70, implementing Article 48(3)(*d*), governs the rights of the worker and his family to remain permanently in the host state, either on retirement, disability, or, in the case of family, the death of the worker. Whilst they do not expressly relate to welfare benefits they will, as will be demonstrated, be highly relevant to the ques-

[45] Art. 2 requires the Union to promote "a harmonious development of economic activities, a continuous and balanced expansion, an increase in stability, an accelerated raising of the standard of living and closer relations between the states belonging to it."

tion of whether, in the event of a claim to benefit, the equality principle will apply. Article 7 of Regulation 1251/70 provides that: "The right to equality of treatment, established by Regulation 1612/68, shall apply to persons coming under the provisions of this Regulation."

Any claim to equality of treatment in the field of social welfare must therefore be based either on the Treaty or the above Regulations, particularly Regulation 1408/71 and Regulation 1612/68. What then is the scope of these Regulations, with regard to the persons covered and the types of benefit to which the equal treatment principle will apply? To what extent has its scope been enlarged by the European Court?

a. *The Legislative Provision*

i. Regulation 1408/71

The aim of Regulation 1408/71, which implements Article 51 of the Treaty, is to promote the free movement of workers, both employed and self-employed, by coordinating, rather than harmonizing, national social security schemes. It achieves this by the application of two principles; the principle of aggregation and the principle of a payment of benefits to persons resident in the territories of Member States in the Union. Rights under this Regulation are attached to worker and members of his family and his survivors.[46] "Worker" is defined in Article (*a*)(*I*) as "any person who is insured, compulsorily or on an optional continued basis, for one or more of the contingencies covered by the branches of a social security scheme for employed persons." "Member of the family" is defined as "any person defined or recognized as a member of the family or designated as a member of the household by the legislation under which benefits are provided."[47]

The benefits to which the Regulation applies are laid down in Article 4(1). These are sickness and maternity benefits, invalidity benefits, old age benefits, survivors' benefits, benefits in respect of accidents at work and occupational diseases, death grants, unemployment benefits and family benefits. The Regulation applies to all general and special social security schemes, whether contributory or non-contributory.

There is an express exclusion in Article 4(4) for "social and medical assistance, benefit schemes for victims of war or its consequences or special schemes for civil servants and persons treated as such." The Regulation offers no definition of social assistance.

Article 3(1) lays down the basic equality provision. It provides:

> subject to the special provisions of this Regulation, persons resident in the territory of one of the Member States to whom this Regulation applies shall be subject to the same obligations and enjoy the same benefits under the legislation of a Member State as nationals of that State.

---

46 Also Stateless persons and refugees residing within the territory of one of the Member States as well as members of their families and their survivors, (Art.2(1).).

47 Art. 1(*f*), not cited in full.

Article 13 lays down the single state principle and the general rule of *lex laboris*. The applicable law governing social security benefits is the law of the State in which the worker is employed. The "competent institution" which will be responsible for payments, is the institution with which the person is insured; the competent state is "the state in whose territory the competent institution is situated." So whilst the social security schemes covered by the Regulation need not be contributory there would appear to be a clear correlation between the fact of insurance and the benefits provided.

Article 10, implementing Article 51 (*a*) EEU, lays down the principle of exportability. It provides:

> Save as otherwise provided in this Regulation, invalidity, old age or survivors' cash benefits, pensions for accidents at work or occupational diseases and death grants acquired under the legislation of one or more Member States shall not be subject to any reduction, modification, suspension, withdrawal or confiscation by reason of the fact that the recipient resides in the territory of a Member State other than that in which the institution responsible is situated.

Rights to equal treatment for both the worker and his family will thus depend on the benefit being of the type covered by the Regulation plus the fact of insurance and residence. With regard to certain categories of benefit, once a benefit is granted, it may not be withdrawn should the recipient transfer his residence to another Member State.

ii. Regulation 1612/68

Like Regulation 1408/71, Regulation 1612/68 applies to EEU workers and members of their family. But "worker" is defined as "employed person,"[48] and the family is expressly defined to include the worker's "spouse and their descendants who are under the age of 21 years or are dependents, and dependant relatives in the ascending line of the worker and his spouse."[49] The Regulation does not cover the self employed.

Title 2 headed "Employment and equality of treatment" provides for equality of treatment for the worker in respect of "any condition of employment and work" including, "should he become unemployed, reinstatement or re-employment."[50] Article 7(2) entitles the worker to "the same social and tax advantage as national workers," and Article 7(3) provides for equality of access for the worker to "training in vocational schools and retraining centers." Article 9 entitles him to "all the rights and benefits accorded to national workers in matters of housing, including ownership of the housing he needs."

Title 3, headed "Workers' families" "gives the worker's spouse and children under 21 or dependant children rights to install themselves with the worker and to take up any activity as an employed person" and Article 12 gives worker's children resident in the host State rights of "admission to that State's general educational, apprentice-

---

[48] Art. 1(1).

[49] Art. 10(1).

[50] Art. 7(1).

ship and vocational training courses under the same conditions as nationals." Member States are also required to "encourage all efforts to enable such children to attend these courses under the best possible conditions."[51]

Prima facie then, both the worker's and his family's rights rest firmly on his economic contribution as a worker (and presumably taxpayer) or insurer, and the family's rights on their relationship to the worker. In both cases, but particularly Regulation 1612/68, the families' rights appear narrower and more specific than the workers'.

Whether intentional or not the legislative scheme outlined above clearly contained lacunae both in regard to the persons covered and the benefits to which the principle of non-discrimination might apply. This factor, plus the wide variation between Member States in what is regarded as social security and social assistance and the absence of any definition or agreed criteria to distinguish between the two, the application in Regulation 1408/71 of different definitions of members of the family, inevitable in the absence of harmonization, was bound to give rise to cases of inequality and injustice, seriously undermining the principle of free movement of workers. It was not therefore surprising that the European Court was quick to fill the gaps and has, over the years, deployed a formidable array of techniques and arguments to remedy the legislative deficiencies.

b. The European Court's Response

i. Regulation 1408/71

It is clear that a worker need not be currently working or contributing in order to claim benefits under the Regulation. Indeed, the Regulation expressly provides for unemployment. As long as he is or has been "subject to the legislation of one or more of the Member States" and is a national of one of the Member States he will be covered by the Regulation.

What was less clear was whether the rights granted by the Regulation attached to the worker or his family only when he moved to another State in order to work. This was held not to be the case in *Hessische Knappschaft v. Singer,*[52] where the Court held that: "It would not be in conformity with [The spirit of Article 51] to limit the concept of 'worker' to migrant workers *stricto sensu* or solely to workers required to move for the purpose of their employment."

However, the main difficulty arising from Regulation 1408/71 with regard to welfare benefits lay in distinguishing between social security, to which the equality principle of Article 3 will apply, and social assistance. Since social assistance is not a term of art, and Member States differ in their categorization of such benefits, States issued a declaration, in accordance with Article 5 of Regulation 1408/71, listing the benefits deemed to be covered by social security. The European Court has opted for the best of both worlds, holding that the fact that a particular benefit is included in a State's declaration is conclusive proof that it is a social security benefit, whilst the fact that it is not so included is not. Arguments based on national legal systems are irrelevant;

---

[51] Art. 12, para. 2.

[52] Case 44/65, [1966] C.M.L.R. 82.

in deciding whether a particular benefit is social security or social assistance, recourse must be had to criteria based on Union law.

The second, subsidiary problem, law in ascertaining whether, even if a particular benefit could be classified as social security the claimant is a person to whom this category of benefit is intended to apply.

A further problem lay in the question of exportability. Assuming that the requirement *ratione personae* and *ratione materiae* are satisfied, is this a benefit to which Article 10 will apply?

The first problem arose before the Court for the first time in *Frilli,*[53] in the context of a claim in Belgium by an Italian, who had worked and retired in Belgium, for a guaranteed income, paid as a supplement to the old age pension. The benefit was non-contributory and payable according to need to men and women over retirement age, to Belgian nationals or persons from countries with which Belgium had a reciprocal agreement. Mr. Frilli's claim was rejected, and he appealed, claiming discrimination, contrary to Article 3.

Advocate General Mayras pointed out the difficulties:

> In view of the developments which have taken place, firstly in social security, a tendency in general to guarantee a minimum income, and secondly in assistance, the recognition of real personal and guaranteed rights, the search for sufficient criteria, enabling a distinction to be drawn between the two concepts appears to yield disappointing results.

The Court, closely following his submissions concluded that:

> Although it may appear desirable, from the point of view of application of the Regulation, to draw a clear distinction between legislation concerning social security on the one hand and assistance on the other, the possibility cannot be excluded that some laws may fall into both of these categories, because of their scope in relation to individual cases of their objectives and of their methods of implementation, and thus escape overall classification. In some of its features, legislation on guaranteed income is akin to social assistance, especially when need is the essential criterion in its implementation and there are no conditions of employment, of affiliation and contributions; but it is nevertheless close to social security in that, by not considering each case on its merits, it gives all beneficiaries a legally defined position giving them a right to benefit similar to old age pensions.
>
> In view of the wide definition of the people entitled to benefit such a legislation fulfills in fact a double function, which is on the one hand to guarantee a minimum income to persons who are entirely outside the social security system, and on the other hand to provide supplementary means to persons whose supplementary benefits are insufficient.[54]

[53] Case 1/72, [1973] C.M.L.R. 386 (claim made under Reg. 3).

[54] Para. 13, 14, 15 the "*Frilli* formula": (cited in full in view of its influence on subsequent case law).

The definition of benefit in Article 1(*s*)[55] must be understood in its widest meaning. The benefit must in this case be regarded as social security.

Frilli represents the first cautious step by the Court in paring down the social assistance exclusion. Contrary to Advocate General Mayras' suggestion that in order to qualify as social security a benefit need not be tied to the claimant's status as a worker, the Court's Judgment was strictly circumscribed:

> *vis à vis* an employee . . . who has performed periods of work in a Member State, permanently resides there and is entitled to a pension, the legislation in question falls within the field of social security . . . even if such legislation falls outside this field so far as concerns another category of beneficiaries.

The reasoning in *Frilli* was followed verbatim in *Callemeyn*,[56] in the context of a claim by Mrs. Callemeyn, a French woman, married to a Belgian and working in Belgium, for a special grant for the handicapped. She was already in receipt of social security, and was claiming the grant as a supplement. The grant was payable independent of contributions or employment to Belgian citizens. Her claim was rejected on the grounds of her nationality, and she claimed discrimination contrary to Article 3 of Regulation 1408/71. Was this social security, an invalidity benefit within 4(1)(*b*), as she claimed, or was it, as the Belgian authorities claimed, social assistance? The Court, applying the *Frilli* formula, found that the benefit in question performed a double function of minimum income and supplementary means and assimilated the grant to an invalidity benefit. As in *Frilli*, eligibility was dependant on her status as a worker.

In *Costa*,[57] the Court was faced with a similar claim for a grant for the handicapped in Belgium, this time by the Italian wife of a Belgian worker. She was denied the benefit on the grounds of nationality and invoked Article 3 of Regulation 1408/71. Clearly she was a member of the family of a worker. But was it a "family" benefit? Entitlement in *Frilli* and *Callemeyn* was expressly confined to workers. For this reason Advocate General Reischl thought her claim was not covered by Regulation 1408/71. This was not a family benefit. "This was purely personal claim based on residence alone." The Court disagreed. Ignoring the limitations of *Frilli* and *Callemeyn*, it again applied the "*Frilli* formula," assimilating the benefit to an invalidity benefit. Since it conferred on the claimant a "legally defined position not requiring a consideration of each case on its merits, a characteristic feature of assistance," it would be deemed to be social security.

The question of eligibility for members of the family was again tested in *Fracas*.[58] This claim too was a claim for a benefit for the handicapped, in Belgium by the 14-year-old son of an Italian worker. The benefit was not prima facie a "family" benefit, nor was it supplementary. It was payable independent of contributions and available

[55] Of Reg. 3, now Art. 1(*t*) of Regulation 1408/71.

[56] Case 187/73, [1974] E.C.R. 553.

[57] Case 39/74, [1974] E.C.R. 1257.

[58] Case 7/75, [1975] 2 C.M.L.R. 442.

to the whole population, subject to a nationality and length of residence qualification. Fracas' claim was rejected. Could he invoke the equality provision of Article 3? If so, would he continue to be eligible when he achieved adult status and was no longer a "member of the family" according to Belgian Law? The limitation of *Frilli* to workers was strongly argued. Advocate General Trabucchi's approach was cautious. He sought to distinguish this benefit from the benefit in *Frilli*; the legislation in question was not intended to have a general application; it applied only to a special, strictly limited category of persons. Fracas *fils* could therefore claim it under Regulation 1408/71. But . . . "There may be obstacles in admitting a principle automatically extending to members of the family all the benefits provided by social security legislation of a general nature. . . ."

The Court in its Judgment expressed no such reservations, and was content to follow *Costa*. The judgment was, however, closely reasoned. The Court invoked Articles 2, 7 and 51 of the Treaty, and argued from the 5th Recital to the preamble to Regulation 1408/71 and Regulations 1612/68 and 1251/70. Since these regulations gave the family a right to reside and, eventually, to remain permanently, neither the worker nor his family must be treated less favorably than nationals of the host state. This must apply even when the child of a worker ceases to be a minor . . . were it not so the worker would be induced not to remain, contrary to the principle of free movement of workers.

Inzirillo[59] was the inevitable sequel to *Fracas*. This time the claim, in France, was for a benefit for the handicapped by the adult son of an Italian working and resident in France. The benefit was payable only to French nationals. His claim was rejected by the French authorities, on the grounds that he was not a French citizen; nor was he entitled to invoke Regulation 1408/71. As an adult he was not a "member of the family" under French law. The Court followed the reasoning in *Fracas*, arguing from Inzirillo's rights to reside in France under Article 10 of Regulation 1612/68 and to remain permanently under Regulation 1251/70. He was therefore entitled to invoke the equality provision of Article 3 (of Reg. 1408/71). In support of their interpretation the Court cited the preamble to Regulation 1408/71 (5th Recital) and Article 7(2)[60] of Regulation 1612/68. Rights under Article 7(2) of Regulation 1612/68 must include, the court held, "every social and tax advantage" granted to workers in the host state.

The last three cases all concerned claims to similar benefits, the problem centering in *Fracas* and *Inzirillo* on their personal right to benefit. Once established in *Callemeyn* applying the *Frilli* formula that the benefits qualified as social security there was no need to pursue the distinction between social security and social assistance. This distinction did fail to be considered however in four subsequent cases, namely *Fossi*,[61] *Tinelli*,[62] *Gillard*[63] and *Even*.[64] All four cases concerned claims arising out of World

---

59 Case 63/76, [1978] 2 C.M.L.R. 596.

60 Entitling immigrant workers to the same "social advantages" as nationals.

61 Case 79/76, [1979] E.C.R. 667.

62 Case 144/78, [1979] 2 C.M.L.R. 735.

63 Case 9/78, [1978] 3 C.M.L.R. 554.

64 Case 207/78, [1980] 2 C.M.L.R. 544.

War II. Two of the claimants, Fossi and Tinelli, both Italians resident in Italy, were claiming special invalidity pensions payable by the F.D.R. to alleviate situations of hardship arising out of the second world war. Payment to persons residing abroad was discretionary. Following refusal of payment both claimed discrimination contrary to Article 3 of Regulation 1408/71. They failed. The Court in *Fossi* looked at the purpose of the provision. The purpose of the German law was to alleviate hardship arising from war. Moreover payment to persons residing abroad was discretionary. "Only benefits conferring a legally defined position involving no discretionary assessment of needs or personal circumstances[65] can be regarded as social security." The benefit lay outside the scope of Regulation 1408/71.

Identical reasoning produced the same result in *Tinelli*. In *Gillard*, closely followed by *Even*, the Court again applied the "purpose" test. Both cases concerned claims for a special rate advance old age pension payable to ex-prisoners of war under French and Belgian law respectively, which they claimed operated in a discriminatory manner against themselves as non-nationals. Gillard was a Belgian, even a Frenchman. They failed, because the purpose of the French and Belgian provision was a "a testimony of national gratitude" for hardships endured in captivity. In addition, their claim fell under the express exclusion of Article 4(4)—this was a scheme for "victims of war and its consequences."

The claimant in *Even*, no doubt daunted by the outcome in *Gillard*, also invoked Article 7(2) of Regulation 1612/68, claiming the facility was a "social advantage," to which he as a worker was entitled. Again he failed. The benefit "was not granted by reason of his status as worker or resident on national territory."

In all four cases the purpose of the provision benefit took it outside the sphere of social security. But there is little indication of what purpose must be served to bring a particular provision within this category. Some help was given in the case of *Vigier*.[66] This case concerned rights under the German reparation act; Mrs. Vigier had been born in Germany, and at the age of 10 had gone as a war refugee to France. She subsequently acquired French nationality and remained in France as a worker. She was affiliated to a French social security scheme. She wished to claim a right under the German Reparations Act, given to those in receipt of reparation compensation, as she was, to contribute retrospectively to a German social security scheme; eligibility depended on the claimant having been insured in Germany for a minimum of 60 months. She was unable to satisfy this condition and complained that the act was discriminatory, invoking Regulation 1408/71. Was this a social security benefit within Article 4(4)? The European Court held that since her rights under the Reparation Act "formed part of the body of law governing social insurance of workers" and did not "depend on a discriminatory appraisal of her personal situation and needs" the benefit was within the definition of social security.

---

65 *Frilli*'s (implied) interpretation of assistance as requiring a "consideration of each case on its merits" becomes one involving "no discretionary assessment of needs or personal circumstances."

66 Case 70/80, [1982] 2 C.M.L.R. 721.

In *Piscitello*[67] the Court reverted to the *Frilli* formula and also, following *Gillard* (*et al.*) looked to the purpose of the benefit and the conditions for its grant in the context of a claim for a "social aid pension" paid under Italian law to Italian nationals of 65 or over living in Italy whose income fell below a specified sum. It was payable alone or as a supplement to an existing but inadequate pension, and granted automatically to those in need and not in receipt of other social security benefits. Mrs. Piscitello, who was Italian, was in receipt of this pension in Italy. She was not claiming it, as was the case in *Frilli*, as a supplemental pension. She went to Belgium to live with her daughter and the pension was withdrawn. She invoked Article 10 claiming that the pension was a social security benefit and therefore exportable under Article 10. The Italian authorities claimed it was social assistance within Article 4(4), having been classified as such by the Italian Constitutional court. The European Court held that that factor was not sufficient in itself to exclude the benefit from the field of application of Regulation 1408/71. Since the legislation fulfilled a double purpose, providing a minimum means of subsistence to persons outside the social security system, and supplementing the income of recipients of inadequate social security benefit . . . since it conferred on the claimant a "legally defined status, not dependent on a discretionary assessment of needs" it fell within the field of social security. This being the case the pension would be assimilated to old age benefit and Article 10 would apply.

Here Mrs. Piscitello was claiming not as a worker, nor as the spouse of a worker. She was not claiming the pension as a supplement. She was entitled to benefit as an Italian citizen. But her claim under Article 10 of Regulation 1408/71 was as a member of the family of her daughter, who was living and working in Belgium. In deciding that she was a member of her daughter's family, Advocate General Mancinni, noting that definitions of member of the family differed according to the benefit concerned, applied the most convenience analogy in Italian social security legislation relating to family allowances.

All the successful cases considered so far have involved benefits which could without difficulty be assimilated to the social security benefits expressly covered by Regulation 1408/71. Their purpose could thus be described as "forming part of the body of law affecting the social insurance of workers." The benefit claimed in *Palermo*[68] was rather different, being a special allowance, non-contributory, payable in France to elderly mothers of large families. Part of the purpose of the provision was said to be to increase the French birth rate. Eligibility depended on both mother and children being of French nationality. Neither Mrs. Palermo nor five of her seven children were French. In refusing to grant her the benefit the French authorities sought to rely not on her (which they conceded they could not) but on her children's nationality.

The European Court on referral under Article 177 held that the benefit in question was social security benefit because it had been included in France's declaration under Article 5 of Regulation 1408/71. This must be accepted as "conclusive proof" of its nature. The nationality requirement for the children was indirectly discriminatory, since

---

67 Case 139/82, [1984] 1 C.M.L.R. 108.

68 Case 237/78, [1980] 2 C.M.L.R. 31.

any nationality qualification required of the children would mean that a mother could only benefit from the allowances in exceptional circumstances, i.e. when the children's nationality did not depend on their parents. Moreover the discrimination could not, as was argued, be objectively justified on the grounds of its purpose which was said to be to increase the French birth rate. "Regulation 1408/71 does not" the Court said "make any distinction between social security schemes to which it applies according to whether those schemes do or do not pursue objectives of demographic policy."[69]

This continual broadening by the European Court of both the categories of, and persons entitled to, benefit, has brought in its wake a third problem, the question of its exportability. If exportable, any refusal on the part of the competent authority to pay the benefit outside the competent state would be unlawful.

The principle, derived from Article 51(*b*) EEU, is stated in general terms in Article 10. But Article 10 is expressly confined to certain benefits, namely invalidity, old age and survivor's cash benefits, pensions for accidents at work or occupational diseases and death grants. The remaining benefits covered by the Regulation are catered for individually.[70]

As the Court pointed out in *Smieja*,[71] the purpose of Article 10 is to "promote free movement of workers by insulating those concerned from the harmful consequences which might result when they transfer their residence from one state to another." To this end the Regulation provides for the payment of benefits by the appropriate national authorities of the Member State in which the claimant resides, and reimbursement by the competent institution. Where long term benefits are concerned the principle of apportionment may operate to spread the cost over all the States in which the claimant has worked.[72]

With the assimilation to social security by the European Court of other "assistance" type benefits, not related to employment, affiliation or contributions, payable according to need, and often tied to the cost of living, came the question of whether these too might not be exportable. *Dicta* in *Frilli* seemed to indicate that rights to the benefit in question depended on residence,[73] although this could be construed as applying only to initial eligibility. However, in *Smieja* the Court found no difficulty in applying Article 10 to a Dutch old age pension scheme, originally, but no longer confined to workers, now available to the whole population. The claim was by a German national who had lived and worked in Holland and returned to Germany on retirement. The decision was, however, limited to its special facts. The questions referred to the Court under Article 177 were exclusively concerned with the meaning of Article 10 and its effect on national law. Also, as Advocate General Trabucchi pointed out, Mrs. Smieja's claim was based on retrospective credit acquired while she was a worker, so it was not to be compared with social assistance. The Court clearly assumed the benefit to be covered

69 A similar view was expressed by the court with regard to Art. 7(2) of Reg. 1612/68.

70 E.g. Sickness, Art. 19; Unemployment, Art. 69; Family benefits, Arts. 73, 74.

71 Case 51/73, [1974] 1 C.M.L.R. 620.

72 E.g. Pensions, Art. 46.

73 "*Vis-à-vis* an employee who . . . permanently resides there."

by Article 10, since it expressly limited the application of that article to "benefits of the type" mentioned therein.

The question of exportability was more fully discussed in *Biason*.[74] Here the claimant was also a worker, an Italian, living in France and in receipt of a supplementary pension payable to persons who received, as she did, disability pension in France. The supplementary pension was classified as social assistance under French law. Eligibility depended on residence in France. Mrs. Biason went to live in Italy and her supplementary allowance was withdrawn. In contesting the decision before the French courts two questions were referred to the European Court: first, was this supplementary pension social security within Regulation 1408/17? and secondly, if so, was it exportable under Article 10? The Court, applying the *Frilli* formula, found that since it conferred a statutorily defined status on the persons concerned, the benefit belonged to the social security system. National definitions were not relevant. With regard to the second question, Advocate General Reischl, clearly influenced by the Commission's opinion, suggested that there was "no question of the general application of the possibility of exportation provided in Article 10 to all cases of supplementary social security payments or guaranteed income." He acknowledged the practical difficulties which would arise for Member States from benefits being exported—"the necessity to assess incomes in another Member State, requiring far reaching collaboration: the fact that recourse may have to be made to the person liable to maintain or to an estate in another Member State." He noted *dicta* in *Frilli* that it was "the duty of the courts to ensure the protection of migrant workers in all cases where such protection is possible *without thereby upsetting national legal systems*." But he concluded that where the right to a supplementary benefit has been acquired, as was in the case here, by a worker resident and entitled in that state to a disablement pension national systems would not be upset and Article 10 would apply. The Court's decision was similarly circumscribed.

Pricitello,[75] already discussed, required an extension of the decision in *Biason* since the benefit in question was not being claimed by a worker, nor as a supplement to an existing pension, and was special old age pension of the type which Advocate General Reischl had thought in *Biason* to be outside Article 10, its application being likely to upset national social security systems. Both the Italian and the United Kingdom government drew the Court's attention to the disruption which would be caused to national systems should such benefits be payable abroad; no legal machinery for assessing income received in other Member States or for sharing costs existed. Advocate General Mancini was not convinced. Both Article 51 EEU and the principles of free movement argued against the restrictive interpretation urged by the Italian and the United Kingdom governments. The Court agreed. Since the benefit was assimilated to old age benefits covered by Article 10, and since the Regulation did not contain specific provisions relating to that pension, it must be presumed to be included.

Miss Biason was claiming as a worker; Mrs. Piscitello as an Italian citizen. Both were able to export their benefit because it fell by a process of assimilation within the

[74] Case 24/74, [1975] 1 C.M.L.R. 59.

[75] Case 139/82, [1984] 1 C.M.L.R. 108.

categories covered by Article 10. Is there any reason in logic why the same right may not be claimed for a similar benefit by a member of the worker's family? In *Fracas* (1974), decided between *Biason* and *Piscitello*, Advocate General Trabucchi was of the opinion that, since the father's residence alone provided the basis for the claim, the son's right would cease were his father to leave the country. Although this statement was hypothetical, in the context of the son remaining in the host state, the argument would apply a fortiori were the son to leave the country with his father.

It is uncertain whether the Court would take the same view today. In reaching a decision on the scope and applicability of Regulation 1408/71 the Court adopts a variety of approaches.

On the question of whether the benefit in question qualifies as social security the Court will examine the purpose of the provision and the conditions for its grant. Does it form part of the body of law governing the social insurance of workers? Does it confer on the claimant a legally defined position, not requiring a consideration of individual needs and circumstances/discretionary assessment of needs in the individual case? Does it fulfill a double function of basic income of supplementary means? Can it be assimilated to an existing social security benefit? If so, it will be deemed to be social security. Even if the purpose of the benefit is to pursue objectives of demographic policy this will not, following *Palermo,* take it outside the sphere of social security.

On this analysis there must be few benefits normally regarded by States as social assistance which would not qualify as social security. Moreover, national gratitude apart, the cases give little indication of what purpose must be demonstrated in order for a benefit to be deemed social assistance. The Court indicates that a benefit requiring a discretionary assessment of needs and circumstances would take it outside the scope of social security. However it could be argued that even discretionary benefits confer on the applicant a legally defined position to be considered for a particular claim according to objective criteria and the Court would be unlikely to countenance a refusal based on the claimant's nationality.

Similarly, on the question of the scope of Regulation 1408/71 *ratione personae*, it seems that a member of the family may now claim any benefit classifiable as social security available to the worker. "Member of the family" is given the widest possible meaning under the social security legislation of the State responsible for benefits, and has even been extended to include any dependent relative entitled to install himself with the worker or to remain permanently following the worker's retirement or death.

Perhaps the most surprising development, raising serious problems for Member States, has been the extension of the exportability principle of Article 10. Here the process of assimilation of social assistance type benefits to existing social security benefits threatens to widen the categories of exportable benefits to an extent which Member States would find administratively unworkable and financially unacceptable, at least in the absence of any machinery for apportionment of costs. Even the Commission in *Biason* commented on the "shocking results" which would stem from a "general application of the possibility of exportation provided in Article 10 to all cases of supplementary social security payments or guaranteed incomes."

ii. Regulation 1612/68

From the beginning, due to the uncertainty and apparent limitations of Regulation 1408/71, Regulation 1612/68 has been invoked as an alternative or supplementary source of rights both by the worker and members of his family. In addition, despite the court's generous interpretation of Regulation 1408/71, it is clear that a number of social benefits and advantages, such as certain kinds of grants, loans, special concessions and facilities cannot be construed as social security, and any rights to equal treatment must lie, if at all, in Regulation 1612/68. In either case the principal question lies in the scope of these rights with regard to the worker and members of his family.

Two questions in particular lay to be tested by the courts; first, just how wide were the rights extended to the worker? Was his right to equality of treatment in particular with regard to "social advantages,"[76] confined within the context of employment? If so, was this context to be understood in the broad or narrow, contractual sense? Secondly, were family rights limited, as they appeared to be, to equality of access to employment[77] and, for the children, *admission* to "educational, apprenticeship or training course?"[78]

Even on a literal interpretation of Regulation 1612/68 the rights accorded to the worker are not confined wholly within the context of employment. Article 9[79] extends to the field of housing, and Article 7(1) and (3) expressly contemplates situations of unemployment. As was to be expected, the European Court has construed the worker's rights equality of treatment in the sphere of employment in the widest possible sense. In *Ugliola*[80] it held, arguing from Article 48 EEU, that Article 7 of Regulation 1612/68 applied to all conditions of work and employment,[81] so that a condition which took account of periods of national service *in Germany*, thereby discriminating indirectly against non nationals, was unlawful. This view was approved and applied in *Marsman v. Rosscamp*[82] in the context of special protection with regard to termination of employment.

More difficult was the question of whether the "social advantages" covered by Article 7(2) were limited to advantages specifically connected with the claimant's status as a worker, i.e. work related benefits, or whether they extended to benefits available to the population as a whole, which the worker could claim by virtue of his status as an employed person. In *Michel S.*[83] both Advocate General Mayras and the court advocated this broad view.

---

76 Art. 7(2).

77 Art. 11.

78 Art. 12.

79 Art. 8 provides that "a worker . . . shall enjoy all the rights and benefits accorded to national workers in matters of housing, including ownership of the housing he needs."

80 Case 15/69, [1970] C.M.L.R. 194.

81 "The legal systems of each Member State must ensure for nationals of other Member States working within its territory all the legal rights it grants to its own nationals."

82 Case 44/72, [1973] C.M.L.R. 501.

83 Case 76/72, [1973] E.C.R. 457.

The question arose for decision by the Court in *Fiorini*,[84] in the shape of a claim in France by an Italian mother, the widow of an Italian who had worked in France, for a special fare reduction card issued by the French Railways to parents of large families. Since cards were available only to French citizens Mrs. Fiorini's claim was rejected. She claimed discrimination contrary to Article 7 EEU and Article 7(2) of Regulation 1612/68. The French Tribunal took the view that Article 7(2) was concerned exclusively with advantages granted to citizens within the ambit of or by virtue of work as employed persons. Since the benefit in this case was not so connected, Article 7(2) was not applicable. On a reference on appeal by the French Cour d'Appel the European Court took a different view, holding that:

> Although certain provisions in Article 7(1) refer to relationships deriving from the contract of employment, there are others . . .which have nothing to do with such relationships . . . Article 7(2) covers *all* social and tax advantages . . .whether or not attached to contracts of employment.

This interpretation was applied in *Even*,[85] where Article 7(2) was invoked as an alternative to Regulation 1408, to support a claim for a special rate advance pension payable to ex-prisoners of war. The claim failed because of the purpose of the benefit; awarded as a token of national gratitude it was not granted "by reason of (the claimants') objective status as workers or by virtue of the mere fact of residence on the national territory and the extension of which to workers who are nationals of other member states therefore seems suitable to facilitate their mobility within the union."

This "purpose" test was invoked subsequently by the defendant bank in *Reina*,[86] as a reason for justifying the refusal of a childbirth loan to a non-national worker and his wife. The loan was State financed, its twin purpose being to relieve poverty and counter the decline in the birth rate. Granting of the loan was discretionary, but limited to German nationals resident in nationality, and they appealed, invoking Article 7(2) of Regulation 1612/68. The bank claimed the facility was not covered by Article 7(2) since:

> (1) There was no connection between the grant of the loan and the recipient's status as worker;
> (2) The refusal of the grant to non-nationals would not affect the mobility of workers;
> (3) Payment of the loan was discretionary; it was not granted as of right;
> (4) It was issued for demographic purposes in the field of political rights.

[84] Case 32/75, *née Cristini*, [1976] 1 C.M.L.R. 573.

[85] [1980] 2 C.M.L.R. 544.

[86] Case 65/81, [1982] 1 C.M.L.R. 744.

Moreover the discrimination was justified on account of the practical difficulties of recovering loans from workers who return to their own countries.

Despite these formidable arguments, the Court, in the most cryptic of judgments, held that the grant was a "social advantage" within Article 7(2). The *Even* test ("granted by reason of the claimant's objective status as a worker or by virtue of the mere fact of residence") was cited, its limitations ("the extension must be suitable to facilitate the worker's mobility") ignored.

In reply to points 3 and 4 the Court held the term "social advantages" covered "not only benefits granted as of right but also on a discretionary basis." The demographic purpose of the grant did not justify discrimination.

Since the term "social advantages" is capable of bearing the widest possible meaning the Court had little difficulty in construing it in the sense most favorable to the migrant worker.

More problematic was the question of the scope of Regulation 1612/68 with regard to "members of the family." Members of the family are not prima facie entitled to the same "social advantages" as the worker, their only express entitlement being to install themselves (Art. 10) and to "take up any activity as an employed person" (Art. 11). Children are entitled to *admission* to the host state's "general education, apprenticeship and vocational training courses under the same conditions as nationals" (Art. 12).

The Court has not been deterred by these limitations. In *Michael S.* arguing from the 5th Recital of Regulation 1612/68 it held that a special benefit in cash or kind to assist in the rehabilitation of the handicapped claimed by the migrant worker on behalf of his severely mentally handicapped son was within Article 12. "The fact that Article 12 does not expressly refer to such benefits is not to be understood as denoting the intention to exclude those arrangements from the scope of the Regulation." Article 12 therefore embraced "measures which allowed the handicapped to realize or improve their aptitude for work, insofar as such measures concern the children of workers." However, both Advocate General Mayras and the Court expressed the view that members of the family were excluded from the application of Article 7(2).

In *Casagrande*[87] the Court was again faced with a claim under Article 12, this time for educational grants for the children of workers. This was an educational benefit, but hardly a matter of admission. Again arguing from the 5th Recital the Court held that Article 12 referred not just to admission to courses but to general measures to facilitate attendance. "The requirement of Article 12 (para. 2) that Member States are to 'encourage all efforts to enable such children to attend these courses under the best possible conditions' is intended to encourage special efforts to ensure that the children may take advantage on an equal footing of the education and training facilities available." This Judgment was followed on very similar facts in *Alaimo*.[88]

In *Fiorini*, contrary to the Court's view of the matter in *Michael S.* a member of the family succeeded in invoking Article 7(2). Advocate General Trabucchi argued by

---

[87] Case 9/74, [1974] E.C.R. 774.

[88] Case 68/73, [1975] 1 C.M.L.R. 262.

analogy with the Court's approach to Regulation 1408, as exemplified in *Fracas*.[89] He suggested that decisions taken under Regulation 1408 had blurred the line between benefits granted to the worker and to his family: the division between Articles 7-9, relating to the worker, and 10-12 relating to families must not be read too narrowly. An "advantage" to the worker was inseparable from an advantage to the family. The Court agreed, concluding that since the worker would have been entitled to claim the benefit during his lifetime it would be contrary to the purpose and spirit of Union rules on freedom of movement for the worker to deprive his survivors of benefit. Since the family had a right to remain under Regulation 1251/70, Article 7 of that Regulation required persons entitled to remain to equality of treatment as provided under Regulation 1612/68.

This Judgment was cited in *Inzirillo*[90] where the court invoked Article 7(2) of Regulation 1612/68 in support of a claim for a general benefit for the handicapped made by a worker father, on behalf of his adult son. The son's entitlement to equal treatment was found by the Court to derive from his right to reside in the host State.

So it seems it may now be possible for members of the family to claim equal treatment to all "social advantages," not only as survivors, but merely by virtue of their legitimate right to residence.

Nevertheless, loopholes still exist. Regulation 1612/68 relates only to employed persons, so the self-employed fall outside its protection. The extent to which members of the family can claim full equality of treatment is still uncertain and vulnerable to a literal interpretation by national courts. In such cases there still remains Article 7 EEU.

It was invoked in *Walgrave and Koch* by two professional self-employed motor cycling "pacemakers" to challenge a nationality limitation imposed by the Association. It is often used to buttress doubtful claims under Regulation 1408/71 and 1612/68. In *Fiorini* Advocate General Trabucchi, prompted by the Commission, pointed out to the Court that Article 7 always remains as an alternative route to Regulation 1612.

In *Forchieri*[91] it formed the basis of a successful claim by a member of the family, the Italian wife of an Italian Union official working in Belgium, who contested the payment of a fee for an educational course in Brussels required from all students who were not Belgian nationals. The same courses were free to Belgians. Mrs. Forchieri claimed the fee was discriminatory, contrary to Articles 7 and 48 EEU, and Article 12 of Regulation 1612/68. The Court, drawing support from Article 48 and the preamble to Regulation 1612/68 (5th Recital) held that:

> Although educational and vocational training policy is not part of the areas allotted to the competence of the Union's institutions, the opportunity for such kinds of instruction falls within the scope of the Treaty.
>
> . . .
>
> Consequently to require of a national of another Member State, lawfully established in the first Member State an enrollment fee which

[89] [1975] 2 C.M.L.R. 442.

[90] Case 63/76, [1978] 2 C.M.L.R. 596.

[91] Case 152/82, [1984] 1 C.M.L.R. 334.

is not required of its own nationals constitutes discrimination by reason of nationality which is prohibited by Article 7 of the Treaty.

c. *Conclusion*

As Advocate General Trabucchi remarked in *Fiorini*:

> Union law concerning social security, whether, as in Regulation 1612/68, it directly relates to the freedom of movement for workers or whether, as in the provisions concerning the coordination of social security, it does so indirectly, works as a dynamic whole, inspired by the same general aims and based on unifying principles. . . .Case law in recent years has developed in a way which reflects the need to achieve full equality of treatment between the union worker and the nationals of the State in which he is an immigrant.

Basing its arguments on the aims of the Treaty and the preambles and general scheme of Regulations 1408/71 and 1612/68 the Court remedies the deficiencies of each Regulation by arguing by analogy from one to the other, reinforcing its case by reference to the worker's right of residence based on Article 10 of Regulation 1612/68 or Regulation 1251/70, and building imperceptibly on its own case law. If the "social assistance" exclusion left an inevitable gap in the protection offered by Regulation 1408/71 in the reduced form of discretionary benefits this has now been filled by *Reina*. Where there is doubt whether either Regulation applies, Articles 48 and 7 of the Treaty remain as a measure of last resort. Moreover, the basis of the right to equality of treatment has shifted from a right attached to the worker and his family to one arising by reason of "lawful residence."

Moreover, where an "assistance"-type benefit can be assimilated to a social security benefit of type covered by Article 10 of Regulation 1408/71 the Court despite the problems, may even permit its export.

Have we reached a point when discrimination, whether direct or indirect with regard to any welfare benefit, against an EEU citizen lawfully resident in the host State will be regarded by the European Court as unlawful, unless the purpose of the benefit is wholly exceptional and inextricably connected in some way with nationality? And once entitlement to benefit is established, providing it falls within Regulation 1408/71 and is assimilable to the benefits covered by Article 10, may a claim to export it be resisted? If this is so, are these developments legitimate?

On a literal interpretation of Union secondary legislation the answer must be no. On an interpretation based on the purpose of the Treaty and the principle of free movement of persons, as well as on grounds of logic, the result must, it is submitted, be a qualified yes. Any exception to the principle of equal treatment would act as a deterrent to the free movement of workers, and any discrimination against EEU workers and their families lawfully resident in territory of another Member State would breach not only the principles of the EEU Treaty but the fundamental human right to equality which is part of EEU law. Similarly, the extension of the exportability principle to benefits not originally within Article 10 of Regulation 1408/71 was perhaps necessary to safeguard migrant workers and their families from the loss of benefits to which they had become entitled. The prospect of such loss would be a powerful deterrent against moving.

The basis of the right to equality of treatment remains economic. An EEU national is entitled to residence by reason of his status as an employed or self-employed person. Should be become involuntarily unemployed during his working life his residence permit need not be renewed beyond a 12 month period of "grace," unless he has acquired the right to remain permanently. His right to remain permanently on retirement or disability, or, in the case of his family, his death, also depends on his having been an employed or self-employed person. As such he will have paid taxes and social insurance contributions. Where unemployment is voluntary his rights of residence cease. The family's rights of residence derive from the worker's. So provision is generous, but there are safeguards against abuse.

Nevertheless, social security entitlement apart, whilst it is right, and consistent with the aims of the Treaty, to guarantee equality of treatment for migrant workers and their families in respect of all welfare benefits available to citizens of the host State, is it right, or consistent with the scheme of Regulation 1408/71, to require the host State to shoulder the financial burden alone? It cannot be denied that the European Court has extended Member States 'and perhaps individuals'[92] obligations towards migrant workers and their families far beyond the limits originally agreed. If States are thus required, in the interests of the Union and the free movement of workers, to provide unanticipated and costly benefits, whether in the form of educational grants or long term social assistance, for all legitimately resident migrant families, equity surely requires some sharing of the burden. Whilst entitlement to benefits in the host State should arise as soon as the migrant family is legitimately resident, should not some minimum period of employment and residence be required to elapse before the State is obliged to foot the bill? Until that time should not the worker's "home" State be required to reimburse the State providing the benefits? Where long term benefits are concerned could not provision be made for some form of apportionment?

Moreover, if it were openly acknowledged that all welfare benefits were to be provided by the host State as of right to EEU workers and their families on the basis of lawful residence, there would no longer be a need to widen the categories of exportable benefits. The only exportable benefits would be the insurance-based benefits explicitly catered for in Regulation 1408/71. Some loss it is true might thus accrue to workers moving from a State where welfare provision is generous. But since there is likely to be provision in all Member State for the same basic categories of benefit, and since "assistance" type benefits are generally cost-of-living-rated, any hypothetical loss to workers is more than outweighed by the practical difficulties involved if such benefits were allowed to be exported.

---

[92] Since the obligations relating to equality of treatment are contained in "directly applicable" Regulations they are capable of horizontal effects; so any institution providing "welfare" benefits, or concessionary rates could be affected. Art. 7 EEU too has been held horizontally effective; see *Walgrave and Koch.*

A system operating along the lines suggested above would, it is submitted, be fair, administratively workable, and consistent with the general scheme of EEU law relating to workers, particularly Regulations 1408/71 and 1251/70. Unless and until some such provision is made, resistance by Member States to the European Court's view of their obligations towards migrant workers and their families is likely to increase, and the gap between theory and practice, between one State and another, to widen. This furthers the interests of neither the worker nor the Union.

3. Competition and State Aid Policy[93]

a. Introduction

When one considers competition law in the European Union ("Union" or "EU"), it is useful to keep in mind the wording of Articles 2 and 3 of the Treaty Establishing the European Union ("EU Treaty" or "Treaty").[94] Article 2 states:

> The Union shall have as its task, by establishing a common market . . . and by implementing the common policies or activities referred to in Article [ ] 3 . . . to promote throughout the Union a harmonious and balanced development of economic activities, sustainable and non-inflationary growth respecting the environment, a high degree of convergence of economic performance, a high level of employment and of social protection, the raising of the standard of living and quality of life, and economic and social cohesion and solidarity among member-States.

Article 3 states that "[f]or the purpose set out in Article 2, the activities of the Union shall include . . . a system ensuring that competition in the internal market is not distorted." The first Chapter of Title V of the Treaty establishes "rules on competition" applying to undertakings and to "aids granted by States." The provisions on competition of the Treaty should also be read in the context of its preamble, in which the founding fathers recognized that "the removal of existing obstacles calls for concerted action in order to guarantee steady expansion, balanced trade and fair competition."

As Helmuth R.B. Schroter stated a few years ago:

> [T]he much broader scope of and plurality of aims pursued by EU competition policy result in making antitrust analysis under Union law a more complicated process than under the antitrust law of the United

---

93 Frederic Yves Jenny, *Competition and State Aid Policy in the European Community*, 18 Fordham Int'l L.J. 525 © 1994. Reprinted by permission.

94 Treaty Establishing the European Community, Feb. 7, 1992, [1992] 1 C.M.L.R. 573 [hereinafter EU Treaty], incorporating changes made by Treaty on European Union, Feb. 7, 1992, O.J. C 224/01 (1992), [1992] 1 C.M.L.R. 719, 31 I.L.M. 247 (1992) [hereinafter TEU]. The TEU, supra, amended the Treaty Establishing the European Economic Community, Mar. 25, 1957, 298 U.N.T.S. 11, 1973 Gr. Brit. T.S. No. 1 (Cmd. 5179-II) [hereinafter EEU Treaty], as amended by Single European Act, O.J. L 169/1 (1987), [1987] 2 C.M.L.R. 741 [hereinafter SEA], in Treaties Establishing the European Communities (EC Off '1 Pub. Off. 1987).

> States which considers 'allocative efficiency/consumer welfare' as the sole valid standard.[95]

These considerations have three consequences that are of particular importance in understanding the way the EU competition law is designed or enforced, and in understanding in particular the enforcement of the provisions on state aids. The first element to bear in mind has to do with the concept of competition, which underlies the EU Treaty. Among other things, competition must be fair. As early as the 1960's, the Court of Justice stated that "the elimination of barriers" and "fair competition" were both necessary to bring about a single market.[96]

As Schroter noted:

> According to the Commission, 'the principle of fairness in the market' place not only requires that equality of opportunity must be preserved for all commercial operators in the Common Market. It also highlights the need to take into account the great variety of situations in which firms carry on business and to pay special regard to small and medium firms. Finally, it demands that competition policy take account of the legitimate interests of workers, users and consumers.

In that sense the EU competition law not only protects the process of competition, but also the competitors. In the area of restrictive agreements, the issue of fairness does not come up very often, but one example quoted by Waelbroeck[97] is the first SABA decision, in which the Commission stated:

> The supply of goods by SABA wholesalers to private customers in Germany would . . . be inappropriate in a multi-level system such as that operated by SABA, with its clear definition of function between wholesalers and retailers. SABA wholesalers would furthermore have an unfair competitive advantage over SABA retailers. This type of unfair competitive advantage would not be protected by Article 85.[98]

Similarly, among the abuses prohibited by Article 86 are "directly or indirectly imposing unfair purchase or selling prices or other unfair trading conditions" and "applying dissimilar conditions to equivalent transactions with other trading parties, thereby placing them at a competitive disadvantage." Commenting on the case law, Thomas E. Kauper states:

> The treatment under Article 86 of refusals to deal by dominant firms . . . has until recently had little to do with economic efficiency in the

---

95 Helmuth R.B. Schroter, *Antitrust Analysis Under Article 85(1) and (3)*, in 1987 Fordham Corp. L. Inst. 645, 661 (Barry E. Hawk ed., 1988).

96 *Italy v. Council*, Case 32/65, [1966] E.C.R. 389, 404, [1969] C.M.L.R. 39, 60 - 61.

97 M. Waelbroeck, *Antitrust Analysis Under Article 85(1) and Article 85(3)*, in 1987 Fordham Corp. L. Inst. 693, 702 (Barry E. Hawk ed., 1988).

98 Commission Decision No. 79/159/EEC, O.J. L 28/19, at 26, P 34 (1976) [hereinafter *SABA*].

> price-output, consumer welfare sense. The Commission and Court of Justice cases concluding that refusals to deal were abusive, like the examples set forth in Article 86 itself, have been based on a concern for fair treatment of distributors (where competitive effects, if any, are to be found at the secondary level), or, in some cases, upon the threatened exclusion of direct rivals (where at least colorable arguments can be advanced to suggest that the refusals increase market power and could therefore impair consumer welfare). In sum, these cases reflect a mix of concerns more common to American antitrust of two decades past, and give Article 86, because it is multi-valued, a highly regulatory quality Section 2 now lacks.

The second element to bear in mind is that the primary goal of the EU competition policy is to unify the common market and to prevent private or public market intervention that is or could be incompatible with such a common market. For example, in the Metro case,[99] the Court of Justice emphasized that the objective of the Treaty regarding competition policy was to ensure "the creation of a single market achieving conditions similar to those of a domestic market." Schroter goes even further when he states that "in the EU competition policy in general and antitrust policy in particular is primarily 'integration policy' aimed at bringing about a maximum of economic interpenetration and thus merging the separate national markets into a single market of the Union." [100]

This means that interventions in the market mechanism, whether private or public, that establish directly a separation between national markets, such as an export cartel or a price discrimination across national borders, are prohibited. This also means that interventions, which establish differences in the economic circumstances faced by potential competitors, are viewed with extreme suspicion to the extent that the competitors affected are located in different countries or that the intervention could apply to competitors located in different Member States because they could directly or indirectly limit the extent of economic inter-penetration between national markets. As Barry Hawk noted:

> The EU market integration goal results in both stricter rules and a different method of substantive analysis than under US law. . . . [T]he market integration goal is not necessarily consistent with other competition policy objectives, notably promotion of efficiency. At the minimum there is tension (and possible trade-offs) between strict legal rules based on market integration goal and efficiencies, at least in the short term.[101]

---

[99] *Metro-SB-Grossmarkte GmbH & Co. KG v. Commission*, Case 26/76, [1977] E.C.R. 1875, [1978] 2 C.M.L.R. 1, 33.

[100] Schroter, supra note [95], at 657.

[101] Barry Hawk, *Un Tour d'Horizon du Droit et de la Politique de Concurrence*, Semaine Juridique, Oct. 15, 1992, at 1.

In this case, the integration goal supersedes the efficiency goal as is suggested by the 1991 report of the Commission on competition policy, which states:

> [C]ompetition policy has been an important Union instrument used both to promote economic integration and to ensure an efficient allocation of resources. Effective competition is the main stimulus to innovation and higher productivity which underpins policies designed to increase economic growth and welfare. Not only does competition lead to higher output but it also enables consumers to obtain a fair share of this growth. Living standards therefore depend on the maintenance of effective competition.

The third important feature of the EU competition law lies in the fact that if the goal of EU competition law is to facilitate the emergence of the common market, then the common market is not an end in itself. Rather, according to Article 2, the common market is a means

> [T]o promote throughout the Union a harmonious and balanced development of economic activities, sustainable and non-inflationary growth respecting the environment, a high degree of convergence of economic performance, a high level of employment and of social protection, the raising of the standard of living and quality of life, and economic and social cohesion and solidarity among Member States.

To achieve these broad goals, Article 3 of the Treaty states, among other things, that the activities of the Union shall include a common policy in the sphere of agriculture and fisheries, in the sphere of transport, in the sphere of the environment, in the strengthening of economic and social cohesion, in the strengthening of the competitiveness of Union industry, and in the promotion of research and technological development.

Two types of trade-offs may thus surface in the application of EU competition law. First, a trade-off between competition in the static sense and dynamic competition, and second, a trade-off between competition and some of the other objectives of the Treaty. Two principles laid out in the provisions of the Treaty related to competition among undertakings allow partial considerations of these trade-offs. First, there is an exemption mechanism that gives a certain amount of flexibility in the enforcement of competition law by allowing some anti-competitive practices that have redeeming values either from the point of view of competition in the long run or from the point of view of the other objectives of the Treaty. Second, such exemptions can only be granted in cases where competition is not eliminated for a substantial part of the products in question.

There is no exemption in the case of Article 86, because, by definition, the anti-competitive abuse by a firm holding a dominant position within the common market restricts competition in a substantial part of the European market. However, practices of undertakings which fall under Article 85(1) may be exempted through Article 85(3) if they "contribute[ ] to improving the production or distribution of goods or to promoting technical or economic progress, while allowing consumers a fair share of the resulting benefit;" if they do not impose on the undertakings restrictions that are not indispensable; and if they do not "afford such undertakings the possibility of eliminating competition in respect of a substantial part of the products in question."

Typical examples of such exemptions would include specialization agreements, research cooperation, or joint ventures through which two or more undertakings combine their capacities and knowledge, when the aim of such arrangements is to improve the efficiency of the firms involved. Additionally, agreements that ensure the existence of a new product or service would be exempt. Discussing the question of the relationship between competition law and industrial policy in the European Union, Manfred Caspari concluded:

> [W]hile the competition rules laid down in the EEU Treaty are applied within the framework of an overall and active competition policy, considerations which in a broad sense may be described as industrial policy considerations enter into a number of decisions. The aim is to create efficient undertakings on markets that fulfill this function, undertakings which are willing and able to engage in fair and active competition.[102]

While the three specific features of European competition law outlined above are well known and have been discussed frequently in the analysis of Article 85 and Article 86 decisions, they are also useful for understanding both the provisions of Article 92, which establish the substantive rules for aids granted by Member States, and the case law.

In the Chapter devoted to Rules on Competition, the first paragraph of Section 3 of Article 92, entitled "Aids Granted by States," provides:
Save as otherwise provided in this Treaty, any aid granted by a Member State or through State resources in any form whatsoever which distorts or threatens to distort competition by favoring certain undertakings or the production of certain goods shall, in so far as it affects trade between Member States, be incompatible with the common market.

The second and third paragraphs of Article 92 detail the exemptions to this rule. Some state aids, including those having a social character, those that compensate for damages caused by natural disasters, and those granted to the economy of certain areas of the Federal Republic of Germany, shall be compatible with the common market. Others may be considered compatible with the common market. Of particular interest is paragraph 3 of Article 92, which states:

> The following may be considered to be compatible with the common market:
>
> (a aid to promote the economic development of areas where the standard of living is abnormally low or where there is serious underemployment;

[102] Manfred Caspari, *1992-EEC Competition Law and Industrial Policy*, in 1989 Fordham Corp. L. Inst. 163, 179 (Barry E. Hawk ed., 1990).

(b) aid to promote the execution of an important project of common European interest or to remedy a serious disturbance in the economy of a Member State;

(c aid to facilitate the development of certain economic activities or of certain economic areas, where such aid does not adversely affect trading conditions to an extent contrary to the common interest. . . . ;

(d) aid to promote culture and heritage conservation where such aid does not affect trading conditions and competition in the Union to an extent that is contrary to the common interest; [and]

(e) such other categories of aid as may be specified by decision of the Council acting by a qualified majority on a proposal from the Commission.

b. State Aids

Although Article 92 does not define state aids, the definition of such aids is clear, if wide-ranging. The Court of Justice has stated:

> The concept of aid is . . . wider than that of a subsidy because it embraces not only positive benefits, such as subsidies themselves, but also interventions which, in various forms, mitigate the charges which are normally included in the budget of an undertaking and which, without, therefore, being subsidies in the strict meaning of the word, are similar in character and have the same effect.[103]

Thus, within the scope of Article 92, state aid can take a variety of forms: subsidies; preferential rates on loans; cash injections to public enterprises; deferrals of tax, social security or other payments; sale or rental of land or property at discounted rates; preferential electricity or natural gas rates; infra-structural projects benefiting identifiable end users; and others. In effect, any intervention by a Member State, i.e., by a state body or through the direction of the state, which intervention benefits a firm or a group of firms by increasing the resources they would normally obtain or by decreasing the costs, including taxes, they would otherwise incur, qualifies as a state aid irrespective of whether the benefit is conferred in money or in kind.

The fact that the aid must favor certain undertakings means that Member State interventions that apply uniformly across the economy cannot be considered state aids. This does not mean that general economic measures, such as rules of depreciation applied to capital equipment or charges on employers and employees to finance social benefits, cannot distort competition, but rather, are covered by other provisions in the Treaty. The only real difficulty concerns the case of capital injections into private or public firms. If the Member State invests in a manner similar to a private investor, expecting a normal return on its investment, then there is no state aid. If the Member

---

[103] *De Gezamenlijke Steenkolenmijnen in Limburg v. High Authority of the European Coal and Steel Community*, Case 30/59, [1961] E.C.R. 1, at 1.

State invests where a private investor would not have invested, then there is a state aid. Thus, when private and public investors inject capital simultaneously and in comparable amounts, it is presumed that there is no state aid. However, when only the Member State injects capital, the Commission evaluates whether a private investor would have been likely to invest given the financial and industrial circumstances of the firm. The hypothetical private investor is assumed to seek a normal rate of return given a reasonable delay.

For example, the Commission's evaluation of a Sicilian regional law concerning in particular the financing of Sitas, a firm engaged in the hotel business, noted that this firm

> is continuing to incur losses despite considerable investment by the region totalling some Lir. 270 billion. . . . There are no prospects of a turnaround, as evidenced by the fact that the management of EMS is seeking to negotiate with the creditor banks and that liquidation proceedings were commenced but not completed, chiefly because of a lack of buyers. No investor operating in a market economy would inject capital under such circumstances or take on the losses of a company without a future.

The Commission concluded that "the sums in question must be regarded as state aid within the meaning of Article 92(1) in so far as they allow a firm with no economic basis to remain artificially in operation."[104]

c. *Distortion of Competition and Effect on Trade*

When comparing the first paragraph of Article 92 to the underlying concept of competition in the Treaty, it is clear that all state aids "distort or threaten to distort competition." Indeed, a state aid gives certain firms an advantage not conferred to their competitors in their own Member State or in other Member States. In that sense, they are discriminatory and unfair. State aids place competitors of the aided undertakings at a disadvantage, thereby distorting competition. As the second report on state aids notes:

> Not only are enterprises in other Member states put at a competitive disadvantage by the aid because the aided enterprises are favored in a way outside the normal fiscal or social security systems that contribute to the equilibrium between Member States, but also enterprises not receiving aid in the same Member State are disadvantaged and pay higher taxes directly or indirectly.[105]

Thus, state aids are treated as per se anti-competitive. In line with this reasoning, the Commission's decision on the financing of Sitas states that "[t]he aid has the effect of distorting competition since it improves the economic position of the recipients in relation to their competitors who do not receive such assistance."

---

[104] C.ommission Decision No. 94/374/EC, O.J. L 170/36, 38-39 (1994) [hereinafter *Sitas*].

[105] Commission of the European Communities, Second Survey on State Aids in the European Community in the Manufacturing and Certain Other Sectors 7 (1990).

The above decision also illustrates one of the disturbing features of the Commission's decisions on state aids. In the landmark Philip Morris case,[106] the Court of Justice ruled that the Commission did not have to determine the relevant market on which competition is supposed to be distorted before establishing that an aid distorted competition, as in Article 85 or Article 86 cases.

An extreme case, which illustrates the dogmatic position of the Commission on the relationship between state aid and competition, is the Commission decision on the proposal to award aid to SST-Garngesellschaft mbH, Thuringen.[107] According to the Commission, the object of this aid was to cover the cost of the installation of new facilities for the production of polyester staple fiber. The entire output of the new plant was to serve as supply for the company's spinning mill for the production of specialized polyester yarn, which is not produced elsewhere in the Union. The Commission then went on to state:

> The aid in question undoubtedly constitutes aid within the meaning of Article 92(1) of the EU Treaty, as it would allow SST-Garngesellschaft mbH to carry out the planned investment without having to bear all of the cost. Furthermore, as there is intra-Union trade in polyester staple . . . , the proposed aid would be likely to distort competition and affect trade among the Member States.

The decision leaves us in the dark as to how the aid would distort competition because the beneficiary of the state aid will be the sole producer in the Union of the specialized yarn it intends to manufacture. The only conceivable cases in which there could be a distortion of competition would be either if the polyester yarn, which the beneficiary planned to produce, was a substitute for some of the other polyester staple produced in the Union, or if there were imports of this yarn. Yet, the Commission indicated that the yarn is specialized, which seems to suggest that it does not have substitutes, and did not mention the existence of imports. Thus, it appears that even when there are no competitors, state aids can be considered to distort competition. In short, there is a clear possibility of conflicts between the interpretation of the concept of competition in Article 85 and Article 86 cases and in state aids cases.

Finally, a state aid within the meaning of Article 92(1) must "affect [ ] trade between the Member States." One should note that the Commission and the Court of Justice have given a broad interpretation of the concept of effect on trade in decisions on state aids, in line with the interpretation of this concept in Article 85 and Article 86 decisions. The Commission and the Court of Justice consider, for example, that even when state aids are not specifically designed to stimulate exports or restrain imports, they nevertheless affect trade if they reinforce the position of an undertaking vis-a-vis competitors in intra-Union trade. When the beneficiary of the state aid exports part of

---

106 *Philip Morris Holland B.V. v. Commission*, Case 730/79, [1980] E.C.R. 2671, [1981] 2 C.M.L.R. 321.

107 Commission Decision No. 94/266/EC, O.J. L 114/21 (1994) [hereinafter SST-Garngesellschaft mbH, Thuringen].

its production, this condition is fulfilled, even if the exports represent a small part, less than 5%, of its total production, or if its exports represent a tiny part, less than 0.03%, of intra-EC trade.

In addition, to appraise the effect of Union trade the Commission not only takes into account the potential advantage that the beneficiary will enjoy on exports markets, it also considers the advantage it may derive from the state aid on its domestic market vis-a-vis foreign importers. For example, in its decision concerning the financing of Sitas, the Commission stated:

> The measures to be regarded as constituting state aid constitute assistance to firms operating in Sicily. They benefit those firms inasmuch as the assistance is not provided outside the region. . . . The aid in question . . . affects trade between Member States. Although it is not possible to assess the full impact of the aid as not all the recipients are known, import and export statistics . . . reveal that a significant proportion of Sicilian products and services is exported to other Member States. In addition, trade between Member States is also affected in cases where the aid favors domestic output and services to the detriment of imports and the provision of services from other Member States.[108]

What is remarkable in this and other decisions is that the Commission relies only on the fact that there is intra-Union trade in the sector in which the beneficiaries of the aid operate to establish that the aid affects trade between Member States.

Furthermore, even in cases in which the state aid is granted to a firm or a group of firms selling a product for which there is practically no intra-Union trade, the Commission may consider that trade is affected if this aid is likely to limit the development of a competing product for which there are significant exports and imports.

Thus, state aid of any significance is automatically deemed to meet the other criteria of paragraph 1 of Article 92 and to be incompatible with the common market. The Commission does not have to elaborate at length over why in the particular case at hand the aid could distort competition, what the market and the affected products are, or whether these particular products as opposed to other products in the same sector are traded among Member States. The Commission, however, considers that Article 92(1) does not apply to state aids grants amounting to less than 50,000 ECU over a three-year period.

d. Exemptions

The main question in state aids decisions, therefore, is whether the aid qualifies for an exemption or, in other words, whether the state aid fulfills some other goal of the Treaty. There are two types of automatic exemptions: Article 92(2) exemptions and various types of discretionary, Article 92(3) exemptions. The two types of automatic exemptions are: first, state aids that have a social character, are granted to individual

---

108 *Sitas*, O.J. L 170/37, at 40 (1994).

consumers, and are granted without discrimination regarding the origin of the product; and second, state aids that are due to exceptional circumstances requiring solidarity, i.e., aids to compensate for the damage caused by national disasters or exceptional occurrences.

Other aids may be exempted. Among these are aids to promote the economic development of severely depressed areas, i.e., areas where the standard of living is abnormally low or where there is serious unemployment. Also included are aids to promote the execution of important projects of common European interest.

Article 92(3)(a) is designed to exempt state aids that compensate for handicaps that would normally deter firms from investing in more backward regions, in which the per capita gross domestic product does not exceed seventy-five percent of the Union average in purchasing power parities. As Manfred Caspari stated, "[s]uch aid is therefore an expression of efforts to create greater equality of opportunity between regions. It is in line with the cohesion requirement . . . incorporated into the EEU Treaty." The granting of an exemption on the basis of Article 92(3)(a) is, however, subject to two conditions. First, the aid must concern one of the regions from a Commission list, which includes the whole of Greece, Ireland, Portugal, the Italian Mezzogiorno, Northern Ireland, various provinces of Spain, and the overseas departments of France. Second, the aid must not lead to the creation of competition-distorting excess capacity in capital intensive industries.

State aids to other regions may be exempted, however, under the provisions of Article 92(3)(c). As far as Article 92(3)(b) is concerned, there are very few cases of "important project[s] of common European interest" justifying an exemption. Those projects are usually associated with programs such as ESPRIT, RACE, or BRITE[109] or with situations in which the Union is confronted by a general threat such as the destruction of the environment. The Commission stated in its 1991 annual report that Article 92(3)(b) could also apply to projects that were important both quantitatively and qualitatively, transnational, and related to the definition of international standards, thus allowing European industry to benefit from the full advantages of a single market. For example, the Commission considered that state aids granted by the governments of France, the Netherlands, and Italy designed to encourage research and development for the definition of a European standard for High Definition Television could be exempted. If the aid examined relates to an important project of common European interest, the Commission also verifies that it does not exceed what is tolerable from a competition policy point of view.

One reason for the Commission's narrow interpretation of Articles 92(3)(a) and 92(3)(b) is that these provisions do not explicitly condition the granting of the exemption on whether the aid will not significantly affect intra-European trade. In the vast majority of cases, the discussion about the possibility of an exemption is based upon Article 92(3)(c), which concerns aids that "facilitate the development of certain eco-

[109] ESPRIT is an acronym for European Strategy Program for Research in Information Technologies. RACE is an acronym for Research and Development in Advanced Communication Technologies for Europe. BRITE is an acronym for Basic Research in Industrial Technologies for Europe.

nomic activities or of certain economic areas, where such aid does not adversely affect trading conditions to an extent contrary to the common interest."

It is not easy to summarize the principles underlying the Commission's reasoning when it applies Article 92(3)(c). Concurrently, one must consider: the wording of Article 92(3)(c); general principles imbedded in other articles of the Treaty; a variety of specific rules established by the Commission in guidelines or frameworks on state aids that are either horizontal, such as the guidelines dealing with regional aids, aids for research and development, aids for the restructuring of firms, aids for small and medium-sized enterprises, and aids for the environment, or sectoral, such as aids for textile and clothing, synthetic fibers, motor vehicles, shipbuilding, coal and steel, agriculture, and food processing; and the case law.

The Commission has enjoyed considerable discretion in interpreting Article 92(3)(c). This situation, however, may change in the future. Leigh Hancher, Tom Ottervanger, and Piet Jan Slot stated that:

> Up until now the Court has generally been prepared to endorse the Commission's discretionary powers to assess the compatibility of individual measures with Article 92(1) as being wide in nature. In only two cases to date has the Court annulled a Commission decision on grounds of a manifest error of fact. Our survey of the Commission's decision making practice suggests that, in certain cases, the factual evidence presented in support of a decision to allow a national aid to be granted could well bear closer scrutiny. Once again parallels may be drawn from the experience gained in the application of Articles 85 and 86. One of the reasons for transferring jurisdiction in appeals against Commission decisions concerning these Articles to the Court of First Instance was to improve the administration of justice in the Union by engaging in more detailed investigation of factual matters. That Court has now developed a particular expertise in dealing with the economic effects of complex factual issues . . . . The transfer of jurisdiction [to the Tribunal, effective August 1993] to review individual challenges to state aid decisions may be one means of stimulating a more critical appraisal of Commission state aid policy.[110]

A necessary, but not sufficient, condition for a state aid to be granted an exemption under Article 92(3)(c) is that it be in the common interest of the Union. This concept is not defined in Article 92. Furthermore, the goals of the Union listed in Article 2 of the Treaty are couched in terms so general that the Commission has a sufficient flexibility to decide what interferences in market mechanisms should be legitimized through state aids and to set Union industrial policy agenda.

Before analyzing the criteria used by the Commission to determine what is in the common interest, it should be stressed that the compatibility with the Treaty must be determined in the context of the Union as a whole and not in the context of a single

110 Hancher et al. , EC State Aids, at 15 (1993).

Member State. This has several implications. The first one is to legitimize the fact that Member States are not competent to apply directly the provisions of the Treaty relating to state aids. Second, it means that Member States cannot justify the granting of state aids solely on the basis of the benefits they expect from such aids. For example, a state aid designed to foster economic development in a depressed region in one Member State may not be in the interest of the Union if the region cannot be considered to be economically depressed when compared to all regions in the Union. Thus, in its Tenth Report on Competition Policy, the Commission stated:

> State aids are in principle incompatible with the common market. The discretionary powers of the Commission should only be exercised when the aids proposed by Member States contribute to the achievement of the Union objectives and interest set out in Article 92(3). The national interest of a Member State or the benefits obtained by the recipient of the aid in contributing to the national interest do not by themselves justify the positive exercise of the Commission's discretionary powers.

Third, it also means that the Commission has reservations about state aids granted to multinational firms. Indeed, because multinational firms often operate on a global level, state aids designed to help them restructure are not necessarily consistent with what would be in the interest of the Union.

At the most general level, one can say that the Commission views four types of aids favorably: aids for small and medium-sized enterprises, aids for regional development, aids for research and development, and aids for the environment.

Regarding aids for small and medium-sized enterprises, the Union Guidelines on State Aid for Small and Medium-Sized Enterprises states that: "there can be no doubt that state aids for [small and medium-sized enterprises] 'facilitate the development of certain economic activities or of certain economic areas.' " At the same time, the Commission considers that aids to small and medium-sized enterprises are less disruptive of competition than aids to larger firms.

State aids for research and development may also be viewed positively to the extent that they relate to the aim stated in Article 130f(1) of the Treaty, which strengthens "the scientific and technological bases of Union industry and [which encourages] it to become more competitive at international level." As the guidelines on research and development make clear, the Commission views favorably state aids for basic industrial research, but limits the state aid to fifty percent of the gross cost of the project or program. The Commission feels, however, that if the research and development is more thoroughly applied so that its output more easily and rapidly influences a product market, then there is a greater risk that the state aid will distort competition. Therefore, the ceiling on the admissible state aid decreases as the research is increasingly applied. The Commission also considers that simple improvement of existing facilities does not qualify for an exemption under Article 92(3)(c). To qualify for an exemption under Article 92(3)(c), the investment benefiting from the state aid must lead to the development of new products or the adoption of new processes. State aids for regional development, when applied to regions that suffer from serious socio-economic disparities with the rest of the Union, are viewed favorably and monitored by the Commission to achieve the goals of promoting a "harmonious and balanced development of economic activities" and "convergence of economic performance" as set out in Article 2 of the Treaty. Thus, for example, state aids to investments in central, industrialized regions, cannot exceed 20% of the total investment, whereas in peripheral, lowly industrialized regions, they can represent a larger proportion of the investment.

Finally, environmental aids, which also relate to the goal of achieving "growth respecting the environment," set out in Article 2 of the Treaty, are viewed favorably if they are necessary to help undertakings adapt to laws or regulations, which impose major new burdens relating to environmental protection. In this instance, an undertaking can get an Article 92(3)(b) exemption. If the aid is intended to promote additional efforts going beyond national standards, then the undertaking may qualify for an Article 92(3)(c) exemption.

In sectors facing serious economic difficulties due to international competition, such as motor vehicles, textiles, shipbuilding, coal and steel, and where Member States may have a natural and growing inclination to grant state aids, the Commission has been concerned with limiting such aids. The aid is limited to projects that improve the efficiency of the industry, allow the conversion of firms to activities outside the industry, or allow existing firms to diversify their production towards products that will place them in a better position on the international markets. Such aids are allowed, however, only to the extent that they will not worsen the difficulties of similar industries in other European countries.

In other sectors, state aids may be allowed if they appear necessary to the development or maintenance of existing strategic industries. Thus, for example, the Commission allowed a state aid by the United Kingdom for the restructuring of the last tin mine in Europe. It also allowed a state aid by the United Kingdom for the purchase of industrial equipment for off-shore exploration when this sector was in an early stage of development in Europe. In 1979, however, the Commission withheld approval of the state aid because by then the sector had developed, and the promotion of this sector no longer had strategic importance. Similarly, the Commission may allow state aids to shipyards for the construction of ships so that they can successfully compete against non-European shipyards. However, in such cases the state aid must not exceed the amount necessary to prevent the order from going to a non-European shipyard.

To qualify for the exemptions of Article 92(3)(c), aids that fit the above mentioned general criteria must also meet at least six conditions: they must be transparent; they must be justified by a market failure or an externality; they must not provide continuous artificial support to non-viable undertakings; they must not create over-capacities; they must be proportionate to the goal they seek to achieve; and the restrictions to competition and trade that they entail must not outweigh the expected benefits at the Union level. The transparency requirement is the easiest to understand. To grant an exemption, the Commission must be in a position to know precisely, both quantitatively and qualitatively, what the aid is all about. In particular, the Commission needs to know who the beneficiaries are, what the mechanism of the aid is, what the goal of the aid is, and what the importance of the aid is, both in absolute terms and in proportion to the total investment. The second condition is more substantive. Exemptions may be invoked only when the Commission is satisfied that without the aid, market forces alone would be insufficient to guide the recipients towards the behavior that the state aid is supposed to encourage and that must be consistent with the other conditions. Thus, on the one hand, the Commission may grant an Article 92(3)(c) exemption for regional aids in certain lagging areas, such as those in which the GDP per inhabitant is in the long run at least fifteen percent lower than the national average, or where the unemployment rate is at least ten percent greater than the national unemployment rate. The Commission must be convinced that without such aids, these areas would not be able to attract sufficient private investment to reduce their deficit. Alternatively, the Commission will refuse to grant an exemption for a state aid to a firm if it is convinced that the proposed investment would be profitable without the aid. The Commission will deny the exemption even if the investment can be considered to have a Union interest, i.e., if it contributes to the development of the firm's region or sector.

State aids designed simply to facilitate the modernization of existing capacities of an unprofitable firm in a sector characterized by existing or potential excess capacity will not be granted an exemption on the basis of Article 92(3)(c) for various reasons. First, the modernization of a firm is, in itself, considered by the Commission to be part of what profit maximizing private investors would normally do, and therefore unrelated to a market failure or an externality. Second, the expansion of capacities or the modernization of a firm in a structurally depressed sector is not likely to alleviate the disequilibrium between supply and demand at the Union level, as would a decrease in capacity or a restructuring of the firm allowing it to redirect some or all of its resources to another sector or to a different market. The profitability of the beneficiary would likely improve from such aids. The burden between supply and demand associated with the structural disequilibrium at the Union level, however, would shift to competing firms of other Member States. Thus, allowing a Member State to grant such aids would eventually give an incentive to other Member States to retaliate by granting aids for the modernization of their firms. Consequently, this succession of aid would not restore the profitability of the sector. The third condition is that state aids must not provide artificial support to unprofitable undertakings. The Commission has repeatedly stated that state aids should not be used to prevent the disappearance of non-viable firms. For example, the Commission, in its decision concerning financing for Sitas, stated:

> With regard to the exceptions provided for in Article 92(3)(c) in respect of aid to facilitate the development of certain economic activities where such aid does not adversely affect trading conditions to an extent contrary to the common interest, the aid is not tied to any restructuring plan ensuring restoration of the firm's viability. It is therefore an operating aid which preserves the status quo by preventing normal market forces from taking effect. The aid cannot, therefore, be considered compatible with the common market.[111]

[111] *Sitas*, O.J. L 170/36, at 41 (1994).

Fourth, the Commission considers that state aids in sectors characterized by existing or potential excess capacities can be tolerated if, and only if, they contribute to a restructuring of the beneficiaries and a decrease of existing capacities, over and beyond the reductions that would be spontaneously forced on the beneficiaries by the normal working of the market. It must be clear that the restructuring will enable the firm to become profitable without further injection of state aid.

This principle is embedded in various sectoral guidelines or codes. For example, investment aids in the steel sector, characterized by severe excess capacity, cannot, in general, qualify for an exemption under Article 92(3)(c). There is a temporary exemption for Greece, Portugal, and the German landers located in the former German Democratic Republic. To qualify for this exemption, capacity reductions must accompany the aids. Similarly, in the synthetic fiber industry, aids for investments relating to the production and texturization of polyester, polyamide, acrylic, and polypropylene fibers can qualify for an exemption only if they are combined with a capacity reduction of the beneficiary. In the automobile sector state aids for unprofitable manufacturers of passenger vehicles must, among other requirements, include a restructuring plan and a reduction in capacity for the beneficiary. Beyond the requirements set in certain sectoral regulations on state aids, other regulations on aids, for rescue aids, or for environmental investments, specify that such aids must be accompanied by reductions of capacity of the beneficiary.

The general concern of the Commission with overcapacity raises several questions. If interpreted strictly, it implies that a new entrant in the sectors or in the markets considered to be having overcapacity cannot benefit from a state aid, because by definition it cannot reduce its existing capacity, whereas established firms could benefit from such an aid in certain circumstances, i.e., if they met the other conditions set by the Commission.

The *SST-Garngesellschaft mbH* decision illustrates this consideration. The object of this aid was to cover the cost of the installation of new facilities for the production of polyester staple fiber. The entire output of the new plant was to supply the company's spinning mill for the production of specialized polyester yarn that is not produced elsewhere in the Union. Having found that this aid violated Article 92(1), the Commission stated:

> Since 1977, aid to the synthetic fibre industry has been subject to constraints. The current version of the Code relates to the production and texturization of four fibers - polyester, polyamide, acrylic and polypropylene - irrespective of the end-use, and to their polymerization where integrated with fibre production in terms of the machinery involved. The Code states clearly that authorization of proposals to grant aid to synthetic fibre producers is conditional on a significant reduction in the production capacity of the prospective beneficiary. SST itself does not currently produce any synthetic fibers so that a capacity reduction is not possible. The aid does not meet the requirements of the Code.[112]

112 *SST-Garngesellschaft mbH*, Thuringen, O.J. L 114/21 (1994).

Perhaps because it sensed that this reasoning led to an economically questionable result in the case at hand, the Commission found a way to authorize it. Despite the fact that the region did not meet the code requirements, the Commission granted the aid because the region could be classified for regional aid by virtue of Article 92(3)(a), and because the investment considered was part of a broader plan to restructure the German Democratic Republic's synthetic fiber industry. The Commission stated that granting the aid would result in a reduction in capacity of twenty-five percent, similar to the reduction in capacity in the rest of the Union since 1978.

The tougher standards used by the Commission to exempt a state aid when there is actual or potential "excess capacity" in the sector, together with the Commission's discretion as to the definition of the market or sector examined, can also lead to striking differences in the standards applied by the Commission in its decisions.

In this respect, it is interesting to compare two decisions: the Commission decision on a state aid granted to Opel for an investment in one of the landers of the former German Democratic Republic,[113] and its decision on the state aid granted to Ford and Volkswagen by the Portuguese government for the creation of a new plant in the Setubal peninsula.[114] In both cases, the aid was for an investment in an automobile plant in an economically depressed area. In the first case, the Commission did not go into details about market segmentation and found that there was overcapacity in the automobile industry. Although it recognized that Opel/GM needed to increase its capacity because it fully utilized its existing capacity, the Commission concluded that the aided investment would increase overcapacity in the sector. In the second case, when it considered the aid granted for the creation by Ford and Volkswagen of a manufacturing plant of monospace cars in Portugal, the Commission considered that there was a separate market for monospace passengers cars. In a related Article 85 decision, the Commission acknowledged the fact that there was some degree of substitutability between monospace cars and other passenger cars, and that there was no overcapacity for this type of cars.[115] In the first case, the Commission required that the aid be limited to the amount or the intensity strictly necessary to compensate for the extra costs incurred by Opel/GM due to the location of its investment. This decision concluded that the aid would create overcapacity, which is far from obvious because Opel needed to increase its capacity, and therefore, would probably have gone ahead with the investment even if the Commission had decided to prohibit the aid, although possibly in a less economically depressed area. In the second case, the Commission used a somewhat arbitrary definition of the market to find that the aid would not create overcapacity. The Commission, adopting a more lenient approach, stated that the aid, which covered the extra cost faced by the investors due to the location of their investment and an additional financial incentive to attract investments in the region, could be exempted.

---

[113] Commission Notice No. 93/C 43/03, O.J. C 43/14 (1993) (regarding German Government proposal to award state aid to Opel Group in support of its investment plans in new lander).

[114] Commission Decision Summary No. 91/C 257/04, O.J. C 257/5 (1991) (raising no objections to aid that Portuguese Government planned to grant to joint-venture of Ford and Volkswagen to establish multi-purpose vehicle plant in Setubal peninsula).

[115] Commission Decision No. 93/49/EEC, O.J. L 20/14 (1993) (Ford/Volkswagen).

The concept of overcapacity, as used by the Commission, is not always economically relevant. For example, the Commission frequently refers to the need to increase the rate of utilization of existing capacities to make European industry more competitive and uses capacity utilization ratios to determine whether or not excess capacity has increased or decreased in a particular sector. Capacity utilization is calculated by the ratio of actual sales by the European manufacturers to their total capacity. Overcapacity is calculated by the ratio of total European demand for a product at a competitive price, whether this demand was met by domestic producers or importers, to total capacity by European manufacturers. Except under strong assumptions, for example, no imports and perfect competition among the European manufacturers, these two ratios are unrelated. Indeed the value of capacity utilization ratios, as opposed to excess capacity ratios, is heavily dependent on the market strategy of the manufacturers.

Reliance on the rate of capacity utilization, to assess the propriety of a state aid, can be extremely misleading from the point of view of what an outside observer could consider to be sound economic reasoning. If total capacity is equal to total demand, in which case there is no excess capacity, but forty percent of the demand is satisfied by more efficient non-European importers, who have developed a new technology not present in Europe, then capacity utilization in the industry will be only sixty percent. It is likely that price competition from the efficient non-European competitors will force the market price below the cost of the non-efficient domestic producers, so that they will incur losses. The requirement that a state aid for an investment, such as one designed to introduce a technological innovation in the production process, to improve the efficiency of the sector, be accompanied by a reduction in the production capacity of the beneficiary clearly favors the importers because it reduces the scope of competition from the new efficient European manufacturer.

Even in cases where there are no significant non-European imports, the concern of the Commission with excess capacity can lead to questionable results from the point of view of competition. If, for example, the excess capacity, as measured by the Commission, is due to weak competition, the requirement that the state aid, designed to encourage the introduction of a technological innovation, be accompanied by a reduction in the capacity of the beneficiary may unnecessarily slow down the adjustment of the sector and stifle competition.

In the decisions of the Commission on state aids, competition in the relevant sector is always, implicitly, assumed to be working satisfactorily, or to be excessive, even though there is practically no analysis of the actual intensity of competition. Therefore, the creation of excess capacity through state aids to investments is never considered by the Commission to enhance competition; it is only considered to distort fair competition. However, there is a growing body of economic literature on the impact of excess capacity and the distribution of such excess capacity among firms, as well as competition in oligopolies. This literature suggests, among other things, that an asymmetrical distribution of excess capacity may, in certain cases, enhance competition. Thus, it is possible that some state aids to investment may have the dual effect of distorting fair competition and contributing to the creation of excess capacity, thereby increasing competition in the marketplace.

The final condition set by the Commission for granting an exemption to a state aid is that it must be proportionate to the problem that it is designed to resolve. This will keep distortion to competition at a minimum and will not affect trading to an extent contrary to the common market.

Whenever the Commission considers state aid for which one of the sectoral or horizontal Codes applies, it verifies that the aid falls within the limit set in the relevant Code. For example, in the case of state aids for research and development, state aids cannot cover more than fifty percent of the gross cost of a project for basic industrial research or twenty-five percent of the cost of a project for applied research and development. Similarly, to benefit from an exemption under Article 92(3)(c), regional aids designed to facilitate the development of certain economic areas cannot amount to more than thirty percent of the investment. Under the Code for state aids to shipbuilding, operating aids for the production of large vessels must be below nine percent of the cost of the vessel, whereas for vessels costing less than ten million ECU, the maximum level of state aid is 4.5%. The maximum levels of state aids for small and medium-sized firms are usually larger than the maximum for larger firms.

In order to benefit from the exemption of Article 92(3)(c), however, the state aid must also be strictly necessary to correct the problem that justifies the exemption. An example is the Commission's decision concerning aid to be provided by the Irish government for the restructuring of the Aer Lingus group, which was facing a serious financial crisis. The Commission first stated that "the genuine restructuring of Aer Lingus contributes to the development of the air transport sector from a Union standpoint." It then asked itself whether the amount of the aid was "adequate and proportionate to the aim of financing the transition and restore the airline's commercial viability." In assessing that the aid was indeed adequate and proportionate, the Commission took into account the fact that "the equity injected into Aer Lingus will not [lead] to an overcapitalization of the airline but will simply bring its financial ratios into more prudent limits, and, therefore, restore the financial balance." "The strategy pursued by Aer Lingus in its restructuring plan is not over-expansionist" because it will not expand its operating fleet or change the general pattern of its operations, and consequently, does not aim at increasing its market share.[116]

Finally, the state aid must not adversely "affect[ ] trading conditions to an extent contrary to the common interest." The Commission does not always make its reasoning explicit, but rather uses its discretionary power to decide whether or not this condition is met or to impose constraints on the granting of the aid so that the condition is met. To establish the extent to which the state aid will affect trading conditions, the Commission takes into consideration a variety of factors, such as whether: the amount of the aid is small when compared to the size of the investment, the market shares of the firms involved are minimal or will decrease, the market is rapidly expanding, there is little intra-Union trade for the product involved, or that the investment will be devoted to the production of goods that will be sold outside the Union.

---

116 Aer Lingus, O.J. L 54/30 (1994).

In its decision on the aid granted by the United Kingdom to SCA Aylesford, a manufacturer of newsprint, the Commission concluded that the investment aid did not adversely affect "trading conditions . . . to an extent contrary to the common interest."[117] The Commission considered that the investment aid would result in an increase in the capacity of production of the firm and that part of the increased production, 100,000 tons or about a third of the increase in capacity, would be sold in other Member States. Nonetheless, the Commission determined that the aid was limited and that although the United Kingdom imported seventy-five percent of its consumption of newsprint, ninety percent of these imports came from non-Union countries.

Similarly, in its decision on a state aid from the German government for the restructuring of Carl Zeiss Jena, Jenoptik, and Jenaer Glaswerk, manufacturers of optical instruments located in the former German Democratic Republic, the Commission considered that the very small scale of the activities of the three firms in the forthcoming years ensured that the aid would not adversely affect trading conditions to an extent contrary to the common interest.[118]

The Commission decisions, however, do not provide clear criteria to assess the extent beyond which the effect of trading conditions due to the state aid will be held to be contrary to the common interest.

e. Conclusion

Manfred Caspari, speaking at the 1989 Fordham Corporate Law Institute conference, remarked that usually lawyers do not take much interest in the subject of state aids. This, in his opinion, was wrong because "[s]tate subsidies can distort competition more, and can create more harm to competing companies which do not get such support than anti-competitive behavior caught by antitrust rules."[119]

The fact is that this apparent lack of interest for the European state aid policy is not unique to lawyers. Economists, even those specialized in market mechanisms and competition, have also been largely silent on the issue. This is all the more perplexing because there are hundreds of decisions by the Commission each year that concern state aids. However, this state of affairs could be explained on the ground that even if the provisions on state aids are part of the rules of competition in the Treaty and even if the Commission produces decisions on state aids as it does when it applies Articles 85 and 86, these two sets of decisions have little in common.

First, as any sizeable aid is considered to threaten or distort competition, market competition or fair competition, there is no real discussion in the decisions of the actual consequences of the aids on the relevant markets or detailed definition of the affected markets. The focus of the decisions on state aids is therefore very different from the focus of Article 85 or 86 decisions in which the reasoning used by the Commission to establish that a particular behavior has restrained competition or to assess the extent to which competition has been affected is explicit and can be challenged.

---

117 Commission Notice, O.J. C 46/5 (1993) (aid to SCA Aylesford, manufacturer of newsprint).

118 Commission Notice, O.J. C 97/7 (1993) (concerning aid awarded by German Government to Carl Zeiss Jena, Jenoptik, and Jenaer Glaswerk).

Second, the formal decisions on state aids mostly deal with the possibility of exemptions for the aids concerned or, in other words, with the potential contribution of these aids to the common interest, the development of certain areas or certain economic activities, etc. The assessment of the contribution of state aids to the promotion of such general and sometimes contradictory goals is, to a large extent, dependent on the policy objectives of the Commission. The Commission has enjoyed broad discretion in making such assessments. In many cases, its decisions do not prove that an aid can or cannot be exempted, but merely state that they do or do not adversely affect trading conditions to an extent contrary to the common interest on the basis of criteria that are not explicit and the validity of which could not be challenged until recently.

Third, over time, the Commission has defined minimal rules in various sectoral or horizontal codes. This effort would certainly be welcome if it contributed to making the decision mechanism more transparent and more predictable. However, not only do the definitions of the rules seem somewhat arbitrary, they constitute a maze rather than an organized body of references. In many cases in which several sets of rules could be applied simultaneously to the same aid with different results, the Commission will choose the one that fits the conclusion it wants to reach.

Thus, one could argue that the relative lack of interest of both lawyers and economists for state aid decisions comes partly from the fact that they do not always appear to be grounded on a predictable economic analysis and that the scope for challenging them is at best limited. Two features that differentiate them from decisions based on Articles 85 and 86.

Echoing these concerns, the authors of the most comprehensive review of EU state aid decisions to date state that

> [n]o one could, for a moment, assume that in an area as highly charged by political and social considerations as state aids policy that one could expect the Commission to apply a rigid, formalistic or mechanistic approach to controlling national state aids. The Treaty itself confers considerable scope upon it to take into account a wide range of factors in reaching its final Decisions. It is, therefore, not so surprising that what appears to be an essentially similar set of facts is capable of yielding quite divergent Decisions in different cases. Yet one is surely entitled to expect some consistency of approach, and at the very least that similar emphasis is given to various factors. One might also expect that especially where guidelines exist these should be applied, and be seen to be applied, in a consistent manner. . . . On the basis of the analysis of Commission Decisions undertaken in the preparation of this study, it cannot be said with any certainty that expectations as to a consistent approach have been or are always likely to be met. The relative lack of institutional constraints on the Commission in this field gives the latter ample scope to draft Decisions in such a way that factual elements which might suggest inconsistency are simply ignored or are only referred to in summary fashion.

It remains to be seen whether the transfer of jurisdiction in appeals against the Commission decisions on state aid to the Court of First Instance will help bring about a more transparent and more predictable decision-making process.

C. European Criminal Jurisprudence[120]

The European Convention for the Protection of Human Rights and Fundamental Freedoms (hereafter the Convention) has been in operation for almost 40 years, the Commission and the court for more than 30 years. In the meantime, recourse to Strasbourg has become a built-in mechanism of judicial review in the Member States. In particular, Art. 25 of the Convention which entitles individuals to plead violation of the Convention has turned into a corner-stone of a working system of human rights protection, since the court's first decision in 1960. Even though the court's output cannot compare to internal state jurisdictions, applications to Strasbourg have risen dramatically over the years.[121] As could have been expected, the Strasbourg institutions for the protection of human rights have attracted substantial academic interest. Everybody seems inclined to pay lip-service to this highly developed international scheme of human right protection. Reaching beyond the surface of lofty oratory we realize though that this interest is—let aside the more spectacular cases which even reach the newspaper headlines—only shared by a limited community of experts. This comes as no surprise: systematic academic teaching of the European human rights protection system is still lagging far behind. The international scope does not facilitate access to the relevant literature published in different countries and different languages. Also, the matter sits uneasily between different branches of law: public international law, European law as well as to criminal law. Even the "inner circle" of experts seems to concentrate on a closed pattern of problems, their preference being guided by the compass of their particular discipline.

The structure of the court's reasoning rather belongs to neglected areas. This may be due to the fact that construction and reconstruction of judgements fall within the domain of jurisprudence. As it seems, jurisprudence though having established a flourishing theory of legal argumentation, is still lacking a firm grip on the functioning international and supranational institutions. . . . We would rather like to join the interdisciplinary and international chorus on a very particular tune which derives its character from a *mélange* of jurisprudence and criminal law. In voicing this duo we may tend to consolidate the notion that the Convention is an academic "no man's land" open for conquests by every discipline. On the other hand, such a commonwealth seems to be the proper platform for interdisciplinary discourse in law. This interdisciplinary approach also dominates a recent and extremely interesting collection of essays in criminal policy and human rights, edited by Mireille Delms-Marty.

---

[119] Manfred Caspari, *1992-EEC Competition Law and Industrial Policy*, in 1989 Fordham Corp. L. Inst. 163, 179 (Barry E. Hawk ed., 1990).

[120] Joxerramon Bengoetxea & Heike Jung, *Towards a European Criminal Jurisprudence? The Justification of Criminal Law by the Strasbourg Court.* 11 Legal Stud. 239-80 (1991).

The links between the Convention and criminal law are manifold. Here we do not intend to follow the criminal lawyers' traditional preoccupation with Arts. 5 and 6 of the Convention and their bearing upon criminal proceedings. Nor are we going to embark on an analysis of the court's judgments as regards the prohibition of torture, or inhuman or degrading treatment or punishment (Art. 3) interestingly developed only recently by the *Soering* case. Nor shall we expand the principle of *nullum crimen sine lege* embodied in Art. 7 or delve into the impact of Art. 2 § 2 for the scope of self-defense.

From a criminal policy as well as from a jurisprudential point of view it may be more promising to tackle those decisions dealing with the state's right to punish. It will be revealing for the court's self-understanding as such to know which course it is steering and which instruments it uses *vis-à-vis* the right to punish as the traditional insignia of state sovereignty. Yet, we do not focus all our attention on the court's supervisory role. We are also interested in assessing the court as a criminal policy maker. In that, we are not primarily concerned with the question whether the court has adopted a more progressive or a more conservative approach. This does not mean that the outcome of the cases is of no relevance to us. What primarily attracts our interest, however, are the court's express, implied or presumable arguments backing a move towards decriminalization or criminalization.

In this sense we are going to elucidate and test the court's argumentative standards within a restricted field. The theory of criminal policy has kept refining on the parameters for criminalization. An abundant literature is available. National courts have set their marks. Hence, in adjudicating on criminalization and decriminalization, the court will draw support from this particular body of domestic standards and doctrinal opinion whether the court is going to opt for its own line of reasoning thus relying on and seeking to enhance its own authority.

Whereas the scope of criminal statutes may have been alluded to on other occasions, the court seems to have dealt with their legitimacy expressly in a handful of judgements only, the *Handyside* case,[122] the *Müller* case,[123] the *Dudgeon* case,[124] the *Norris* case,[125] and *X and Y v. The Netherlands*.[126] Such scarcity does not really facilitate our task; it requires caution with regard to far-reaching generalizations as well as consideration of how the strategy of justification adopted in these cases fits its general strategy of justification, if indeed it has one. We also have to consider the joint fabric of the Strasbourg human rights protection system involving not only the court, but also the Commission and the Committee of Ministers which have also voiced their opinion on related issues.

---

[121] Up to the end of 1989 the court has handed down 205 judgments, 20 of them between 1959 and 1975, 185 of them between 1976 and 1989.

[122] Series A No. 24.

[123] Series A No. 133.

[124] Series A No. 45.

[125] Series A No. 142.

[126] Series A No. 91.

On the other hand, this small group of cases is of a particular fascination: for one, the court arrived at antagonistic results, in *Dudgeon* and *Norris* calling for the revision of a criminal statute, in *X and Y v. The Netherlands* requesting criminal legislation, in *Handyside* and in *Müller* tolerating the concrete application of a domestic criminal statute. The first three deal with norm-making, the last two with norm-application and in this sense they are more in line with the court's general judicial approach. In all these cases the question boils down to the same problem structure, i.e. striking the balance between legitimate state interference and the right to privacy or freedom or expression, proclaimed in the Convention by Arts. 8 and 10 respectively.[127]

1. The Facts of the Cases

Several decisions touched on criminalization issues. This holds true in particular for the abortion cases *Paton v. UK*[128] and *Brüggemann and Scheuten*.[129] Yet, let aside the fact that both these cases did not reach the court, they both fall short of really entering into the criminalization debate. In *Paton v. UK* the Commission dismissed a breach of Art. 2 of the Convention in case of a so-called medical indication and otherwise denied the applicant, who wanted to prevent his wife's abortion, procedural standing of his own with regard to Art. 8 of the Convention. In the case of *Brüggemann and Scheuten* the Commission and the Committee of Ministers, starting out from the assumption that abortion is not merely the pregnant woman's private affair, did not have to go very much into detail to find that the German abortion legislation in question did not impinge on the woman's right to privacy. The court's *The Sunday Times*[130] decision was concerned with the English law relating to contempt of court and thus with a criminal matter. Even though the court tried to avoid considering the English law on its merits, the case will still be of interest to us in relation to our criminalization cases, and more particularly in relation to our study of interpretation. Nonetheless, the details of the case need not be presented here.

It all started with *Handyside* in 1976. The applicant's firm had published The Little Red Schoolbook, an adapted English translation of a Danish book. The book was

---

[127] Text of Art. 8: "(1) Everyone has the right to respect for his private and family life, his home and his correspondence. There shall be no interference by a public authority with the exercise of this right except such as is in accordance with the law and is necessary in a democratic society in the interests of national security, public safety or the economic well-being of the country, for the prevention of disorder or crime, for the protection of health or morals, or for the protection of the rights and freedoms of others."

Text of Art. 10: "(1) Everyone has the right to freedom of expression. This right shall include freedom to hold opinions and to receive and impart information and ideas without interference by public authority and regardless of frontiers. This article shall not prevent States from requiring the licensing of broadcasting, television or cinema enterprises. (2) The exercise of these freedoms, since it carries with it duties and responsibilities, may be subject to such formalities, conditions, restrictions or penalties as are prescribed by law and are necessary in a democratic society, in the interests of national security, territorial integrity, or public safety, for the prevention of disorder or crime, for the protection of health or morals, for the protection of the reputation or rights of others, for preventing the disclosure of information received in confidence, or for maintaining the authority and impartiality of the judiciary."

[128] 8416/79: 19 DR 244 (Commission Decision).

[129] 6959/75: (Decision of the Committee of Ministers) 17-II-78.

[130] Series A No. 30.

meant to be used as a reference book for schoolchildren from age 12 onwards. Translations of the book had appeared and had been circulating freely in the majority of the Member States. The English authorities intervened on the ground of an alleged violation of the Obscene Publications Act. In summary proceedings before the magistrate, the applicant was found guilty. The court also ordered the books to be destroyed by the police. On appeal, the imminent danger that this book could "deprave and corrupt" a significant number of children was confirmed. Mr. Handyside argued principally a violation of the right to freedom of expression (Art. 10 of the Convention). The issue at stake was the interpretation of Art. 10 § 2 which allows *inter alia* for restrictions or penalties prescribed by law and "necessary in the democratic society." In defining the legal set-up the court pointed out that

- the domestic laws of the various Contracting States do not share a uniform conception of morals:
- the national authorities have priority in assessing the pressing social need and, in doing so, enjoy a margin of appreciation:
- it is up to the court to give the final ruling on whether a "restriction" or "penalty" is reconcilable with freedom of expression as protected by Art. 10.

In using the "supervisory power" the court could however, "on the strength of the data before it," detect a breach of Art. 10.

The *Müller* case which was decided some 12 years later followed a somewhat similar pattern in as much as the application of the Swiss obscenity statute (Art. 204 Swiss Criminal Code) to a painter's artistic expression was put into question. The applicants, among them the Swiss painter Josef Felix Müller, had been sentenced for publishing obscene material. Three paintings were confiscated. The paintings, in dispute for their crude depiction of sexual activity, had been exhibited at an exhibition of contemporary art in Fribourg (Switzerland). On appeal, the verdict was upheld, since the paintings aroused "repugnance and disgust." The Cassation Division of the Swiss Federal Court emphasized the overall impression conveyed by the paintings being such as to be morally offensive to a person of normal sensitivity. Hence it could detect a breach of Union law. In 1988, the confiscation order of 1982 was discharged and the paintings were subsequently returned to Mr. Müller, a move of the Swiss judiciary which may have had something to do with the fact that the case was pending before the Strasbourg court.

The applicants complained that their conviction and sentence to a fine as well as the confiscation of the paintings in dispute amounted to a breach of Art. 10 of the Convention. The Commission agreed as regards the confiscation, but denied a violation of Art. 10 in respect of the conviction. The court found no breach of Art. 10 at all. It boiled down to the question whether the interferences were "necessary in a democratic society." The court, in exercising its power to give the final ruling on the existence of a "pressing social need," started out by underlining the demands of plurality, tolerance and broadmindedness as well as artists' contribution "to the exchange of ideas and opinions which is essential for a democratic society" (§ 33). Yet, it considered artists not to be immune from the possibilities of limitations as provided for in § 2 of Art. 10, thus dismissing the idea of a general exemption from criminal liability for artistic expression. Notwithstanding the fact that conceptions of sexual morality have changed, the court accepted the view taken by the Swiss local and federal courts that these paintings were "liable grossly to offend the sense of sexual propriety of persons of ordinary sensitivity." The court rejected the argument that the confiscation was in breach of Art. 10 since the applicant Müller could have applied earlier to have his paintings returned. Judge Spielmann dissented, dwelling on the relativity of the notion of obscenity and referring to the historic *Baudelaire* case.

The *Dudgeon* case concerned the law in Northern Ireland with regard to homosexual conduct. The applicant complained that the relevant provision in Northern Ireland, in punishing sexual practices between consenting male adults, violated his right to respect for his private life, in breach of Art. 8 of the Convention. The applicant had been the object of police investigations destined to bring about a prosecution for the offense of gross indecency between males. Even though the Attorney General had decided that the prosecution was not within the public interest, the applicant, who had previously been engaged in a campaign to liberalize the existing law, brought the case to Strasbourg. He claimed *inter alia* that the existing law in Northern Ireland relating to male homosexual conduct and the police investigation violated Art. 8 of the Convention. The Commission held in its report that the legal prohibition of homosexual acts between consenting adults was in breach of Art. 8, though it did not object to prohibitions incriminating homosexual acts involving male persons under 21 years of age.

The court started out by scrutinizing the law, the law reform perspectives and the practice with regard to such conduct in the UK, also considering Northern Ireland's particular constitutional and political situation. At the time when the applicant lodged his complaint, in 1976, homosexual conduct between consenting adults no longer constituted a criminal offense in England and Wales, subject to certain exceptions. The Criminal Justice (Scotland) Act 1980 followed suit, after a period of a policy of non-prosecution. Similar moves for reform of the law in Northern Ireland came to a standstill. The position is best summarized by a statement on the part of the Secretary of State for Northern Ireland in 1979 quoted by the court: "Consultations have shown that strong views are held in Northern Ireland both for and against change in the existing law. Although it is not possible to say with certainty what is the feeling of the majority of the people in the province, it is clear that a substantial body of opinion there (embracing a wide range of religious as well as political opinion) is opposed to the proposed change . . . " (§ 26).

Again, the court located the seed of the problem in the "necessity clause" of Art. 8 § 2 of the Convention allowing for restrictions and penalties which are "necessary in a democratic society" for the protection of morals. They followed their own formula of a "pressing social need," used for the first time in *Handyside.*

The court considered it self-evident that some degree of regulation of homosexual conduct by means of the criminal law can be justified as necessary. It further conceded that the national authorities make the initial assessment of the pressing social need. On the other hand, it reserved for itself, in conformity with *Handyside,* the position to review the reasons given for that interference spelling out review parameters such as proportionality and relevance of interests at stake. The court accepted the argument that the national authorities would, within the framework of Art 8 § 2 of the Convention, have to take into account the particular socio-cultural and moral background of a specific community. Yet again, the court was not prepared to sanction total relativity. Referring to the "marked changes which have occurred in this regard in the domestic law of the Member States" (§ 60), these being the result of a more rational and tolerant approach towards different forms of sexual behavior—the court in the end held that the reasons brought forward to justify such offenses were not sufficient.

The *Norris* case pertaining to the criminal law governing homosexual behavior in Ireland is the almost exact replica of the *Dudgeon* case, the only relevant factual difference being that the application had not been subject to any police action at all. Consequently, the court only had to re-affirm the stand it took in the *Dudgeon* case.

X and Y v. The Netherlands also concerned the area of sexual offenses. A mentally handicapped girl (Y) who had been living in a privately-run home for mentally handicapped children was forced by the son-in-law of the directress of the institution to have sexual intercourse with him. At the time of the incident she had just become 16. Since Y was, due to her mental state, unable to file a complaint, her father (X) did so on her behalf. However, the prosecutor's office did not open proceedings. Judicial remedies failed: the Court of Appeal held that it was doubtful whether the charge of rape could be proved. With regard to the specific crime of sexual abuse (Art. 248 of the Netherlands Criminal Code), the father's complaint was considered invalid, since his daughter, being over 16, would have been the only person legally empowered to file a complaint, even though she was, in the concrete circumstances, incapable of doing so. Mr. X instituted proceedings in Strasbourg claiming *inter alia* that, due to this lack of protection by the Netherlands sexual offenses system, the right of both his daughter and himself to respect for their private life, guaranteed by Art. 8, had been violated. The proceedings centered around this alleged violation of Art. 8 and around the necessity of a criminal law protection. In justification of this lacuna, the Netherlands government referred to alternative civil remedies which were available and to the legislator's dilemma in the sense that a criminal provision might itself have been challenged under Art. 8 of the Convention as a form of "unacceptable paternalism" (§ 25). Neither the Commission, nor the court were prepared to follow this line of argument. The court, recalling that Art. 8 of the Convention could require positive measures designed to secure respect for private life, found protection by criminal law provisions indispensable in this case. The relevant passage of the court's reasoning (§ 27) reads as follows: "The court finds that the protection afforded by the civil law in the case of wrongdoing of the kind inflicted on Miss Y is insufficient. This is a case where fundamental values and essential aspects of private life are at stake. Effective deterrence is indispensable in this area and it can be achieved only by criminal law provisions: indeed, it is by such provisions that the matter is normally regulated. Moreover, as was pointed out by the Commission, this is in fact an area in which the Netherlands has generally opted for a system of protection based on the criminal law. The only gap, so far as the Commission and the court have been made aware, is as regards the persons in the situation of Miss Y: in such cases, this system meets a procedural obstacle which the Netherlands legislature had apparently not foreseen." The court therefore held that the lacuna in the Netherlands criminal law constituted a breach of Art. 8 of the Convention. It ordered that a compensation of 3,000 guilders be paid to Miss Y under Art. 50 of the Convention.

2. Some Remarks on Legal Justification

a. The Sonderfall Thesis

Justification consists in giving "good" reasons in support of an action or a decision. Legal justification consists in giving "legally good" reasons in support of a legal decision. We take judicial justification to be the paradigm of legal justification: the justification advanced by the parties and by the Commission will be modeled upon the doctrine or strategy of justification generally adopted by the court. In this sense, courts generally provide ideal types of operative interpretation used by practitioners.

Legal justification is seen as a special case *(Sonderfall)* of justification in practical discourse. It is special because it is highly institutionalized; there is a limit to the grounds (sources) that can be advanced in support of a legal claim and juridical procedures are highly regulated. The rules governing legal justification are accepted by a social interpretative practice—by authoritative and expository doctrine—and are regulated, at least in part, by jurisdictional and procedural norms mainly Art. 51 of the Convention and Art. 52 § 1 of the Rules of Procedure. According to these, legal arguments must be ultimately grounded on sources of law which count as reasons of authority. This need to connect with accepted legal norms makes the structure of legal justification deductive *sensu largo*: the decision is *presented* as applying the law (as interpreted by the court) to the facts (as established and qualified by the court).

b. Rational Reconstruction

The method we follow in the analysis of the court's justification is that of *rational reconstruction*. Our attention focuses on the justificatory arguments offered by the court and on the deep structure of justification. By "deep structure" we mean the moves from established law to the concrete law applying decisions which need not necessarily be made explicit in the judgments. Rational reconstruction is in this sense a descriptive method: it tries to capture the arguments which are explicitly or implicitly used by the court. These arguments are then systematized and discussed from a theoretical point of view, i.e., from the standpoint of recent theories of legal reasoning as developed by, for example, Aarnio, Alexy, Bell, MacCormick, Peczenik, Wróblewski, etc.

The aim of rational reconstruction is the elaboration of the operative theory of justification in a given court, in our case, of the European Court of Human Rights. The materials from which such a doctrine will be reconstructed are:

- the enacted norms that regulate certain aspects of justification as interpreted and elaborated on by the court;
- the explicit pronouncements of the court as to how interpretation should proceed (these can be called explicit *directives* of interpretation);
- the *criteria* of interpretation implicit or resorted to by the court in its interpretative activity;
- doctrinal works on the methods of interpretation used by the court.

We believe it is possible to reconstruct the doctrine of justification (or interpretation) operative at the Strasbourg court relying on these materials. The descriptive import of our reconstruction can be checked and controlled in different ways. The main control consists in assessing whether our reconstruction helps to understand the court's activity in a clear light, whether it provides new insights into the work of the court. Our reconstruction can be further checked by those who are in close contact with the court and well-acquainted with its working methods. What they will ask is whether our analysis in any way captures what they see the court as doing. If these tests fail, then we can conclude that our reconstruction is wanting. In saying this we are calling for further discussion and criticism.

But rational reconstruction also has a critical import: in reconstructing the court's operative doctrine of justification at a more general remove we are at the same time elevating it to the level of a model or a landmark against which particular justifications of the court can be assessed and criticized. For instance, if we hold that the court interprets the Convention according to the principle of *effet utile* (or effectiveness) i.e., making sure that the rights and obligations laid down therein are constructed so as to achieve their full realization, then the court can be criticized according to its own standards if, in a given case, it adopts an interpretation of the Convention which does not lead to its full effectiveness. Of course, dwelling on this critical task of rational reconstruction presupposes an acceptance of the underlying values of consistency and coherence and universalizability over time and over cases which are predicated of any rational agent. Otherwise any internal systematic criticism would be futile.

c. *Stages of the Law-Applying Decision*

The court's application of the Convention will characteristically follow four stages:

(1) *Selection or determination of the applicable article(s) of the Convention or the Protocols.* This task will normally be facilitated by the applicants and the Commission who will frame the dispute in legal terms expressing which article(s) of the Convention call for consideration. But the court is not bound by such characterizations and it can examine the facts submitted to its examination and characterize them in law *ex officio*, in the light of the Convention as a whole (*Handyside*, § 41). The determination of the applicable article(s) of the Convention is fairly unproblematic: the law which the court is called on to apply is not scattered in a congeries of sources. It is contained in one basic text, the Convention (and the Protocols). In this sense the Strasbourg court contrasts with the Luxembourg court which often has to decide hard cases regarding the determination of the applicable norm.

(2) *Determination of the meaning of the applicable norm.* Two situations might exists. If the meaning of the norm is clear as regards the facts at stake, this will probably mean that the court has already taken a decision on a similar issue and that the case at hand raises no novel issue. In this case the Commission will normally decide the case without referring it to the court. This amounts to saying that the court will usually receive hard cases only, i.e., cases that raise novel and hard points of law. But it does not follow that all the aspects of the cases decided by the court will be hard, nor that the cases decided by the Commission are always

clear. Besides, the Commission plays an important role regarding hard cases, first by centering the legal dispute and secondly by facilitating friendly settlements. Also, in deciding a case without referring it to the court, the Commission may be trying to avoid placing the court in a difficult position. This is the case in *Paton v. UK* decided by the Commission and in the *Brüggeman and Scheuten* case decided by the Committee of Ministers; both cases deal with the abortion issue.

In *Norris* the only novel issue was whether the applicant could count as a "victim" and it is probably because of this issue that *Norris* reached the court. As for the substantial issue raised in this case, the court dealt with it applying *acte clair* doctrine. The court applied the *Dudgeon* principles to *Norris* in a way which clearly resembles the European Court of Justice's handling of the *Da Costa* case. In other words, *Norris* is to *Dudgeon* what *Da Costa*[131] is to *van Gend en Loos*[132]: both the Luxembourg and the Strasbourg courts treat their own jurisprudence as authoritative and previous decisions *in practice* work as precedents within these courts.

It is in this second state that the court interprets the Convention resorting to some implicit or explicit doctrine of interpretation. In order to justify its proposed interpretation, the court will provide some arguments or reasons, which, although they frequently overlap, can be roughly classified in three groups:

(a) authority reasons based on the text of some legal norm or on the logical consequences that derive from it according to some conception of the logic of norms;
(b) arguments derived from the Convention as a whole, as a legal system, or from the purposes, aims or objectives which it seeks to achieve, or from the principles which it embodies;
(c) substantive arguments that regard the Convention as a living instrument to be interpreted according to the changing conceptions of the day. The debate on criminalization and decriminalization can be located here. These substantive arguments can be of different types: arguments from moral or political principles, arguments from consequences, arguments from the specific legal discipline, policy arguments, etc.

(3) *Determination of the facts of the case and their characterization in law.* This step is extremely important. Whereas this state is usually associated with truth finding procedure, we focus our attention on the court's choice of the facts as being relevant. In making this choice the court is guided by a notion of narrative coherence. The court will normally be presented the facts by the Commission, which, in its turn will have established them having regard to the proceedings in domestic courts. The court will characterize or qualify these facts in law and will formulate them in the appropriate legal language with a view of their subsumption under the application norm. The facts will be presented by the court as *particular* instantiations of the *universal* categories predicated in the applicable norm.

---

[131] Case 28-30/62 [1963] ECR 31.

[132] Case 26/62 [1963] ECR 1.

(4) *Determination of the consequences*. In many cases the law provides a single solution, but in others, e.g., sentencing in criminal law or, as regards the Convention, awarding compensation according to Art. 50, the law allows for a scope of discretion in the determination of consequences. The decision on consequences is presented as the conclusion of the reasoning.

d. Two Aspects of the Justification of Judicial Decisions

The justification of the judicial decision is twofold: the reasoning and the premises have to be justified.

(1) The decision will be formal-logically justified if it can be shown to follow from established premises, i.e., if the logical transformations leading from the premises to the conclusion are formally valid. This aspect of legal justification is interested in the reasoning without looking at the content of the premises. These transformations are roughly deductive.

(2) The decision will be materially justified when the different premises (stages (1) to (4) above) are themselves regarded as justified or *richtig*. This is the most important aspect of justification. By calling it material all we mean is that the elaboration of the premises is not itself a process governed by logics, but is a matter of (legal) substance and that implies a certain range of *choice* on the part of the judge. Logics do not govern the choice of this or that applicable norm, nor do they determine the qualification of facts as being relevant and the determination of consequences when there is leeway. Logics are only concerned with the formal aspect of reasoning.

e. The Role of Discovery in the Explanation of Justification

We focus our attention on the process of justification of the decision, i.e., on the arguments offered by the court as grounds for the decision. This process may or may not coincide with the process of discovery of the decision, i.e., the heuristic process which leads to it. It may be the case that, as a matter of fact, the court first considers the possible consequences of a tentative decision within the legal system and within the environment of the legal system, and then formulates the premises environment of the legal system, and then formulates the premises accordingly with a view to obtaining the desired consequences or else, reformulates the premises, chooses a different norm to govern the case or interprets the same norm in a different way or qualifies the facts in a different way, if the foreseen consequences are undesirable or could not be acceptable to a given audience. It may also be that the reasons which actually led the court to take this or that decision are not reflected in the motivation publicly offered.

The focus on discovery can provide a better understanding of justification; it can give us clues as to which reasons are being considered by the court and why of all these only some are given in the public justification. In this respect discovery adds a certain sociological tune to the explanation of justification without which decision-making cannot be properly accounted for. But this does not mean that the public justification is itself unimportant or irrelevant. Of course, from the standpoint of a critical normative theory of justification we can postulate that the public justification offered by the court should reflect the arguments and considerations that *in fact* lead to the decision. We wish to argue that this requirement of sincerity or transparency of the motivation is necessary for the rational acceptability of the decision. The problem will then be a methodological one: how can we know which reasons actually led to the decision if judicial deliberations are private and secret, and we are not judges of the court? We seem to be condemned to speculate on the basis of hypotheses, Art. 19 of the rules of Procedure making an empirical enquiry of these factors practically impossible.

It is interesting to note in this respect that the court's judgments contain two elements which contribute to the view that the court does face a plurality of arguments in its deliberations. The possibility of drafting separate opinions is the first interesting pointer to such plurality. Art. 51 of the Convention allows the publication of separate opinions. These contribute to the clarity and depth of judicial debate. It is sometimes argued that the possibility of drafting separate opinions diminishes the authority of the court's justification; we subscribe to Ost's point of view that separate opinions can reinforce the court's authority, "*si du moins on vent rendre à l'obligation de motivation son sens véritable et faire dériver l'autorité d'un arrêt de sa rationalité intrinsèque plutôt que de l'usage de l'"argument" d'autorite.*" Secondly, as a matter of practice, the court presents some of the arguments put forward by the parties and usually addresses those arguments in detail, presenting counter-arguments and sometimes even indicating to what extent it considers them persuasive. The very existence of these two elements supports the view that the court is usually confronted with an arsenal of arguments among which it will select those which will appear in the public justification. Series B of the European Court of Human Rights provides valuable clues as to the parties' pleadings, as do the parties' memorials at the oral hearings.

Indeed, replying to the arguments put forward by the parties can be considered a feature of rational practical discourse as theorized by, e.g., Alexy. It can also serve as a basis for criticizing and assessing the court's decision-making practice. Thus the court can be criticized in *The Sunday Times* case for refusing to consider one of the main contentions of the applicants: that their right to freedom of expression had been violated, not only by reason of the injunction granted by the English courts, but also by reason of the continuing restraints to which they were subjected as a result of the over-extension and lack of precision of the law on contempt of court. This second part of the claim was supported by the Principal Delegate of the Commission at a hearing on 24-4-78, but it had not been included in the Commission decision of 21-3-75 declaring the application admissible. According to the court, it is this formal decision which determines the object of the case brought before the court. The court relied on an extremely formalistic argument to conclude that it had to examine only whether there had been a violation of the Convention by reason of the judgment of the House of Lords, and refused to consider the English (common) law of contempt of court on its merits, i.e., whether it was too broad, uncertain and ambiguous. This clearly contrasts with its own, less formalistic, decision in *Handyside* where the court said that "once a case is duly referred to it, the court may take cognizance of every question of law arising in the course of the proceedings (§ 41). In *The Sunday Times* the court avoided having to address the legally and politically hard case whether the English common law on contempt of court satisfied the requirements of Art. 10 § 2, thus placing itself in a position where it might have to require the UK to adopt precise legislation on contempt of court (this the UK did later on in 1981).

It might be interesting to point out that the court adopted the more formalistic attitude in a case where it found in favor of the applicants and the less formalistic attitude in a case where it found in favor of the respondent government. It is not possible to say how far this is the result of a conscious implicit policy, but at any rate, it is thought provoking, and a similar compromising attitude can be found in the European Court of Justice.

By concentrating on the context of justification we do not intend to downplay the relevance of the context of discovery. Yet, we are not persuaded by the argument that the public presentation of the decision is only a façade legitimation. Rather, the justificatory reasoning of the court represents a self-conscious effort to achieve rationality. The court will try to articulate the reasons that support its decision, to address this decision to an audience and to present this decision as legally correct, as discursively as possible. The addressees of the decision will be able to control the rationality and acceptability of the decision precisely by examining the reasons offered by the court in support of its decision. The court will therefore try to achieve the rational acceptability of its justification because it is precisely the rationality of the court's justification which enhances its own authority and legitimacy.

3. The Court as a Social Agent

Many aspects of the context of discovery—covering the psychological process of decision-making and also socio-political factors of judicial decision-making—are relevant for a better understanding of justification. Perhaps the most important aspects are those regarding the court as a social agent, i.e., as an institution engaged in social action. As a social agent the court is self-conscious of the role it plays within the Strasbourg system for the protection of Human Rights. The role of the court is a function of the task assigned to it by the Convention and of the expectations which the legal and political environment of the court have developed, i.e., a function of what the Commission and the Committee of Ministers and the Contracting Parties expect from the court. The expectations of the larger audiences of the court are also to be considered. These audiences include the legal audience, practicing and academic lawyers, the applicants and the public at large, usually mediated by the mass media. Taking all these elements into account, the court will mold its own self-perception.

The court is assigned the task of interpreting and applying the Convention. By means of its dynamic approach to interpretation the court can, to some extent, develop the Convention. By dynamic we mean a cluster of arguments: teleological interpretation, its use of the principle of effectiveness, its resort to general principles of law and to evolutionary interpretation in the light of changing social conditions (see *infra*). But there are practical limits to this development: the very text of the Convention and the acceptability of its interpretation among the audiences. It is not possible to determine *a priori* exactly when the Contracting States will consider that the court is engaging in dangerous policy-making, thus overstepping its role. The court will, at any rate, try to present its interpretation as based on the letter and spirit of the Convention.

The court does not enjoy primary political authority, i.e., the authority to create law anew. This primary authority is held, in the Strasbourg system, not by an institution but by a document, by the Convention which can be modified or added to only by agreement of the High Contracting Parties. The court enjoys only a secondary or derived authority, i.e., an authority to interpret and apply the law of the Convention.

In this sense the Strasbourg system differs from the legal system of the European Union. In the EU primary authority lies in the foundational Treaties (and also indirectly in the Member States), but, and this is where it differs from the Strasbourg system, there are institutions whose express task it is to develop the (programmatic) law laid down in those Treaties. These institutions are the Council of Ministers and the Commission (to a lesser extent) of the EU. The result is that the body of law is ever growing in the EU. Law-making in the Union is essentially dynamic: the objectives laid down in the Treaties (especially in the Treaty establishing the EEC) being the source of such dynamism. The European Court of Justice, the Luxembourg court, applies and interprets a complex and mounting corpus of norms scattered in different documents which derive their legal validity from the Treaties. By contrast, the Strasbourg court has to interpret and apply one legal document: the Convention (including its Protocols and the Rules of Procedure of the court), even though it will, in support of its interpretation not only refer to the Convention, but will at times also hold recourse to conventions of the Council of Europe as evidence of common European standards. This focus on one document makes the task of determining the applicable norm and of systematizing the law considerably easier. But the Convention is a corpus of legal norms which resemble principles more than strict rules. The very area of Human Rights is a "fuzzy" set of the law, *flou du droit*, as Mireille Delmas-Marty has brilliantly explained. Rules have an "all or nothing" character, as Dworkin says whereas principles have a dimension of weight, they are formulated in a general, sometimes ambiguous, way which calls for interpretation; all the more so because they are the result of a complicated process of weighing and balancing differing rights and interests. The human rights of the individual are weighed against the state authorities' interference with those rights when certain conditions obtain. Not surprisingly, the interpretative task of the court will also imply weighing and balancing the interests at stake in particular cases and defining ever more the conditions and limits in which state interference can be tolerated or can be called for (criminalization) or cannot be considered legitimate (decriminalization). In that sense, "decisions about human rights are not a technical exercise in interpreting texts, but judgments about political morality." This can clearly be seen in the cases we are concerned with here.

Although the court tries to restrict its discussion to the possible violation of the Convention by a law-applying decision taken by domestic authorities, the examination of domestic law on its merits is sometimes unavoidable. This supervisory activity, whereby the court almost has a "judicial review" function, takes place especially with regard to criminal law. However, it can also bear on civil law, as the recent case of *F v. Switzerland* indicates. There the court held that the disputed measure (a three year prohibition on re-marriage imposed by the Lausanne District Civil Court on the basis of Art. 150 of the Swiss Civil Code) violated Art. 12 of the Convention which protects the right to marriage. This was indirectly a decision to the effect that the said Art. 150

violated Art. 12 of the Convention, "but the court notes that the Convention does not give it jurisdiction to order Switzerland to alter its legislation" (§ 43).

In making such decisions, the court is supervising states' interferences with the rights of the individual. States find themselves having to justify their own policies before the court. Herein lies the relevance of the court as a socio-political agent. Surely, the court realizes that it cannot go too far and upset the Contracting parties. But at the same time it has to make sure that the rights proclaimed in Section One of the Convention do not become dead letter. But precisely where the limit lies is something that cannot be determined *a priori*.

The decisions we are concerned with present precisely this dilemma. In *Handyside* and in *X and Y v. The Netherlands* the court expressly states that it is in no way its task to take the place of the competent national courts in the interpretation of domestic law. In *X and Y v. The Netherlands* the court regarded it as established that in the case in question criminal proceedings could not be instituted. The court took it for granted that the Arnhem Court of Appeal had interpreted domestic law correctly: there was a gap in the Netherlands criminal law, and this gap could not be filled by analogy nor by broad interpretation leading to incrimination. This strategy is a generally rejected argument—a *may-not* source—in most legal systems, and it is also forbidden by the Convention (Art. 7). So, the court is clearly sticking to its own competence. In *Dudgeon* the court admitted that the UK had acted in good faith in taking into account that in Northern Irish society there was a strong body of opposition to changes in the law relating to homosexuality and in *Handyside* the court recognized that "by reason of their direct and continuous contact with the vital forces of their countries, State authorities are in principle in a better position than the international judge to give an opinion on the exact content of those [moral] requirements" (§ 48 of *Handyside* also quoted at 52 of *Dudgeon*). Here the court is faithful to the established international principle of *comity*.

But, at the same time, the court is willing to assert its own authority and to proclaim that it is competent to decide whether the state interferences in question were proportionate to the social need as claimed by the respondent government. In other words, the court is saying that the state authorities do not have an unlimited power of appreciation; the court is reserving for itself the final say. As Merrills has eloquently put it, "the margin of appreciation is a way of recognizing that the international protection of human rights and sovereign freedom of action are not contradictory but complementary." Where the one ends, the other begins, or, as the court said in *Handyside*, the domestic margin of appreciation goes hand in hand with a European supervision (§ 49, recently recalled in *Müller* § 32).

The court faces a similar dilemma in considering whether to construct *European standards* of morals or whether to respect the possibly diverse views prevailing in each Member State and even in the different nations which make up the Member States. This second option was taken in *Handyside*. The court accepted that the state interference was aiming at the protection of the morals of the young as understood by the domestic authorities according to domestic standards within their margin of appreciation (§ 54). Five years later the court moved closer to the idea of European standards. Thus in *Dudgeon* the court said that it could not "overlook the marked changes which have occurred in this regard [homosexual practices between consenting adults] in the domestic law of the Member States" (§ 60). But it might be interesting to point out that in this case too, the court admitted a certain degree of paternalism as regards the young. Whereas it stated that it was not concerned with making any value judgment as to the morality of homosexual relations between adult males (§ 54), it also acknowledged the legitimate necessity in a democratic society for some degree of control over homosexual conduct notably in order to provide safeguards against the exploitation and corruption of those who are especially vulnerable by reason, for example, of their youth (§ 62) and the court referred back to the idea of European standards: "in practice there is legislation on the matter in all the Member States of the Council of Europe" (§ 49).

In toying with the idea of European moral standards it is approaching a slippery slope, which explains why the court is moving with extreme care. It is aware that reference to such standards as a justificatory reason itself requires justification: some empirical proof that there are such standards, and some reasons why they are considered relevant to the case at hand. In those matters where there has been a given legislative trend in several Member States of the Council of Europe it might seem possible to try to distill certain European standards. This is the case regarding the trend of decriminalizing homosexual conduct between consenting adults in private or, as in the recent *Soering* case, the practical abolition of the death penalty. But in other matters, the court might not be willing to have recourse to the idea of European standards: e.g., as regards obscene publications in the *Handyside* case where the court did not dispute the domestic court's application of the moral-legal standard of English law, i.e., "tendency to deprave and corrupt" to the "Little Red Schoolbook," or in *Müller*, where the court recognized, as did the Swiss courts, that conceptions of sexual morality have changed in recent years [but] in the circumstances, having regard to the margin of appreciation left to them under Art. 10 § 2, the Swiss courts were entitled to consider it "necessary" for the protection of morals to impose a fine on the applicants for publishing obscene material (§ 36). The court was not persuaded by the applicants' argument that similar works by Müller had been freely exhibited in other parts of Switzerland. These decisions recall the familiar discussion about community standards as a yardstick to judge pornography, much debated in particular in the USA.

The dilemma between allowing the state authorities a "margin of appreciation" and not questioning state action on the one hand and, on the other hand securing individual human rights thus building upon a European supervision is reflected in the court's interpretative activity. There is a basic choice between an interpretation favorable to the fundamental rights of the individual (this position is especially defended by the Commission) and an interpretation weighted towards state sovereignty (this approach has been defended by Judge Fitzmaurice). The court usually sides with the Commission in opting for the effectiveness principle.

The idea of European standards also reflects this tension. It is related to the criterion of the autonomous meaning of Convention notions. This difficult balance can be clearly seen in *Öztürk*[133] where the court elaborated the autonomous notion of "criminal charge" or "*matière pénale*" in relation to Art. 6.

---

[133] Series A No. 73.

4. The Deep Structure of Justification in our Cases

The cases analyzed all share a similar deep structure of justification which can be called deductive. Such structure can be reconstructed in the following manner:

(1) The first question the court might deal with is that of the admissibility of an action. This question will arise whenever the defendant contests the capacity of the applicant to institute proceedings, and the dispute will usually turn on the question whether the applicant counts as a "victim" within the meaning of Art. 25 of the Convention. *Norris* provides a good example. The court found that Mr. Norris could claim to be a victim of a violation of the Convention, because, although no police action had been taken against him, he was in substantially the same position as Mr. Dudgeon in that he ran the risk of being directly affected by the challenged legislation (§ 32-34). This preliminary question is especially relevant in this case since six judges dissented from the court's decision precisely and only on this point. They held Mr. Norris could not claim to be a victim because no action was taken against him by the authorities. A question on the interpretation of the word 'victim' arises here. The approach followed by the court in this respect is guided by the effectiveness principle allowing individuals to question criminal statutes as such. A similar wide approach has been adopted by the Commission and the Committee of Ministers (see, e.g., the *Brüggemann and Scheuten* decision).

(2) The second step of the justification is not usually present in the presentation of the court's justification, but it underpins such justification. It consists in a syllogism which runs:

- major premise: Art. 1 of the Convention: "the High Contracting Parties shall secure to everyone within their jurisdiction the rights and freedoms defined in Section One of this Convention," i.e., Art. 2-18;
- minor premise: *a* (i.e., the Netherlands, Switzerland, the UK or the Republic of Ireland in our cases) is a High Contracting Party; the applicant *b* (i.e., Mr. Handyside, Mr. Dudgeon, Mr. Norris, X and Y, Müller and others, and *The Sunday Times*) is within *a*'s jurisdiction; and *c* (i.e., the freedom of expression defined in Art. 10 and the right to privacy defined in Art. 8) is a right or freedom defined in Section One of the Convention;
- conclusion: High Contracting State *a* shall secure right *c* to *b*.

This is the underpinning syllogism which makes it technically possible for the court to formulate the *dispositif* of its judgment: *a* has (or has not) violated the Convention in so far as it has not (or it has) secured to *b* a right *c* defined in Section One of the Convention.

Of course the most difficult and interesting questions of legal justification are not amendable to classical binary logic, but rather to the interpretation of the applicable norm and to the qualification of the facts, and the two are ultimately a matter of choice or discretionary judgment (see *supra*). The crux of the matter consists in determining what exactly the article of the Convention requires, and in deciding whether the facts of the case are covered by the applicable article. Perhaps extended multivalue logics can account for some of these operations.

(3) The next step consists in determining the applicable provision: which article of the Convention is under discussion. We are focusing our attention on Arts. 8 and 10 which are the main articles upon which the applicants base their pleadings. This third step is governed by paragraph one of Arts. 8 and 10, and it amounts to determining whether there has been a violation of the right of privacy (Art. 8) or of the freedom of expression (Art. 10). The violation can originate in:

- existing legislation (as in *Dudgeon* and *Norris*);
- the non existence of legislation protecting such rights (as in *X and Y v. The Netherlands*). In this case the breach of the Convention originates in a non-action, i.e. in a lack of the protection due to the individual. This almost revolutionary possibility, inspired in the idea of states' *Schutzpflichten*, was first recognized in *Airey*;
- the decision of a state authority in application of the existing law, in which case the law *en soi* may not be the matter in dispute but can be implicitly contested (as in *Handyside, Miller* and *The Sunday Times*).

(4) The final and most important step consists in determining whether that violation which the court has found can be justified by the three cumulative conditions laid down in paragraph two of Arts. 8 and 10:

- the interference has to be in accordance with the law;
- the interference must be necessary in a democratic society;
- the interference must have an aim which is legitimate under this paragraph: for our purposes: the protection of morals or, as in *The Sunday Times*, maintaining the authority and impartiality of the judiciary.

These conditions are framed in ambiguous terms which call for interpretation. In the next section we shall examine how the court has interpreted them and what reasons it has offered in support of such interpretation. The court's interpretative activity is only one aspect of its discretionary decision-making. The other aspect is its qualification of the facts as being relevant to the case and to the norm. Interpretation is the *process* through which the court determines the meaning of the applicable norm and qualification the process through which the court establishes and formulates the facts of a case with a view to their subsumption under the applicable norm, once a certain interpretation (*as result*) has been given to it. Thus qualification pragmatically follows interpretation, although, heuristically, there is a feed-back between the two guided by a certain "*Vorverständnis.*"

5. The Court's Doctrine of Interpretation

As we stated above, the court provides three main types of reasons for its interpretative decision: authority reason, canons or arguments of interpretation *stricto sensu* and substantive reasons. Authority reasons are specially protected reasons, e.g. arguments drawn from the "clear" text of a legal provision or, more commonly, from precedent. There are few provisions in the Convention which can be considered clear in a pre-interpretative sense, that is following a linguistic understanding of the provision for the purposes of communication. But many provisions of the Convention have already been interpreted in previous decisions given by the court. Such decisions pragmatically operate as precedents, and the court makes extensive use of these: the *Norris* judgment is a carbon copy of *Dudgeon*. *The Sunday Times* keeps going back to *Handyside* as do *Dudgeon* and *Müller*.

Even *X and Y v. The Netherlands*, which has a structure clearly distinguishable from the other judgments, makes use of two "precedents": *Airey* and *Handyside*. Actually, its distinctiveness flows from a combination of these two decisions. *Handyside* elaborates on the margin of appreciation. *Airey* is very important because in that case the court held that, although the object of Art. 8 is essentially that of protecting the individual against the arbitrary interference of public authorities (negative obligation of the State), in addition there may be positive obligations which "may involve the adoption of measures designed to secure respect for private life [*Schutzpflichten*] even in the sphere of the relations of individuals between themselves." Thus, a breach of Art. 8 can also come about from a lack of protective positive measures (§ 23 of *X and Y*, and § 32 of *Airey*). It does not become apparent from the judgment whether the court is extending the meaning of interference within Art. 8 § 2 to a lack of positive protective measures or whether it is extending the possible breach of Art. 8 § 1 to cover not only interferences—narrowly interpreted—but also non-action. The fact that the court did not qualify the arguments brought forward by the Netherlands government as a "reverse test" of Art. 8 § 2—non-interference with the right of the accused to private life—would support the narrow meaning of interference.

Substantive reasons will be dealt with in the next section, especially as regards the (de)criminalization debate. Let us now concentrate on the arguments of interpretation used by the court in the case we are discussing.

On some occasions the court explicitly states how interpretation is to proceed; in other words, the court provides *directives* of interpretation which have a prescriptive illocutionary force. On other occasions the court follows or uses certain criteria of interpretation which can be reconstructed by the observer by looking at the meaning ascribed to a certain provision (interpretation as result). The court's *directives* of interpretation can be found in *Golder* where the court closely follows Arts. 31-33 of the Vienna Convention on the Law of the Treatise.

a. Established Methods of Interpretation

1. Criteria of Interpretation

(1) *Semiotic criteria of interpretation*

The court first resorts to semiotic or linguistic criteria in order to interpret a provision. Of course, even when interpretation *stricto sensu* is not present, linguistic understanding always is, and roughly follows the same scheme as other forms of pragmatic understanding for the purpose of verbal communication. But when it comes to interpreting the words of the Convention, if puzzled about their meaning, the court will resort to some semiotic argument of interpretation.

In the cases analyzed we have detected one explicit semiotic directive: in *The Sunday Times* (§ 48) the court is faced with the interpretation of the words "prescribed by law" or, in French "*prévues par la loï*." The court mentions other articles of the Convention where a similar expression is found (systemic contextual criterion) and then states: "thus confronted with versions of a law-making treaty which are equally authentic but not exactly the same, the court must interpret them in a way that reconciles them as far as possible and is most appropriate in order to realize the aim and achieve the object of the treaty." In support of this directive the court mentions its own decision in *Wemhoff* and Art. 33 § 4 of the Vienna Convention. Thus it seems that the court considers teleological criteria as the most important. The court also refers to its own case law on the interpretation of "prescribed by law" in *Müller* (§ 29). The court states that this notion is related to the principle of foreseeability of the law but recognizes that foreseeability cannot be absolute. The need to avoid excessive rigidity and to keep in pace with changing circumstances means that many laws are drafted in vague terms. In saying this the court is developing ideas on the origin of interpretation.

It is common opinion that words can have an ordinary language meaning or a specialized meaning. The court has followed the ordinary language criterion in *X and Y v. The Netherlands* (§ 22) where it held that "private life" covers the physical and "moral integrity of the person, including his or her sexual life." In *Handyside* (§ 48) the court faced the interpretation of the word "necessary" which appears *inter alia* in para 2 of Arts. 8 and 10. The court said it is not synonymous with "indispensable" but neither has it the flexibility of such expressions as "admissible," "ordinary," "useful" or "desirable." The court mentioned the articles of the Convention where these expressions are contained and concluded by giving this word a special Convention meaning: the notion of "necessity" implies a "pressing social need." This interpretation is confirmed in its later judgments, especially in *Dudgeon* (§ 51), and it can therefore be affirmed that the notion has acquired an autonomous meaning within the Convention. In *Norris* the Irish government contested this interpretation, but the court confirmed its previous interpretation and saw "no reason to depart from the approach which emerges from its settled case law . . . ." The court gave a further reason for rejecting the wider interpretation proposed by the government, a reason of authority in an *a contrario* argument: to accept the government's contention that the court is precluded from reviewing Ireland's observance of its obligation not to exceed what is necessary in a democratic society "would run counter to the terms of Art. 19 of the Convention, under which the court was set up in order 'to ensure the observance of the engagements undertaken by the High Contracting Parties'" (§ 45). This interpretation in *Norris* is also inspired by effectiveness and systematic criteria, but it is dealt with here because the main point is the construction of an autonomous Convention meaning.

This notion of autonomous meaning can further be detected in *The Sunday Times* where the court insisted, once again, on the special meaning of necessity: "If and to the extent that Art. 10 § 2 was promoted by the notions underlying either the English law of contempt of court or any other similar domestic institution, it can not have adopted them as they stood: it transposed them into an autonomous context. It is 'necessity' in terms of the Convention which the court has to assess, its role being to review the conformity of national acts with the standards of that instrument" (§ 60).

The importance given to the autonomous meaning of Convention notions and the "unimportance" of recourse to *travaux préparatoires* are two sides of the same coin: dynamic interpretation. Recourse to preparatory material normally only features in more "conservative" separate opinions. The closest any of our cases comes to the *travaux préparatoires* is the mention by the court of the intentions of the drafters of the Convention in *The Sunday Times* (§ 47).

(2) *Systemic criteria of interpretation*
These criteria can be divided into two groups: arguments drawn from the context of the particular provision which is being interpreted and arguments drawn from the conception of the Convention as a system, i.e from the systemic relationships between the different provisions of the Conventions.

(a) We have already mentioned some contextual arguments used in support of semiotic criteria. Let us now mention three further uses of contextual criteria.

In *Dudgeon* (§ 53) the court said: "in Art. 8 *as in many other articles of the Convention*, the notion of 'necessity' is linked to that of a 'democratic society.'"

In *The Sunday Times* (§ 55) "the court first emphasized that the expression 'authority and impartiality of the judiciary' has be to understood 'within the meaning of the Convention.'" The court cited the *König* judgment[134] in support of this autonomous meaning and added: "For this purpose, account must be taken of the central position occupied in this context by Art. 6 which reflects the fundamental principle of the rule of law." Here, as in most cases, a contextual argument is used not as a sufficient argument in itself but rather in order to bring in a new argument: in this case an argument from a general legal principle which operates as an authority reason: the rule of law.

Finally in the same judgment (§ 59) the court held that the notion of the "authority" of the judiciary is more objective than that of the "protection of morals," and in support of this view the court referred to a comparative law argument (*prima facie* authority reason): "The domestic law and practice of the Contracting State reveal a fairly substantial measure of common ground in this area," and to a contextual argument: "this is reflected in a number of provisions of the Convention, including Article 6, which have no equivalent as far as 'morals' are concerned."

(b) In this very paragraph the court used a systematic argument of analogy: "In the different, but to a certain extent comparable, contexts of Arts. 5 § 3 and 6 § 1, the court has on occasion reached conclusions different from those of the national courts on matters in respect of which the latter were also competent and qualified the initial assessment." The court mentioned the judgments where it has done so. The aim of this argument was to support the view that the court has the last word even where the states have a margin of appreciation.

A further systemic criterion is the principle that exceptions to the principles recognized by the Convention are to be narrowly interpreted, also found in *The Sunday Times* (§ 65). The court first proclaimed that "freedom of expression constitutes one of the essential foundations of a democratic society" and it later added: "The court is faced not with a choice between two conflicting principles but with a principle of freedom of expression that is subject to a number of exceptions which must be narrowly interpreted," and mentioned *Klass*[135] in support of this systematic principle.

---

[134] Series A, No. 27, § 88.

[135] Series A, No. 28, § 42.

(3) *Dynamic criteria*
Dynamic criteria is again a general term which covers different types of argument: teleological, functional and consequentialist.
(a) *Functional* arguments are drawn from the value-laden conception that the Convention and its provisions are to be interpreted in such a way that they function effectively. The most common such argument is that of *effet utile*. An example has already been given above in relation to the autonomous meaning in *Norris*. Further examples are found in the court's broad interpretation of the meaning of "victim" within Art. 25, and in general in all our cases on the question of the states' margin of appreciation, which is not absolute, and can be supervised by the court.
(b) *Teleological* arguments are drawn from the objectives which the Convention or its provisions explicitly formulate or are reputed to be pursuing. Thus, in *X and Y v. The Netherlands* the court recognizes that the object of Art. 8 is essentially that of protecting the individual against arbitrary interferences by public authorities, but in this case it does not draw an *a contrario* argument from this main objective because it also sees the article as covering *Schutzpflichten* on the part of the state (§ 23).

In *The Sunday Times* the court interprets the expression "maintaining the authority and impartiality of the judiciary" as having a purpose *inter alia* of protecting the rights of litigants.

Besides considering the aim of the Convention or of its articles the court also considers the aims of domestic laws but, in this case, not in order to draw arguments of interpretation, but rather in order to assess whether those aims are in accordance with the Convention. This assessment of supervision is required by para 2 of Arts. 8 and 10.

A variant of the teleological argument is the argument drawn from the intention of the drafters of the Convention. In *The Sunday Times* (§ 47) "the court observes that the word 'law' in the expression 'prescribed by law' covers not only statute law but also unwritten law . . . it would clearly be contrary to the intention of the drafters of the Convention to hold that a restriction imposed by virtue of the common law is not 'prescribed by law' on the sole ground that it is not enunciated in legislation: this would deprive residents of a common law State which is Party to the Convention of the protection of Art. 10 § 2 and strike at the very roots of the State's legal system." This is a good example of dynamic interpretation: the court provides two arguments in support of its interpretation of the word "law" as covering the common law: first comes a teleological-historical argument which adopts the form of an apagogic or *ad absurdum* reasoning. Then comes a consequentialist argument which also adopts an *ad absurdum* reasoning: excluding the common law would bring along unacceptable implications within the legal system of the Convention and would amount to questioning a High Contracting Party's legal system. The court would thus engage in an intolerable policy making role.

(c) Arguments drawn from the consequences to which a proposed interpretation of the Convention or of its articles leads can be called *consequentialist* and they usually adopt the logical form of *ad absurdum* reasonings:

- the interpreter has a certain interpretation in mind (interpretation 1);
- the interpreter postulates as a hypothesis the opposite interpretation (interpretation 2);
- the conclusions from this interpretation 2 are drawn;
- these consequences are evaluated as either incompatible with existing law (consequences as implications within the law) or else as undesirable according to some axiological criteria (consequences as behavioral outcomes in the law's environment);
- the interpreter then rejects interpretation 2.

An example of consequences as juridical implications has already been mentioned above. Consequences as behavioral outcomes are usually evaluated according to axiological criteria. *Dudgeon* (and *Norris*) provide a good example: "On the issue of proportionality, the court considers that such justifications as there are for retaining the law in force unamended are outweighed by the *detrimental effects* which the very existence of the legislative provisions in question can have on the life of a person of homosexual orientation like the applicant" (§ 60 of *Dudgeon*, emphasis added). The court points out that its decision on the issue of proportionality consists of weighing the consequences of alternative interpretations.

2. On the role of axiology in support of interpretation

Whereas the methods of interpretation lend themselves to a systematic analysis, we can detect a layer of arguments operative in the interpretative process which are hard to classify. This may have to do with the fact that these arguments will adopt the form of dynamic methods. However, the weight of these considerations would be underestimated if we just look at their form. The points at one of the crucial issues in today's theory of legal argumentation which however can not be dealt with in depth here. A few hints underpinned by examples derived from the court's practice must suffice.

(1) *Evaluations backing interpretation*

In support of its interpretations the court can draw arguments from legal principles, or from a given axiology, or from social reality or even from a specific legal field. An example is the above mentioned principle of the *rule of law* which governs the court's interpretation of the term "prescribed by law," or as in *Müller* (§ 42): "A principle of law which is common to the Contracting States allows confiscation of 'items whose use has been lawfully adjudged illicit and dangerous to the general interest,'" a principle elaborated on in *Handyside* in relation to the interpretation of Art. 1 of Protocol No. 1 on the right to property, and which is not discussed in this article. However, these arguments from legal principles, operate more like reasons of authority than like interpretative reasons.

Arguments drawn from the specific legal field will be discussed separately in relation to the (de)criminalization debate. We are left with those arguments which refer to social reality as considered in, e.g., *Handyside* (§ 54-57) and in *Müller* (§ 36).

In *Handyside* the applicant and the minority of the Commission put forward four evaluations which the court downplayed: they drew attention to the fact that the original edition of the Schoolbook was the object of no proceedings in Northern Ireland, the Isle of Man and the Channel Islands, and of no conviction in Scotland and that, even in England and Wales, thousands of copies circulated without impediment; that the revised edition was not the object of proceedings in England and Wales; that in addition to the original Danish edition, translations of the "Little Book" appeared and circulated freely in the majority of the Member States of the Council of Europe; and finally that a host of publications dedicated to hard core pornography and devoid of intellectual or artistic merit allegedly profit by an extreme degree of tolerance in the United Kingdom. In addition, the applicant also claimed that the real motive behind this prosecution was political. Similarly, in *Müller* the applicants claimed that the confiscated paintings had given rise to no public outcry and that similar paintings by Müller had been exhibited in other parts of Switzerland (§ 36).

The court replied to these arguments referring to the national (national in the sub-state sense) or even local margin of appreciation and to the optional nature of the "restrictions" and "penalties" referred to in Art. 10 § 2. The court had special regard to the sector of the public to which the Schoolbook was addressed (schoolchildren) and accepted that the domestic authorities were guided by the aim of protecting the morals of that "vulnerable" sector of the public (axiological-moral argument), and in *Müller* the court said that argument of the applicants did not prove that Müller's conviction in Fribourg did not respond to a genuine social need (§ 36).

(2) *Evaluation in the qualification of facts*

A further axiological criterion resorted to by the court is the idea that "in assessing the requirements of the protection of morals in Northern Ireland, the contested measures must be seen in the context of Northern Irish society"[136] but this implied directive does not guide interpretation as much as it guides the qualification of the facts: account must be taken of the social conditions in which the law operates (environment of the law).

Unfortunately, legal theory has not, so far, developed analytical models for the study of qualification, perhaps because this subject is not amenable to a systematic analysis in the way which the study of interpretation is where the scope of discretionary judgment is not as great. We shall only make a very general comment in this regard.

As Weidmann has pointed out[137] the court does not acritically accept the qualification of the facts made by the domestic courts. This can be clearly seen in *Handyside* and in *The Sunday Times* where the court carried out an autonomous evaluation of the circumstances of the cases in line with its autonomous interpretation of the Convention. Of course, this does not mean that the court will necessarily differ from the domestic courts in the qualification of the facts; only that, although it respects the state authorities' margin of appreciation, it wishes to have the last say on the matter. The idea underlying the notion of the margin of appreciation is that the law does not operate in a vacuum but rather in a certain social setting, and that since state authorities are in closer contact than the court with the social reality where the law operates, it falls

[136] *Dudgeon*, Series A No. 45, § 56.

[137] K. Weidmann, *Der Europaïsche Gerichtshof für Menschenrechte auf dem Weg zu einem europaïschen* Verfassungsgericht, Frankfurt am Main 1985, conclusions.

on them to make the initial assessment of what legal action is to be pursued in the relevant circumstances. This can be even more clearly seen in *Müller* (§ 36) where the court said that the paintings in question depict in a crude manner sexual relations, particularly between men and animals, they emphasized sexuality in some of its crudest forms and were liable grossly to offend the sense of sexual propriety of persons of ordinary sensibility (here the court was using something close to the standard of the "reasonable person"). For these reasons and considering that the public had free access to the paintings, the court, following the general principles developed in *Handyside*, regarded the measures of the local Swiss authorities—i.e., conviction and confiscation—as proportional to the aim pursued—i.e., the protection of morals.

b. The Court's Strategy of Interpretation

We shall conclude this section on interpretation with some general comments on the court's strategy of interpretation. Our findings are in accordance with the findings of recent works on the court, mainly with Ost's, Merrills' and Weidmann's. In particular Ost's more comprehensive survey supports our findings and this may partly be due to the fact that we share a similar theoretical background. This points to the idea that the subject matter of the cases at hand does not require a specific interpretative approach. Of course the methods of interpretation do not dictate the outcome of a case, that is a matter of discretionary judgment but they do serve a function: textual or semiotic criteria act as negative tests: a decision will not be accepted if it contradicts the text of the Convention as understood in a pragmatic context (interpreted in a large sense), but strict literal interpretation does not determine the outcome of a case. Systematic and dynamic criteria are very useful in that they can present a bold decision as being inspired in the Convention as a whole and/or in its objectives and in the need for the Convention to be effective. The European Court of Human Rights makes extensive and imaginative use of such systemic and dynamic criteria which, as our examples show, are usually combined and tend to overlap in a complex network of interpretative reasons.

This is a feature which it shares with the Court of Justice of the European Communities, which deals with a rather different set of legal questions, even though it also deals, on occasion, with human rights. Both European courts have developed similar techniques of justification. So, the operative justificatory practice of both European courts is closer to that of state constitutional courts than to that of, say, the International Court of Justice, which abides by the more restrictive interpretation proper to public international law. It might be that the dynamic strategy of interpretation adopted by the Strasbourg court is demanded by the dynamism inherent in the very subject matter with which it deals.

6. The Substantive Reasoning from a Criminal Policy Point of View

By now a criminal lawyer may have become impatient. Instead of dwelling on patterns, structures and features of judicial reasoning he might prefer to assess the criminal policy impact of these decisions. Yet, the jurisprudential efforts and a criminal policy review go hand in hand and back each other reciprocally in the attempt fully to elucidate the court's argumentative approach to the justification of criminal law.

a. The Issues Raised

From a criminal lawyer's point of view the issues have a striking similarity. Let aside *The Sunday Times*, they all pertain to the larger area of sexual offenses. The field of sexual offenses is know for its strong moral impact. In fact, it has become standard procedure since the Enlightenment to draw from this reservoir when illustrating the borderline and interchange between morality and law. The close linkage to institutional morality accounts for the fact that sexual offenses tend to reveal socio-cultural differences perhaps more than any other matter of criminal law, or, to look at the other side of the coin, tend to be the appropriate testing-field for the existences of common standards. Bearing this in mind, the court's pre-occupation with cases of sexual morality—"*affaires de moeurs*" as Koering-Joulin calls them[138]—comes as no surprise. Being particularly liable to cross-cultural disparities, sexual offenses entail a wider potential for harmonization than would be felt with regard to the technicalities of theft and robbery. Also, the criminal law reform movement has brought about remarkable changes within this field over the last 20 years. The reform in this or that country would of course give backing to critics of a different legal set-up in another. In that sense, major reform movements in criminal law will rarely be limited to one country, but may operate as a catalyzer elsewhere. Such repercussions may also point in an underlying international wave of social change.

However, we should not overestimate the uniformity of the category "sexual offenses": pornography, homosexuality and the sexual abuse of the mentally handicapped offer, though somewhat related, clear dissimilarities as well. In particular, pornography relates to a different cluster of associations such as freedom of expression whereas the cases of homosexuality and sexual abuse of the mentally handicapped boil down to a somewhat similar problem structure, i.e., the justification and limits of state interference with sexual behavior. Yet again, the "*Leitmotiv*" of the protection of juveniles or otherwise not fully competent persons runs throughout *Handyside, Dudgeon, Norris* and *X and Y v. The Netherlands* thus reminding us of one of the widely accepted foundation layers of any system of sexual offenses.

It will be of interest to note whether the court swims on the wave of international criminal policy moves, to what extent it produces new or reproduces familiar lines of argument and whether it has itself had a sizeable influence on the formulation of national or international criminal policy standards.

(1) The liberalization of the law related to *homosexuality* has been the logical consequence of the more rational approach to the justification of criminal law, which, as a late off-spring of the Enlightenment, came to supersede moral "left-overs" from the late 1950s onwards. Hanack's renowned assessment for the reform of the sexual offenses in the Federal Republic of Germany ranked the non-qualified homosexuality within the category of emotionally based crimes protecting the general moral sentiment only. Referring to new scientific knowledge about homosexuality he argued against discrimination of homosexuals and saw no case for the criminalization of homosexual

---

138 R. Koering-Joulin, *Affaores de moeurs* (pp.121-144).

behavior among consenting adults; protection of the young and protection against force and pressure remaining as the only legitimate purposes for criminalization. Hanack's proposals were in line with and expanded the position taken by the Wolfenden Committee which had, ten years earlier, recommended in its report that homosexual practices between consenting adults in private should no longer be a crime. References in *Dudgeon* show that the Wolfenden Report exercises some persuasive power on the court (§§ 17, 49). The famous controversy on law and morality between Hart and Lord Devlin which also dwells on the Wolfenden Report is alluded to in Judge Walsh's partially dissenting vote in *Dudgeon* (§ 8).

In view of the general criminal policy climate with regard to homosexuality the court was not particularly adventurous when it called for a decriminalization of homosexual acts between consenting adults. On the other hand, Judge Walsh's objections to the development of a "Euro-norm in the law concerning homosexual practices" (§ 16) illustrate the difficult stand of the court. From this point of view Merrills' labeling of *Dudgeon* as an "activist approach" may have some justification after all. It should not be overlooked that the court condoned criminalization within a more restricted field inasmuch as it accepted some degree of control over homosexual conduct "notably in order to provide safeguards against the exploitation and corruption of those who are especially vulnerable by reason, for example, of their youth," (§ 49) leaving the details, however, to the discretion of the domestic authorities. All in all, the court favored a position which narrows the gap between the public control of heterosexual acts on the one hand and homosexual acts on the other.

(2) *Handyside* and *Müller* touch on another controversy of old standing: the legal treatment of *pornography*. This is neither the place to rehearse the whole pornography debate nor to register its different oscillations on the criminal policy seismograph, in particular the most recent ones provoked by a review of the matter from a feminist point of view. Nor can we delve into the underlying empirical issues which are far from being settled. *Handyside* and *Müller* allow for, even demand, a selective approach to the topic: the legitimacy of some form of obscenity law is more or less taken for granted by the court. At least the court did not touch on the legitimacy of the domestic regulations as such which may have to do with the fact that the applicants themselves did not attack the general validity of the regulation. The special features of the cases, i.e., the issue of child protection on the one hand and the conflict between art and obscenity on the other, impose themselves commandingly upon the subject, thus cutting short the general debate. However, even the treatment of such specialities hints at some of the characteristic features of the general debate. In particular, the court takes a firm stand on the legitimacy of "local morality" within the field of pornography almost to the extent that it cannot conceive of a uniform standard. The communicative element of obscenity certainly justifies, even requires, the consideration of local standards but does not back the notion of total relativity. Such relativity seems particularly questionable as regards a work of art. Let aside the outcome of the particular case, the court's emphasis on the "local perspective" in *Müller* (see in particular § 36) tends to disregard the universal approach to works of art. Judge Spielmann arrived at this very conclusion in his dissenting vote criticizing that such an assessment be left to a Canton or a municipal authority (§ 10).

The court's denial of immunity from criminal liability to artists meets no objection. Such limits of artistical expression flow from the respect for other high ranking values and do not contradict the special role artists play within a democratic society. However, the court is not only not prepared to give artists a "carte blanche," it also tends to be extremely vague as to the criteria which should govern the balancing of the interests involved. At least one cannot derive much guidance from the formula that "the court cannot overlook this aspect of the matter" (§ 34). The cryptic reference to the duties and responsibilities "of those who exercise their freedom of expression," previously used in *Handyside* lacks precision as well. Hopefully future decisions should adhere, for the sake of art and artists, to Judge Spielmann's emphasis on the relativity of values in art.

(3) *X and Y v. The Netherlands* raises somewhat different problems. This is not so much a consequence of the matter involved. Rather, it has to do with the fact that what is being questioned is the lack of criminal legislation and not its existence. Even though recourse is being had to the same Art. 8 of the Convention also invoked in *Dudgeon* and *Norris*, this different starting point accounts for the distinctiveness of the case. Whereas *Dudgeon* and *Norris* are concerned with the compatibility of an *existing* criminal statute with the Convention, *X and Y* centers around the individual's right to criminalization. Robbers therefore calls this case the decisive step on the way towards a right to personal protection by the state.[139] Still the decision, controversial as it may be, did not come as a total surprise. *Airey* paved the way: the court put acts and omissions on an equal footing. Also, the German Federal Constitutional Court had, in its abortion case, established the state's duty to grant protection by way of criminalization in certain cases. *X and Y v. The Netherlands* has carried this line further by taking up a position which comes close to an individual's right to criminal protection. A rights-oriented approach will rather welcome this clarification. On the other hand, the open flank of both decisions lies in the state's margin of appreciation. The "margin of appreciation" in the sense of a "Spielraum" comes in at two different levels. It concerns the question whether the good deserves protection as such, as well as the question how this protection should best be afforded, which again may require complex forecasts. It is a matter of debate how far such imponderables are compatible with a concept of "rights." Ultimately, they do not concern the right as such, but fall within the realm of enforceability. Thus the procedural aspect of the right eclipses its material aspect: in most instances, the margin of appreciation will indeed reduce the material potential of such a right almost to nil. It did not do so in *X and Y v. The Netherlands*. Even if one approves of the outcome of the case, the court's laconic reasoning in such a controversial and far-reaching issue may be misunderstood so as to convey the false message that criminal statutes offer better protection *per se*, thus unduly fueling repressive law and order debates.

---

139 G. Robbers, *Sicherheit als Menschenrecht*, Baden-Baden 1987, p. 25.

b. The Court's Express or Implied Approach to the Pre-requisites of Criminal Law

(1) *Morality versus harm*

At present, we undergo a certain re-appraisal of the role of morality in criminal law. The guiding potential of the Enlightenment's harm principle is somewhat blurred by perennial disagreement on how to satisfy its demands. Also, one has to concede that it is infiltrated by moralism which can be shown time and again in the discussion of borderline cases such as ours.

Much is to be said in favor of retaining the harm principle as the starting point of any criminalization debate. But this is not the point we are aiming at. It is the court's terminology which attracts our primary interest. It consistently refers to the protection of the moral ethos and speaks of the legitimate aim of protecting morals. Only in *X and Y v. The Netherlands* the court seems to pay tribute to the harm principle when it alludes to the necessity of an effective protection. Certainly, terminology may be revealing at times. In this case, the frequent references to morality do not allow the inference that the court wanted to take position in the familiar dialectic between criminal law and morality. The court simply abides by the Convention which in Art. 8 § 2 refers expressly to the protection of morals, as a legitimate ground for interference. In using the word "morals" the Convention reflects existing cross-cultural differences and a certain moral back-drop of law. Neither the Convention nor the court are engaged in domestic academic criminal law debates and will therefore not need to pay too close attention to their niceties but rather develop their own concept which has to fit the international and cross-cultural scope of the Convention's Member States and has to bear in mind that the guarantees of the Convention are not restricted to criminal law. In fact, not even *X and Y v. The Netherlands* can serve as a genuine example of a harm oriented approach. Rather, this term does not come into the picture at all, since the court is referring to the protection of individual rights of others which is not necessarily identical with the notion of harm of the body social ("*Sozialschädlichkeit*"). All this would support Mireille Delmas-Marty's view that the concept of criminal policy might have an autonomous meaning within the Convention.

Seemingly the court does not hold that the protection of existing moral standards *per se* is a sufficient ground for criminalization. At least in *Dudgeon*, alluding to the controversy about the interaction between (criminal) law and morality (§ 61), the court states: "In particular, the moral attitudes towards male homosexuality in Northern Ireland and the concern that any relaxation in the law would tend to erode existing moral standards cannot, without more, warrant interfering with the applicant's private life to such an extent." Its next sentence strikes a tune which sounds very familiar to those who have followed the reform of the abortion legislation: "Decriminalization does not imply approval, and a fear that some sectors of the population might draw misguided conclusions in this respect from reform of the legislation does not afford a good ground for maintaining it in force with all its unjustifiable features."

(2) *The role of criminal law within the system of social control*

Criminal law is understood to be the last resort of all mechanism of social control. This *ultima ratio* or subsidiary function of criminal law is actually an off-spring of the proportionality principle. Whereas every criminal lawyer would subscribe to this in principle, the realization of *ultima ratio* is overshadowed by the hazards of evaluation. It can be argued that still too ample a use of criminal law derives from this predicament.

Sedes materiae, in terms of the Convention, is the Contracting States' margin of appreciation. Whereas in *Engel and others*[140] the court had stated *obiter* that "the Convention leaves the States free to designate as a criminal offense an act or omission not constituting the normal exercise of one of the rights that it protects" (§ 81). It accepts in *X and Y v. The Netherlands* that recourse to criminal law is not necessarily the only answer (§ 24). Existing civil remedies are being discussed, but are ultimately dismissed as insufficient (§§ 25, 26). The fact that fundamental values are at stake calls, in the eyes of the court, for an effective deterrence which ". . . can be achieved only by criminal-law provisions . . . ." By this matter-of-fact reference to the effectiveness of deterrence via criminal law the court avoids going into the details of the deterrence debate. One could certainly not have expected a re-appraisal of the whole criminological body of knowledge on the subject. On the other hand, by taking the deterrence mechanism and, in the last instance, the priority of criminal law for granted, the court circumvents the most crucial issue of the case. The court is not unaware of potential alternatives but does not really enter into their discussion. Having denied the civil remedies a preventive function, the court simply invokes an existing tradition, within this particular field, to hold recourse to criminal law. This only proves the difficulty of how to handle in practice widely accepted, but in their details and dimension still contested working assumptions of the criminal justice system. Not surprisingly, the German abortion decision overcomes this slippery ground with the same authoritative rhetoric as to the integrative function of criminalization.

Ultima ratio, alternatives to criminal law and the selective nature of criminal law protection all flow from the principle of proportionality. It is a matter of doubt whether the court has sized up the full potential of these basic criminal policy axioms. At least, the selective nature of criminal law does not appear as a reference point in the line of argument. Rather, the court concludes from the existing sexual offenses that this gap should be filled, too. Of course, it is possible to draw such a conclusion and, again, one cannot expect the court to enter into a criminal law "name calling business." On the other hand, it would have improved the acceptance of *X and Y v. The Netherlands* if the court had at least considered the axiom that not every behavior worth punishing ("*Strafwürdigkeit*") needs to be punished ("*Strafbedürftigkeit*").

(3) It could well be argued that these aspects rather fall under the general heading "substantive quality of the court's criminal policy arguments." In fact, the court cannot be blamed for not sticking to domestic criminal law concepts in particular if, at least in their details, these concepts vary from Member State to Member State. What counts in the end is the depth, the differentiation and the completeness of the substantive arguments with regard to the protection of human rights in a criminal law context. In that sense formulae such as that of "margin of appreciation" and "pressing social need"

---

140 Series A No. 22.

may of course pass as the proper standard for the discussion of criminal policy aspects. It would be counterproductive if one were tempted to transplant the domestic criminal policies' categories in their pure state to the interpretation of the Convention. Yet, on the other hand, the interpretation of the Convention cannot completely disregard such categories.

From this point of view the court's reasoning reveals at least three aspects which deserve further scrutiny:

- the "Euro-norm" perspective shows up in the line of argument, but is being handled very prudently. In particular, the court hesitates to rely on an automatism in the sense that the last in line *must* follow suit. The socio-cultural differences are being used as a counter-balance. In comparing *Handyside* and *Müller* on the one hand and *Dudgeon* and *Norris* on the other, one is tempted to speculate that the "Euro-norm" argument gains in importance with the dimension and weight of the charge of potential infringement on individual rights;
- the court's reasoning has a society dimension in that it frequently refers to societal conditions and social change. Instead of expressly referring to the social sciences as a path-finder, leading official documents like the Wolfenden Report will act as a welcome transfer agent. In a way, referring to *flou*-notions like "social change" is a rhetorical device to avoid having to proceed on a deeper analysis. This relative reluctance to assess social reality following the social sciences is however no peculiarity of this court;
- the more crucial the issue, the more laconic the language of the court will become. Such scarcity and economy could be a direct consequence of the fact that the judges of an international court will have to compromise. Such compromises tend to favor the procedure of leaving out rather than of adding an extra word or an extra consideration. Merrills invokes the picture of the judges "bargaining over words" and concludes: "The above practice not only makes the court's judgments less interesting than they might be, but also ensures that they rarely display either the forcefulness or depth of juridical analysis characteristic of the best individual opinions." Also one should bear in mind that the belief in the increased authority of the longer judgment may be a domestic idiosyncracy and may perhaps also reflect a different perception of the authority of judges.

c. *The Court as a Criminal Policy Maker?*

(1) The court's judgments are addressed at the Member States. Notwithstanding the intricacies of and controversies about their inner-state bearing, the court's statement that there is a breach of the Convention cannot nullify the relevant domestic statute, nor does the court act as a domestic law making agent. Rather the states are obliged to change the domestic law which is in breach of the Convention. It may therefore be of interest to take a closer look at the implementation of the decisions by the domestic authorities and their concrete impact on the domestic criminal law. All in all, the Member States have reacted more or less promptly:

- The *Netherlands* had even anticipated the court's ruling in *X and Y v. The Netherlands*. In February 1985, the decision was handed down in March, the relevant provisions concerning the filing of a complaint were revised to fill the gap (of Art. 65 to the Netherlands Criminal Code);
- *The Sunday Times* gave rise to the Contempt of Court Act 1981 destined to bring the British law into conformity with Art. 10 § 2 of the Convention;
- The *UK* decreed by the Homosexual Offense (Northern Ireland) Order 1982 that homosexual acts between consenting adults no longer constituted an offense in Northern Ireland, thus complying with *Dudgeon*;
- the *Irish* legislature has yet to react to *Norris*. O'Malley speculates about possible repercussions extending beyond the issue of homosexuality and even sexual offenses in general, since the Irish substantive criminal law—according to him—"remains rooted in the nineteenth century and is often derived virtually unchanged from earlier centuries . . ."[141] In that *Norris* could serve as a general impulse to reduce the ethical impact in the Irish system of criminal law, *Müller* has had a different form of impact on *Swiss* domestic criminal law in as much as the court's judgment has stabilized a "reductive interpretation" of Art. 204 No. 3 of the Swiss Criminal Code which provides that the confiscated objects be destroyed. The court condoned the temporary confiscation as the less imposing alternative which up to that point, despite an existing precedent, had not been a firmly established practice in Swiss criminal law.

(2) It goes almost without saying that the court's role to guarantee a working system of human rights protection has a policy impact. The certain programmatic overload of the human rights concept even increases the policymaking potential. Due to the weight which is being attached worldwide to the human rights question the court's verdict operates like a motion of censure on the international scene. In a way, this moral background underpins the position of the court. On the other hand, the court has to strike a delicate balance *vis-à-vis* the domestic legal systems. It is not called upon to reach out for uniformity, but for compatibility which in actual fact amounts to avoiding disparities. Internationalization of legal standards does not mean uniformization. The Commission and the court will therefore be reduced to operating within a certain margin of harmonization. Overstepping this margin will tend to undermine the acceptability of this international system of human rights protection on the side of the Member States. On the other hand, not using this margin will diminish the court's moral authority and thus weaken its influence. The court can neither disappoint those who have vested their hopes in this legal *instrumentarium* for the promotion of human rights; nor does the international context allow it to deal continuous blows in the face of the states which have subscribed to this system of international judicial review of domestic acts.

Such ambivalence can only be captured by relying on allegorical speech. Speaking of the court's "filter function" might come close to the truth. Filter function

[141] O'Malley, *Norris v. Ireland—An Opportunity for Law Reform*, Irish Law Times 1988, pp. 279, 281.

alludes to the decision making process in as much as the court will have to select from the input which comes from different legal traditions and assess the merits of the issue with its own increasingly potent litmus paper. The sensitivity of this device depends on the ability of the judges who apply it. Whereas the court may by now rely on the orientation of 30 years of adjudication, new cases tend to call for differentiations, which make path-finding more difficult instead of easing it.

Selecting implies power and calls for control of power. As it seems the court controls itself: the merger of different legal traditions and judicial temperaments as well as a certain judicial self restraint contribute to the court's careful maneuvering. Even should the court eventually turn against the domestic authorities, it may try to sweeten the bitter pill as can be seen in *Dudgeon* where the court emphasized that the UK had acted in good faith (§ 59). Speaking of selection and filter function it is worth noting though that the court has no control over the cases referred to it. Rather, the input is predetermined.

Up to now we have just been rehearsing the role of the court as a social agent. The court's potential as a policy maker will primarily pertain to human rights issues, the very essence of its scope of adjudication. Criminal policy implications will only come in under this disguise. On the other hand, since criminal justice represents the traditional testing-field for human rights, we may not be altogether mistaken in asking for criminal policy implications. Again it seems necessary to recall that the court cannot be measured with the yard stick of domestic criminal law standards. It may however still be of interest to note whether and how far the court's judgments fit into the pattern of "international mainstream criminal policy." Our task is further complicated by the fact that it may not be all that easy to detect and describe an international mainstream criminal policy, if it exists at all. We shall therefore concentrate on very few points which flow more or less naturally from the relevant cases and which, though vague, still allow a meaningful evaluation.

(3) It will not takes us very far to dwell on the question whether the court has taken a "progressive" or a "conservative" stand. As we know, even a dynamic approach need not necessarily bring about a progressive result. There is no common understanding of the term progressive. In very general terms it can be submitted that a court which has been assigned the task of protecting human rights will, from the individual rights' point of view, at least have a progressive potential. In applying the *effet utile* on the protection of human rights the court has been making use of this potential.

Otherwise the court tends to formulate positions which rely on a solid backing by a rational criminal policy. Such has been the case with *Dudgeon* and *Norris*. In that sense the court will not tend to condone experiments, but rather tend to hold recourse to a form of criminal policy "common sense." *X and Y v. The Netherlands* forms a certain exception to this rule. However, the German abortion decision had somehow paved the way and, if one expands the *effet utile* principle, the concept of a "right to criminalization" no longer seems totally incompatible with an advanced system of human rights protection.

Of course, one is tempted to relate the decisions to the development of international criminal policy. In this sense, *Dudgeon* and *Norris* could be related to the liberalization of criminal law which has taken place from the 1960s onwards. They fall within the larger scope of decriminalization, a criminal policy issue which has *inter alia* been taken up by the European Committee on Crime Problems. Whereas no direct links between its Report which came out in 1980[142] and the two decisions are to be detected, the time link—the decision in *Dudgeon* was handed down in September 1981—is still noteworthy. In discussing the consequences of a withdrawal of criminal protection, the court expressly speaks of "decriminalization" (§ 61). Otherwise, the court has referred *obiter* to the decriminalization debate in *Öztürk,* its primary concern there being the scope of the Convention's guarantees as regards "*Ordnungswidrigkeiten.*"

X and Y v. The Netherlands leads to speculation as to whether the court sensed the turn of the policy tide due to the victimological approach which has gained momentum. At least, the correction of the Netherlands system of prosecuting sexual offenses which the court called for is well in line with the move towards more victim protection. More than the outcome of the case, what proponents of the victim movement will appreciate is the refined tool to bring a state to court if personal safety is at stake. *Norris* should also be welcomed by victimologists, since the court has advocated a wide interpretation of the term "victim" allowing for a review of the criminal statute as such, whereas ordinarily the mere existence of a relevant statute does not give a sufficient procedural basis.

The Court's reluctance to interfere with local standards on pornography in *Handyside* and *Müller* gives the notion of "relative obscenity" some additional backing. Therefore these decisions could one day turn into an unwanted precedent, since the international circulation of pornographic material may call for a more harmonized international approach. Yet, we must remember that the court, in both these decisions, did not deal with the statutes as such, but with their application by local authorities. From this point of view our critique loses some of its bite, since it cannot be the purpose of judicial review under the auspices of the Convention to reach out for total uniformity of domestic decisions.

7. Conclusion

Our study has concentrated on a small segment of the body of decisions which have so far been handed down by the Strasbourg court. Such a topical approach does not allow for far-reaching generalizations. In particular, we cannot and do not pretend to come forward with *the* theory of justification pertaining to the Strasbourg court. On the other hand, approaching relevant court decisions in criminal matters with the instruments which have been developed for the assessment of judicial reasoning in general may have introduced a special note even if it only consists in re-arranging existing knowledge about the court and its justification processes under a somewhat different, though not altogether new, perspective.

Our study has been selective in yet a different sense: we have been focussing our attention primarily on the court and have been touching on the Commission's and the

---

[142] Council of Europe, *Report on Decriminalization,* Strasbourg 1980.

Committee of Ministers' activity only in passing. Of course, we are aware of the fact that the Strasbourg system of human rights protection can only be evaluated properly if all its organs are included. This general statement also applies to the field of judicial reasoning. It would even be of special interest to find out to what extent the court, the Commission and the Committee of Ministers coincide in their approach and where and how they differ. Though, having to take a closer look at the interrelationship and interaction of the three institutions would give such a study a momentum of its own which deserves to be dealt with separately.

Our findings, though related to a special field of court activity, confirm the general perception of the court's judicial reasoning which derives its idiosyncrasy from the fact that domestic laws have to stand the human rights test. This calls for a comprehensive scope and a selective perspective, a combination which resembles that of constitutional courts. On the other hand, the international context of the protection system makes for differences. Here, the Luxembourg court comes into the picture. Somehow situated between both these concepts and also sharing somewhat the tradition of international courts, the court has had to find its own way and has impressively done so.

In the Strasbourg court's interpretative paradigm dynamic elements excel. This comes as no surprise. The Convention's expressed aim of consolidating traditions in key respects, the rising relevance of the human rights perspective to which the court has itself contributed as well as the need to consider social changes, have together favored a dynamic approach. In that, decisions in criminal matters form no exception, even though the court tends to maneuver very carefully within this field.

Due to its particular human rights protection perspective the court will have to leave domestic criminal law standards behind and reach out for new international parameters. They might be more abstract, yet on the other hand less nominalistic. They should be truly international. No domestic system should be favored on account of the language used by the court and the legal tradition to which its wording is indebted. The fact that the formulation of some of the Convention's guarantees cannot disguise the traces of the British legal tradition does not seem so far to have prejudiced the court in this regard. It cannot be overlooked though that the official languages used by the court may transport or favor a specific juridical ambience. Guidance may be derived from comparative criminal law, and criminology as well as sociology of criminal law. They help in finding the structural seed of the problem. Judicial reasoning at this level is faced with the challenge to apply and shape standards which excel in their "majestic vagueness" and their forceful persuasion at the time. Even though one might disagree with this or that concrete decision, the court should be encouraged to continue on its way towards establishing the framework of a European Criminal Jurisprudence.

D. Extension to Central and Eastern Europe[143]

1. The Feasibility of Extending the ECHR

The Statute of the Council of Europe was signed in London on 5 May 1949 on behalf of ten states.[144] In the preamble the contracting parties declared that they were "reaffirming their devotion to the spiritual and moral values which are the common heritage of their peoples and the true source of individual freedom, political liberty and the rule of law, the principles which form the basis of all genuine democracy."

There was then a clear recognition that the values which were common to those ten countries formed the basis—almost the philosophical justification—for the new venture. As Ralph Beddard observed, "[o]ne of the explanations for the success of the Convention is that European States make up a culturally identifiable unit and their like-mindedness has meant easier agreement on what are considered to be basic human rights."[145] This emphasis on shared cultural values is hardly surprising because at the time of the setting up of the Council of Europe there was an enormous ideological conflict between Eastern Europe and Western Europe. We should not forget that the European movement was at that time driven not only by an inherent desire for unity after World War II and a revulsion against the atrocities committed during that war, but also by Western Europe's reaction to the threat posed by the Communist bloc in Eastern Europe. This view of the philosophical basis of the ECHR is shared by those who implement it. Judge Rudolph Bernhardt, a judge of the European Court, said:

> The main reason for the effectiveness of the European Convention and Court is the considerable measure of homogeneity among European states. The member states of the Council of Europe and the parties to the Convention have recognized that the interpretation and the application of the European convention can contribute to uniform European standards. . . . [T]here is a feeling among the states that there exists a common European standard and that this standard should be further developed.[146]

If it is true, as the preamble to the statute setting up the Council of Europe implies, that our sense of individual liberty springs from shared cultural and religious values and a common heritage of moral beliefs, it must be dangerous to assume that a convention based on a particular set of values is necessarily capable of being

---

[143] David Seymour, *The Extension of the European Convention on Human Rights to Central and Eastern Europe: Prospects and Risks,* 8 Conn. J. Int'l L. 243 (Spring, 1993).

[144] Belgium, Denmark, France, Ireland, Italy, Luxembourg, Netherlands, Norway, Sweden, and the United Kingdom.

[145] Ralph Beddard, *Human Rights and Europe* 1 (2d ed. 1980).

[146] Rudolph Bernhardt, *Commentary: The European System*, 2 Conn. J. Int'l. L. 299, 299-300 (1987) (adapted from the text of an address delivered at the Conference on International Courts and the Protection of Human Rights held at the University of Connecticut School of Law in October 1986).

adopted in countries beyond the original confines of Western Europe. As Pascal observed in the mid-seventeenth century, "three degrees of latitude reversed the whole of jurisprudence; a meridian decides about the truth."

The values and philosophy which gave rise to our sense of individual liberty and human rights are rooted in our culture and pre-date the rise of professional government in the eighteenth century and the emergence of Western European democracy. We do not owe our concept of human rights (as opposed to their practical guarantee) to elected governments of the modern era. So a change in government or of a system of government will not necessarily change the fundamental values or expectations of a society or the conditions and customs which gave rise to them. In these circumstances one uncomfortable proposition that needs to be addressed is whether such a uniformity of shared values exists that we can assume that the ECHR can be successfully transplanted beyond Western Europe. The fact is that there is no single universally held view on the substance of fundamental human rights. For example, in some countries corporal punishment can form part of a sentence and is currently permitted in many countries, some of which were formerly British colonies to which the ECHR was extended. Also permitted under Islamic law in some countries is punishment by way of amputation of the left hand or fingers for repeated property-related crimes. Article 1 of the Sixth Protocol to the ECHR provides that the death penalty should be abolished, but it is provided for by law in more than one hundred countries. Even within Western Europe there are fundamentally different views on human rights issues. For example, there is much debate in the West about women's rights. Article 41.2 of the Constitution of the Republic of Ireland provides that:

> The State recognizes that by her life within the home, woman gives to the State a support without which the common good cannot be achieved. The State shall, therefore, endeavor to ensure that mothers shall not be obliged by economic necessity to engage in labor to the neglect of their duties in the home.[147]

That is not a view of women's role in society which most countries would now incorporate in their constitution were they drawing up a new one. Issues relating to divorce, abortion, contraception, pornography and HIV testing are issues raising fundamental questions of human rights—but differences of view remain. Divorce is still prohibited under the Irish Constitution. The 1930 Irish statute banning the sale, advertising and importation of contraceptives was only struck down as being a violation of the marital right of privacy by the Supreme Court of Ireland as recently as 1974. Within little more than a decade of that decision many countries in Western Europe engaged in expensive programs of education and advice positively encouraging the use of contraceptives as a protection against the increasing spread of HIV and AIDS.

The area of education is another realm about which there is debate and difference. Many people in the United Kingdom consider that private education is wrong in principle, although it is widely accepted as being a right guaranteed by the ECHR.

---

[147] IR. Const. art. 41.2.1 - 41.2.2

Cases before the European Court have often raised fundamental issues and in the course of those proceedings it has become clear that even within the confines of a single Member State there are serious differences of view about the nature of the rights guaranteed.

In these circumstances it is dangerous to assume that there is a consensus about the nature of fundamental rights. As Jeremy Bentham said in the eighteenth century, the constitution maker should be aware of "the old conceit of being wiser than all posterity."[148] Moreover, we should not take for granted, as the jurisprudence of the ECHR develops and is refined, that the end product, even if it is acceptable in Western Europe, is necessarily a product ready to be exported and transplanted in other countries which do not share the same cultural heritage. As Judge Brian Walsh, a judge of the European Court of Human Rights observed:

> These concepts [the Universal Declaration of Human Rights], originally derived from the Greeks, reflect the common traditions and heritage of Western European countries. It cannot be claimed, for instance, that should one attempt to implement the European Convention in some other part of the world it would necessarily take root. The underlying philosophy and heritage of Western Europe [sic] civilization is intricately woven with the recognition of the inalienable and absolute rights of the individual.[149]

General declarations of human rights are often agreed to by Governments for political reasons. However, it is clear that the ECHR, with its accumulation of over thirty years of jurisprudence is not necessarily capable of being embraced by other countries who were not involved in its authorship or the development of its jurisprudence and who may not—only time will tell—share the same views as the original member states on some of the difficult and substantive issues which the European Court of Human Rights addresses.

2. Interstate Cases

As the map of Eastern and Central Europe is redrawn, and the ECHR expands, one aspect of ECHR procedure which merits attention is the interstate application under Article 24. Under that provision any High Contracting Party may refer to the Commission any alleged breach of the ECHR by another High Contracting Party. It is important to note that this procedure is significantly different from the right of individual petition conferred under Article 25 for a number of reasons. First, in an interstate case, there are no procedural filters. For example, there is no requirement that there be a "victim" before a case is brought—the complaint can be merely about the

---

[148] Jeremy Bentham, *Anarchical Fallacies*, in *Works of Jeremy Bentham* 489, 494 (Jon Bowring, ed., 1962).

[149] Brian Walsh, *The European Court of Human Rights*, 2 Conn. J. Int'l L. 271, 273 (1987) (adapted from the text of an address delivered at the Conference on International Courts and the Protection of Human Rights held at the University of Connecticut School of Law in October 1986).

incompatibility of national legislation or of an administrative practice with the ECHR without there being a specific allegation or violation against any individual person. Secondly, there is no need for a state to show that any of its nationals is adversely affected or even that the state has any special interest in the alleged breach. In this respect, the interstate procedure represents a departure from the normal principles of international law whereby a state can take action against another only when a right of the former state is at stake or when that state takes up the case of one of its nationals whom it considers to have been treated by the other state in a way contrary to the rules of international law. Thirdly, the Commission has no power to reject such an application if it is substantially the same as one which has already been dealt with either by the Commission or some other body, or if it is manifestly ill-founded or an abuse of procedure—these are powers which the Commission has under Article 27 only in relation to an individual application under Article 25. Fourthly, there is no need for a state to show even prima facie evidence of breach at the admissibility stage. Finally, an interstate case can relate to any alleged breach of the Convention and not just the substantive Articles.

The philosophy behind the interstate case is that members of the Council of Europe have a collective interest in the maintenance of human rights. However, as commentators have observed, the interstate procedure has not proved to be as successful as the right of individual petition. As Ralph Beddard said, the interstate procedure "was bound to be founded for the greater part on unfriendliness in the relations between States."[150] Professor Francis Jacobs was of the same view when he argued that interstate applications would never be successful as a means of protecting human rights because they were never brought solely for humanitarian (as opposed to political) reasons.[151] Only eighteen such applications have been brought in thirty-seven years and they relate to only six situations. The last application was brought by Denmark, France, the Netherlands and Norway against Turkey in 1982 and a friendly settlement was reached in 1985.

One can speculate about why there have been no interstate applications during the past eleven years. However, with the expansion of the ECHR to Eastern and Central Europe, the potential scope for more use of this procedure by new members is obvious—particularly if new members are slow to recognize the right of individual petition. In particular, the existence throughout Central and Eastern Europe of minority groups with cultural and ethnic ties to neighboring states, as opposed to the country of their nationality or residence, might give rise to political pressure on individual countries to invoke the procedure in Article 24 against their neighbor.

If the problem of minorities in Central and Eastern Europe cannot be resolved there is a risk that countries might—for political reasons—resort to the interstate procedure to draw the attention of the rest of Europe to perceived breaches of human rights. This might provoke retaliation in kind. In these circumstances and in the absence of any

---

150 Ralph Beddard, *Human Rights and Europe* 7 (2d ed. 1980).

151 Francis G. Jacobs, *European Convention on Human Rights* 273-74 (1975).

procedural filters, there has to be concern that the limited time and resources of the Commission and Court might be further strained by such applications and that the resulting caseload would do little to enhance the general reputation of the Strasbourg machinery.

3. The Process of "Strasbourg-Proofing" Domestic Law

The original members of the Council of Europe have had over thirty years to adjust their domestic law to the requirements of the ECHR. They decided themselves what substantive rights the ECHR would embrace in 1949 and some played a significant part in drafting the final document. Moreover, the jurisprudence has evolved gradually over a period of decades and member states have influenced that jurisprudence by the representations they have made before the Commission and Court. Yet still, as the experience of the United Kingdom demonstrates, the European Court has on many occasions found the domestic law and practice of member states to be in breach of the ECHR. If this is the case for founding members of the ECHR then one wonders how easy will it be for the new members of the Council of Europe to adapt their laws and practices to ensure compliance with the requirements of the Convention and its sophisticated jurisprudence. It is well known that Hungary, in particular, has gone to considerable lengths to bring its domestic law into line with current Strasbourg jurisprudence. In September 1990 the Hungarian Center for Human Rights was set up in Budapest. The Center's task is to advise on the drafting and application of new laws to ensure that they are in accordance with international standards. At a recent meeting in Strasbourg with Central and Eastern European countries the representative from Hungary explained that for almost two years Hungary had systematically reviewed its national legislation to ensure conformity with the requirements of the ECHR and had carried out a thorough analysis of ECHR case law. A detailed study of the review process was prepared by the Minister of Justice for use by the Hungarian Government and an English translation is to be made available to other governments. To what extent can such an ambitious program be successful?

The United Kingdom was the first country to ratify the ECHR in 1951 and by 1953 had extended its obligations under Article 63 to forty-two of its dependent territories. Sir David Maxwell Fyfe, later Lord Chancellor, was one of the ECHR's main authors and at the time of its drafting and for many years thereafter the view in the United Kingdom was that domestic law in the United Kingdom complied with the requirements of the ECHR. Professor S.A. de Smith, one of the most distinguished of British constitutional lawyers, was able to write in 1964 that it was possible for the United Kingdom "to accede to the Convention without any undue straining of conscience. The rights and freedoms there proclaimed were, to a very large extent, already recognized in English law—not as formal constitutional or statutory guarantees but as residual rights, liberties and immunities of the individual." Professor de Smith added, by way of a footnote, that "[i]t is doubtful whether any subsequent change in English law is directly attributable to the United Kingdom's accession to the Convention." Thirty years after that view was expressed a fresh assessment needs to be made. It is clear that the critical turning point was in 1966 with the United Kingdom's recognition under Article 25 of the individual's right of petition. Since 1966 the United Kingdom has had to amend its law and/or practice on many occasions in order to meet its obligations under the ECHR. Moreover, as the jurisprudence of the Commission and Court evolves, it becomes increasingly necessary for new laws to be examined carefully, before they are passed, to ensure that they are not in breach of the ECHR.

The European Court's purposive approach to the interpretation of the ECHR has resulted in the rendering of judgments in a number of areas and on a wide range of issues which might not have been in the contemplation of the original signatories to the Convention. The jurisprudence of the ECHR is now very sophisticated. It draws subtle distinctions in response to each different set of facts. The permitted grounds for interfering with guaranteed rights (e.g., to the extent "necessary in a democratic society in the interests of national security, public safety or the economic well being of the country for the prevention of disorder or crime, for the protection of health or morals or for the protection of rights of freedoms of others") and the doctrine of "margin of appreciation" invite subjective judgment on which reasonable people may disagree. Moreover, whatever the domestic law may provide, the European Court has made it clear on a number of occasions that they will not consider national legislation in abstracto but only the application of that law to the particular facts of any given case. So even if domestic law is identical to the ECHR, or if the ECHR is incorporated into domestic law, there is no guarantee against an adverse judgment in Strasbourg. That is not to say that governments should not strive to ensure that the ECHR implications of any proposed legislation or administrative action are fully considered. But that process has to be undertaken in the realistic knowledge that Strasbourg jurisprudence is not static and is capable of overtaking domestic legislation however conscientious a national government may be when drawing up its own laws.

4. Practical Issues

On a practical level there remain problems which may well be exacerbated by the rapid extension of the ECHR to the rest of Europe. Domestic legal systems tend not to be receptive to outside influences and in the United Kingdom it has taken a long time for knowledge of the existence of the ECHR, let alone its jurisprudence, to permeate through to practitioners. This is understandable to some extent because the United Kingdom has not incorporated the ECHR into its domestic law and therefore its practitioners have no experience of taking ECHR points before domestic courts. In turn, those courts have no experience of interpreting or applying the jurisprudence of the European Court. The normal course of events in the United Kingdom is for domestic remedies to be exhausted (as required by Article 26) without either side addressing the ECHR dimension. The case is then referred to Strasbourg where a metamorphosis takes place. The arguments deployed suddenly become ECHR arguments drawing on jurisprudence which simply was not in play before the domestic courts. On occasions, even the parties to the action change since the respondent in Strasbourg is always the United Kingdom Government (because it is they who have undertaken under Article 1 "to secure to everyone within their jurisdiction the rights and freedoms defined in [the] Convention") whereas the proceedings before the domestic courts may not have involved the government at all.

However, the lack of awareness of ECHR jurisprudence amongst domestic courts and practitioners is not confined to the United Kingdom. Even in countries which have incorporated the ECHR into their domestic law the same problems appear to arise. As Andrew Drzemczewski observed, if there is an international legal norm and a conflicting internal text, the natural inclination and professional training of the bench and the bar will cause the latter to prevail.[152] He concluded that "[t]his is probably so for the simple reason that both majority at the bar and the bench of most member states of the Council of Europe are completely unaware of, or unfamiliar with, the published case law emanating from Strasbourg."[153]

There are a number of reasons for this. The Strasbourg jurisprudence is a response to the actual cases brought before the Commission and Court. All sorts of factors—including the friendly settlement procedure—determine whether a case results in a published judgment of the Court. The reports of the Commission and the judgments of the Court appear only in French and English. The obligation of each state under Article 53 is only to abide by the decision of the Court "in any case to which they are parties." Consequently, there is no requirement that member states monitor all the jurisprudence of Strasbourg and change their laws periodically to reflect it. The ECHR is not a comprehensive set of rights and in the United Kingdom it is probably true to say that it is not perceived as the main instrument for protecting civil liberties. Despite a wealth of academic literature there is a shortage of authoritative and up-to-date textbooks for the practitioner on ECHR jurisprudence. Moreover, legal aid is not normally available in Europe for applications to the Commission in Strasbourg. The Commission's own legal aid scheme becomes operative only at the point where an application is declared admissible or the government has been invited to submit written observations upon it. Thus in 1991 the Commission received 1,648 applications concerning individual applications of which 217 were declared admissible—but in the same period the budgetary appropriation for the Commission's legal aid scheme was only FF324,000 and only 54 applicants benefitted in 1991 from this scheme. In many countries, including the United Kingdom, domestic law makes no provision for legal aid to be made available to applicants who bring cases before the Commission.

All these factors combine to make life difficult for practitioners who wish to specialize in ECHR law and represent applicants in Strasbourg. It will inevitably take many years before the ECHR system takes root in the new member states of the Council of Europe. However, there are grounds for supposing that that process may be completed more quickly in Central and Eastern Europe than it was in Western Europe. There will be less complacency than there was amongst the original member states of the Council of Europe that domestic law complies with the ECHR. Accession to the ECHR has coincided with a fundamental change in the system of government. Accession to the ECHR and incorporation of its values and standards into the domestic life of the countries of Eastern and Central Europe will not be perceived, as it was in West-

---

[152] Andrew Drzemczewski, *The European Convention on Human Rights in Domestic Law* 336 (1983).

[153] *Id.*

ern Europe, as a mere reflection of pre-existing national values—but rather as a challenge which consciously has to be met with energy and vigor. This approach is reflected in the extensive work now being undertaken in the human rights field by the countries of Central and Eastern Europe. The Council of Europe has provided specific resources to strengthen and develop democratic reforms in the countries of Central and Eastern Europe by creating a special budget for contacts and co-operation with the countries of Central and Eastern Europe. Moreover, in 1990 the Council of Europe set up a specific program of co-operation and assistance ("the Demosthenes Programme") to strengthen the reform movement and the progressive integration of these countries into the Council of Europe family and the institutions of European cooperation. Under the auspices of this program an enormous amount of work is now being undertaken in the human rights field including the production of documents in the languages of Central and Eastern Europe and visits and meetings for government officials, professionals and individuals. For example, a meeting of experts to examine Articles 5 and 6 of the ECHR (the right to security of person and the right to a fair trial) for the purpose of enabling the Hungarian authorities to take into account Strasbourg case law in the preparation of the Hungarian draft code on penal procedure, took place in Budapest on 12 and 13 June 1990. The workshop was organized by the Hungarian Ministry of Justice in cooperation with the Council of Europe's Directorate of Human Rights. The representatives from the Council of Europe included the President and Secretary of the European Commission of Human Rights together with a judge of, and the secretary to, the European Court of Human Rights. Other meetings and sessions included discussions on the ECHR for members of the legal profession and law students in Budapest and Miskolc in November 1990; a delegation from the Supreme Court and the Constitutional Court of Hungary to Strasbourg in the same month; an external session of the International Institute of Human Rights attended by the sixty practicing lawyers and officials in co-operation with the Hungarian Human Rights Center and the Ministry of Justice in Budapest in April 1991; an expert mission to Budapest in August 1990 to carry out consultations on the new Hungarian media legislation in the light of Article 10 of the ECHR (freedom of information and expression).

Such measures will go some way to increase awareness of the ECHR in Hungary. However, as the United Kingdom's experience shows, such a process takes time and the single most influential factor in generating that awareness is a well publicized "government defeat" in Strasbourg and a consequential change in domestic law. That is a process which all Governments have to come to terms with and accept as an integral part of their constitutional arrangements.

5. The Impact on Strasbourg Procedure

The extension of the ECHR to Central and Eastern European states is likely to have a significant impact on the procedure of the European Commission and Court of Human Rights. The unique procedure established by the ECHR has worked well for thirty years. It was, however, designed for a small number of member states and it is, even now, struggling to cope with the increasing number of individual cases submitted to it. As has often been said by a number of commentators, the ECHR system has become a victim of its own success.

The statistics are revealing. In 1955 the Commission received a total of 138 applications, only five of which were introduced through a lawyer and with seventeen percent of the applicants being detained or interned. In 1991 the Commission received 1,648 applications, nearly half of which (713) were introduced by lawyers. The percentage of applicants who were detained or interned remained constant at fifteen percent. These statistics illustrate the increase in the Commission's case load. The increased involvement of lawyers, together with the accumulated jurisprudence of thirty years is a testimony to the increasing sophistication and complexity of the applications, and the fact that 250 detainees have cases pending before the Commission in Strasbourg illustrates the urgency of many of these applications. The backlog of cases pending before the Commission in July 1992 was 2,397, more than 1,530 of which had not yet even been considered by the Commission. As of July 1992, 363 cases had been referred to the Court of which 67 were pending. Up to 1988 the largest number of cases referred to the Court in any one year was 25 but in 1991 the number of cases referred was 93. These numbers will no doubt continue to increase as more applicants invoke the Strasbourg procedure. This natural growth will be exacerbated by the operation of the 8th Protocol (which enables the Commission to operate two Chambers), by the entry into force of Protocol Number 9 (which enables individual applicants to refer their case to the Court) and the addition to the Council of Europe of a number of Central and Eastern European countries. It is quite possible that by the year 2000 there may be forty member states and the potential pool of applicants may double in number.

The problems caused by the increasing case load and back log have already been addressed by the existing member states. The implementation of the 8th Protocol in 1990 enabled cases which were capable of being dealt with on the basis of established case law or which raised no serious questions affecting the interpretation of the Convention to be dealt with by Chambers of the Commission. It also introduced a system for the summary dismissal of clearly inadmissible cases. Moreover, the Commission and the Court have become semi-permanent bodies and the Commission's sitting time has increased to sixteen weeks per annum. It is expected that the new chamber system will lead to an increase in productivity of about thirty-three percent. It may well be that further delay can be prevented by further administrative measures. For example, there could be an increase in the number of the Commission sittings and, particularly when the number of member states is increased to thirty, there could be an increase to three in the number of Commission Chambers. The Court could work in simultaneous chambers and the Court's sessions could be extended.

However, there is now a debate about whether there should be a more fundamental change in the Strasbourg procedure in order to cope with the demands that will be made upon it in the foreseeable future. One proposal is that the Commission and Court should merge and that there should be a single body to implement the ECHR. It is argued that none of the other major international judicial bodies such as the International Court of Justice provide for a two-tier system. A single court in Strasbourg could be split up into three or more chambers of between seven or nine judges. It would of course be necessary to try to establish a geographical balance in the representation of the chambers. It would be necessary for a judge of the respondent state to be represented in each chamber. It would be necessary for important, controversial or exceptional cases to be dealt with by the plenary Court. The argument against such a merger is that it would do away with the opportunity for important cases to be looked at twice, it might reduce the possibility of achieving effective friendly settlements, and there would be a risk of inconsistency in the jurisprudence which would emerge from a system comprising a number of chambers of equal standing consisting of different judges. An alternative to the merger proposal is a compromise, the main features of which are that there should remain a two-tier system with the decision of the Commission being final in most cases but with important cases being referred to the Court. There would be difficulties with this compromise unless a respondent government retained the ability to refer a case to the Court for an authoritative ruling on a politically sensitive matter.

The need for reform of the system is widely recognized throughout the Council of Europe. Discussion has continued in Strasbourg for almost a decade. The system needs to be streamlined; the procedure simplified; the duration of the proceedings shortened and costs must be kept down. Most importantly, however, the high quality of judgments must be maintained. As the President of the European Court of Human Rights, Judge Ryssdal said last year:

> There is acute awareness that the length of Strasbourg proceedings from the introduction of an application before the Commission until the final judgment of the Court is too long and that the authority of the Convention will be jeopardized unless there is a radical change in the protection machinery. The challenge which confronts us is to adapt that machinery so as to enable cases to be heard within a reasonable time—without forgetting that the Convention community may soon number 35 if not more. Hardly surprisingly, it is therefore broadly accepted today that a radical reform of the Convention's control machinery is called for and that the procedure which it established has to be simplified.[154]

However, beneath what appear to be dry and technical arguments about efficiency and output lies a fundamental debate about the nature and purpose of the ECHR. The discussions about merger reflect a difference of philosophy and approach towards the whole concept of a supra-national system for the enforcement of the ECHR. Is the Strasbourg machinery to be an extension of domestic proceedings or it is to be viewed as separate and distinct? Expressing a personal view, the President of the Court has stated that the opponents of merger appear "to fail to appreciate fully the spirit and philosophy of the Convention system." With the imminent expansion of the ECHR to Central and Eastern European countries, those who support a merger believe that it will be essential for there to be a full time European Court of Human Rights but

---

[154] Rolv Ryssdal, Address at the Conference of Presidents and Attorney Generals of the Supreme Courts of the European Community (Brussels, May 19-22, 1992).

not the present two-tier system with its own appeal mechanism. The President's conclusion is that:

> The European Court of Human Rights has to be an integral part of the European judicial landscape and has to be perceived as such by our domestic courts. Judicial protection of human rights and fundamental freedoms does not and cannot begin in Strasbourg; it begins in proceedings before the judge in each of our countries and may subsequently require the intervention of appeal court judges and supreme court justices. Ultimately and in specific instances a decision of the European Court of Human Rights may be necessary and must therefore be available but no European Court of Human Rights can be expected to do more than assist the domestic courts and in particular the supreme court in our countries in their task of affording protection for the fundamental rights of the individual. Two instances at the European level would not guarantee that the final decision is of higher quality but would doubtless lead to longer proceedings and thereby to less efficient protection. It is significant that none of the contracting states which have instituted a specific mechanism of human rights protection have opted for a system with two levels of jurisdiction.[155]

So the extension of the ECHR to Central and Eastern European countries will take place at a time when those who have participated in the system for many years are themselves asking fundamental questions about the way forward and the relationship of the ECHR to the national legal systems. The debate about procedure has reopened—albeit obliquely—the vexed question of whether member states should incorporate the ECHR as part of the national law. So it is a time of uncertainty—made more uncertain by speculation about the likely impact of the extension of the ECHR to Central and Eastern Europe.

6. Conclusion

I want to draw together some of these thoughts into a conclusion which takes the form of a very basic question. The success of the ECHR system is attributable to the fact it has evolved over a number of years; with the participation of a gradually increasing number of member states; with a Commission and Court interpreting a limited range of specific rights which are closely defined at least by the standards of international instruments; and against the background of cultural homogeneity and, critically, political stability. Given the imminent expansion of the ECHR to Central and Eastern Europe what sort of regional system for the international enforcement of human rights would best serve the whole of Europe?

Do we want a system which is an expanded version of the present arrangements—a supra-national constitutional court determining a limited range of civic and political rights; refining its already sophisticated jurisprudence in the application of the limited

---

[155] *Id.*

rights set out in the ECHR; continuing its purposive approach to that document enabling it to address wider issues; striving for what Judge Bernhardt called "a common European standard"; relying on the doctrine of the member states' "margin of appreciation" to accommodate differences when the European standard cannot be reached in the expanded ECHR system; and, either adopting lower standards to accommodate new members or risking disruption by imposing unrealistically high standards for which new member states are not prepared and cannot reasonably be expected to meet. The fact is that Strasbourg has not had to deal with widespread human rights abuses of the kind it was originally set up to prevent. Rather it has devoted much of its time to a quest for a common European standard in the enjoyment of certain civic and political rights. This is the consequence of having a regional enforcement system operating in a politically stable and democratic part of the world. As Thomas Buergenthal, the President of the Inter-American Court of Human Rights observed, "Europe has, for all practical purposes, transformed an international human rights system into a regional constitutional system with the European Court, assisted by the Commission, performing the functions that constitutional courts perform on a domestic level." Is this the future for Strasbourg in an expanded Europe?

Alternatively, would it be more appropriate for the Strasbourg machinery to devote its undoubted reputation and limited resources to examining and policing the abuse of those human rights which are recognized by everybody as abuses whatever their cultural heritage. As was noted earlier, the ECHR was established partly as a response to the atrocities of World War II. It is these situations which most often render domestic courts powerless and we need a respected international body to adjudicate on these matters. Mere uniformity across a wide geographical area in the application of the ECHR and the quest for a common standard in the maintenance of constitutional guarantees may not be the most valuable service which the Strasbourg machinery could render to an enlarged Europe struggling to come to terms with new political systems and redrawn national boundaries. Thomas Buergenthal tells the story of the Inter-American Court of Human Rights visiting Strasbourg and being present at the public hearing of the Campbell case which involved a claim that the practice of corporal punishment in British schools violated the European Convention.[156] At one point during the argument one of his Latin American colleagues whispered to him, "If the time ever comes when we have these problems to worry about we will have solved our human rights problems."[157]

My personal hope is that in taking stock at this critical time member states of the Council of Europe will address two related issues, namely whether—given its limited resources—the Strasbourg machinery should concentrate its efforts more on the larger human rights issues and whether it is realistic to continue in its quest for common standards in every area of public and private life which the ECHR has now permeated.

---

[156] Case of Campbell and Cosans, 48 Eur. Ct. H. R. (ser. A) (1982); Case of Campbell and Cosans, 60 Eur. Ct. H. R. (ser. A) (1983).

[157] Thomas Buergenthal, *Human Rights in the Americas: View from the Inter-American Court*, 2 Conn. J. Int'l L. 303, 304 (1987) (adapted from the text of an address delivered at the Conference on International Courts and the Protection of Human Rights held at the University of Connecticut School of Law in October 1986).

Chapter 7

Environmental Law

I. European Union Environmental Law and Policy: Introduction[1]

With the democratization of Central and Eastern Europe, the establishment of a common market in the European Union, and the creation of pan-European organizations such as the European Economic Space, a geographic realignment of Europe is emerging. This realignment is uniting European nations by establishing a common front for pursuing social, economic, and political activities. As Europe unites, environmental protection is emerging as a pervasive social issue which will be at the forefront of future European political and economic policy-making.

II. An Overview of EU Environmental Law and Policy

The existence of three separate European regional groups—the EU, the European Free Trade Association (EFTA), and the Central and Eastern European nations—has created great disparity in environmental policy- and law-making throughout the European continent. Of the three groups, the EU is the only organization to confront environmental affairs on a regional scale. EFTA and Central and Eastern European nations leave environmental protection efforts to national jurisdiction and provide little guidance regarding environmental protection on a regional scale. The role of the EU has expanded beyond its original economic and trade mandates and now includes provisions for the integration of environmental protection.[2] The EU first began to address environmental issues in 1973, when it passed the first of four environmental action programmes.[3] It was not until 1985, however, that the Single European Act (SEA) incor-

---

1 Cynthia B. Schultz and Tamara Raye Crockett, *Developing a Unified European Environmental Law and Policy*, 14 B.C. Int'l & Comp. L. Rev. 301-319 (1991). © 1991 Cynthia B. Schultz and Tamara Raye Crockett. Reprinted by permission.

2 Treaty Establishing the European Economic Union, Mar. 25, 1957, 298 U.N.T.S. 11, at arts. 130r-130t [hereinafter EEU Treaty].

3 Declaration of the Council of the European Communities and of the Representatives of the Governments of the Member States meeting within the Council on the programme of action of the European Communities on the environment (1973-1977), O.J. C112/1 (1973) [hereinafter First Environmental Action Program].

porated Title VII, titled Environment, into the EEU Treaty.[4] Title VII clearly establishes the Union's authority to initiate environmental law- and policy-making activities, signifies the EU's commitment to environmental protection, and reaffirms the Union's right to pursue a cohesive environmental policy.

The new environmental provisions delineated under articles 100A and 130r-130t of the EEU Treaty establish environmental protection as a Union priority and require the EU member states to take action to protect environmental quality within their domestic jurisdictions. Thus, the Union and the member states share responsibility for environmental protection.[5] Article 130r(4) provides that, based solely on the nature of the issue, the Union should address some environmental protection issues, while others should be left to the member states. These new environmental provisions have prompted the EU to pursue a stronger, more consolidated environmental policy.

A. Development[6]

It appears that there have been three periods in the development of the Union legal order: a *Foundational Period*, from 1958 to the mid-1970s; a *Mutational Period*, from 1973 to the mid-1980s; and the *Single European Act Period*, from the mid-1980s onwards. The development of the Union environmental law closely follows this periodic development. However, given the absence of any express provision concerning environmental protection in the Treaty of Rome, environmental issues were not themselves the driving force behind the developments during the Foundational Period.

Union environmental law came into its own during the Mutational Period. Although there had been a few, isolated acts of secondary legislation with environmental implications in the earlier Foundational Period, the 1972 United Nations Conference on the Human Environment in Stockholm was a major catalyst for the development of Union environmental law. This Conference led directly to Union consideration of environmental matters and an October 1972 Declaration on the Environment by the heads of state and governments of the then nine Union members. The Union adopted its first Action Programme on the Environment in early 1973.

By 1987, when the Single European Act amendments to the Treaty of Rome came into effect, the Union had already adopted more than 150 acts of secondary environmental legislation; and it was into its third Action Programme on the Environment. Between 1973 and 1987, the Union adopted an extensive body of substantive environmental rules covering water, air, and noise quality, the control and management of waste and hazardous substances, and the protection of flora, fauna, and countryside.

---

4 Single European Act, Feb.17, 1986, O.J. L169/1 (1987) [hereinafter SEA]. Articles 100A, and 130r-130t of the EEU Treaty incorporate environmental protection into Union law and policy. EEU Treaty, supra note 2, at Arts. 100A, 130r-130t.

5 EEU Treaty, *supra* note 2, at Art. 130r.

6 Philippe Sands, *European Community Environmental Law: The Evolution of a Regional Regime of International Environmental Protection,* 100 Yale L.J. 2511-23 (1991). © 1991 Philippe Sands. Reprinted by permission .

It also introduced various environmental protection procedures, including environmental impact assessments and mandatory notification to the Commission of certain environmentally harmful activities. The Union also signed a number of international environmental treaties during this period, and its approach to the development of regional rules of environmental protection began attracting the rest of the international Union's interest.

Union environmental law during this period was largely motivated by a desire to remove nontariff barriers to intra-Union trade by harmonizing member states' environmental laws. It was thus rooted clearly within the original intent of the Treaty of Rome to regulate trade and competition, rather than to regulate environmental protection as an end in itself. By 1985, however, with a large body of Union environmental rules already adopted, the Euro pean Court held that, even absent express reference in the Treaty of Rome, the protection of the environment was one of the Union's "essential objectives" justifying certain limitations on the principle of free movement of goods. The Court stressed that these limitations must not "go beyond the inevitable restrictions which are justified by the pursuit of the objective of environmental protection." The SEA completed the establishment of environmental protection as an express end in itself.

The development of Union environmental law in this period reflects the process of mutation Professor Weiler describes as "expansion"—"in which the original legislation of the Union 'breaks' jurisdictional limits"[7]—rather than "extension," "absorption," or "incor poration." However, the legal basis for the explosion of environmental legislation between 1973 and 1987 was not only Article 235, but also Article 100.

Environmental legislation's rapid expansion supports Weiler's general thesis that, in this period, "the principle of enumerated powers as a constraint on Union *material* jurisdic tion (absent Treaty revision) substantially eroded and in practice virtually disappeared." Contrary to Weiler's general assertion, however, in the environmental field the process did not go "largely unnoticed when it occurred"; rather, it resulted from the direct and express will of all the member states, as manifested in comprehensive Action Programmes on the Environment, from which no member state dissented. Nonetheless, with regard to environmental law, Professor Weiler is undoubtedly correct that "its far-reaching consequences and significance were not appreciated at that time."

Only very recently have some member states felt the consequences of much of the environmental legislation adopted in this Mutational Period. In the late 1970s and early 1980s, the legislative momentum developed a life of its own. It became politically impossible to oppose legislative expansion into other areas, such as environmental impact assessment, to ensure the effective application of the earlier environmental legislation.

Significantly, much of the legislation adopted in the Mutational Period, usually in the form of Directives, mandated neither implementation into national law nor compliance with its provisions until very much later. Thus, some member states, like the

---

7 Weiler, *The Transformation of Europe*, 100 Yale L.J. 2403 (1991).

United Kingdom, could support Union environmental legislation, that did not impose significant short-term costs and was supported domestically, without looking to the long-term costs. In this context, the Union was seen "more as an instrument in the hands of the governments than as a usurping power."[8] Consequently, in certain areas, including water quality, the Union adopted Directives establishing standards of protection which were relatively high compared to then-existing standards in some member states. Only now are these decisions returning to haunt these member states.

Therefore, despite the fact that perceptions of the importance of environmental protection differed greatly among the member states, some of whom were actively trying to hold back the tide, Union environmental law continued to grow as member states negotiated the SEA. The changes the SEA implemented simply added to the momentum of, until then, a relatively discrete area of Union policy. The SEA transformed the somewhat marginal body of environmental policy and law into one of central importance, bringing environmental considerations to bear in previously unimaginable ways on areas of the law including incorporations, tax, financial services, broadcasting, and civil procedure.

The SEA's addition of Title VII, on "Environment," to the Treaty of Rome went beyond mere codification of environmental law. Title VII established a formal and express legal basis for the future development of Union environmental law, effectively bringing all Union activities within the scope of environmental lawmaking. The Treaty now provides that Union action shall be preventive, that environmental damage should as a priority be rectified at its source, that the polluter should pay for damage, and that the Union may participate in international environmental agreements. Under this title, all action is taken by the Council acting unanimously, unless otherwise agreed by the Council. Significantly, where measures are taken under Title VII, member states may maintain or introduce "more stringent protective measures compatible with this Treaty."[9]

The Title VII change gives environmental policy a formal and express status, as well as greater centrality, in the Union order. The Commission, and in particular Directorate General XI (DG XI), which is responsible for environmental policy, now occupies a central and powerful position. DG XI has taken a leading role in setting an ambitious environmental agenda for the next decade, contributing to the "eruption of significant proportions" to which Professor Weiler refers.

Since 1987, environmental legislation in the Union has become ever more ambitious. One of the SEA's most significant effects has been to encourage the extension of environmental lawmaking into new substantive areas. For example, the Union has passed legislation prohibiting television advertisements which encourage behavior prejudicial to the protection of the environment, proposed legislation on eco-labeling and on civil liability for waste, and considered strategies for corporate environmental audits, environmental taxes, and other fiscal measures.

---

8 *Id.* at 2449.

9 SEA, Art. 130T.

The SEA has also led to significant changes in Union institutions. The Union has adopted legislation establishing a European Environment Agency and an environmental monitoring and observation network. The Commission has also sought to improve public access to environmental policy decisionmaking by promulgating a Directive on Freedom of Access to Environmental Information and establishing a working group to study the harmonization of citizen suit provisions in member states' environmental laws.

However, even after the SEA came into force, environmental lawmaking under Title VII still required unanimous voting, resulting in protracted negotiations and watered down provisions. Moreover, as the Commission became increasingly ambitious in its environmental program, particularly enforcement measures, the legislative process slowed down even further as some member states sought to limit the adoption of expensive environmental legislation.

The new Article 100A provides a means to overcome this institutional foot dragging. For measures "which have as their object the establishment and functioning of the internal market," Article 100A allows qualified majority voting, rather than unanimous voting.[10] Furthermore, it assures that those measures which relate to the environment "will take as a base a high level of [environmental] protection."[11] The combination of these two provisions in Article 100A creates, for the first time in the Union's history, the possibility of adopting environmental legislation under qualified majority voting.

In this context, it is not surprising that, in September 1989, the Commission proposed that the Directive on Civil Liability for Waste be based on Article 100A, which is primarily concerned with removing barriers to trade, in spite of the Directive's clear environmental objectives. This decision placed the Commission in direct confrontation with a number of member states as well as the Economic and Social Committee, all of which considered the Directive to be more properly based on Article 130S. This conflict heralds a new round of wrangling in the environmental field, focused on the constitutional basis for environmental measures, and presents further obstacles to the progress of the Commission's legislative agenda.

B. Union Environmental Law as International Environmental Law

The Union legal order, including its environmental law, remains a part of the old order of public international law from which it grew. Its approach is rooted in an international agreement, the Treaty of Rome, whose validity and effect continue to be governed by the traditional rules of international law. In the case of *Van Gend en Loos*, the European Court called the Union "a new legal order *of international law.*" As such, the Union joins other specialized legal orders of international law, such as the European

10 *Id.*, Art. 100A(1).

11 *Id.*, Art. 100A(3).

Convention on Human Rights' regional human rights law and the international administrative law that international administrative tribunals apply.

The Union legal order is innovative, however, and it has significantly moved the "goalpost" of traditional international law. It extends the scope of possibilities available under international law. One important achievement is the wholesale change in our perceptions of how international law can work as a dynamic and effective force. The Union legal order has done so most notably by granting to nonstate actors rights that they can enforce before national courts and the European Court of Justice, by applying the doctrines of direct effect, supremacy, and implied powers, and by instituting a decisionmaking process based on qualified majority, rather than unanimous, voting. While, as Professor Weiler recognizes, each of these doctrines existed under traditional international law, the Union legal system and the European Court have given them flesh.

Whether one believes that state responsibility is a substantive rule of international law or simply "a general term for all the consequences of wrongdoing," it exists in the Union legal order as in any other discrete international legal order. Neither application of Union law in the national courts nor recourse to Article 177 can force a member state to remedy a breach of the Treaty of Rome. Rather, recourse to Articles 169 and 170, which give the European Court of Justice jurisdiction over alleged wrongdoing and breaches of the Treaty of Rome by member states, will provide, at a minimum, attempts at remedies. The European Court has compulsory jurisdiction, and its powers under Articles 169 to 172 in contentious proceedings involving issues of state responsibility are similar to those of the International Court of Justice.

The Union legal order differs from general international law in that the Union allows nonstate actors to trigger action by an independent international actor (the Commission) which then alleges the breach of an international legal obligation (a Union law) before the compulsory jurisdiction of an international court (the European Court). Despite this procedure's weaknesses, it is unique both in its scope and in bringing into the enforcement process members of the international union other than states.

The Union legal order is an important step in the progressive development of international law. It builds up the historic foundations of traditional international law. As such, the Union's rules on environmental protection constitute a part of international environmental law and can contribute to its progressive development, whether in the Caribbean, the South Pacific, the Americas, or globally.

C. Union Environmental Law and Participatory Democracy: The Role of Environmental Groups

Pressure groups—or "common interest groups," in Union parlance—and other interested nonstate actors have long been involved in Union environmental law and policy. Even prior to the SEA, Brussels was home to a number of national, regional, and international environmental groups. The legislative lobbying process in which they were involved became increasingly sophisticated by the late 1980s, focusing on the Commission, the Parliament, and individual member states. At this time, environmental groups also became involved in the enforcement process, often notifying the Commission and other member states of breaches of environmental laws. The SEA then transformed the Union into a "necessary, legitimate, and at times effective locus for direct constituency appeal," often replacing the individual member states as the focus of lobbying efforts.

In response to the SEA, the lobbying process has become ever more sophisticated, with groups such as Greenpeace International establishing specialized, Brussels-based units to focus exclusively on influencing the Union's legislative and decisionmaking process. The lobbying process seeks to influence not only legislation and decisionmaking under the jurisdiction of DG XI, but any legislation on matters of environmental significance, including agriculture, energy, transportation, and fisheries.

Environmental groups have played a major role in integrating environmental considerations into all areas of Union activity. The lobbying process has already achieved significant results, such as the European Parliament's amendment of the Broadcasting Directive to prohibit advertisements which encourage behavior prejudicial to the protection of the environment. Moreover, the Commission is receptive to legislative suggestions from environmental groups. In July of 1990, it responded to the recommendations of a meeting of academic and environmental group lawyers by establishing a working group on the harmonization of citizen suit provisions in member states' environmental laws. This move was only a precursor to yet wider formal involvement of environmental groups.

Particularly in the enforcement of Union environmental law, the environmental groups are breaking new ground. They have a variety of tools to aid enforcement, including notification of breaches to the Commission, formal written complaints of breaches, legal proceedings in national courts based upon causes of action founded upon Union environmental law, and use of Article 177 to enforce Union environmental objectives. None of these methods is generally available to nonstate actors under traditional international environmental law, supporting Professor Weiler's view that the Union legal order's enforcement and compliance procedures "represent a quantitative change of such magnitude that it is qualitative in nature."[12]

D. Conclusion

European Union environmental law represents the first attempt of any region in the international union to legislate widely on transboundary environmental issues. In seizing jurisdiction over the internal affairs of member states by regulating environmental matters which do not raise *prima facie* transboundary issues, Union environmental law goes even further. It effectively says that the member states of the Union share a single, indivisible environment.

[12] Weiler, *The Transformation of Europe*, 100 Yale L.J. 2403 (1991).

Although Union environmental law may still rightly be criticized for establishing weak standards in certain areas, it is unmatched as a manifestation of international law in both its substantive and procedural content and in bringing a wide spectrum of the international union into the international legal process.

III. The Influence of EU Environmental Law and Policy Throughout Europe[13]

Until recently, the EU and EFTA member nations have interacted with one another more than they have interacted with the Central and Eastern European nations. Central and Eastern European nations have historically focused most of their trade relations on the Soviet Union. The opening of Central and Eastern Europe in 1989, however, has turned the attention of many of these nations away from the Soviet Union and toward Western Europe. The interest in a united Europe has spurred the national governments of various European countries to create a common European economic market and to encourage political stability and environmental protection throughout the European continent. The nations of Central and Eastern Europe, however, face the difficulty of developing democratic systems and converting their economies into capital markets. These changes require significant reformation of economic, legal, and environmental institutions. While European free trade and foreign investment are the primary areas of focus, concern for environmental protection is significantly increasing.

Partially by default, and partially due to its successes in uniting its member states, the EU is emerging as the model structure for uniting Europe and creating a federation of states devoted to environmental, political, economic, legal, and social integration. Of the two currently existing European regional organizations—the EU and EFTA—the EU is the only organization with a mature supranational structure capable of bringing the diverse European nations together.

The EU's role in uniting Europe, however, is not clearly defined. The EU, therefore, has decided to strengthen its economic and political ties to non-EU nations. For example, the EU has pursued negotiation of a Joint Declaration with the Council of Economic Mutual Assistance (COMECON) trading bloc, and bilateral economic cooperation agreements with the EFTA member nations and several Central and Eastern European nations. These preliminary agreements have taken various forms and are legally binding. They do not, however, assure non-EU signatories a preference for or guaranty of membership in the EU.

The EU is interested in expanding its role throughout the European continent, but has found achievement of this goal to be arduous. As an interim solution to granting full EU accession, the Union is pursuing two alternatives: creation of the European Economic Space (EES, also commonly referred to as European Economic Area) and

[13] Cynthia B. Schultz and Tamara Raye Crockett, *Developing a Unified European Environmental Law and Policy*, 14 B.C. Int'l & Comp. L. Rev. 301, 304. (1991).

negotiation of individual agreements with non-EU European nations, many of which include environmental provisions.

Concurrent in their efforts to create the EES, EFTA and Central and Eastern European nations will probably enter into association agreements with the EU. Negotiating an association agreement is difficult because the EEU Treaty does not provide clear direction in this regard. In fact, as a result of overwhelming interest in full accession to the EU, the Commission of the European Communities (Commission) has decided to draft a new proposal that would more clearly define the law of accession to the EU. These "third-generation association agreements" will address more than just trade issues—they will also focus heavily on protection of the human environment and scientific research and development. Utilizing these association agreements, the EU should pledge to make its environmental programs and agenda available to nations seeking association.

As the EES gradually develops and the association agreements are redefined, the EU should take the immediate step of negotiating protocols to existing bilateral economic cooperation agreements. The bilateral economic cooperation agreements that currently exist between the EU, EFTA, and Central and Eastern European nations do not adequately address environmental concerns. Therefore, it would seem appropriate for the EU to adopt protocols to these agreements to provide financial and environmental development assistance as well as to promote harmonization of environmental policies.

IV. Expanding EU Environmental Law and Policy Throughout Europe

In attempting to centralize environmental policy, the EU has expressed an interest in extending its environmental controls to non-EU nations. To achieve this goal, the Union has undertaken at least two notable steps. First, the EU has initiated expansion of its environmental law and policy. For example, the EU has offered membership to non-EU nations in its newly-created European Environment Agency (EEA), which is designed to gather and access European environmental information. Expansion of the EEA would facilitate European-wide administration of essential EU environmental law and policy, access to environmental information, and completion of environmental impact assessments. Second, the EU has actively supported the creation and funding of a multinational development bank, which is responsible for funding Central and Eastern European development, with an eye toward environmental protection and restoration.

A. Gathering and Accessing European Environmental Information: European Environment Agency

Unlike the U.S. Environmental Protection Agency (EPA), the EEA is primarily designed to verify and coordinate member states' environmental standards. Although the exact role of the EEA is still uncertain, the Union has asserted that the EEA will be largely responsible for the EU's environmental research activities, coordination of the environmental information programs of both the EU and its member states, and possible implementation of a Union-wide environmental impact assessment program. These types of activities—research, information dissemination, and environmtal impact assessments—could form the basis of a unified European environmental law and policy.

1. Research Programs

The EU focuses much of its environmental protection efforts on defining and identifying environmental problems. Union environmental research programs are an integral component of this effort[14] and continue to receive funding and support from the EU.[15] Such support encompasses the proposed establishment of an EU environmental research laboratory and accompanying guidelines for research practices.

2. Freedom of Access to Environmental Information

Unlike the situation in the United States, information regarding environmental conditions and governmental activities affecting the environment is not readily available in most European nations. The Council, however, has adopted Directive 90/313 to ensure the availability and free exchange of environmental information throughout the Union.[16] This directive mandates free public access to all environmental information held by public authorities and strictly limits the prerogative of member states to deny access to such information.

This directive may become a cornerstone for a unified European environmental program because it reflects the importance of providing free access to environmental information in developing environmental law and policy. Certainly, the success of unified European environmental law and policy depends on the availability and free exchange of environmental information.

---

[14] The First Environmental Action Program expressly created provisions for research projects concerning protection of the environment, which subsequently have been carried forth in the Second, Third, and Fourth Environmental Action Programs.

[15] Regulation 1872/84, Council Regulation on Action by the Union relating to the environment, O.J. L176/1 (1984) (appropriating Union funding for specific environmental measures and research and development programs relating to the environment and raw materials at the Union level).

[16] Directive 90/313, Council Directive of 7 June 1990 on Freedom of Access to Information on the Environment, O.J. L158/56 (1990).

3. Environmental Impact Assessment

Directive 85/337 concerning environmental impact assessments of significant public and private projects stresses that comprehensive environmental law and policy must aim to prevent environmental pollution and nuisances. Assessment of the environmental impacts of these projects will aid European legal integration by forcing consideration of potential environmental harm in the early phases of planning and decision-making.[17] The individual member states control the implementation, oversight, and enforcement of this directive. Regardless of the member states' role, however, the EEA should be the mechanism for ensuring that all projects within the EU and under EU supervision are subject to environmental impact assessments. This procedure and the ensuing role of the EEA would provide for a Union-wide, and potentially, a European-wide implementation of the environmental assessment directive.

B. European Bank for Reconstruction and Development

The EU fashioned the newly-created European Bank for Reconstruction and Development (EBRD) as a major source of its financial aid to Central and Eastern European development. The EBRD was created in 1990 as a multilateral development effort to support social, economic, and environmental reforms in Central and Eastern Europe. The EBRD represents the political and financial commitment of Western Europe to changes in Central and Eastern Europe. The EU has a powerful influence in the EBRD. The creators of the bank include a unique group of nations and organizations totaling 44 charter members, with both the EU and the European Investment Bank, an institution of the EU, having membership in their individual capacities. The EU holds a 51 percent majority interest in the EBRD, establishing EU control over its policy-making and lending activities.

Although the EBRD is not expected to begin issuing loans until mid-1991, financial assistance will be dedicated to both public and private sector projects, and will include support for infrastructure projects as well as environmental clean-up and restoration projects. The EBRD's enabling legislation includes a mandate for balancing Central and Eastern European environmental problems with concerns for economic development. Several Western European nations and the EU insisted on this provision, thus establishing environmental protection and sustainable development as direct responsibilities of the EBRD. In short, the EU will utilize the EBRD as a primary mechanism for channeling financial assistance to the emerging democracies of Central and Eastern Europe and promoting the EU environmental program at the European level.

---

[17] Directive 85/337, Council Directive of 27 June 1985 on the assessment of the effects of certain public and private projects on the environment, O.J. L175/40 (1985). The Second Environmental Action Program, adopted in 1977, specifically identified the need for environmental assessments to carry out the objectives and principles set forth under the First Environmental Action Program.

V. Prospects for Unified European Environmental Law

As the nations of Europe increasingly cooperate under the auspices of the EU, environmental protection will be catapulted to the forefront of a united Europe's policy agenda. In an effort to move closer to integration with the EU, Central and Eastern European governments are "anxious to bring their environmental legislation and practice into line with EU guidelines."[18] Similarly, the EFTA nations have strong domestic interests in environmental protection. Given that EFTA environmental standards are generally higher than EU standards, however, it is not clear whether EFTA nations will agree to the lower EU compliance level.

Ultimately, all European nations should adopt environmental laws and policies which complement the needs and desires of a united Europe. Accomplishment of this task, however, will not be easy, and it will not be achieved in the near future. Although the nations of Europe have many incentives for integration, these nations are extremely diverse. A successfully integrated European environmental law and policy must overcome intense cultural, economic, and governmental diversity.

The EES should develop the institutional mechanisms necessary to carry out such an environmental mandate. With final agreement on the EES expected by January 1, 1993, details as to the amount of non-EU involvement and participation in the decision-making process on policy and legislative levels remain unresolved. One of the major points of contention in the EES negotiations remains environmental regulation. The EU would prefer that all goods freely circulate throughout the EES in compliance with EU environmental protection standards. The EFTA nations, however, argue that they should be allowed to maintain restrictions on products that do not meet their own more stringent standards. Thus, without effective institutions, the EES may prove to be little more than a one foot in, one foot out approach that may, in the long term, thwart European integration.

The EU has positioned itself as the mechanism for overcoming this diversity. The EU and its individual member states have a strong commitment to environmental protection. EU environmental law and policy could expand throughout the region as, first, environmental protection within the EU becomes more centralized and coordinated, and second, as the EU begins to intensify relations with non-EU European nations.

In its attempt to unify European environmental law and policy, the EU has undertaken several interim mechanisms to expand its influence over environmental issues. Establishing the EEA and the EBRD are significant first steps in this expansion. The EEA and the EBRD could develop into complex institutions with comprehensive oversight and administrative authority for EU environmental law and policy. Ultimately, the EEA's tasks should expand beyond research, information monitoring, and environmental impact assessments to include implementation and enforcement of EU environmental standards. Vesting these responsibilities in the EEA would centralize European-wide application of EU environmental law and policy. Similarly, EU influence could ensure that the EBRD will incorporate environmental provisions into all levels of its activities.

---

[18] Dempsey, *Eastern Europe Lacks Incentives*, Fin. Times, Mar. 13, 1991, at 2, col. 5.

While these goals may seem lofty, the EU could approach expansion of its environmental agenda in a calculated and meticulous manner. First, the EU should allow non-EU nations to participate in developing European environmental law and policy. Second, the EU should give substantial financial assistance for environmental protection to Central and Eastern European development. This financial assistance should include specific procedural provisions, and funds earmarked for environmental protection and restoration. Third, the EU should negotiate environmental protocols to its current bilateral cooperation agreements with non-EU nations. At a minimum, these protocols should call for the establishment of joint research and monitoring programs, free access to environmental information, and preparation of environmental impact assessments.

VI. Role of Court of Justice in EU Environmental Law[19]

There are four scenarios for issues of environmental law to come before the ECJ. First, if a Member State fails to comply with environmental protection obligations imposed by EU law, it is the Commission's responsibility under Article 169 to commence proceedings for an infringement of Treaty obligations (EEU TREATY Art. 169). Second, in the absence of a Commission action, a Member State may proceed under Article 170 (EEU TREATY Art. 170). Third, issues of EU environmental law may also arise in institutional battles brought pursuant to Article 17 (EEU TREATY Art. 173). Finally, environmental issues also may reach the ECJ on an Article 177 reference from cases instituted against a Member State in the national courts (EEU TREATY Art. 177).

There are few areas of EU law and policy that have been shaped and influenced more positively by the jurisprudence of the ECJ than the area of environmental protection. Union environmental policy is "a monument to a pragmatic or flexible approach to the interpretation of the aims of the European EEU Treaty."[20] For example, the ECJ recognized the Union's competence to adopt legislation on matters of environmental protection despite the conspicuous absence of the word "environment" from the original text of the Treaty Establishing the European Economic Union (EEU Treaty or Treaty).[21] The ECJ later went on to declare environmental protection a "mandatory requirement" of Union law.[22] Single European Act case law reveals the ECJ's willingness to look beyond the plain meaning of language in Treaty articles[23] and

---

[19] Matthew L. Schemmel and Bas de Regt, *The European Court of Justice and the Environmental Protection Policy of the European Community,* 17 B.B. Int'l Comp. L. Rev. 53-83 (1994). © Matthew L. Schemmel and Bas de Regt. Reprinted by permission.

[20] David Freestone, *European Union Environmental Policy and Law,* 18 J.L. & Soc'y 135 (1991).

[21] Joined Cases 91 & 92/79, *Commission of the European Communities v. Italian Republic*, 1980 E.C.R. 1099, 1099 [hereinafter Joined Cases 91 & 92/79, 1980 E.C.R. 1099].

[22] Case 302/86, *Commission v. Denmark*, 1988 E.C.R. 4607, 4630.

[23] Upon an Article 177 reference, the ECJ held:

> [A]rticle 37 can achieve its purpose only if it is interpreted to mean that it requires the Union to be furnished with the general data concerning a plan for the disposal of radioactive effluents *before* such disposal is finally authorized. Such an interpretation, which is *able to safeguard the necessary effect of the provision*, must be given priority in accordance with the Court's settled case law. EURATOM TREATY Art. 37 (emphasis added).

EU secondary legislation[24] to give effect to the Union's environmental protection policies. Thus, Union institutions, Member States, Union citizens, and the lawyers that represent them should expect the ECJ to take a dynamic approach to the interpretation and application of Union environmental laws when ensuring the effectiveness of a Union environmental protection policy.

A number of the ECJ's "landmark" decisions, some of which specifically address environmental issues and others that indirectly affect Union environmental policy, illustrate this dynamic approach. This Article examines some of these decisions and discusses their implications for the continuing development of an effective Union environmental protection policy. Despite Denmark's and England's intransigence in ratifying[25] the Maastricht Treaty (Maastricht), its provisions recently have become part of Union law.[26]

A. Legal Basis of EU Environmental Legislation

1. Before the Single European Act

The Union's secondary legislation must have a legal basis identifiable in an Article of the Treaty. The ECJ held that the choice of a legal basis must be grounded in objective criteria subject to judicial review. And yet, as Ludwig Kramer stated, "Union environmental policy developed and flourished in the absence of explicit powers in the original EEU treaty."[27]

The combined cases in *Commission v. Italy* illustrate how the ECJ approved the Council's choice of a legal basis for Union environmental policy, even though there was no explicit reference to the environment in the original EU Treaty. The Commission instituted an action against Italy for its failure to implement Directives on detergents and the amount of sulphur in liquid fuels. The Council selected Article 100 as the Directive's legal basis. Italy argued that it was not clear from the Treaty that the Union had the power to legislate on matters of environmental protection and that the measures at issue were actually international agreements in the form of Directives. The Commission argued that the Directives, which were part of a Council program to eliminate

---

Case 187/87, *Saarland v. Minister of Industry*, 1 C.M.L.R. at 542.

[24] *See* Case 359/88, *Zanetti* 1990 E.C.R. I-1518, I-1518, 1522. The ECJ held that for purposes of Council Directives 75/442 and 78/319, the term "waste" must be broadly construed to include materials that were incapable of being put to an economic "re-use" and also materials that were capable of being recycled or re-used in some way. *Id.* at 1522. The Italian implementing legislation sought to define "waste" more restrictively, so as to exclude materials that were capable of being recycled or put to some other economic use.

[25] *See* EEU Treaty Art. 236. Article 236 states: "[t]he amendments [to the Treaty Establishing the European Economic Union] shall enter into force after being ratified by *all* the Member States in accordance with their respective constitutional requirements." EEU Treaty Art. 236 (emphasis added).

[26] *See* Robert Rice, *High Court Rejects Maastricht Challenge*, Fin. Times Weekend, July 31/Aug. 1, 1993, at 7.

[27] Kramer, EEU Treaty and Environmental Protection 31-35 (1990).

technical barriers to trade, were based on Article 100 because they had a direct effect on the establishment and function of the common market. The ECJ held that basing the Directives on Article 100 was indeed proper, reasoning that they were part of a program to eliminate trade barriers. But the ECJ also recognized the Commission's argument that measures concerning the environment may impose burdens on undertakings and thus distort competition in the absence of harmonization of national provisions. Kramer argued, "[t]he correct interpretation of the Court's judgements must therefore be that, if the Union by adopting [environmental] action programmes has documented its political view on the measures that are to be the subject of Union legislation, there is no need for further proof of the necessity for Union action." But regardless of what the Union wants to achieve, there always must be a proper legal basis for Union secondary legislation.[28] Thus the ECJ's decision in *Commission v. Italy* is of central importance, as it implicitly invited the Union institutions to develop a more comprehensive environmental protection policy on the basis of Article 100.

2. Legal Basis and the Single European Act

The word "environment" finally appeared in the written corpus of Union law with the adoption of the Single European Act,[29] and in particular with the incorporation of Title VII, Articles 130r, 130s, and 130t. Perhaps the most significant aspect of Title VII is that it provides an explicit legal basis for the creation of Union environmental legislation.[30] The Council subsequently adopted important Union environmental measures based upon Article 130s. When a piece of secondary legislation is based upon Article 130s, it must be adopted by a unanimous vote of the Council. The Parliament, however, only needs to be consulted for an opinion on the substance of the measure. Member States also retain the power to introduce more stringent national environmental measures than those taken pursuant to Title VII, as long as the national measures are compatible with the Treaty.

In addition to the new Maastricht provisions, the other possible legal basis for adopting Union environmental measures exists under Article 100a, which amended Article 100 and is intended to achieve the objectives set out in Article 8a, namely the progressive establishment of the internal market. Article 100a clearly was intended to serve as a potential legal basis for Union environmental protection measures. Article 100a(3) states that proposals on "environmental protection" shall "take as a base a high level of protection," while Article 100a(4) allows Member States some discretion as

---

[28] The Court noted that the Directives were adopted within the Environmental Action Programme but also that they were adopted under the General Programme for the elimination of technical barriers to trade which result from disparities between the provisions laid down by law, regulation or administrative action in Member States adopted by the Council on May 28, 1969. In this sense said the Court, '*it is validly founded upon Article 100.*' Case 45/86, *Commission v. Council.*

[29] See AMENDED EEU TREATY Art. 130s.

[30] AMENDED EEU TREATY Art. 130r(1). "Action by the Union relating to the environment shall have the following objectives: to preserve, protect and improve the quality of the environment; to contribute towards protection of human health; to ensure a prudent and rational utilization of natural resources." AMENDED EEU TREATY Art. 130r(1).

to the application of national measures on "protection of the environment."[31] Some of the Union's secondary environmental protec tion legislation has been based on Article 100a. The most significant implications of basing Union environmental policy on Article 100a, as opposed to Article 130s, are (1) that environmental measures which help achieve the functioning of the internal market may be adopted by qualified majority voting and (2) Parliament must be allowed to "cooperate" with the Council on the substance of that legislation.

Thus, the choice of a legal basis for Union environmental legislation is not a purely academic exercise.

> The legal basis of an act [100a or 130s] indicates not only the objective and nature of the measure which the Union can adopt [100a, measures affecting the functioning of the internal market or 130s, measures to protect the environment], but also the procedural requirements for its adoption [100a, the cooperation procedure or 130s, the consultation procedure], the Union institution competent to adopt it [greater Parliament participation under 100a] and, . . . the voting majority in the Council [100a, qualified majority vote, or 130s, unanimity].[32]

The Treaty does not indicate when Article 100a or Article 130s should serve as the legal basis of Union environmental policy.

3. The ECJ's Titanium Dioxide Decision

The ECJ addressed this issue in the case of *Commission v. Council (Titanium Dioxide).*[33] In 1983, the Commission presented the Council with a proposed Directive on harmonization of Member State programs for the reduction of waste from the titanium dioxide industry. The proposed Directive was based upon Articles 100 and 235. Subsequent to the Single European Act, the Commission changed the legal basis of the proposed Directive to Article 100a. The Council, however, rejected Article 100a and in its "common position" decided to base the Directive on Article 130s. The Council consulted the European Parliament pursuant to Article 130s and the Parliament, in agreement with the Commission, stated that the Directive should have been based on Article 100a, not 130s. Nevertheless, the Council ultimately adopted the Directive by a unanimous vote under Article 130s. The Commission, with the European Parliament's intervention, brought an action to annul the Directive on grounds that it had been adopted on an improper legal basis.

The Council and Commission agreed that in order to meet the ECJ's mandate that a legal basis must be founded on objective criteria amenable to judicial review, it was

---

[31] Often referred to as the "Thatcher Clause," in reference to former British Prime Minister Margaret Thatcher's insistence that it be included in the text of the Single European Act, Article 100a(4) nevertheless limits the Member States' ability to apply national environmental provisions to cases where it can show a major need, i.e. those exceptions, like public security, that are listed in Article 36.

[32] Bradley, *The European Court and Basis of Union Legislation,* 13 Eur. L. Rev. 379-402 (1988).

[33] *Titanium Dioxide*, Case C-300/89, *Commission v. Council*, 1991 E.C.R. I-2878 [hereinafter *Titanium Dioxide*].

necessary to establish the measure's "center of gravity." The "center of gravity" test assumes that a measure may be designed to meet more than one Union objective, but the legal basis should be founded in the Treaty article most compatible with a measure's primary objective. The Council argued that while the Directive sought internal market/competition policy objectives, the primary objective of Directive 89/428 is the reduction and ultimate elimination of pollution caused by titanium dioxide production and therefore should be based on Article 130s. Conversely, the Commission and European Parliament argued that Article 100a was the proper legal basis. The Directive's primary objective was to establish a level playing field for competition between titanium dioxide producers, thereby improving conditions for achieving the internal market.

The ECJ scrutinized the language of Directive 89/428 and found that the provision addressed both the need to reduce/eliminate waste from the titanium dioxide industry as well as the need to harmonize titanium dioxide production so as to improve competitive conditions. Thus, rather than having a "center of gravity" or primary objective, the ECJ found that the Directive had a dual, inextricably connected concern for protecting the environment and achieving an effective internal market.

Citing its own case law, the ECJ stated that the Directive, which had characteristics of an environmental measure adoptable under 130s and an internal market measure adoptable under 100a, ordinarily would be based on both relevant Treaty provisions. The ECJ ruled, however, that the Directive lawfully could not be based on both 130s and 100a, because a concomitant reliance on the respective articles would deprive the European Parliament of essential institutional powers granted to them under the "cooperation procedure" in Article 100a. Under the cooperation procedure, as required by Article 100a, the Council only needs to reach a qualified majority vote to adopt the European Parliament's proposed amendments to the Council's common position. If the Council's common position is rejected by the European Parliament or the Council wishes to amend the Commission's second proposal, re-drafted in light of the European Parliament's amendments, the Council must act unanimously. But, as the ECJ noted, if both 100a and 130s were relied upon as the Directive's legal basis, the Council still would be required to vote unanimously in accordance with Article 130s's requirements, thereby effectively avoiding the European Parliament's input under the cooperation procedure. The ECJ recognized that the cooperation procedure enhanced the European Parliament's ability to affect the substance of Union legislation and reflected a "fundamental democratic principle" of citizen participation through its directly elected Union institution. Thus, the ECJ concluded that to maintain the powers extended to the European Parliament under the Treaty, it was necessary to determine whether Article 100a or 130s was the appropriate legal basis of the Directive. The ECJ, in a characteristically dynamic approach, held that the Council improperly based Directive 89/428 on Article 130s and should have selected Article 100a as the appropriate legal basis. The ECJ reasoned based on Article 130r(2), that a measure need not be based on Article 130s for the sole reason that it contains a concern for environmental protection. The ECJ also pointed to the language of Article 100a(3), which states that measures adopted to achieve the internal market shall take a high level of protection with regard to health, safety, and the environment. Thus, the ECJ concluded that the goal of environmental protection articulated in Article 130s could be achieved effectively under Article 100a. Most importantly, the ECJ stated that measures which are required to protect the environment can, in the absence of harmonized national laws, distort competition. Therefore, the ECJ determined that a measure like Directive 89/428, intended to approximate national laws in a specific industry and thereby avoid distortions in competition, contributes to the establishment and function of the internal market, and therefore should be based on Article 100a. The ECJ subsequently declared the Directive void.

The judgment in *Titanium Dioxide* exemplifies the ECJ's dynamic approach to inter preting the Treaty and may contribute to a strengthened Union environmental policy. First, it seems clear that the Commission will seek to base a significant amount of future and pending Union environmental legislation on Article 100a. The Commission increasingly may draft its proposals with language that sets out the dual objectives of environmental protection and the avoidance of unfair or distorted competition. The Commission can argue persuasively that a significant number of Union measures intended to protect the environment share the dual aim of achieving the internal market, as even the slightest difference among national laws arguably may distort competition within particular industries. Additionally, in light of Denmark's, England's, and Germany's Maastricht ratification battles, it is significant that the *Titanium Dioxide* case may extend qualified majority voting in the area of Union environmental policy, as required by Article 100a. Qualified majority voting may aid the efficient adoption of stronger environmental policy as it will prevent one or even two large Member States, England and Italy for example, from vetoing tough environmental measures.

Third, the ECJ's enthusiastic "endorsement" of the cooperation procedure may not only mean greater powers for the European Parliament, but indirectly may result in strengthened Union environmental measures. The European Parliament has shown "Green" inclinations. Thus, it may use the cooperation procedure to influence the Council for greater environmental protection measures.

Finally, as stated above, the power of the Member States to take unilateral action after the Union has adopted an environmental measure is clearer under Article 130t than it is under Article 100a(4). Thus, the *Titanium Dioxide* decision represents a diminution in the Member States' power via the Council. Furthermore, the decision is a victory for the proponents of establishing environmental protection standards at the Union level.

4. One Step Up, Two Steps Back?

Common responses to the ECJ's *Titanium Dioxide* decision ranged from caution[34] to criticism.[35] With the recent decision in a subsequent case involving the legal basis of

---

[34] Derrick Wyatt & Alan Dashwood, *European Union Law*, 369 (3d. ed. 1993), "It would be premature to conclude from the *Titanium Dioxide* judgement that any Union measure for the protection of the environment which has a tendency to equalise conditions of competition must, for that reason, be based on Article 100a."

[35] Scott Crosby, *The Single Market and the Rule of Law*, 16 Eur. L. Rev. 451 (1991).
In *Titanium Dioxide*, the Court of Justice gave a wide but not all embracing interpretation to Article 100a. This judgment, however, does not invalidate but tends to confirm the arguments supporting the thesis that Article 100a is being misused. A reversal of this dangerous trend is necessary in the interest of the rule of law and the Union.

the Union's amended Directive on waste,[36] there is bound to be a flood of new commentary. Arguably, the ECJ's recent decision in *Commission v.Council* (*Waste Directive*) refines the principles adumbrated in *Titanium Dioxide* rather than reverses them.[37]

In *Waste Directive*, the Commission and Parliament brought an action for annulment[38] of the EU's amended Directive on the elimination of waste. The Commission and Parliament invoked the identical arguments they successfully relied upon in *Titanium Dioxide* to assert that the amended *Waste Directive* should have been adopted under Article 100a as opposed to 130s. The Commission and Parliament reasoned that the Directive sought to impose a common arrangement among the Member States for the removal and elimination of waste, and it therefore contained the dual aims of achieving both environmental protection and an internal market. As in *Titanium Dioxide*, the Council argued that the amended *Waste Directive* was concerned primarily with environmental protection and therefore was based properly on Article 130s.

The ECJ began its decision by reiterating that the choice of a Directive's legal basis must be based on the objective criterion of content and aim and must be amenable to judicial review. In considering the language utilized in the Directive's preamble, the ECJ determined that it was intended to apply to the removal and elimination of all types of waste regardless of its source, that Member States are obliged to control the removal of waste, and that waste should be eliminated as close to its source as possible.

The Commission's argument that the Directive should have been based on Article 100a largely hinged on the fact that waste must be considered a "good" in accordance with Article 30, and is thus subject to the rules on the free movement of goods. But the ECJ concluded that environmental protection is a mandatory requirement of EU law and that in such circumstances limitations of the free movement of goods are allowable. Although the ECJ admitted that some elements of the Directive would have some affect on the functioning of the internal market, it concluded that this was merely a "side effect" of the overarching goal of establishing an effective system for the processing and elimination of waste. The ECJ also held that basing a Directive on Article 100a is not justified merely because some elements may effect the functioning of the internal market. Thus, the ECJ held that Article 130s was the proper legal basis and dismissed the action. The *Waste Directive* decision is significant for numerous reasons. First, the ECJ has breathed new life into Article 130s. After the decision in *Titanium Dioxide*, it was unclear whether Article 130s would maintain any significance as a potential legal basis for secondary legislation. But the *Waste Directive* decision represents a firm acknowledgment that measures which are concerned primarily with environmental protection most likely will be based on Article 130s.

---

[36] Council Directive 91/156, EEU on Elimination of Waste, amending Directive 75/442, 1991 O.J. (L 78) 32 [hereinafter Waste Directive].

[37] Case 155/91, 17 March 1993.

[38] *Id.* ¶ 3.

Second, although some commentators may disagree,[39] the ECJ's decision in *Waste Directive* has not overruled the reasoning and decision in the previous *Titanium Dioxide* case. In *Waste Directive*, the ECJ is careful to distinguish its reasoning from that employed in *Titanium Dioxide* and acknowledges that the facts surrounding the two decisions are crucially different. The factual distinction of the greatest importance is that the Directive interpreted in *Titanium Dioxide* concerned a very specific type of pollution and a very specific source, namely the titanium dioxide producing industry. In circumstances where an EU Directive singles out a specific industry and thereby seeks to regulate the production of a specific type of product, the fairness and equality of the competitive business environment is effected immediately and unequivocally. This fact underlined the ECJ's reasoning in *Titanium Dioxide*, and led the Court to conclude that the aims of maintaining competitive equality in the titanium dioxide industry and enhancing the environment could not be separated, but were in fact dual aims of the Directive.

In contrast, the Directive interpreted in *Waste Directive* constituted a general scheme for the processing and elimination of waste without regard to its source. Further, the ECJ emphasized that the Directive's preamble made explicit reference to the fact that pollution should be processed close to its source and that Member States should place limits on its movement. Not only are intra-industry competitive pressures left unaddressed in the ECJ's interpretation of the *Waste Directive*, but by its very language the Directive seeks to place certain limitations on the free movement of goods. Under these factually distinctive circumstances, it was proper for the ECJ to distinguish its *Waste Directive* decision from *Titanium Dioxide* and to conclude that Article 130s is the *Waste Directive*'s proper legal basis. In *Waste Directive*, however, the ECJ left the door open for its reasoning in *Titanium Dioxide* to be used at a later date and under factual circumstances closer to those present in that case. The decision is bound to have an effect on the propriety of choice of a legal basis after the coming into force of the Maastricht Treaty.

5. Legal Basis and the Maastricht Treaty

The *Titanium Dioxide* and *Waste Directive* cases allowed the ECJ to clarify some questions and ambiguities about the proper legal basis of Union environmental legislation. With the Maastricht Treaty as a component of Union law, however, there are new, even more vexing questions surrounding the legal basis of Union environmental policy that the ECJ will have to resolve. The Maastricht Treaty substantially amends the language in Articles 100a, 130r, 130s, and 130t. As a result, there are now at least four different ways to adopt secondary Union legislation on the environment. First, the procedural structure articulated in Article 100a of the Single European Act has been extended to Article 130s(1) of the Maastricht Treaty. Consequently, the Commission will be able to draft proposals primarily or even exclusively intended to pursue goals of environmental protection, and in most cases the Council will be obliged to adopt such proposals by a qualified majority vote in cooperation with the European Parlia-

[39] *See* Ann Wachsmann, 31 C.M.L.R. 1051, 1062-63 (1993).

ment. If the *Waste Directive* decision represents a setback for the scope of qualified majority voting in the environmental protection area, the amended Article 130s restores its strength.

Second, Article 130s(2) of the Maastricht Treaty entails certain "sensitive" areas where Union environmental policy still will be adopted by a unanimous Council vote, in mere consultation with the European Parliament. Arguably, Article 130s(2) reflects the Member States' unwillingness to give up control over what are deemed traditional state functions, i.e. the power to impose taxes, to establish an energy policy, and the powers of eminent domain. Additionally, amended Article 130s(3) introduces the concept of a "co-decision" between the Council and the European Parliament on measures concerning the Union's general environmental action programs. These measures shall be adopted by a qualified majority vote. The co-decision procedure represents a significant strengthening of the European Parliament's powers, insofar as it allows the Parliament to veto measures it deems unsatisfactory. Before a proposal is vetoed, however, the procedure provides for the creation of a Conciliation Committee, where the Council and an equal number of European Parliamentarians will meet and attempt to reach a consensus.

The fourth legal basis for Union environmental legislation exists under Maastricht amended Article 100a. Article 100a still will require the Council to adopt measures by qualified majority vote, but will replace the cooperation procedure with the co-decision procedure. The incorporation of the co-decision procedure is arguably the Union's most earnest effort to reduce the so-called "Democratic Deficit."[40]

The Maastricht amendments ultimately will lead to litigation between Union institutions regarding the proper legal basis of Union environmental protection legislation. Once again, the ECJ will be called upon to interpret the Maastricht amendments. Union institutions should expect the ECJ to continue to interpret them in a way that furthers the effectiveness of the Union's environmental protection policy.

For example, potentially the Commission and the European Parliament may bring an action against the Council for the annulment of a measure the Council adopts pursuant to the amended Article 130s(2), as opposed to 130s(1). Amended Article 130s(1) should be relied upon as the primary legal basis for most Union environmental legislation, as the language of 130s(2) states that it is to be used in derogation of the former and only under limited circumstances. The language used to delineate when Article 130s(2) may be used is, however, general and unclear. The Council surely will interpret the categories that fall within Article 130s(2) broadly, as reliance on Article 130s(2) requires unanimous voting, allows Member States to retain veto power, and the Parliament only needs to be consulted. Thus, the Council may attempt to base environmental protection provisions that would be adopted under Article 130s(1) on Article 130s(2) instead. Arguably, the ECJ would rule in favor of the Commission and/or

[40] The "Democratic Deficit" in the European Union stems from the perception that unelected officials, mainly the Commis sion and the ECJ, have too much power over the shape of EU policy, whereas the directly elected European Parliament has very limited powers. The extension of the European Parliament's veto power to the great amount of EU secondary legislation that will be based on the amended Article 100a significantly increases its institutional powers.

the European Parliament if they should be confronted with such an action for annulment. The ECJ consistently has held that derogations and exceptions within the Treaty should be construed strictly and applied narrowly. Conversely, the ECJ demonstrated its willingness to interpret the Treaty in a way that makes Union environmental policy effective. Because Article 130s(2) increases the power of a single Member State to veto certain types of secondary legislation concerning the environment, only a strict interpretation of Article 130s(2)'s applicability would be consistent with the ECJ's jurisprudence in the area of Union environmental protection policy.

The Commission, in reliance on the ECJ's decisions in *Titanium Dioxide* and *Waste Directive*, will continue to rely on the amended Article 100a as the legal basis for some of its proposals on Union environmental legislation. Nevertheless, the Council may disagree with the Commission and instead seek to adopt a measure on the basis of the amended Article 130s(1). Although both articles oblige the Council to act by a qualified majority vote, under the amended Article 100a the European Parliament has co-decision rights, and thus a veto power. Under 130s(1), however, the Council only needs to cooperate with the European Parliament. If the Council adopts an environmental measure under 130s(1), and the Commission or Parliament subsequently brings an action for annulment, the ECJ will employ a *Titanium Dioxide/Waste Directive* analysis. The ECJ probably will annul the measure if the challenging party can show that achievement of the internal market by reducing distortions in competition is a serious goal and not merely a "side effect." Of course, the ECJ will have to refine what level of concern a particular piece of legislation must have with regard to establishment of the internal market in order to clear the "side effect" threshold, and thereby be deemed a genuine "aim" of the Directive.

The major battle cry will be sounded when the Commission proposes that a carbon tax, or some other economic instrument aimed at environmental protection should be based on the amended Article 100a, and the Council proceeds to adopt the measure under the amended Article 130s(2). The Commission may bring an action for annulment arguing that amended Article 100a is the appropriate legal basis for measures on carbon taxes and economic instruments that address source and industry-specific pollution. Additionally, such a Directive is necessary because only a harmonization of environmental tax measures will prevent distortions in competition within the common market. The ECJ's decision in *Waste Directive*, specifically its distinction of the facts and reasoning employed in that case from the facts and reasoning in the *Titanium* decision, cuts in favor of the Commission, as such a tax is essentially source and industry specific and a failure to harmonize measures would create a serious distortion in competition with regard to the costs incurred by carbon producers. The Council, on the other hand, will argue that taxes and economic instruments are "measures primarily of a fiscal nature" and therefore must be adopted under Article 130s(2).

Both the Commission and the Council have sound reasons for arguing that a proposed environmental tax or other economic instrument should be based on amended Article 100a or 130s(2) respectively. It would be disingenuous for the Commission to argue that environmental tax measures are not primarily fiscal in nature and therefore not within the competence of 130s(2). The Commission, however, can make a strong argument that the function of the internal market would be affected directly and significantly by such a measure. Thus, if confronted with a choice between amended Article 100a and amended Article 130s(2), the ECJ should promote the democratic principles enshrined in the co-decision procedure, and therefore choose amended Article 100a. Although the Council will argue that the plain language of amended Article 130s(2) undoubtedly gives them the power to adopt an environmental tax, the ECJ most likely will interpret the Maastricht amendments in a way that gives effect to the Union's environmental policy and spurs movement towards democratic accountability. In the case of a carbon tax, the rationale for acting at the Union level should be based on the obvious concerns of maintaining the Treaty's dedication to a level, competitive economic environment. Thus, it is possible that the ECJ will overlook the clear language of 130s(2) and hold that amended Article 100a is the proper legal basis for a carbon tax and for other economic instruments designed to protect and preserve the environment.

B. Environmental Policy and Economic Growth

1. Reconcilable Goals?

As discussed above, a provision of Union law may aim to achieve the goal of environmental protection and the goal of establishing an internal market simultaneously. Thus, arguably, the Union's environmental and economic concerns are potentially compatible. On the other hand, one can argue that "despite the affinity which exists between them, the mutual inter ests of economic integration policy and environmental policy do not always coincide, so that progress in integration policy can, as a result, represent a setback for environmental protection."[41] For example, steady economic growth and increased productivity (constitutionally enshrined as primary goals of the EU) easily could cause harm to the environment, as more factories and more products often create more pollution and waste.

The EU's first attempts at implementing a policy for environmental protection resulted indirectly from the regulation of competition and the desire to achieve the common market. But achieving environmental protection goals through measures designed to achieve the functioning of the common market exposes a new lacuna in the Union legal structure: what happens when economic and environmental goals conflict? The ECJ filled this gap. Accordingly, when there is a confrontation between the demands of an effective Union environmental protection policy and the fundamental Union doctrine on free movement of goods, the ECJ settles in favor of the environmental policy at issue.

2. *Waste Oils* and *Danish Bottles*

In the *Waste Oils* case, the ECJ held that a Council Directive on the disposal of waste oils, which included provisions allowing Member States to set up a system of zones

[41] Owen Lomas, *Environmental Protection, Economic Conflict and the European Union*, 33 McGill L.J. 507 (1988).

and permits for the collection and disposal of waste oil, did not contravene fundamental principles of Union law, i.e., free movement of goods and freedom of trade. The ECJ acknowledged that principles of free movement, free competition, and fair trade as fundamental rights are "general principles" of Union law that must be ensured. The ECJ stated, however, that the right to fair trade is not unlimited and may be restricted by measures which pursue an objective of "general interest" to the Union. Despite the fact that the word "environment" was not in the Treaty text at the time of its decision, the ECJ concluded that environmental protection was an "essential objective" of Union policy, and that the *Waste Oils* Directive sought to ensure that objective in a proportionate and non-discriminatory manner. Finally, the ECJ held that the French implementing legislation, which prohibited the burning of waste oils outside state approved facilities, was intended to protect the environment and did so without using unnecessarily restrictive methods. The French law therefore was held to be consistent with the aims and scope of the Waste Oil Directive.

The decision in *Waste Oils* illustrates the ECJ's willingness to promote the aims of environmental protection, despite the plain language of the Treaty. The ECJ, however, did not address specifically the language of Article 30, nor did it spell out clearly the test it would utilize in cases where it is confronted with a conflict between the "essential" EU objective of Union environmental protection and free movement principles.

In the *Danish Bottles* case, the ECJ built on and clarified the approach taken in *Waste Oils*, while concomitantly vaulting environmental protection into the forefront of Union consciousness. Denmark created a compulsory deposit and return system for the re-use of drink containers and included a requirement that only containers which had been approved previously by the national environmental agency could be marketed in Denmark. There was an exception for producers to import up to 3,000 hectoliters per year in unapproved containers and foreign producers could "test" the Danish Market with a limited number of unapproved cans. The Commission, with the United Kingdom intervening, argued that the Danish System violated Article 30. The ECJ held that the bulk of the Danish System was compatible with Union law. The ECJ reasoned that a recycling program was a necessary measure to protect the environment and that a compulsory deposit and return system was an essential and proportionate means of implementing the program. The ECJ concluded, however, that the pre-approval requirement did have a disproportionate effect despite the 3,000 hectoliter exception. Additionally, the ECJ held that any restrictions on trade that resulted from the compulsory deposit and return system did not violate Article 30.

The ECJ's decision in *Danish Bottles* advanced the cause of environmental protection in at least three ways. First, the ECJ declared that environmental protection was a "mandatory requirement" under Union law; thereby in effect limiting the application of Article 30.

The ECJ articulated the doctrine of "mandatory requirements" in the *Cassis de Dijon* decision, where the ECJ held that in the absence of Union legislation, Member States may adopt measures regarding the marketing of products that result in a restriction on free movement in order to satisfy mandatory requirements "relating in particular to the effectiveness of fiscal supervision, the protection of public health, the fairness of commercial transactions, and the defense of the consumer."[42] Thus, although environmental protection is not among the derogations to free movement listed in Article 36,[43] is not mentioned anywhere in the original EEU Treaty or in the language of *Cassis de Dijon*, the ECJ used the *Danish Bottles* decision to read environmental protection into the "mandatory requirements" doctrine.

Second, the ECJ articulated a three part test to clarify what types of environmental measures lawfully may restrict the fundamental Union provisions on free movement. The ECJ reasoned that: a) the measure genuinely must be intended to protect the environment and not be a disguised restriction on trade; b) the measure must be indistinctly applicable; and c) the measure must fall within the EU law principle of proportionality. This test will provide certainty for Member States as they strive to develop tough environmental protection policies.

Third, the ECJ's decision strengthens the power of Member States to enact stringent national environmental policies, thereby providing a spur for tougher policies at the Union level. Advocate General Sir Gordon Slynn concluded that the Danish measures were disproportionate and that other methods could have achieved a "reasonable standard" of environmental protection without seriously impinging Article 30. In taking a course of action different from that recommended by the Advocate General, the ECJ implicitly rejected the "reasonable standard" approach and opted for a more effective approach to environmental protection, even at the expense of a fundamental Union policy on free movement. One can argue that the answer to *Danish Bottles* is to take tougher, more comprehensive action at the Union level. It will be more difficult for Member States to justify taking unilateral action under Article 100a(4) or 130t if the Union already has acted under one of those provisions to achieve a high level of environmental protection.

3. Maastricht: Environment and Economic Development

a. Sustainability

The development of a strong European economy was one of the most important forces behind the creation of the EEU Treaty. As noted above, a concern for the environment was not reflected in the original Treaty text. After the word "environment" finally was incorporated by the Single European Act, environmental protection remained a secondary concern to economic development.

---

[42] Case 120/78, *Rewe Zentral AG v. Bundesmonopolverwaltung für Branntwein*, 1979 E.C.R. 649, 662 [hereinafter *Cassis de Dijon*].

[43] EEU TREATY Art. 36. Article 36 states:

> [t]he provisions of Articles 30 to 34 shall not preclude prohibitions or restrictions on imports, exports or goods in transit justified on grounds of public morality, public policy or public security; the protection of health and life of humans, animals or plants; the protection of national treasures possessing artistic, historic or archeological value; or the protection of industrial and commercial property. Such prohibitions or restrictions shall not, however, constitute a means of arbitrary discrimination or a disguised restriction on trade between the Member States.

EEU TREATY Art. 36.

It is arguable that the inclusion of the principle of "sustainability," as articulated in the Maastricht Treaty, raises concern for the environment to the same level as has been accorded to economic development.[44] The purpose of sustainable development is to set the pace of economic growth according to the capacity of the environment to absorb the adverse consequences of that growth, thus sustaining the health of our ecosystem. The logical corollary is that if the environment cannot sustain further development appropriately, further development should not be pursued. Arguably, however, most forms of economic development will cause some environmental damage, and hence the line at which it becomes unsustainable is a difficult one to draw. Based upon the approach taken by the ECJ, it most likely will define and apply the concept of sustainable development in a way that provides greater protection of the environment, even where the evidence of actual or potential environmental damage is not 100 percent conclusive.

b. *Subsidiarity*

In the *Danish Bottles* case, Denmark adopted legislation in the area of recycling in the absence of a Union measure. The power of a Member State to take unilateral action and pass measures of environmental protection was enshrined in the Treaty by the Single European Act. At first glance, the Maastricht Treaty seems to reaffirm, if not expand, the powers of the Member States to act unilaterally by including the principle of subsidiarity. The principle of subsidiarity requires Union institutions to take action only where the measure cannot be adopted more effectively at a national level, and such action must be done in the least restrictive manner.

Without prejudice to other areas of EU law, the principle of subsidiarity should not result in a shift of power away from EU institutions in the area of enacting environmental legislation. The problems of environmental protection cannot be addressed adequately within the rigid system of separate sovereign states. Subsidiarity really is about protecting sovereignty, but "the notion of sovereignty which underlies the current regime poses insurmountable obstacles when the problems to be addressed are transnational in scope." Because problems of environmental protection are largely transboundary in nature (pollu tion does not recognize a nation's sovereign border), there are compelling reasons for developing environmental protection policies primarily at the Union level. The ECJ's approach to the ambiguities and lacunae in EU law almost always results in a decision that strengthens the effectiveness of a Union environmental protection policy. Thus, when the ECJ is confronted with the principle of subsidiarity within the context of Member State and Union environmental protection policy, it is likely to give it a narrow application and rule that the Union institutions, not the individual Member States, are the appropriate bodies for adopting environmental legislation.

---

[44] *See, e.g.,* Maastricht Treaty, supra note 2, tit. VII, Art. 2, 31 ILM at 256-57. Article 2 states in pertinent part: "[t]he Union shall have as its task . . . to promote throughout the Union a harmonious and balanced development of economic activities, *sustainable and non-inflationary growth respecting the environment. . . " Id. (emphasis added).*

C. The Doctrine of Direct Effect and Environment

Application of the doctrine of "direct effect" is particularly important in the area of environmental protection, as a large majority of EU environmental policy is implemented in the form of Directives. The ECJ consistently has held that Directives which impose sufficiently precise, clear, and unconditional obligations upon a Member State, without requiring further Member State action, may give rise to rights and obligations that individuals can rely on in actions before their national courts. Additionally, a Member State may not rely, as against individuals, on its failure to perform obligations which a Directive entails. Thus, enforcement of EU environmental legislation may be achieved substantially by individuals and common interest groups bringing actions against Member States, and emanations thereof, before their national courts.

An individual may rely on the provisions of a directly effective Directive in bringing an action against a Member State in a national court. In *Foster v. British Gas*, the ECJ gave a broad interpretation to what constitutes the "State," and included certain utilities operators. The ECJ's ruling in *Foster* represents a significant development for the enforcement of Union environmental laws, as such a broad definition of the "State" potentially could reach the actions of gas, nuclear, coal, and other energy suppliers, as well as the water companies. For example, an individual that suffers harm from drinking water provided by the State run water authority will be able to bring an action in the national court against that authority if the water is not up to Union standards.

A recent ECJ decision raised the possibility that an individual, like one harmed from drinking impure water, may be able to recover damages as a remedy. In the joined cases of *Frankovich and Bonifaci v. Italian Republic,* the ECJ held that individuals who were owed back-pay by their insolvent employer could collect money damages from the State. In this case, Italy failed to implement a Directive on the approximation of Member State laws relating to the protection of employees whose employers become insolvent. Although the ECJ held that the Directive did not give rise to directly effective rights, it further held that Italy's failure to implement the Directive infringed EU law, that the applicant's injury flowed directly from that infringement, and that the applicant therefore was entitled to money damages. Although the Treaty does not contain any language about the awarding of money damages, the ECJ concluded that the principle of liability of the State for damage caused to individuals by infringements of Union law is inherent in the scheme of the Treaty.

This decision fills a lacuna in EU law. The ability to award damages when a Member State fails to meet its obligations under EU law essentially provides "teeth" to the ECJ's powers under articles 169 and 170. Thus, if a Member State fails to implement a Union Directive aimed at environmental protection and an individual suffers harm from exposure to the part of the environment which the Directive was meant to regulate, that individual will have a strong case for collecting damages from the Member State. The prospect of financial liability will in turn prompt Member States to implement environmental Directives in a timely and proper manner.

D. Summary

The net result of the ECJ's jurisprudence has been an increase in Union awareness of environmental issues and an increased effectiveness of Union measures designed to protect the environment. The ECJ's judgments in *Titanium Dioxide* and *Waste Directive* clarify some of the controversy surrounding the proper legal basis of Union secondary environmental legislation. The ECJ's decisions will have a generally positive effect on EU environmental policy. Article 100a will remain a viable legal basis for environmental legislation, thus potentially extending qualified majority voting. The ECJ most likely will interpret the new Maastricht legal basis provisions in a manner consistent with its previous jurisprudence, while simultaneously promoting the European Parliament's new co-decision powers with the Council. The ECJ's decisions in *Waste Oils* and *Danish Bottles* illustrate a willingness to promote the EU's environmental protection policies, even when they may conflict with another fundamental principle of EU law. Thus, Maastricht's incorporation of the principle of sustainability raises environmental protection to co-equal status with the EU's policy on economic integration. On the other hand, Maastricht's inclusion of subsidiarity is not very significant from the perspective of the environmental protection policy because the inherently transboundary nature of pollution and other dangers to the environment requires the continued development of environmental protection policy primarily at the Union level. Finally, the ECJ's decisions in *Foster* and *Frankovich* will have a profound influence on the way EU environmental policy is enforced. Both cases expand the category of potential Member State defendants in actions brought by individuals before the national courts, and create the possibility of collecting money damages from Member States who fail to implement Union environmental Directives properly.

VII. Conclusion

The EU, EFTA, and Central and Eastern European nations have identified the environment as a common problem and are seeking common solutions. The development of EU environmental law and its expanding influence over environmental affairs throughout Europe has fostered the recognition of the need for a unified European environmental law and policy. Although the EU will continue to have a prominent role in this process, all European nations must act together to reallocate resources, technology, and cultural understanding in order to enter the next stage of European-wide environmental protection—namely, harmonization, compliance, and enforcement.

Chapter 8
Intellectual Property

I. The Beginning and Early Developments[1]

An understanding of the European Union's present and probable future role in the field of intellectual property would be incomplete without some reference to the past.

To begin, we should recall that the European Union is an association of states engaged in a process of political and economic integration based on a single internal market. The realization of this internal market is in turn based on four fundamental freedoms laid down by the Union Treaty: the freedom to supply goods, the freedom to render services, the free movement of persons and the free movement of capital. In addition, the Union Treaty proscribes anti-competitive behavior such as cartels, abuses of dominant position and subsidies. It also provides for a common commercial policy and common action on other matters of mutual concern in relation to the outside world. Finally, in addition to the Treaty's provision, the Union may adopt secondary legislation through a legislative procedure involving the Commission, the European Parliament, the Economic and Social Committee and the Council in order to realize its objectives. Some of this legislation, particularly legislation pertaining to the realization of the internal market, requires a qualified majority for adoption.

However, as to intellectual property, the EEC Treaty contains no specific mandate or program. On the contrary, it includes possible restrictions on the extent to which the Treaty provides that the Treaty provisions on the free movement of goods shall not prejudice the intellectual property laws of the Member States. Similarly, Article 222 specifies that the Treaty may in no way prejudice the rules in the Member States governing their respective systems of property ownership. Finally, there is no provision which is equivalent to Article 1, Section 8 of the U.S. Constitution. These restrictions have had the unfortunate effect of lending comfort to those who have argued from time to time that the Union has no or very limited power to legislate on or otherwise affect intellectual property.

Very rapidly after the Union's foundation, however, developments occurred which demonstrated that the Union did in fact possess important powers which would enable it to address intellectual property in a variety of ways. First, the European Court of Jus-

1 Robert J. Coleman, *The 1991 Horace S. Manges Lecture—Intellectual Property and the European Community After 1992*, 15 Colum.-VLA J.L. & Arts. 117-33 (1991). © 1991 Robert J. Coleman. Reprinted by permission.

tice began to define the limits of Treaty provisions like Articles 36 and 222, discussed above, which might have been thought to insulate national intellectual property rights and the way in which they had traditionally been exercised from the Union principles of free movement of goods and services. And second, work began on legal instruments to address the needs of those persons who wish to see their inventions and creations protected in a more coherent way throughout the territories of the Member States.

A. The Case Law of the European Court of Justice

The main principles developed by the Court can be summarized as follows. Article 36 provides that Treaty requirements ensuring the free movement of goods—in particular, Article 30—do not preclude restrictions on imports justified by the need to protect industrial and commercial property, including copyright and neighboring rights. However, the court held early on that once goods have been lawfully placed in Union market, either by the right holder or with his consent, national intellectual property rights cannot be used to prevent the goods from entering another Member State. In such a case the intellectual property rights in question have been "exhausted" and cannot be used to partition territorially the Union's internal market. The importation of copyrighted goods cannot be prevented. Right-holders cannot claim any difference between royalties payable for goods first marketed in the importing state. On the other hand, where copyrighted goods have been lawfully placed on the market but without the consent of the right-holder, for example, where the length of protection in one member State is shorter than in another, then the right-holder can rely on his copyright to prevent the importation or sale of the goods in the state in which his right still exists.

Articles 59 to 66 protect the freedom to provide services, including those subject to copyright (such as broadcasting). The European Court of Justice has ruled that these provisions must also be interpreted as not prejudicing national intellectual property regimes, although there is no explicit provision in the Treaty parallel to Article 36. Moreover, while the Court has maintained that certain aspects of the way in which rights are exercised may be incompatible with the free movements provisions, it has limited the exhaustion doctrine significantly in relation to works which are exploited through public performance or rental. The Court has done this on the grounds that the right-holder has a legitimate interest in receipts from successive performances or rental transactions. Therefore, permission given to perform the work on occasion does not exhaust these rights, nor are they exhausted by placing a recording of the work on the market. Accordingly, the re-transmission of television broadcasts via cable may be prohibited; a supplementary mechanical right royalty may be required for the public performance of recordings placed on the market in a state where the supplementary right does not exist; and a rental right may be invoked to prevent the rental of audiovisual works placed on the market in another State which does not recognize such a right.

The Court has further ruled on a number of occasions that, in the absence of secondary legislation, Union law does not limit the freedom of Member States to determine the character of intellectual property rights and the conditions or procedures under which they are granted. However, the Court has at the same time held that the national rules in question must not be contrary to the last part of Article 36 by constituting "a means of arbitrary discrimination or a disguised restriction on trade between Member States." Such discrimination has been detected by the Court in the case of a national rule in the patent field.

Moreover, an impressive body of case law has developed defining the circumstances in which the use of intellectual property rights constitutes an "arbitrary discrimination" or a "disguised restriction" because such use violated the competition provisions of the Treaty, in particular Articles 85 and 86. It suffices to note here that in the design field, the Court has in recent years confirmed that neither the acquisition of an intellectual property right nor its exercise in and of itself constitutes an abuse of a dominant position, even where the objects in question are spare parts for which there is no alternative source of supply. Some further element of abuse must be shown, such as predatory pricing or a refusal to supply.

Finally, Article 222 on property ownership has been held not to limit the Court's power to ensure that intellectual property rights are used in conformity with the Treaty. Its function being simply to reserve Member States' questions of public or private ownership of the means of production, Article 222 has never been used to challenge the Union's capacity to legislate on intellectual property rights, a capacity which several of the Court's judgments confirm although without detailed examination or definition.

To summarize, the Court's case law guarantees that copyrighted goods may circulate freely once they have been placed on the market, either by the right-holder or with his consent, anywhere in the Union. Rights may thus not be used to partition the Union market. On the other hand, rights can be used to oppose the free circulation of goods which are lawfully marketed but without the consent of the right-holder due to differences in protection offered by the laws of the Member States. Also, the placement on the market of a recording or a work, either by a right-holder or with his consent, does not exhaust the right-holder's rights with respect to subsequent public performance or rental of the work in other Member States. Rights may not, however, constitute or be used to effect arbitrary discrimination or a disguised restriction on trade between Member States, in particular, where such a use would violate the Treaty's provisions on anti-competitive agreements and abuses of dominant position. Member states are free within these limits to fix the characteristics of their intellectual property regimes to the extent that the Union has not adopted legislation harmonizing those provisions. The Union's legislative competence in the field is thus clearly recognized, Article 222 notwithstanding, although the precise limits remain to be determined.

B. Legal Instruments

Early preparatory work on legislation concentrated on industrial property—patents, trademarks, designs and models—and not on copyright and neighboring rights. There was less immediate need for action in the latter area since copyright and similar protection in the Member States was automatic, not being dependent on registration. In addition, all Member States were parties to the Berne Convention and on that basis had adopted laws which were felt to have much in common. The same was not true, however, for industrial property rights. Different registration formalities frequently had to be followed. Moreover, important differences between national regimes were perceived to exist as the Paris Convention had not produced sufficiently convergent solutions.

The initial approach was also markedly cautious with regard to use of the Union's own legislative powers. Work on European and Union patents was not based on specific provisions in the EU Treaty but on the inherent power of the Member States to conclude other agreements which do not conflict with the Treaty. This approach avoided the risk of a confrontation on the competence issue and had the added advantage of allowing participation in the work by interested European Free Trade Association (EFTA) countries, particularly the United Kingdom, which at the time was a member of the Union. At the same time, of course, this approach perpetuated uncertainty about the Union's own powers in the field. Also, because of the procedural weakness of intergovernmental conventions as a legislative technique, this approach did not maximize the changes of the regime's entering into force. Despite the proven success of the European patent granting mechanism, the Union patent is still on the horizon and, like some mirage, continues to retreat as we try to approach it.

In the early 1970's, however, with the weaknesses of intergovernmental procedures already apparent and with growing confidence in the EEC Treaty's capacity to address all issues relevant to the proper functioning of the Common Market, the Commission took the plunge and suggested that trademarks be dealt with on the basis of the Treaty itself, i.e., the harmonization of national laws (Article 100) and the creation of a uniform Union trademark system (Article 235). Both articles require agreement between the Member States in Council, and as a consequence, work was slow. But at least the machinery of the Council, with its regular ministerial meetings on matters affecting the internal market, and the involvement of the European Parliament guarantee that a certain pressure for agreement is maintained. Also, once agreement is achieved, the enforcement mechanisms of the Treaty will be available to ensure that the measures are given effect sooner rather than later.

In 1988, the directive on trademark harmonization was agreed upon. The regulation on the Union Trademark is now also final. In reality, only disputes concerning highly political issues, like the site of a number of Union institutions and bodies, including the future Union Trademark Office, are difficult.

In the meantime, however, two events had occurred which combined to put an end to any doubts about the Union's power to legislate on intellectual property, including copyright and neighboring rights, and radically improved the Union's effective capacity to do so.

In 1986, the Council adopted the first piece of Union legislation on intellectual property: the directive on the legal protection of semiconductor topographies. It is worth noting that this exercise in fact catapulted the Union rather unexpectedly into copyright, albeit in a technical area, since a number of Member States considered that semiconductor designs were already protected by their national copyright laws, or might turn out to be so. It is also notable that the Council acted on the Commission's proposal in less than a year given the clear need to respond quickly to the initiative taken by the U.S. Congress in the area. The speed of events was also a measure of the way in which intellectual property issues were emerging as issues of high policy, no longer the almost exclusive domain of experts working assiduously for years at a time.

An event of more general significance also occurred in 1986; the Single European Act, which entered into force on July 1, 1987, and empowered the Union to legislate by qualified majority to establish the internal market by December 31, 1992. The trademark directive was the first intellectual property instrument to be adopted on this basis. More significantly, it has become clear that majority voting has transformed the efficacy of the legislative machine. Under the old unanimity regime, important pieces of internal market legislation would take on average ten years from conception to adoption, with all that such almost geological time scales imply for the attitudes and morale of those involved. The average time period has now dropped to two to three years. Those involved in the initial preparation of an initiative now have the satisfaction, and the added sense of personal engagement and responsibility, that comes from knowing that they will still be involved when ministers reach a final decision.

II. The Emergence of Intellectual Property as a Political Priority

The developments in the Union's legislative machinery have coincided with the emergence of intellectual property as a political priority for the Member States and the Union's legislative institutions. This increased interest has been due in large part to changes which have been occurring in the world economy involving important structural changes, not the least of which involve the industrialized countries.

First, there has been a continuing shift in the economic activity of industrialized countries away from the production of goods having the character primarily of staple commodities and towards the production of goods and the provision of services to which considerable value has been added through the application of technology, skill and creativity. The superior performance and non-material attributes of such goods, such as their design, expression or image, constitute their main competitive advantages. If some or all of those features can be readily appropriated by others through copying for commercial purposes at a fraction of the cost of developing a competing original, then the production and marketing of such high added-value goods is put at risk.

Second, the industrialized countries' manufacturing activities have often proved less dynamic than those of the service sector, of which the information and entertainment industries form an important part. Copyrighted goods and services account for three to five percent of the gross domestic product of western economies. More significantly, that share of GDP has in the recent past been steadily growing. However, at the same time, these activities are also particularly vulnerable to damage through misappropriation, particularly by unauthorized copying. Thus, the very activities which offer the best hope for economic expansion, and which are consequently the subject of considerable new investment, are those which are particularly exposed to losses through copying and accordingly need appropriate forms of protection, including suitably adapted copyright laws.

Third, new technologies such as satellites, digital communications, electronic storage and the development of easy access to telecommunication networks, as well as the continued economic integration of the European Union itself, have strongly emphasized the transnational way in which many creative works are exploited. The frontiers of the Member States have become permeable, particularly those borders that they share in common. Solutions limited to national territories are partial solutions. If nothing is done, those who create will see their work inadequately protected, and sometimes even completely unprotected, in important parts of their home market, with all that this implies for the future development of their activities, particularly in fields which demand considerable "up front" investment.

Fourth, in the European context, these challenges are not seen solely in economic terms, although the economic dimension of the problem looms necessarily large. The maintenance and development of Europe's cultural diversity and richness, for which a solid economic foundation is a prerequisite, is regarded by many as a vital task, even a solemn duty. This goal applies not only within the boundaries of the Member States but also to the place of European culture in the larger Europe that is emerging and indeed in the world at large.

In these circumstances, it is not surprising that intellectual property issues, for all their technical complexity, have long since ceased to be the concern only of specialists and those directly interested. Intellectual property issues have increasingly been recognized as political priorities and even, for example, in the case of royalties for blank recording tape or the limits of copyright protection for computer programs, have become subjects for popular political dispute.

III. Intellectual Property and Competition[2]

A. Introduction

Although the European Economic Community Treaty (EU Treaty) does not give a clear indication of what is to be understood by the term "common market," its characteristics can be deduced from those provisions of part two of the EU Treaty that refer to the foundations of the European Union (EU). These characteristics were articulated in 1985 by the European Commission's White Paper entitled "Completing the Internal Market," and include the free movement of goods, free movement of labor, freedom to provide services, and free movement of capital. These basic freedoms of the common market can only be realized by approximating the laws of the EU's Member States, thus installing a system through which all obstructions to competition are removed.

[2] Victor Vandebeek, *Realizing the European Community Common Market by Unifying Intellectual Property Law: Deadline 1992,* 1990 B.Y.U. L. Rev. 1605. © 1990 Victor Vandebeek. Reprinted by permission .

Competition policy is not an end in itself. Nevertheless, competition is not only the condition *sine qua non* for a steady improvement of well-being and welfare but also the instrument to achieve a single product market of 320 million consumers. Here, reference should be made to intellectual property rights with respect to the Community competition rules because intellectual property rights guarantee a perfect competitive model by creating market transparency, which protects both the consumer and the producer. It is of tremendous importance that the Community take the necessary steps to unify the national intellectual property laws of individual EU Member States in order to bring the internal market into existence by December 31, 1992. The difficulties surrounding intellectual property rights within the EU arise from the fundamental disparity between the EU freedoms which eliminate all barriers among the Member States and the monopolies resulting from the territoriality principle of intellectual property rights.

B. Trademark Law

1. Consistencies Between National Trademark Laws and Community Competition Rules

Article 30 of the Treaty of Rome prohibits quantitative import restrictions and all measures with equivalent effect. Exceptions to this prohibition are set out in the first sentence of Article 36, which expressly includes industrial and commercial property.

In the early eighties, the European Court of Justice first decided on the proper application of the restriction on slavish imitation. Both in *Dansk Supermarket v. Imerco*[3] and in *I.D.G. v. Beele,*[4] the Court of Justice held that Article 36 should be included in the law of unfair competition and based its decision on the reasonable character of the national laws in question.

The court's decisions confirm that national intellectual property laws, which are generally used to prevent trade, do not conflict with the free movement of goods under Article 30 "provided that those rights are only used to what is strictly necessary to attain the specific objective against precise imitation which is to avoid needless confusion as to a product's origin."

Articles 85 and 86 of the Treaty of Rome refer to the effects of an agreement assigning trademark and prohibit companies from abusing a dominant position. At first sight, an intellectual property right gives the owner a degree of monopolistic power because he can prevent another producer from marketing products. At the same time, however, trademarks outweigh any possible monopolistic consequence. The Court of Justice confirmed this thesis for the first time in 1970 in *Sirena v. Eda*[5] when it stated that:

---

3 1981 E. Comm. Ct. J. Rep. 181, 32 Comm. Mkt. L.R. 590.

4 *Industrie Diensten Groep v. J.A. Beele Handelmasschappij*, 1982 E. Comm. Ct. J. Rep. 707, 35 Comm. Mkt. L.R. 102 (hereinafter I.D.G.)

5 1971 E. Comm. Ct. J. Rep. 69.

> The owner of a trademark does not enjoy a dominant position under Article 86 merely because he can prohibit third parties from marketing products bearing the same mark in the territory of a Member State. It is also necessary that he should be in a position to prevent effective competition in a considerable part of the market in question.

Therefore, intellectual property rights alone, *a priori*, should not be considered an aggravating component of a dominant position. An examination of Community competition policy with respect to intellectual property law reveals that there are no inconsistencies between the two bodies of law and that intellectual property law must be considered an integrated part of competition law. In fact, intellectual property law contributes to greater transparency of the product market by protecting both the consumer and producer. However, it took the Commission several years (until 1984) to realize that intellectual property law can be used effectively to create and guarantee a free internal market.

On August 31, 1984, the Commission adopted a proposal for a Council Regulation for establishing a Community trademark (CTM). The proposed regulation would establish a single trademark valid throughout the entire EU and create an EU Trademark Office.

It sets out the legal rules and procedures necessary for registering and using a CTM. While some consensus has been achieved among the Member States, a few substantive decisions must still be made. For example, the location of the CTM Office headquarters and the official working language must be decided. The only remaining legal question is whether the CTM Office would be responsible for monitoring former national trademarks.

CTMs may consist of personal names, designs, letters, numerals, combinations of colors, shapes, packaging, or any other sign or symbol which is capable of distinguishing the goods or services of one enterprise from those of other enterprises. The CTM is a mark of origin and will be examined and accepted based on origin. The European Commission wrote that "[a]ny regulation of the trademark law depends totally upon the questions which functions are given to the trademark. The origin function is pre-eminent. All other functions are derived from this basic function."[6]

EU trademark law does not replace the trademark laws of the Member States. National trademarks are still necessary for companies that do not require EU-wide trademark protection. The CTM will therefore be of greater use to those with real and effective industrial or commercial establishments throughout EU territory. Multinational enterprises will benefit from CTMs because CTMs are valid throughout the entire EU and CTMs are more practical and less expensive than requesting individual national trademarks.

CTM rights are obtained by registration only and will be refused if the trademark is not distinctive, lawful or available. CTM applications must be filed at the CTM office along with the appropriate documentation. If approved, a CTM is valid for ten

---

[6] New Trademark System for the Community, Bull. E.C., May, 1980.

years from the date of filing and may be renewed. The CTM Office may withhold registration if the trademark conflicts with another CTM, the owner of prior CTM rights has opposed the registration, and all efforts to produce an amicable settlement have failed. The owner of a prior non-registered right may also oppose a CTM once the CTM Office informs him of a conflicting application. Member States can request information on new applications from the CTM Office and can conduct searches in their own national registers. The CTM Office must notify both the applicant and the owner of prior rights when a registration is accepted or rejected.

CTM protection is limited to similar goods, services and signs. Contrary to the Commission's 1980 proposal, a CTM owner can prohibit the use of an identical trademark without proving that there is "serious likelihood of [consumer] confusion between the goods or services. Industry put a lot of pressure on members of the European Parliament to change the 1980 proposal's confusion standard. Parliament discussions also made it clear that the confusion standard would jeopardize the preeminence of the similarity standard.

CTM infringement and validity conflicts will be governed by the national law of the Member State as applied by the court hearing the action. Decisions, however, will be binding in the entire EU to ensure CTM uniformity. Furthermore, CTM owners may challenge trademarks under both CTM law and national law. This practice is similar to an owner's ability to pursue a counterfeit goods claim under unfair competition law and criminal law. The owner of a national trademark or an unregistered common law right may also oppose the use of a later CTM by instituting proceedings in a national court. However, when a CTM owner also owns an identical or similar national trademark, the plaintiff must choose a single forum.

The proposed regulation avoids the plurality of national procedures, which even enterprises owning international registrations under the Madrid Agreement may encounter. Furthermore, although most national registrations are canceled if not used in their territory for five years, a CTM remains valid once it has been used in at least one Member State. However, the Community registration procedure can fail if successfully opposed by an owner of an earlier and similar trademark in one or more of the ten territories.

Since industry opposed any kind of search at either the community or national level because it believed the system would become unworkable, a proposal which eliminated searches was worked out on January 23, 1986 for a Council Regulation implementing the CTM Council Regulation. The purpose of the latter proposal was to ensure the smooth operation of the main CTM procedural rules and registrations. The implementing rules (1) classify CTMs, (2) simplify formalities, (3) establish a fee system, (4) select the language, (5) develop opposition rules, (6) provide an appeals process, and (7) establish revocation and invalidity procedures.

A CTM is undoubtedly of interest to both producers and consumers since it creates market conditions within the EU similar to an internal national market. Indeed, as long as national trademarks exist, their geographical application will be limited to a single EU Member State. Consequently, many conflicts may arise between identical or similar trademarks because of differing legislation. In contrast, a CTM granted by the CTM Office will be valid throughout the entire EU and will be founded on a single piece of Union legislation.

The objective of the CTM proposal is not to approximate the different national laws. The proposal's objective is merely to create an EU level system to unify national trademark law. If this results, producers will enjoy equal protection for their products on a larger geographical basis. They will be able to extend the commercial promotion of their products and enjoy all of the benefits of scale, such as lower production costs. Consumers will be able to select from a wider variety of products with little risk of confusion between the products. Furthermore, the CTM will be less expensive in the long run since the cost of obtaining a trademark in each EU country will be eliminated.

2. Trademark Directive

On December 21, 1988 the Council issued a Directive designed to approximate the trademark laws of the Member States.[7] The Directive facilitates the free movement of goods on the Community level by approximating the main provisions of national trademark laws. The Directive does not eliminate all of the differences among the trademark laws but attempts to eliminate those differences which impede the free movement of goods or distort competition within the internal market. Therefore, the Directive merely complements the CTM Regulation. Full scale approximation can only be reached through additional directives.

The 1988 Trademark Directive delineates two grounds for refusing or invalidating trademarks. The first ground concerns the trademark itself; a trademark may be invalidated or refused if it is devoid of any distinctive character, is contrary to public policy or accepted principles of morality, or deceives the public. The second ground concerns conflicts with earlier rights: a trademark may be invalidated or refused if it is identical to an earlier trademark, it covers goods or services protected by an earlier trademark, or there is a likelihood that consumers will be confused. By derogation, however, if a prior trademark owner consents, a Member State may find a subsequent, identical trademark valid. Interested parties may challenge a trademark in judicial or administrative proceedings when the trademark has not been used for five consecutive years, it has become a common name after its registration, or it is capable of misleading the public as to the quality or geographical origin of the goods or services.

The exclusive rights granted a trademark allow the owner to prevent any authorized use of an identical or similar mark if it leads to a "likelihood of confusion" for consumers. The distinctiveness of a mark is judged on a country by country basis and not on an EU level. Thus, the Commission makes it practically impossible for the Member States to extend the geographical protection of a national trademark.

---

[7] First Council Directive 89/104 to Approximate the Laws of the Member States Relating to Trademarks, 32 O.J. Eur. Comm. (No. L 40) 104 (1989).

C. Patent Law

1. EU Patent Convention

Despite the Commission's 1985 White Paper, there is currently no EU patent law which ensures EU-wide patent protection. Member States still maintain their own, non-unified patent laws. Although various attempts were made to unify the EU patent system, the attempts failed due to a lack of EU interest and to strong national sentiment among the Member States.

The EU Patent Convention of 1975 (CPC), which was supplemented by a second Convention in 1985, outlines an agreement among Member States relating to EU-level patent law. The CPC provides for a supranational patent but is not yet in effect. The advantages of a single EU patent include uniform laws and procedures, such as a single patent renewal fee. The EU Patent (CP) also has a unitary character with equal effect throughout the entire EU.

The CP System, however, merely complements the individual patent systems—it does not replace them. Indeed, the CPC provides that each contracting State may decide what conditions will invalidate a national patent. Therefore, simultaneous protection by a CP and a national patent will exist unless otherwise provided by the contracting State.

The CPC also sets up an European Patent Office (EP Office), which is entitled to collect fees and revenues. The EP Office will supervise both the financial matters and the effects of a CP within the EU. It will deal with examination claims, revocation or opposition proceedings, and applications for renewal, which are required every two years.

The EU Patent Agreement of December 4, 1985 embodies protocol for settlement of litigation concerning infringement and validity of EU patents and protocol for the statute of the Common Appeal Court (COPAC). Appeals are initially heard by the Revocation Divisions and the Patent Administration Division. Further appeals can be lodged with the COPAC but only for questions of validity and infringement of an essential procedural requirement or any rule of law relating to its application. Actions based on national law, like injunctions and damages, must be lodged with the national courts where the defendant or his business resides or where the patent was infringed. In both cases, the European Court of Justice retains jurisdiction to give preliminary rulings in accordance with Article 177 of the Treaty of Rome.

Infringement proceedings are currently split into two parts: (1) validity proceedings before the COPAC and (2) injunction proceedings before the national courts. Before the CPC can be ratified, the final legal restraints within the Irish and Danish constitutions must be overcome by developing a more flexible approach to infringement proceedings. This new approach could combine the validity and injunction proceedings and grant jurisdiction to national courts. The COPAC could then act as an international court with jurisdiction to give preliminary rulings. Under this proposal, all Irish and Danish constitutional restraints would vanish since judgments would be rendered by national courts and their decisions would have effect in the entire EU.

The burden and costs of translating patents could easily be resolved by publishing the CP in only one of the official languages used on the application form. This would require the applicant to use the national language of the decentralized patent office where the application is filed.

The goal for a supranational patent system, however, has not been abandoned because of these problems. The potential benefits of a community patent, as illustrated in the next section, prove that such a system would be worthwhile.

2. European Patent Convention

The European Patent Convention (EPC) was signed in 1973 and became effective in 1977. While the CPC applies only to EU Member States, the EPC is open to any European country. Therefore, the EPC has been drawn up by experts from twenty-one European countries. This led to the creation of a European patent (EP), which has the effect of a national patent in any contracting State. All EU Member States have ratified the EPC except Denmark, Ireland and Portugal.

It is important to examine the fundamental differences between the two patent systems. As discussed above, the EP's scope is broader than the CP's scope. Furthermore, EPC membership is voluntary, while the CPC is an obligatory system for all EU Member States, and it imposes a single unitary patent in addition to national patent legislation. The EPC, on the contrary, does not impose upon national law, but grants a bundle of national patents in a rational, centralized system without approximating different national laws.

The EP system is unique because once an EP is granted, it will be considered a national patent in all respects. In fact, it grants several national patents via one application. Therefore, it is possible to choose the number of countries in which the patent will apply. Due to the EPC's flexibility, industry and most EU Member States prefer the EP system. In order for the CPC to be successful, the Commission must adopt more flexible procedures and limit translation costs. Unless these problems are resolved, the CPC will only be achieved at great expense to the internal market.

While the EPC is a success, it merely rationalizes and simplifies the miscellaneous national patent procedures. In order to create a single, uniform patent protection system between the EEC Member States, the territoriality principle of patent rights must be transcended. Consequently, a free internal trade of patented products will only be realized if there is a unified patent law with equal effect and meaning in all EU Member States. The preamble of the CPC states that the "creation of such a Community patent system is therefore inseparable from the attainment of the objectives of the Treaty." This objective as regards the free movement of goods protected by patents will only be achieved by the creation of the CP System.

In the absence of a supranational patent law, patent rights will remain confined to the territory where a patent was granted. A supranational patent right, however, would be enforced throughout the entire Community regardless of the different national laws and would avoid the unjustified differences among the states and the uncertainty that this causes patentees.

In addition to the general legal and economic policy of the Commission mentioned above, there are practical benefits to the creation of the CP System. The CPC will considerably limit the costs of obtaining a patent. The applicant will only have to pay one fee instead of a separate fee for each country designated in the EP application form. The renewal fee will also be lower than the sum of the renewal fees for each country.

The CPC will also simplify legal proceedings since all competitors and patentees will have the right to institute revocation and infringement proceedings. Most important, however, the patentee will receive Community-wide patent protection via one application and one fee. Furthermore, patent protection will be equally enforced in all fifteen Member States contrary to the EPC where the enforcement continues to depend on the national laws, which leads to unjustified differences and uncertainty for the patentees.

Criticism that the CPC is too complex cannot be denied. Nevertheless, the advantages of a EU-wide patent clearly outweigh this disadvantage. Thus, the patent will be accepted in due time despite new rules and a corresponding adjustment period.

3. Biotechnological Inventions

Since the CPC is not yet in force and encompasses a general approach to the issue, on January 13, 1989 the Commission drew up a proposal for a Council Directive specifically dealing with the legal protection of biotechnological inventions.[8] The Commission considered this matter of fundamental importance to the EU industrial development since biotechnology and genetic engineering are playing increasingly important roles in the economy. The Directive will adapt the CPC to specific industries and newly developed technologies. The Directive is an answer to the pressures of the biotechnology industry, which felt the need for a harmonized patent protection system.

Because some EU Member States do not provide legal protection for biotechnological inventions and national governments will soon provide for their protection, the Commission was forced to submit this Proposal in order to obtain consistent treatment among the EU Member States. The Directive must not be perceived as harmonizing all EU patent law. Rather it should be seen as a specific response to industry's specific, practical need to protect their biotechnological inventions at the EU level, especially against the U.S. and Japan. The Directive also ensures that enterprises will be offered effective, EU-wide legal protection, and it safeguards the results of their research activities in the entire EU.

The proposal covers micro-organisms and microbiological processes or products other than plants or animals. The protection of plants and animals will not be discussed because they are regulated by very technical provisions, which are beyond the scope of this article. However, protection is provided for biotechnological products which are novel, inventive, and have industrial application. It is not necessary that the entire process be considered biotechnological. Rather, if one step is micro-biotechnological, the whole process may be patented. In addition, patents obtained for experimental inventions will be extended to new or improved products to the extent they are used for private or experimental purposes. Finally, biotechnological techniques of animal production that are industrial or commercial in nature and are not therapeutic will also

8 Proposal for a Council Directive on the Legal Protection of Biotechnological Inventions, 32 O.J. Eur. Comm. (No. C1013) 3 (1989).

be patentable. Industry fears that legal protection for plants and plant varieties in the EU will continue to lag behind the level of protection provided by the U.S. and Japan.

Another controversial problem in the European Parliament is the moral implication of the Directive. Some members of the European Parliament with strong religious backgrounds still oppose the Directive because of the potential consequences of genetic experiment involving human life.

4. The Pharmaceutical Industry

The sector of the pharmaceutical industry that involves patent law represents almost one percent of the European Gross Domestic Product. It has been subjected to numerous regulations and measures with respect to market authorization, premarket testing, pharmaceutical pricing, and health insurance arrangements. Since the European pharmaceutical industry is investing heavily in research and development, it desires to protect its new products with an efficient patent system. However, despite an abundance of legislation, the Commission has not yet provided this system.

Presently, only the EPC provides protection by granting a twenty-year patent from the date of application. Twenty years is insufficient, however, because it includes a three- to five-year delay for product authorization. A fifteen year extension is necessary to create an exclusive patent right.

The Commission must take measures to preserve the position of the European pharmaceutical industry in the world market. Competition with the U.S. and Japan will increase because pricing is unregulated in their markets. The Commission's incentive objective is not to catalyze harmonization of all EU patent law, but to respond to an economic need.

5. Conclusions

The ECJ has repeatedly emphasized that its role is not to apply the EU Treaty but only to interpret it. Article 177 of the EU Treaty refuses to give the ECJ more power. Indeed, there is no provision for a direct appeal to the ECJ from a decision of a national court. Therefore, the ECJ cannot rule on whether decisions by national courts conform to the EU Treaty or ensure the uniform application of Community law through direct proceedings.

Article 177 reduces the role of the ECJ and makes the patent system entirely dependent upon the cooperation of the national courts. Since the role of the ECJ is confined to interpreting Community law, the ECJ can merely deal with the real consequences of the solutions offered by the Commission. In contrast, the Commission will continue to be the most important institution because it provides regulations which are aimed at reaching Treaty objectives. This reiterates the differences between basic continental principles and the Anglo-Saxon system.

D. Copyright Law[9]

1. Green Paper on Copyright

Following the 1985 White Paper on Completing the Internal Market, the Commission outlined the Green Paper on Copyright and the Challenge of Technology.[10] The Green Paper sets goals to ensure the proper functioning of the common market. Manufacturers and suppliers of copyrighted goods and services must be able to treat the Community as a single internal market. This requires eliminating obstacles and legal differences between national copyright laws that may disrupt the EU market.

Looking back, one can already see that the approach was heavily conditioned by two pressing and related considerations; the need to justify the Union's competence to legislate on these matters and the political imperative of completing the internal market by 1992. These factors were related because insofar as an initiative could be shown to be necessary for the completion of the market, it would automatically fall within the Union's legislative jurisdiction. The results of this consultative phase can be summarized as follows.

First, the exhaustive analysis of Union competence effectively put and end, at least for the time being, to tiresome challenges to the authority of the Commission to make the proposals that it was preparing. Second, rapid follow-up with formal legislative proposals was possible for both television and computer programs, the latter instrument now being close to final adoption. Third, the relatively narrow focus of the approach, with its emphasis on the proper functioning of the internal market, produced a sharp reaction, even a backlash. The proposed provisions on legal licensing to facilitate cross-frontier television broadcasts failed to win a qualified majority in Council and were separated from the rest of the proposal. A new consultative exercise is now under way to try to develop an approach which can command more support. More generally, the approach to copyright was strongly criticized in some quarters as being unduly narrow and unbalanced, giving excessive emphasis to the interests of those who produce, invest in or distribute copyrighted works as opposed to those who actually create them. The Commission was accused of being simply Philistine. One may agree or disagree with the critics, but it cannot be denied that the criticism was strongly felt and strongly voiced, in some cases in politically influential circles. The result was a pause for reflection and a new work program which seeks to incorporate the lessons learned from the consultative phase.

2. The Current Program

The main features of the current program are the following. First, the approach is a *global* one. It seeks to address the broad range of interests that are affected by the creation of a single market in copyrighted goods and services. Accordingly, it will

---

[9] Robert J. Coleman, *Intellectual Property and the European Community after 1992,* 15 Colum.-VLA J.L. & Arts. 117-33 (1991). © 1991 Robert J. Coleman. Reprinted by permission.

[10] Copyright and the Challenge of Technology, 1988 Eur. Com. Doc. (COM No. 88) (1988) (*hereinafter* Green Paper).

address not only the priority issues which were discussed in the Green Paper on copyright and the challenge of technology, but also other issues that emerged during the discussion of that paper, including concerns which are of particular importance to creative authors and artist, as well as the concerns of the enterprises which produce cultural goods and services. Thus, the issues of term of protection, moral rights, reprography and "droit de suite" or resale rights (the right to an interest in the proceeds of sales subsequent to a work's first transfer) have been added to the work program as a direct response to those who criticized the Green Paper as being too narrow in its approach.

The program also looks beyond the frontiers of the Union in recognition of the fact that the interests concerned are vitally affected by the protection available to them, or in some cases not available to them, in countries outside the Union. In addition, of course, the continued application of the principle of national treatment laid down in the Berne Convention means that improvements in protection within the Union can actually aggravate existing imbalances in protection unless other action is taken to promote similar advances in other countries. Initiatives to this end are already being pursued in the General Agreement on Tariffs and Trade (GATT), in the World Intellectual Property Organization (WIPO), in association negotiations with EFTA or East European countries and bilaterally. These efforts will be continued and indeed reinforced.

As to the measures already formally launched, the starting point is the proposal for all Member States to adhere to at least the two basic contemporary conventions on copyright, namely the Paris Act of the Berne Convention of 1976 and the Rome Convention of 1961. Most Member States are already party to these international instruments, but all are not. Belgium and Ireland are parties to the earlier Brussels Act of the Berne Convention of 1948. As to the Rome Convention, seven Member States are parties: Denmark, France, Germany, Ireland, Italy, Luxembourg and the United Kingdom. The other states are not, although Spain and Portugal have passed legislation recently on neighboring rights. Belgium and the Netherlands are also considering legislation which would put them in a position to ratify the Convention, and Greece has recently initiated work for the same purpose. The Commission's proposal is designed to speed up the process of ratification and implementation of these Conventions by using the Union's capacity to make decisions of a binding nature by qualified majority if necessary. Indeed, it is worth recalling that an earlier attempt in 1984 based only on a non-binding resolution failed to produce the desired result. In this way, the Union can rapidly establish a common foundation for copyright in all Member States on the basis of which further steps can be taken, both within and without the Union, to improve the level of protection and strengthen the fight against piracy. It is clear that the political will necessary to take this first step exists for it is seen as indispensable to the completion of the internal market.

As for improvements in the level of protection, another measure already proposed in the form of a directive concerns minimum protection for certain neighboring rights which goes beyond, in particular, the requirements of the Rome Convention. This proposal, which again can be adopted by qualified majority, will require the Member States to provide certain rights in favor of authors, phonogram producers, film producers, broadcasters and performing artists.

The rights in question concern authorization of fixation, reproduction and distribution. The proposal also provides a regime for commercial rental and public lending. Thus, the proposal goes significantly beyond the minimum requirements of the Berne and Rome Conventions. One main goal is the creation of both a solid legal basis throughout the Union for the legitimate exploitation of works and recorded performances and a legal environment in which piracy can be successfully repressed.

However, according to the Green Paper, Union legislation should be restricted to that which is necessary to carry out the tasks of the EU. Indeed, a great consensus has already been achieved since all EU Member States are contracting parties to the Berne Convention for the Protection of Literary and Artistic Works and to the Universal Copyright Convention, to which the U.S. also adheres.

The 1986 International Convention for the Protection of Literary and Artistic Works (Berne Convention) has been an important approximating factor for copyright law among EU Member States. It called for adhering States to "sacrifice, in some measure, their rigid national conceptions and bend their internal legislation to general rules that were internationally recognized. Two problems demanded solution: conflicts of laws had to be adjusted and differences between national legislation bridged, if not eliminated." The first problem was solved by extending national treatment to foreign works and authors. The second problem was solved by uniform standards for copyright content, scope, and duration.

These general results of the Berne Convention received wider application in the Universal Copyright Convention (UCC) of September 2, 1952, to which the U.S. and other countries of the American continent adhere. While the Berne Convention sought to protect the rights of authors, it has been supplemented by the UCC, which extended copyright protection to the sciences and arts, as well as works of the human mind. Other benefits that accrue to authors through the UCC are: (1) equal protection for foreign and national works unrestricted by reciprocity, (2) formalities simplification, and (3) author control over translation rights.

As stated earlier, an important part of approximating copyright law within the Community was realized through the two Conventions mentioned above. Nevertheless, some substantial problems remained, and the EU Commission had to intervene. These problems were due to the fact that the original Berne Convention was amended and supplemented seven successive times in 1896, 1908, 1914, 1928, 1948, 1967 and 1971. At the EU level, complications arose since not all EU Member States accepted all the revisions. Some countries kept the level of protection provided in the Rome version of 1928, others the Brussels version of 1948, and still others one of the remaining versions. These changes can be characterized as the continuous expansion of copyright protection.

The Berne Convention came up with solutions for many, but not all, copyright law issues. It achieved a fundamental approximation of the EU Member State laws, but other issues impacting the internal market remained unsolved. Therefore, most issues were left for regulation by national laws within the framework of the Berne Convention, while issues relating to Union matters required a EU approach.

Therefore, the scope of the Commission's Green Paper was consciously limited to the following: (1) private, home copying of sound and audio-visual works, (2) distribution and rental rights for sound and video recordings, (3) legal protection of computer programs, (4) legal problems relating to the operation of data bases, and (5) external aspects of copyright protection.

The Green Paper seeks to obtain a final approximation of the EU Member State copyright laws based on the principles of the Berne Convention and to resolve some specific matters that affect the functioning of the internal market. Thus, the Green Paper is not only a confirmation of, but also a complement to, the Berne Convention that is limited to specific Union issues.

Manufacturers and suppliers of copyrighted goods and services should be able to approach the EU as a single internal market without the obstacles that disrupt the market or distort competition. The Commission dealt with several fundamental obstacles to inter-state trade of goods and services protected by copyrights. These obstacles were caused by differences in copyright laws which adversely affect the Common Market by distorting competitive conditions. Illegally copied works, for example, can be manufactured cheaper than originals and can undercut the latter in a free market system. A direct negative impact on Member States offering weak copyright protection is that illegally copied works capture a bigger market share than they do elsewhere.

At the same time, the need to take action against imported, illegally copied works tends to perpetuate controls within the EU. Inevitably, these controls adversely affect the free movement of legitimate goods. Different copyright laws not only affect trade flows but also the scale and nature of the connected manufacturing activities and the investments therein. The following example emphasizes the advantage of the non-territoriality principle in competition law.

Copyright exhaustion occurs when the copyright holder sells a copy of his copyrighted work. The holder must authorize the sale, but once the sale has occurred, the copyright is exhausted. Once this occurs, the work can be sold again, but without copyright protection. This is true of patent and trademark rights as well.

When a work copyrighted in Germany and Belgium is sold in Germany, only the corresponding German copyright is exhausted. The two rights remain independent of each other in accordance with the Territoriality principle. One negative impact that this has on the market is that the German proprietor of the unexhausted Belgian right may still prohibit any unauthorized importation of German products into Belgium. Thus the German proprietor has a monopoly in Belgium, creating boundaries between the EU Member States. This type of monopoly can be used to set up price differences.

The Green Paper has also generated a proposal for a Council Directive on the legal protection of computer programs. This directive will be examined in the following section.

3. Legal Protection of Computer Programs

On January 5, 1989 the Commission submitted a proposal to the Council on the legal protection of computer programs. This proposal seeks to provide copyright protection for computer programs equal to that existing for literary and artistic works under the Berne Convention. Copyright is the best way to protect computer programs because the inventive step usually contains algorithms which, like mathematical principles and natural law, are unpatentable.

The proposal does not, however, define "computer program." Experts warn that any definition would soon become obsolete as technology progresses. Copyrights do not protect ideas, but the expression of ideas. Therefore, by copyrighting a computer program, it will be protected as a whole rather than its underlying principles, logic, algorithms or programming. Originality is the only criterion a program must meet before it can be copyrighted.

As with literary and artistic works, copyrights for computer programs are granted only to the person(s) who created the program. Computer programs are often created by freelance programmers who obtain the exclusive copyright. However, when an employee creates a program during his office hours and within the company organization, the company is entitled to the copyright.

Only the copyright holder may authorize reproduction, distribution and adaptation of the program. However, these rights can be limited by a written agreement between the holder and user. The right to control distribution is exhausted once the program has been marketed, unless otherwise agreed by the copyright holder and user. Copyrights continue for fifty years from the date of creation and do not need to be registered. Unfortunately, the Commission did not follow the Berne Convention, which grants protection for the lifetime of the author plus fifty years.

Industry unanimously supports this proposal to protect computer programs. While this protection is already available in four EU Member States (France, Germany, Spain and the UK), protection will soon be available throughout the entire Union.

4. Conclusion

The abolition of trade limitations must be realized within the fixed institutional background of each national Member State. Therefore, the process of unifying national laws and increasing the EU's supranational power will not occur without problems. One major problem is how to unify the different intellectual property laws in a professional manner. This problem must be solved, however, because trademark, patent, and copyright protection is crucial to the creation of a smooth-operating internal market. Of course, some problems still await solutions. This is especially true in those sectors of industry, like the pharmaceutical and biotechnological industries, where the welfare of the populace depends upon those problems being solved. From 1992 on, those problems will sharpen as borders vanish.

All EU Member States agree that a common market based on free competition is an improvement over the current system. In spite of this consensus, important steps must be taken in order to achieve a common policy. Therefore, the Commission anxiously seeks for the adoption of its proposals on intellectual property rights. The adoption of these proposals are imperative for industrial development and commercial extension of trade between Member States. The Union still has a long way to go to achieve the aims outlined in the EU Treaty.

IV. Intellectual Property and External Power of the EU[11]

The EU tends to extend its external competence before having a clear authority for doing so and only later provides a *post hoc* rationale. This observation suggests that the justification, not the propriety, of a newly acquired external competence is the question. Nowhere is this *modus operandi* better illustrated, or more sorely tested, than by the EU's growing involvement with and pursuit of international intellectual property issues.

Indeed, not only has the EU begun to act before having an obvious or agreed upon legal basis, but it also does so in the face of argument that it cannot.

The parameters of the EU's external powers vis-à-vis the Members States' defy easy definition. Generally stated, once the EU exercises external competence in a particular field, the Member States' power correspondingly decreases. Actual practice, however, presents a far more complicated picture. There exist two sources for external Union power: explicit, which are based upon provisions within the Treaty of Rome (the Treaty), particularly Article 113; and implicit (or implied), which are derived from internal Union competence. External powers derived from explicit sources are exclusive to the Union; no Member State may pursue actions that may affect explicit Union external competence. The exclusivity of implicit powers, external powers, however, is far more problematic. Implicit external powers stem from internal Union provisions that necessarily require an external power in order to realize the internal goals. Exclusivity of such external powers depends upon the extent such powers are exclusive internally or, in other words, upon the intensity of the internal arrangement. Ultimately, the issue becomes a question of interpretation. Nevertheless, if the Union acts internationally regarding intellectual property issues, the Member States should refrain from undertaking any domestic or international actions that might affect the Union's endeavors. In short, they cannot pursue their own agendas. This, however, has not happened.

Although the Union pursues intellectual property issues, the Member States also continue to act internationally. The majority belong to organizations such as the World Intellectual Property Organization (WIPO) and are also parties to the Berne and Rome Conventions. More significantly, the Treaty of Rome refers to intellectual property, or "industrial and commercial property," only in Article 36, which specifically permits Member States to derogate from the single market ideas to protect their intellectual property rights. The Court of Justice observed that the Member States still determine the rules and conditions for intellectual property protection while the Community's intellectual property law is "characterized by a lack of harmonization or approximation."

Despite the Member States' international activity, the Union has pursued international intellectual property matters since the mid-1980s, including the negotiations on trade-related aspects of intellectual property rights (TRIPs) in the recently concluded

---

11 A. David Demiray, *Intellectual Property and the External Power of the European Community: The New Extension*, 16 Mich. J. Int'l L. 187 (1994).

Uruguay Round of the General Agreement on Tariffs and Trade (GATT). Although the EU initially was reluctant to endorse the GATT approach to intellectual property protection, the Union has emerged as a "major demandeur, perhaps stimulated by the ambitious submissions from the private sector and other participants." In a significant development for its partners, the EU also has begun to retaliate against nations that do not protect Union producers' intellectual property and has required recognition as well as acceptance of intellectual property standards in its trade treaties. Furthermore, the EU makes tariff preferences contingent upon adequate intellectual property rights for its goods. In January 1991, the Commission proposed a Council Decision that all Member States that had not done so accede to the Berne and Rome Conventions. It flatly declared, "the subject matter of the Berne Convention . . . . and the Rome Convention falls within the competence of the Community." The Council did enact a resolution on May 14, 1992, but did not adopt the broad language or claims of the Commission. All these actions imply exclusive Union competence, yet no Member State has either changed its behavior regarding intellectual property matters or objected to the behavior of other Member States. Naturally, the immediate reaction to this is: "something is wrong." As one commentator remarked in reviewing the Court of Justice's jurisprudence regarding the Union's external competence, "[o]ne inescapable conclusion is that with a single-minded purpose, the Court has gradually enlarged the scope of the Union's external competence and has correspondingly diminished that of the Member States. Moreover, it is reasonable to expect that this trend will continue."[12] The trend will likely continue in light of the extensive EU activity regarding intellectual property and the chaos that would result if deprived of this authority. Accordingly, the more correct reaction would be: "something is not yet right." This does not mean that the Member States will be *non plus* about the legal foundation, which could have enormous implications for their sovereignty. Arguably, it progressed thus far regarding intellectual property because its actions had no obvious direct effect upon Member State power despite the theoretical implications. In other words, the Member States simply did not consider the consequences. The deliberations on the legal basis for the Council Decision regarding the Member States' accession to the Berne Convention, however, indicate the Member States have begun to do so. Because every expansion of Union external power means a decrease in Member State authority, the Member States will be careful not to endorse a legal basis which surrenders too much power. The larger Member States especially will resist relinquishing too many powers because they fear that the Union's policy would be flawed or unenforceable and that the Member States' external identity would be compromised. According to one commentator, "Member States are only impressed by *a priori* exclusive Union powers."[13] Finally, the issue of whether the Union, as an international entity, or the Member States individually have competence regarding intellectual

[12] F. Burrows, *The Effects of the Main Cases of the Court of Justice in the Field of External Competencies on the Conduct of Member States,* in Division of Powers Between The European States in the Field of External Relations 15 (C.W. Timmermans and E.L.M Völka eds.1981), at 111, 111-12.

[13] C.D. Ehlermann, *The Scope of Article 113 of the EEC Treaty*, in Etudes de Droit des Communautés Européennes 145, 146 (1984).

property issues (or other trade issues, for that matter) has consequences for their respective international obligations, particularly within the GATT.

Ultimately, the EU must square Member State prerogatives under Article 36 with external Union competence in the same arena: theory must catch up with circumstance. Resolving this question requires examining intellectual property within the Union and the international arena as well as examining the basis for EU external power. In short, one must determine what relation Article 36 has to external Union competence either based on the common commercial policy or derived from other powers.

The Treaty offers no guidance in determining the relation of Article 36 to external Union competence, and while secondary Union law and the Court's case law provide some clues about the external effect of Article 36 derogations, they are inconclusive. Consequently, this inquiry identifies both the ill-defined division of powers between the Member States and the Union and the limitations of the theories of EU external competence. This does not suggest that there are no justifications for extending EU power; rather, among them is sheer practicality. Still, until the Court and Council decide on the appropriate foundation, they remain only arguments. Nonetheless, the Union's progression thus far without a clear legal foundation reveals much about the dynamics of exercising external competence: namely, that it grows less from design and more from opportunity and need. The growth of external competence through need has been possible because the scope of the EU's external power has defied precise definition. The EU's actions with respect to intellectual property, however, may force the Union to better define the scope of its powers vis-à-vis the Member States. All things considered, the EU probably would have preferred to avoid this situation.

In any event, the current situation cannot endure. The Court of Justice has held that Union acts must include:

> a statement of the facts and law [that] led the institution in question to adopt [the acts], so as to make possible review by the Court and so that Member States and the nationals concerned may have knowledge of the conditions under which the Union institutions have applied the Treaty. . . .
>
> It must be observed that in the context of the organization of the powers of the Union, the choice of the legal basis for a measure may not depend simply on an institution's conviction as to the objective pursued but must be based on objective factors [that] are amenable to judicial review. [14]

---

[14] Case 45/86, *Commission v. Council*, 1987 E.C.R. 1519-20. The Court has consistently held that:
[t]he question whether the conclusion of a given agreement is within the power of the Community and whatever, in a given case, such power has been exercised in conformity with the provisions of the Treaty is, in principle, a question which may be submitted to the Court of Justice, either directly, under Article 169 or Article 173 of the Treaty, or in accordance with the preliminary procedure of Article 228.
Opinion 1/75, *Opinions of the Court Given Pursuant to Article 228 of the EEC Treaty,* 1975 E.C.R. 1355, 1361.

Beyond this, the Union's trading partners will want to know whether the EU or its Member States possess the power to negotiate and enforce agreements. As intellectual property's international trade implications continue to grow, if the EU claims to represent European economic interests abroad it will need authority over intellectual property issues and therefore must find a legal justification. The present difficulty stems from events outrunning theory. The EU will play catch-up; the only question is how much this route will strain credulity.

A. Intellectual Property and the Union's External Competence

The EU has two sources of external power: explicit provisions and implied powers. Of the three explicit provisions only Article 113 could possibly provide a basis for external competence in intellectual property because the other two, Articles 111 and 238, cover tariffs and association agreements. The implied external powers, on the other hand, flow from the internal powers that are necessary for reaching specific Treaty or legislative goals. Unlike explicit powers, derived competencies are not necessarily exclusive. Consequently, neither source possesses a well-defined, all-inclusive scope that gives EU external competence its essential evolutionary and adaptable character. Bearing this in mind, one cannot *a priori* exclude international intellectual property issues from the Union's competence. Determining whether either source can reach intellectual property depends, however, upon different considerations.

B. The New Concept: Intellectual Property Protection as an International Trade Issue

The following will show that intellectual property issues have evolved from primarily national concerns to international trade questions and that the EU, recognizing the trade implications of intellectual property, has long acted to protect EU interests abroad.

The international trade dimension of intellectual property is a relatively recent phenomena that international organizations have been slow to appreciate. In spite of the TRIPs negotiations, GATT Article XX has permitted the contracting parties to derogate from the principle of free trade to safeguard intellectual property interests. Thus, this intellectual property based exception to trade liberalization can be invoked when entering agreements with third countries that are contracting parties to GATT. Even within free trade areas or customs unions, the GATT does not prohibit trade restrictions between and among members as long as the restrictions protect intellectual property rights. Before the Uruguay Round negotiations ended, the GATT intellectual property provisions, as well as other international conventions, were "minimal and permissive."

Though varying in details, intellectual property laws throughout the world essentially seek to ensure that the creator is rewarded for his or her inventiveness and to motivate further creativity. These laws protect the creator from rival enterprises and competitors pirating the creator's process or idea. Since the creation of the GATT, however, intellectual property has undergone a fundamental conceptual change: the emphasis has moved away from sovereign matters—e.g., one of protective norms restricted to the territority of the state—to issues of adequate protection of intellectual property rights abroad. As the economic importance of exports has increased, so have the needs for improved extra-territorial protection of intellectual property rights. This is particularly true for inventors and producers of technological goods who, having spent great sums in research and development, demand that their national governments protect their investments from pirating and the subsequent undermining of their competitive positions. "As such, it was no longer the existence but rather the absence of, or deficiencies in, intellectual property protection which became the central issue in the international trade debate. . . ."[15] While strong intellectual property rights were once believed to create possible trade barriers, today the international exchange of goods is threatened by insufficient or nonexistent intellectual property rights.

The international dimension of intellectual property is not altogether new, however. The Berne Convention on Copyright protection has existed for over one hundred years and similar treaties have been adopted, including the Universal Copyright Convention and the Rome Phonograms Conventions. In addition, organizations largely provide permissive regulatory protection based upon the reciprocity of national treatment. What is new, however, is the awareness of the effect that intellectual property protection may have on international trade and an active desire to protect these rights abroad. It has been discovered that the absence of adequate protection of intellectual property or the existence of excessive protection can undermine the benefits derived from the elimination of high tariffs and the reduction of non-tariff barriers. The growing interdependence of national economies in the increasing globalization and regionalization of markets has revealed insufficiencies in the present international regulatory framework. Many current market factors combine to demonstrate a growing need for effective transnational protection of intellectual property rights. As indicated above, intellectual creation and know-how increasingly comprise the value of products and services as well as represent substantial cost in research and development. Given the relative ease that modern technology permits intellectual creation of know-how to be copied, inadequate international intellectual property safeguards hinder investment recoupment and inhibit further research and development. Furthermore, without intellectual property protection, the producer or supplier of services will find itself at a disadvantage in the highly competitive foreign market. This situation is exacerbated considering the trend toward research and development in one country and licensed development in another. One commentator noted that "[t]he present state of law in international intellectual property protection increasingly impairs or even nullifies acquired benefits accruing under the [GATT]."[16]

---

[15] Inge GoVaere, *Intellectual Property Protection and Commercial Policy,* in the European Community's Commercial Policy after 1992: The Legal Dimension 197, 205-206 (Marc Marescean ed., 1993).

[16] Thomas Cottier, *The Prospects for Intellectual Property in GATT*, 28 C.M.L. Rev. 383, at 384 (1991).

In its Green Paper on copyrights and neighboring rights, the Commission observed that new technologies during the last ten years have created the need for a "global approach" to intellectual property (in this case, copyrights). The Commission cited three main developments: 1) copyrights and neighboring rights in western economies play an increased role; 2) the use made of goods and services with links to copyright had undergone profound changes; and 3) questions of copyright and neighboring rights have become international as the new technologies have blurred national borders thus making domestic protection inadequate. Because the new uses of copyright and neighboring rights are often practiced on an international scale, the EU must recognize this new dimension and take a multilateral approach to intellectual property.

The international trade realities explained above have compelled the EU to act to secure its intellectual property rights abroad. This new development in international trade is the sort to which the Court of Justice intended Article 113 to adapt. As some commentators have noted with respect to the international provision of services:

> If negotiations in the GATT take place on matters such as the international provision of services and international establishment in an international trade organization such as the GATT and such matters become a permanent concern of the GATT then it is not conceivable that the concept of a common commercial policy would not also embrace these subjects in the long run.[17]

Similarly, it is inconceivable that the common commercial policy would not also embrace intellectual property.

---

[17] P.L.G. Kapteyn & P. Verloren Van Themaat, *Introduction to the Law of the European Communities* 773-74, at 781 (Laurence W. Gormley ed., 2d ed. 1990).

Chapter 9

EU Interactions With GATT[1]

Introduction

In a dark corner of the GATT negotiations lurks a fundamental issue of international trade relations unlikely to find a peaceful resolution in the near future. It is clear that through the middle of 1990 scant attention was paid to the relationship which would exist between the GATT and the European Union ("EU"), or the GATT and any other regional group, subsequent to the incorporation of the so-called "new areas" into the GATT regime, and with respect to the scope of preferential arrangements or discriminations that these regional trading arrangements ("RTAs") might be allowed.[2]

The most current round of international trade negotiations under GATT[3] auspices was designed in large measure to bring trade in services, investment measures and intellectual property rights protection within the framework of GATT regulation. Developments in the international economy make the GATT somewhat anachronistic in that it concerns itself only with the trade of goods, while a large portion of inter-

---

1 Frederick M. Abbott, *GATT and the European Community: A Formula for Peaceful Coexistence*, 12 Mich. J. Int'l L. 1-58 (1990). © 1990 Frederick M. Abbott. Reprinted by permission.

2 As will be elaborated in this article, considerable scholarly attention has been paid to regional trading arrangements in the GATT framework with respect to the GATT's historic role in regulating world trade in goods. See Dam, *Regional Economic Arrangements and the GATT: The Legacy of a Misconception*, 30 U. CHI. L. REV. 615 (1963); R. Hudec, THE GATT LEGAL SYSTEM AND WORLD TRADE DIPLOMACY 211-26 (2d ed. 1990); J. Jackson, THE WORLD TRADING SYSTEM 141-43 (1989); J. Jackson, WORLD TRADE AND THE LAW OF GATT 575- 623 (1969) [hereinafter LAW OF GATT]; FREE TRADE AREAS AND U.S. TRADE POLICY (J. Schott ed. 1989). Particularly with respect to the pre-Uruguay Round relationship between the European Community and the GATT, see THE EUROPEAN COMMUNITY AND GATT (M. Hilf, F. Jacobs & E. Petersmann eds. 1986) [hereinafter EC AND GATT]. An excellent critique of the GATT treatment of regional trading arrangements which suggests reexamining the existing legal mechanism is in Cottier, *Die Bedeutung des GATT* im PROZEBETA DER EUROPAISCHEN INTEGRATION, EGRECHT UND SCHWEIZERISCHE RECHTSORDNUNG (O. Jacot-Guillarmod, D. Schindler & T. Cottier eds. 1990).

3 General Agreement on Tariffs and Trade, opened for signature Oct. 30, 1947, 61 Stat. A3, T.I.A.S. No. 1700, 55 U.N.T.S. 187. The "GATT" is commonly used to refer both to an international organization [hereinafter "GATT"] and to the General Agreement on Tariffs and Trade [hereinafter "General Agreement"], which is its charter document. The history of the GATT is so well-chronicled and its operations so extensively analyzed that these undertakings will not be repeated in this article except as specifically relevant to its subject matter. Primary sources for description and analysis of the GATT are R. Hudec, *Id.*, J. Jackson, *Id.*, Law of GATT, *Id.*, and EC AND GATT, *Id.*; K. Dam, THE GATT: LAW AND INTERNATIONAL ECONOMIC ORGANIZATION (1970); J. Jackson, J. Louis & M. Matsushita, IMPLEMENTING THE TOKYO ROUND: NATIONAL CONSTITUTIONS AND INTERNATIONAL ECONOMIC RULES (1984); O. Long, LAW AND ITS LIMITATIONS IN THE GATT MULTILATERAL TRADE SYSTEM (1985).

national economic flows are made up of services, the sale and transfer of intangible technologies and direct investment. Many years and much effort have been spent to reconcile the GATT with international trade reality, and there are good prospects for at least limited success. Moreover, even if the Uruguay Round negotiations should fail as a whole (crashing on the shoals of agricultural subsidies perhaps), the major international trading powers may well reach an accommodation on the problem of liberalizing cross-border trade in services.

Significant is the relationship between the GATT, the European Union and other RTAs as and when trade in services and other "new areas" are incorporated into the GATT framework.

Succinctly stated, the central issue is whether RTAs should be permitted to adopt rules which derogate from the National Treatment principle of the GATT in the application of new agreements covering trade in services and other "new areas," and therefore be allowed to discriminate in favor of member country enterprises for reasons having to do with the formation or maintenance of the RTAs. If so, by what legal standard should such derogations be evaluated? This issue is not a mere abstraction. The EU clearly has in mind that it will be enabled to liberalize its internal market for the benefit of domestic service providers without extending the benefits of that liberalization directly to non-Member State enterprises.[4] Such discrimination would necessarily involve derogations from the National Treatment principle to which parties to a new GATT Services Code would otherwise be subject.

I. Regional Trading Arrangements at the Conceptual Level

A. Politics

A waiver permitting the formation of RTAs and condoning certain RTA discriminatory practices was incorporated in the GATT General Agreement in 1949 because of a belief that RTAs might be economically desirable,[5] and because of post-war perceptions of

---

[4] The following draft clause is taken from the EC's proposal for a GATT Services Code:

> Subject to the conditions [sic] that the resulting regime is on the whole no more restrictive than that resulting from previous commitments set out in its schedule, this Agreement shall not prevent any party from being a party to an agreement aiming at a higher degree of liberalization of trade in services in the framework of a customs union or free-trade area within the meaning of Article XXIV paragraph 8 of the GATT, or to adopt an interim agreement leading to the formation of a customs union or free-trade area whose scope would include trade in services.

Proposal by the EC: A Draft, General Agreement on Trade in Services, Art. III(1), GATT Doc. MTN.GNS/W/105 (June 18, 1990) [hereinafter EC Services Proposal].

[5] Jackson notes that the United States officially supported the RTA exception on the grounds that such arrangements are desirable, with the proviso that they do "not cause any disadvantage to outside countries, in comparison with their trade before the customs union [was] effected." Law of GATT, *supra* note 2, at 577.

> If a single adjective were to be chosen to describe article XXIV, that adjective would be 'deceptive.' First, the standards established are deceptively concrete and precise; any attempt

the potential advantages for regional political stability which might be achieved through economic integration. There was then and remains a strong political/military motivation for encouraging European integration in particular.[6] Then and now, these political/military motivations may outweigh all but the most compelling economic arguments against an RTA like the EU.

B. Economics

Economists, on the other hand, have not been able to provide a definitive perspective on the welfare benefits and costs of RTAs because of their enormous complexity and dynamism. In 1950 economist Jacob Viner described the basic economic impact of the RTA,[7] and his observations remain at the core of RTA economic analysis. Viner observed that RTAs may both create trade among RTA members by shifting production and imports from higher-cost RTA members to lower-cost RTA members, and divert trade by shifting production and imports from non-RTA member country exporters (with former cost advantages) to member country producers/exporters awarded cost advantages by new preferences. Whether an RTA would produce an economic welfare benefit would depend upon whether its trade creating (i.e., new trade between the member countries) or trade diverting (i.e., member country trade which is substituted for third-country trade) forces were predominant. Though not so assumed by Viner, Dam (among others) concluded after Viner's observations on RTA effects were published that it would be possible to predict whether a particular RTA would, as a whole, be trade creating or trade diverting and therefore beneficial or detrimental to global economic welfare.

Forty years following Viner's pathfinding work there seems to be some consensus that predicting or even determining after the fact the trade creating/trade diverting impact of an entire RTA is no easy matter and, moreover, that the determination of the so-called "welfare effects" of the RTA should involve an analysis of factors other than trade effects. A recent Note prepared by the GATT Secretariat which reviews the literature on the trade creation and trade diversion effects of RTAs suggests that as eco-

---

> to apply the standards to a specific situation reveals ambiguities which, to use an irresistible metaphor, go to the heart of the matter. Second, while the rule appears to be carefully conceived, the principles enunciated make little economic sense. Third, the dismaying experience of the Contracting Parties has been that no customs union or free-trade area agreement presented for review has complied with Article XXIV and yet every such agreement has been approved by a tacit or explicit waiver.

Id. at 619.

6 It has been observed that:

> The idea of the 'United States of Europe' . . . which would be a faithful partner of the United States of America, could be seen behind the Marshall Plan, the American decision to take part in the defense of Europe (the Vandenberg Resolution), and U.S. support for the process of neo-functional integration after 1950.

Elazar & Greilsammer, *Federal Democracy: The U.S.A. and Europe Compared, A Political Science Perspective,* in 1 INTEGRATION THROUGH LAW 71, 88 (M. Cappelletti, M. Seccombe & J. Weiler eds. 1986).

7 J. Viner, THE CUSTOMS UNION ISSUE 41-81 (1950).

nomic analysis has become increasingly sophisticated and the dynamic effects of market manipulating mechanisms have become better understood, the complex effects of trade barrier adjustment on local production and consumption, external production and consumption, employment, social welfare, monetary policy (including balance of payments effects), etc. challenge the most sophisticated empirical and modeling capacities of the economist. Beyond that, an evaluation of RTAs involves "public choice" issues which are not answerable by economic modeling alone.

Following a thorough review of economic studies with respect to the economic impact of RTAs (including the EU) and an identification of the more prudent and realistic of these studies, the Note observes, inter alia, a "considerable variation" in the estimated trade creation and trade diversion effects of the EU. The Secretariat adds that "with few often striking exceptions . . . most studies [of customs unions] have produced estimates of substantial absolute values for TC, net TC and/or welfare gains, which nevertheless are extremely small as percentages of national income or GNP," and that the difficulties encountered by leading economists in estimating after the fact the impact of the creation of an RTA "underlines the limits in the logic and practice of ex ante prediction of TC-TD [trade creation-trade diversion]."

The GATT Secretariat's survey of the global economic welfare effects of RTAs suggests that there are no conclusive answers to these key questions: (a) from a global economic welfare standpoint, are RTAs as a general proposition good or bad? (b) from a global economic welfare standpoint, are particular RTAs good or bad? While there are opinions on all sides of these questions, the economic costs and benefits of RTAs appear to remain largely indeterminate at present. There does appear to be some consensus that the tools of economic analysis are not yet sufficiently developed to permit conclusive predictions about the welfare effects of prospective RTAs.

C. Arguments Against RTAs

There are a wide range of additional perspectives as to the merits of RTAs beyond those founded on political/military stabilization or pure analytic economics. The concerns of those who believe that global economic welfare is best served by an open trading system as embodied in the GATT, and who are concerned that a preoccupation with regional arrangements will undermine the open system, are articulated by Professor Riesenfeld:

> Let me remind you that the basic blueprint of a new world order designed at Bretton Woods was that of a peaceful, nondiscriminating, and open system of economic and trade relations of global dimensions and that both bilateralism and regionalism were viewed, at best, as an exception and transitional phase in the realization of the ultimate goal. Thus the General Agreement on Tariffs and Trade (GATT), which survived as the remnant of the idea of the International Trade Organization planned in Havana, was instituted as the instrument governing worldwide liberalized, if not free, trade.

> It was clear from the beginning of that system that the building of a free global trade system would not be easy and would take a sequence of negotiating rounds. For that reason and to accommodate perceived benefits of customs unions and free trade areas, Article XXIV of GATT excepted arrangements of that type from the sweep of the most favored nation treatment requirement which is the central provision of the system. . . .
>
> Regional cooperation in trade and resource conservation and sharing is both necessary and desirable. Nevertheless, regionalism should not be at the expense of a global perspective of the ultimate needs of mankind.[8]

Those who believe that world economic welfare is maximized by the broadest opening of national markets, giving the widest room for the functioning of the laws of comparative advantage, naturally view RTAs with suspicion. RTAs by their very nature distort international markets because they create preferences for intra-regional trade. It is only second-best to argue that comparative advantage is at least extended beyond narrow national borders into a region when the best alternative of extending comparative advantage on a global basis is available.

Second, countries which form RTAs are often geographically contiguous and at relatively comparable stages of economic development. If regional preferences are granted among a group of countries at an advanced stage of economic development, this may only widen the schism between more and less developed countries by permitting those with existing advantages to enhance their status without extending the benefits of expanded trade opportunities to the less developed. In this sense RTAs may function to widen the gap between rich and poor.

Third, smaller countries which are not part of a natural alignment in a geographic region or which are part of a region in which their particular attributes are not rewarded are threatened by RTAs. This threat may be of a political nature, as when a particular country finds that it lacks the leverage necessary to secure equitable treatment from the regional partners with which it finds itself aligned. Some countries may, by virtue of geography or political incompatibility, be excluded from whatever benefits RTAs have to offer.

Fourth, transnational business enterprises are concerned that regional trade preferences will inhibit their access to markets. Protectionist policies intended to foster the development of regionally-based industries are a threat to the global enterprise, which thrives in the open market. Much of the adverse effect which protectionist policies may have on transnational enterprises may be ameliorated by extending to them the right to establish themselves and take on a local character within the RTA.

Individuals, either as consumers or employees, certainly have interests in the question whether RTAs create global welfare benefits. If the U.S.-Canada Free Trade Agreement and the EU experience are illustrative, the most significant individual con-

---

[8] Riesenfeld, *Pacific Ocean Resources: The New Regionalism and the Global System*, 16 ECOLOGY L.Q. 355-56, 359 (1989).

cerns with respect to the establishment of RTAs are expressed by employees whose job security is threatened by the liberalization of markets and regional operation of comparative advantage. More abstract concerns about whether RTA comparative advantage or global comparative advantage is the better alternative for economic prosperity are left for senior government officials to ponder.

Finally, it is easy to be concerned that a marked trend toward the solution of economic problems on a regional level will undercut efforts to resolve economic problems on a global level. A form of regional isolationism could emerge and diminish the authority of global institutions such as the GATT. Even if regional groups at the outset express a commitment to long-term participation in an open global trading system, enthusiasm for that system might well be undermined by a preoccupation with more immediate regional concerns.

D. Arguments for RTAs

There are forceful arguments in favor of RTAs. First, if it were true that the global economic system functioned as the harmonious interplay of 160 sovereign States negotiating the progressive liberalization of trade barriers to the ultimate benefit of all mankind, it might be difficult to promote the RTA concept. However, the world trade community is not functioning in this utopian sense, leaving RTA proponents to argue that the best road to the eventual utopia is through the formation of RTAs, whose members gain experience in economic cooperation through the formation of regional institutions, the intra-regional reduction of trade barriers, and the creation and operation of effective dispute resolution bodies. By demonstrating the advantages of market liberalization on a smaller scale, the RTAs promote liberalization on a larger, universal scale. If the current system can be portrayed as one in which cooperation is difficult because of widely divergent national interests which are difficult to resolve on a country-to-country basis, the better idea may be to encourage the formation of a dozen regional groups which will thereafter negotiate on the basis of regional interests in a less fragmented environment. The EU can be pointed to as an example of regional cooperation in the formation of institutions, removal of barriers, creation of dispute mechanisms and promotion of a common trade policy which makes the Union easier to deal with than twelve independently negotiating European nations. Whether the EU experience can be replicated in other regions is an interesting and difficult question. Other RTAs have not been nearly so successful. A particularly significant feature of the EU that may provide a model for other regional arrangements, and, ultimately, the global trading system, is the direct applicability of Union law to the individual and the extension to the individual of direct access to the judiciary for the purpose of challenging Union regulation.

Second, RTAs can be viewed as the engines which will drive global economic development. If it is true that a regional group of economically advanced countries will accelerate intra-group development beyond that achievable by a more economically disparate and geographically diverse universe of countries, it may be preferable to encourage this advancement which can then be used to improve the lot of the less economically fortunate. Just how this economic bootstrapping will occur remains to be seen, but mechanisms surely are conceivable.

Finally, RTAs are a reality. Although the EU is evolving at a rapid pace and both its immediate and longer-term structural futures are unclear, it would be somewhat disingenuous to propose the dismantling of the EU because RTAs are not a demonstrated virtue. Even a cautionary message to the Heads of State of the Western Hemisphere who seem to have collectively concluded that bilateral and regional free trade areas will further their collective interests would be unlikely to turn the tide of history. The more limited ambition of this article is to attempt to define a rule or rules which will help to constrain the post-Uruguay Round policies of RTAs within limits which are reasonably consistent with the concept of a liberal global trading system, and thus are less likely to lead to a disintegration of that system.

II. RTAs in the Existing GATT Framework

The General Agreement is tolerant of the formation of RTAs. Provided that the members of a prospective RTA notify the GATT Contracting Parties and meet a requirement that their formation measures will involve "substantially all the trade" among them, they are permitted under Article XXIV of the General Agreement to ignore the GATT's Most Favored Nation treatment principle and grant each other tariff preferences which need not be extended to non-RTA members (as well as, in the case of a "customs union," to form a common tariff wall). The incidence of tariffs affecting non-members of a customs union is not to exceed "on the whole" the tariffs which were applicable to them prior to the formation of the RTA. Tariffs affecting non-members of a free trade area ("FTA") should be no higher than those applied to them by each member of the FTA prior to its formation. The GATT Contracting Parties have never refused an Article XXIV waiver to a prospective RTA.

Most Favored Nation and National Treatment Derogations

1. The MFN Principle

Article XXIV permits discriminatory preferences with respect to "duties and other regulations of commerce" maintained in each of the constituent territories of an RTA. Though Article XXIV is decidedly vague, this reference appears to be directed at permitting only derogations from the GATT MFN principle, specifically as it requires each GATT Contracting Party that grants a tariff benefit to any country to extend immediately and unconditionally the same benefit to all GATT Contracting Parties. Under this narrow construction, preferential arrangements under Article XXIV are limited to the discriminatory reduction or elimination of intra-RTA tariffs and should not extend to the discriminatory reduction or elimination of non-tariff barriers such as internal sales taxes (e.g., the removal or reduction of taxes only in favor of regionally-produced goods). The latter type of preferential treatment would involve derogation both from the GATT MFN principle (regarding equivalency of treatment for all GATT Contracting Parties) and from the GATT National Treatment principle.

2. The National Treatment Principle

The National Treatment principle is a fundamental tenet of the GATT. Each Contracting Party agrees to treat goods from each other Contracting Party on a level comparable to those produced in its own territory for the purposes of internal sale. Article XXIV does not expressly address deviations from the National Treatment principle and there is no good reason to conclude that the drafters of the General Agreement intended that RTAs be permitted to grant internal preferences to locally produced goods. However, on a purely semantic level, a case for an interpretation of Article XXIV which permits derogation from the National Treatment principle can be made, though such interpretation is by no means widely accepted. This is not to say that there is absolutely no scholarly support for the proposition that Article XXIV permits derogations from provisions of the GATT other than the MFN principle as it applies to tariffs and related charges and regulations, or that the EU (for example) has not from time to time adopted and been challenged for adopting regional internal discriminations with respect to locally-produced goods.

3. Application of Article XXIV to Services

Assuming that Article XXIV is intended only to permit exceptions to an RTA's MFN obligation with respect to tariffs, in its current formulation it is not usefully applied to trade in services. In the context of regulating trade in goods, an RTA typically subjects non-member goods to a tariff as they cross its external border. An RTA extends a preference to regionally-produced goods by not imposing a tariff on them. Foreign or external goods are acted upon on the basis of their origin—i.e., coming from outside the RTA's external border. Similarly, "preferred" goods—those which were either produced within the RTA or have already paid the entry fee or tariff—are not acted upon because they are within the tariff wall. In sum, Article XXIV permits RTAs to favor local production by removing intra-RTA tariff barriers without eliminating external barriers (and, in the case of a customs union, by erecting a common external wall).

The regulation of trade in services is a more complex matter. Because services are routinely provided by persons "at the site," they are generally not subject to "border measures" such as tariffs (although there are border measures affecting services, such as employee visa requirements). External service providers are typically regulated (and discriminated against) both on a national and RTA level by internal regulations such as licensing requirements which establish, either expressly or through their operational effect, different standards of treatment for local (or "national") and foreign (or non-RTA member country) service providers. The trade regulation of "foreign" service providers, then, occurs not necessarily (or even generally) at an RTA's external border, but rather internally where rules and regulations may be either expressly or operationally discriminatory. A local service provider licensing requirement, in order to discriminate against a foreign service provider, need not expressly preclude the foreign service provider from operating locally if such a licensing requirement provides, for example, that the provider must possess certain local academic credentials which cannot reasonably be obtained by a person seeking to enter the market (and which are not a reasonable requirement for the license). Insurance and banking enterprises might be discriminatorily impaired from providing services across borders as a result of disparate capital or reserve requirements which are arbitrary or unjustified. Thus, trade restrictions based on nationality may be "disguised" in the form of licensing or other regulatory requirements which do not expressly contain reference to nationality. To the extent that such regulatory requirements are arbitrary or unjustified, they are the equivalent, from a trade regulation standpoint, of denial of National Treatment.

A recent Gatt Panel Report, which involves a claim by the EU against the United States arising out of the discriminatory impact of section 337 of the Tariff Act of 1930, makes clear that compliance with the National Treatment principle is not to be confined by reference to the language of rules or regulations. An inquiry into the application (or potential application) of the rules or regulations is appropriate. An analysis of legal rules should not be confined to instances of their application, but should take into account their "potential impact" as well.

If foreign services (and service providers) were regulated/dutied by individual countries or RTAs only when they literally crossed borders, much foreign or external trade would go unregulated because it would in fact be provided locally. In the services context, differential treatment must to some extent be based (expressly or by operational effect) on the nationality of the service provider, and any such differential will involve the National Treatment principle.

4. The Need to Modify Article XXIV

If RTAs are to be permitted to discriminate in favor of services of local/regional origin, such permission must therefore be couched at least partially in terms of derogation from the National Treatment principle. An amended form of Article XXIV will therefore be needed in a GATT agreement on services to incorporate the concept of derogation from the National Treatment principle (in addition to derogation from the MFN principle) if certain RTA discriminations in the services sector are to be permitted. This article is concerned with the conceptual underpinnings to and the potential form of such an amended provision. Moreover, it is a premise of this article that the adoption in a GATT services agreement (or other "new area" agreement) of a new formula for evaluating RTA discriminations will not put an end to debate over the appropriate limits of that formula. Because of the innumerable potential mechanisms of non-tariff barrier trade discrimination and the wide array of services, investment mechanisms, etc., it is difficult to imagine that any formula will permit a neat evaluation of all potentially discriminatory measures which RTAs might adopt.

III. Services Liberalization Within the GATT

Both the United States and the EU have prepared and submitted to the GATT Negotiating Group on Trade in Services a specific proposal for an agreement on trade in services. These proposals followed the adoption by the Contracting Parties of a services Framework Agreement at the Uruguay Round Mid-Term Review. The U.S. and EU proposals demonstrate much more clearly than the very general Framework Agreement the type of commitments more likely to emerge from the services negotiations. Both the United States and the EU submitted their proposals in the form of a separate GATT agreement or Code rather than an amendment to the General Agreement, reflecting an assumption that, with respect to services, the two-thirds majority of the Contracting Parties necessary for an amendment to the General Agreement itself will not be forthcoming at the conclusion of the Uruguay Round. Both Code proposals envisage that separate "Annexes" will be adopted to add specificity to, clarify or modify the Code with respect to the regulation of trade in specific sectors such as financial services and telecommunications.[9]

Regardless of the ultimate outcome of the negotiations, the U.S. and EU proposals are of comparative interest from the standpoint both of their points of convergence and their points of divergence. Both would incorporate the fundamental principle of National Treatment as a litmus test of liberalization. Thus, each party to a Services Code would agree, under both proposals, to grant to service providers of other Code parties treatment equivalent to that of their own nationals. Application of the National Treatment principle assumes, of course, that service providers are effectively enabled to enter the local market (i.e. are granted market access) in the first place. Both proposals envisage that Code party governments will, in spite of the National Treatment provisions, retain the right to apply different regulations to foreign service providers than to domestic providers when such regulations are required for public policy reasons, but each would in its own way preclude the application of differential regulations intended as artificial barriers to liberalization. Both proposals would permit derogation from the National Treatment principle in the area of government procurement (not intended for resale), a matter which presumably will be further dealt with in revisions to the Government Procurement Code.

Both proposals would incorporate a Most Favored Nation provision, so that benefits granted to any party to the Services Code will be made available to all other parties to the Code. The U.S. and EU proposals each take a different approach to the question of derogations from the MFN obligation with respect to liberalization commitments beyond those initially agreed to, though these differences appear to be more a matter of form than substance. Under each proposal, it appears to be envisaged that each Code party's initial schedule of liberalization commitments will apply to all other parties to the Code. The U.S. proposal seems to suggest that additional benefits provided by each party under the Code will be the subject of separate Protocols (for added liberalization to covered sectors) or Special Agreements (for non-Code-covered sectors). The EU proposal appears to contemplate progressive rounds of multilateral liberalization negotiations and agreements pursuant to which any party entering into a liberalization commitment beyond that to which it was previously subject may choose not to extend that commitment to another party "when it considers that the level of commitment of the other party is not in keeping with the particular characteristics of that party's market and its degree of liberalization."

---

9 *EC Services Proposal; supra* note 4, at Art. XVIII.

The United States and the EU follow somewhat different approaches to establishing the universe of services to be liberalized under the Code, although both are variations of a so-called "negative" listing approach. Under the U.S. proposal there will be a collectively agreed-to list of service sectors covered by the Code, to which each party may independently adopt its own exclusions.[10] Under the EU proposal the assumption is made that all traded services will be covered by the Code, except those that each party independently elects to reserve through enumeration on a separate schedule. Under a "positive" listing approach (used by neither the United States or EU), parties would be expected to liberalize only those sectors which they individually designated. A positive approach would presumably result in a lesser degree of overall liberalization.

One of the major differences between the U.S. and EU proposals concerns recognition of the "right of establishment." The U.S. proposal would specifically require each Code party to agree that persons of other parties could establish or expand a commercial presence on the territory of that party on a basis no less favorable than that of the party's national persons.[11] The EU proposal makes a reference to measures affecting "commercial or professional presence" as being subject to the Code,[12] but does not otherwise specifically address the right of establishment. This difference could be read merely as one of shading, or nuance, since the general National Treatment provision in each Code proposal could be construed so as to require the equivalent treatment of applications for establishment. If such is the intended construction, the EU might be faulted for subtlety or the United States criticized for overconscientious specifity. Further supporting the "mere nuance" hypothesis is the fact that the U.S. National Treatment provision is directed at service providers "whenever market access has been achieved,"[13] while the EU National Treatment provision more broadly refers to "service providers of other parties."[14] However, since National Treatment can only truly become meaningful to a service provider which is able to enter a market, and since the right of establishment in an RTA like the Union is of paramount importance to foreign providers, the absence of specific mention of this right in the EU proposal may understandably give rise to questions of intention from participants in the negotiating process.

Both Code proposals envision transparency of regulations, equivalent treatment by government monopolies, balance of payments measures, freedom of currency movement and (at least temporary) mobility of key labor as elements of an eventual Services Code. Both proposals make specific provision against harmful subsidies, and the EU proposal also envisages antidumping procedures and makes allowance for restrictive

---

[10] *Communication from the United States: Agreement on Trade in Services,* GATT Doc. MTN.GNS/W/75 (Oct 17, 1989) [hereinafter *U.S. Services Proposal*].

[11] *U.S. Services Proposal, Id.,* at Art. 4.

[12] *EC Services Proposal, supra* note 4, at Art. I(1)(c).

[13] *U.S. Services Proposal, supra* note 10, at Art. 8.1.

[14] *EC Services Proposal, supra* note 4, at Art. IV(1).

business practices regulation. In addition, both proposals would permit the imposition of measures relating to such matters as public morals and health, protection of privacy and the prevention of deceptive practices.

Although it is not apparent whether the proposed provisions are intended to supplant or merely supplement those provided in the Technical Standards Code (and this requires clarification from the Union), the EU proposal addresses (certainly in more detail than the U.S. proposal) the topic of "rules, standards and qualifications."[15] The EU proposal permits the adoption of standards based on public policy considerations as well as objective requirements, using international standards where appropriate. According to the proposal, the standards adopted should not render inoperative a commitment to grant market access. Standards requirements may be waived where the rules of the provider's home territory guarantee equivalent regulatory conditions. The proposal also emphasizes that measures should be formulated in a transparent, uniform, impartial and reasonable manner, and neither the formulation nor administration of such measures should constitute an arbitrary or unjustifiable discrimination or a disguised restriction on trade in services. Interestingly, the EU Code proposal takes note of an interrelationship between its general provision on standards and the EU's draft RTA waiver. The Union appears to envisage that it will have the right, pursuant to its RTA waiver, to conclude intra-Union standards agreements under the conditions of the RTA waiver, and not the generally applicable provisions of the Services Code.

IV. The EC's Proposal for an RTA Waiver

Article III(1) of the EU Services Code proposal states:

> Subject to the conditions [sic] that the resulting regime is on the whole no more restrictive than that resulting from previous commitments set out in its schedule, this Agreement shall not prevent any party from being a party to an agreement aiming at a higher degree of liberalization of trade in services in the framework of a customs union or free-trade area within the meaning of Article XXIV paragraph 8 of the GATT, or to adopt an interim agreement leading to the formation of a customs union or free-trade area whose scope would include trade in services.

The EU's RTA waiver proposal permits individual member countries of an RTA to enter into agreements among themselves "aiming at a higher degree of liberalization." In the context of the Services Code, this involves a right of derogation from both the Most Favored Nation and National Treatment principles. First, comparable to Article XXIV of the General Agreement regarding tariff barriers applicable to trade in goods, the member countries of an RTA will be entitled to grant more liberal service trade terms to each other without immediately and unconditionally extending these benefits

[15] *U.S. Services Proposal, supra* note 10, at Art. 7 (regarding only licensing and certification); *EC Services Proposal, supra* note 4, at Art. V.

to each non-RTA party to the Services Code—that is, the MFN principle will be waived. Second, because the "liberalization" commitments of parties to the Services Code will distinctly involve the grant of National Treatment rights to other Code parties, the waiver permitting RTA members to adopt more liberalizing agreements among themselves (without extending these agreements to other Code parties on an MFN basis) means that they will also not be granting equivalent—i.e., National—treatment to non-members. It is the right to derogate from the National Treatment principle which is of great concern because it involves a significant departure from prior GATT law. As discussed previously, the Article XXIV waiver concerns only the right to grant intra-RTA tariff preferences on a non-MFN basis. While a waiver of the obligation to apply the National Treatment principle is not expressly stated in the EU proposal, it is necessarily implicit in it. If it were to be assumed, conversely, that National Treatment would remain a constant governing principle regardless of the waiver proposal, there would be no apparent point to the waiver, since the benefits of internal liberalizing measures ("higher" or otherwise) would automatically be passed on to non-RTA members by virtue of the principle.

In the EU proposal there appear to be only two limitations on the rights of the RTA to derogate from the National Treatment principle. The first is that the intra-RTA agreement must be "aiming at a higher degree of liberalization." This is only to say that the RTA member countries may not enter into a more restrictive, i.e., de-liberalizing, agreement among themselves in derogation of their obligations under the Code. Reasons why RTA members might want to inhibit their own internal trade (while perhaps extending more liberal trade terms to non-RTA members) might be postulated, but it seems sufficient here to note that the EU concedes that RTA members will not be permitted to do so. The second limitation is established by the first clause of the proposal, which subjects the waiver to the condition that the "resulting regime is on the whole no more restrictive than that resulting from previous commitments set out in its [each member's] schedule." This clause appears to be directed at establishing a condition that while an individual RTA member may, by virtue of an intra-RTA "liberalization" agreement, adopt measures which are in fact more restrictive than its commitments as set out in its Code schedule, the sum of RTA member liberalizing measures will be as favorable to non-RTA members as would have been the separate member country commitments under the Code. The reference to "previous commitments set out in its schedule" must be viewed as limiting each individual country's more generalized National Treatment commitment to those specific commitments set forth in its schedule. If this were not the case, a right extended to RTA members to enter into more highly liberalizing agreements would not be meaningful, since the benefits of such agreements would automatically be extended to non-RTA members.

The "on the whole" language in the EU's draft waiver is borrowed from the basic Article XXIV exemption which says that an RTA (customs union) external tariff wall may not "on the whole" exceed the tariff wall of each member state prior to the formation of the common external tariff wall. When the EU first erected its common tariff wall, much controversy arose with respect to how multiple Member State tariff walls should be aggregated to determine a common "on the whole" tariff barrier involving a myriad of products crossing a multiplicity of boundaries. In the context of a Services Code, the potential practical application of the "on the whole" test staggers the imagination. There appears to be an underlying assumption that it is possible to determine what the existing economic impact of service barriers are and, in addition, to determine on an objective basis what the effect of eliminating these barriers would be. This is not the case. Professor Jackson employs an element of understatement in his recent book when he observes that "[s]cholars have tried to estimate the 'tariff-equivalent' effect of the various non-tariff measures, but have found this to be no easy task."[16]

It is clear that the most sophisticated analytic tools are unable to describe with accuracy either the current effect of non-tariff barriers ("NTBs") on trade in services or the impact of removing these barriers. The United States Trade Representative ("USTR"), with tremendous incentive to quantify foreign NTBs affecting trade in services, is perhaps the most articulate spokesperson for the impracticability of the task.[17] In its 1990 Foreign Trade Barriers Report, following a lengthy discussion of the difficulties inherent in attempting to estimate the impact of NTBs on U.S. exports of goods, the USTR states:

> The same limitations that affect the ability to estimate the impact of foreign barriers upon U.S. goods exports apply to U.S. services exports. Furthermore, the trade data on services exports are extremely limited and of questionable reliability. For these reasons, estimates of the impact of foreign barriers on trade in services are also difficult to compute.[18]

Starting with the understanding that the quantitative impact of NTBs on trade in services are not presently determinable and that there is no reason to believe that this situation will be remedied in the near future, it does not require an immense leap of logic to conclude that it is impracticable to evaluate the impact of the NTBs of each RTA member in order to determine whether an RTA's non-tariff barriers "on the whole" are no more restrictive than the individual commitments of its member states. For this reason the EU's proposal is unworkable.

Even if it were possible to calculate in some manner the Union's "on the whole" services barriers and thereby establish an objective minimum level of service liberalization which the EU would agree to extend to non-Member countries, allowing the Union as a regional entity to liberalize its internal market without any apparent limitation on the extent to which it may refuse to pass this liberalization on to non-Members—except that the EU must "on the whole" meet its specific minimum Services Code commitments—raises important questions: Why should the United States (with an internal market roughly comparable to that of the EU) liberalize its market for the benefit of Union service providers beyond the United States' "on the whole" com-

---

16 J. Jackson, THE WORLD TRADING SYSTEM 130 (1989).

17 *See* Office of the United States Trade Representative, 1990 National Trade Estimate on Foreign Trade Barriers 3 (1990) [hereinafter USTR FTB Report].

18 *Id.*, at 3-4.

mitment in its Services Code schedule if the United States could get by with the minimum commitment set forth in its schedule? Why should Japan? If the international trading system is based on reciprocity, would not the United States and Japan be acting reasonably in refusing the EU National Treatment beyond that level committed in the Services Code so long as the EU based its participation on an "on the whole" commitment?

There is a sharp distinction between the RTA exemption when applied to the trade of goods and when applied to the trade of services. When Article XXIV permitted the EU to remove internal tariff barriers while erecting a common tariff wall, the goods of the United States and Japan were affected only to the extent that they were subject to a one-time entry fee into the internal market (payable at the border) to which goods produced within the EU were not subject. Goods produced in the EU achieved a cost advantage only to the extent that they moved between Member countries in a manner that they had not previously, while goods produced for consumption within a particular Union Member and consumed there obtained no new advantage. A foreign producer shipping goods into a discrete Union Member State was affected little if at all by the change to a common tariff wall; it was disadvantaged only to the extent that its intra-Member State competitors were able to achieve better economies of scale in their intra-Union export operations. Once a foreign producer had paid the common external tariff and its goods had entered a Union Member State, that producer and its goods enjoyed the benefits of tariff-free transit throughout the Union and was subject to no additional disadvantage.

Failure to grant National Treatment in the context of the services market means something entirely different. If National Treatment is not provided in the Union country in which services are introduced from abroad, this will give rise to an immediate disadvantage in that market, equivalent to an immediate common external tariff disadvantage. Moreover, the immediate entry barrier disadvantage will not necessarily be compensated for by unrestricted access on a National Treatment basis to "transshipment" markets elsewhere in the Union. If the National Treatment requirement is not adhered to, external service providers might be treated in a discriminatory manner on a continuing basis for the duration of their presence in the Union, both within their country-of-entry and in other Member States, and therefore achieve no particular advantage from having entered the market. The continuing impact would not likely be measurable by an objective yardstick, such as the percentage duty imposed by an external wall tariff charge. It might instead be composed of innumerable and hardly measurable intangibles such as subjection to prolonged licensing procedures, inability to obtain Union-wide licensing, lack of access to leased telecommunications lines on an equivalent basis, continuing higher public telecommunications rate charges and other factors. An RTA waiver formula which permits the EU to adopt additional liberalizing measures with no limitation on the extent to which such measures may discriminate in favor of local enterprises may lead to a significant actual or perceived imbalance between the benefits and obligations pertaining to RTA members and those pertaining to non-RTA members.

A perception by the United States, Japan and other EU trading partners that the Union is refusing to grant access to its liberalized market beyond the strict terms of the

Services Code, based on the RTA waiver in article III of its proposal, would lead most likely to a reversion to strict reciprocity as a basis for future services liberalization concessions. Both the United States and Japan would abide by their strict commitments in the Code, but refuse to grant external parties access to further liberalized markets without reciprocal concessions. While such a result would not spell the end of the GATT trading system (which involves a high degree of dependence on "global reciprocity"), it would certainly slow the process of global liberalization. Each country undertaking a liberalization of its internal market would find itself negotiating with each of its trading partners to determine the overall new balance of reciprocal concessions. An alternative formula for evaluating discriminatory RTA measures is required.

V. A New Formula for Evaluating RTA Measures

A. Premises

This proposal for a new formula by which to evaluate RTA measures involving trade in services (and other GATT regimes not involving trade in goods) is based on certain premises. First, as discussed above, the proposal put forward by the EU in the GATT services negotiating group is both unworkable and unwise. It is unworkable because it would be exceedingly difficult to evaluate the impact of service liberalization regimes in individual RTA members as required to make a determination that the total RTA liberalization package is "on the whole" compatible with each individual RTA member's schedule of commitments. It is unwise because internal barriers to trade in services brought about by derogations from the National Treatment principle may have a far more pervasive impact than derogations from the MFN principle with respect to tariff barriers and trade in goods. The implementation of such derogations, without meaningful limitation, is likely to cause either an actual or perceived imbalance vis-a-vis the EU's trading partners which would be likely to lead in turn to a system of liberalization based on strict reciprocity. Since strict reciprocity is more easily determined on a bilateral rather than multilateral basis, a liberalization program based on case-by-case reciprocity may result in a shift from the GATT goal of comprehensive global liberalization to one of fragmented country-by-country and region-by-region liberalization. One of the principal goals of and justifications for the GATT system is the avoidance of country-by-country negotiations focusing on narrow interests.

A second premise underlying the evaluation criteria proposed below is that evaluating RTA discriminatory acts in new areas by invoking the classic economic criteria of whether such discrimination is predominantly "trade creating" or "trade diverting," while elegant in concept, would be at least as unworkable as the EU proposal. The state of the art in economic analysis simply does not permit an objective "scientific" determination—and certainly not a determination in advance—of the extent to which the imposition either of a discrete non-tariff internal discrimination or a complex system of internal discriminations will affect service providers in the three relevant markets (i.e., the territory in which services are at present locally provided, the RTA territories from which services might be provided if discriminations in the first territory were removed on an intra-RTA basis, and the non-RTA territories from which services into the first territory are currently provided or would be provided but for the preferences granted to providers within the RTA). It is therefore impractical to suggest that RTA discriminatory preferences be approved or disapproved on the basis of a determination of whether their predominant effect will be trade creating or trade diverting.

The third, and perhaps most important, set of premises is that: (a) RTAs will require some measure of flexibility to adopt intra-RTA preferences which are not extended to external territories, and (b) it is preferable to limit RTA internal discrimination in order to preserve the liberal international trading system embodied in the GATT. This set of premises is most important because it is possible to conclude from the foregoing discussion that any RTA derogation from the National Treatment principle is unwarranted. By excluding an RTA waiver provision from its Services Code proposal, the USTR impliedly signalled its adoption of such a conclusion. This conclusion, however, may ignore certain legitimate interests of RTAs such as the EU.

The general principle of the GATT mandating National Treatment for goods of foreign origin is applicable to GATT Contracting Parties, a term which, at least at the formation of the GATT, referred only to individual countries. Each of these individual members of the GATT was and is presumed to be competent within its own territory for the implementation of GATT commitments. Each member is thus obliged to apply the National Treatment principle throughout its territory, even though this does not (as in the case of the United States) preclude the adoption of internal regulations respecting different subterritories of the "federal" state so long as such disparate treatment applies alike to nationals and non-nationals. For purposes of the GATT, individual countries like the United States are considered unitary actors which have since the inception of the arrangement had the authority and power to liberalize their internal market and to extend National Treatment to foreign countries.

Prospective members of an RTA, on the other hand, are considering the mechanisms by which they may achieve some form of market unification and perhaps some degree of federalization of authority. RTAs do not share the same goals. Some, such as the EU, may envision a centralization of decision-making authority in institutions such as the EU Council and Commission. Others, such as the U.S.-Canada Free Trade Agreement may envision very little in the way of centralized decision-making authority. No RTA, however, prior to its inception, has central authority with the power to mandate unitary regulation through different national territories; and only after the inception of the RTA can its institutions initiate the process (in light of its goals) of unifying the internal market and applying (to the extent contemplated by its members) uniform trade regulation in a manner to which the federal State is accustomed. Thus, during the process of its unification and federalization, an RTA cannot be (and perhaps therefore should not be) considered the precise equivalent of an individual GATT Contracting Party, because its institutions lack the authority and power to accomplish what the institutions of a separate country may achieve.

As an RTA acts to unify, federalize and liberalize its market, it encounters certain risks. One of these risks, viewed from the internal RTA standpoint, is that enterprises in whose interests the liberalization efforts are primarily made, i.e., those located within the RTA, will face immediate competition for shares of a unified internal market from enterprises coming from outside the RTA. A certain anxiety is likely to arise on the part of RTA officials—and this appears to be the case with the EU Commission—that foreign enterprises with greater experience operating in larger domestic markets (as well as international markets) will be able to react to market unification and liberalization measures more quickly than RTA-based enterprises, and may overwhelm existing and emerging RTA enterprises if new internal regulations assume that all enterprises will be treated on an equivalent basis.

It may well be argued that fear of market liberalization and opening—even if reasonable—should not justify an RTA's derogation from immediate fulfillment of the GATT's National Treatment principle. Each individual GATT Contracting Party has its own anxiety about the impact of market opening, which does not translate into justification for failing to apply the National Treatment principle. The essential question is this: does the global trading system gain an incremental measure of value from the unification and liberalization of a formerly fragmented market such as to justify granting that new union some remedial measure in fulfilling its ultimate GATT obligations?

If the answer is no and the GATT as a whole elects to deny the RTA any temporary measure of special treatment, then the RTA which nevertheless wishes to pursue market unification and trade liberalization policies has three basic alternatives: first, it may follow the generally applicable GATT rules and accept the risk; second, it may withdraw from the GATT framework and concentrate on its own development priorities; and third, it may pretend to accept the GATT rules yet ignore them in practice. Only the first of these outcomes would appear to have any appeal with respect to non-member countries; yet, even if preferable, it may be that such an outcome is not very likely in view of political and economic factors affecting RTA decision-makers.

On the other hand, if non-member countries perceive a long-term benefit from a unified and liberalized RTA market, then the grant of a temporary waiver from strict adherence to the National Treatment principle may be an acceptable, if not strictly preferred, alternative. In other words, if a group of independent, sovereign countries decides to undertake the "federalization" of its trading system, to expand the size of and liberalize the regulatory environment within its completed market (and these activities will involve significant inter-RTA variations in degree), it may be preferable to permit the group a period during which to undertake these activities with some relief from the external demands to which the GATT Contracting Parties are normally subject. An underlying assumption behind such limited tolerance is that the unification or harmonization of trade regulation is ultimately beneficial to the global trading community as a whole, or is at least not harmful to the community, and that the potential short-term adverse consequences arising from the creation of temporary internal preferences can be kept to a bare minimum by placing strict constraints on discriminatory measures.

A waiver during the period of market unification and federalization must be viewed as a temporary measure, i.e., limited in duration. If the justification for permitting an RTA to derogate from certain fundamental GATT principles is that the RTA is undergoing a positive transformation the benefits of which will ultimately inure to non-RTA members, the justification loses its force as the transformation takes effect. Therefore, in no event should extension of a right to derogate from a principle as central to the GATT as that of National Treatment extend beyond an initial phase of the RTA's formation, after which it would be deemed to be "completed," except with respect to very strictly confined circumstances involving safeguard justifications already recognized by the GATT. Because of the risks to the global trading system associated with creating isolated regions with special and more beneficial rules, derogations must be strictly limited to those which are demonstrated by the RTA to be essential to its completion. It is on the basis of the foregoing premises that the following proposal is made.

B. A New Formula

On the surface, the following proposal is quite straightforward. It is suggested that RTA discriminations in new areas such as services and investment measures be evaluated by the criteria of "necessity." An RTA exemption in a new GATT Services Code might read:

> Code Parties which are members of customs unions and free trade areas (within the meaning of paragraph 8 of Article XXIV of the General Agreement) (hereafter "regional trading arrangements") shall be entitled to adopt as between themselves agreements for the purpose of achieving more liberalized internal markets and shall be entitled to implement those agreements by means of laws and regulations when such agreements are necessary to the formation or maintenance of said regional trading arrangements. The benefits of the aforesaid agreements shall be extended (by complete application where possible and otherwise progressively) to Code Parties which are not members of the regional trading arrangements which have adopted them as soon as the necessity for limiting their general application has expired. Liberalization agreements which have as their predominant purpose the creation of preferences in favor of enterprises established within regional trading arrangements shall be presumed to be not necessary within the meaning of this paragraph.

In addition to the foregoing, a new RTA waiver would include: (a) a provision requiring notification of an agreement to the appropriate parties (e.g., parties to the Services Code); (b) an avenue for parties opposed to the agreement to make recommendations addressing objectionable provisions or to refuse a waiver to the agreement; and (c) a dispute settlement procedure afforded either by the Code in question or the GATT General Agreement structure so that issues arising out of adopted but allegedly "unapproved" discriminations could be addressed. The policy premise favoring the minimization of RTA derogations from fundamental GATT principles leads to a further recommendation that, within the framework of the selected GATT dispute settlement procedure, the burden of proving the necessity of a specific RTA activity should be placed on the RTA seeking to justify its conduct.

In notifying a "derogating" agreement to the appropriate parties, an RTA should be required to include a binding commitment with respect to the maximum duration of the discriminatory feature(s) of such agreement, beyond which time the agreement would be presumed to violate the RTA's GATT commitments. Such a notification of commitment as to duration might also include a timetable (where feasible) for the progressive elimination of discrimination.

C. Defining Necessity

The proposed formula incorporates the concept of necessity as the test according to which RTA discriminations will be evaluated. The word "necessary" is subject to many meanings depending on the context of its use, ranging from "absolutely indispensable" to the accomplishment of a task to "convenient or desirable" in the accomplishment of a task. In the context of determining the permissibility of RTA derogations from the rules of a GATT Services Code, "necessary" should be synonymous with "indispensable to the accomplishment of the formation and maintenance of an RTA." However, even if necessity might generally be defined as constituting an essential or indispensable requirement (evidencing a far more compelling justification than mere desirability), it is obvious that "necessary" will not through this sole clarification become self-defining. Rather, some general guideposts in the form of supplemental legislative history or regulation will be required, and decisions by authoritative decision-makers such as RTA government officials, the Code Parties and GATT panelists should be expected to flesh out the concept. Given the complex nature of the integration process and its relationship to the global trading system, it would be unproductive to attempt to set out in advance and attempt to evaluate all of the types of discrimination in each economic sector in which they might arise. Nevertheless, it may be useful to discuss some general ideas about the areas in which discriminatory acts might be justified as necessary.

First, the effective establishment of RTA political institutions may require regional discriminations directed toward the creation and support of institutions such as parliaments, executive councils, and administrative and judicial bodies which might well be justified as "necessary." If, for example, the creation of an effective regional central banking administration required that regionally-owned banks be given emergency access to funds that could not reasonably be extended to banks owned by foreign nationals, then discrimination in favor of providing such access only to banks owned by regional nationals might be justified during a transition period in which regional banking stability was to be achieved.

Second, if an RTA were to adopt a common foreign and defense policy, regional discriminations for security reasons would be justified by necessity. For example, service consultants to the common defense establishment might be limited to "regional nationals" for security reasons.

Third, regional preferences established to promote the economic development of impoverished areas or peoples might be justified by necessity. Therefore, certain service industry sectors or contract opportunities in designated impoverished regions might be limited to members of a specific regional class.

Fourth, regional discriminations adopted as emergency safeguard measures for reasons set forth in the EU Services Code proposal, such as the prevention of immediate and severe economic dislocations or the resolution of a balance of payments crisis, might be justified by necessity. Also, RTA discriminations necessary to remedy abuses of dominant position may be justifiable.

Derogations from the National Treatment principle will, virtually by definition, operate in favor of RTA-based enterprises and give them some measure of comparative advantage vis-a-vis non-RTA-based enterprises. With this in mind, it is important and difficult to consider a basis for distinguishing RTA measures which have as their motive a successful completion of the internal market and those which are intended as protectionist. There may be a fine line between measures which legitimately take into account local infrastructure requirements and economic conditions (and which may operate temporarily to facilitate adaptation by locally-based enterprises to a completed internal market), and those measures intended to block foreign enterprises from fair access to the same completed market. Generally speaking, an RTA should be encouraged to use its competition laws to protect local enterprises (and consumers) from abuses of dominant position by foreign enterprises. Competition laws are far preferable to trade laws as a mechanism for protecting local enterprises because competition laws minimize trade distortion by affecting only the oppressive actors. Protectionist trade measures taken in the name of local ownership distort trade and capital flows which should otherwise produce the optimum allocation of global resources. The protection of RTA enterprises from foreign competition should not as a general proposition be a legitimate goal of an RTA waiver. On the other hand, measures which may have as their effect the maintenance of a "level playing field" for an interim period may be tolerated, if not encouraged. With this fine distinction in mind, the proposed RTA waiver formula provides that measures with the predominant purpose of protecting local enterprises will be presumed to be unnecessary. This brief formula will, however, require additional elaboration, perhaps aided by analogy to other trade laws intended to maintain level playing fields, e.g., anti-dumping and subsidy laws. Anti-dumping laws which distinguish "fair" and "unfair" foreign trade necessarily have a protectionist impact vis-a-vis foreign traders seeking to elude the basic laws of competition. In the anti-dumping area, there is a fine line between fair aggressive competition and unfair below market value cut-throat competition. With respect to RTA activities permitted by the proposed waiver, necessity relating to positive attempts at market unification, as opposed to "mere expediency" at the expense of foreign competition, should guide decision-makers in their evaluation of legitimacy.

D. The EC as a Model

In the balance of this article, discussion will largely focus on the policies of the European Union. The EU is by far the most successful model of large-scale regional economic integration. It has developed refined decision-making institutions at the legislative, executive, adjudicatory and administrative levels, developed a coordinated external trade policy, and presented proposals with respect to the post-Uruguay Round treatment of RTAs within the GATT framework. Moreover, there is every indication that the size and influence of the EU will continue to expand. Already far more influential in the sphere of trade policy than its twelve member countries would suggest (by virtue, inter alia, of the EFTA and Lome arrangements), the EU figures prominently in the economic plans of the emerging Eastern European economies.

E. Telecommunications as a Case

In addition to narrowing the scope of the following discussion to the EU, this article will focus on efforts within the GATT to liberalize the international telecommunications trade and the relationship between that process, the EU telecommunications liberalization process and non-EU telecommunications sectors. International trade in telecommunications is a useful analytical tool because it involves: (a) trade in both goods and services; (b) an area historically subject to intense government regulation (including outright government ownership); (c) substantial issues of public policy (involving, e.g., employment and security); (d) disparity between developed and developing countries; and (e) an area in which the EU has been implementing significant measures to liberalize its internal market.

VI. The Telecommunications Issues

The establishment of a readily accessible and efficient global telecommunications network would generate obvious benefits for global economic efficiency as well as the distribution (and presumably the creation) of knowledge. There can be little doubt that each country in the global community will be better off if its scientists and engineers have ready access to databases in other countries and the capacity to exchange information freely with each other; that global business will be more efficient if enterprises are able to transmit and receive information concerning production and shipping schedules, inventory levels, sources of supply and pricing more rapidly; and that individuals will be more knowledgeable, and perhaps better able to maintain more lasting interpersonal relations, if all are enabled to communicate more freely. A multitude of blessings seem to be inherent in an open and efficient global telecommunications network.

Without doubt, not everyone perceives the global network as an unalloyed good and, of course, much depends on who controls the network and how it is used. Certainly there is a "dark side," in which the efficient telecommunications network becomes the most important tool of "Big Brother." The potential for mischief points to certain areas where regulation, even in a relatively harmonious world, is to be expected. Individuals will want to ensure that they are not listened to by uninvited intruders (be they governmental or otherwise), businesses will wish to avoid the misappropriation of their proprietary knowledge, and, of course, all but a few will wish to avoid the concentration of power to control the global network in the hands of a dominant provider.

While some regulation will always be required, the telecommunications sector is one in which the benefits of ultimate global liberalization seem indisputable. The issue is not whether this liberalization is ultimately desirable from a public welfare standpoint, but how it can be achieved within a framework of entrenched interests which include not only government owners, but vast numbers of employees who may be dependent on certain features of the existing regimes. This is certainly true in the EU, where the vast majority of telecommunications providers are government-owned monopolies—PTTs and RTTs, also referred to as telecommunications administrations ("TAs")—which represent one of the largest single pools of employment in the Union.

A. Basic Structure in the EC

A few basic observations about the structure of the telecommunications industry in the EU are necessary for an understanding of its relationship to the international trade regulatory scheme. The telecommunications market is divided between goods and services. Goods include infrastructure equipment such as telephone cables and switching equipment, user equipment such as terminals (e.g., telephones) and processing equipment (e.g., computers) which is used both by service providers and users. Services are divided into two primary categories: basic services and value-added services ("VAS"). Although the dividing line is not universally agreed upon, it is understood that basic services have at their core voice telephony. Basic service providers argue that rudimentary additional services such as voice mail should be included within the definition of basic services. Value-added services include everything that is not part of basic service, such as data processing, electronic banking, electronic shopping, and the furnishing of databases.

In the EU until recently, the telecommunications market was virtually the exclusive province of government-owned monopolies. The TAs owned the infrastructure equipment and had a monopoly on the provision of basic services, the supply of terminal equipment and terms of access to third-party VAS providers. In recent years the market has been significantly liberalized. The U.K. government privatized its TA (while continuing to allow it part of a basic services monopoly), and there has been some additional movement toward privatization. In 1988, the Commission issued a Directive aimed at fully opening the terminal equipment market to competition, depriving TAs of an important, long-standing equipment monopoly. The Commission has decreed that TA monopolies may extend only to voice telephony and that third-party providers must be given equitable access to the TA networks. The Commission has decreed that TA equipment procurement must be open to suppliers throughout the Union. At the suggestion of the Commission, the European Technical Standards Institute ("ETSI") was established (with membership open to members of a variety of European organizations) to develop common technical standards for the Union network. These measures, some of which have not been received enthusiastically by the Member States, have as their end the promotion of a more open and efficient EU telecommunications network.

The Commission's efforts to liberalize the telecommunications market began with a few general references in the White Paper on Completion of the Internal Market in 1992, which were elaborated upon in great length in its Green Paper on Completion of the Telecommunications Sector. The Commission seems determined to create a telecommunications infrastructure in the Union which will enhance the entire process of integration.

B. Basic Structure in the GATT

The telecommunications sector is a peculiar creature in the existing GATT framework. Moving into the Uruguay Round, trade in services has not been covered by the GATT. The GATT has therefore not concerned itself with whether foreign service providers (either basic or value-added) have access on any set of terms to the EU telecommunications market. Since the preponderance of EU telecommunications equipment purchases are made by government-owned monopolies, such purchases would theoretically be covered by the GATT Government Procurement Code. However, the Government Procurement Code does not cover sectors in countries which have not chosen to list them on an annex, and up until a recent listing by Japan, no country had listed its telecommunications sector in the annex, so that the EU TAs have not been subject to GATT government procurement regulation. In theory, the promulgation of technical standards is governed by the GATT Technical Standards Code. However, while under that Code the EU (as a "central government") as well as "regional bodies" within the EU (with respect to technical standards) are covered, so- called "non-governmental" bodies are not directly subject to the Code (although the Code parties are to take reasonable measures to assure the compliance of non-governmental parties).[19] It is likely, though the matter is not free from doubt, that the EU's new technical standards body, ETSI, will be considered a non-governmental body and therefore only indirectly subject to the Technical Standards Code. Moreover, as currently drafted the Technical Standards Code refers to standards as they affect imported "products," so that technical standards with respect to the provision of telecommunications services are not covered. In sum, while isolated pockets of EU telecommunications activities have been subject to the GATT regulatory scheme prior to the Uruguay Round (the recent coverage of the terminal equipment market stands out), for most intents the Uruguay Round effectively represents the potential commencement of GATT coverage of the telecommunications sector.

---

[19] Pursuant to Article 4.1 of the Code:

Parties shall take such reasonable measures as are available to them to ensure that non-governmental bodies within their territories comply with the provisions of Article 2 [covering technical standards]. . . In addition, Parties shall not take measures which have the effect of, directly or indirectly, requiring or encouraging such non-governmental bodies to act in a manner inconsistent with any of the provisions of Article 2.

C. Equipment in the GATT

Telecommunications equipment constitutes goods which have historically been covered by the GATT and therefore are not a "new area" in the Uruguay Round. All GATT Contracting Parties, the EU included, are required to adhere to the fundamental GATT principles in the regulation of equipment imports. No country or region should receive treatment more favorable than any other country or region, except that in consequence of article XXIV, the EU countries may apply lower tariffs on imports of telecommunications equipment from Member State territories than they apply to equipment imported from outside the Union. An equipment producer located within the EU, therefore, may have a cost advantage over a producer located outside the EU on the basis of a GATT-authorized measure to promote regional integration. As discussed previously, whether this preferential tariff arrangement creates global economic welfare benefits is an open question, but these relatively benign preferences have not to date appeared to do any great harm, and the elimination of regional arrangement tariff preferences is not an issue which will be addressed in this article.

A recently adopted EU government procurement Directive permits discrimination in favor of Union-based telecommunications equipment suppliers. This type of discrimination is clearly prohibited by the GATT Government Procurement Code, except that the telecommunications sector is currently not covered by the Code. A Commission representative has publicly stated that the local content discriminations are on the bargaining table at the Uruguay Round negotiations and are part of a "negotiating position."[20] Thus, while government procurement-related local content discrimination is anathema to free trade (and the National Treatment principle), the Commission is within its GATT rights in maintaining such discrimination until the Procurement Code is amended, while recognizing the desirability of negotiating away this discrimination in the Uruguay Round. The EU's local content discrimination is based not on a special exemption for RTAs, but on a well-recognized gap in GATT coverage which the Uruguay Round will presumably eliminate. The equipment procurement issue is therefore not of special interest.

D. Telecommunications Services Liberalization in the EC

The EU is taking steps to ensure that, insofar as the internal market is concerned, there are a minimum of barriers to the cross-border provision of telecommunications services through, inter alia, the adoption and implementation of the "Council Directive on the Establishment of the Internal Market for Telecommunications Services through the Implementation of the Open Network Provision ("ONP")."[21] The ONP Directive

---

[20] Statement by Anna Snow of the EC Commission Delegation to the United States at Deloitte & Touche/Admerca Conference in Washington, D.C. (Feb. 28, 1990), *reported in 'Local Content' Restrictions Subject to GATT Discussion, Official Says*, 56 TELECOMM. REP. (BRP) (No. 9) 22 (Mar. 5, 1990).

[21] *Council Directive on the Establishment of the Internal Market for Telecommunications Services through the Implementation of the Open Network Provision (ONP),* 33 O.J. Eur. Comm. (No. L 192) 1 (1990) [hereinafter *ONP Directive*].

envisages the adoption of harmonized rate structures, usage conditions and technical standards on the Union level. Its purpose is to create conditions of "open and efficient" access to the public telecommunications network[22] based on conditions guaranteeing equal and nondiscriminatory access, transparency and objectivity. Deviations from these conditions will be permitted only for the essential requirements of security of network operations, maintenance of network integrity, interoperability of services and protection of data. With the implementation of the ONP Directive, value-added telecommunications service providers will be assured of equivalent treatment in each of the Member States on conditions designed to promote the most efficient exchange of data between the Member States.

The ONP Directive is expressly addressed to affording the benefits of the completed internal market to enterprises established within the Union, and explicitly provides that the extension to third-country providers of the benefits of the internal market will be dependent on reciprocal market opening. The Directive states a preference for achieving external market opening through multilateral negotiations in the GATT.

The potential adverse impact of the ONP Directive on non-EU countries largely depends, first, on the extent to which the Union acts to deprive third-country service suppliers of equivalent access to the Union telecommunications network. It is, of course, one thing for the Union to reserve the power to discriminate in favor of locally-established enterprises and another thing entirely for the Union to use that power. For example, does the Union actually intend to propose two telecommunications rate structures—one applicable to local service enterprises and another applicable to non-Union service enterprises? To date, there is no indication that such a bifurcated approach might be taken. Second, the impact of the Directive will also largely depend on whether the Union adopts supplemental regulations defining what it considers to be an enterprise "established in the Union." It is the present perception of the Commission and industry observers that the opening by a foreign telecommunications enterprise of an office within the territory of the Union is adequate to constitute "establishment" for purposes of the telecommunications sector. If this is true and remains so, then the larger players in the telecommunications services sector will not be affected by discrimination against non-Union providers because large players will not find it burdensome to establish a presence in the Union. The impact of a de facto establishment requirement on smaller service suppliers would, of course, be more significant.

The area of potential Union discrimination which is most troubling to third-country service (as well as equipment) providers appears to involve Union standards-setting activities. Outsiders are concerned that the Union will have the capacity through the exercise of seemingly "objective" and "scientific" powers to alter the balance of economic power in favor of local/regional industry, at least for a period of time long enough to preclude these external suppliers from taking advantage of current market leadership. By defining technical interface standards which are not those currently used

---

[22] *Id.* at Art. 1.

by industry leaders—who are, perhaps coincidentally, not EU-based—the Commission could force major changes to be implemented in the equipment and software of foreign suppliers which may take years to accomplish. Some concern has been expressed that EU-based companies will be given more immediate access to these standards so that they would have an advantage in implementation. Even if this proves false, merely placing competing companies at the same starting line would represent a substantial gain for the EU telecommunications industry because of the lead currently held by its U.S.- and Japan-based competition. Moreover, if the standards adopted in the EU are not generally accepted international standards, foreign equipment and service providers will lose some of their economy of scale advantage.

A major segment of the U.S. telecommunications industry contends that "market-driven" standards-setting is preferable to government (or government-directed) standards-setting. According to this view, service providers should adopt the standards set by market-leading providers because the development of workable standards has already been accomplished. This approach would obviously favor current industry-dominant participants, who would have both a lead in the provision of network services (as well as equipment) and perhaps be in a position to collect royalties from users of the standards. The Commission may well take a dim view of the "market-driven" approach to standards-setting, considering that it might be more appropriately referred to as a "dominant actors" approach.[23]

E. U.S. and EC Telecommunications Annex Proposals

The draft Telecommunications Annex provisions to the GATT Services Code proposals of both the United States and the EU do not materially alter the general Services Code proposals. The Annexes state in greater detail the kinds of entities which will be considered "public" (e.g., including private providers acting as common carriers) and indicate that terms of access to the services of these public entities will be nondiscriminatory. The definition of "reasonable access" in telecommunications terms is specified: the availability of leased lines at cost-based, flat rate prices. There is the widely anticipated provision in each Annex permitting parties to reserve the "basic services" sectors to public entities (including chartered monopolies), provided that these basic services are made available in a nondiscriminatory manner. With respect to standards, the U.S. Annex proposal states that no party shall require a customer to "use any mandatory or designated standards or protocols, except as such standards and protocols establish interfaces to public, switched telecommunications transport networks, or as may be required to prevent technical harm to a public telecommunications transport network." The U.S. proposal thus envisages that each party will be permitted to adopt its own protocols for access to its public "basic services" transmission network, but not to adopt standards for services unrelated to transmission on the public

---

[23] Commission officials note that standards-setting in the U.S. telecommunications industry has historically been accompanied by a few dominant industry enterprises.

network. The EU Annex provides that standards may be adopted to ensure "network security" and "network integrity, particularly with regard to the normal interworking of all network components and network termination points." Both of these proposals regarding the adoption of telecommunications standards should be read in light of the more general provisos in the U.S. and EU services code proposals that standards or protocols may not be adopted as a disguised restraint on trade.

F. Evaluating Commission Action under the EC's RTA Waiver Standard and the "Necessary" Formula

This article has analyzed the EU's proposed standard for evaluating whether an RTA will be justified in witholding the benefits of internal market liberalization from non-RTA parties and suggested that the formula is unworkable (and unwise). It may now be illustrative to consider how the EU's waiver formula might work with regard to hypothetical telecommunications sector regulation.

Assume, hypothetically, that in the Services Code telecommunications annex each party agrees to provide non-discriminatory access (which precludes the charging of discriminatory rates) for the basic telecommunications transport services of public network operators. Assume that this agreement does not extend to providing non-discriminatory access to the transmission services of public cellular telephone networks, which prior to the adoption of the Code are regulated within the EU on a Member State to Member State basis. Assume, further, that existing Member State public cellular system regulation generally permits the adoption of rate structures which discriminate between enterprises based in the regulating Member State and enterprises not based within that Member State (including EU-based enterprises not based within the regulating Member State). Consider that following the adoption of the Services Code, the EU Commission mandates that all public cellular transmission system operators provide non-discriminatory access to their basic transmission services; but it extends this mandate only to benefit system users that are based in Member States. Public cellular network operators in the EU, which prior to the adoption of the new regulations charged system users different rates depending on whether they were intra-State or external enterprises, adjust their rate structures to apply uniformly within the Union (using the old intra-Member rates), leaving the "old" external rates applicable to non-EU Member State enterprises.

Analyzed under the EU waiver formula, the EU cellular telephone regulations would presumably give rise to a higher degree of liberalization in the Union than was existing prior to their adoption because more competitive conditions in the Union are created, at least as regards EU Member State enterprises. The EU's higher degree of liberalization test does not specify that improvements in the Union may not adversely impact enterprises based outside the Union. The resulting "regime" does not appear to be more restrictive "on the whole" than the Code commitments of each individual Member State, because the Member States did not specifically undertake to establish

National Treatment with respect to public cellular telecommunications transport services in their schedules of commitments and, moreover, appear not to have made conditions worse for non-Member State enterprises which remain subject to a previously existing two-tier structure. The above described hypothetical Union measures therefore appear to be permitted by the EU's proposed RTA waiver.

Assume, alternatively, that there are no common technical standards for the telecommunications industry in the EU. Assume also that each Member State of the EU agrees in its schedule to the Services Code that its adoption of technical standards will be based on objective scientific criteria, using international standards where reasonably appropriate. Following the adoption of the Code, at the instigation of the Commission, the European Technical Standards Institute adopts telecommunications interface standards applicable to all public telecommunications network providers in the Union. Assume that in doing so it rejects standards widely adopted in the United States and Japan (and which may generally be considered to be international standards) on the grounds that a majority of Union-based service providers deemed these standards incompatible with European scientific objectives in the development of an integrated Union network. In response to objections from the U.S. and Japanese governments, the Commission concedes that the international standards would have been adequate, but were nevertheless not wholly consistent with with its plans for the integration of the Union telecommunications industry. As a result of the adoption of the new standards, U.S. and Japanese network service providers must reprogram all telecommunications-related software to enable it to interconnect with the EU public network. Have the Union and its Member States derogated from their commitments under the Services Code?

The action instigated or taken by the Commission appears to be "liberalizing" from the Commission's standpoint, since prior to the adoption of new standards there were no standards generally applicable throughout the Union. Intra-Union access to the telecommunications services network is enhanced for EU enterprises which have not developed their own proprietary standards. Each Member State will contend that its actions in adopting the new EU standards are consistent with its Code obligation to adopt international standards where reasonably appropriate and to avoid the unjustifiable adoption of standards as a disguised barrier to trade in services. There is no readily apparent yardstick for determining whether the resulting "regime" is more or less restrictive "on the whole" than if each Member State either pursued its own standards-setting or adopted alternatively available international standards. Pan-EU standards would in most instances appear to be less restrictive than the adoption of separate standards by each member country, and it might be difficult to demonstrate that each Member State should have adopted a particular international standard. The "on the whole" test may therefore provide little guidance in this context. Ultimately, it appears that the RTA waiver formula proposed by the EU will have little to do with determining whether pan-EU standards are found to be compatible with the obligations of the EU or its Member States under the Services Code. That decision will more likely be based on a determination of whether the EU or its Member States have adopted standards as a disguised barrier to trade in the context of the substantive rules of the Code.

G. Application of New Formula to the Telecommunications Sector

From the standpoint of non-Member State service providers, the EU's most important regulatory activities will be undertaken pursuant to the ONP Directive. On its face, the ONP Directive is inconsistent with the National Treatment requirement because the benefits of the Directive are expressly addressed to service providers established within the Member States. If the Council and Commission did not contemplate that the EU Member States would pursue policies which discriminated in favor of local service providers, they could as easily have drafted the ONP Directive to address its benefits to services enterprises without qualification. Since the Union can readily extend the benefits of the ONP Directive to enterprises established within specific trading partners, the reservation of the right to discriminate in the ONP Directive may be perceived by the EU as a bargaining chip in the Uruguay Round negotiations, or as a long-term discrimination tradeable in reciprocity negotiations. It is assumed by both the United States and the EU that the GATT Services Code will not be adhered to by all GATT members, so the retention by the EU of its discriminatory legislation will not be contrary to its GATT obligations and may, after a Services Code is agreed upon, be amended to reflect its accommodation to parties to the Code. Only by maintenance of its discriminatory characteristics vis-a-vis parties to a GATT Services Code would such EU legislation be subject to evaluation under the test of necessity.

The two hypothetical cases of prospective EU discrimination against non-Member State service providers that were previously considered under the EU's proposed waiver formula might now be examined under the test of necessity.

The adoption by the EU and its Member States of a cellular telephone transmission regulatory structure which maintains rate discrimination as between Member States and third-country providers would not easily be justified as necessary to the formation or maintenance of the EU. A contention that discriminatory rates based on the nationality of service providers (or the country of origin of services) are necessary to the financial viability of the completed internal cellular network would be easily countered by the observation that rates necessary to establish or maintain the network could just as easily be spread over all users of the system regardless of national origin. If the Union could demonstrate that certain costs were incurred only in the provision of access to users based outside the Union, a surcharge might be justified, but the likelihood of such a cost differential appears remote. Furthermore, discriminatory access charges based on the nationality of the service provider (or country of origin) are unlikely to be supportable for reasons relating to establishing political institutions, maintaining regional security, providing assistance to impoverished regions or as a safeguard measure.

Evaluation of the adoption of "discriminatory" intra-EU telecommunications standards is likely to be more problematic. In the first place, the EU certainly has the inherent right to adopt (or cause the adoption of) telecommunications standards in order to assure the public welfare and protect regional security interests. The absence of established standards might seriously interfere with the provision of vital government services, in addition to harming the less compelling interests of the private sector. The more difficult question is whether, and to what extent, the Commission should be entitled to ignore existing "market-driven" standards and adopt pan-EU standards developed by ETSI. To some extent, resolution of this issue may depend on the attitude of foreign market players. Currently, many telecommunications network standards are owned by private sector entities. Refusal by these entities to make their standards available to the public at a nominal price might in itself justify the Union in adopting regionally developed standards, because the Union should be under no obligation to adopt regulations which would require local enterprises to make significant payments to private business enterprises, either local or foreign.

Suppose, however, that foreign private industry offered to make its proprietary standards publicly available at nominal cost. If ETSI then elected to adopt pan-EU standards which were not justifiable as a technical advancement over standards widely adopted and available in the private market, the adoption of such standards would not be "necessary" and might well represent a disguised barrier to the market advantages of foreign service providers.

The adoption of technical standards by the EU is likely to become mired in controversy over the "scientific" merits of ETSI technical advances, and even the most sophisticated GATT panel might well have trouble sorting fact from fiction. In these circumstances, the scales of trade justice would be forced to tip either in favor of the inherent right of government to regulate or the promotion of open markets. The right of government to regulate is likely to have the advantage in such a balancing test, if for no other reason than the fact that the balancing test would ultimately be performed by government regulators.

Adopting "necessity" as the test for an RTA waiver from the National Treatment principle and other GATT rules will not provide a ready answer for all questions of whether or not a derogation is appropriate. In the limited context of considering two prospective EU derogations, one set of facts may seem to present a "bright line" answer and the other a close question. Because the political nature of the GATT favors compromise, close questions are likely to be resolved in favor of taking no action—i.e., in permitting derogation to take place. A formula based on a flexible concept like "necessity" will not be satisfactory to parties looking for clear-cut answers. On the other hand, analyzing barriers to trade in services is no simple matter, and a seemingly simple objective test of permissible RTA derogations that places no meaningful limitation on discriminatory regulations and is unworkable in practice will not promote peaceful coexistence between the GATT and RTAs. A subjective test, allowing GATT parties to weigh competing interests, is most appropriate in these circumstances. What must be clear, however, is that RTA derogations from the rules generally applicable in the GATT should be limited to those which are indispensable to the formation or maintenance of an RTA, and that are, to the maximum extent feasible, limited in duration. A more liberal standard would threaten to undermine the foundation of the GATT.

H. Conclusion

Political leaders appear to be wedded to the concept of regional economic integration. Agreements to lower regional trade barriers provide an easy and highly visible answer to economic problems. Regional arrangements such as the EU provide political and military stability which may outweigh all but the most severely adverse economic effects they create for non-RTA members. Nevertheless, while such arrangements may accelerate development on a regional basis, yield political benefits and provide models for future global economic institutions, they also pose risks to the liberal global trading system.

RTA discriminations in new areas such as services will create effects which are presently incapable of measurement. As such discriminations will be continuing measures based on the nationality of service providers as opposed to one-time border measures, their effect is likely to be greater than that of border measures (e.g., tariffs). Such measures should be limited to the extent feasible in order to prevent the global trading system from reverting to a reliance on bilateral reciprocity determinations. Narrow reciprocity as a basis for trade liberalization is inimical to the most fundamental principles of the GATT, such as Most Favored Nation and National Treatment, which appear to have played a substantial role in the expansion of world trade in the late twentieth century.

Liberalization of trade within regional groups without extending the benefits of this activity to the global trading system as a whole would reflect a movement toward isolationism and protectionism—both of which tendencies have had ill effect when practiced on a national level. Regional liberalization as a transition to global liberalization may produce certain economic benefits and may aid in the development of valuable "prototype" trading systems. Regional development, particularly in the industrialized countries, must not be allowed to become a substitute for global development. It is in the enlightened self-interest of the industrialized countries to aggressively promote economic development throughout the world. Regional systems narrowly promoting local interests should not become substitutes for national policies of protectionism. Regional preferences in "new areas" of trade regulation should be adopted and implemented with the greatest restraint.

Chapter 10

Judicial Remedies

I. Introduction[1]

The institutional mandate of the European Court of Justice (ECJ) is to interpret and apply the Treaties of the European Communities for the purpose of ensuring that the Member States, the Council of the European Communities (Council), the Commission of the European Communities (Commission) and the European Parliament act in conformity with European Community (EC) law. The ECJ also must ensure that Member States comply with the provisions of Council regulations and implement Council Directives in a timely and proper manner. The ECJ has not been accorded policy-making powers under the Treaties, as the responsibilities for proposing and adopting Community legislation is reserved for the Commission and Council respectively.[2] For an example, see the ECJ's jurisprudence in the area of EEC Treaty articles 30-36. The ECJ has insisted that article 36 must be interpreted strictly and does not extend to justifications not mentioned specifically in its language.[3]

II. Background to the Community System of Judicial Review[4]

The hierarchy of norms within the European Union is typical of a nonunitary system. The Higher Law of the Union is, of course, the Treaty itself. Neither Union organs nor the Member States may violate the Treaty in their legislative and administrative actions. In addition, Member States may not violate Union regulations, directives, and decisions. Not surprisingly, then, the Union features a double-limbed system of judicial review, operating on two levels. Two sets of legislative acts and administrative

---

1 Matthew L. Schemmel and Bas de Regt, *The European Court of Justice and the Environmental Protection Policy of the European Community*, 17 B.C. Int'l & Comp. L. Rev. 53-58 (1994). © 1994 Matthew L. Schemmel and Bas de Regt. Reprinted by permission.

2 EEC TREATY Art. 189. Article 189 states: "[i]n order to carry out their task the Council and the Commission shall, in accordance with the provisions of this treaty, make regulations, issue directives, take decisions, make recommendations or deliver opinions."

3 Case 7/68, *Commission v. Italy*, 1968 E.C.R. 423.

4 Joseph H.H. Weiler, *The Transformation of Europe*, 100 Yale L.J. 2419-2422 (1991). © 1991 Joseph H.H. Weiler. Reprinted by permission.

measures are subject to judicial review: (1) the measures of the Union itself (principally acts of the Council of Ministers, Commission, and the European Parliament), which are reviewable for their conformity with the Treaties; and (2) the acts of the Member States, which are reviewable for their conformity with Union law and policy, including the above-mentioned secondary legislation.

A. Judicial Review at the Community Level

Either the Commission or an individual Member State may, in accordance with Articles 169-72 of the EEC Treaty, bring an action against a Member State for failure to fulfill its obligations under the Treaty. Generally, this failure takes the form either of inaction in implementing a Union obligation or enactment of a national measure contrary to Union obligations. The existence of a mandatory and exclusive forum for adjudication of these types of disputes sets the Union apart from many international organizations.

The role of the Commission is even more special. As one commentator noted, "[u]nder traditional international law the enforcement of treaty obligations is a matter to be settled amongst the Contracting Parties themselves. Article 169, in contrast, enables an independent Union body, the Commission, to invoke the compulsory jurisdiction of the European Court against a defaulting Member State."[5]

At the same time, the "intergovernmental" character of this procedure and the consequent limitations on its efficacy are clear. Four weaknesses are particularly glaring:

(1) the procedure is political in nature; the Commission (appropriately) may have nonlegal reasons not to initiate a prosecution;

(2) a centralized agency with limited human resources is unable adequately to identify, process, and monitor all possible Member State violations and infringements;

(3) Article 169 may be inappropriate to apply to small violations; even if small violations are properly identified, dedicating Commission resources to infringements that do not raise an important principle or create a major economic impact is wasteful; and finally, and most importantly,

(4) no real enforcement exists; proceedings conclude with a "declaratory" judgment of the European Court without enforcement sanctions.

B. Judicial Review at the Member State Level

The weaknesses of Articles 169-172 are remedied to an extent by judicial review within the judicial systems of the Member States in collaboration with the European Court of Justice. Article 177 provides, inter alia, that when a question concerning the interpretation of the Treaty is raised before a national court, the court may suspend the

[5] Evans, *The Enforcement Procedure of Article 169 EEC: Commission Discretion*, 4 Eur. L. Rev. 442, at 443 (1979).

national proceedings and request a preliminary ruling from the European Court of Justice in Luxembourg on the correct interpretation of the Treaty. If the national court is the court of last resort, then it must request a European Court ruling. Once this ruling is made, it is remitted back to the national court which gives, on the basis of the ruling, the opinion in the case before it. The national courts and the European Court are thus integrated into a unitary system of judicial review.

The European Court and national courts have made good use of this procedure. On its face the purpose of Article 177 is simply to ensure uniform interpretation of Union law throughout the Member States. That, apparently, is how the framers of the Treaty understood it. However, very often the factual situation in which Article 177 comes into play involves an individual litigant pleading in a national court that a rule, measure, or national practice should not be applied because it violates the Union obligations of the Member State. In this manner the attempts of Member States to practice selective Union membership by disregarding their obligations have become regularly adjudicated before their own national courts. On submission of the case, the European Court has rendered its interpretation of Union law within the factual context of the case before it. Theoretically, the European Court may not itself rule on the application of Union law. But, as one scholar notes:

> [I]t is no secret . . . that in practice, when making preliminary rulings, the Court has often transgressed the theoretical border line. . . . [I]t provides the national judge with an answer in which questions of law and of fact are sufficiently interwoven as to leave the national judge with only little discretion and flexibility in making his final decision.[6]

The fact that the national court renders the final judgment is crucial to the procedure. The binding effect and enforcement value of such a decision, coming from a Member State's own court, may be contrasted with a similar decision handed down in declaratory fashion by the European Court under the 169 procedure. A national court opinion takes care of the most dramatic weakness of the Article 169 procedure: the ability of a Member State, in extremis, to disregard the strictures of the European Court. Under the Article 177 procedure this disregard is impossible. A state, in our Western democracies, cannot disobey its own courts.

The other weaknesses of the 169 procedure are also remedied to some extent: individual litigants are usually not politically motivated in bringing their actions; small as well as big violations are adjudicated; and, in terms of monitoring, the Union citizen becomes, willy-nilly, a decentralized agent for monitoring compliance by Member States with their Treaty obligations. The Article 177 system is not complete, however [as the following discussion will illustrate]. Not all violations come before national courts and the European Court of Justice; and Member States may, and often have, utilized the delays of the systems to defer ruling.

---

6 Ramussen, *Why is Article 173 Interpreted Against Private Plaintiffs?*, 5 Eur. L. Rev. 112, at 125 (1980).

On the other hand, the overall system effect of the judicial remedies cannot be denied. The combination of the "constitutionalization" and the system of judicial remedies to a large extent nationalized Union obligations and introduced on the Union level the habit of obedience and the respect for the rule of law which traditionally is less associated with international obligations than national ones.

It is at this juncture that one may speculate about the most profound difference between the Union legal order and international law generally. The combined effect of consti- utionalization and the evolution of the system of remedies results, in my view, in the notion (and doctrinal apparatus) of exclusive state responsibility with its concomitant principles of reciprocity and countermeasures. The Union legal order, on this view, is a truly self-contained legal regime with no recourse to the mechanism of state responsibility, at least as traditionally understood, and therefore to reciprocity and countermeasures, even in the face of actual or potential failure. Without these features, so central to the classic international legal order, the Union truly becomes something "new."

At the end of the day, the debate about the theoretical difference between international law and Union law may have the relevance of some long-lasting theological disputes—i.e. none at all. Whatever the differences in theory, there can be no argument that the Union legal order as it emerged from the Foundational Period appeared in its operation much closer to a working constitutional order, a fact which, as will shortly emerge, had a fundamental impact on the way in which it was treated by its Member States.

III. Federalism, Courts and Legal Systems: The Emerging Constitution of the European Community[7]

The European Community is not a federation, though it may one day become one. It nevertheless possesses a number of distinctly federal elements, a fact which had led writers to coin the neologism "supranational" to describe it. The United States and Canada, both mature federations, will be used as a "control group" to provide an example of what true federalism requires. By concentrating on these features (clearly the most interesting) the impression might be given that the European Community is more developed, and more nearly federal, than is the case. This is particularly so in view of the fact that it is precisely those parts of the Community constitution which are concerned with the legal and judicial system that are most federal; the parts concerned with the political system, on the other hand, are still firmly rooted in the pre-federal milieu of inter-governmental diplomatic co-operation. Thus, the main Community legislature (the Council) is not elected by the people of the Community: its members are mere delegates of the Member States and they vote on the instructions of their gov-

[7] Trevor C. Hartley, *Federalism, Courts and Legal Systems: The Emerging Constitution of the European Community*, 34 Am. J. Comp. L. 229-47 (1986). © 1986 Trevor C. Hartley. Reprinted by permission.

ernments. (The European Parliament is directly elected by the people of the Community, but it has no legislative power, though it does have significant powers over the Community budget.) Moreover, though the Treaties envisage qualified majority voting for the exercise of many of the Council's powers, a rule of unanimity prevails in most situations in practice. Secondly, the legislative powers of the Council are insufficient by federal standards. For instance, defense, foreign policy (except as regards international trade), monetary policy, citizenship and immigration into the Community (though not intra-Community immigration) are wholly or mainly outside the competence of the Community legislature. Thirdly, the tax powers of the Community are insufficient for its purposes. Fourthly, the Community Executive (the Commission) is not fully responsible to the elected representatives of the people (the European Parliament). These factors (which have been discussed elsewhere) are in themselves sufficient to prevent the Community from being a federation. However, when one looks at the judicial and legal aspects of the Community, a different picture emerges.

What are the essential features of a federation, as far as the courts and the legal system are concerned? First, obviously, there must be a federal constitution which delimits the respective spheres of the federation and the units (states, provinces, etc.). Secondly, there must be a federal supreme court which has jurisdiction to give authoritative rulings on the interpretation of the constitution; there may also be other federal courts. Thirdly, the federation must have power to enact legislation within its proper sphere and this must be supreme over state law and effective throughout the federation; it is probably also essential that the federal supreme court should have ultimate power to interpret this legislation and to rule on its validity; there may, or may not, also be a unified system of common law throughout the federation, and there may, or may not, be provision for the constitutional protection of fundamental rights. Fourthly, the federation should have the right to conduct diplomatic relations with foreign states and to conclude treaties with them. Finally, there may be federal rules limiting the jurisdiction of the courts of the states and providing for recognition of their judgments on other states. These are the judicial and legal characteristics of federalism: how far are they possessed by the European Community?

A. The Community Constitution

It goes without saying that a federation must have a constitution which must be in written form. (A largely unwritten constitution of the British type would hardly be feasible outside the very special circumstances of the United Kingdom.) The Constitution of the Community takes the form of a series of international treaties. There is no reason to believe that this form, in itself, disqualifies the Constitutive Treaties from being regarded as a constitution. It is true that they are undoubtedly acts of the Member States, and not an act of the people, as is the Constitution of the United States, but this is not determinative of their status: the Canadian Constitution originated as a series of statutes of another country, the United Kingdom.

The Community Treaties fulfill most of the requirements of the constitution in that they establish the legislative, executive and judicial organs of the Community and grant them their powers. They do not, however, grant any powers to the Member States: it is assumed (quite correctly) that the Member States already have their power from another source. The consequence of this is that all powers not granted to the Community remain with the Member States.

Moreover, it would be a mistake to think that the circumstance in which the Community Constitution was adopted means that sovereignty resides wholly with the Member States: in the *van Gend en Loos* case the European Court held that the institutions of the Community are "endowed with sovereign rights" and that the Member States have "limited their sovereign rights, albeit within limited fields."[8] Thus the European Court has rejected the view that the Treaties simply delegate power to the Community from the Member States: in its view a transfer of sovereignty has taken place within certain fields. This may be an overambitious claim, but it is undoubtedly still the view of the Court.

Another essential requirement for the constitution of a federation is that it should be supreme law and override any law of the states. The Community Treaties contain no such clause and it is far from certain that their framers intended them to be supreme. In spite of this, the European Court has created a supremacy clause by judicial decision: according to the European Court, any provision of Community law, provided it is "directly effective," whether contained in the Treaties or in Community legislation, prevails over any provision of the law of the Member States, including the constitutions of the Member States. In the *Simmenthal* case[9] the European court sought to justify this principle on the ground that "any recognition that national legislative measures which encroach upon the field within which the Community exercises its legislative power or which are otherwise incompatible with the provisions of Community law had any legal effect would amount to a corresponding denial of the effectiveness of obligations undertaken unconditionally and irrevocably by Member States pursuant to the Treaty and would thus imperil the very foundations of the Community." The establishment (and defense) of this principle—which is by no means to the liking of all the Member States—is one of the most important achievements of the European Court.

B. Community Law

A basic requirement of a federation, so basic in fact that it is often overlooked or taken for granted, is that federal law should constitute a separate legal system, separate both from the law of the states and international law. This means, among other things, that it cannot be amended or repealed by any state legislature. In the Community, the European Court has always insisted that Community law constitutes a separate "legal

---

[8] *Van Gend en Loos v. Nederlandse Administratie der Belastingen* (Case No. 26/62), 1963 E. Comm. Ct. J. Rep. 1, 12 (Preliminary Ruling).

[9] *Italian Finance Administration v. Simmenthal* (Case No. 106/77), 1978 E. Comm. Ct. J. Rep. 629, 643 (Preliminary Ruling).

order," distinct from both Member State law and international law. This view has been explicitly accepted by the courts of at least some Member States.[10]

Community law is, therefore, an independent legal system. It is not, however, foreign law in the Member States: it is valid law in the land and it can directly confer rights on private citizens which must be recognized and enforced by the Courts of the Member States. This characteristic of Community law, which applies to both the Treaties and to Community legislation, is largely the result of decisions of the European Court. The only relevant Treaty provision is EEC Article 189, which covers only regulations and statutes that are "directly applicable" in all the Member States. However, the European Court has ruled, in a series of decisions, the Treaty provisions and all forms of Community legislation can give rights directly to the individual without any legislative or executive action by the Member States. Community law will not in all cases have this characteristic of directly effect, and there is a not inconsiderable body of learning devoted to the elucidation of the rules which decide the question, but in practice any provision will be directly effective if it is feasible for it to be applied by the courts without any further enactment. The ultimate authority on the question whether any particular provision is directly effective is, of course, the European Court: the preliminary reference procedure (discussed below) applies also to the question.

C. The Supreme Court of the Community

There is no doubt that a supreme court is essential for any federation in order to settle disputes as to the interpretation of the constitution and the respective powers of the federation and the states. The Community also has a court, the European Court of Justice. How far does it fulfill the requirements of federal supreme court?

Perhaps we should begin by noting that the judges of the European Court hold office for a limited term of only six years and are then subject to re-appointment. Moreover, they are appointed, not by the Community, but by the Governments of the Member States. They do, however, have security of tenure during their six-year period of office and a European Court judge may be removed only if, in the unanimous opinion of the other judges and advocates general, "he no longer fulfills the requisite conditions or meets the obligations arising from his office."[11]

1. Judicial Review of Community Legislation

The European Court is the final authority on the interpretation of the Community Constitution (the Treaties) and Community legislation. It is also the final authority on the validity (constitutionality) of Community legislation. These questions may arise both

---

10 *Internationale Handelsgesellschaft mbH v. Einfuhr-und Vorratsstelle fur Getreide und Futtermittel*, 14 C.M.L.R. 540 (*Bundersverfassungsgericht* 1974): Community law is neither a component part of the national legal system nor international law, but forms an independent system of law flowing from an autonomous legal source.

11 See Art. 6 of the Statute of the Court of Justice of the EEC, (annex to the EEC Treaty, and Art. 6 of the Statute of the Court of Justice of EURATOM.

in proceedings originally begun in the European Court and in proceedings originally begun in the courts of the Member States. There is no right of *appeal* from a Member State court to the European Court on any of the questions; there is only provision for a *reference*. Under this procedure, the initiative lies not with the parties but with the court from which the reference is made: it must certify questions for the European Court on the interpretation of the Treaties or the validity interpretation of Community legislation. Such a reference is obligatory where the case is pending before a court "against whose decisions there is no judicial remedy" under the law of the Member State; in other cases it is optional. When a reference is made, the court will stay the proceedings and send the case to the European Court. The latter will rule on the questions certified, after it has held a hearing, and return the case to the court which made the reference. The case will then continue along its normal course. The courts of the Member State are bound by the European Court ruling.

This procedure is different from an appeal because, first, it can be set in motion only if the Member State court decides to make the reference and, secondly, because the European Court can never decide the *case* but only the *questions* of Community law: the final judgment must always come from the Member State court. This, in turn, gives rise to two dangers: a Member State court may refuse to make a reference when it disagrees with the ruling that it thinks the European Court will make; and it may refuse to follow the European Court's ruling once it has been made. Each of these possibilities has actually occurred: the French *Conseil d'Etat* (the highest administrative court in France) and the *Bundesfinanzhof* (the highest tax court in Germany) have each refused to make a reference in cases in which their own holdings were plainly contrary to the established case-law of the European Court. In another case the French courts refused to follow a ruling of the European Court after they had made a reference to it. Here, the French court asked the European Court to rule on the validity of a Community measure imposing an export tax payable to the French customs. The European Court held that the measure was invalid but, going beyond the questions asked, ruled that money already paid under the tax could not be recovered. The French courts accepted the first part of the ruling but asserted that the European Court had no jurisdiction to rule on the second point. They therefore refused to follow it, and ordered the French customs to repay the money.

In addition to cases where the validity of Community legislation arises incidentally in the course of proceedings in Member State courts or in the European Court, it is also possible for an action to be brought directly and specifically for the annulment of Community legislation or of a Community executive act. The European Court has exclusive jurisdiction in such actions, which may be brought by a Member State, the Commission, the Council or, in certain cases, by a private individual. There is also provision for an action, somewhat akin to mandamus, for obtaining a remedy where the Community has wrongfully refrained from acting.

2. Judicial Review of Member State Legislation

The power of a federal supreme court to review the constitutionality of state legislation is much more crucial from the federal point of view than the power to review federal legislation. It is significant that the Treaties do not directly give the European

Court this power. It does, however, have indirect power to review Member State legislation (as well as executive and judicial acts). The power is indirect because the European Court cannot declare Member State legislation invalid: all it can do is to declare that in enaction or maintaining in force the measure, the Member State has "failed to fulfill an obligation" under the Treaty. This is not quite the same thing as a direct power of judicial review, though it comes very close to it since the offending Member State is obliged by the Treaty to "take the necessary measures to comply with the judgment of the Court of Justice." Actions of this kind are brought against the delinquent Member State, by another Member State, or more usually, by the Commission (the Community Executive). The European Court has original jurisdiction and there is no appeal from its judgment.

The preliminary reference procedures discussed previously provide another, even more indirect, means of ensuring that Member State legislation is in according with Community law. This takes place when it is argued in proceedings in a Member State court that Member State legislation is invalid because it conflicts with Community law. In this situation, the Member State court cannot ask the European Court to rule on the validity of the Member State statute, but it can ask it to interpret the provision of Community law with which it is alleged to conflict and the questions can be framed in such way as to be determinative of the validity of the statute. If the European Court's ruling has the effect of rendering the statute invalid, the Member State court will then declare that it is not to be applied. In some ways this procedure is more effective than that mentioned in the previous paragraph because there is normally no difficulty in ensuring that the judgments of the Member State court are obeyed. It is, however, subject to the general weaknesses of the preliminary reference procedure.

D. The Member State Courts

The Community Treaties say very little about the Member State courts and their powers. As has already been explained, it was through the efforts of the European Court that it became established that Community law is to be applied by the Member State courts and that it overrides any conflicting provision of Member State law. The European Court has been able to lay down these principles by means of its jurisdiction to give preliminary rulings on a reference from a Member State court, a procedure which also enables it to police the activities of the Member State courts. The advantages and weaknesses of this procedure have already been discussed.

Except where they are obliged to make a reference to the European Court, Member State courts are free to interpret Community law for themselves and even to decide on the validity of Community legislation, though they would normally hesitate to declare a Community provision invalid without a reference to the European Court.

Article 211 EEC provides that the Community has full legal capacity in all the Member States, including the capacity to own property and be a party to legal proceedings. Article 183 EEC allows the Member State courts to take jurisdiction in cases to which the Community is a party, except where the European Court would itself have jurisdiction. This means that the Community has no blanket immunity from the jurisdiction of the Member State courts, but any jurisdiction in this regard expressly given to the European Court is exclusive. Since almost all the heads of original jurisdiction of the European Court are concerned with actions by or against the Community, the original jurisdiction of the European Court is in practice exclusive. Such cases include actions against the Commission or Council to annul a Community measure or to obtain a remedy for failure to act, and actions in tort against the Community. The European Court also has exclusive jurisdiction where there is a provision to this effect in a contract to which the Community is a party. It appears to be standard practice for Community contracts to contain a clause giving such jurisdiction to the European Court with regard to disputes arising out of the contract. Since these cases cover almost all the situations in which proceedings are likely to be brought against the Community, the jurisdiction of the Member State courts over the Community is in practice almost non-existent.

In the Community, actions by the Commission against a Member State for an infringement of the Treaties could, for the reasons explained above, be brought only in the European Court. The European Court also has jurisdiction in cases brought on similar grounds by one Member State against another. Since EEC Article 219 prohibits Member States from submitting a dispute concerning the interpretation or application of the Treaty to any method of settlement other than those provided in the Treaty itself, this jurisdiction is exclusive.

E. Community Common Law

The position in the Community regarding Community common law, owing to the fact that the Member States clearly do not share a common legal tradition and in many of them the very idea of common law in the Anglo-American sense is rejected: for them, judicial decisions can never, in theory, constitute a source of law, though knowledge of the latest cases may be important to the practicing lawyer. In view of this, it might be thought surprising that a Community common law exists and, indeed, thrives. It is not of course called this and is disguised, though not very effectively, under the rubric of "general principles of law." The doctrines that have emerged under this head are of great importance to Community law and are entirely due to the creative jurisprudence of the European Court. In developing Community common law, the European Court is in no way bound by the principles applicable in Member State law, though in important cases the European Court will consider the position in the law of each Member State before giving a ruling.

This body of law does not merely fill in the gaps in Community legislation. Whole areas of law, of which tort law is but one example, are entirely based on Community common law. The willingness of the European Court to take on the task of creating a Community common law is obviously of great significance for the future development of the Community, especially in view of the deficiencies in the legislative process in the Community.

F. Fundamental Human Rights and Civil Liberties

The Constitutional protection of fundamental rights, though not essential to federalism—is nevertheless often regarded as desirable. This is not only for reasons which would apply equally well in a unitary state, but also for particularly federal reasons: the political stresses which necessarily result from divided sovereignty are considerably lessened if the powers of the federation and states are limited, not only on the basis of subject matter, but also on the basis of generally-accepted values.

There is no Bill of Rights in the Community Treaties or in any legislative enactment. Nevertheless, the fundamental rights of the Community citizen are protected by the European Court on the basis of the theory of "general principles of law" discussed above. The origins of the development aptly illustrate the inter-relationship between fundamental rights and federalism: the doctrine that fundamental rights are part of Community common law was first enunciated by the European Court in direct response to the evident danger that German courts would not apply Community legislation where it was found to violate the concept of fundamental rights embodied in the German Constitution. It was in an attempt, only partially successful, to head off this threat to the uniformity and supremacy of Community law that the European Court first held that there existed a Community concept of fundamental rights, separate from, but influenced by and, in practice, embracing, the concepts in the constitutions of the Member States.

Under this doctrine the European Court will declare invalid (unconstitutional) any Community legislation or administrative decision that infringes fundamental rights. However, the Community doctrine of fundamental rights applies only to Community institutions. So far the European Court has made no attempt to apply it to the Member States.

G. Treaties with Third Countries

What powers does the Community have to enter into treaties with non-member states and to ensure that they are implemented? This is clearly an important question for determining how far down the road to federalism the Community has advanced.

The Community power is a rather feeble thing. The Commission does not even claim that the Community should have treaty-making power over areas within the internal jurisdiction of the Member States; so no problem of implementation in this respect can arise. All it asks is that it should have external jurisdiction (treaty-making power) which is co-extensive with its internal jurisdiction. The EEC Treaty does not give it even this, though the Euratom Treaty does. However, the European Court has again stepped in and, by a series of decisions of remarkable boldness, has established the doctrine of "parallelism," under which the EEC enjoys implied treaty-making power in all areas where it has internal authority, a power which is normally exclusive of the Member States, at least once the Community has taken action in the area either by adopting internal measures or by entering into a treaty.

The European Court has also extended the doctrine of direct effect to cover treaties with third countries so that they can be self-executing in the same way as in the United States. The European Court applies the doctrine of Community supremacy to them so that, where they are self-executing (directly applicable), they override any inconsistent Member State law or Community law. By a judicial amendment to EEC Article 177, the European Court has ruled that the preliminary-reference procedure applies to them, so that it has the final say (within the Community) as to their interpretation.

However, in spite of this impressive progress (which has not always met with the approval of the Member States), the treaty-making power of the Community still falls short of what one would expect in a federation.

H. Full Faith and Credit

Full faith and credit to judgments exists in the Community, though in a separate instrument from the Community Treaties—the Convention on Jurisdiction and the Enforcement of Judgments in Civil and Commercial Matters.

In the Community the jurisdictional rules for Member State courts are laid down by the Convention. However, these rules do not constitute merely the outer limit of Member State jurisdiction: they constitute (subject to one very important exception mentioned below) the *whole* of it. In other words, the jurisdictional provisions of the Convention are the equivalent of both the constitutionally-imposed minimum contacts doctrine and the state-law rules of jurisdiction, whether they be of common-law origin or contained in a state long-arm statute. The most important rules are set out in Article 1 of the Convention, which states that the courts of the defendant's domicile have general jurisdiction (irrespective of where the cause of action arose) and Article 5, which lays down rules of special jurisdiction analogous to those found in state long-arm statutes. The greater clarity and simplicity that result from this arrangement have already been subject to favorable comment.

If the Community system has certain advantages as regards clarity and simplicity, it is subject to a very considerable defect which might justifiably give rise to charges of juridical chauvinism: the "constitutional" limitations on Member State-court jurisdiction apply only where the defendant is domiciled in another Contracting State. A defendant domiciled outside Europe has no protection under the Convention from exorbitant jurisdiction: in his case, Member State courts may reach out as far as they like to take jurisdiction. Yet the obligation on other Contracting States to recognize and enforce such judgments applies in exactly the same way as in the case of judgments against Contracting-State domiciliaries.

I. Conclusion

Enough has been said to show that, in the limited area under consideration, the European Community has already acquired many of the features one would expect to find in a federation. This is largely due to the efforts of the European Court, which has not hesitated to remodel the law even when this has entailed adopting a solution different from that envisaged in the Treaties. The role played by the European Court in the development of the Community Constitution recalls that of the United States Supreme Court in the days when John Marshall was Chief Justice. The vital difference, however, is that the political foundations of federalism already existed at that time in the United States; in Europe, on the other hand, they have yet to be established.

IV. The Nature Of Articles 169 And 170 EEC[12]

Legal action may be taken against a Member State which fails to fulfil an obligation under the EEC Treaty by the Commission under Article 169[13] and by another Member State under Article 170.[14] A corresponding remedy is provided by Article 141 and 142 EURATOM. The ECSC Treaty deals with Member State violations somewhat differently.

Under both Article 169 and Article 170 EEC the procedure falls into two distinct phases. In a first "administrative" phase, the Commission receives observations on the allegation of non-compliance from the Member State (or in proceedings under Article 170, the Member States) concerned and defines it own position in a reasoned opinion. An attempt is made to reach a satisfactory settlement without resorting to litigation, and in the great majority of cases this has proved possible. Where it is not, an action is brought by the Commission or by the complaining Member State in the European Court. The aim of the action is to obtain a declaration by the European Court that the defendant Member State has failed in a specified manner to fulfil its obligation under specified provisions of Community law. The Member State will be bound under Article 171 EEC to take the necessary measures to comply with the judgment.

The procedure under Article 169 represents a considerable advance on the rules that normally apply in public international law where a state fails to fulfil its obligation under a treaty. In the first place, a right to prosecute infringements is given to the

---

[12] Alan Dashwood and Robin White, *Enforcement Actions Under Articles 169 & 170 EEC*, 14 E.L. Rev. 388-413(1989). Reprinted with permission.

[13] Article 169 EEC provides: If the Commission considers that a Member State has failed to fulfil an obligation under this Treaty, it shall deliver a reasoned opinion on the matter after giving the State concerned the opportunity to submit its observations.

If the State concerned does not comply with the opinion within the period laid down by the Commission, the latter may bring the matter before the Court of Justice.

[14] Article 170 reads:

A Member State which considers that another Member State has failed to fulfill an obligation under the Treaty may bring the matter before the Court of Justice. Before a Member State brings an action against another Member State for an alleged infringement of an obligation under this Treaty, it shall bring the matter before the Commission.

The Commission shall deliver a reasoned opinion after each of the States concerned has been given an opportunity to submit its own case and its observation on the other party's case both orally and in writing.

If the Commission has not delivered an opinion within three months of the date on which the matter was brought before it, the absence of such opinion shall not prevent the matter from being brought before the Court of Justice.

Commission, an institution specifically charged with protecting and promoting the interests of the Community as a whole. This makes it much more likely that effective action will be taken than if the decision depended exclusively on Member States' estimation as to what would best serve their particular interests. Secondly, by virtue of their adherence to the EEC Treaty, Member States accept the compulsory jurisdiction of the European Court. No express declaration of acceptance is required; and no reservations or time limit may be imposed. These special features of the procedure are explained by the vital role the Member States are called upon to play in the concrete implementation of Community policies and rules.

However, the procedure does not go so far as to allow an action to be brought in the European Court by individuals or firms whose interests have been harmed by a Member State's failure to fulfil an obligation under the EEC Treaty. Two courses are open to a private party in such circumstances. One would be to lodge a complaint with the Commission, which might lead to the initiation of proceedings under Article 169 EEC. The other would be to bring proceedings in the courts of the Member State concerned, assuming the Community provision in question is a directly effective one, and an appropriate national remedy is available. To help establish the infringement, it may be necessary to ask the national court to make a reference to the European Court under Article 177 EEC for a preliminary ruling on the interpretation of the Community provision.

A. Failure to Fulfil an Obligation under the EEC Treaty

1. Source of the Obligation

Articles 169 and 170 speak of non-fulfillment by a Member State of "an obligation under this Treaty." This phrase clearly covers, in addition to the obligations imposed on Member States by provisions of the EEC Treaty itself, those arising under acts which the institutions of the Community are empowered by the Treaty to adopt.

The action will also lie for the infringement of provisions in treaties concluded pursuant to Article 228 EEC between the Community and a third country or countries. It is expressly laid down in Article 228(2) that such agreements "shall be binding . . . on Member States."

The same, it is submitted, must be true of the general principles of law, including the protection of fundamental rights, since these are integral to the legal order established by the Community Treaties.

A more difficult case is that of the various formal and informal agreements between the Member States themselves that complement the main Treaties. One class of such agreements are conventions under Article 220 EEC, like the Convention on Jurisdiction and the Enforcement of Judgments in Civil and Commercial Matters. Since Article 220 EEC lays an obligation on Member States to enter into negotiations with a view to securing a number of specific objectives, it is arguable that conventions representing the fruit of such negotiations fall within the scope of the present action. That, in our view, cannot be the position where an agreement is legally entirely independent of the EEC Treaty, though it may pursue parallel aims. An example is the Community Patent Convention.

2. Source of the Infringement

Actions are brought under Articles 169 and 170 to enforce the obligations of Member States, not their governments. There is a case in the *European Court Reports* where the defendant is identified as the "Government of the Italian Republic," but this seems to have been an error. The judgment of the European Court assumed that the case was against the Italian Republic.

It will, therefore, be no defense that responsibility for the alleged infringement lies not with the government but with some other organ of the state, such as the legislature. In a case relating to a discriminatory tax on imported wood, the Belgian Government argued that its best endeavors to secure the amendment of the offending legislation had been frustrated by the dissolution of Parliament and by further delays in the new Parliament. Rejecting that excuse, the European Court said:

> [t]he liability of a Member State under Article 169 arises whatever the agency of the State whose action or inaction is the cause of the failure to fulfil its obligations, even in the case of a constitutionally independent institution.

Another kind of "constitutionally independent institution" is found in Member States with federal or devolved systems of government. It is well settled that infringements of Community law by autonomous provincial or regional authorities, like the *Lander* of the German Federal Republic or the Sicilian regional administration, can give rise to proceedings under Article 169.

The behavior of courts can amount to an infringement by a Member State of its obligations under the Treaty. However, it is important to be clear as to what such judicial infringements might entail. Merely mistaken application of Community law would not be enough, since that is just one of the hazards of adjudication: there would have to be behavior amounting to a refusal by the national court in question to fulfil its role in the legal order of the Community or to acknowledge the pre-eminent place of the European Court in that order. The Commission believes such behavior to be actionable, but it has shown a preference hitherto for exercising informal pressure on the governments concerned.

Lastly, the responsibility of a Member State may be engaged through a private body whose activities are subject to direct or indirect governmental control. The *"Buy Irish"* case[15] concerned a campaign to encourage Irish consumers to buy more home produced goods. The campaign was run by a body called "The Irish Goods Council," which had the legal status of a company limited by guarantee. That did not prevent Ireland's being found guilty of infringing the principle of the free movement of goods enshrined in Article 30 EEC, since the Irish Government appointed the

---

15 Case 249/81, *Commission v. Ireland* [1982] E.C.R. 4005.

chairman and members of the Council, provided most of its funds and laid down aims and the broad outline of the promotion campaign.

3. Modes of Infringement

An infringement may be committed by a Member State through the enactment or maintenance in force of legislation incompatible with provisions of Community law or through failure to take the legislative steps necessary for the implementation of such provisions. Or it may be the result of administrative action within a framework of legislation which is not in itself objectionable. It may even be the result of taking too narrow a view of the interpretation of Community law. The United Kingdom was found to have infringed the EEC Treaty by its reliance on a literal interpretation of the English text of a regulation, where there was a divergence between the language versions of the regulation. In such cases, the European Court held, the Community instrument must be interpreted by reference to the purpose and general scheme of the rules of which the regulation forms part.

A common form of infringement over the years has been the adoption of measures that directly or indirectly restrict imports from, or exports to, other Member States, contrary to Article 30 and 34 EEC. Since the measures in question are fundamentally incompatible with the common market, they have usually been presented in a respectable disguise, such as that of restrictions imposed for the protection of human, animal or plant health which, if genuinely necessary, receive exemption under Article 36 EEC from the prohibition in Article 30, or as not falling with the regime of the free movement of goods at all. What is clear is that effective, rather than purely formal compliance is required.

One example of a purported reliance on Article 36 EEC is the *Turkey* case[16] against the United Kingdom. The Case concerned legislation ostensibly enacted for the control of Newcastle disease, which affects poultry. In furtherance of a change from a policy of vaccination to one of slaughter of infected flocks, a ban was imposed on imports of poultry and eggs in the United Kingdom except from countries which applied a similar slaughter policy, while prohibiting vaccination against the disease. The effect of the ban was to preclude the importation into the United Kingdom of poultry from all the Member States other than Denmark and Ireland. In its judgment the European Court referred to a number of factors supporting the inference that the real aim of the legislation was to protect the British poultry industry against competition, notably from French producers. Nor could it be shown that a complete ban on imports from countries satisfying the conditions in the legislation was necessary to protect the poultry flock in the United Kingdom. Less drastic means, such as inspection at the time of importation, would have been sufficient. The European Court concluded that the legislation entailed a disguised restriction on trade between Member States, to which the animal health exception in Article 36 could not apply. The United Kingdom was accordingly in breach of its obligations under Article 30.

---

[16] Case 40/82, *Commission v. United Kingdom* [1982] E.C.R. 2793, noted at (1983) 8 E.L. Rev. 119.

Breaches can also arise where legislation leaves doubt as to whether exports are permissible. In the *Waste Oils Case*[17] the European Court held that where national legislation leaves some doubt as to whether or not it contains a prohibition on exports, it must be regarded as having an inhibitory effect on export trade and may therefore constitute a distortion of trade contrary to Article 34 EEC.

The maintenance in force of legislation incompatible with Community law may amount to an infringement, even if the legislation is not applied in practice. This was made clear in the case of the French *Code de travail maritime*.[18] Under the *Code* there were strict limits imposed on the employment on French merchant vessels of seamen who were not French nationals. The terms of the legislation conflicted with the right under Article 48 EEC of the equal access to employment for nationals of all Member States. The French Government contended, however, that, since verbal instructions had been given to the naval authorities that Community nationals were to be treated for the purposes of the *Code* as French nationals, no actionable breach of obligations under the EEC Treaty was taking place. The European Court disagreed. The existing text of the *Code* was liable to give rise to uncertainty among seamen from other Member States as to their precise legal position. The European Court said: "This uncertainty can only be reinforced by the internal and verbal character of the purely administrative discretion to waive the application of the national law."

The lesson of this case is that legislation can produce effects incompatible with national obligations independently of its application by national authorities.

The indirect or potential effects of legislation are, therefore, enough to found an action under Articles 169 and 170. On the other hand, an incompatibility that exists purely on paper, having no practical effects whatsoever, will not give rise to liability. One of the infringements alleged against Italy in the *Cocoa* case[19] was of this kind. It concerned the imposition of excise duty on the shells and husks of cocoa beans in a way that appeared to discriminate against imports, contrary to Article 95 EEC. The European Court found, however, that the duty has deliberately been fixed at levels which rendered the products in question unsalable. The point of this was to ensure that shells and husks would only be used in certain applications, for the purposes of which both imports and domestic products were exempt from duty. Since there was no market at all in Italy for products subject to the duty, the unequal rates that were chargeable in theory did not entail any practical discrimination.

Non-fulfillment of the obligation to transpose a directive into national law may involve, as well as complete failure to take implementing action within the time limit fixed by the directive, the adoption of measures failing short of the result to be achieved. The European Court has stated that governments of Member States participate in the preparatory work for directives and must, therefore, be in a position to prepare within the time prescribed, the draft national legislative provisions necessary for

---

17 Case 173/83, *Commission v. France* [1985] E.C.R. 491.

18 Case 167/73, *Commission v. France* [1974] E.C.R. 359.

19 Case 28/69, *Commission v. Italy* [1970] E.C.R. 187.

their implementation. A Member State is not, of course, obliged to act, if the requirements of a directive are already embodied in its laws and administrative practice. But there is a natural tendency for governments to leap too readily to the conclusion that nothing further need be done. The United Kingdom Government, for instance, appears not to have suspected that the practice of stamping passports of Community nationals with leave to remain in the United Kingdom for an initial period of six months might not comply with Directive 68/360, as the *Pieck* case[20] was to show. But in a recent case[21] against Belgium the European Court differed from Advocate General Jacobs in concluding that the practice of the Belgian immigration authorities in conducting certain checks on entry into the country did not breach the requirements of Community law.

The United Kingdom Government also seems wrongly to have assumed that the means provided by the Equal Pay Act 1970 for determining whether work is "of equal value" were adequate for the purposes of Directive 75/117. In *Commission v. Denmark*[22] the European Court said, in relation to the implementation of Directive 75/117/EEC[23] on equal pay:

> The principles of legal certainty and the protection of individuals thus require an unequivocal wording, which would give the persons concerned a clear and precise understanding of their rights and obligations and would enable the courts to ensure that those rights and obligations are observed.[24]

Occasionally the Commission is too strict in its view of what is required to implement a directive; it must show that the deficiency in implementation will have a negativing effect on the result required by the directive, not merely that some detail has not been transposed. So the European Court in the *Animal Feed* case dismissed the Commission's application where the Commission could not prove that the absence of the transposition of certain definitions contained in the directive into national law had any effect on the achievement of the required result.

The strictness with which the European Court requires Member States to implement directives has been mitigated by recognition of a principle of *force majeure*. In the *Statistical Returns* case[25] the Italian Government sought to argue that its failure to comply with a directive providing for annual statistical returns in respect of the carriage of goods by road had been caused by the destruction of the data in a bomb attack. The European Court conceded that a Member State which has encountered insurmountable difficulties outside its control may plead *force majeure* to justify a failure to implement a directive, but this applies only during the time needed to overcome the

---

20 Case 157/79, *R. v. Pieck* [1980] E.C.R. 2171.

21 Case 321/87, *Commission v. Belgium* Judgment of April 27, 1989.

22 Case 143/83, [1985] E.C.R. 427.

23 O.J. 1975 L45/19.

24 Case 143/83, *Commission v. Denmark* [1985] E.C.R. 427, para. 11 of decision, at 435.

25 Case 101/84, *Commission v. Italy* [1985] E.C.R. 2629.

difficulties caused by the event and cannot be relied upon to justify a continuing failure to implement the directive.

Regulations are not, like directives, instruments that operate by way of securing the adjustment of national law and administrative practices to the objectives of the Community. They apply with direct legal force in all the Member States. Indeed, a Member State that "naturalizes" a regulation by re-enacting it, thereby concealing its Community character, is guilty of an infringement of the EEC Treaty. However, it is often the case that implementing steps have to be taken by Member States to give concrete effect to a scheme laid down by a regulation. Thus in *Slaughter Premiums*[26] the European Court held that Italy had failed to adopt the administrative and financial mechanisms necessary for the application on its territory of a scheme designed to reduce the output of dairy products. Similarly, the United Kingdom was found in the *Tachograph* case[27] to have infringed the relevant Community regulation by making the introduction and use of tachographs in vehicles engaged in road transport optional rather than compulsory.

A regulation that calls for action by Member States will very often specify a time limit, in the manner of directives. Where there is no express provision, time limits are to be inferred "from the content of [the regulations] and the aims of the system established by them."[28] The European Court said this in a case concerning Italy's failure to implement a scheme of premiums for the grubbing of fruit trees. Guidance in that case was obtained from the fact that the normal time for grubbing was between the end of the harvest and the renewal of growth in the spring.

An example of administrative action in breach of the EEC Treaty was found in the *Italian Wine* case[29] against France. Between April 1980 and March 1982 the French customs authorities had adopted various practices which had the effect of restricting imports of wine in bulk from Italy. In particular, there was minute examination of customs documents, with any irregularity resulting in the rejection of the documents or in a lengthy investigation during which the wine was held at the frontier. The European Court ruled that pursuant to Regulation 1153/75 the customs authorities of the importing Member State were only entitled to reject documents in cases of material irregularity, for instance where no country of origin was stated or where the health certificate was missing: purely formal errors did not justify rejection.

Even a failure to co-operate in a *bona fide* manner with an enquiry undertaken by the Commission and to supply the Commission with information it legitimately requests may amount to a failure to fulfil the obligation in Article 5 EEC.

---

26 Case 39/72, *Commission v. Italy* [1973] E.C.R. 101.

27 Case 128/78, *Commission v. United Kingdom* [1979] E.C.R. 419.

28 Case 30/72, *Commission v. Italy* [1973] E.C.R. 161, at 170.

29 Case 42/82, *Commission v. France* [1983] E.C.R. 841.

B. Proceedings under Article 169: The Administrative Phase

1. The Steps in the Procedure

Action can only be taken by the Commission on cases of Member States' failure to fulfil Community obligations which become known to it. That some infringements will go undetected for years seems inevitable.

Complaints from individuals, companies, trade associations and governments provide the Commission's main sources of information about possible infringement. Questions in the European Parliament may also suggest a line of enquiry, while new legislation in the Member States is kept under review through scrutiny of official publications. The task of monitoring the transposition of directives into national law is made easier by the inclusion in the text of a requirement, which is now standard, that the Member States notify the Commission of the implementing measures they have taken.

Formal action under Article 169 is normally preceded by informal contacts with the Member State concerned in which the Commission seeks further information and explores the possibility of reaching a friendly settlement. These contacts are initiated by a letter from the Director-General responsible for the sector in question to the Permanent Representative of the Member State in Brussels. The letter will request a reply within a stipulated time. If the Member State responds (which is by no mean always the case) meetings may take place between national and Commission officials.

The formal opening of proceedings is signaled by the dispatch of a letter in which the Commission invites the Member State, pursuant to Article 169, to submit its observations on the alleged infringement. The letter will be signed on behalf of the Commission by the official in whose areas of responsibility the matter falls and will be addressed to the Foreign Minister of the Member State concerned. The Commission aims to move from initial complaint to a decision whether or not to issue an Article 169 letter within a year of the matter being raised with it.

The purpose of the Article 169 letter is to delimit the subject matter of the dispute and to give the Member State the information it needs to prepare its defense. The European Court has stressed that the opportunity to respond to the Article 169 letter is "an essential guarantee required by the Treaty" observance of which "is an essential formal requirement of the procedure under Article 169."

The Member State's reply to the Article 169 letter may raise points that call for further exchange of correspondence at Director-General to Permanent Representative level. If, however, a settlement acceptable to the Commission remains elusive, the administrative phase of the proceedings will culminate in the issuing of a reasoned opinion. The purpose of the opinion is twofold: it provides a final opportunity for the Member State to remedy the infringement before the matter is taken to the European Court; and, if the Member State remains obdurate, it defines the subject matter of the dispute which the European Court is called upon to resolve.

The Commission is required to provide a coherent statement of the reasons which led it to conclude that the Member State has failed to fulfil an obligation under the EEC Treaty. While the opinion must not raise objections on which the Member State has not been invited to comment, it may be more detailed than the Article 169 letter and may reflect any reconsideration of the matter which the response to the letter may have provoked. The reasoned opinion must also inform the government of the Member State of the measures the Commission considers necessary to bring the infringement to an end. Finally, the opinion must stipulate a time limit sufficient to enable to Member State to regularize its position. The time limit stated in the reasoned opinion is definitive. Subsequent dealings with the Commission cannot justify a Member State in concluding that the time limit laid down in the reasoned opinion is suspended. Member States are usually allowed one to two months in which to take the prescribed action but a shorter period may be justifiable.

2. The Discretion of the Commission

Article 155 EEC places a general duty on the Commission to ensure that the provisions of the EEC Treaty and the measures taken by the institutions pursuant thereto are applied. How is that duty to be discharged within the framework of Article 169? Is the Commission required to take action wherever it encounters a possible infringement of Community law by a Member State and, if it cannot achieve a settlement, to follow each stage of the proceedings through to judgment in the European Court?

The first paragraph of Article 169 appears to create an obligation by using the words "it *shall* deliver a reasoned opinion" but this is conditional on a discretionary judgment made clear by the earlier words "if the Commission *considers* . . . ." The language of the second paragraph makes it clear that, if the Member State fails to comply with the reasoned opinion within the stipulated time, the Commission has a discretion as to whether an application should be made to the European Court. In a case brought under the corresponding provision of the Euratom Treaty Advocate General Roemer expressed the view that any automatic application of the procedure or compulsion to initiate it must be ruled out; and the European Court said:

> [B]y reason of its nature and its purpose, this procedure involves a power on the part of the Commission to consider the most appropriate means and time limits for the purposes of putting an end to any contravention of the Treaty.

The answer therefore seems to be that, while the Commission is bound to work actively for the removal of infringements, it has discretion to decide what steps should be taken for this purpose, and when they should be taken.

C. Proceedings under Article 169: The Judicial Phase

1. The Nature of the Proceedings

The European Court has full jurisdiction to determine whether the alleged infringement of Community law took place. This may be contrasted with the power of judicial review under Article 173 EEC which enables the European Court to control the legality of acts of the Community institutions. If the European Court finds an act of an institution to be defective in one of the respects specified by Article 173 EEC, it does not substitute its own view as to how the matter should be decided, but simply annuls the act. Here the proceedings are not for the review of the reasoned opinion. The Commission appears not in defense of its opinion but as the applicant for a declaration that the defendant Member State has failed to fulfil an obligation under the EEC Treaty. The European Court considers afresh all the relevant issues of fact and law and, in the light of these, either grants the declaration or dismisses the application. But the scope of the proceedings is strictly delimited by the matters complained of in the reasoned opinion; the Commission may not widen the scope of the action during the course of the proceedings.

The decision the European Court is called upon to make is one as to the position of the defendant Member State in strict law. It is not concerned with factors that might explain or even excuse the act or omission of the defendant; or that might limit its liability to other Member States or to private parties, if that were in issue.

Three lines of defense on which Member States have sometimes sought to rely are thus doomed to failure.

The first is that the infringement was not the result of wrongful intent or negligence on the part of the Member State concerned but of internal difficulties that could not be overcome in time. Mere acknowledgment of the existence of the violation does not exculpate the Member State. Whatever the difficulties invoked, whether constitutional, administrative, political or economic, the defense is consistently, repeatedly and invariably rejected by the European Court. The furthest the European Court has been willing to go is to recognize that a limited delay in failing to implement a directive caused by *force majeure* may be forgivable.

Secondly, the European Court has held that a Member State cannot in any circumstances plead the principle of reciprocity and rely on a possible infringement of the EEC Treaty by another Member State to justify its own default.

Thirdly, it is no defense that the institutions of the Community may have failed to take steps that they were required to take under the EEC Treaty. Means are provided by the EEC Treaty itself to deal with such lapses, and the Member State may not resort to self help. It is also immaterial that no action has been taken by the Commission against other Member States allegedly guilty of the same infringement as defendant Member State.

2. The Burden of Proof

The burden of proof in an action under Article 169 falls on the Commission. It has the responsibility of producing the information necessary to enable the European Court to find that the alleged failure by the defendant Member State to fulfil an obligation under the EEC Treaty actually occurred.

A Member State's failure to inform the Commission, pursuant to an obligation imposed by a directive, of the steps it has taken to transpose the measure into national law may, in itself, provide grounds for an action under Article 169. However, the Commission is not entitled to assume from the silence of the Member State that nothing has been done.

3. The Judgment

Judgment against a Member State is given in the form of a simple declaration that, by the act or omission specified, it has failed to fulfil an obligation under the EEC Treaty. The European Court has no power to impose sanctions on the Member State in default. Nor does it have the power to stipulate that the Member State do or abstain from any particular thing in order to eliminate the infringement.

The Member State is, however, required by Article 171 EEC to take the necessary measures to comply with the judgment. It discretion for this purpose is limited by the nature of the infringement found by the European Court. The chosen measures must be appropriate and sufficient to bring the infringement to an end. The implementation of the judgment must be started immediately and be completed with proper expedition if the Member State is not to find itself in further breach of its obligations under the Treaty.

Within the Member State's own legal order the consequences of an infringement of Community law depend on whether the provision in question is directly effective. If it is, then the act or omission to which the judgment relates would already have been subject to a prohibition of which the national courts were bound to take cognizance. The effect of the judgment would be to prove authoritative confirmation of the prohibition. Any national court before which the issue arose would be required either to accept the European Court's interpretation of the relevant Community provision or if it felt any doubts, to seek further guidance from the European Court by requesting a preliminary ruling under Article 177 EEC. On the other hand, a judgment in proceedings under Article 169 will not render a provision directly effective if it is not already so.

D. Proceeding under Article 170

The initiative in bringing a defaulting Member State before the European Court may be taken by another Member State under Article 170. Before making an application to the European Court, however, the complaining Member State must bring the matter before the Commission. An opportunity must be given to each of the Member States involved to put its own case and to comment on the other's case both orally and in writing and the Commission will then deliver a reasoned opinion. If it has not delivered an opinion within three months of the notification of the complaint, proceedings in the European Court may be started without further delay.

The role of the Commission in proceedings under Article 170 is that of an umpire and conciliator, not that of an accuser. The terms of Article 170 make it clear that compliance with the reasoned opinion by the respondent Member State has no bearing on the complainant's right of action. The Commission is not, therefore, required to identify the measures it considers necessary to bring the infringement to an end nor to fix a time limit for the purpose; though it may do so in order to keep open the option of proceeding under Article 169.

In the judicial phase of the proceedings there are only two requirements going to admissibility: that the Commission was notified of the complaints; and that either three months have elapsed or a reasoned opinion has been delivered. The burden of proof is on the complainant Member State and the Commission may intervene in support of one side or the other. The judgment will have the same effect as in proceedings under Article 169.

E. Article 177 EEC[30]

In addition to Articles 169 and 170 EEC, Article 177 EEC, concerning preliminary rulings of the Court on the validity and interpretation of Community law on the request of a national court, provides for a second procedural means to rule, although only indirectly, on the constitutionality and compatibility of the law of the Member States with Community law.

As the Court held in the *van Gend & Loos* case, Article 177 EEC gives the Court jurisdiction to rule independently from Articles 169 or 170 on the interpretation of all Community law, including the establishing of direct effect and supremacy over national law of rules of Community law.

According to the Court of Justice, Article 177 EEC supplements the supervision of national law by the Commission under Articles 155 and 169 with the "vigilance of individuals concerned to protect their rights."

The starting point of this indirect constitutional review of the laws of the Member States under Article 177 EEC is the consistent case law of the Court of Justice that "under Article 177 the Court only interprets the Community law and refrains from any decision concerning the compatibility of national law with Community law." However, the Court felt able in *SAIL, Rewe, van den Hazel, Mirepoix and Schumacher* to "provide the submitting national courts with all such matters relating to the interpretation of Community law as will be necessary to enable the national court to decide the issue of compatibility in the case before it." Therefore the Court cannot rule directly on the compatibility of national law with Community law as the constitutional courts in federal states are able to do. The Court can only indicate the compatibility of national law with Community law by ruling on the direct effect of Community law. It is for the national courts to draw the appropriate inferences from the ruling given by the ECJ and to give full effectiveness to the judgment in the national legal system. However, the judgments of the Court are generally followed by national courts as far as the ruling on the direct effect of a certain Community rule is concerned. In practice, the European Court's rulings under Article 177 have therefore the same effect as a concrete (*inter partes*) review of state law in a federal state by the federal constitutional court.

This practical point of view is backed up by the fact that the Court of Justice sometimes rules under Article 177 more or less directly on the compatibility of national law with Community law and is often asked by the national courts to do so. To rule more or less directly on the compatibility of national law with community law, always paying lip service to the rule that the Court cannot do so, the European Court uses a method which might be described most appropriately as the "relative abstract method."

---

[30] J. Rinze, *The Role of the European Court of Justice as a Federal Constitutional Court*, (1993) Public Law 426-43.

Within the context of Article 177 EEC, the Court of Justice cannot interpret Community law in an absolutely abstract way, in the way that a federal constitutional court can do in the abstract *(ex parte)* a review of state law as to its compatibility with federal law on the application of a competent authority. The Court interprets Community law always in view of a particular case and certain questions referred to it by the national court. As the case pending before the national court depends on national law called into question on grounds of individual Community law rights, the Court of Justice has to interpret Community law in its relationship to certain rules of national law. In order to avoid ruling on the compatibility of *concrete* national law with Community law, while at the same time indicating its incompatibility with Community law, the Court of Justice often rules that a certain provision of Community law *must be interpreted to mean* that certain legislative measures of Member States (abstract) of the type at issue (relative) are incompatible with Community law.[31]

Not only does the Court of Justice use Article 177 EEC to rule more or less directly on the compatibility of national law with Community law, but the whole concept of supremacy of Community law was developed by cases brought to the Court under Article 177 EEC.[32]

However, the effectiveness of Article 177 depends not only on the "vigilance of individuals" but also on the readiness of national courts to co-operate[33] with the Court of Justice. National courts have to provide the ECJ with preliminary references (there is no individual appeal to the European Court[34]) and have to implement the interpretation of Community law given by the Court in the national legal systems. Yet national courts are very willing to co-operate with the ECJ, although there has been some resistance to do so as well.[35] Should the national court not adhere to the ruling of the European Court, this would establish a breach of a Community obligation which could be brought before the European Court under Article 169 EEC if the

[31] *E.g.* case 215/87, *Schumacher* [1989] E.C.R. 617 at 638, 640, [1990] 2 C.M.L.R. 465; case 111/76, *Van den Hazel* [1977] E.C.R. 901 at 909, 912, [1980] 3 C.M.L.R. 12; case 125/88, *Nijman* [1989] E.C.R. 3533 at 3547, [1991] 1 C.M.L.R. 92; case 60/75, *Russo* [1976] E.C.R. 45 at 55, 56; compare as well *Bridge* [1982] AALR 130 at 144, 145, and *Mancini* [1989] C.M.L. Rev. 595 at 606.

[32] See case 6/64, *Costa v. ENEL* [1964] E.C.R. 585, [1964] C.M.L.R. 425; case 106/77, *Simmenthal* [1978] E.C.R. 629, [1978] 3 C.M.L.R. 263; case 11/70, *International Handelsgesellschaft* [1970] E.C.R. 1125, [1972] C.M.L.R. 265.

[33] See case 283/81, *CILFIT* [1982] E.C.R. 3415 at 3428: ". . . The obligation to refer a matter to the Court of Justice is based on *co-operation* . . ."

[34] Lower national courts decide on their own, if they refer a question of interpretation to the Court of Justice; see *Mancini* [1989] C.L.M. Rev. 595 at 605; case 283/81, *CILFIT* [1982] E.C.R. 3415 at 3428, [1983] 1 C.M.L.R. 472. However, lower national courts are obliged to refer a question of validity of Community law to the ECJ, see case 314/85, *Foto-Frost* [1987] E.C.R. 4199 at 4231, 4232, [1988] 3 C.M.L.R. 57.

[35] *Bridge* [1982] Anglo-Am. L. Rev. 130 at 145; *Hartley* [1986] American Journal of Comparative Law 229 at 236; Schermers and Waelbroeck (*op. cit.*, n. 4), para. 565, p. 323; *Mancini* [1989] C.M.L. Rev. 595 at 597, 605; as for example for a long lasting resistance against co-operation with the ECJ by the German *Bundesfinanzhof* and the French *Conseil d'Etat* see Meier, *Europäische Zeitschrift für Wirtschaftsrecht* (EuZW, 1992), 11 with case law in nn. 7 and 8 on p. 11.

national court deliberately ignored Community law.[36] Nevertheless, in practice, the Community has been very reluctant to institute proceedings under Article 169 for infringement of Community law by a national court, because of the implications for the independence of the judiciary.

The necessary co-operation between national courts and the European Court is also acknowledged and protected by at least one constitution of a Member State: it is considered to be unconstitutional in Germany if a court, against whose decision there is no appeal, arbitrarily decides not to refer questions of Community law to the European Court of Justice.[37] In favor of the effectiveness of Article 177 in general and in favor of the effective protection of individual rights one should construe broadly the obligation of national courts "against whose decisions there is no judicial remedy. . ." (Art. 177(3)EEC) to make a reference to the Court of Justice. Article 177(3) EEC must therefore be interpreted as binding not only courts against whose decisions there is *generally* no appeal, but also any national court against whose decision there is no appeal in the particular *concrete* case.

Furthermore, the procedure under Article 177 depends on the existence of national procedural means under which individual rights can be invoked before national courts. Therefore, it has been the policy of the Council, the Commission and the Court of Justice to place an obligation on the Member States to establish appropriate national procedures under which individual Community law rights can be invoked.[38]

It can therefore be concluded that the Court of Justice, although depending on the co-operation of national courts, uses Article 177 EEC as an effective means to guarantee the constitutionality of the laws of the Member States.

F. Conclusion

The continued existence of the Community would be imperilled if the Court of Justice did not have jurisdiction under Article 169, 170 and 177 EEC to rule on the constitutionality of the laws of the Member States. The methods used by the Court of Justice do not so resemble in their practical effects, despite all differences in theory, very much the concrete and abstract review of state law in federal states by federal constitutional courts. Corresponding to the process of the European Community developing more and more to a federal state, the European Court of Justice will use more and more inten-

[36] Opinion of A.-G. Warner in case 30/77, *Bouchereau* [1977] E.C.R. 2020, [197?] 2 C.M.L.R. 800.

[37] *BV erfGE* 73, 339 at 367 on October 22, 1986 and *BV erfGE* 75, 223 at 233, 234 on April 8, 1987 (*BV erfGE* = Collection of the decisions of the German Federal Constitutional Court). The German Federal Constitutional Court refers to Art. 101(1) 2 of the German federal constitution which reads: "No one may be removed from the jurisdiction of his lawful judge." Compare similar provisions in the constitutions of Belgium (Art. 8), Greece (Art. 8), Italy (Art. 25), Luxembourg (Art. 13) and the Netherlands (Art. 17).

[38] *E.g.* case 69/90, *Francovich* [1992] 21 I.R.L.R. 84, rec. 42; case C-208/90, *Emmoit* [1991] 3 C.M.L.R.·894 at 914, 915; see as well as examples Art. 14(4) 3, 38 or the regulation No. 2137/85 of July 25, 1985, [1985] O.J. L199/1 or Art. 6 of the directive 76/207, [1976] O.J. L39/40.

sively those judicial competences which are based on similar provisions concerning constitutional courts in existing federal states, especially those in the Federal Republic of Germany.

V. Action Before the Court of Justice Against Member States

A. Introduction[39]

There has been a great increase recently in the use by the Court of Justice of Article 5 of the EEC Treaty, and the corresponding Articles in the other Treaties. Of over 120 judgments in which these Articles have been cited, more than half have been given since 1st January 1985. Article 5 reads:

> Member States shall take all appropriate measures, whether general or particular, to ensure fulfilment of the obligations arising out of this Treaty or resulting from action taken by the institutions of the Community. They shall facilitate the achievement of the Community's tasks.
>
> They shall abstain from any measure which could jeopardize the attainment of the objectives of this Treaty.

Article 5 applies to all national authorities, executive, legislative and judicial, to State enterprises, to regional and local authorities, and to private bodies to which State powers have been delegated. Each Member State may decide which national authority is responsible for carrying out any given duty under Community law.

Article 5 applies to national courts, subject to Article 177, in particular when they decide whether to give effect to any rule of national law which may be contrary to the State's duties under Community Law. The distinction between directly applicable Community rules and rules which are not directly applicable may be less important than it would appear, since national courts are bound by Article 5 to comply with all the obligations of the Member State. Article 5 obliges every national judge to be a Community law judge. Member States are not free to carry out a Community law duty in such a way that it is incompletely or ineffectively applied by national courts.

Article 5 contains two general duties and one general prohibition, the content of which depend on provisions elsewhere in the Treaty or arising from Community measures, even when they are not directly applicable. But "Article 5 does more than merely set out a programme which is relevant solely in the determination of the objectives of the other provisions of the Treaty."[40]

---

[39] John Temple Lang, *Community Constitutional Law: Article 5 EEC Treaty*, 27 C.M.L.R. 645-681 (1990). © 1990 Kluwer Academic Publishers. Reprinted by permission .

[40] Case 231/83, *Centre Leclerc v. Au Blé Vert*, [1985] ECR 1, conclusions of the Advocate General.

According to several judgments[41] the duties of cooperation imposed on Member States by Article 5 "may under certain circumstances transcend specific legally binding duties laid down elsewhere."[42] It is possible to deduce from the general scheme of the Treaty or from other relevant sources a definition of the general duties laid down in Article 5.

There are limits to the implications of Article 5. The Commission could not use it to create new kinds of obligations for Member States. "An obligation on the Member States to adopt specific measures cannot be created by a Commission memorandum in the absence of a particular provision in the Treaty or in binding acts adopted by the institutions."[43]

Article 5 has nevertheless been underestimated, because some of its practical effects are set out in specific Articles, and because the Court does not always refer to it expressly even when it clearly has it in mind.

In the Community, Member States have wide powers. Article 5 is particularly important because the Community, unlike most federations, has no clear or fixed boundary between Community and State powers, and because the Community depends much more than most federations on having its policies carried out by Member States.

B. The Duties Imposed by Article 5

1. The Duty to Enforce and Give Full Effect to Community Law

Article 5 imposes a positive obligation on Member States to take all measures, legislative, administrative and judicial, which are necessary to give full effect to Community law.

> According to the general principles on which the Institutional system of the Community is based and which governs the relations between the Community and the Member States, it is for the Member States by virtue of Article 5 of the Treaty, to ensure that Community regulations, particularly those concerning the common agricultural policy, are implemented within their territory. Insofar as Community law, including its general principles, does not include common rules to this effect, the national authorities when implementing Community regulations act in accordance with the procedural and substantive rules of their own national law. However . . .this rule must be reconciled with

[41] *See e.g.*, Case 78/70, *Deutsche Grammophon v. Metro*, [1971] ECR 487, 499, para. 5; Case 13/77, *INNO v. ATAB*, [1977] ECR 2115, 2144-45, paras. 30, 31, 36, 37; Case 141/78, *France v. UK*, [1979] ECR 2923, 2942, para. 8.

[42] Case 231/83, *supra* note 40, conclusions of the Advocate General; Case 2/73, *Geddo v. Ente Nazionale Risi*, [1973] ECR 865.

[43] Case 229/86, *Brother Industries v. Commission*, [1987] ECR 3757 at p. 3763.

> the need to apply Community law uniformly so as to avoid unequal treatment of procedures and traders. . . .[44]

In the *Italian fruit trees* Case, the Court said that

> A Member State cannot plead the provisions or practices of its internal order to justify failure to observe obligations and time-limits arising from Community Regulations.
>
> It falls to a Member State in accordance with the general obligations imposed on Member States by Article 5 of the Treaty, to recognize the consequences, in its internal order, of its adherence to the Community and, if necessary, to adapt its procedures for budgetary provisions in such a way that they do not form an obstacle to the implementation, within the prescribed time-limits, of its obligations within the framework of the Treaty.[45]

This duty means that "all the institutions of the Member State concerned must . . . ensure within the fields covered by their respective powers, that judgments of the Court are complied with."[46]

This obligation, which also derives from Article 171 EEC Treaty, requires parliaments to repel or amend legislation which is contrary to Community law, and requires all other bodies to use their powers in the areas for which they are responsible so as to achieve the results required by Community law.

This duty also imposes negative obligations. Member States must *not* enforce arbitral awards which are unenforceable under, or contrary to, Community rules, such as competition rules. The duty to give full effect also obliges Member States not to interfere with the exercise by companies of rights given by Community law. They may not, for example, make the exercise of those rights conditional on waiver or loss of other rights or acceptance of extra obligations, or penalize or unfairly pressurize companies exercising or seeking to exercise their rights.

The duty to give full effect to Community law also means that national courts must act even on rules which are not directly applicable. In particular, they must interpret national law adopted to implement a directive, or said to be sufficient to comply with

---

[44] Joined Cases 205-215/82, *Deutsche Milchkontor GmbH v. Germany,* [1983] ECR 2633, 2665-67, also 2680, 2683 (conclusions of the Advocate General); Case 54/81, *Firma Wilhelm Fromme v. Bundesanhalt für land wirtschaftliche Marktordnung*, [1982] ECR 1449, 1469, 1477-78 (conclusions of the Advocate General); Case 137/80, *Commission v. Belgium*, [1981] ECR 2393, 2407, para. 9, 2413, 2414, 2416 (conclusions of the Advocate General); Case 30/70, *Scheer v. Einfuhr-und-Vorrasstelle Getreide,* [1970] ECR 1197, para. 10; Case 85/85, *Commission v. Belgium*, [1986] ECR 1149, paras. 22-23 (duty to implement Protocol on Privileges); Case 239/85, *Commission v. Belgium*, [1986] ECR 3645, para. 7 (Article 5 imposes a duty to implement a directive by a legally binding measure); Case 68/88, *Commission v. Greece*, judgment dated 21 September 1989 (the enforcement procedures and the diligence with which they are applied must be the same as for breached of national law).

[45] Case 30/72, *Commission v. Italian Republic*, [1973] ECR 161, 172; see also Case 93/71, *Leonesio v. Ministry for Agriculture and Forestry*, [1972] ECR 287, 295-296; Case 130/78, *Salumificio di Cornuda*, [1979] ECR 867, para. 27; Case 45/85, *Verband der Sachversicherer v. Commission*, [1989] ECR 405, at para. 20.

[46] Joined Cases 314-316/81 & 83/82, *Procureur de la Republique v. Waterkeyn*, [1982] ECR 4337, para. 14.

the requirements of a directive, in the light of the wording and the purpose of the directive, interpreted as the Court would interpret it, and not necessarily as the national court would interpret it if it was a purely national measure.

Article 5 obliges national courts "to ensure the legal protection which persons derive from the direct effect of provisions of Community law . . . any provision of a national legal system . . . which might impair the effectiveness of Community law by withholding from the national court the power to do everything necessary . . . to set aside national legislative provisions which might prevent, even temporarily, Community rules from having full force and effect are incompatible with those requirements." This includes a duty to set aside national rules preventing interim relief. In other words, if Community law gives a right, whatever the nature of the right (to damages, injunction, interim relief, a declaration) national courts *must* provide an appropriate, complete and effective remedy—the fact that national law does not itself provide it, or says that it should not be provided, is irrelevant. Procedures and national remedies must be adapted as far as necessary to protect fully the right given by Community law.

Article 5 obliges all Member States' authorities to ensure that everyone complies, within their jurisdiction, both with Community law and with national measures implementing Community obligations. In the *Nordsee* case, the Court said:

> The Federal Republic of Germany, as a Member State of the Community responsible for the performance of obligations arising from Community law within its territory pursuant to Article 5 and Articles 169 to 171 of the Treaty, has not entrusted or left to private individuals the duty of ensuring that such obligations are complied with . . . Community law must be observed in its entirety throughout the territory of all the Member States; parties to a contract are not, therefore, free to create exceptions to it.[47]

This means that Member States are required to legislate to create sanctions, and to provide administrative and enforcement procedures and personnel, which are adequate to ensure effective application and enforcement of Community rules.

The duty to enforce Community law includes an obligation to recover from companies all money which has been paid to them contrary to Community law, e.g. unlawful State aids, or money improperly paid under CAP rules.

In the *Fromme* case the Court said:

> Actions for the recovery of sums which have been wrongly paid under Community law must be decided by national courts in accordance with their own national law in so far as Community law has not provided otherwise. In particular, it is for the national authorities to settle all ancillary questions relating to such recovery, such as the question of payment of interest . . . [This requirement] does no more than confirm expressly an obligation already incumbent on the Mem-

[47] Case 102/81, *Nordsee Deutsche Hochseefischerei*, [1982] ECR 110-11.

ber States by virtue of the principle of cooperation enunciated in Article 5 of the Treaty.[48]

The duty of national courts to enforce Community law includes a duty to enforce the rights of private parties against the public authorities of the State itself. This has been stated in a series[49] of cases involving claims for repayment of taxes imposed contrary to Community law.

However, the language of the Court seems deliberately broad. It is not limited to tax cases. It extends to actions for declarations, and to claims for damages against public authorities for breach of directly applicable rules of Community law.

In *Rewe*, the Court said:

> Applying the principle of cooperation laid down in Article 5 of the Treaty, it is the national courts which are entrusted with ensuring the legal protection which citizens derive from the direct effect of the provisions of Community law. Accordingly, in the absence of Community rules on this subject, it is for the domestic legal system of each Member State to designate the courts having jurisdiction and to determine the procedural conditions governing actions at law intended to ensure the protection of the rights which citizens have from the direct effect of Community law, it being understood that such conditions cannot be less favourable than those relating to similar actions of a domestic nature. In the absence of . . . measures of harmonization the right conferred by Community law must be exercised before the national courts in accordance with the conditions laid down by national rules.
>
> The position would be different only if the conditions and time limits made it impossible to exercise the rights which the national courts are obliged to protect.
>
> This is not the case where reasonable periods of limitation of actions are fixed.[50]

The duty of national courts to protect the rights of private parties under Community law *against the State* is not limited to rights given by directly applicable rules.[51] There does not seem to be any reason to doubt that national courts are obliged to enforce all rules of Community law binding Member States, according to their terms, against all State authorities, and to provide sufficient remedies in all cases of infringement.

---

48 Case 54/81, *Fromme*, [1982] ECR 1449, 1463-64; Joined Cases 146, 192 & 193/81, para. 23.

49 Case 33/76, *Rewe*, [1976] ECR 1989 at pp. 1997-98.

50 *Id.*, See Case C-213/89, (a national court is obliged not to apply an Act of the national legislature if it is inconsistent with a Community law right).

51 Member States may not rely on, and national courts may not apply, against privatc parties rules of national law which are inconsistent with even non-directly applicable rules of Community law: Case 148/78, *Ratti*, [1979] ECR 1629; Case 8/81 *Becker*, [1982] ECR 53; Case 23/70, *Haseldorst*, [1970] ECR 881 at para. 5; Case 130/78, *Salumificio di Cornuda*, [1979] ECR 867 at para 27. This principle must also apply in proceedings brought by a private party against a state authority.

The importance of these judgments cannot be overestimated and it is not easy to see why it has not been more clearly understood. What they seem to mean is that every time a Member State adopts a measure which is in breach of a directly applicable rule of Community law, it is liable to an action for an injunction or damages, or both, in its own Courts, brought by every individual or company which can show that it has suffered or is likely to suffer loss as a result. If Member States realized the huge potential cost of infringements of directly applicable Community rules, they would be very much more careful to avoid infringing them. But of course until individuals and companies (and their lawyers) claim damages and seek injunctions regularly in such cases, Member States will not have to pay the full cost of their infringements. If use is made of this principle, no more effective way of ensuring that Community law is respected by Member States can be imagined, because the powers of national courts would be mobilized to enforce the judgments of the Court of Justice.

In the case of Community law rules which are not directly applicable, the situation is more complicated, since the rights of the individual or company can be relied on only in litigation against the State or State bodies, and it is not always procedurally convenient or possible to arrange litigation in such a way that such rights can be claimed. But in principle individuals and companies can also rely on these rights based on such rules also.

National courts must also provide appropriate, complete and effective remedies for those injured by breaches of directly applicable Community rules binding on the private parties against which the remedies are claimed.

National law rules, both procedural and substantive, must not make it excessively difficult for private parties to obtain evidence of or procedurally to prove a breach of Community law. It has for example been suggested that Article 5 might alter the rule allowing governments to withhold official papers, and the rule allowing companies to refuse to incriminate themselves when sued for breach of Community competition law.

Since national courts have a duty to apply Community law, they must raise questions of Community law on their own initiative even if they are not raised by the parties.

2. The Duty of Member States to Comply with Fundamental Rights Rules and the "General Principles of Law" Binding on Community Institutions.

Article 5 obliges Member States to abstain from measures which could jeopardize "the objectives of the Treaty." A necessary condition for fulfilling these objectives is the operation of Community law. Under Article 164, the Court is required to ensure that, in the interpretation and application of the Treaty, "the law is observed." The law to be applied by the Court includes principles of fundamental rights and also includes a number of "general principles of law," including the principles of proportionality, legal certainty, non-discrimination, the right to be heard, the right to obtain legal advice, and the right to judicial review.

In the Community law sphere, under Article 5 both fundamental rights principles and "general principles of law" also bind national authorities. The Court has not so far said this in general terms.

However, there are a number of reasons of principle for believing that this must be so, and in every one of the numerous cases in which the Court has been faced with the question whether national authorities, in the Community law sphere, must comply with one or more of these principles, the Court has answered that they must. The "Community law sphere" means, for example, when Member States are implementing Community measures or policies, are acting on behalf of the Community, or are using powers which are regulated by the Community. However, Community law does not oblige national authorities to comply with these principles in the purely national law sphere.

In *Jongeneel Kaas*[52] the Advocate General's conclusions were very clear:

> The . . . question is concerned with the general principles of Community law, and in particular, with the principle of proportionality. The national court wishes to ascertain whether that principle is directly applicable in a case such as that pending before it.
>
> The answer to that question must be in the affirmative. The general principles elected by the Court from the primary and secondary provisions of Community law, and in particular from those fundamental values which are common to the legal systems of the Member States, form part of the Community legal order and may therefore be relied upon by individuals before the national court *which, as is well known, is also a Community court*. However, that is subject to the limitation that such principles may come into operation only in cases where the application of substantive rules of Community law is involved. To be more explicit, those principles may be relied upon by individuals and will be taken into account by the courts not in any circumstances but only in cases which display some connection with the legal order of the Community . . .
>
> The general principles of law and, in particular, the principle of proportionality have direct effect. Accordingly, they must be applied by national courts if the circumstances in relation to which they are relied upon display a connection with the Community system. (emphases supplied)

Once again, the importance of these principles in the administration of Community law by national authorities cannot be over stressed. We are progressively building up a Europe-wide body of rules for the protection of the rights of individuals and companies, applying to both national and Community institutions, in the ever-widening Community law sphere. Community law contains a wide range of ethical as well as economic principles: Community law now clearly has moral as well as economic objectives.

---

52 Case 237/82, *Jongeneel Kaas*, [1984] ECR 483 at p. 520 (conclusions of the Advocate General).

3. The Duty to Implement Community Objectives

Article 5 imposes a duty on Member States to implement Community objectives when the objective and the required action are sufficiently clear. The objectives can be legal, found in or derived from the Treaties, or policy objectives adopted by the Community institutions, such as conservation of biological resources. In *Thieffry*, the Court stated:

> [F]reedom of establishment, subject to observance of professional rules justified by the general good, is one of the objectives of the Treaty.
>
> In so far as Community law makes no special provision, these objectives may be attained by measures enacted by the Member States, which under Article 5 of the Treaty are bound.[53]

When the question arose whether a Member State had a legal duty under Article 5 to adopt measures to conserve a fish stock, when scientists advised that a ban on fishing was needed, the Court stated:

> There are several factors which, when taken together, lead to the conclusion that the United Kingdom was under a duty to take conservation measures in the zone in question . . . It is not is dispute that according to the available scientific opinions recognized by all parties a total ban on fishing was required for the conservation of the Mourne stock . . . both Article 102 of the Act of Accession and Council Regulation (EEC) No. 101/76 . . . are based on the twofold assumption that measures must be adopted in the maritime waters for which the Community is responsible so as to meet established conservation needs and that if those measures cannot be introduced in good time on a Community basis the Member States not only have the right but are also under a duty to act in the interests of the Community.[54]

So if there is clear scientific advice that a given measure is necessary for the conservation of a biological resource which the Community aims to conserve, such as maritime biological resources or wild birds, Article 5 imposes a legal obligation to adopt the measure. The same might be true of e.g. measures needed to protect human health, or to protect the environment, or any other type of measures if the objective was undisputably a Community objective and if the scientific advice as to what was needed was sufficiently clear, or had been accepted by Member States as requiring action, or had been adopted by the Commission if it was competent to determine Community policy on the question (e.g. competition policy).

---

[53] Case 71/76, *Thieffry v. Conseil De L'Ordre des Advocats à la Cour de Paris*, [1977] ECR 765, 777-78, para. 15-18 and 22.

[54] Case 32/79, *Commission v. U.L.*, [1980] ECR 2403, 2437-38 and 2460-61 (conclusions of the Advocate General in which the duty is described as a real legal duty to develop the Communities).

If a Community measure envisages supplementary Community measures, and none have yet been adopted, Article 5 requires Member States to adopt measures on behalf of the Community even if Member States no longer have powers of their own to adopt national measures.

Article 5 also can impose a duty to ratify conventions negotiated by the Community or under Community auspices, whether between Member States or between Member States and non-Member States, such as the Montreal Protocol to the Vienna Convention on the Protection of the Ozone Layer. This duty arises when it is sufficiently clear, from the circumstances in which the convention in question was negotiated or otherwise, that it is Community policy that all Member States should ratify it. This duty can also arise in the case of a convention which Member States are asked to ratify to complete the internal market, such as the Berne Convention for the Protection of Literary and Artistic Works.

If one aim of a Community measure is to end distortions of competition, and distortions will arise if exchange rates alter significantly, Member States are obliged to take appropriate counter-measures. This duty can only be based on Article 5.

4. The Duty Not to Interfere with the Operation of Community Law Rules

The duty of Member States not to adopt any measures which conflict with, or interfere with the operation of, Community law is stated in a long line of cases, mostly involving the Common Agricultural Policy.[55] This duty arises from Article 5. This rule may be, or sometimes is, one of competence rather than conflict.

National authorities must avoid measures which could conflict with the uniform application of Community law, or with the "practical effectiveness" of Community law in particular cases. If a national authority has adopted a measure that conflicts with a Community decision, the authority must do whatever is necessary to end the conflict. To determine what the aim of a Community measure is and how it is intended to operate in practice, one should look in the first instance at the recitals in the measure itself.

In *Leclerc*, the Court stated:

> The rules on competition are concerned with the conduct of undertakings and not with the national legislation of Member States. However, as the Court has recently ruled in its judgment of 10 January 1985, in . . . Leclerc . . . Member States are nonetheless obliged under the second paragraph of Article 5 of the Treaty not to detract, by means of national legislation, from the full and uniform application of Community law or from the effectiveness of its implementing measures; nor may they introduce or maintain in force measures, even of a legislative nature, which may render ineffective the competition rules applicable to undertakings.[56]

---

55 Case 31/74, *Deuka v. Einfuhr-und Vorratsstelle Getreide*, [1975] ECR 421, 427.

56 Case 231/83, *Cullet v. Centre Leclerc Toulouse*, [1985] ECR 305, paras. 16-18.

In another *Leclerc* case, the Court said:

> The purely national systems and practices in the book trade have not yet been made subject to a Community competition policy with which the Member States would be required to comply by virtue of their duty to abstain form any measure that might jeopardize the attainment of the objectives of the Treaty. It follows that, as Community law stands, Member States' obligations under Article 5 of the EEC Treaty, in conjunction with Articles 3(f) and 85, are not specific enough to preclude them from enacting legislation of the type at issue on competition in the retail prices of books, provided that such legislation is consonant with the other specific Treaty provisions, in particular those concerning the free movement of goods.[57]

In other words, once the policy of the Commission (which is responsible for Community competition law) was clear, Member States could not adopt legislation that would jeopardize the objectives or defeat the purpose of that policy.

In a fisheries case, the Advocate General said that when the Council has power to adopt conservation measures but has not yet done so, Member States are bound

> under Article 5 of the EEC Treaty, to take the necessary conservation measures *in the general interest* and having regard to the substantive and formal requirements of Community law . . . The interim decisions of the Council . . . are merely to be considered as *specifying the duty of cooperation* of the Member States in accordance with Article 5 . . . [i]f the Council fails to act the Commission is competent to grant that approval regardless of whether the decisions in question are considered a restoration of powers to the Member States or, on a more correct view, a specification of their obligations under Article 5 of the EEC Treaty . . . these decisions . . . merely render specific the Member States' duty of cooperation, which they undertook in accordance with Article 5 of the EEC Treaty by the accession to the Community.[58]

The duty not to interfere with the operation of Community law is not limited to substantive conflicts. They duty was held, in the *Variola* case, to mean that it was unlawful for a Member State to enact national measures reproducing the terms of a Regulation, because this interfered with the direct application of the Regulation, concealed the Community nature of the legal rule, and interfered with jurisdiction of the Court under Article 177.

Yet another example of the duty not to interfere with the operation of Community law was the *Deville* case[59] in which the Court held that, after a judgment of the Court

---

[57] Case 229/83, *Centre Leclerc v. Au Blé Vert*, [1985] ECR.

[58] Case 124/80, *Officier van Justitie v. Van Dam & Zonen*, [1980] ECR 1447, 1463-65 (emphasis in original).

[59] Case 240/87, *Deville*, judgment dated 29 June 1988.

holding certain national tax measures contrary to the Treaty, national procedural rules may not be adopted making it more difficult for taxpayers to recover tax improperly collected.

5. The Duty Not to Interfere with the Operation of a Community Institution

Article 54 created a duty not to interfere with the operation of a Community institution. The Court in the *Lord Bruce* case said:

> Community law lays down certain limits . . . which the Member States must observe in the enactment of taxation laws applicable to Members of the Parliament. Those limits arise in particular from Article 5 of the EEC Treaty which . . . includes the duty not to take measures which are likely to interfere with the internal functioning of the institutions of the Community.[60]

In the case of *Luxembourg v. Parliament* the Court stated:

> When the Governments of the Member States make provisional decisions they must, in accordance with the rule imposing on Member States and the Community institutions mutual duties of sincere cooperation, as embodied in particular in Article 5 of the EEC Treaty, have regard to the power of the Parliament to determine its internal organization. They must ensure that such decisions do not impede the due functioning of the Parliament.
>
> Furthermore the Parliament is authorized, pursuant to the power to determine its own internal organization . . . to adopt appropriate measures to ensure the due functioning and conduct of its own proceedings. However, in accordance with the above mentioned mutual duties of sincere cooperation, the divisions of the Parliament in turn must have regard to the power of Governments of the Member States to determine the seat of the institutions and to the provisional decisions taken in the meantime.[61]

The duty not to interfere with the operation of a Community institution, it has been said, might invalidate the "Luxembourg agreement," under which the Council would act only by unanimity even when qualified majority voting is envisaged by the Treaty.

The duty not to interfere with Community institutions applies when the Council has not yet adopted common rules or when the Commission has submitted proposals for urgently needed Community measures. For example, Article 5 may prohibit Member States from entering into international agreements with third States while Council discussions are in progress or imminent, if this would make the Council's discussions more difficult. It would also prevent a Member State insisting on "linkage"

---

60 Case 208/80, *Lord Bruce of Donington*, [1981] ECR 2205, 2218-2219, para. 14.

61 Case 230/81, *Luxembourg v. European Parliament*, [1983] ECR 255, 287, para. 37.

between unrelated measures and insisting that one measure should not be adopted by the Council until another unrelated measure had been agreed.

In *Hasselblad (GB) Ltd. v. Orbison*, Hasselblad sued for defamation based on statements by Orbison in a letter to the EEC Commission saying that Hasselblad had infringed Article 85 EEC Treaty. The English Court of Appeal said:

> Since this country is a Member of the European Community, there is a public interest in ensuring that the Commission, as the primary authority of the Community [in the area of competition law] should not be frustrated in the duty imposed on it by the EEC Treaty and Council Regulation 17 of enforcing compliance with Articles 85 and 86.[62]

If such a claim could be made in a national court, the Commission would find it harder to investigate breaches of Articles 85-86 if complaining to the Commission exposed complainants to libel actions, the supply of information to the Commission would be significantly reduced. The English court added "it cannot be right that national courts and Community institutions shall both independently weigh the force of particular evidence with the possibility of inconsistent results."

The argument that the Commission's functioning should not be interfered with is similar to the rule in *Lord Bruce*.[63] The other risk, that of inconsistent decisions of national courts and of Community institutions, arose in *Walt Wilhelm*.[64] The *Hasselblad* judgment extended the duty not to interfere with the internal working of a Community institution to the ability of the institution to receive information supplied voluntarily by members of the public. This principle might also apply to e.g. submissions to the European Parliament. The principle would also prohibit e.g. improper efforts to interfere with the independence of members of the Commission.

Below, reference is made to the cases in which the Court has said that the duty to cooperate binds Community institutions as well as Member States, and has accepted new court procedures to facilitate this. If the institutions are also legally obliged to cooperate with one another, as they almost certainly are, the principles discussed here usefully supplement whatever may result from the 1990-1991 Intergovernmental Conference, and should facilitate the working of all the institutions. One can expect that the European Parliament will make use of the principle that the other Community institutions are legally obliged to cooperate with it, and may seek to use the Court's new informal procedure, also mentioned below, to ensure this when necessary.

6. The Duty Not to Encourage Breaches of Community Law or to Defeat its Purposes

Member States have a duty, derived from Articles 5 and 90, not to encourage, facilitate or confirm a breach, by either public authorities or private enterprise, of any rule

62 *Hasselblad (GB) Ltd. v. Orbison*, [1984] 3 CMLR 540, 679 at p. 692.

63 Case 208/80, [1981] ECR 2205.

64 Case 14/68, [1969] ECR 1.

of Community law, or to allow their courts to be used to facilitate any such breach, or to deprive any rule of Community law of its useful effect (*effet utile*). This principle could be regarded as a special case of the duties already outlined, but because of its importance in relation to rules of competition law which apply primarily to enterprises, it seems worth mentioning separately. It was first stated by the Court in *GB-INNO v. ATAB*.[65]

> The second paragraph of Article 5 of the Treaty provides that Member States shall abstain from any measure which could jeopardize the attainment of the objectives of the Treaty . . . Article 90 provides that, in the case of public undertakings and undertakings to which Member States grant special or exclusive rights, Member States shall neither enact nor maintain in force any measure contrary *inter alia* to the rules provided for in Articles 85 to 94 . . . Likewise, Member States may not enact measures enabling private undertakings to escape from the constraints imposed by Articles 85 to 94 of the Treaty. At all events, Article 86 prohibits any abuse by one or more undertakings of a dominant position, even if such abuse is encouraged by a national legislative provision. In any case, a national measure which has the effect of facilitating the abuse of a dominant position capable of affecting trade between Member States will generally be incompatible with Articles 30 and 34.

So it is clear that the principle prohibits measures encouraging breaches of *any* rule of Community law, or defeating the purpose of any such rule.

In *Buys*[66] the Advocate General said that "a Member State would be in breach of Article 5 it if enacted legislation calculated to bring about or to encourage agreements, decisions or concerted practices" contrary to Article 85. In one of the *Leclerc* cases the Advocate General said:

> If by encouraging behaviour prohibited by Article 85 and 86 [a national measure] is, in addition, capable of affecting trade between Member States . . .it will amount to an infringement of Article 3(f) and the second paragraph of Article 5, read with Article 85 or 86 . . .
>
> [A] national measure which deprived of practical effectiveness the prohibition directed to undertakings by Articles 85 and 86 or frustrated action by the Commission under Article 87 would be in direct conflict with the second paragraph of Article 5 inasmuch as it would prejudice the objective assigned to the Community by Article 3(f), which aims at the institution of a system of effective competition in the Common Market . . .[T]hose considerations bring closer to its proportions the objection that Article 3(f) merely outlines an aim while the second

---

65 Case 13/77, *NV GB-INNO-BM*,[1977] ECR 2115, 2144-45, paras. 30-33.

66 Case 5/79, *Procureur Général v. Buys*, [1979] ECR 3203, 3226, 3230-31.

> paragraph of Article 5 is too general. It is true that Article 3(f) lays down an objective for the Community, but it also sets forth a principle, the fundamental nature of which I have just emphasized. As for the second paragraph of Article 5, *it makes the transfer of powers effected by the Treaty irreversible*. The Member States must comply with the provisions in question, so as not to render nugatory the rules of the Treaty which provide for its implementation.
>
> Every time a Member State prevents those provisions from being applied, *its action is liable to deprive individuals of the rights that they might derive therefrom* and prevent the Community institutions from exercising the prerogatives that the Treaty confers on them.
>
> I consider that to be the sense of the court's judgment in *INNO v. ATAB*: a national measure which encourages behaviour in restraint of competition or, more generally, deprives of practical effect the prohibition laid down in Articles 85 and 86 of the Treaty is incompatible with Article 3(f) and the second paragraph of Article 5, read together with Articles 95 and 86.[67]

The *Leclerc* case just cited is one of the most important of what is now a long line of cases making it clear that Article 5 prevents Member States from encouraging, approving, confirming or extending restrictive agreements which are contrary to Article 85, or otherwise preventing Community competition law from being effective. The same principles also apply to Article 86, although the Court has had fewer opportunities to clarify the implications of Article 5 in relation to Article 86, and they are harder to state because the situations covered are more varied and more complicated. Member States' obligations under Article 5 not to enact legislation or any other measures which encourage infringements of Community competition law extend to State authorities. Article 90 EEC Treaty, which is only a specific example of the general principle stated in Article 5, also shows this.

It follows from this principle that Member States must not enforce arbitration awards which have been made without applying Community law, including in particular Community competition law, when it should have been applied to the case before the arbitrator. Indeed it is not yet clear whether, and if so how far, Member States can permit issues of Community law to be put to arbitration, in particular to arbitration outside the Community, where the result is to deprive the Court of jurisdiction under Article 177 over any issue which may arise.

Article 5 has direct effects when it prohibits national legislation that interferes with the operation of rules of Community law that themselves have direct effects. The duty of Member States under Article 5 not to enact legislation that encourages State authorities to breach Community law is a directly applicable rule; Article 90 of the EEC Treaty, which is directly applicable, is an example of this rule.

---

[67] Case 229/83, [1985] ECR 1, paras. 14, 20 (obligations of Member States not yet specific enough because Commission policy not formulated).

7. The Duty to Clarify the National Law Position in Relation to Community Law

Article 5 imposes a duty on Member States to clarify their national laws, if necessary by amending or repealing national measures, to avoid or resolve conflict or uncertainty, and to make clear the legal position which Community law was designed to bring about. This could be regarded as an aspect of the duty of national authorities, mentioned above, to comply with the principle of legal certainty, but it includes a duty "not to conceal the Community nature and legal effects of any legal provision from the persons to whom it applies."[68] The duty to clarify also obliges national courts to refer questions of Community law to the Court under Article 177, if there are conflicting national judgments on the issue (including national judgments in different Member States) in order to establish a uniform interpretation of Community law, especially where rights and duties of private parties are involved. National courts also have a duty to use Article 177 if there is any serious doubt as to whether a national court decision by which they are bound is compatible with the case law of the Court in Luxembourg.

8. Article 5 Had the Effect of Making Certain Acts Binding

The Court often says that specific provisions of the Treaties or of Community legislation are particular examples of the general duties resulting from Article 5. When the specific provisions are legally binding and directly applicable, the fact that Article 5 also applies may not affect the practical result. Article 5, because it binds national courts, may create direct effects from non-directly applicable rules, in litigation to which State authorities are parties; this question has been raised above.

A specific measure which would not otherwise be legally binding may be an example of a general duty imposed by Article 5, and if it is, it derives legally binding force from that Article. In the leading case[69] certain resolutions of the Council said that Member States should consult the Commission and seek its approval when adopting fisheries measures. As a part of a resolution, this would not normally have been legally binding. But the Court said:

> The Commission has rightly claimed that the resolution, in the particular field to which it applies, makes specific the duties of cooperation which the Member States assumed under Article 5 of the EEC Treaty when they acceded to the Community. Performance of these duties is particularly necessary in a situation in which it has appeared impossible, by reason of divergences of interest which it has not yet been possible to resolve, to establish a common policy and in a field such as that of conservation of the biological resources of the sea in which worthwhile results can only be attained thanks to the co-operation of all the Member States.

---

68 Case 50/76, *Amsterdam Bulb*,[1977] ECR, paras. 5, 7, 8.

69 Case 141/78, *France v. UK*, [1979] ECR 2923, 2942 at para. 8; Case 804/79 *Commission v. UK*, [1981] ECR 1045 at pp. 1090-1091 (conclusions of the Advocate General).

A resolution makes specific the duties resulting from Article 5 if, for example, it sets out a procedure for organizing cooperation, in particular where effective cooperation is necessary to achieve satisfactory results or to avoid harm to Community interests, or where it says *how*, substantively, any of the duties resulting from Article 5 are to be carried out.

9. Duties of Member States in the Sphere of External Relations

Article 5 is particularly important in the area of external relations, because both the Community and Member States have and exercise treaty making powers, and because the exercise of those powers gives rights to States which are not bound by Community law. If, then, a treaty is made which is inconsistent with Community law, it is difficult, time-consuming and perhaps embarrassing to revise or terminate it.

Under Article 234, Member States are obliged to eliminate conflicts between the Community Treaties and treaties they entered into before they became Member States. This applies *a fortiori* to obligations entered into after they became Member States. Under Article 5, Member States have a duty to cease being parties to conventions that are inconsistent with, or oblige them to act inconsistently with, Community law.

Similarly, Article 5 and Article 228 require Member States not to do anything that would cause the Community to be in breach of its obligations under any treaty to which it is a party. Member States must refrain from any action that would make it more difficult for the Community to have an effective international negotiating position. A Member State could breach Article 5 by prejudging or compromising the result of internal discussions on the negotiating position of the Community, or by weakening its negotiating position in any way.

Article 5 also binds Member States to use every legal and political means at their disposal to ensure the participation of the Union in international conventions when the Union must do so in the exercise of its exclusive competence, or when the Council has decided or is likely to decide that the Union should participate. Member States must enable the Union to exercise its powers and therefore should not agree to the terms of a draft convention or rules of procedure for negotiations unless they contain provisions enabling the Union to become a party on conditions compatible with Union law. In some circumstance, Member States are also obliged to act on behalf of the Union, by Article 5. If a Member State is bound by any of these duties, it may also be bound under Article 5 to consult the Commission beforehand about how to behave, and not to act unilaterally.

VI. Action Before the Court of Justice Against Union Institutions[70]

In two recent cases, the Court of Justice has ruled on two fundamental issues of the reference procedure under Article 177 EEC Treaty. The case of *Foto-Frost* raised the issue

[70] Gerhard Bebr, *The Reinforcement of the Consstitutional Review of Community Acts under Article 177 EEC Treaty* (Cases 314/85 and 133 to 136/85), 25 C.M.L.R. 667-91 (1988).

of jurisdiction of lower courts of the Member States to review the validity of Community acts—a power which appears inconsistent with the Court's exclusive jurisdiction to review the legal exercise of Community powers under Article 173 EEC Treaty.[71] This case is a remarkable constitutional decision which in its importance and implications may well surpass rulings the Court has so far rendered on fundamental problems of the reference procedure. The second case, the *"Berlin Butter"* case, prompted the Court to address the relationship between EEC Treaty Articles 173 and 177 as far as the legal protection of individuals is concerned.[72]

A. The Court's Exclusive Jurisdiction to Review the Validity of Community Acts under Article 177(2)

1. Facts and Background of the *Foto-Frost* Case

In this case the Court asserted, for the first time, its exclusive jurisdiction to review the validity of Community acts to the detriment of lower courts of the Member States. The main issue before the referring *Finanzgericht* (Finance Court) Hamburg concerned the execution of a Commission decision obliging the competent German authorities, pursuant to Article 5(2) of Council Regulation 1679/79, to request a post-clearance recovery of import duties on goods originating in the German Democratic Republic but purchased from traders established in Denmark and the Netherlands. The goods were dispatched from customs warehouses in Member States under the external transit procedure. In this case, the plaintiff impugned the decision of the German customs authorities which had requested subsequent payment of the duties on the basis that the relevant Commission decision was invalid.

In its reference, the Finance Court raised the question whether a lower national court may, under Article 177(2), review the validity of a Commission decision addressed to the Federal Government. In case the *Finanzgericht* lacked such jurisdiction, it requested the Court of Justice to review the validity of the Commission decision.

The Finance Court assumed, as it had already done in a preceding reference, that it lacked power to review the validity of the decision which, in its view, was within the exclusive jurisdiction of the Court. Nevertheless, it referred the question of jurisdiction to the Court of Justice with the aim of obtaining an authoritative ruling. Notably, this is one of the rare instances in which all participants in a preliminary proceeding were in agreement on the fundamental constitutional issue that national courts lack jurisdiction to review the validity of Commission decisions; such jurisdiction, by implication, belonging to the Court of Justice.

---

71 Case 314/85, *Foto-Frost v. Hauptzollamt Lübeck-Ost*, preliminary ruling of 22 October 1987.

72 Cases 133 to 136/85, *Walter Rau and Others v. Bundesanstalt für landwirtschaftliche Marktordnung*, preliminary ruling of 21 May 1987.

2. Reasoning and Findings of the Court of Justice

The question whether lower courts may review the validity of Community acts was, in the view of Advocate General Mancini, one of the most difficult questions ever submitted to the Court. The fact that the Court considered it necessary to rule on this question *in plenum* already underlines the importance of the issue involved.

The Court introduced its reasoning with the surprising statement that Article 177(2) did not determine decisively whether lower courts may review the validity of Community measures. The reason and justification for such a statement will be examined later on in the following evaluation of this remarkable ruling. The Court recognized the power of lower courts to confirm the validity of Community measures challenged by the parties to the litigation, adding significantly that such a review does not endanger "the existence" of these measures. However, it denied lower courts the power to declare a Community measure invalid on grounds which are largely based on its well established case law and on the system of legal protection as provided for by the EEC Treaty.

The Court based its ruling on two fundamental requirements of the Community legal order. First, the uniform application of Community law by all national courts—a requirement in support of which the Court referred to its ruling in *International Chemical Corporation.* This requirement, reasoned the Court, is particularly imperative if the validity of a Community measure is questioned. Moreover, the Court stressed in this connection the need for the fundamental requirement of legal certainty which, in its view, would be at stake if lower courts could individually and exclusively review the validity of Community measures.

The second fundamental requirement of the Community legal order, according to the Court, is the cohesion of the Community system of legal protection. A reference for review of Community measures controls in its proper form and function their legality as does an action for annulment. Referring to its ruling in *Parti écologiste "Les Verts"* the Court stated that ". . . in Articles 173 and 184, on the one hand, and in Article 177, on the other, the Treaty established a complete system of legal remedies and procedures designed to permit the Court of Justice to review the validity of measures adopted by the institutions." The Court reasoned that under Article 173 it has an exclusive jurisdiction to annul a measure of a Community institution. Consequently, the cohesion of the Community legal system required that it also have exclusive jurisdiction to declare a Community act invalid under Article 177.

Finally, the Court justified its exclusive jurisdiction by a practical consideration, highlighting the nature of the reference procedure and its potential for facilitating an adequate review of validity—concluding that it is in the best position to undertake such an examination. Moreover, the Court observed, the reference procedure enabled, on the one hand, the Community institution to "defend" the act in question, while providing, on the other, an opportunity to the Court to request all necessary information from other Community institutions. Thus the Court implicitly suggests that national procedure is inadequate to provide the necessary procedural safeguards for the Community institution to properly defend the validity of its act.

Interestingly, in the case of an interlocutory proceeding the Court would appear inclined to admit, in principle, an exception to its exclusive jurisdiction. Unfortunately, the Court does not elaborate its view on this point—presumably because it was not raised by the referring court.

The second question of the Finance Court concerned the validity of the Commission decision. Two points are to be noted. First, the plaintiff did not lodge an action for annulment impugning the Commission decision addressed to the Federal Government—although such an action would have been most likely admitted by the Court since the plaintiff was directly and individually concerned under Article 173(2). Instead, the plaintiff questioned the validity of the Commission decision later on in the case before the referring Finance Court. This raises the question of the relationship between EEC Treaty Article 173 and Article 177 which was not examined by the Court in the given instance—a problem to be discussed in the second part of this note.

Secondly, this case throws some light on the true nature of a reference procedure when reviewing the validity of a Community act. The Court clearly states that in such a preliminary review procedure it may ascertain the existence of facts on which a Community act was based if some factual errors are pleaded. For example, in the present case, the Commission decision in question refused to waive a post-clearance recovery of customs duties because the conditions required by Article 5 of Council Regulation 1697/79 for such a waiver were not satisfied in the given instance and the competent German customs authorities were, therefore, obliged to proceed to collect them. According to this provision, three conditions are required for such a waiver. First, the customs authorities must have failed to collect the customs duties at the time the goods were imported; secondly, the importer should have acted in good faith; and finally, a proper customs declaration should have been completed. The validity of the Commission decision, therefore, depended on the fact whether these conditions were actually satisfied. It is obvious that the Court could not have reviewed the validity of the decision unless it also examined and evaluated the relevant facts.

Unlike Advocate General Mancini, the Court found that the customs authorities had erred in their failure to apply the appropriate provisions at the time the customs declaration was made. Moreover, according to the Court, the importer acted in good faith as he could not have detected such an error of the customs authorities. In support of its view the Court mentioned the fact that even the referring Finance Court doubted whether the import in question was subject to customs duties because it could be considered as being part of purely internal German trade and as such exempted from customs duties according to the Protocol on internal German trade. This uncertainty, together with the fact that the importer had previously imported the same goods free of any customs duties, led the Court to believe that, under such circumstances, the importer could not have assumed or discovered such an error of the customs authorities. Since even the third condition was in its view satisfied, the Court found the Commission decision to be invalid and the plaintiff's claim for a waiver of a post-clearance recovery of customs duties justified.

Advocate General Mancini took an opposition stance. In his view, an importer regularly engaged in trade with Eastern European countries must have been fully aware that such triangular transactions, as in the present instance, could not be considered as part of internal German trade and, therefore, subject to customs duties as found by early decisions of the highest German courts. For this reason he concluded that the importer was not acting in good faith. Since one of the conditions for a possible waiver was not fulfilled, he proposed to uphold the validity of the decision.

3. Critical Evaluation and Implications of the Ruling

The great importance of this ruling may properly be evaluated only if the complex and delicate nature of the problem which the Court had to resolve in this instance, is examined. As is well known, Article 177 EEC distinguishes between the competence of lower courts and the obligation of courts of final instance to refer questions of interpretation or validity of Community acts to the Court of Justice. Article 177, therefore, pursues two basically different objectives by the same procedure under the same conditions. This distinction between the discretion of lower courts and the obligation of courts of final instance to refer is adequate and justified in the case of interpretation of Community rules. However, what appears entirely adequate, as far as the interpretation of Community rules is concerned, becomes inadequate, and indeed inconsistent with the Community system of rule of law, if its result is that lower courts are then free to declare a Community act invalid. There is no need to speculate any further whether the drafters of the EEC Treaty really intended to introduce such a glaring inconsistency or whether this Treaty provision was the result of a mere oversight or of negligent drafting.

Whatever the reason for this unfortunate and misconceived provision, the fact remains that its application would have had serious consequences for the cohesion of the Community legal order. It is therefore hardly surprising that, as Advocate General Mancini observed in his opinion, the prevailing view in early academic literature was that there should be a mandatory reference of lower courts for review of the validity of Community acts. Article 41 of the ECSC Treaty, it may be noted, already established an exclusive jurisdiction of the Court to review the acts of the Commission and of the Council. Similarly, the ill fated EDC Treaty laid down the exclusive jurisdiction of the Court in such instances.

Advocates General have clearly pleaded for a mandatory reference of lower courts. Advocate General Capotorti observed ". . . under the Treaties the invalidity of a Community measure *cannot* be established other than through proceedings before the Court of Justice (under Articles 173 or 177 of the EEC Treaty) and that until such a ruling is given every measure is presumed to be lawful and has effect. . . ."[73] Similarly, Advocate General Darmon insisted that ". . . the exclusive jurisdiction of the Court is based on the system of remedies established by the Treaty: Articles 173 to 176 of the Treaty concerning the application for a declaration that a measure is void and Article 177 concerning preliminary rulings on validity clearly imply that the Court has the *sole* power to decide on the legality of secondary legislation."[74] Both advocates General drew the logical consequences from the incoherent provision of Article 177(2). They

[73] Case 101/78, *Granaria v. Hoofdproduktschap voor Akkerbouwprodukten*, [1979] E.C.R. 640, 642 — Emphasis added.

[74] Case 112/83, *Société des produits de maïs v. Administration des douanes et droits indirects*, [1985] E.C.R. 720, 724 — Emphasis added.

stressed the need for an exclusive jurisdiction of the Court in matters of legality or validity of Community measures without, however, explicitly stating that as a consequence of this exclusive jurisdiction of the Court lower national courts are obliged to refer questions of validity to the Court of Justice.

The Court was, of course, aware of the deficiency of Article 177(2) and its potential danger to the coherence of the Community legal system; having already suggested with respect to the European Union that "a provision should be included to prohibit national courts from treating a Community act as invalid unless the European Court, having already considered the matter, has declared the act invalid."[75]

The grounds which the Court invoked for closing the alleged gap of Article 177(2) and for asserting its exclusive jurisdiction in reviewing the validity of Community acts are powerful indeed and their logic unassailable. In fact, arguably the Court could not have ruled otherwise if it wished to do justice to the nature of the Community legal order and respect the fundamental principles and requirements it has developed.

The grounds advanced are already sufficient for recognizing the exclusive jurisdiction of the Court. There is, however, an additional ground, inherent in the very nature of the Community legal order which is neither mentioned by Advocate General Mancini nor invoked by the Court: the autonomous nature of the Community legal order which the Court has stressed from the very beginning. This nature of Community law carries in the present context a particular weight. The power of a lower court to review the validity of a Community act, which is a higher source of law enjoying supremacy in the national legal order, is indeed incompatible with and clearly contrary to the autonomous, independent nature of the Community legal order.

The review of the validity of Community acts is, as Advocate General Mancini observed, a delicate task. Obviously, such a review may not be carried out in an abstract manner. The Court dispelled the myth of the non-contentious nature of a preliminary review procedure by recognizing, for the first time, that such a review requires the relevant facts to be ascertained. In *Foto-Frost* the Court inquired as to the reasons for which the goods had not been directly imported from the German Democratic Republic to the Federal Republic and as to the final destination of these goods—questions which subsequently became irrelevant as the Court declared the Commission decision invalid. A matter which did remain relevant, however, was the question addressed to the Commission concerning the plaintiff's alleged failure to properly complete the customs declaration—one of the conditions required for a possible waiver for a post-clearance recovery of import duties by the customs authorities.

Foto-Frost is bound to have far-reaching implications. It will promote the uniform application of Community law; enhance legal certainty; reinforce the rule of law within the Community and ultimately strengthen the legal protection of individuals. In particular, it means that a mandatory reference will clarify the question of validity of a Community act as soon as it is raised—even at the lowest level of litigation, thereby enhancing legal certainty and possibly shortening the dispute. The exclusive jurisdiction of the Court, so forcefully and unequivocally stated, refutes an interpretation

---

[75] Report of the European Union, 9/75 Supplement, Bulletin of the European Communities, 17, 21.

according to which national courts are obliged to refer only if they had serious doubts about the validity of the act. Similarly, national courts may not claim jurisdiction and avoid their obligation to refer even if the invalidity of an act was manifest. In both instances, the exclusive jurisdiction of the Court must be respected.

Another aspect of the judgment is that it fosters the protection of Community fundamental rights of individuals, since any presumed infringement of such rights by a Community act obliges any national court to request a review of such an act. Finally, a possible infringement of this widened obligation of national courts to refer widens also the right of appeal of individuals, under national law, to a higher court to have this obligation respected.

Unquestionably, *Foto-Frost* is one of the most important constitutional rulings. It reinforces the cohesion of the Community legal order and, at the same time, strengthens the indirect constitutional review which ensures a wider legal protection of individuals. The Community system of legal protection has become more coherent and legally watertight as far as the relationship between Articles 173 and 177 is concerned since only the Court of Justice may review the legality or validity of a Community act either on an action for annulment of a party or on a reference of a national court.

The difficulties and obstacles the Court had to overcome to reach such a conclusion should not be underestimated and deserve to be duly recognized and appreciated. If the Court had not given this remarkable ruling in response to an explicit question of the Finance Court, and had not asserted its exclusive jurisdiction to review the validity of Community acts, it is respectfully submitted that it would have abdicated an important part of its function as a constitutional court of the Community.

This far-reaching judgment may, at first, meet some opposition or at least be seriously criticized, as Advocate General Mancini fears. So far the fundamental rulings of the Court have been ultimately accepted and followed by national courts. It may, therefore, be reasonably expected that this ruling will be respected as well. In this context it may be noted that in comparison with cases cited by the Advocate General in which lower courts reviewed the validity of Community acts themselves, there is a far greater number of instances in which lower courts have requested a review of validity even though, at the time, they were not obliged to do so.

B. Articles 173 and 177 EEC: The Relationship Between Direct and Indirect Remedies of Individuals

1. Introduction

For the Court the procedure under these Articles constitutes two mechanisms for reviewing the legality of Community acts.[76] This general statement does not, however, clarify the relationship between these two remedies. Are they complementary or

[76] Case 112/83, *Société des produits de maïs v. Administration des douanes et droits indirects*, [1985] E.C.R. 743, 747 (Ground No. 17).

autonomous? In particular, this raises a special problem as far as the legal protection of individuals is concerned. There are two means of redress individuals may apply for: one within the Community legal order before the Court under Article 173, limited in time and restricted to Community decisions (direct remedy); the other within the national legal system before a national court under Article 177 (indirect remedy). This difference in remedies may primarily be explained by the fact that, apart from very few exceptions, Community law is by and large implemented, executed and applied by national authorities. Thus the review of legality of such national implementing measures clearly falls under the jurisdiction of national courts.

In a case before a national court an individual may challenge, according to national law, the national measures for lack of legal basis arguing that the Community act which the national authorities have executed and applied, is invalid. This raises the question whether an individual may still challenge the validity of a Community act before a national court which he did not challenge timely by a direct action for annulment under Article 173—or where such an action failed. This problem arises only in instances in which an individual contests the validity of a decision addressed to him or to a third party against which he could have lodged an action for annulment; or where such an action was declared by the Court inadmissible or unfounded.

Cases in which the validity of a regulation or directive is at stake before a national court raise, in this respect, no particular problem since an individual lacks a right of action under Article 173 to challenge such a Community act. For the Court the absence of such a right has never been an obstacle to review of the validity of regulations; it has reviewed them without any further examination whether or not an individual had a right of action. The following discussion focuses, therefore, on the specific situation in which the validity of a decision is questioned before a national court.

One clarifying remark may be added. The expression "indirect remedy" is somewhat imprecise. An individual may merely question the validity of a Community act before a national court but it is up to that court whether to apply the act or request the Court of Justice for a review of its validity. Thus an individual has a mere "right" of initiative which need not necessarily be followed by the national court.

2. Facts and Background of the "*Berlin Butter*" Case

In the case under review the plaintiffs, margarine producers, lodged an action before a German Administrative Court seeking to prohibit the German intervention agency from executing a Commission decision. As a measure for expanding the butter market and for reducing the surplus stock of butter, the decision obliged the intervention agency to release a limited quantity of butter form public stocks and put it, free of charge for a short period of time and under specific conditions, on the West Berlin market. This measure was intended to create a test case and to provide a basis for a study pursuing two objectives: to determine the possible extent of a price reduction which would result in increased butter consumption and, at the same time, a decrease in the costs of the intervention system. As to the origin and background of the case it is sufficient for present purposes to note that the plaintiffs, parties to the main proceeding before the referring national court, subsequently also lodged an unsuccessful annulment action against the Commission decision which the Court of Justice found in admissible.[77] Thus the plaintiffs challenged the Commission decision before two jurisdictions—the Court of Justice and the referring German court.

In its reference the Administrative Court requested the Court of Justice to review the validity of the decision on several grounds of a presumed infringement of some general principles of law and of fundamental rights: freedom to pursue trade and profession; freedom of competition and the principle of proportionality. For the present analysis, the only relevant question is the request for the Court to interpret Article 183 EEC. According to this Treaty provision a national court remains competent to deal with cases to which the Community is a party except where the Treaty establishes an exclusive jurisdiction of the Court. The referring court inquired whether this Treaty provision is to be so construed that the right of an individual to challenge the Commission decision under Article 173 precludes him from bringing an action before a national court contesting the relevant national measure, on the ground that the Commission decision was invalid.

3. Reasoning of the Court

In formulating its question, the referring court obviously misunderstood the meaning and purpose of Article 183, as the Community was not, in the given instance, a party to the litigation, as required. The Court merely briefly observed that no answer to the question raised may be deduced from this Treaty provision. The actual problem which preoccupied the referring court, as the Court anticipated, essentially concerned the relationship between the national and Community legal remedies.

On the point the Court made two brief but revealing observations. First, there is no Community rule which would preclude an action before a national court contesting a national measure taken in execution of a Community decision—provided such an action meets the necessary requirements of national law. Second, a national court may (according to the ruling in *Foto-Frost* now it must) request the Court for review of a Community act if such a question is relevant to the outcome of the case. Significantly, the Court added that a national court may do so without examining whether the plaintiff in the main action may directly challenge the decision before the Court of Justice.

4. Critical Evaluation of the Judgment

The Court has clarified an important and complex question. In general, the judgment is to be welcomed as it has interpreted the scope of the indirect remedy widely and independently of a direct action under Article 173. Curiously, the Court stated its view without offering any reason for such an interpretation; an expectation which is arguably not unreasonable since the judgment was delivered *in plenum* by the Court.

The following conclusions may be drawn from the nature of the reference procedure for the review of validity as an autonomous legal remedy. First, an individual may contest the validity of any Community act before a national court; there are no restrictions in this respect as in Article 173. Second, he may do so regardless of whether or

---

[77] Joined Cases 133 to 136/85, *Union Deutsche Lebensmittlewerke, Walter Raul and Others v. Commission*, 21 May 1987.

not he could have impugned the act, in due time, before the Court. Third, the nature and function of this indirect legal remedy precludes the application of the requirement of individual and direct concern, as required by Article 173 for the admission of an annulment action of an individual contesting a decision addressed to a third party—be it another individual or a Member State. It is not an individual who may request a review of validity but a national court; and with regard to national jurisdiction such a requirement makes no sense. Moreover, the essential point is whether a national implementing measure is based on a valid Community act—in this context such a requirement is misplaced. Indeed, a practical consideration precludes the application of such a requirement. If the admission of a reference for review depended on a prior finding of whether the plaintiff was directly and individually concerned by the contested decision addressed to a third party, this would place a national court in an extremely difficult position. Facing such a situation, a national court could either itself examine such a question of admissibility—a paradoxical situation if a national jurisdiction is to determine whether an action would have been admitted by the Court; or, request a preliminary interpretative ruling from the Court of Justice on this point—a no less unsatisfactory solution as the Court would have to rule on this notion of direct and individual concern in an abstract manner. A fourth point of criticism is that if an individual had to show in support of his challenge of the validity of a decision that his action would have been inadmissable, this would lead to a great number of precautionary annulment actions. Finally, the application of the requirement of admissibility as required by Article 173, would lead to discrimination. For example, an individual whose action would have been admitted if lodged, could, because of this omission, no longer contest the validity of a Community decision before a national court. An individual, however, whose action would have been inadmissible because he was not directly and individually concerned by a decision could still contest its validity before a national court.

These considerations may make it clear that in the process of challenging a Community decision before a national court it is irrelevant whether an individual has a right of direct action and if so whether his action would have been admitted. One minor point remains to be clarified, however. If an annulment action of an individual against a Community decision has failed on *substantive* grounds, can the individual still contest its validity later on before a national court?

C. Conclusion

According to established case law of the Court, individuals may question the validity of regulations and directives before a national court even though they have no right to lodge an annulment action against such acts. In the present case the Court goes one step further by recognizing such a right even in cases of decisions which an individual may challenge by direct action before the Court. Community decisions addressed to Member States are an important instrument for the application of Community law by national authorities. Under such circumstances it was essential to extend the indirect remedy of individuals even to decisions. Without such a remedy, individuals would hardly be able to contest the national measures taken in their execution of application. This indirect legal remedy available before national courts, however, may not obscure the true nature and function of a reference for review of the validity of Community acts as a constitutional review initiated by national courts. It is primarily a remedy in the nature of an objective control of ensuring a rule of law within the Community from which individuals may, however indirectly, benefit.

VII. The Future of the ECJ—Introduction of the Court of First Instance[78]

As the European Union approaches the twenty-first century, it finds itself confronted by a number of major challenges: the effects of recession, the accession of new member States, making a success of economic and monetary union, dealing with the civil war in the former Yugoslavia, its relationship with the emerging democracies of Central and Eastern Europe, to name but a few. These issues are the stuff of headlines, but there is another challenge, apparently more mundane in nature, which poses a serious threat to the first pillar of the Union: the pressure on the Court of Justice caused by its burgeoning workload. Upon the solution to that problem may depend the continued existence of a Union based on the rule of law.

A. The Workload of the Court of Justice

It is appropriate to begin by considering whether the Court of Justice performs effectively the task attributed to it by Article 164 of the EC Treaty, that of ensuring that the law is observed in the interpretation and application of the Treaty. The basic features of an effective court are not controversial: such a court is one which, within a reasonable period of time, gives just and intellectually compelling decisions. To what extent does the Court of Justice satisfy that test?

In 1980 it took the Court of Justice nine months on average to deal with a reference for a preliminary ruling and 18 months to dispose of a direct action. The Court's workload is such that, by the end of 1992, those figures had risen to nearly 19 months and nearly 26 months respectively. Figures for the early part of 1993 showed that they were continuing to rise. The days (perhaps apocryphal) when the arrival of a new case would be greeted with the popping of champagne corks are a distant memory.

Just over two years for a direct action may not compare unfavorably with some national courts or with the European Court of Human Rights, although it must be remembered that, in actions under Article 169 of the EC Treaty, the pre-litigation procedure has to be added. Asking a national court to wait in excess of 18 months for a preliminary ruling raises a more serious problem. The time spent in Luxembourg has

---

[78] Anthony Arnull, *Refurbishing the Judicial Architecture of the European Community*, 43 Int'l & Comp. L.Q. 296-316 (1994). © 1994 Anthony Arnull. Reprinted by permission.

to be added to the time spent in the domestic forum, so a delay of that magnitude may act as a serious disincentive to national judges contemplating a reference.

The pressure on the Court caused by its workload has an adverse effect on the quality of its judgments in two ways. First, the Court does not generally have time to investigate the factual background to the cases brought before it. When it does decide to do so, the consequence may be excessive delay. In most cases, the Court is forced to resolve factual disputes by strict application of the rules relating to the burden of proof, sometimes supplemented by written questions, or requests for the production of documents, or by questions at the hearing. It generally approaches such disputes essentially in the role of umpire, simply deciding which side's claim is the more plausible.

Second, even where the facts do not require further investigation, it can no longer be said that the Court's judgments are invariably the product of mature reflection. The Court may as a result overlook the implications of some of its rulings, as appears to have happened in *Barber* and the Sunday trading cases. As further result, it may feel reluctant to address apparent inconsistencies in its case law.

B. The Establishment of the Court of First Instance

It was in an attempt to address some of these problems that, in 1985, the Court proposed an amendment to the Treaties providing for the establishment of a court of first instance. As a result of that proposal, Article 168a was inserted into the EC Treaty by the Single European Act. That provision conferred on the Council, acting at the request of the Court and after consulting the Commission and the European Parliament, power to establish a court of first instance. The new body was not to be a separate institution but was to be attached to the Court of Justice, to which there was to be a right of appeal "on points of the law only." It was to have jurisdiction in "certain classes of action or proceeding brought by natural or legal person." Actions brought by Member States or by Community institutions and references for preliminary rulings under Article 177 of the EC Treaty were expressly excluded from its jurisdiction.

In 1987 the Court duly requested that a court of first instance be established. As far as the jurisdiction of the new body was concerned, the Court was faced with a choice between a general transfer of jurisdiction to the maximum extent permitted by the Treaties and a transfer in certain specific areas only. The Court took the view that the latter approach presented a number of advantages; first, it would enable the Court to foresee with some degree of certainty the number of cases involved: second, it would exclude from the new court's jurisdiction certain cases which it was considered ought to remain with the Court of Justice; third, it would reduce the risk of related cases being brought before both courts simultaneously.

The Court therefore proposed that the new body should be given jurisdiction to hear four categories of cases brought by natural and legal persons, namely:

(1) staff cases;

(2) actions for annulment and failure to act concerning the competition rules applicable to undertakings and trade protection measures in the field of dumping and subsidies;

(3) certain categories of actions brought under the Coal and Steel Treaty; and
(4) actions for damages arising out of an act or failure to act which was the subject of a challenge by the applicant under one of the first three heads.

With regard to the first category, the Court had suggested as long ago as 1974 the creation of an administrative tribunal to deal with staff cases. The limited importance of such cases made them an ideal candidate for transfer to the new body. The other categories of cases which it was proposed to transfer were characterized by the detailed factual nature of the issues they often raised.

The Court's request was implemented by the Council's decision of 24 October 1988 establishing a court of first instance. That decision departed from the Court's request in one important respect: the Court of First Instance was not at the outset to have jurisdiction to deal with dumping and subsidy cases. Although such cases nearly always involve consideration of complex and voluminous material of a factual nature, and may therefore be considered ideally suited to the CFI, their transfer was opposed by the Commission and by France, on the basis, *inter alia*, that the principles applicable were not yet sufficiently developed. In its decision, however, the Council undertook to re-examine the matter "in the light of experience, including the development of jurisprudence, and after two years of operation of the Court of First Instance."

The CFI commenced operations on 31 October 1989. In practice, its case load initially consisted almost exclusively of competition and staff cases, cases under the Coal and Steel Treaty having practically disappeared following the abolition of the steel quota regime.

The CFI's special responsibility for investigating factual matters is reflected in the preamble to the Council's decision of 24 October 1988 and in the CFI's Rules of Procedure, which entered into force on 1 July 1991. Article 64 of those Rules makes provision for the adoption by the CFI of so-called "measures of organization of procedure," with the object of ensuring that "cases are prepared for hearing, procedures carried out and disputes resolved under the best possible conditions." There is no direct counterpart to Article 64 in the Rules of Procedure of the Court of Justice, although strictly speaking it seems that all the measures of organization of procedure enumerated in the Rules of Procedure of the CFI could be adopted by the Court of Justice, either as measures of enquiry under Article 45 of its own Rules or under Articles 21 and 22 of the Statute. Be that as it may, the CFI makes extensive use of the powers conferred on it by Article 64, in particular by "summoning the parties' agents or the parties in person to meetings" before the chamber responsible or the judge rapporteur, at which the possibility of a friendly settlement or the conduct of the hearing is discussed. It may also be noted that hearings before the CFI sometimes last much longer than is customary before the Court of Justice. There is therefore no doubt that the CFI exercises its inquisitorial functions with gusto. One may be forgiven for doubting whether the Court of Justice would have uncovered the catalogue of procedural errors which led the CFI to find a Commission decision non-existent in the *PVC* cases.

C. Expanding the Jurisdiction of the Court of First Instance

The conclusion was an obvious one: the jurisdiction of the CFI should be expanded. Accordingly, in October 1991, the Court submitted a request to the Council for an extension of the CFI's jurisdiction to embrace all actions for annulment, failure to act and damages brought by natural and legal persons. The Court's request would have practically exhausted the possibilities presented by Article 168a of the Treaty as it then stood.

The response of the Commission, the European Parliament and the majority of the member States to the Court's request was on the whole a favorable one. The approval of the Commission was, however, made subject to agreement by the Council on simplification of the procedure for imposing anti-dumping and anti-subsidy duties. Both the Commission and the Parliament proposed that the CFI should also be given jurisdiction to hear actions brought by natural and legal persons arising out of arbitration clauses, within the meaning of Article 181 of the EC Treaty, contained in contracts concluded by or on behalf of the Community. Such actions are relatively few in number, but they can be problematic as they involve the application of the relevant national law. IT was envisaged that the jurisdiction of the CFI would arise only in respect of contracts concluded after the proposed decision had entered into force. Actions brought by the Community on the basis of such clauses would for the time being continue to be heard by the Court.

1. The Council's Decision of 8 June 1993

The Court's request was implemented on 8 June 1993, when the Council adopted a decision amending its decision of 24 October 1988. Broadly speaking, the new decision gave effect to the Court's request, subject to the amendments proposed by the Commission and the Parliament. However, as far as dumping and subsidy cases are concerned, the entry into force of the new measure was deferred until a date which the Council is to fix by unanimous decision. The remainder of the decision entered into force on 1 August 1993. Its main effects were as follows.

First of all, all actions for damages against the Community under the second paragraph of Article 215 now fall within the jurisdiction of the CFI. It will be recalled that only a restricted category of such actions was originally transferred to the CFI. The reason for this was that, although such cases often raise complex factual issues, they also sometimes involve an assessment of the validity of normative acts of general application. It was originally felt that such assessments should be reserved to the Court, but that body is now content for them to be made by the CFI. The disruption that might be caused were a decision of the CFI declaring such a measure void subsequently reversed by the Court is minimized by the second paragraph of Article 53 of the Statute. Under that provision, and by way of exception to the general rule that appeals to the Court do not have suspensory effect, decisions of the CFI declaring a regulation void do not take effect until the period for bringing an appeal before the Court of Justice has expired or, if an appeal is brought, until it is dismissed.

In addition, actions brought by natural and legal persons against the Commission in the field of State aid now fall within the jurisdiction of the CFI. Such actions were originally excluded from the jurisdiction of the CFI because they are frequently accompanied by proceedings against the Commission by the member State concerned. These would have to be brought before the Court. A similar situation may also arise, however, in cases involving the application of the Treaty competition rules to public undertakings. Moreover, under the third paragraph of Article 47 of the Statute, where the validity of the same act is called in question in proceedings before both the Court and the CFI, the latter may decline jurisdiction or stay the proceedings until the former has given judgment. There is therefore little risk that contradictory rulings will be delivered.

The failure of the Council to fix a date for the entry into force of the new decision in so far as it extends to dumping and subsidy cases can only be deplored. Closer scrutiny of the facts of such cases would reinforce both the rule of law and the competition policy of the Community by subjecting the Council and the Commission to a stricter standard of judicial review. None the less, the decision resulted in the transfer to the CFI of about 450 cases and therefore made a considerable dent in the backlog of cases pending before the Court.

2. The New Text of Article 168a

In the interval between the Court's 1991 request and the Council's decision of 8 June 1993, the text of Article 168a was replaced by the Treaty of Maastricht. Under the new version of that provision, the only category of cases which is expressly excluded from the jurisdiction of the CFI is references for preliminary rulings under Article 177. The question therefore arises whether further transfers of jurisdiction to the CFI should be contemplated.

It is clear that the answer to that question is "yes", for the seemingly inexorable growth in the Court's case load is likely to continue. It is salutary to list some of the most important sources of future work. First of all, there is the huge body of legislation adopted to implement the Single Market programme, which is likely to give rise to a large volume of litigation in the national courts; the number of references from national courts in some of the new Member States can be expected to increase as their courts become accustomed to using the preliminary rulings procedure; moreover, new member States are likely to accede the Union in the foreseeable future. The Court will also have to deal with issues arising out of the Treaty of Maastricht, the Agreement on the European Economic Areas, the Rome Convention on the law applicable to contractual obligations, the Agreement relating to Community Patents and the proposed Council regulation on a Community trade mark. At the same time, it seems likely that the CFI will still have some spare capacity, or at least that it will be less overworked than the Court itself. What further extensions to its jurisdiction might therefore be envisaged?

a. Direct Actions

One solution would be to give the CFI jurisdiction in essentially all direct actions, leaving the Court with responsibility for dealing with references for preliminary rulings, appeals and special procedures, such as requests for opinions under Article

228(6) of the EC Treaty (formerly the second paragraph of Article 228(1) of the EEC Treaty) on the compatibility with the Treaty of proposed international agreements. This would have the not inconsiderable merits of simplicity and clarity, but would neglect the fundamental distinction between the roles of the Court and of the CFI. While it is right that the latter should have responsibility for dealing at first instance with cases which are factually complex, or which are considered inappropriate for the supreme court of the Union, the Court itself is the proper forum for direct actions raising issues of constitutional significance.

It follows that disputes between the institutions should continue to fall within the exclusive jurisdiction of the Court. Such disputes typically raise important issues about the institutional balance. Moreover, they do not normally require detailed examination of complex factual issues and little would therefore be gained in terms of the quality of judicial review by transferring them to the CFI. It may be noted, however, that the number of such cases can be expected to increase in view of the introduction by the Treaty of Maastricht of a new legislative procedure.

Certain disputes between the institutions and the Member States are also likely to have important constitutional implications. There are, however, a number of discrete classes of action brought by Member States which might usefully be transferred to the CFI. Actions by Member States for the annulment of measures taken by the Commission in the field of public undertakings and State aid are obvious candidates, since the CFI now has jurisdiction to deal with actions brought by natural and legal persons in these fields. Disputes over Commission decisions on the clearance of accounts in respect of the EAGGF also seem ideally suited to the CFI's forensic microscope.

It will be observed that cases such as these nearly all involve challenges to decisions. It might therefore be suggested that this provides a suitable criterion for distinguishing actions brought by Member States which should go to the CFI from those which should remain with the Court. It is true that it is actions by Member States for the annulment of normative acts (regulations, directives) that are perhaps most likely to raise important constitutional issues, such as the balance between the Community and the Member States. However, it would be going too far to suggest that such issues are never raised in actions for the annulment of other types of acts, such as decisions and so-called acts *sui generis*. An example is the migration policy case, which involved the validity of a Commission decision and which raised important questions about the scope of the Commission's powers under Article 118 of the EC Treaty. Another is *France v. Commission*, which concerned the validity of internal instructions issued by the Commission to its officials concerning the sampling and analysis of products for the purposes of the management and control of the EAGGF. If the CFI is to be given jurisdiction in certain types of direct action brought by Member States, it would therefore be preferable for the categories concerned to be specified as precisely as possible.

It may be doubted whether the time is yet ripe for the transfer to the CFI of jurisdiction to hear actions brought by the Commission under Article 169. It is true that actions of that nature which are essentially uncontested, or which are contested on purely factual grounds, could, in principle, be dealt with by the CFI. But some actions under Article 169 raise issues of great importance. Moreover, under the new version of Article 171, the Court has the power, at the request of the Commission, to impose financial sanctions on any Member State which fails to comply with an earlier ruling against it under Article 169. It is unlikely that the Member States would accept that the power to impose sanctions should be conferred on the CFI and it would be undesirable to attribute that power to a court other than that which dealt with the original breach. The possibility that the Commission might subsequently ask for sanctions also seems to exclude the possibility that the Court might be given a power to delegate simple Article 169 actions to the CFI on a case-by-case basis.

It may, however, be possible to rationalize the way in which the Court deals with actions under Article 169. At present, the Court allows the Commission to pursue actions under Article 169 where the Member State concerned complies with its obligations after the expiry of the deadline laid down in the reasoned opinion. The justification for this is that the Court's ruling may be relevant in subsequent proceedings by third parties against the Member State arising out of the breach. The Court's attitude in proceedings under Article 169 may be contrasted with its approach in proceedings under Article 175. Where the defendant institution takes the steps sought by the applicant over two months after being called upon to do so but before judgment is given, the Court will decline to give a ruling on the ground that "the subject-matter of the action has ceased to exist." The hypothetical possibility that the institution's failure to act might give rise to a claim against it under the second paragraph of Article 215 is not treated as relevant. It is submitted that this approach should be extended to actions under Article 169, so that compliance by the Member State with its Treaty obligations before the Court gave judgment would normally be treated as depriving the action of its subject matter. In these circumstances, the proceedings may be considered to have served their purpose of securing respect for the Treaty. The potential liability of the Member State to third parties should be left for another occasion.

The file in Article 169 cases will typically contain the Commission's letter of formal notice and the Member State's reply, the reasoned opinion, the application, the defense, a reply and a rejoinder. Sometimes there will be a written complaint to the Commission and additional correspondence between the parties. In most cases, it is not necessary for the issues to be rehearsed so many times. It is therefore suggested that the parties should be entitled to submit a reply or a rejoinder only where the President of the Court considers further pleadings necessary. It may be noted that, on an appeal from the CFI, only one round of pleadings is permitted in the absence of permission from the President.

A more radical possibility would be to remodel Article 169 along the lines of Article 88 of the Coal and Steel Treaty, giving the Commission power to record the defendant Member State's failure in a binding decision, which the Member State could then challenge before the Court. Since Member States could be expected not to go to the Court where the breach was essentially uncontested, a reform of this nature might lead to some reduction in the Court's workload. It is perhaps doubtful, however, whether such a reform would be acceptable to the Member States.

Article 14 of the Agreement relating to Community Patents gives the Court jurisdiction to rule on disputes between the contracting States concerning the interpretation or application of the Agreement. It would be unrealistic, at least for the time being, to propose that the CFI should be given jurisdiction to hear such actions. The same is true of actions under the new Article 180d introduced at Maastricht, which will give the Council of the European Central Bank the power to bring proceedings before the Court against national central banks which are said not to have fulfilled their obligations under the Treaty.

It is not entirely clear whether the CFI will have jurisdiction in actions brought by natural or legal persons against the European Central Bank under Articles 173 or 175 of the EC Treaty or under the second and third paragraphs of Article 215. By virtue of Article 35 of the Protocol on the Statute of the European System of Central Banks and of the European Central Bank, adopted at Maastricht, jurisdiction in such actions is conferred on "the Court of Justice." Moreover, the transfer of jurisdiction to the CFI effected by the Council's decision of 8 June 1993 is expressed to take effect "save as otherwise provided in an act setting up a body governed by Community law." It is submitted, however, that since Article 35 of the Protocol contains no mention of the CFI it cannot be construed as "providing otherwise" for the purposes of the Council decision. It follows that the jurisdiction conferred on the Court of Justice by that provision will be exercised at first instance by the CFI, unless the act of the Member States which results in the establishment of the European Central Bank itself provides otherwise. It would perhaps be desirable for that act to do so, at least on a temporary basis.

b. References for Preliminary Rulings

Much of the foreseeable increase in the Court's workload will take the form, not of direct actions, but of references for preliminary rulings. Where these are made under Article 177 of the EC Treaty, they will remain excluded from the jurisdiction of the CFI, even under the new version of Article 168a. The reasons for this are a mixture of pragmatism and principle.

By definition, references under Article 177 are concerned only with questions of law. The uniform application of Community law, properly construed, is of fundamental importance to the proper functioning of the Union and can be ensured only by the Court itself. Were jurisdiction to give preliminary rulings to be conferred on the CFI, it would not be feasible to allow for an appeal to the Court, which would therefore be deprived of the opportunity to supervise the way in which that jurisdiction was being exercised.

Transferring all references under Article 177 to the CFI therefore seems out of the question. Might it none the less be desirable to transfer to it certain categories of such reference? The problem with that approach would be the difficulty of defining the classes of reference falling within the CFI's jurisdiction. Assigning them according to their subject matter seems impractical, as they often concern several different areas of Community law. Another possibility would be to take account of the status of the referring court, but this approach seems thoroughly undesirable; the seniority of the national court is not a safe guide to the importance of the questions raised.

An alternative would be to permit the Court to delegate to the CFI on a case-by-case basis power to deal with simple references. This solution also has a number of disadvantages. To some, it might seem inconsistent with the principle of the *juge legal* or *gesetzlicher Richter,* according to which the parties to a case should know in advance who has jurisdiction to decide it. It is doubtful whether that principle has any place in the Community legal order, but in any event the idea suffers from a number of other drawbacks. It would require someone in the Court, probably the judge rapporteur and the advocate general, to study the file as soon as the deadline for submitting written observations has expired, in order to establish whether it is suitable for transfer to the CFI. Yet if the case is a simple one, the delivery of a judgment might not entail a great deal of extra work. In any event, the importance of a case might not become apparent until a later date, perhaps at the hearing when oral observations may be submitted by, for example, a Member State or by a party to the main action which did not submit written observations. Is the CFI to be expected to transfer the case back to the Court at that stage, with all the extra delay [that] that would inevitably cause?

It therefore seems right that references under Article 177 should remain the exclusive preserve of the Court. The solution to the likely growth in the number of such references must be sought instead in the way in which the Court deals with them. That subject is considered below.

It may be noted that Article 168a would not prevent the CFI from being given jurisdiction to deal with references on the interpretation of the Brussels and Rome Conventions, since such references are made, not under Article 177 of the Treaty, but under special protocols. The rules contained in those Conventions, while important, may be considered to fall outside the central core of Community law and it may in due course be appropriate for jurisdiction to give rulings on their interpretation to be conferred on the CFI.

References to the Court of Justice by courts and tribunals of EFTA States which have ratified the EEA Agreement will be made, not under Article 177, which can be invoked only by a court or tribunal of a Member State, but under Article 107 of, and Protocol 34 to, that Agreement. Such references are not therefore excluded *a priori* from the jurisdiction of the CFI by Article 168a. From the point of view of the Community, however, the Agreement constitutes an act of one of the institutions. References on the interpretation of EEA rules by courts and tribunals of the Member States will therefore be made under Article 177. Moreover, the right of EFTA courts and tribunals to make references to the Court of Justice under Protocol 34 will arise only in respect of provisions of the Agreement "which are identical in substance to the provisions of the Treaties establishing the European Communities, as amended or supplemented, or of acts adopted in pursuance thereof." It would therefore be entirely inappropriate to confer on the CFI jurisdiction to deal with references by courts and tribunals in EFTA States. The question is perhaps an academic one, however, since EFTA States will not be obliged to apply Protocol 34 to their courts and tribunals. For constitutional and political reasons, it seems unlikely that any of them will choose to do so.

The Agreement relating to Community Patents gives the Court jurisdiction to accept references from the Community patent appeal court, otherwise known as the Common Appeal Court, as well as from certain national courts. References by the former are expressed by the Agreement to be made "in accordance with Article 177" of the EC Treaty, but this seems incorrect, for the Common Appeal Court is not a court or tribunal of a Member State and the Agreement itself falls outside the scope of the first paragraph of Article 177. If references by the Common Appeal Court are not made under that Article, the CFI could, within the terms of the new version of Article 168a, be given jurisdiction to hear them. None the less, this would probably be inappropriate, since such references may require the EC Treaty itself to be interpreted. It would probably be undesirable to treat references made by the Common Appeal Court differently from references made by national courts, so these too should remain with the Court of Justice, at least for the time being.

D. Dealing with Cases

It is appropriate at this point to turn to the way in which the Court deals with the cases brought before it. The following changes, which have recently been made to the Court's working methods to help it deal more expeditiously with its case load, may be noted.

(1) In 1990 oral delivery of the advocate general's opinion in its entirety was abandoned. Generally it is now only the recommendation at the end of the opinion that is read out to the Court. This is usually done in French, the Court's working language, prior to the hearing in another case by the advocate general to whom that case has been assigned, rather than by the author of the opinion.

(2) The Court now has the power, subject to certain conditions, to dispense with a hearing. In direct actions, this can be done only "with the express consent of the parties." In references for preliminary rulings, the rule is slightly more flexible, for the Court may decide not to hold a hearing if none of those who are entitled to submit observations has asked to present oral argument.

(3) The Court also has the power to deal with references for preliminary rulings by reasoned order, where a question referred "is manifestly identical to a question on which the Court has already ruled."

(4) Under an amendment made at Maastricht to Article 165, the Treaty now requires the Court to sit in plenary session only "when a Member State or a Community institution that is a party to the proceedings so requests". It is to be hoped that three- and five-judge chambers will become the rule, the full Court very much the exception.

All these changes promise to have some effect in improving the Court's productivity, but more could be done.

The experience of the CFI in hearing cases without an advocate general, except when sitting in plenary session or when "the legal difficulty or the factual complexity of the case" is such that the assistance of an advocate general is considered desirable, raises the question whether it is always necessary for the Court to be assisted by an advocate general. The general importance of the office of advocate general is widely acknowledged, but a fully reasoned opinion is not necessary in simple cases.

It is therefore proposed that cases assigned to three-judge chambers should be dealt with without an advocate general. If the hearing too was dispensed with, the result would be a considerable saving of time. An alternative would be for the decision to proceed without an opinion to be taken on a case-by-case basis at the administrative meeting. Either approach would mean that the decision would not be taken until the judge rapporteur and the advocate general initially assigned to the case had perused the file. The result might be that references on the interpretation of the Common Customs Tariff, for example, would be dealt with by a three-judge chamber sitting without any advocate general, perhaps without a hearing too, unless they raised issues of general importance.

Where an advocate general does deliver an opinion, there is scope for the Court to place more reliance on it. For many years judgments of the Court contained no reference to the advocate general's opinion. Nowadays the Court sometimes refers to the opinion where it agrees with a particular view expressed in it. This enable the Court to avoid dealing with the point in detail. The Court could make greater use of this practice, only giving the briefest judgment where it agrees with the result proposed by the advocate general and with the broad lines of his argument. It could be made clear perhaps in something like a practice direction, that the Court's ruling was not necessarily to be taken as an endorsement of everything contained in the opinion. A precedent for such an approach can be found in the practice of the French Counseil d'Etat, the decision of which may need to be read in conjunction with the *conclusions* of the *commissaire du gouvernement.*

It may be doubted whether much would be gained from giving the Court power to reject a request from a member State or a Community institution, being a party to the proceedings, that a case should be heard by the Court sitting in plenary session. Such an innovation would mean that the Court would have to hear argument on the matter, which might outweigh the potential benefits. For the present at least, it seems preferable to rely on the member States and the institutions to exercise restraint in making such requests.

In any event, since there are no parties in references for preliminary rulings, the Treaty now gives the Court absolute discretion to assign such references to the formation it considers appropriate. If a corresponding amendment is made to the Rules of Procedure, a member State or an institution will no longer be nettled to insist on a reference being heard by the full Court for purely political reasons.

It does not yet seem necessary to introduce a requirement that leave be obtained before an appeal can be brought against a decision of the CFI. This device, which is familiar to British and North American lawyers, can be an effective way of limiting appeals in relatively unimportant cases, but it is not in keeping with the civil law tradition, according to which the right to appeal is a subjective one belonging to the parties. Moreover, dealing with a case on appeal is less time-consuming than hearing it at first instance, for the facts will already have been established and the issues in dispute clarified. In any event, the number of appeals brought before the Court is probably not yet high enough to merit the introduction of a requirement that leave be sought. For the moment at least, an adequate safeguard against frivolous appeals is provided by Article 119 of the Court's Rule of Procedure, which enables the Court to dismiss by reasoned order any appeal which is "clearly inadmissible or clearly unfounded." None the less, the question may have to be reviewed if there is a large growth in the number of appeals.

It is sometimes suggested that the Court's workload could be reduced simply by appointing more judges, but this does not seem likely to have the desired effect. One result would be a proliferation in the number of chambers and a consequent increase in the need for the Court to sit in plenary session in order to preserve consistency in its case law. The larger the Court, the less effective it is at delivering prompt and intellectually compelling judgments. In any event, the prospect of new accessions means that the number of judges will inevitably increase. The logistical problems this will cause would only be exacerbated if additional judges were appointed from among the existing Member States. Indeed, it is possible that the Member States will in future have to be limited to one member each, either a judge or an advocate general.

The CFI, however, has no general responsibility for preserving consistency in the decisions of its chambers. That responsibility belongs to the Court of Justice in the exercise of its appellate jurisdiction. It was for this reason that the Court's 1987 request made no provision for the CFI to sit in plenary session. It may therefore be possible to relieve the pressure on the CFI, should this prove necessary, simply by increasing the number of judges.

The Court has never made use of its power to propose to the Council the appointment of assistant rapporteurs. Such rapporteurs could provide an important source of additional assistance, although care would need to be taken to specify their function. In particular, overlap with the role of legal secretaries and that of the Research and Documentation Division would need to be avoided.

In view of its growing jurisdiction, it is perhaps unfortunate that no provision has been made for assistant rapporteurs to be attached to the CFI. The more active inquisitorial role played by the CFI would seem to offer greater scope for the involvement of such officials. Extra help could also be provided by the appointment of additional legal secretaries to assist the members of the CFI, although any more than three per judge would probably be unmanageable.

Many of the suggestions put forward above would affect all proceedings brought before the Court, but the way in which references for preliminary rulings in particular are dealt with calls for some additional comments. It is now clear that such references will be rejected by the Court as inadmissible if the national court does not give an adequate explanation of the background to the case. The Court may even take this step by reasoned order under Article 92 of its Rules of Procedure. This change of direction offers some scope for eliminating speculative and ill-though-out references, although the Court will have to be careful not to discourage the use of Article 177 where there is a genuine question of Community law at issue.

Further flexibility would be introduced if the Court were given greater freedom to deal with references—albeit admissible—by reasoned order. It is not often that a question referred can be considered "manifestly identical to a question on which the Court has already ruled." At present, references are sometimes withdrawn following a letter from the Court's registrar drawing the attention of the referring court to a previous ruling, but national procedural rules may not permit this to be done. It is therefore suggested that the Court should be able to respond to a reference by reasoned order where the question referred is in substance the same as a question on which the Court has already ruled. Although a previous proposal by the Court to similar effect failed to secure the approval of the Council, the matter may have to be reconsidered if the delay in dealing with references is to be significantly reduce.

E. Conclusion

It may be helpful to summarize in broad terms the extension in the jurisdiction of the CFI proposed in this Article. First, an early date for the transfer of dumping and subsidy cases to the CFI should be fixed by the Council. This should be done regardless of whether agreement has been reached on reform of the procedure for imposing duties. Second, the CFI should be given jurisdiction in actions brought by member States pursuant to the second paragraph of Article 173 and the first paragraph of Article 175 in respect of the following categories of act:

(1) decisions concerning the competition rules applicable to undertakings and aids granted by States;
(2) decisions concerning the clearance of the accounts presented by Member States in respect of the expenditure of the Guarantee Section of the EAGGF.

Finally, the CFI should be given jurisdiction in actions brought by the Community pursuant to Article 181 of the EC Treaty.

The Court of Justice should retain exclusive jurisdiction for direct actions brought by the institutions, direct actions brought by the Member States other than those referred to above, and references for preliminary rulings under Article 177. Consideration should be given to conferring on the CFI jurisdiction for some other categories of reference, such as those concerning the interpretation of the Brussels and Rome Conventions.

In combination with the internal changes suggested above, these reforms could be expected to make some contribution to improving the effectiveness of the Community's judicial structure. If the pressure on the CFI became too great, there are two simple ways in which it could be significantly reduced. The possibility of increasing the number of judges in the CFI has already been mentioned. Another possibility would be to remove staff cases from the jurisdiction of the CFI and transfer them to a new tribunal specially established to deal with them. It would be preferable if the decisions of such a tribunal were to be final, but a right of appeal on points of law, either to the CFI (sitting in such cases as a tribunal of last resort) or directly to the Court of Justice, might perhaps be envisaged.

In the longer term, however, more radical solutions may have to be considered: the introduction of a right of appeal to the CFI against decisions of national authorities taken in application of Community rules; the creation of further specialist tribunals on the model of the Community patent appeal court, and even regional courts of first instance.

Chapter 11

New Challenges and Problems

Part I: Integration: Eastern Europe and the European Union

Editor's Note: In May 1996, Member States of the European Union had the Intergovern mental Conference in Turin, Italy. One of the more important issues on the agenda of the conference, was the integration of Eastern European States into the European Union. There have always been problems in this respect, particularly in terms of political and economic differences, not to mention the cultural differences between EU states and the Eastern European countries. This Chapter is intended to map out the development of the EU relations with Eastern Europe.

Following the Introduction, a historical point of view of the evolvement of EU-Eastern Europe relations is set out in Section II, ranging from the early trade relations when the Council of Mutual Economic Assistance represented the Eastern European states, to the Generation Agreements after the liberalization from CMEA. Particular emphasis is placed on relations with former Communist countries such as East Germany, Romania, Hungary, the USSR and Poland.

Section III focuses on the Europe Agreements which provide a far more extensive and reciprocal relationship between EU and the Eastern European states. The Europe Agreements represent a giant step in implementing the objectives of the EU, such as free movement of trade and workers, reciprocal right of establishment, to mention a few, in the Eastern European states upon integration.

Section IV represents the viewpoint of the Eastern European integration from the other end of the stick: the EU Commission in Brussels. A particular opinion in some of the more affluent Western European states is that the integration of Eastern Europe should be more gradual and implemented after appropriate adjustments to the economies of the Eastern European states. It is proposed that a transitional stage such as membership via the European Free Trade Association (EFTA) should be set for Eastern European states. In this sense, integration is more likely to be smoother than a sudden, disruptive change. This sets the stage for the discussion in Sections V and VI for proposed future relationships between the European Union and Eastern European states, among the more prominent is via the route through membership in the European Economic Area (EEA).

The final Section, Section VII, provides Eastern Europe's view of integration into the EU. There are obvious benefits from joining the EU, whereby the poorer Eastern European states can share the wealth of the industrialized Western European states. But as indicated before in Section IV, the problems Eastern Europe faces are the qualifications for membership, as it is not an easy task to adjust age-old policies and established economies to suit the qualifications for membership.

I. Introduction[1]

The dramatic political changes in Eastern Europe over the past years have been accompanied by legal, technical, institutional and financial efforts to link the countries emerging from communist rule to the structures of the European Union (EU). From both sides of Europe, the motivations for these efforts have mixed political and economic considerations, ranging from consolidating the Westward political orientation of a reunified Germany to supporting the economic development of market structures in the East.

The recent history of trade relations between the EU and the Eastern European members of the Council for Mutual Economic Assistance (CMEA) highlights the continuity between the liberalization efforts underway before the recent political changes and what have been seen as responses to those changes. Indeed, the initial responses from Brussels to those changes have been a surprisingly *ad hoc* and modest combination of trade and aid initiatives familiar from previous relations with the East or with other third countries. Even as the aid programs have become increasingly generous in recent months, the path for political and economic integration between Eastern Europe and the EU has become by no means clear.

The EU has indicated that these initiatives are to be continued and expanded in the context of a broader institutional or "architectural" approach to Europe as a whole. The Eastward expansion of the EU's influence may be institutionalized in a variety of ways. Those (including many in the EFTA countries) who consider membership an exclusive path to integration with the EU underestimate the range of the possible no less than those (including many in Brussels) who consider country-by-country association agreements the only approach for the Eastern European countries. Although the specific approach currently being taken toward the old Eastern bloc countries fits within the historic ebb and flow of Western European integration, this approach may not provide the most advantageous structure from the point of view of the Eastern European nations.

Beyond statements about potential membership in various Western European institutions, the Eastern European countries have focused on attracting foreign investment and integrating themselves into the international trade system. While their recent legislative initiatives relating to foreign investment vary in emphasis, they all seek to attract project investment and promote exports to the West. Although the

[1] David Kennedy & David E. Webb, *Integration: Eastern Europe and the European Economic Communities,* 28 Colum. J. Transnat'l L. 634-75 (1990). ©1990 David Kennedy & David E. Webb. Reprinted by permission.

tools for domestic industrial policy available in each country vary in sophistication, the governments in the East have not focused on the relationships among microeconomic policies, economic freedoms and harmonization initiatives associated with participation in the EU.

It is difficult to know where this combination of an integrative single-market orientation in the EU and a focus on foreign investment, export promotion and democratic constitutional reform in the East will lead. In some respects, these are simply two political visions of economic modernization. The negotiations will be particularly sensitive because these two visions, taken together, may result in only the most technocratic dimensions of EU politics being extended Eastward while the East relates to the EU primarily as a developing and dependent economy. This is precisely the model of integration and the approach to politics which has proven least satisfactory elsewhere.

II. Prior Economic Relations Between the European Union and Eastern Europe

The EU's current intentions toward Eastern Europe should be understood as the latest stage in an evolving history of EU-Eastern European trade relations. Although the political and economic changes in 1989 and 1990 have no doubt caused the EU to accelerate its policy of improving its bilateral relations with the countries of Central and Eastern Europe, this process pre-dates recent upheavals.

Perestroika and the collapse of communist rule in the Soviet Empire cannot be considered as the starting point in the Community's relationship with the countries of Eastern Europe.[2] Foundations had been laid early as 1963 when the Community addressed an *aide- mémoire* to the Soviet Union on the normalisation of relations. However, little came of this overture as the Soviet Union was steadfast in its perception of the Community as NATO's economic arm. The Soviet Union's refusal to recognise the Community had both economic and political consequences for the other States who were members of the Council for Mutual Economic Assistance (CMEA) since these States were thereby prevented from recognising the Community and ultimately denied the opportunity of access to the Common Market.

The EC's relations with Eastern Europe can be divided into three essential phases:[3]

- an initial phase in which there are limited bilateral or multilateral links between the EC and its Member States and the Council for Mutual Economic Assistance (CMEA) and its members, with the EC applying a technical set of rules for state-trading countries devised under the Common Commercial Policy (CCP)

---

[2] Lynn E. Ramsey, *The Implications of the Europe Agreements for an Expanded European Union*, 44 Int'l & Comp L.Q. 161-71 (1995).

[3] David Kennedy & David E. Webb, *The Limits of Integration: Eastern Europe and the European Communities*, 30 C.M.L.R. 1095-1117 (1993).

- a second phase, in which the EC takes the lead in orchestrating the Western re sponse to the fall of the Soviet bloc and contemplates the "normalization" of trade relations;
- the current phase, in which the EC, challenged by internal conflicts and a debate over enlargement, manages "association" relationships with Hungary, Poland, the Czech Republic, the Slovak Republic, Bulgaria and Romania (the Association Countries), which are designed gradually to deepen economic, legal and institutional links.

A. Phases One and Two: The Normalization of Trade Relations[4]

Prior to the 1980 agreement with Romania, no formal trade links existed between the EU and other Comecon[5] or its Eastern European member countries beyond a limited number of sectoral agreements and common membership with Romania, Poland, Hungary and Czechoslovakia in the General Agreement on Tariffs and Trade (GATT). Actual trade with these countries was also limited.

Following an initial period of hostility to European integration, Comecon made repeated efforts to commence direct negotiations for a comprehensive trade agreement with the EU. The EU refused on the basis that Comecon lacked the competence to conclude a trade agreement on behalf of its members. Instead, the EU applied a trade regime to each of the countries of Eastern Europe which included a number of import restrictions and provided neither preferential treatment nor EU aid.

The real breakthrough in Community/Comecon relations came with the conclusion of the Joint Declaration on the Establishment of Official Relations in 1988. [And] Romania's decision to break ranks with the Comecon opened a second sate of EC-Eastern European relations. During this phase, Eastern European countries endeavored to "normalize" their trade and commercial relations with the EU through bilateral agreements independent of other Comecon members. Czechoslovakia and Hungary concluded such agreements in 1988, Poland and the Soviet Union (USSR) in 1989 and East Germany and Bulgaria in 1990. The focus of these agreements has been the elimination of commercial and legal barriers to trade.

From 1976 to 1980 negotiations took place between the Community and the CMEA.[6] The fundamental stumbling block in these negotiations proved to be the dif-

---

4 David Kennedy & David E. Webb, *Integration: Eastern Europe and the European Economic Communities,* 28 Colum. J. Transnat'l L. 634-75 (1990), at 635. © 1990 David Kennedy & David E. Webb. Reprinted by permission.

5 COMECON was the old name for the Council for Mutual Economic Assistance. It is now known by its new acronym CMEA.

6 Lynn E. Ramsay, *The Implications of the Europe Agreements for an Expanded European Union*, 44 Int'l & Comp. L.Q. 161-171 at 162 (1995).

fering expectations of the parties. The Community sought the conclusion of a framework treaty that is, an agreement establishing the legal basis for relations where the substantive detail is agreed subsequently. Conclusion of a framework treaty would enable the Community to conclude agreements directly with individual CMEA States. The CMEA, on the other hand, did not wish to weaken its bargaining position, and instead sought bloc-to-bloc negotiations leading to the conclusion of a substantive agreement. There was, prior to 1988, virtually no institutional framework for trade relations between the EC and Eastern European countries other than common GATT membership in the cases of Hungary, Poland, Czechoslovakia and Romania, as the EC refused on both legal and political grounds to negotiate trade matters with CMEA.[7] In building the tools for implementation of the CCP, the EC adopted into Community legislation the various quantitative restrictions imposed by the Member States on imports from state-trading countries.

The real breakthrough in Community/CMEA relations came with the conclusion of the Joint Declaration on the Establishment of Official Relations in 1988. [8] The Joint Decla ration had two main consequences. First, it established official relations between the Community and the CMEA and by implication, a recognition by the Community of the individual CMEA States. Second, it provided the legal basis for co-operation between the two organizations in fields falling within their competence.

B. The First-Generation Agreements

The establishment of official relations gave individual CMEA States the freedom to negotiate with the Community and hence the way was clear for the conclusion of the "first-generation" agreements. The first of these were signed in 1988 and first-generation agreements exist with Hungary, Poland, (East Germany), the Soviet Union, Bulgaria and Romania.

The agreements share three main features. First, and arguably the most important, are the provisions concerning commercial co-operation. Under this title the parties commit themselves to the most-favoured-nation principle as defined by Article 1 of the 1946 General Agreement on Tariffs and Trade. Moreover, the Community commits itself to the gradual abolition of quantitative restrictions which operate in relation to goods originating in the associated State. Second, the agreements contain provisions relating to trade co-operation whereby the parties undertake to "promote, expand and diversify their trade on the basis of reciprocity and non-discrimination." Finally, provisions are included which created a framework. Joint committees were established to ensure the proper functioning of the agreement.

---

7 David Kennedy & David E. Webb, *The Limits of Integration: Eastern Europe and the European Communities*, 30 C.M.L.R. 1095-1117 at 1100 (1993).

8 Lynn E. Ramsay, *The Implications of the Europe Agreements for an Expanded European Union*, 44 Int'l & Comp. L.Q. 161-171 at 162 (1995).

Even a cursory glance through the first-generation agreements reveals that they are fairly limited in their scope. This becomes apparent in the legal basis under which the agreements were enacted. By employing Articles 133 and 235 of the original EEC Treaty the Community emphasized the limited nature of these agreements. This was to have been expected given the political context within which the agreements were formed and the speed at which they were concluded after the 1988 Joint Declaration. However, it must be accepted that these agreements do create precise and legally binding obligations, such as the abolition of quantitative restrictions. These agreements are therefore significant because of the sharp contrast they provide to the mutual suspicion and limited contact of the Cold War decades. Indeed, in the final analysis the true value of these agreements will perhaps prove to be the foundation which they have established for the Europe Agreements.

Current EU-Eastern European relations have been built on these agreements.[9] Indeed, despite the virtual end of communist regimes throughout Eastern Europe, so far there has been only modest progress beyond the trade agreement stage. For Poland and Hungary, "normalization" of trade relations has been virtually assured under the Poland/Hungary Assistance for Economic Restructuring (PHARE) program and the two countries have been granted certain preferential treatment and aid. For the remaining countries, as of this writing, the process of eliminating trade restrictions is still underway with aid only now forthcoming on the basis of the EU's recent decision to extend PHARE to Czechoslovakia, East Germany, Bulgaria and Yugoslavia.

C. The EU's Trade Regime for Eastern Europe before Bilateral Relations: The Common Commercial Policy

The EU's approach to trade with Eastern Europe prior to the recent changes differed from its approach to market economies in matters of form and detail but not in structure. The differences were more technical than political and their effects were felt primarily as special restrictions and duties on particular products, the traditional substance of technical trade disputes, rather than as a more dramatic ideological rupture.

Article 113 of the Treaty of Rome (EU Treaty), pursuant to which the EU has exclusive competence to conduct a common external commercial policy on behalf of the Member States, provides the basis for its trade relations with Eastern Europe. On the basis of Article 113, Member States may not independently impose tariffs or quantitative restrictions on products originating in third countries. Further, they may not enter into voluntary export restraint or other trade agreements with third countries. This centralization of trade competence has led to the distance between Member State political alignments and the technically constituted EU commercial policy.

---

[9] David Kennedy & David E. Webb, *Integration: Eastern Europe and the European Economic Communities,* 28 Colum. J. Transnat'l L. 634-75 (1990), at 637.

The EU's common commercial policy is pursued within the context of the GATT, which both permits customs unions and provides a framework for their trade relations with third countries. Within that framework, third countries are generally to be treated on a "most favored nation" (MFN) basis, although some are given special "preferences" as part of the Generalized System of Preferences (GSP) intended to assist developing countries. The GATT also permits derogations in certain cases and provides for more restrictive treatment of state-trading countries. Non-GATT members benefit only from whatever bilateral arrangements they have negotiated. In general, the EU applies the same tariffs to imports from all third countries, including those in Eastern Europe, except those countries that have either negotiated special tariff reductions (such as Israel, Turkey and the EFTA countries) or those that participate in the GSP.

1. Quantitative Restrictions

The EU's approach to quantitative restrictions has traditionally differentiated third countries with market economies and those with state-trading economies. Significantly, however, a structurally similar institutional and legal process has been established for both systems.

Member States of the EU are authorized to impose only a limited number of quantitative restrictions on their imports from market countries. This open regime is subject to two important general limitations. The EU Commission may, on its own initiative or at the request of a Member State, impose restrictions on products whose import would injure Union producers. Such measures expire after three months absent further action by the EU Council. Where, following a request by a Member State, the Commission does not submit a proposal for Council action, a Member State may act unilaterally to restrict imports on an interim basis or in accordance with a bilateral agreement between it and the third country in question. Furthermore, as a matter of EU law, the EU can impose Union-wide quotas, although this is unlikely to be done except perhaps in highly sensitive sectors such as steel, textiles, or automobiles for which imports are currently limited by bilateral and multilateral voluntary export restraint agreements.

The Member States have been authorized to maintain a much greater number of specific quantitative restrictions on imports from state-trading countries. A Member State maintaining such a quantitative restriction might limit imports of these goods directly into its territory from the third country in question. It may not restrict imports of these goods which have lawfully entered another Member State, except in accordance with a specific measure under Article 115 of the EU Treaty. In addition, the Commission is required to consider the economic characteristics peculiar to state-trading countries when reviewing requests by Member States to impose surveillance or protective measures. The basis for these additional safeguards and restrictions is the presumed potential for state-trading countries to harm EU industries by rapidly increasing exports in accordance with centralized planning decisions not dependent on market forces. The EU has not specified the characteristics of a state-trading country, but has simply indicated that the restrictions permissible under this regime apply to the Comecon countries (other than Cuba), Albania, North Korea and the People's Republic of China.

The EU's tolerance of significant quantitative restrictions imposed by the Member States has until recently applied equally to all Comecon countries, notwithstanding the GATT membership of Czechoslovakia, Hungary, Poland and Romania. Quantitative restrictions are permitted by the protocols of GATT accession for Hungary, Poland and Romania, as an exception to the general prohibition against quantitative restrictions contained in Article XI of the GATT. However, progress on the EU's elimination of quantitative restrictions imposed by its Member States has been clearly slower than contemplated at the time of Hungary, Poland and Romania's accession to GATT. In the case of Czechoslovakia, one of the original GATT signatories, there is no explicit justification for the EU's continued application of quantitative restrictions.

2. Anti-Dumping

The EU's anti-dumping rules, applicable to imports from both market and non-market economies, have placed the greatest burden on exports from Eastern Europe. The reason for this disparity is the EU producers have easily been able to argue that the lower prices at which products from Eastern Europe are sold in the EU are not determined by market forces and should therefore be subject to an anti-dumping duty. The EU's basic anti-dumping legislation establishes specific rules for imports from state-trading countries. As in the EU's quantitative restrictions legislation, there is no definition of "state-trading country," but rather a list which includes all of the Eastern European Comecon countries.

The most important point to be noted is that the greatest difference between the approaches taken by the EU to market and non-market economies involves a method of technical calculation. In determining the "normal" value of a good for comparison with its sales price to determine if the product was dumped, the Commission or Council may select the price at which a like product is sold by a market economy producer in either the exporter's domestic market or in a third country, the constructed value of a like product in a market economy, or the Union price for a like product. Prices on the exporter's home market for like products are rarely selected as the normal value because of the presumption that these prices are subsidized. As a result, prices or constructed values in market countries are generally selected, leaving the Eastern European exporters with little input in this determination. Since the third country selected is often more developed than the Eastern European country concerned, the advantages of lower wages and other production costs that the Eastern European producers are likely to enjoy can be eliminated.

As in the case of quantitative restrictions, negotiations on normalization with the newly created free market economies may ease these potential negative effects for specific exports. In any event, the EU has traditionally used the anti-dumping proceedings as a tool of the industrial policy in both market and state-trading situations. Thus, in the technocratic environment within which anti-dumping decisions are made, particular dumping determinations will continue to depend upon a variety of factors in particular cases, rather than upon any general ideological shift on the part of the exporting nation. Improved ties with the EU may enhance the Eastern European countries' input into the EU anti-dumping process, and the Commission may reduce its anti-dumping measures activity with respect to Eastern European products as a form of indirect aid. Such a policy could then be reversed if, for example, Korean and Japanese companies were to exploit the relaxation of trade restrictions on Eastern European products and the low cost of production in Eastern European countries to supply the EU market from new operations in Eastern Europe.

D. EU-Eastern European Trade Agreements

The central theme of the trade agreements between the various Eastern European countries and the EU is the elimination of EU quantitative restrictions on imports from these countries. Prior to the EU agreements with the USSR, East Germany and Bulgaria, all parties to the agreements were GATT members and the agreements sought to resolve the problem of quantitative restrictions largely in the manner already provided for under GATT. The agreements with these three non-GATT members apply a similar approach.

From the EU's perspective, the trade agreements purport to assure its producers access to Eastern European markets. In fact, the key legal barriers to EU exports to Eastern Europe are the import licensing systems authorized under GATT and used by various Eastern European countries to limit their balance of payments deficits, and the Coordinating Committee (CoCom) restrictions on the export of certain products to Eastern Europe. Hungary is the only Eastern European country which has significantly liberalized its import licensing system. It did so as part of a general economic reform, rather than in response to obligations under its trade agreement with the EU. Similarly, the loosening of CoCom restrictions is not coming about in the context of trade negotiations. In any event, non-legal barriers to EU exports to Eastern Europe and, in particular, the lack of convertible currency in Eastern Europe, are more important than any legal barriers.

Because the EU negotiates trade matters individually with each Comecon country, relations between the EU and Eastern Europe have not been uniform. Czechoslovakia and Romania signed so-called "first generation" trade agreements which cover only industrial products and did not contain a firm commitment to eliminate all discriminatory quantitative restrictions set by these countries on exports to the EU. The EU signed "second generation" trade and commercial cooperation agreements first with Hungary in 1988 and with Poland in 1989. The USSR, East Germany, Czechoslovakia and Bulgaria signed second generation accords with the EU in 1990 and the EU and Romania have initialed a second generation accord. These agreements cover all products other than textiles and European Coal and Steel Community (ECSC) goods and contain a firm commitment for the abolition of quantitative restrictions by a certain date. In addition, the agreements establish joint committees to consider commercial cooperation possibilities. East Germany stands apart from this third group of countries because of its special trade relationship with West Germany.

1. First Generation Agreements

a. Romania

The agreement on trade in industrial products between the EU and Romania (EU-Romania Agreement) entered into effect in 1981. The obligations of each party primarily reflect those assumed under GATT. In particular, the EU agreed gradually to reduce quantitative restrictions against Romanian imports authorized by Romania's GATT Protocol of Accession. The agreement incorporates a list of priority products for which the EU agreed to lift quantitative restrictions immediately. Subsequent liberalization has been negotiated in the context of an EU-Romania joint committee. In addition, Romania was, until the PHARE program, the only Eastern European country to benefit from the GSP regime. In exchange for these commitments from the EU, Romania agreed to increase and diversify its imports of EU products at the same rate as for other GATT contracting parties, including several Comecon countries. In addition, the Romanian authorities undertook to ensure that Romanian goods were delivered in the EU at "market-related prices."

Romania's aggressive export policy and limitations on internal consumption, coupled with the reduction in restrictions made by the EU under the trade agreement, led to a consistent surplus of Romanian exports to the EU over imports from the EU. This fact, together with the greater attention given by many EU Member States in recent years to human rights abuses under the Ceaucescu regime, prevented Romania from obtaining the complete elimination of EU discriminatory quantitative restrictions and a commitment by the EU to negotiate a commercial cooperation agreement.

b. Hungary

The EU-Hungary Agreement entered into force on December 1, 1988. The basis for the EU-Hungary Agreement is the EU's lack of progress in eliminating discriminatory quantitative restrictions on Hungarian exports to the EU following Hungary's accession to GATT. At the 1986 review of Hungary's accession to GATT, the Hungarian delegation contended that the EU had only eliminated ten percent of the quantitative restrictions applied by its Member States to Hungary. The 1988 agreement resolved this issue by adopting a schedule for the abolition of the quantitative restrictions permitted by Hungary's Protocol for Accession to GATT, with the last restrictions to be abolished by the end of 1995.

Consistent with the terms of Hungary's GATT accession, the EU did not require Hungary to commit to increasing its imports from the EU. Hungary does not impose specific quantitative restrictions on EU goods and is required to administer its tariff system in a manner consistent with its GATT obligations. Accordingly, the EU obtained a promise that Hungary would administer both its import licensing system, sanctioned under GATT because of its balance of payments deficit, and its global quota for consumer goods in a non-discriminatory fashion.

In the agricultural sector, the agreement contains a simple covenant for a joint EU-Hungary committee to consider "the possibility of granting each other reciprocal concessions on a product-by-product basis." Although this provision is not a legally enforceable obligation, the trade agreement appears to be a framework pursuant to which the EU is prepared to consider reducing the application of tariffs, levies and quantitative restrictions on Hungarian agricultural exports in contrast to its generally conservative approach to agricultural trade matters.

c. *Poland and the USSR*

The EU-Poland Agreement, which entered into effect on December 1, 1989, closely parallel the EU-Hungary Agreement. Article 9 of the EU-Poland Agreement provides for the EU, "subject to exceptions, progressively and regularly to increase . . . quotas with a view to elimination by the end of 1994 to the quantitative restrictions" authorized by the Polish GATT Protocol of Accession. Poland did not waive its right to deviate from its substantially equivalent trade obligations following the reinstatement of quantitative restrictions by the EU.

In the case of the EU-USSR Agreement, the EU agreed to eliminate all discriminatory quantitative restrictions (outside the ECSC, textile and agricultural sectors) by the end of 1995 except for "those concerning a limited number of products which might be deemed to be sensitive." Unlike the EU's agreements with Poland and Hungary, the EU and the USSR did not make a specific commitment to achieve mutual concessions with respect to agricultural products, although the agreement is generally applicable to agriculture. The EU has therefore indicated its intentions to act more cautiously in reducing barriers to Soviet products than it did with respect to Poland and Hungary.

The EU-USSR Agreement is of particular significance because the USSR is not a GATT member. Thus, while the MFN treatment promised by the parties in the Romanian, Czechoslovakian, Hungarian and Polish agreements was merely a reiteration of an obligation already assumed under GATT, it has greater legal significance in the EU-USSR Agreement. As with the recent EU-Czechoslovakia Agreement, the arrangement also includes an agreement between the European Atomic Energy Community (Euratom) and the Soviet Union on cooperation in matters relating to nuclear energy.

2. Former East Germany

The quantitative restrictions imposed by the EU Member States on East German goods have been less detrimental to East German exports than those imposed on goods of other East European countries. East German products have been accepted into West Germany, the EU's largest market, on a strictly regulated basis and treated as domestic products pursuant to West Germany's Basic Law. This practice is recognized by the EU Treaty's Protocol on Inner German Trade. Shortly before the East German elections in March 1990, the EU and East Germany agreed on a trade and commercial cooperation pact modeled on the second generation agreements between the EU and Hungary, Poland and the USSR. A more important development, however, has been the clear choice by the East German voters of immediate union with West Germany and the acceleration of this process both at the German and EU levels. As a result, trade and aid are increasing together with the creation of a common German monetary system as of July 1, 1990 and the extension of the freedoms and policies of the EU Treaty. The financial and bureaucratic resources involved, although still a matter of estimate, are certain to be much greater than the trade concessions and aid packages offered to the other Eastern European countries. The East German situation is interesting as a demonstration of what can be done to integrate and stabilize a Union neighbor.

Although the EU thus responded quickly to the developments in Eastern Europe, the key word was "normalizing" not innovating.[10] Trade and political were placed on the same footing as those with other unstable and impoverished third countries. Despite the early rhetoric, the limits of what the EU was prepared to do for Eastern Europe appeared quickly.

E. Initiatives after the Governmental Changes: PHARE[11]

At the summit, the EU Commission was given a mandate to coordinate aid for Poland and Hungary on behalf of all the countries of the Organization for Economic Cooperation and Development (OECD) under the Poland/Hungary Assistance for Economic Restructuring (PHARE) program.

In February 1990, the OECD countries decided that aid programs (PHARE) would in principle be extended to include Czechoslovakia, East Germany, Romania, Bulgaria and Yugoslavia, subject to continued progress in economic and political reform in those countries. This wait-and-see approach primarily required each country to establish economic restructuring programs sanctioned by the International Monetary Fund (IMF) and to undergo successfully the transition to a government selected through multi-party elections.

The PHARE program is significant in two respects. First, the program unifies a variety of quite different initiatives and places Brussels at the center of relations with the East. The EU's aid programs are primarily being determined and implemented independent of the OECD process, with EU procedural rules often attached as conditions. This approach recognizes the importance of the EU as a "pole of attraction" for the Eastern countries, while fixing Western initiatives within the technocratic and unification-oriented political processes in Brussels. Second, the PHARE program offers the Eastern countries precisely the mix of trade concessions, aid and investment guarantees that were available as models from pre-existing EU negotiations with the East and with developing countries. Despite the bureaucratic and monetary costs involved, this initial program sets relations between the East and West in Europe on a path of continuity and provides for only modest integration (excluding the case of East Germany).

The PHARE program is a grab bag of initiatives ranging from emergency food aid to Poland to the establishment of a European Bank for Reconstruction and Develop-

---

[10] David Kennedy & David E. Webb, *The Limits of Integration: Eastern Europe And The European Communities*, 30 C.M.L.R. 1095 (1993), at 1101. © 1993 Kluwer Academic Publishers. Reprinted by permission.

[11] David Kennedy & David E. Webb, *Integration: Eastern Europe and the European Economic Communities,* 28 Colum. J. Transnat'l L. 634-75 (1990), at 648. © 1990 David Kennedy & David E. Webb. Reprinted by permission.

ment (EBRD). The most significant achievement to date is the reduction or elimination of the EU's historical barriers to, and in certain cases, the granting of special treatment in favor of, Polish and Hungarian products exported to the EU. [It] has surpassed the EU's trade agreements with Poland and Hungary by abolishing all specific quantitative restrictions imposed by the Member States on Hungarian and Polish products (excluding textiles and agricultural products as well as goods governed by the ECSC), giving Poland and Hungary treatment equal to that accorded to most of the EU's other GATT trading partners.

In addition, the EU adopted a regulation suspending for 1990 the application by the Member States (other than Spain and Portugal) of non-specific quantitative restrictions on Polish and Hungarian goods, putting Hungary and Poland in a better trading position than most of the EU's other GATT trading partners for exporting products for which Member States maintain quantitative restrictions, such as cars, shoes and toys. Also in the context of PHARE, the EU has extended to Poland and Hungary the GSP system of preferential tariff concessions on imports from developing countries.

Outside of the trade area, much of the EU aid currently being made available is either emergency food and medical assistance or direct loans to Poland and Hungary. A significant portion of funds committed are being used to purchase agricultural products in the EU at market prices for shipment to Poland. Local proceeds from the sale of food, which is donated by the EU, are being used to establish counterpart funds to finance the modernization of local agricultural production. The remainder of these aid funds are being divided among grants for industrial "infrastructure," training programs and environmental projects. The Hungarian and Polish joint venture laws give some indication as to which projects Hungary and Poland are likely to select, [such as] special tax benefits to joint ventures in, among others, the pharmaceutical, electronics, packaging, machine tools and waste recycling fields. An *ad hoc* EU committee chaired by the Commission is responsible for award ing the related contracts.

The PHARE program illustrates that the EU is prepared to relinquish trade barriers against Eastern European products, except perhaps in certain "sensitive" sectors such as agriculture, textiles, coal and steel. Outside of the trade area, however, the EU appeared unable to find a coherent, programmatic expression of its view that the opportunity has arrived to reverse the post-World War II division of Europe through bold action. The PHARE initiatives contain few surprises and repeat many aspects of prior development programs, including lengthy bureaucratic procedures for each ECU spent and a bias toward purchases of EU agricultural surpluses.

III. The Europe Agreements[12]

Very soon after the initial rash of association agreements came plans for a much wider-reaching and more ambitious form of agreement, the Europe Agreement. Agreements were initiated with Poland and Hungary in December 1991, and both entered

[12] Lynn E. Ramsay, *The Implications of the Europe Agreements for an Expanded European Union*, 44 Int'l & Comp. L.Q. 161-171 (1995). © 1995 Lynn Ramsay. Reprinted by permission.

into force in February 1994. The agreements with the Czech, Slovak, Bulgarian and Romanian republics were initialed in 1993 but have not at the time of writing entered into force. Each of the agreements share a common framework, the principle features of which are:

(a) a common legal basis and form;
(b) political dialogue and institutions of association;
(c) free movement of trade;
(d) free movement of workers;
(e) the right of establishment;
(f) the provision of services;
(g) completion provisions and State aids;
(h) the approximation of legislation;
(i) economic co-operation;
(j) cultural co-operation; and
(k) financial co-operation.

A. Legal Basis and Form

The Europe Agreements are extensive and involve far-reaching, reciprocal obligations. This is reflected in the legal basis under which the agreements were enacted. Clearly, the Europe Agreements may be classified as a form of mixed agreement since they encompass areas for which the Community has exclusive competence, such as commercial policy, and areas which remain largely within the competence of the member States, such as culture. The agreements therefore require ratification by the member States' parliaments. This has proved to be a time-consuming process and, in order to ease the delay, interim agreements have been enacted in relation to certain topics falling wholly within the Community's competence.

The agreements provide for a staggered development divided into two five-year phases. The Community's justification for this "softly softly" approach is that of necessary protectionism; the need to protect the associated States from the full rigors of a market economy and to create a breathing space in which their industries and democratic practices may develop.

Whilst many of the Eastern Europe countries currently face a common set of problems they do so to differing degrees. In the newly established Czech and Slovak Republics, it may be discerned that Slovakia is experiencing much greater problems moving from a command to a market-based economy. The Czech Republic is benefiting from the fact that its industrial base and economy were already fairly diversified. Slovakia, on the other hand, was overly dependent on heavy industry and armaments, both of which were aimed at the guaranteed, and of course now defunct, CMEA market. The fact that Poland and Hungary are economically stronger than many of their neighbors is reflected in the earlier entry into force of their Europe Agreements. Whilst the agreements do contain a common framework, each therefore contains sections designed to reflect the particular requirements of each individual associated State.

B. Political Dialogue and the Institutions of Association

An institutional framework is included to oversee the operation of the agreements and in particular to facilitate political dialogue. The aims of political dialogue are threefold:

(a) to assist the associated States in their transition toward democracy;
(b) to increase convergence between the Community and the associated States on international issues; and
(c) to strengthen security in Europe.

Three Institutions of Association are to be established: an Association Council, an Association Committee and an Association Parliamentary Committee. These institutions are broadly based on the Community model but have a much more restricted role. Whilst the Association Councils have a limited degree of decision-making powers, their real function is to monitor the implementation of the agreements. The Association Councils may also delegate powers to the Association Committees. The Association Parliamentary Committees have the weakest role of all three institutions: essentially they fulfil the function of a "talk-shop" providing the opportunity for the exchange of views. However, any resolutions made by them will be non-binding.

C. Free Movement of Trade

The most important aspect of the agreements for the associated States therefore must surely be the establishment of a free trade area based on reciprocal and balanced obligations. However, faced with a poor infrastructure and goods of inferior quality the associated States run the risk that higher quality goods from the Community will flood their markets and wipe out any existing or new industries. Whilst the main thrust of the agreements is the establishment of a free trade area, its establishment will be mutual but asymmetrical: the Com munity will make greater and more immediate concessions, the associated States more gradual and initially less extensive concessions.

To complete the free trade area, the Europe Agreements provide for the abolition of measures having equivalent effect to quantitative restrictions. The abolition of these impediments to free movement of goods will take place progressively, with more rapid advancement in relation to non-sensitive products than in relation to products which are of particular importance for the associated States' economies.

As with the EC Treaty, provision is made for derogation from the principle of free movement on the grounds of public health, public policy and public security under Article 36. Derogation under these conditions is to be treated as an exceptional and temporary measure and must not discriminate on the ground of nationality.

D. Free Movement of Workers

The agreements enshrine the principle of non-discrimination based on the ground of nationality. This principle applies not only to workers but also to spouses and families.

The Community is required to give full effect to the non-discrimination principle as soon as the agreement enters into force.

Action in relation to the free movement of workers is to take place in two phases of five years. The first phase concentrates upon laying the necessary foundation by requiring the creation of a social security system effectively co-ordinated with that of the Member States. During the second phase, consideration will be given to both the social and economic situation, the requirements of the associated State and to the employment situation in the Community.

Whilst the inclusion of a title on the free movement of workers is undoubtedly of symbolic importance the freedom to move afforded under this title is more apparent than real. These agreements seek primarily to improve the situation of workers from the associated states who are already legally established in the Community, leaving the Member States free to establish their own immigration policies. The limited scope of this provision may also have the knock-on effect of reassuring those employers and government officials in the East who feared a mass exodus to the West by nationals enticed by higher wages and an apparently superior standard of living. This title is significant because it lays the foundations for future co-operation on free movement of workers; however, it is clear that future developments will depend not merely upon the degree of progress made by the associated States but on factors beyond their control, principally unemployment within the Member States.

E. Right of Establishment

Provision is made under this head for non-discriminatory [national] treatment to be granted to nationals and companies by the signatory States. The associated States will, over ten years, gradually implement the non-discriminatory treatment so that their most sensitive industries are afforded a transitional degree of protection.

The Association Councils are charged with the task of easing the barriers to establishment, in particular by articulating the steps necessary for the mutual recognition of qualifications. In its absence, barriers to the freedom of movement may exist: for example, a professional regulatory body may require a detailed knowledge of the country's language. Mutual recognition of qualifications within the Community has taken one of two forms. The initial route taken by the Commission was to harmonise individual professions. The advantage of this approach is that true harmonization occurs from the grassroots level up since it first co-ordinates education and then deals with professional training. The great disadvantage with this approach is the length of time taken to reach agreement; harmonization of standards for architects necessitated some 16 years of negotiation. The alternative approach is the mutual recognition of all professions through a single instrument; basically this is the notion that professional qualifications gained in one Member State should in principle be recognised in all Member States. Clearly, this approach obviates the requirement of protracted negotiations with each professional body in each Member State. On the other hand, the broad-brush treatment does not provide for harmonization of each profession and therefore there may still be considerable difficulties experienced by professionals seeking to establish themselves in another Member State; for example, lawyers seeking to establish themselves in another Member State may discover that the divergence between the law degree programmes in their own State and the host State is such that true freedom of movement is denied them. Given that these measures have had an extremely limited impact within the Community, and that a number of practical difficulties exist with both approaches, it is likely that the creation of a system for the mutual recognition of qualifications will not be a priority for the Association Councils.

F. Provision of Services

Provisions relating to the supply of services between the Community and the associated States do not lay down a detailed timetable for implementation; rather, it is left to each Association Council to take "the measures necessary to progressively implement the provisions." The liberalism process is designed ultimately to permit the temporary movement of individuals providing the service who are "key personnel." Progress in this area will depend upon the degree of development of the services sector in the associated State.

G. Competition Provisions and State Aids

[T]he provisions on competition law and State aids follow the same design as those contained in the EEC Treaty [and] where questions of interpretation arise they should be assessed by the same criteria applied to the existing EC Treaty provisions. Initially, the associated States will be partly shielded from the full rigors of competition policy since in relation to State aids the associated States will be classified as areas of low income. Under Article 92(3)(a) EC, where areas of low income exist it is possible for development-orientated State aids to be authorized. This consistency of approach is favorable to the associated States' bid for full membership since it fosters compliance with the *acquis communautaire*, which is one of the prerequisites to full membership.

H. Approximation of Legislation

[T]he associated States are to ensure that their existing and future legislation is consistent with Community law, particularly in relation to customs law, company law, banking law, company accounts and taxes, intellectual property, protection of workers in the workplace, financial services, rules on competition, protection of health and life of humans, animals and plants, consumer protection, indirect taxation, technical rules and standards, transport and the environment. Comparison with the European Economic Area (EEA) Agreement is instructive. By comparison the Europe Agreements provide that technical assistance should be made available to assist the associated States implementing these measures. The requirements of technical assistance would suggest that associated States may have difficulty in complying even with this limited scale of approximation of legislation.

I. Economic Co-operation

Economic co-operation is designed to assist the associated States in their efforts towards economic restructuring and development. The co-operation covers all areas of mutual interest and includes important areas such as industrial co-operation, investment promotion and protection, science and technology, environment, telecommunications and broadcasting.

J. Cultural Co-operation

Cultural co-operation has only recently been introduced into Community law by virtue of Title IX of the Treaty on European Union. Its inclusion in the Europe Agreements is interesting for two reasons. First, it has symbolic importance. The title does not seek to expunge the national cultural identity of the associated State: rather, it aims to strengthen the common links between the parties. Provision is made for co-operation in cultural events with a European character. The motivation here is to promote a sense of European identity in the associated States in place of an identity as a member of the Soviet Union. Second, it has importance for the success of future applications for full membership. The inclusion of a recent innovation in Community law ensures that these agreements develop in line with the *acquis communautaire*.

K. Financial Co-operation

The Community undertakes to provide the associated States with a degree of financial support to assist them in achieving the agreements' objectives. [G]rants and loans provided by the Community under these agreements represent only one component in a range of financial assistance supplied both by the Community and the wider international community.

The Europe Agreements represent an important stage not only in the economic and democratic development of the associated States but also in the expansion of the European Union. The preambles of the agreements clearly state that full membership of the European Union is the ultimate objective of the associated States. The success of [Eastern European application for membership in the EU] will depend upon a number of factors including the degree of democratic stability and the level of economic development in the applicant State.

Generally, the Europe Agreements have established a framework for the development of a much deeper and more structured co-operation between the Community and the associated States than had hitherto been possible. They have also laid the foundations for an expanded European Union. In the final analysis, the Europe Agreements [have] come to be classified as but stepping stones to full membership of the European Union for the countries of Central and Eastern Europe.

IV. Integrating Eastern Europe: The View from Brussels[13]

In recent [years], it appears that much of the EU's collective energy is focused on Eastern Europe and yet an institutional cautiousness remains, particularly on matters of trade and political integration. The EU has set an ambitious agenda for removing internal barriers to trade, creating economic and monetary union as well as setting an unofficial goal of making inroads into U.S. and, to an even greater extent, Japanese competitive advantages. From this perspective, the demands by Eastern Europeans for participation in putatively "Western" institutions pose a problem.

The problem is that Eastern reformers have been demanding a form of democracy and a form of market freedom which the EU has increasingly abandoned for a more technocratic political culture and industrial policy. It is ironic that the European Communities' 1992 program coincided with demands for mass democracy in Eastern Europe. Precisely as Eastern Europeans demand more democratic political forms at home, the EU has bid the cumbersome legislative, judicial and administrative structures of national democratic government farewell for a more flexible and technically sophisticated approach to government. As a result, the Western European response to developments in the east shows a mix of encouragement and anxiety, for the democracy of mass parties in both its Western and Eastern form seems strangely antiquated.

For all these reasons, Western Europeans are right to be wary about admitting new members from the East, and the range of *ad hoc* measures they have proposed may well suit their own unification aims. At the same time, however, it has been difficult for those outside the EU to imagine a form of association not dominated either by the objective of EU membership or by the acceptance of the particular trade and aid concessions currently being advanced.

The EU has said that the countries of Eastern Europe are neither politically nor economically prepared for EU membership. Instead, it has proposed association agreements with each of the countries of Eastern Europe, other than the Soviet Union, achieving an unspecified level of political and economic reform. The precise nature of the basis for the establishment of a "free trade zone" and for the extension of EU aid. The EU has stressed that association would not determine any eventual application for EU membership.

"Association" is provided for in Article 238 of the EU Treaty. [T]his term has had different meanings for different countries. For Greece, association was intended to and did serve as a prelude to EU membership. Association is, however, neither a prerequisite to, nor a guaranty of, EU membership. In contrast to Greece, the twenty-five year old EU-Turkey association agreement (EU-Turkey Association Agreement) has functioned primarily as a preferential trade agreement, with some direct financial aid for infrastructure projects in Turkey.

---

[13] David Kennedy & David E. Webb, *Integration: Eastern Europe and the European Economic Communities,* 28 Colum. J. Transnat'l L. 634-75 (1990), at 652. © 1990 David Kennedy & David E. Webb. Reprinted by permission.

Association, therefore, is simply the agricultural title given by the EU to its future initiatives with respect to Eastern Europe. The promise of association agreements does not itself constitute a coherent program. [It is agreed] that there is no formula for undoing forty years of totalitarianism and planned economics to enable the countries of Eastern Europe to participate in a world economy dominated by market economies. However, framing the problem in this way easily leads to misunderstanding, for the situation in the Eastern European countries is neither uniform nor simply marked by government presence in the economy, any more than Western economies are uniformly developed or innocent of government.

Each Eastern European country is, to a greater or lesser extent, substantially industrialized, while at the same time completely unprepared to compete with the West because of technological underdevelopment, lack of experienced managers, chronic indebtedness, severe balance of payment deficits and intrusive legal rules regarding economic operations. Moreover, Eastern Europeans have never experienced the mass-marketing of consumer goods that has been experienced by the Western public since World War II.

These semi-industrialized countries, conscious of their cultural affinity and economic attraction to Western Europe, might use negotiations with the EU as an opportunity to address the *sui generis* nature of these economic problems, rather than responding primarily to the unification-motivated Western proposals.

V. Proposed Relationships Between the EU and Eastern Europe

A. The Conventional Road to Accession[14]

Article O [of] the Treaty of European Union (TEU) provides that 'Any European State may apply to become a member of the Union.' The conditions required for accession are not articulated, instead they are to be the 'subject of an agreement between the Member States and the Applicant State.' At the Copenhagen Summit of June 1993 the members of the European Council outlined the conditions which it considered necessary for accession to the European Union as follows:

(1) the need for stability of institutions guaranteeing democracy, the rule of law, human rights and respect for the protection of minorities;
(2) the ability to take on the obligations of membership including adherence to the aims of political, economic and monetary union;
(3) the Union's capacity to absorb new members, while maintaining the momentum of European integration; and
(4) the existence of a functioning market as well as the capacity to cope with competitive pressure and market forces within the Union.

[14] Lynn E. Ramsay, *Towards A Wider European Union: A Commentary on the Possible Accession of Hungary and Poland to the European Union* (1995) European Public Law, Vol.1 Iss. 2 189-200.

To establish a framework for integration, this article briefly considers four different examples of relations between the EU and third countries: accession, the EU-EFTA free trade agreements and the prospective establishment of the European Economic Space (EES), the EU-Turkey Association Agreement, and the Lomé Convention.

B. Enlargement: Integration through Membership

Membership has been the traditional means to integrate neighboring countries into the EU. Britain, Denmark, Ireland, Spain, Portugal and Greece have been admitted as members since the formation of the Union. The membership process has been used to integrate neighbors of varying levels of development, with greater and lesser degrees of political and democratic stability and experience. Indeed, for Spain, Greece and Portugal in particular, membership has been seen as a tool to solidify democratic and free market commitments and to bring about economic development.

EU membership permits a country to participate in the decision-making processes of the Union while subjecting it to the growing body of Union law and policy administered in Brussels. The participation of the new member is a structural one and, as a result, microeconomic and regulatory processes are more important than simple trade and aid concessions. The key is acceptance of existing Union legislation and the extension of the EU Treaty's freedoms and policies to the territory of the new member. Moreover, a member may receive huge transfer payments as part of either normal EU programs or special "cohesion" initiatives for under-developed regions, and may experience sharply increased trade with an investment from the Union.

The accession process has also proven to be extremely flexible and capable of accommodating long and complex transitional arrangements, [accommodating] currency conversion restrictions, local aid arrangements, historic insulation from free market forces and various competitive weaknesses. Historically, the accession process has started with the formulation of certain legislation and the negotiation of a trade agreement, followed by lengthy negotiations concerning transitional arrangements and other special accommodations. Thereafter, the new member begins participation in the administration and legislative processes of the Union, with the transitional periods acting as incentives to bring about the economic restructuring necessary for eventual open competition within the EU.

From the Eastern European point of view, much political and legal independence would need to be sacrificed for EU membership. The costs would be particularly high for EFTA countries that might achieve a great deal of participation in the internal market and policy structure of the EU through an appropriate arrangement on the European Economic Space (EES). Country-by-country membership negotiations would also prevent the development of a common Central European unity, just as membership would largely prevent the achievement of an independent political middle way between East and West.

More important resistance to membership, however, comes from the EU itself and should be understood as a matter of bad timing. Although resistance to membership is defended in terms of the inability of Eastern European countries to survive the transition to membership, the resistance results more from the particular politics of integration prevalent within the EU at the moment. Integration of the East is shaped by concerns for integrating the West.

As the Union extended integration, the substantive opposition of existing members—often those admitted in the first wave—became increasingly frustrating for the Europeanists. The Single European Act, moreover, did not fully abolish unanimity. Even countries content with the current weighted voting scheme might hesitate to see their participation in a qualified majority vote diluted by new members.

As a result, the extension of the Union has come to be seen in Brussels as a threat to its success, particularly if the Bonn-Paris axis were to be either diluted or distracted by concerns in the East. It is in this context that Commission President Delors proposed the alternative of a Europe of "concentric circles" on the basis of which neighboring countries could share some of the glow of EU integration without being invited on stage. It was a vision born of the drive for EU unification, not of an interest in integrating the countries of the East.

C. Integration Without Membership: The European Free Trade Association

In terms of trade and trade relations, the EFTA countries are at the other end of the spectrum from Eastern Europe and the EFTA countries together form the EU's largest trading partner. On the basis of trade agreements between the EU and each of the EFTA countries, industrial products circulate among the eighteen member countries of the two organizations generally without tariffs or quantitative restrictions.

The EFTA countries also differ from Eastern Europe because they are deemed by the EU to be its economic and political peers. Although certain of the EU-EFTA trade agreements afford the EFTA countries additional protection in a few selected areas, such as in the fishery sector for Iceland, they are non-preferential agreements pursuant to which the EFTA countries are required to reduce trade barriers at the same rate as the EU. The EU provides no aid to the EFTA countries as it does under its trade or association agreements with virtually all other countries, including Israel, Yugoslavia, Turkey, and the Maghreb, Mashrak and Lomé countries.

The EFTA countries, unlike the countries of Eastern Europe, are thought to be fully prepared for EU membership. Some of them reject the prospect of EU membership because they fear the loss of political independence and the opportunity to develop their own local industrial policy. They also fear that their agricultural sector will suffer if merged into the EU's Common Agricultural Policy. For its part, the EU has proposed the negotiations toward EES as an alternative to EU membership for EFTA countries. This is an effort to avoid diverting bureaucratic energy from work on the internal market to arduous accession negotiations and the process of accommodating new members with long individualist traditions.

The current EU-EFTA trade agreements reflect the EU's dominance over the negotiation process which, some EFTA observers fear, may be extended to EES. Although ostensibly the result of individual negotiations, the trade agreements are virtually identical. As a striking example, Article 23 of each agreement contains little-used competition law provisions which are taken virtually verbatim from Articles 85, 86 and 92(1) of the EU Treaty.

The EU-EFTA agreements are limited almost exclusively to trade matters. A separate joint committee oversees implementation of each agreement. In advance of the current EES negotiations, there was some effort to expand the scope of EU-EFTA integration, partly through negotiations between the EU and individual EFTA countries. The most recent and comprehensive example is the EU-Switzerland non-life insurance treaty, which seeks to guarantee the reciprocal rights of EU and Swiss insurers to establish themselves and provide cross-border services on each other's territories. The EU and EFTA also have some joint institutional memberships. In particular, all the EU and EFTA countries are members of the European Committee for Standardization (CEN), the European Committee for Electrotechnical Standardization (CENELEC) and the European Telecommunications Standards Institute (ETSI), the three European technical standards bodies.

Establishment of the EES would essentially extend the five freedoms of the EU Treaty (free movement of goods, of capital and of workers, right of establishment and freedom to provide cross-border service) to the EFTA countries. As a corollary to the five freedoms, the EU and the EFTA countries would likely develop common policies in such areas as competition law, environmental protection and worker safety. Extending EU freedoms and policies to the EFTA countries means, as a practical matter, the necessity of accepting a great deal of the existing and prospective rules of Union law by which those freedoms are implemented (the "*acquis communataire*"). In the 1992 program, the free movement of goods or services has come to mean much more than reciprocal open borders. It also means a harmonization of regulatory provisions and the establishment of common minimum standards. Similarly, if the common policies are to become more than articles in an association agreement, there must be coordinated administrative and judicial action.

In exchange for submitting to the Brussels legislative and judicial machinery, the EFTA countries have demanded input into the decision-making process. Although the form for such input remains unclear and is treated with much trepidation in Brussels for its tendency to complicate an already difficult decision-making process, it is clear that some joint institutional framework must be devised to give EFTA members input into the legislative and administrative process and the right to reject individual pieces of EU legislation if the EES approach is to become a viable alternative to membership. Without such a system, an EFTA country would sacrifice more sovereign independence as a participant in the EES than it would as a participant in the EU.

Regarding the free movement of goods, the *acquis communautaire* means the adoption by the EFTA countries of the growing body of harmonization directives. Under these directives, the Member States have relinquished their authority to prevent imports from other Member States on the basis that the goods do not satisfy their own quality and safety rules, so long as the goods comply with the EU rules set forth in the directive or with the rules of a Member State deemed to be an equivalent by the Commission. This integration goes well beyond the abolition of tariffs and quantitative restrictions, because it calls for the EFTA countries to modify their legislation, at least as it applies to imports from other EES countries. Like certain EU Member States, many EFTA countries maintain standards that may be higher than the common denominator reached by the EU for a given group of products. For EFTA countries such as Austria, which has gradually been preparing itself for EU membership, the harmonization process is already well under way. Even where the EFTA countries can agree to accept the existing Union rules on the free movement of goods, the implementation and modification of these rules, as well as the development of rules for additional products or new technologies, calls for joint dispute resolution and decision making institutions.

The other areas in which these institutional issues are raised dramatically is the freedom to provide cross-border services provided for in Articles 59 to 63 of the EU Treaty. Implementation of this freedom, particularly in highly regulated industries like banking and insurance, has proven to be difficult for the EU. It has long been the view of the Commission that an EU insurer, for example, should be entitled to do business throughout the EU without any obligation to establish a local branch under the insurance regulatory rules of its home Member State as long as these rules meet a common standard. Faced with resistance from Member States eager to protect local insurers and consumers, the EU has only partially achieved this goal over a period of almost two decades. Extension of this policy to the EFTA countries would certainly be difficult and, moreover, would require adequate institutions for its development and enforcement.

The solution to this institutional dilemma is by no means clear. Both sides may come to feel comfortable with the creation of an EES court with judges from both EU and EFTA member countries, although the compatibility of such a court with current EU law is difficult to ensure. Much more difficult problems are joint executive actions, such as those performed by the EU Commission in the competition area. Given the EU reluctance to offer EU membership to harmonization and economic and monetary union more difficult, the EU is unlikely to agree to structure which would delay or impede its decision-making.

One solution which would accommodate both this concern of the EU and the desire of the EFTA countries to decide individually whether to adopt individual EU measures would be to permit EFTA countries the full opportunity to participate in the decisionmaking process except that current EU rules regarding adoption of measures would continue to apply and EFTA countries would be free to accept or reject any measures adopted without their support. In practice, however, this alternative could lead either to a gradual drift away from the common rules established at the time of creation of the EES or to the EFTA countries feeling compelled to adopt legislation for which their input was not valued equally. The dilemma for the EFTA countries therefore is how to reconcile their desires for political independence and economic integration when the EU by both deliberate action and sheer geographical and bureaucratic vastness, has written much of the script.

The EU-EFTA relations probably cannot serve as a model for EU-Eastern European association agreements. The Eastern European countries will have to dismantle their export licensing systems and reduce tariffs on EU goods on a gradual basis pursuant to preferential agreements on the basis of which the EU reduces tariffs on an accelerated basis. In addition, the restructuring process calls for substantial and sustained aid from the EU of the kind never made available to the EFTA countries. However, in order to avoid the limitations traditionally associated with the EU's relations with less-advanced countries, such as those with Turkey and the Lomé countries, Eastern European countries should insist that they be treated like peers of the EU in areas of commercial and legal cooperation. This would include immediate participation in CEN and CENELEC, in EU-EFTA research and develop ment projects and in meaningful consultation on measures to be taken by the EES which may affect their exports.

The EU-EFTA negotiations are significant as illustrations of the advantages and difficulties of pursuing integration with the EU at the levels of industrial and microeconomic policy as well as trade. In particular, some Eastern European countries may want their own association agreements with the EU to reflect progress with respect to the free movement of goods between the EU and the EFTA countries and joint decision making and consultation between the EU and EFTA institutions. The EU-EFTA negotiations demonstrate the difficulty, even for well-developed neighbors acting together, of resisting the standardized pressure simply to accept Brussels legislation. In any event, the outcome of these negotiations are of interest to Eastern European countries because, upon satisfaction of certain criteria of political and economic stability, they may in the future be invited to join the EES.

D. Association: Turkey

The EU-Turkey Association Agreement was signed in 1963. A 1970 Protocol (the Protocol) contains detailed provisions for its implementation. The EU-Turkey Association Arrangement is, with good reason, viewed as the most comprehensive model for the EU-Eastern European association agreements. Its scope is quite broad, ranging from trade to the free movement of workers. Moreover, it is a preferential agreement in that Turkey is authorized to lift trade restrictions on EU products at a slower pace than the EU does for Turkish products and Turkey is granted special derogations such as with respect to the liberalization of payments and state aids. Finally, in the context of association, the EU has awarded the Turkish government and, in certain cases, private Turkish companies, financial aid for economic development.

Except in the area of quantitative restrictions and tariffs, the EU's obligations under the various agreements and protocols which make up the association arrangement require further action by the parties on which there has been little progress. The long-standing Greece-Turkey dispute, political instability in Turkey, slow progress in Turkey's economic development and requests for protection from Turkish exports by Union producers have all served to retard this progress. Turkey has now deemed itself ready for accession to the EU at a time when the Union has determined that further expansion is against its interests. Further, Turkey's strategic importance has declined as a result of the opening up of Eastern Europe.

Like the EU-EFTA agreements, the Protocol draws its inspiration from the EU Treaty. It provides for the elimination of quantitative restrictions and tariffs as the initial goal and for the gradual implementation of other aspects of the free movement of goods as well as the remaining four freedoms. It also provides for the harmonization of competition rules, economic policies and other laws relevant to the association relationship. On an institutional level, integration between the EU and Turkey is much less than that contemplated for EES, although the potential for joint action is in principle greater than is traditionally the case through the EU's trade and cooperation agreements. In addition, the agreement explicitly contemplates consideration of Turkey's accession to the EU after a certain period. Significantly, these institutional aspects of the EU-Turkey arrangement are virtually identical to those contained in the EU's pre-accession association agreement with Greece.

In general, it would appear, with the Greek example as a guide, that the legal relationship between Turkey and the EU contains the promise for gradual political integration of Turkey into the EU and significant EU investment in Turkey's economic development to facilitate its eventual accession to the EU. This promise is far from being realized as a result of the lack of follow-through on the part of both Turkey and the EU.

In non-sensitive sectors, the EU has eliminated quantitative restrictions and tariffs on Turkish products in accordance with the Protocol. For many years, Turkey abandoned its tariff reduction obligations and is at this date many years behind the schedule established in the Protocol. There has been no significant progress in other areas covered by the Protocol, most dramatically with respect to the free movement of workers. In the context of Union enlargement (for Greece, Spain and Portugal) and the EU's extension of preferential trading agreements (to the Maghreb and Mashrak countries, for example), the prospect of cooperation between the European and Turkish Parliaments has been largely unrealized.

Turkey's experience with EU association can serve as both a lesson and a model for Eastern European countries interested in integration with and eventual accession to the EU. In the area of trade, Eastern European countries may want to consider negotiating up front a schedule for increased access of their products to the EU market in sensitive sectors rather than leaving it to open negotiation under the association agreement. Trade concessions for Eastern Europe may never be more popular than they are today. Eastern European countries would also want to "upgrade" the Turkish model to incorporate aspects of EU-EFTA relations, such as to include equal participation in programs regarding research and development, environmental protection and the elaboration of technical standards, which are as important for helping to achieve the integration of Eastern Europe into European economic and political affairs as for their substantive aspects. Real progress on the free movement of workers may also be a priority for some Eastern European countries. Finally, in the area of aid, Eastern Europe will want to make an effort to obtain more money than has been made available to Turkey and to ensure that it is available to local businesses without requiring guarantees from the Eastern European governments.

E. Development Assistance: The Lomé Convention

The Lomé Convention (Lomé), first signed in 1975 between the EU Member States and forty-six African, Caribbean and Pacific countries (the ACP States), is the EU's most comprehensive preferential trade and financial aid arrangement. In its current version, Lomé IV, the arrangement extends to sixty-eight ACP States, all of whom qualify as less or least developed countries. Lomé is quite detailed: it covers three main areas: preferential trade arrangements; export stabilization; and financial and technical aid. One of the drawbacks characteristic of Lomé in each of these areas is that dependency on exports to the EU, particularly of raw materials, is encouraged.

Lomé's preferential trade regime is the most liberal afforded by the EU to any third countries. The EU has eliminated tariffs on a vast number of imports from ACP States with no reciprocity obligations on the part of the ACP States and has agreed to special rules of common origin. Unlike Turkey or the EFTA countries, the ACP States for the most part supply the EU with products not available from Union sources. On the other hand, in the few cases where Union-producers have complained about competition from ACP States, such as textiles, the ACP States have faced barriers to market access similar to those faced by Turkey.

The total expenditures by the EU and its Member States over the years for development aid under the Lomé Conventions have been significant. [H]owever, this aid has only made a limited contribution to the development of the production sector in the ACP States. The Union has previously sought to limit aid to those countries following development policies approved by the EU. From an institutional point of view, the Lomé Conventions have successfully provided a forum for consistent contacts between the EU and the ACP States. This consultation process has prevented the gaps in relations which have characterized EU-Turkey relations.

There is little danger that the EU will seek to copy the Lomé model directly for the integration of Eastern European countries. Eastern European countries have few raw materials in demand in the EU and, indeed, Eastern European and Union producers compete in a number of sectors. There is, however, some danger that the economic woes of Eastern Europe may lead certain countries in this region to accept a different kind of dependency relationship which would resemble EU-ACP relations except for the overall higher standard of living enjoyed by Eastern Europeans. Eastern Europe may well be tempted by a hard currency export led model of growth which emphasizes industries and sectors which neither compete with Western producers nor contribute to intra-East trade and development. For example, eager to obtain foreign investment, Eastern European countries might be tempted to accept (and maintain existing) industrial facilities deemed undesirable in Western Europe because of hazards to the environment and worker safety. Similarly, Eastern Europe may become a favored spot for Western companies to establish low technology industries which only contribute in a limited way to improving the region's self-sufficiency and standard of living. The dangers increase to the extent the EU and Eastern Europe focus on trade and aid—even infrastructure aid—without considering the microeconomic aspects of the integrated markets based on the EU Treaty's economic freedoms and common policies.

The experience of the ACP countries clearly marks the limits of dependency on the EU. For Eastern European countries with EU integration as a goal, however, the initial terms of association are crucial in creating the conditions for integration rather than dependency as an outsider. With respect to aid, the Eastern European countries need to focus not only on increasing the volume, but the means of distribution so that aid does not become an instrument for the EU to determine the sectors to be developed. The countries of Eastern Europe, despite their economic problems, may be well advised to establish themselves as "insiders" in political, economic and technical cooperation. Finally, Eastern European countries, either collectively or individually, may wish to insist on institutional links with the EU which will promote the continued integration of their micro-economic policies as well as make it harder for the EU to restrict market access in sensitive sectors.

VI. The Case for Eastern European Accession to the European Economic Area[15]

When the EU anticipated requests for membership from members of the European Free Trade Association (EFTA), it concluded the European Economic Area (EEA) with the potential applicants. The EEA goes much further than the Europe Agreements (EA), reflecting the EU's reluctance to provide for the integration of Eastern European States. Although the *substantive* benefits of the EEA could be gradually extended to the EA States within the framework of the EAs, the EEA's institutional provisions, especially the incorporation of the Court of Justice's case law, would be essential to the associates' future integration into the EU. Although the EAs may serve well as an interim measure while the EA States become familiar with the EU legal system, a comparison of the EEA with the EAs will demonstrate that membership in the EEA is the best way of preparing EA States for EU membership.

A. Joining the EEA

The three largest EEA signatories intend to join the EU on 1 January 1995, leaving the EEA an empty shell regulating the EU's relations only with Iceland, Norway and soon Liechtenstein. However, the EU has confirmed that it will continue to operate the EEA, even if there are only three members. The Eastern European States will still have to join EFTA first before they join the EEA, no matter how many members remain in the latter. Since each EA State already has an FTA with EFTA, similar to the EAs signed with the EU, joining EFTA would be a simple procedure for the EA States as long as the transitional provisions of these FTAs were incorporated with membership. Similarly, the provisions of the Central European Free Trade Area (CEFTA) between four of the EA States could be incorporated into EFTA and EEA membership, with Romania, Bulgaria and future EA associates joining separately. The hurdle would then be negotiating admission to the EEA and adaptation to its more advanced substantive and institutional provisions.

---

[15] Steve Peers, *An Ever Closer Waiting Room?: The Case for Eastern European Accession to the European Economic Area,* 32 C.M.L.R. 187-213 (1995).

B. Summary of Substantive Provisions: The EAs and the EEA

Both the EEA and the EAs establish free trade in industrial goods with the EU. The dif-fer ence is that the EEA States already enjoyed free trade with the EU before the agreements were signed, while the EAs give the associates ten years to phase in free entry for all EU goods and seven years for the EU to phase in entry of textiles, coal and steel trade and several "sensitive" items from the associates. Agriculture is liberalized slightly under the EAs and the EEA, under either agreement to eventual full liberalization or greater integration into the CAP. However, the EEA commits the EU to more regular reviews and negotiations on agricultural trade than do the EAs. The EA States would also benefit from the EEA Annexes adopting the EU's veterinary and phytosanitary legislation, which might prevent the imposition of measures like the EU's widely-criticized temporary ban on Eastern Europe's meat and dairy exports in spring 1993. The EA States, all actual or potential agricultural exporters, have a greater need to secure access to the EU market than do EFTA States, most of which are net agricultural importers.

The EEA States are almost fully incorporated into the remaining areas of the EU's internal market, with the exception of tax harmonization and monetary coordination. They have also adopted most of the EU's flanking policies. The EAs, in contrast, extend free establishment of companies, and integrate the associates into the EU's public undertakings, procurement and intellectual property policies, but contain only limited provisions for movement of workers, call for negotiations on services and transport, and postpone free movement of capital. Flanking policies are to be harmonized eventually.

The provisions for cooperation are similar in both agreements, allowing EEA or EA States to join in EU programmes where the EU decides. The intent is to draw upon the expertise found in the developed EEA States and to ease the transition to a market economy for the EA States. The Eastern European States will be offered access to EU programmes "taking as a point of departure those programmes which are already open for participation by the EFTA-countries".

Finally, the EAs offer one extra element of integration that the EEA does not: cooperation with the EU on foreign and home policy measures. Foreign policy cooperation does not extend to an offer of NATO or WEU membership, but does allow the EA States regular consultation with the EU on political issues. The home policy cooperation provisions associate the EA States with anti-drug, crime, or immigration policies of the EU which significantly affect their vital interests. These cooperation provisions could be preserved if the Eastern Europeans enter the EEA by adding them as an additional Protocol to the EEA (with opt-outs offered to the initial EEA members if they did not wish to participate).

C. Trade Laws, Competition, Safeguards and Dispute Settlement

Although there will be delays before the Europe Agreements come fully into effect, the Agreements' terms on free trade in industrial goods are being implemented swiftly and efficiently. Yet there is a catch: Eastern European States know well that no matter how open their *de jure* access to EU markets, their *de facto* access will remain sharply limited. The genuine openness of the EEA is a stark contrast.

De facto access to EU markets will be limited by the continuing existence of the Union's anti-dumping duties, countervailing (anti-subsidy) duties, measures against "illicit commercial practices," voluntary export restraints (VERs) and safeguards. In particular, the EU's frequent use of anti-dumping duties has been criticized for its inadequate procedural safeguards and limited judicial review, with conclusion that anti-dumping law is being used as a form of protectionism. The Uruguay Round amendments to the GATT Anti-Dumping Code are not expected to transform the EU's anti-dumping laws, although observers expect some improvements. It remains to be seen whether the transfer of anti-dumping cases to the Court of First Instance (CFI) will improve the judicial scrutiny of the EU authorities' direction. Any improvements resulting from these developments may well be off-set by the Union's decision to speed up investigation of anti-dumping cases (but not "sunset" reviews of existing duties) and to allow for the imposition of duties by a simple majority, rather than a qualified majority vote.

The EEA prohibits the use of all anti-dumping and countervailing (anti-subsidy) duties and of measures against "illicit commercial practices." The reason for this almost unprecedented mutual disarmament of trade weaponry (paralleled only within the EU itself and between Australia and New Zealand) is that the EEA extends the EU's legislation on competition and state aid in its entirety to all its signatories, along with an institutional structure for enforcing this legislation. An effective system of competition law substitutes for anti-dumping actions, because businesses can take their case against predatory pricing of imports to a supranational authority instead of national trade investigators. Similarly, since the EEA bans all state aid, except that specifically approved by its supranational institutions, there is no need to levy national countervailing duties on state-subsidized imports.

Additionally, it is essential that a multilateral system (concurrent with national law) is established to monitor violations of competition law in the associates, and to enforce that law. This is necessary to ensure consistent interpretation and enforcement of competition legislation. Even if each associate adopts the precise wording of EU competition legislation, the application of the legislation is sure to diverge from that of the EU and the other associates, given the different circumstances the competition authorities will have to analyze. There will also be an urge to relax competition law to back "national champions." This divergence might lead to trade disputes between the associates, and retaliation from the EU.

Furthermore, competition law must be applied multilaterally to ensure that competition is not restricted by cartels or dominant companies operating across borders.

The growth of multinational investment in Eastern Europe makes this threat a strong possibility. The EEA's competition system was designed to address these two concerns.

Under the EEA competition system, the EFTA Surveillance Authority is to review transactions that take place largely within the EFTA States and apply the EU's competition and state aid rules to them. Judicial review of the Authority will be provided by the EFTA Court. These new institutions will work in parallel to and in collaboration with the EU's Commission and Court of Justice. Although these provisions are complex, they have freed the EEA signatories from the threat of three of the EU's four trade defence mechanisms.

The only weapon left in the parties' trade protection armory is the safeguard action. Safeguards may be applied under the EEA if there are "serious economic, societal or environmental difficulties of a sectorial or regional nature liable to persist." GATT Article XIX, echoed in all other EU trade agreements, allows for safeguard action by a signatory when "a product is being imported . . . in such increased quantities and under such conditions as to cause or threaten serious injury to domestic producers in that territory of like or directly competitive products." The broader definition in the EEA is due to its broader coverage: the GATT covers only trade in goods (excluding textiles and clothing, and *de facto* excluding most trade in agricultural goods until implementation of the Uruguay Round), while the EEA covers the entire field of trade, including services, intellectual property, and procurement. Because neither safeguard provision specifies the level of import penetration (or equivalent societal or sectoral injury under the EEA) at which the safeguard provision is normally triggered, the different wording may not result in different interpretation in practice.

The GATT and the EEA both provide for consultations to settle disputes. Under the EEA, unless there are "exceptional circumstances requiring immediate action," there is a one-month consultation period, and there are consultations within the EEA Joint Committee every three months with a view to early abolition of the measures. Retaliation may be undertaken by the other parties to the agreement to compensate for this withdrawal of benefits.

Although the EU and the EEA signatories found a method of settling most trade disputes, the EU was unwilling to accept any reduction in the arsenal of contingent protection devices it has erected against Eastern European goods. For the associates' exporters, the EU's trade mechanisms are the equivalent of two paper tigers and two nuclear weapons. The paper tigers are the EU's "illicit practices" legislation and its option of imposing countervailing duties. The former is not likely to be used against the EA States. Although the Europe Agreements provide for levying countervailing duties, they also grant the associated States status as undeveloped areas under the EC Treaty's state aid rules. This automatically authorized substantial state aid by the associates and so significantly reduces the threat of anti-subsidy action. The EU and the associates are to adopt common rules on state aid, and in the interim the field is governed by the GATT Subsidies Code, which grants a separate exemption to ex-communist States. However, EU anti-subsidy law would pose little threat to the associates even without these exemptions, for the EU very rarely applies or threatens to use its anti-subsidy legislation.

For Eastern Europe, the real threats to free access to EU markets are the possibility of safeguard actions and the near-certainty of anti-dumping actions. Provisions for operation of these actions are found in all EU trade treaties bar the EEA. States facing these barriers often agree to accept VERs on the disputed products instead.

The EAs provide for general safeguards in terms similar to GATT Article XIX and the EEA safeguard provision. However, since the EA safeguard article is part of the provisions on goods trade, it cannot apply to other forms of trade. Moreover, textiles are subject to a separate safeguards procedure, while special safeguards exempt agricultural trade almost entirely from the bar on new or more restrictive trade measures, with the exemption of the specific concessions in the agreement. In each case, there is a requirement to contact the Association Council, which may take a decision to settle the dispute; but if it does not decide on a way to avoid safeguards within thirty days, the parties may adopt or apply "appropriate measures". Regular consultations are held (rather than the review every three months which the EEA provides for) with the aim of terminating the safeguard.

The EU faces no restriction on its anti-dumping actions under the EAs. Although the EA States are obliged to adopt EU competition rules, the EU is encouraging them to adopt equivalent competition *policy*, rather than identical competition *law*. Since the EAs do not provide for joint surveillance and execution of harmonized competition law, the EU is reluctant to drop its anti-dumping actions.

The Commission has proposed that the EU gradually phase out its anti-dumping duties against Eastern Europe, if the associated States and the EU can successfully coordinate their competition policies. Even if the Member States accept this suggestion, its intent will be difficult to achieve without the institutions provided for in the EEA. How could competition policy be coordinated without a mechanism to adopt and enforce policies within the associates (the EFTA Surveillance Authority) or to settle disputes (the EFTA Court)?

With the safeguard provisions, the anti-dumping duties, and the VERs adopted to avoid them, estimates by economists suggest that the associates' exports still face considerable barriers under the EAs. This "contingent protection" that the EU can employ may restrict the growth of the most competitive Eastern European industries, deterring investment and reducing confidence in the region. Barriers have been imposed against a number of Eastern European products since 1991. Despite the asymmetrical trade liberalization of the Europe Agreements, the EU has benefitted more to date from increased trade with the associates than have the supposed beneficiaries.

The two treaties share more benign safeguard provisions in common. The EC Treaty's "official authority" and "public health, public security, and public morality" exemptions apply in the fields of services, establishment, and procurement, and there is an equivalent to Article 36 EC. Finally, in addition to the safeguard clause allows the associates to take actions of their own to protect infant industry, under certain limited conditions, and they have special safeguards against establishment and capital liberalization.

The safeguard provisions suggest that the liberal access promised by the Europe Agreements may only be honored if Eastern Europe is relatively unsuccessful at exporting to the European Union. However, the Union's Member States recognize that their more protected industries must open up to Eastern Europe's exporters eventually, if only to provide a more prosperous market for the EU's own exports. For now, the EU has offered an overall "package" of eventual free access for industrial goods, limited access for agricultural goods, regular political consultations, financial aid, access to cooperation programmes, and future harmonization with the internal market and flanking policies. These provisions differ from the EEA only in their timing and their level of detail. The EU's continuing hostility to cheap Eastern European imports in "sensitive" areas could be ended by an agreement to link the associates' national competition authorities with the Commission and to terminate anti-dumping actions against the associates' goods. The Europe Agreements are flexible enough to allow for liberalism instead of protectionism, if the EU's political spirit were willing.

Yet even if the political will existed, there is no doubt that such immediate accession to the EU's internal market would place an intolerable strain on both the associates and the EU. If a "slow lane" to the EU must be taken, there are two different options. The associates could either adopt EU law under the Europe Agreements, whenever the EU felt ready to open its markets, or they could join the EEA with blanket derogations from its Annexes. "Entry" into various provisions of the Annexes could be negotiated between the parties later. On the face of it, the two procedures may appear to have much in common. But the effects of joining the EEA would be entirely different. New entrants would have access into both the decision-making structure of the EEA and the EEA's institutional provisions.

D. EEA and Europe Agreement Institutions: Decision-making and Harmonization

The chief institutional feature of the EEA is its extensive provision for harmonization with both the EU's *acquis* and its developing legislation. Each EEA Annex includes extensive lists of EU legislation which the EEA signatories must adopt, but that is where the Treaty's harmonization requirements begin, not where they end. The EFTA States realized that EC law, like the law of any legal system, consisted not only of legislation but also of an extensive and developing body of case law. Therefore the EEA provides for the adoption of previous ECJ case law relating to each field and sets up a mechanism for adopting new case law as part of the agreement. Since the EFTA States also wished to integrate with later internal market measure and to gain a say in the decision-making for later measures, the EEA provides for consultation with the EEA States on new EU legislation in the fields of the EEA. These provisions have the effect of granting full access to the internal market for the EEA States, as EEA businesses will be able to enforce their rights under the agreement in the courts of the EU under the established *corpus* of EU case law.

The harmonization provisions will be coordinated by an EEA Joint Committee, buttressed by other institutions modeled on those of the EU. An EEA Council, consisting of members of the EC's Commission and Council of Ministers and members of the EEA States' governments, will meet twice a year, to give "political impetus" to the EEA's operations (like the EU's Council of the Union).

In contrast, the EA States have a general obligation to harmonize their legislation with that of the EC, with no structure for this harmonization provided for in the EAs themselves. Under the EAs, decisions will be taken by Association Councils (ACs), but these will only meet once a year, not once a month. Initially, the President of each EA associate was to meet "as appropriate" (not twice a year) with the President of the European Council and the President of the Commission, but for "political dialogue" only. A task force of Commission and Member State representative will be set up to "co-ordinate and direct" law and procedure. Worker protection, the environment, and consumers are suggested priorities "from the point of view of accession". There is no provision, in the EAs or the Copenhagen summit amendments, for the adoption of the case law of the ECJ. Even if the EA Association Councils met far more frequently than anticipated, in an effort to match the EEA's pace, they could not arrange effectively for harmonizing the associates' laws with the EU's. Firstly, the multilateralism of the EEA offers advantages over the bilateralism of the EAs. If all harmonized laws are adopted bilaterally by individual ACs, it will be difficult for businesses to keep track of which provisions have been adopted by which country. The reason the EEA negotiations adopted a multilateral approach (instead of the bilateral approach of the 1972-73 FTAs with EFTA States) was to ensure that each and every signatory applied common rules and shared common obligations.

Multilateralism also ensures that signatories will apply obligations in relations with *each other* as well as with the EU. Given the likely expansion in trade among the nations of Eastern Europe, multilateralism is essential. In the absence of multilateralism, there would have to be multiple negotiations to extend the effect of EU legislation: first within each EA Association Committee, then within the EFTA States, and then between the EFTA States and the non-EFTA EA States. Unless these multiple negotiations were coordinated successfully, trade flows would be encouraged between the EU and the EA associates to the exclusion of trade flows between the associates themselves.

A multilateral approach would also allow the EA States to present concerns as a group. Of course, the EA States will not always share a common interest on every issue, but at present, where some or all of them wish to argue a case together, they must issue a joint declaration or wait for a multilateral summit meeting. The EEA offers an institutionalized series of regular meetings, covering a broad array of policies, at which the EA States could coordinate their approach to the EU's proposals.

Secondly, unlike the EEA signatories, the EA States now have little chance to comment on proposals at early stages, While this right would only be valuable if the EU were willing to consider the objections of the EA States, at the very least it would present an opportunity for the associates to influence EU law-making not now available to them. Advocates of greater links with Eastern Europe have suggested that the EAs might be "multilateralized," with more frequent meetings and amendments to ensure that decision-making and harmonization extends to all States. While "multilateralization" of the Europe Agreements would doubtless ameliorate many of their inadequacies, the associate States would still not receive the full benefits of the EEA. The EEA decision-making mechanism can be copied, but it inhabits a different legal environment from that of the EAs. While the EA States can count on the ECJ enforcing certain provisions of the Europe Agreements, there is no common legal space with the EU. The EEA's provisions on legal integration are the heart of the treaty. Without the means to enforce and interpret the treaty, the EEA would be, like other trade agreements, dependant upon the vagaries of political discretion, not the certainty of the rule of law.

E. Conclusion: Towards Membership of the Union

It has often been predicted that it would take many years for the Eastern European States to join the EU. If this wait is inevitable, for political and economic reasons, the EU has to determine the best available substitute.

While the Europe Agreements are well-intentioned, and could assist Eastern Europe's transition if implemented flexibly, the EEA is the best medium-term instrument for transition to the EU. Although the associates could continue to adopt legislation equivalent to the EU's unilaterally, with assistance from the EU (the current approach), this method of integration falls short of the benefits of the EEA. The present approach will exclude the Eastern Europeans from exemption from the EU's anti-dumping law; prevent the adoption of effective, multilateral competition policy; shut the associates out of the bulk of the EU's decision-making; impair the effectiveness of the associates' attempts to harmonize their legislation with the EU's; exclude multilateralism; and preclude the associates from relying upon the full protection of EU law. Any one of these exclusions would set back the associates' integration into the EU. All six of them might seriously impair it.

First, the continued application of the EU's anti-dumping policy would deter investment in the associates and would poison trade relations between the Union and its eastern neighbors. Since Eastern Europeans will purchase increasing amounts of the Union's exports as their economies grow, it would be foolish for the EU to maintain barriers against its associates' most competitive industries. The EFTA Surveillance Authority and the EFTA Court replicate the EU institutions, whose effective application of competition law have relegated anti-dumping duties to the ash-heap of Western European economic history.

The eventual hope is that the EU may suspend anti-dumping duties and other trade protection practices against its associates' products by use of competition law. Yet this goal is quixotic without a Court to settle disputes or a Surveillance Authority to supervise consistent adoption and interpretation of competition law, and to ensure enforcement. Divergent application of competition policies could result in trade disputes and contribute to investors' uncertainty.

Integration will also be delayed if the associates are not fully consulted about the development of EU law and policy. The extensive advance consultation provided for in the EEA would allow the associates to suggest necessary amendments to proposed EU measures before they have gathered political momentum. Extended advance notice would also allow the associates more time to plan for the adoption of legislation equivalent to the EU's and will reduce the risk that the associates would always be lagging behind developments in EU policy.

Continued consultation with the EU is also essential if the Eastern European States are to meet their obligation to harmonize their legislation with the Union's. Harmonization is likely to be piecemeal and ineffective unless it is implemented as rigorously and precisely as the EEA prescribes, and will frequently be meaningless without simultaneous adoption of the ECJ's case law. Harmonization by the associates without the EEA's legal structure will lead to uncertainty over how legislation is to be applied by the associates' courts.

There will be even more uncertainty over which legislation applies in which associate State without the EEA's multilateralism. Divergent approaches to competition law present special problems, as discussed [before]. Yet divergent approaches to the rest of the *acquis* will be nearly as damaging. Integrating Eastern Europe into the European Union demands a multilateral approach because the EA States need to expand their trade with each other, as well as expand their exports to the EU. The Commission has expressed support for the goal of intra-regional cooperation, but concluded that there is little that the EU can do to foster it. Clearly inter-regional trade and cooperation *could* receive a substantial boost if the associated countries adopted their *own* internal market as the same time as integrating with the EU's. The structure and institutions of the EEA are tailored to achieve precisely this objective.

Finally, the story of European integration has been the story of integration through law. The ECJ has propelled the integration of the EU by consistent interpretation of its legislation and founding Treaties. If the Eastern Europeans are to have any hope of ever joining the EU, they should be given the opportunity within the EEA to import the ECJ's judgments into their legal system, to approve and incorporate new judgments by the ECJ, and to operate a parallel Court that enforces disputes between their own nationals. The complex task of harmonizing with thousands of pages of legislation is unlikely to succeed without effective judicial machinery.

The European Union has set itself the task of completing a substantial eastward expansion. It has opened its market to its associates and has required them to harmonize their legislation with its own. For a plethora of political and economic reasons, full membership of the EU is not open to the Eastern associates until the end of the century or beyond. Yet in the meantime, the EU could extend many of the advantages of its internal market to its associates, increasing legal certainty, investor confidence, regional trade, effective competition law, and economic integration—all essential precursors to membership of the European Union. A mechanism for this process already exists, in the form of the EEA. The European Union should select the best means to achieve its ambitious goal of eastward expansion, and accept Eastern Europe into the European Economic Area.

VII. Joining The West: The View from Eastern Europe[16]

A. Membership in Western Institutions

The agenda for institutional discussions between the EU and the Eastern European countries has largely been set in Brussels. Initial efforts to integrate these countries into the Western European economic and political structure have been designed and motivated by the experience and ambitions of the European Unions. The East has so far responded within the framework offered, negotiating country by country trade and aid packages and, in some cases, making clear their interest in eventual EU membership. There has been only modest discussion about alternative and more long-term approaches to integration with the Unions and very little attention to the relationship between internal microeconomic reform and integration with the EU. Unlike some EFTA countries, such as Austria or Norway, which have long-standing internal debates about the forms and conditions of membership in the EU, the Eastern European countries have largely left the institutional form for their relations with the EU as well as issues of regulatory compatibility without comment for the moment.

The most important institutional exceptions have been strong interest, particularly in Hungary, in the human rights institutions of Western Europe, and efforts, led by Czechoslovakia, to promote both an extension of the Helsinki process and development of a Central European alternative to COMECON with at least Poland and Hungary. These later efforts would be important for relations with the EU, if only because they would make it more difficult to deal with the Eastern countries one by one, rather than jointly, as the EU has been advocating for EFTA. This, in turn, might lead to greater political participation by the Eastern countries in the integration process.

These political developments, while encouraging, will not by themselves lead to Eastern European participation in the many other areas of cooperation, such as those being discussed by the EU and EFTA, which are ultimately more vital to their economic restructuring. In the absence of any concrete proposals for sustained interaction outside of trade with the EU, East Europeans have sought integration with the free markets of Europe not primarily through institutional means, but through economic and legislative reform at home.

B. Foreign Investment and Industrial Policy

So far, the East's primary strategy for integration with the economies of the West has been to encourage foreign investment. East Germany, Romania and the USSR have adopted "first generation" investment laws, prior to which there existed no clear legal basis for foreign investment. Bulgaria, Czechoslovakia, Hungary and Poland had prior foreign investment laws, which have been modified as part of their economic

[16] David Kennedy & David E. Webb, *Integration: Eastern Europe and the European Economic Communities,* 28 Colum. J. Transnat'l L. 634-75 (1990) at 668. © 1990 David Kennedy & David E. Webb. Reprinted by permission.

restructuring programs. The Hungarian and Polish laws in particular deserve the title "second generation" in that they have settled such issues as the right of a company with foreign investment to own property, the right of a foreign investor to repatriate profits and the independence of companies with foreign investors from the centrally planned economy.

In addition to removing historical impediments to foreign investment, these laws also seek to promote foreign investment, primarily through a variety of tax incentives. Foreign investors have further learned that additional benefits and investment protection can often be obtained through negotiations with government entities in each country.

Three aspects of Hungary's foreign investment law render it the most favorable to foreign investors in Eastern Europe. First, foreign investments of up to fifty percent of the equity of a company do not require government approval. Second, the National Bank of Hungary will convert the local currency (forint) dividends paid to foreign investors into the hard currency of the foreign investment for repatriation. Third, the law targets various sectors in which companies with foreign investment will receive special tax incentives. The joint venture law was accompanied by a reform of Hungarian corporate law, which resembles modern Western European laws, and a law on the privatization of State-owned enterprises. In addition, for a number of years Hungary has been pursuing a system of liberalizing foreign trade both by permitting non-state enterprises to engage in foreign trade and by limiting the need for import and export licenses.

There has been some backlash in Hungarian public opinion with respect to the Hungarian government's foreign investment policy. In particular, on several occasions it has been widely believed that privatized companies were sold too cheaply. In response to this, a central government agency has been established to review the fairness of privatizations. Interestingly, some Czechoslovakian government officials who are advocating large-scale reforms in that country have criticized the Hungarian approach, which has in fact been developed for a number of years by communists and reformers, as being too cautious in adopting free market principles.

Under the Polish foreign investment law, all foreign investments require authorization from the Agency for Foreign Investment, but the authorization procedure is relatively transparent and reliable. The law provides that authorization is to be granted for investments (up to one hundred percent) that introduce new technologies and management methods, manufacture goods for export, improve the supply of high quality goods for the domestic market or are involved in the protection of the environment.

The more severe economic situation in Poland has led the Polish government to impose greater restrictions on companies with foreign participation than the Hungarian law. Foreign parties must invest at least $50,000 and acquire twenty-five percent of the company's equity. Fifteen percent of a company's hard currency earnings must be converted into local currency (zlotys). When the Polish law was first implemented in 1988, the Polish Central Bank did not undertake to convert zloty dividends into hard currency for repatriation. In December 1989, the law was amended to permit repatriation in hard currency of fifteen percent of local currency profits. Because all foreign investments require authorization, unlike in Hungary, it remains to be seen how reluctant the Polish government will be to approve foreign investments in companies that will not have substantial hard currency earnings because of this repatriation obligation.

In the area of tax incentives, the Polish law, at least initially, was clearly designed to stimulate foreign investment which can result in exports to hard currency countries. Polish corporations are generally subject to a forty percent tax. A tax holiday of three years is granted to companies with foreign investment. The tax holidays can be extended for up to an additional three years for companies operating in preferred sectors, such as construction, telecommunications and transport.

For the most part, Eastern Europe has shed the reluctance to accept foreign investment and private enterprise which were characteristic of communist rule. Foreign investment remains more highly regulated than in the West, which can be attributed to two independent factors. First, uncontrolled foreign investment could exacerbate Eastern Europe's already critical balance of payments and debt situation. Second, there is a strong sense that governmental control is required to direct foreign participation in economies which are still predominantly state-owned even if the companies with foreign participation are permitted to operate independently of the planned economy. In addition, the free market aims of most current Eastern European leaders face resistance from those who remain in significant positions long after the fall of the communist leaders and who either seek to block or to benefit from the reform process.

Aside from these different currents in the procedures for permitting foreign investment, the Hungarian and Polish foreign investment laws seem to mix export-oriented development with internal restructuring in an ambivalent fashion.

What appears to be underrepresented in Eastern Europe's general approach to the EU countries is a recognition that integration with the West is not wholly dependent on the attraction of foreign investment and on expanding exports to the West. In order to avoid the isolation experienced by Turkey and the dependency of the ACP countries, the countries of Eastern Europe might well use regulatory and institutional integration with the West (and with each other) in such areas as the free movement of workers, the provision of cross-border services, standardization, environmental protection and legal harmonization as a tool for internal microeconomic development. The PHARE program, with its emphasis on large infrastructure programs, suggests that the EU has not yet decided to commit itself to opening up the EU to the East in these other areas. For this reason, EU aid may actually encourage Eastern Europe to neglect the development of internal competitive conditions by concentrating too narrowly on exports and on developing large scale Western-style institutions like stock exchanges.

VIII. Conclusion

European countries face two distinct dangers in pursuing economic modernization and integration into the institutional and economic structures of Western Europe. On the one hand, they could become a new third world, a region of stagnant, often unstable dependent economies. On the other, as they accede to the first world, they may find themselves subject to a technocratic political and legislative machinery in Brussels which is incompatible with their current aspirations for democratic governance and market freedom. It is against these dangers that the preliminary approaches to integration—from both East and West—may be measured.

The EU and its new Eastern partners have approached their new relations in strangely similar ways. From both sides we find a continuity with programs and initiatives which predated the revolutionary governmental changes that purportedly inspired them. We find continuity with both familiar models of development and ongoing negotiations concerning East-West trade and aid. Indeed, in both Brussels and the East we find a focus on trade, aid and investment rather than on microeconomic restructuring and legislative or administrative harmonization. Both sides seem to accept an inevitable chronology of macro and microeconomic policy. And on both sides we find an eagerness to negotiate on a country-by-country basis rather than collectively.

The basis for alternative approaches to integration: approaches which focused on reciprocal political relations and placed participation in microeconomic policies and freedoms ahead of export and investment driven growth.

Although pursuit of a more balanced program of relations with the EU may be advisable for the countries of the East, there is little that can be done to avoid the technocratic political vision of the Union legislative structure. Indeed, the closer neighbors come to membership, the more wary they might rightly become about accession to the politics of 1992. Joining the European Unions means a large scale and largely irreversible transformation of a nation's substantive law, governmental structure and international status. By pursuing an assertive policy of association with the internal market of the West as an expression of newfound democratic and economic freedom, the new neighbors find a technocratic administrative apparatus driven to strengthen its own economic mechanisms through governmental regulation and intervention. This is perhaps the irony of Eastern European integration into the West: finally to seek integration into democracy and the free market, only to discover that these concepts have been transformed in their absence.

Part II: Fiscal and Monetary Unification in the European Union

I. The EMU and Fiscal Policy in the New European Community: An Issue for Economic Federalism[17]

A. A European Monetary Union?

The Maastricht Treaty creating an EMU was successfully negotiated in December 1991 and received final approval of all Member States in October 1992. The [T]reaty seeks to ensure more open borders for Member States in the movement of goods, labor, and capital, and a common monetary policy for all Member States through a European

---

[17] Robert P. Inman and Daniel L. Rubinfeld, *The EMU and Fiscal Policy in the New European Community: An Issue for Economic Federalism*, Int'l Rev. L. & Econ. 147 (1994). © 1994 by Butterworth-Hetwemann, a division of Reed Publishing (USA), Inc. Reprinted by permission.

Monetary Union with a single currency and a single central bank. While evidence seems conclusive on the advantages of more open borders, the economic pros and cons of an EMU are more controversial. We briefly review the evidence here.

1. The Benefits of Monetary Unification

The benefits of monetary unification are fourfold. First, with a common currency, the EMU should lower the transactions costs of doing business in the EU. While this gain is not large, it is clearly significant. The Commission of the European Communities (1990) estimates the current costs of monetary conversion to be approximately 0.1% of gross domestic product (GDP) for large states, but as high as 1% for small, open, less-developed economies. Second, the EMU has the potential to ensure greater overall price stability in EU countries. Whether it will do so or not depends substantially on whether (1) national central banks will be prevented from engaging in excessively expansionary monetary policies, and whether (2) the European Central Bank (ECB) under EMU will achieve a degree of political independence that is comparable to that of the German Bundesbank.

A third potential benefit from EMU relates to market integration; EMU could further encourage trade among EU Member States. While there is little disagreement that the gains in [an open-European economy] are large, the marginal benefits of EMU remain hotly debated. The benefits of EMU are substantial, because the value of exchange-rate stability increases as economies become more open; [there are, however, some critics who believe they are overstated]. Fourth, and finally, to the extent that a common currency leads to exchange rate stability, increased capital formation in the EU may result. The stability of exchange rates within EMU can reduce currency exchange risk and therefore encourage capital mobility among EMU Member States. These capital flows can be expected to increase overall productivity in the EU.

2. The Costs of Monetary Unification

There are clearly well-defined benefits associated with EMU, and they may be substantial. The costs of EMU are more problematic. One important advantage of a decentralized exchange rate system is that nations can devalue their currency in response to an economic shock. If economic shocks affect all or most of the EU countries similarly, then a common exchange rate controlled by the EMU can serve effectively the same function. However, to the extent that the shocks are country specific, asymmetric, and substantial as they may be for members of the new EU, then the loss of country-specific monetary policy may be very costly.

The costs to the individual Member States of the EMU of losing control over domestic monetary policy depend first on whether those policies now effectively stimulate aggregate demand in times of localized recessions. Such policies have been effective in the larger countries of the EU. [On the other hand] in the small, open economies of the EU the ability of monetary policy to reduce temporary unemployment is considerably less. If [the current] monetary policy is ineffective in reducing the adverse consequences of asymmetric demand shocks, then the costs of losing that policy to an EMU are zero. The small, open economies of the EU—Ireland, Belgium, The Netherlands, Portugal—should therefore be supporters of an EMU; indeed, this appears to be the case. For the larger EU countries, the potential benefits of the EMU come at a price, however, the loss of effective monetary policy to manage country-specific recessions. This cost could be reduced if the use of fiscal policy were an effective alternative policy, as it might well be in the larger EU countries.

The aggressive use of local fiscal policy to control local unemployment has its own risks, however. [The argument is that] when capital is mobile, an expansionary fiscal policy in one country may lead to higher interest rates in that country and elsewhere if that country's demand for funds is large relative to the relevant capital market. As a consequence, interest rates may increase throughout the EU as one member adopts an expansionary fiscal policy. Inefficiencies will then be created to the extent that other nonexpansionary governments are forced to raise distortionary taxes to finance the interest charges on their own debt.

Second, if capital markets anticipate a central government "bailout" of large local government debts, then there are moral hazard reasons to expect excessive local government borrowing. Such bailouts are most likely when the country is large and its debt becomes an important part of other member country portfolios. Both arguments suggest that there may be important negative spillovers from the use of decentralized deficit policies for managing unemployment risk.

There is an alternative fiscal policy strategy that will reduce the costs of the EMU to large country members and provide an added benefit to small country members. This is a central government policy of cross-country fiscal assistance in times of country specific recessions. Such assistance can be paid as grants to the ailing country or directly as assistance to families in unemployment. Transfers would be paid from a centrally managed fund into which all EU-member countries make contributions. To the extent possible, contributions should be experience rated based on each country's cyclical history of employment. In effect, such policies are insurance policies among Member States in which the Member States pool their risks of country-specific, asymmetric unemployment shocks. Here is an example of a positive spillover among all EU countries—risk pooling—that central government fiscal policy can internalize.

Currently, the EU does not have the fiscal capability to effect substantial intergovernmental transfers, however. The EU budget is only about 1% of EU gross domestic product and 5% of the government spending of individual EU members. If the EU is to engage in the provision of substantial intergovernmental transfers, a number of important options must be considered. First, the EU must decide whether transfers are to be person specific or region specific. Region- (or state-) specific transfers are less desirable since they run the risk of perpetuating permanently depressed regions and consequently discouraging the efficient location of economic resources. Structural funds that are aimed at regions such as southern Italy are unlikely to be effective in the long run. Person-specific transfers are to be encouraged.

Second, the EU should consider the introduction of a system of EU unemployment insurance. There are risks, of course, since insurance creates moral hazard, as, for example, when domestic labor unions push for higher wages, knowing that the costs (unemployment) will be borne by the central government. But, we believe that the program can be worthwhile.

[The conclusion is] that the potential net benefits from centralizing European monetary policy are positive if a suitable alternative policy can be implemented to neutralize the adverse employment consequences of country-specific, asymmetric shocks to aggregate demand. Country-specific fiscal policy is likely to be ineffective for the small, open economies of the new EU. For the larger members of the EU, [whose] own fiscal deficits may have adverse negative effects on fiscal efficiency in neighboring countries and may create a moral hazard incentive when the risks of default are shared within the Community, rather than country-specific fiscal policies, EU-wide fiscal policies might be considered. One such policy involves cross-country risk sharing through a centrally administered, experience-rated transfer program. This program can either compensate countries via EU grants-in-aid tied to country unemployment rates or compensate individuals via individual-based unemployment insurance payments. At the moment, however, the EU lacks both the tax structure and the fiscal institutions needed to implement such schemes.

B. Private Control of Country-Specific Economic Shocks

[There are] three alternative nongovernmental responses that might arise to help EU nations respond to asymmetric economic shocks following entrance into an EMU. They are (1) private labor market responses that lower wages or reallocate workers; (2) private market insurance for country-specific unemployment; and (3) negotiated labor management coordination across EU countries to adjust wages and employment in times of offsetting booms and recessions.

1. Labor Market Responses

In a fully responsive private economy one would expect a recession in one country, say, Italy, to lead to a decline in the demand for workers there, a fall in wages, and an outmigration of workers to other countries where wages are higher and jobs are more plentiful. A consequence of this outmigration is that wages in Italy will rise to a new equilibrium level. Both migration and wage adjustments mute the effect of the adverse shock on Italy, in effect, by sharing its negative impact on labor incomes among the workers of the other nations in the EU.

How effective are these private labor market responses in the EU likely to be? We are not optimistic. Even in a fully open economy such as the United States, we found that labor market adjustments were relatively slow. Moreover, even if border controls were eliminated in the EU, cultural and language barriers would still be likely to limit international labor mobility. In addition, wages are less flexible in Europe than in the United States. On balance, therefore, it seems unlikely that labor market responses to adverse economic shocks will be satisfactory from the point of view of the EU.

2. Private Unemployment Insurance

If labor markets do not fully adjust to the uncertain swings in aggregate demand, workers may seek to purchase private insurance against spells of unemployment. Three problems must be overcome before such a market can function efficiently. First, insurers must be informed about each worker's risk of unemployment. If not, the problem of adverse selection in which bad risks drive out the good risks may preclude writing profitable policies. Second, insurers must be able to monitor worker behavior to distinguish periods of valid unemployment from unwarranted quits. If not, such worker moral hazard may again undo firm profitability.

Finally, private firms must be able to pool the risks of unemployment using the premiums from workers who remain employed to pay the benefits of workers who fall into unemployment. Importantly, this will mean insurance companies must be allowed to write policies across all, or at least several, EU countries. While current insurance regulations have limited this option, new EU market regulations should permit such cross-country insurance pooling. Regulatory restrictions aside, there is the deeper economic problem of the likely inability of private firms to insure against unemployment during major EU-wide recessions of long durations, as, for example, Europe is now experiencing. In this case firm assets may be exhausted, and EU central government bailouts will be necessary. While such events may be rare, the fact that they can occur creates a new moral hazard problem, now between private insurance firms and the EU central government as the insurer of last resort. When are bailouts justified and when are they not? Detailed government regulation of private firm performance might be required to answer this question. In the end, what we are likely to observe is private insurance in name only.

3. Labor-Management Coordination

If private markets are unlikely to respond efficiently to adverse economic shocks, there is an alternative solution to the externality that is created, Coasian bargains across private actors in the EU. Coordinated wage bargaining (CWB) across unions and employers in the EU might be imagined. CWB is a system of informal agreements between employer associations and centralized trade unions to smooth employment shocks across industries. One would expect, other things being the same, that coordination can substitute for the market. When an adverse economic shock affects one region or industry, unions and employers can agree to adjust wages downward in that sector and to the extent possible to offer jobs elsewhere. Unions would encourage workers to migrate to those jobs, and employers would agree to hold wages down so that new workers can be absorbed. To the extent that the bulk of the adjustment occurs through increased migration, CWB should lower overall unemployment rates and reduce wage dispersion.

Recent empirical studies of average levels of unemployment across OECD countries with varying degrees of wage coordination generally support the view that CBW can have a positive effect in lowering the national rate of unemployment. Countries with centralized labor organizations that coordinate bargaining have lower average levels of unemployment. The mechanism that lowers unemployment in the centralized labor countries appears to be a form of informal cross-sector employment insurance facilitated through countrywide moderations in wages.

Wage dispersion is much less in the countries with coordinated wage bargaining. Interestingly [enough], countries with the most competitive labor markets also have low average levels of unemployment. Here wage adjustments and labor mobility ensure low rates of unemployment; allowing for coordination on the employer side as well. Coasian bargains should be most likely when there are centralized employer associations dealing with centralized labor associations. There is evidence that suggests that coordinated wage bargaining confirms previous results and improves the fit of the relationship between labor market coordination and low unemployment. The evidence also suggests that coordinated wage bargaining does appear to lower unemployment rates in within-member EU countries where labor and management work together. Unfortunately, however, the labor-management institutions required for similar coordinated wage bargaining across EU countries are not yet in place. Until those institutions develop, the Coasian solution to the problem of asymmetric, country-specific employment shocks is not available.

II. The Political Management of Centralized Fiscal Policies in the EU

The success of a centralized fiscal policy depends crucially on the makeup of the authority responsible for making policy and on the political incentives that it faces. [Following] likely politics of a centralized fiscal authority, we evaluate the potential for successful fiscal policy in the EU.

A. The Political Institutions of EMU and EU Economic Policy-Making

The political structures of the EU and of EMU seem especially complex. While there is no formal EU constitution, the legal system in the EU treats the 1958 Treaty of Rome and the Single European Act like a constitution. The European Parliament is constituted similarly to the U.S. House of Representatives. Its 518 members are elected, each representing citizens of one of the EU Member States. At the moment, however, the most important institution in deciding issues relating to the EU economic affairs is the European Council of Ministers. The Council of Ministers is composed of representatives from each of twelve EU countries. Voting is weighted, with Great Britain, France, Germany, and Italy having ten votes, Spain eight, five each for Belgium, Greece, the Netherlands, and Portugal; three for Denmark and Ireland, and two for Luxembourg. Fifty-four of the seventy-six votes constitutes a qualified majority. Finally, a European Court of Justice performs a monitoring function, much as a U.S. Federal Court would monitor an administrative agency. It is not entirely clear which political body—the Council of Ministers or the Parliament—will have primary responsibility for managing a centralized fiscal policy. Current rules favor the Council of Ministers. While formal power over fiscal policy is granted by Article 103 of the Maastricht Treaty to the heads of state from each EU country meeting as a body called the European Council, this body receives its agenda from the Council of Ministers. The Coun cil of Ministers drafts guidelines for the economic policies of member countries and reports its findings to the European Council. In addition, the Council of Ministers can monitor economic conditions (by Article 104c) and policies in individual countries and make recommendations to national governments. If the Council of Ministers' recommendations are not heeded, the Council can impose sanctions. It can have the European Investment Bank halt lending to the country at issue; it can require non-interest-bearing deposits with the Community, and it can impose fines. The continued institutional preeminence of the Council of Ministers is not certain, however. If EU fiscal policy becomes important and Community legislation is required for implementation, the European Parliament assumes a more central role in the policy process. Through a process called the Cooperation Procedure the Parliament has the ability to first comment on and to then approve, amend, or reject Council legislation. The Council is then given the opportunity to override the Parliament's amendments or rejections, but the override requires unanimity of the Council, not just a qualified majority. As the fiscal agenda of the EU grows with the development of the EMU, so too should the influence of Parliament over domestic fiscal policy.

B. The Politics of Fiscal Policy and the EU Agenda

Expanding centralized fiscal authority within the EU requires a careful consideration of the nature and performance of the EU's political institutions that will be assigned this added responsibility. As the new political economy has made clear, there is no guarantee that majority rule—or qualified majority rule—legislatures will allocate public resources efficiently. There are two solutions to this problem. The first is simply to exclude significant fiscal policy from the domain of responsibility of the central government. Such an approach may give away too much. One would hope that a second strategy that seeks to improve the allocative performance of majority-rule legislatures might be fashioned. Understanding the U.S. congressional experience is helpful, for in periods of strong party rule or with strong presidential leadership, the propensity of the U.S. Congress to adopt inefficient fiscal policies was significantly curtailed. Such results make sense, for centralizing institutions such as political parties and the president are exactly what is needed to control individual legislators' incentives to overspend.

Fortunately, the current EU political structure through the Council of Ministers offers such a centralizing institution for the control of EU fiscal policies. This relatively small legislative body is likely to be tied closely to country, rather than localized, political interests, thereby muting the incentives to overprovide public goods and transfers. While individual countries retain some incentive to overspend on country-specific public goods using an EU-wide tax base, the bias here will be far less than anything now existing in the U.S. Congress or that might hold in the European Parliament. Further, the weighted voting of the Council favors the larger and wealthier countries of the EU, enhancing their ability to resist subsidized and inefficient overspending. For fiscal efficiency, this is as it should be, for the larger and wealthier countries will bear a disproportionate share of any EU-wide taxes.

The preeminence of the Council of Ministers in fiscal affairs would give way, however, if the newly proposed "Co-decision" Procedure of the Maastricht Treaty (based on Section 189b) were used instead of the current "Cooperation" Procedure that presently governs the internal market. Under the Co-decision Procedure, the European Parliament will be given a veto power over Council policies. As a large and decentralized political body, Parliament's incentives for the formation of fiscal policy will eventually, closely mimic those now found in the U.S. Congress. The Council will have to be responsive to those preferences when shaping fiscal policy, for under the Co-decision Procedure its powers are limited to being the agenda setter to a decentralized legislature. Not surprisingly, the added influence of the decentralized Parliament under the Co-decision Procedure is likely to make fiscal policies less efficient. Still, such diminished Council powers are strongly preferred to no Council powers at all and the complete dominance of Parliament over fiscal affairs.

To the extent, then, that EU fiscal policy remains the legislative responsibility solely of the Council of Ministers—or even, if modified to agenda power only—we are optimistic that such policies can be fashioned to minimize the excesses of more decentralized legislative processes. High on the Council's agenda should be policies to insure against temporary unemployment. To the extent that the Parliament alone assumes responsibility for EU fiscal policies, we would become significantly more cautious in our recommendations. In this instance, the costs of centralization may significantly outweigh the benefits in the provision of fiscal policy.

III. Implications for European Federalism

The adoption of the EMU raises important—and as yet not carefully considered—issues of economic federalism. If adopted, the EMU will deny members of the EU access to country-specific monetary policies to soften the consequences of adverse country-specific economic shocks. Member States can look to their own managed fiscal policies as an alternative policy tool, but such deficit policies are likely to be ineffective for smaller members and perhaps the source of adverse negative externalities for all Community members if adopted by the larger countries of the EU. A centralized, EU-wide fiscal strategy of insurance against negative demand shocks is an attractive alternative, run either as experience-rated transfers and taxes to countries or as experience-rated unemployment insurance for individuals. Both options will require the implementation of significant EU-wide taxes and transfers, however. Consideration must be given to the ability of central government fiscal institutions to efficiently manage such a program. A centralized political process with legislative power concentrated in the hands of the Council of Ministers is the most promising of the current EU alternatives. The analysis here has implications that go beyond questions relating to just the joint management of monetary and fiscal federalism. Many of the same concerns and lines of thought apply to economic federalism in the EU more generally. The EU has struggled with the meaning of economic federalism since the signing of the Maastricht Treaty. The focus has been on the principle of "subsidiarity," which would determine which economic functions should be kept solely at the state or country levels.

When considering the question of whether EU economic functions ought to be centralized, our analysis recommends that we begin by asking whether decentralized domestic economic policies generate substantial spillovers. If the answer is yes, we then ask whether market mechanisms or coordinated Coasian solutions are possible to overcome those spillovers. Only if this answer is no, do we pursue the centralization of economic policy further. Third, and finally, before accepting centralization, we must evaluate the political process by which centralized decisions are made. Can a central government political institution be created that will implement more efficient economic policies? If yes, then and only then do we favor centralization. It is in answering these three questions that the principle of subsidiarity becomes operational.

IV. EC Banking Laws and the Banking Systems[18]

Member States have developed different banking systems as a result of different traditions, historical experiences and legal systems. The "universal banking" system and the "dual banking" system alone are not representative of the variety of systems which exist. For example, the Italian banking system is still influenced by the Depression of the Thirties and thus is severely restricted in its powers. First, the Italian banks may only conduct deposit, credit and investment business for the accounts of others. Entrepreneurial participations in commercial enterprises and, vice versa, are prohibited. Second, the banks are divided into two big groups. On one side there are the so-called ordinary banks (aziende di credito ordinario), which are primarily engaged in short term lending for up to eighteen months. On the other side, there are the special banks (instituti di credito) which are engaged in medium and long term credit transactions of eighteen months to four or more years.

In contrast to this restrictive banking system, the universal banking system has existed for a long period of time in the Federal Republic of Germany. German banks may not only engage in investment banking, real estate transactions, and act as agents for insurance corporations (insurance brokerage), but may also offer any other type of nonbanking business. For example, a German bank may act as a travel agent, engage in gold-trading, or sell agricultural machines and fertilizers, as many cooperative banks do.

Three models of universal banking can be distinguished. In the first model, banks are allowed to offer securities, but only through subsidiaries. This model is based on the idea of building corporate "firewalls" between the holding and the subsidiary to avoid a conflict of interest. However, banks are not permitted to invest in other corporations, such as a car manufacturer or a chemical producer.

In the second model, banks may engage in all banking and securities activities directly. The conflict of interest is partly minimized through firewalls between the departments, for it is thought that as long as firewalls work, it matters not whether they are built between subsidiaries or between departments. Furthermore, the conflict of interest is minimized by special rules in the law of bank transactions.

---

[18] Uwe H. Schneider, *The Harmonization of EC Banking Laws: The Euro-Passport to Profitability and International Competitiveness of Financial Institutions,* 22 Law & Pol'y Int'l Bus. 261, 279-288 (1991). © 1991 Uwe H. Schneider. Reprinted by permission.

In the third model, banks are not only allowed to provide a full array of financial services, but are also allowed to engage in other forms of business. For example, German banking law allows banks to conduct many types of nonbanking business. While German banks may not underwrite insurance policies, it is not the banking supervisory law, but the insurance supervisory law, which restricts corporations that underwrite insurance policies to only engaging in the insurance business.

A. Strong Tendencies Toward Universal Banking

The new developments must be viewed in the context of different banking systems. Credit institutions which sought business in other Member States previously had to cope with the regulatory system of the host country. They had to compete with the credit institutions of the host country's banking system, and they had to submit to local business restrictions. This was changed by the Second Banking Directive. The Directive does not mandate a specific banking system, but leaves it to the Member States to determine to what extent they restrict the banks that they authorize. At the same time, the principle of mutual recognition results in several rules.

First, credit institutions which are not restricted by the law of their home country may, in the future, do business to some extent in other Member States, even though credit institutions of the host country may not conduct such business. Article 18 of the Second Banking Directive states that:

> [A]ctivities listed in the Annex [to the Directive] may be carried on within their territories, . . . either by the establishment of a branch or by way of the provision of services, by any credit institution authorized and supervised by the competent authorities of another Member State, . . . provided that such activities are covered by the authorization.

The following activities are examples of the activities listed in the Annex to the [Second Banking Directive]:

> [F]inancial leasing, . . . trading for own account or for the account of customers in (a) money market instruments (checks, bills, CDs etc.), (b) foreign exchange, (c) financial futures and options, (d) exchange and interest rate instruments, (e) transferable securities, participation in share issue and the provision of services related to such issues, . . . portfolio management and advice, safekeeping and administration of securities.

Second, the Directive allows participation in the profits and operations of other corporations, and therefore credit institutions may have holdings in nonbanking corporations. Thus, insurance corporations, car producers, and other nonbanking corporations may participate in the profits and operations of banks, or may even own banks as subsidiaries. As already stated, however, this does not prohibit the Member States from restricting the participation of the banks authorized in their own country. Articles 5 and 11 of the Directive act as a minimum standard establishing information requirements as prerequisites for participation in a bank. These requirements will also apply when anyone is acquiring a qualifying holding in a bank.

The acquisition of a qualifying holding in a bank may also be prohibited if, in view of the need to ensure sound and prudent management of a credit institution, the host Member State is not satisfied as to the suitability of the shareholder. The acquisition of such holdings is common in several Member States, not only in the Federal Republic of Germany. For example, a leading Spanish bank, Banesto, recently concentrated all of its industrial participations into one holding corporation. Their holdings are worth 2.5% of the total market value of all stocks registered at the Madrid Stock Exchange.

Any qualifying holding binds the equity of the bank to some extent. That is, if the corporation in which the bank has a holding defaults, this may cause a crisis for the bank was well. For this reason, the Second Banking Directive contains a rule which provides that the holdings of banks in nonbanking corporations are limited to fifteen percent of the bank's own funds. Exceptions exist for temporary holdings during a financial reconstruction or rescue operation, during the normal course of underwriting, or with respect to funds held in an institution's name on behalf of others.

The ongoing process of harmonization recently came under fire by critics. The conditions and duties posed by the banking supervisory law are an important element of competition across the European Community. Thus, competition sometimes is not determined by a bank's marketing but by the legal department. Banks have taken this into account in their willingness to accept the consequences of harmonization measures on the competition in the Common Market. Good examples of this acceptance are the proposal for a Directive on Investment Services in the Securities Field and the proposal for a Directive on Capital Adequacy of Investment Firms.

The Member States with a universal banking system, where credit institutions may engage in investment business, are afraid of a balkanization of the supervisory law, a balkanization of the supervisory authorities, and ultimately, a balkanization of the whole banking system. The different structures within the Member States clarify this point. The United Kingdom and France have specialized securities firms. In Great Britain, these securities firms were independent corporations until recently. Today most of the big banks such as Barclays, National Westminster, Midland and Lloyds have investment firms as subsidiaries. By contrast, in Germany, banks not only receive deposits and grant loans, they are also directly involved in securities trading often through special departments of the same legal entity. As was mentioned before, institutions which are involved in securities trading are regarded as banks.

As the First Banking Directive has a very narrow definition of "credit institution," it would have been possible to widen the definition for investment services firms. Instead the Commission went a different direction. It proposed the Directive on Investment Services in the Securities Field and the Directive on Capital Adequacy of Investment Firms. This means that two different sets of rules would exist.

The Investment Services Directive corresponds to a great extent with the Second Banking Directive. In the future, to do business Eurowide and to open branches in other Member States without applying for another authorization by the host-country, it will be sufficient for an investment firm to be authorized by one Member State.

However, the first Proposal of a Capital Adequacy Directive for investment firms was very different from the Directives on Credit Institutions' Own Funds and on a Solvency Ratio. The standards for banks certainly are more rigid. For example, it was foreseen that for banks, subordinated loan capital may not exceed a maximum of 50% of the primary capital. For investment services firms, it may not exceed a maximum of 250%. For banks, subordinated loan capital, to the extent which it may rank as own funds, must be gradually reduced during at least the last five years before the repayment date. For investment services firms, no such restriction was provided. So the basic problem was whether banks which engage in both banking and securities activities should be subject to the rules for investment firms as well as those for banks.

If both rules did apply, this would mean that tougher rules would have to be applied to the German style universal bank. It probably would result in a shift of the securities activities into subsidiaries by the large banks (balkanization), and it would mean the end of business for those banks which are not allowed to have subsidiaries. This means that the same business would be regulated in different ways. The principle of "same business, same risk, same rule" would be hurt. Now it is said that the securities activities of banks should be regulated in the same way as the securities activities of investment firms. This is sort of functional regulation although the general concept of the Commission is an institutional regulation.

Several lessons may be learned [here]. First, the process of legal harmonization is not restricted to the harmonization of operational rules. It may change sub-systems, such as the banking system or even whole systems of financial intermediaries, directly or indirectly. Second, the process of legal harmonization may not distort the competition between different systems and different financial intermediaries. Third, deregulation by harmonization for one legal system may lead to reregulation for another legal system, which has been more liberal in the past.

B. New Developments in the Banking Industry

The potential "balkanization" certainly is not the only effect of the new European legislation. Generally, it has created a new "Euro-optimisme." One can imagine that "1992" is not only a great challenge for lawyers, but it is also a great challenge for corporate management and for business consultants. New strategies are being developed and a new financial industry is foreseen. Of course, there will be no sudden change between December 31, 1992 and January 1, 1993. There will be an evolution and the psychological impact of "1992" will be as great as the strain caused by the new European banking law.

Seven developments should be noted:

(1) a strong tendency towards universal banking;
(2) a need for new financial services;
(3) rising competition;
(4) increasing concentration;
(5) growing diversification;

(6) an intensified international cooperation; and
(7) the growth of new competitors.

C. A Strong Tendency Towards Universal Banking

It is true that under the new European banking law every country may keep its own banking system and every Member State may limit national bank activities by regulation. However, since foreign banks may carry on all the activities listed in the Annex of the Second Banking Directive throughout the Community, the restricted banks must compete with foreign universal banks.

This competition of different banking systems will lead to a universal banking system in all Member States in the long run. The universal banking system does not mean that banks are obliged to offer all kinds of services. They have an option to offer those services which they believe are profitable. Therefore, at first, universal banks from one country will be specialized banks in other countries, for they will only offer special services. Thus mixed banks will only slowly develop into Eurowide universal banks.

D. New Financial Services

For a long time, multinational corporations have not thought of frontiers as barriers to business. However, export duties, and the establishment of branches and subsidiaries in foreign countries were expensive and time consuming. In every Member State there was another law. For the production and distribution of products, specified consulting licenses were needed. Corporations had to be knowledgeable about the market structure, the distribution lines, and the consumers' desires.

These problems could only be overcome by big corporations. Now, the situation is changing. The European internal market particularly helps small and medium-sized corporations of all countries, and it helps the individual customers to do Eurowide business. This creates a new demand for financial services such as international payment, financing arrangements in international trade, export factoring, leasing in export transactions, handling bills of exchange, etc. It also creates a new demand for information and advice, for example, how to organize a distribution system in other countries, or how to finance a foreign subsidiary. This growing demand for information is one of the reasons that, for instance, Deutsche Bank Group wants to become Europe's largest information broker.

E. Rising Competition

Banks, which follow their customers, not only have to compete with foreign banks in their market, but also have to face foreign banks on their own traditional hunting ground. A sharp increase in competition can be observed in all Member States, but there are still niches where admirable profit can be made. One of these niches certainly is financial advisory services and portfolio management. For example, Europe actually sees a change in generations, as the active post-war generation passes away and leaves money which has to be reinvested. It is estimated that in Germany within the next ten years, estates totaling 2.3 trillion deutsche marks will be transferred. There is a need for consulting and there is a lot of capital to be invested, for the new generation certainly is going to use other forms of investment. The new generation will be grateful for a little help, which banks can provide.

F. Increasing Concentration

The demand for new, especially international, financial services, new competition, and rising costs lead to an increasing concentration in the banking industry. Smaller banks certainly have their advantages. Size is not necessarily a good indicator of performance, but on the other hand, only large banks can finance a Eurowide or global service, build up international experience, and create the new international services required in a global market.

In all Member States, there is still a considerable amount of small or medium-sized regional banking. Some of these small banks are highly profitable, in part because they did not give loans to less developed countries. However, it is a general opinion that concentration is needed, and it does take place. Among the small but strong German cooperative banks, there are more than 350 mergers every year; this means that nearly everyday there is one merger. The concentration process, however, is not restricted to the local level of savings and cooperative banks. Large national institutions may also be merged into international banks to meet the new challenges since a bank which is large in its region may be small in the European market.

G. Growing Diversification

In recent years, savings have flowed in increasing amounts away from banks towards life insurance, mutual funds, and other alternative forms of investment. At the same time, profit figures are under strain on some classical banking areas such as retail banking and loans to large corporations. Therefore, banks are looking for new business areas. They have increased their securities and investment banking arm, and since British, French and German banks are now allowed to be involved in more than just banking services, they are entering the insurance industry, managing mutual funds, engaging in real estate brokerage, opening travel agencies, and even contemplating opening golf courses. Banks may grow into financial conglomerates or, from a customer's point of view, they may provide a one-stop financial center.

H. Intensified International Cooperation

In order to provide the new services, different strategies are followed. Some global banks want to open branches everywhere in Member States, while other large banks open branches or form subsidiaries only in the financial centers of each Member State.

The smaller banks, such as savings banks and cooperative banks may intensify the cooperation by working with their partners in the other Member States.

I. The Growth of New Competitors

At the same time, we see the growth of new competitors in the financial markets. Insurance corporations, car manufacturers, department stores and other businesses have bought or founded banks as subsidiaries. For example, Opel, a subsidiary of General Motors, owns one of Germany's largest retail banks, specializing in the financing of sales and car leasing. These new competitors, including leasing firms and factoring firms, have taken over a portion of the financial market.

J. U.S. Bank Activities in the European Communities

What is the impact of these legal and structural developments for United States bank activities in the European Community?

First, in a global banking market, local, regional, national and multinational banks compete. But within the market, banks are still linked to national laws. In this framework the national banking laws and the banking system become important factors for competition between U.S., Japanese and European banks. If, for instance, the banks of one country have a higher standard for their own funds and if they contribute to a broader deposit insurance scheme, they have higher costs. This may be a problem, but in a world of well-informed and risk-minded depositors, it also can be an advantage.

In a global financial market, at least a minimum standard must be assured. The competition of legal systems takes place on several levels. In the U.S., this kind of competition is well known in the area of corporation law. While it may have positive effects, in the banking supervisory law it is problematic. An international "competition by laxity" not only poses problems to the soundness of the whole system, but also to individuals, who are not able to weigh the safety of an institution. It is not only a problem for the taxpayer, who has to pay for the lifeboat, it is also an unfair method for international competition. Also for this reason, the process of harmonization must not be restricted to the European Community. Efforts [should also be made] to harmonize the U.S. and European supervisory laws as well.

Second, it is true that the concept of the four freedoms only applied to individuals and firms of the EC, and not to U.S. firms. However, it is also true that the European Community, as a general rule, guarantees free access to the market for foreign firms, and the four freedoms are guaranteed to all subsidiaries once established in the Community. The question of reciprocity was highly overrated.

Articles 8 and 9 of the Second Banking Directive merely acknowledge and repeat the global concept within the GATT System. The concept is based on the principle that a party will only be granted access to a national market if the home state of the party opens its own barriers.

Third, if a U.S. bank establishes a subsidiary in one Member State, the bank may provide all the cross-border services within the Community which are allowed by the relevant national law. This favors countries with a universal banking system. Subsidiaries of a U.S. bank may even offer services and engage in activities which are forbidden to the parent bank. So, for instance, subsidiaries of U.S. banks trade securities in Germany, and a large U.S. bank based in New York owns a successful life insurance corporation in Düsseldorf.

Fourth, U.S. banks have to compete with the national banks, and they certainly have great opportunities to do so in retail and wholesale banking. U.S. Banks have been very innovative and have served customers with new financial products. The international success of credit cards is a very good example. For wholesale banking there are mainly two targets, the U.S. corporations doing business in Europe and the European corporations doing business in the United States. For a long time, U.S. banks followed their customers into Europe. They followed and served American multinationals, such as IBM, Coca-Cola, GM, Ford, Hewlett Packard, Exxon and General Electric. Many of the largest corporations in the country are subsidiaries of foreign, particularly U.S. multinational corporations. Generally speaking, the German industry is a multinational industry, and multinational banks are the natural allies of those corporations. That is why U.S. multinational banks already hold a large portion of the business volume of all non-German banks.

Fifth, some U.S. banks such as Citibank are also very successful in retail banking. Citibank bought German banks, including the business expertise, the reputation, and the customers, as did English and Spanish banks. The subsidiary of Citibank is successful in consumer loans, the issuance of credit cards, and insurance brokerage.

V. EUROFED: Toward a European System of Central Banks and A European Central Bank[19]

This Note explores the rationale behind the new EC central monetary authority. It then analyzes the EC drafted statute for the central monetary authority, focusing on the statute's objectives, guiding principles, structure, and functions. Next, the legal ramifications of this new institution, and its role in the context of the EC's movement toward economic and monetary union (EMU), are analyzed. The Note concludes with an analysis of the practical effects of the central monetary authority in both the EC and the international community and a discussion of what remains to be accomplished before the new institution is established.

A. Introduction

The European Council, meeting in the Dutch town of Maastricht on December 9th and 10th, 1991, agreed upon a Treaty on Economic and Monetary Union (Treaty on EMU), which includes provisions for a central EC monetary authority. The new cen-

[19] Christopher A. Whytock, *Eurofed: Toward A European System of Central Banks and a European Central Bank*, 23 Law & Pol'y Int'l Bus. 469-501 (1992). © 1992 Christopher A. Whytock. Reprinted by permission.

tral monetary authority will formulate and implement a single monetary policy for the EC by taking control of the money supply, key interest rates, minimum reserve requirements, the issuing of notes and coins, and other functions typically associated with the work of national central banks.

B. A Central Monetary Authority: The Rationale

There are economic, political, and legal arguments for the creation of a central monetary authority for the EC. The principal economic argument expresses the fear that the European Monetary System (EMS), as presently structured, would be unable to guarantee financial and monetary stability in a fully integrated European market, and that the liberalization of capital flows would make the current EMS collapse. This argument presumes that fixed exchange rates, free capital mobility, and independent monetary policies cannot simultaneously exist. However, adjustable fixed exchange rates already exist in the context of the EMS, and free capital mobility will be part of the common financial market planned for the end of 1992. Since 1965, an individual nation's ability to use exchange rates and capital controls has prevented a breakdown of the EMS that would otherwise have been caused by speculative attacks and financial crises. Such controls, however, are inconsistent with the free capital mobility of the common financial market. For this reason, national monetary policies will not be able to continue to function independently; they will have to be fully converged. This is tantamount to the implementation of a single monetary policy that would have to be managed by some EC central monetary authority.

A second argument in favor of a central monetary authority is based on the political favor for a monetary union as already expressed by EC members. This goal has been frustrated by the past enactment of provisions designed to preserve monetary sovereignty. A central monetary authority would provide the institutional framework necessary for the achievement of monetary unification by formulating and executing a common European monetary policy and effectively bypassing the sovereignty of national monetary authorities.

A third argument is raised by those who advocate the separation of monetary policy decisions from other government policies. Their objective is to "get control of the money supply . . . out of the hands of politicians" or to "use economic policies to promote political integration." The establishment of a central monetary authority would require national authorities to relinquish their monetary autonomy, thus minimizing government influence on monetary policy.

A fourth argument advanced in favor of a central monetary authority is that the creation of such an institution would help remedy problems associated with the existing asymmetric exchange-rate mechanism. At present, smaller EC members with weaker currencies are forced to follow the monetary policies of members with stronger currencies, even when these policies are inconsistent with their national objectives. Consequently, the burdens of exchange rate, interest rate, and trade adjustment fall more heavily on these members. A central monetary authority provides a mechanism to resolve this problem of asymmetrical adjustments.

The fifth argument focuses on the absence of a clear legal framework for EC monetary cooperation. With the monetary system's functioning governed by a mix of regulations and decisions, agreements between central banks, and a European Council resolution, the EMS's legal basis is ambiguous. In particular, members are under no legal obligation to participate in the exchange-rate mechanism (ERM) and the rules governing the narrowing of the margins between currencies are unclear. As one commentator has stated, "[t]he situation is sufficiently confused at the legal level to bolster supporters of institutional progress."

C. The Draft Statute of the European System of Central Banks and European Central Bank

In June 1989 the European Council, meeting in Madrid, asked the competent EC bodies to prepare for an Inter-Governmental Conference (IGC) on EMU. The Committee of the Governors of the central banks of Member States (the Committee), in preparation for this conference, engaged in extensive discussions on the monetary aspects of EMU. These discussions resulted in the promulgation of a draft statute for a European System of central banks (ESCB) and for a European Central Bank (ECB). The Draft Statute specifies both the ESCB's and ECB's (collectively known as the System, or as Eurofed) objectives, guiding principles, structure, and functions.

1. Objectives

According to the Committee, the Draft Statute focuses entirely on the achievement of EMU: a situation in which exchange rates between participating EC currencies are irreversibly locked and a single currency is subsequently issued to replace existing national currencies. The primary objective of the System is to maintain price stability. Without prejudice to the objective of price stability, a second objective is to support the EC's general economic policy. Third, the System envisioned by the Committee will be compelled to adhere to the fundamental principle of a market-based economy. In order to ensure that these objectives are met, the Draft Statute embodies a number of central principles and defines the System's structure and functions.

2. Principles

According to the Committee, the principles of the indivisibility and centralization of monetary policy, federalism, subsidiarity, democratic accountability, and autonomy are "indispensable cornerstones of a system committed to the maintenance of price stability." Thus, these ideas have been "fully embodied in the statute."

3. Indivisibility and Centralization of Monetary Policy

"The single most important characteristic of monetary policy is that it is indivisible and that the responsibility for monetary policy cannot be shared out between autonomously acting bodies." This principle dictates that monetary policy decision-making be centralized. National authorities should not be able to pursue separate monetary policies. Instead, a Community institution should formulate a single internal and external monetary policy for the entire Community.

4. Federalism

The System should have a federal structure. This principle not only reflects the federative structure of the EC, but also takes into account the historical experience of national central banks—a history which suggests that monetary policy cannot be regionalized. Decisions should therefore be based on the Community's interest as a whole rather than on regional considerations, but distinct national and Community legal entities should be maintained. Under this principle of federalism, the new monetary institution would encompass the existing national central banks and a central body.

5. Subsidiarity

Closely related to the principle of federalism is the idea of subsidiarity: that central institutions should take advantage of national institutions to the greatest extent possible. In the context of a European system of central banks, this principle implies a reliance on national central banks as the operational arms of a central policy.

6. Independence

The new Community monetary system should be independent vis-à-vis both national governments and other Community bodies. In particular, if the of price stability is to be credible, the central monetary decision-making body must remain neutral so as not to be influenced by considerations that might conflict with the price stability objective.

7. Democratic Accountability

The Community monetary institution should be democratically accountable for its actions. This principle is a necessary corollary to ensuring the acceptability of the new institution's policies to both national political representatives and the EC public-at-large. The national parliamentary bodies' ratification of the treaty and statute, which would create the new Community monetary institution, would partially ensure its democratic legitimacy.

8. Structure

Eurofed will have two basic components: the participating national central banks (NCBs); and the ECB, which would be comprised of an Executive Board and a Council. The Executive Board would be a full-time body consisting of a president, vice-president, and four other members (each of whom serve eight year terms) who are to be appointed by the European Council, following consultation with the European Parliament.

The ECB Council, which will meet at least ten times each year, will consist of the Executive Board members and the governors of national central banks. The Council members who are not Executive Board members will have five year tenures. Members of the Council may only be removed for serious personal misconduct and only by the European Court of Justice.

9. Functions

Eurofed will have the exclusive responsibility for formulating and implementing all EC monetary policy. The System will also conduct foreign-exchange market operations in accordance with the prevailing exchange rate regime, as well as hold and manage the official foreign reserves of the participating countries. Further, the System is to have a role in the following areas: clearing and payment systems, prudential supervision, and maintenance of the financial system's stability. A simplified amendment procedure will allow Eurofed to undertake other responsibilities as needed.

The ECB will implement Eurofed's agenda either by using ECB resources through its own activities or through the NCBs. In particular, the ECB Council will be the supreme decision-making body on all matters relating to System tasks, including all strategic monetary policy issues, such as intermediate monetary objectives, key interest rates, the supply of the System's reserves, and the establishment of guidelines for the use of those reserves. The daily execution of monetary policy must be responsive to market developments; therefore, the full-time Executive Board is responsible for operational decisions.

The NCBs will act in accordance with instructions and guidelines issued by the ECB. Nevertheless, the NCBs will be able to perform functions other than those assigned to the System, if the Council finds that such functions do not interfere with the System's objectives and tasks.

In addition to these more general responsibilities, the System has specific advisory, monetary, prudential, financial, regulatory, and statistical functions to execute.

10. Advisory Functions

The Council will play an advisory role in all matters directly or indirectly relating to its field of activity. Community and national authorities will be obligated to consult the ECB before adopting any legislation that relates to Eurofed's sphere of activity. While political authorities will make decisions relating to the exchange-rate regime, the ECB must be consulted before any such decisions are made, so as to achieve a consensus consistent with the objective of price stability.

11. Monetary Functions

The ECB Council will have the exclusive right to authorize the issuance of notes, and only notes issued by the ECB and the NCBs will have legal tender. The ECB will also issue coins—in volumes and denominations to be determined by the Council. Coin holdings by the ECB and NCBs shall be kept to a minimum so as to avoid significant lending to the issuers of such coins.

As will be illustrated below, the ECB and the NCBs will be able to regulate money and credit market conditions indirectly, without resort to administrative controls or restrictions. Further, the ECB will have the ability to require credit institutions to hold minimum reserves in accounts with the ECB and NCBs under conditions and terms established by the Council. Neither the ECB nor the NCBs may provide direct monetary financing to the public sector. This implies that operations by NCBs in the primary market of government securities will no longer be possible. However, outside the realm of monetary policy operations, the ECB and NCBs will be permitted to purchase government securities on the secondary market. These rules do not apply to publicly-owned credit institutions; such institutions may obtain credit from the ECB or from the NCBs in the same way as private credit institutions.

The role currently performed by NCBs with respect to clearing and payment will be extended to the System as a whole. Further, the ECB and NCBs will be empowered to perform all external operations necessary to oversee the EC exchange rate policy and the management of foreign exchange reserves. Finally, the ECB will be permitted to create and develop its own operational and administrative infrastructure and provide banking services for its employees.

12. Prudential Supervision

The ECB will act as an advisor and consultant with respect to the interpretation and implementation of Community legislation that relates to supervisory policies involving Eurofed's field of activity. NCBs will still be able to exercise their own supervisory functions to the extent that these are consistent with the System's overall objectives.

13. Financial Responsibilities

All assets and liabilities relating to Eurofed's operations will be recorded on the balance sheets of the ECB and the NCBs, as well as on a single, consolidated balance sheet. In order to ensure the comparability of financial data, the Eurofed ECB Council will establish rules aimed at harmonizing the accounting and reporting of operations undertaken by NCBs. Auditing will be performed by independent external auditors who are to be appointed by a procedure in which the EC Council of Ministers participate.

Voting on financial matters will be weighted. The Executive Board members in the ECB Council will have no vote on financial matters. The key for weighting the remaining votes will be the same as that used for subscription by the NCBs to the capital of the ECB and for their contributions of foreign reserve assets to the ECB. According to the Committee, this key should be based on objective criteria such as gross national product and population.

The NCBs will be the sole subscribers to and holders of the ECB's capital. Capital, which could include gold, would be paid out of the NCBs' assets to prevent them from incurring additional liabilities. The ECB Council will be authorized to increase the ECB's capital from time to time and to determine the extent to which and the form in which this capital is to be paid out. As stated above, the distribution of capital shares shall be conducted based on the same key as that used for weighting votes. Capital shares are to be reallocated following a change in the key for weighting, as established by the Council.

In addition, the ECB will receive foreign reserve assets from the NCBs. The amount of foreign reserve assets to be transferred to the ECB depends on the Community's exchange rate regime and on current international monetary and financial conditions. However, such assets must be enough at least to ensure the credibility of the System's exchange-rate policy. The Council is charged with deciding the amount of foreign reserve assets to be transferred initially to the ECB, as well as any amounts to be subsequently transferred. Notwithstanding this responsibility, the Council must remain within limits set by the Statute of the ESCB and ECB. These mandatory transfers of foreign reserve assets will consist of foreign convertible currencies and possibly gold, but not International Monetary Fund (IMF) Special Drawing Rights

(SDRs). Some foreign reserve assets might remain in NCBs, but all NCB use of these assets for purposes other than those of the System must be approved by the ECB.

14. Regulatory Powers

The Council and the Executive Board have the power to issue binding regulations and decisions necessary for the performance of the System's tasks as outlined in the Draft Statute.

15. Collection of Statistical Information

The ECB will have the authority to govern the collection, compilation and distribution of statistics relating to the System's field of competence. NCBs will carry out this task to the extent possible.

VI. Legal Issues

A. General Considerations

The Committee proposed that Eurofed's statute (the Statute) be annexed as a protocol to the Treaty on EMU that was agreed upon in Maastricht. As such, the Statute will have the status of primary Community law. Due to this primary Community law, the Statute could only be amended by using the formal negotiation and ratification procedure required by EEC Treaty Article 236. However, the Statute contains provisions of a very technical nature that demand flexibility. Therefore, the Committee proposes that a simplified amendment procedure be introduced, which would apply only to the more technical provisions while excluding all fundamental features of the System. Before a simplified amendment procedure can be drafted, however, the outcome of the IGC on political union, which led to revision of Community decision making and legislative procedures, must be assessed.

While the ECB and the NCBs will have separate legal personalities, the ESCB (Eurofed, or the System) will not. For this reason only the ECB and the NCBs, and not the System as such, can own, buy, and sell assets; conclude contracts; or be a party in legal proceedings. Consequently, the ECB will be liable for Council and Executive Board acts and decisions.

In order to ensure that the general provisions relating to existing Community institutions will not apply to the ECB or the ESCB, the proposal classifies neither the ECB nor the System as a "Community Institution" under Article 4 of the EEC Treaty. The Committee instead proposes that a new paragraph be added to Article 4 that would contain general provisions specifically designed to govern both the ECB and ESCB. The proposal exempts the ECB from any form of national taxation. The Committee has intimated that, depending on the provisions governing the allocation of income among NCBs, it might be necessary to consider constraints on national taxation of NCBs as well. The same level of judicial control that applies to existing EC institutions will apply to the System. In particular, the System may submit statements of a case or written observations to the European Court of Justice and intervene in cases pending before the Court.

Four additional factors are necessary to clarify the legal ramifications of Eurofed's creation: the legal basis for the System's statute, the need for amendments to the EEC Treaty, the role of EC legislation, and the problems associated with harmonizing national legislation with the System's statutes.

B. Inadequate Legal Sources

The "timidity" of the EEC Treaty's provisions in the monetary field prior to the enactment of the Single European Act is striking. In order to promote coordination of the monetary policies of Member States, the EEC Treaty did create an advisory Monetary Committee. Article 105 enabled this Monetary Committee to review the monetary and financial situation of Member States and report regularly thereon to the Council and the Commission. However, the objective of monetary union was not explicitly mentioned in the EEC Treaty. Nor did any terms impose obligations and constraints on the Member States' monetary policies.

The Single European Act (SEA), signed in 1986 and entering into force in 1987, introduced a new Chapter on "Cooperation in Economic and Monetary Policy (Economic and Monetary Union)" under Title II (Economic Policy) of the EEC Treaty. The Chapter's single Article 102A recognizes that convergence of monetary policies "is necessary for the further development of the Community" and contemplates the necessity of institutional changes in the field of monetary policy. Thus, the SEA has given the EC a "monetary capacity" by confirming the monetary competence of its institutions and the objective of EMU.

C. Need for Treaty Revisions

Despite the EC's confirmed monetary capacity, the EC Commission concluded that the creation of EMU based on a design including Eurofed would require that important modifications be made to the EEC Treaty. Article 235 of the EEC Treaty allows the Council of Ministers, unanimously on a proposal from the Commission and after consulting the European Parliament, to take measures appropriate and necessary to attain a Community objective. This provides a sufficient legal basis for the development of EMU, but only to the extent that the proposed development does not involve institutional changes. Article 102A, however, states in relevant part: "Insofar as further development in the field of economic and monetary policy necessitates institutional changes, the provisions of Article 236 shall be applicable. The Monetary Committee and the Committee of Governors of the central banks shall also be consulted regarding institutional changes in the monetary area." Article 236 states:

> The Government of any Member State or the Commission may submit to the Council proposals for the amendment of this Treaty. If the Council, after consulting the Assembly and, where appropriate, the Commission, delivers an opinion in favor of calling a conference of representatives of the Governments of the Member States, the con-

> ference shall be convened by the President of the Council for the purpose of determining by common accord the amendments to be made to this Treaty. The amendments shall enter into force after being ratified by all the Member States in accordance with their respective constitutional requirements.

Thus, the creation of Eurofed will require the ratification of treaty amendments. These amendments were agreed upon by the Member States at the Maastricht Summit in December 1991.

Analysis of the Draft Statute reveals that a number of specific amendments will be necessary. First, the EEC Treaty must include provisions that refer to the System's establishment as it relates to the ECB and the NCBs, its objectives, its tasks, its powers, and its independence. The EEC Treaty must also contain a provision stipulating that all foreign reserve assets be transferred to the NCBs from any other official bodies which may hold official reserves in the Member States. Further, to give the System access to the European Court of Justice, the Protocol on the Court's statute must be modified.

Additional provisions must be introduced to the EEC Treaty to allow the ECB to represent the Community in international monetary institutions and to conclude agreements on behalf of the Community. In particular, the pooling of SDRs by the ECB would require the Member States to make decisions, which should be reflected in the EEC Treaty, to appoint the ECB as their agent at the IMF. Further, the EEC Treaty must be amended to accommodate both the simplified amendment procedure (for provisions which do not embody the fundamental principles of the System) and a complementary Community legislation procedure.

D. The Role of Community Legislation

The Draft Statute provides a special complementary procedure to be followed when acts of Community legislation are required or are made possible by the Statute. Although the Committee has not yet made a concrete proposal for this complementary procedure, such a procedure would facilitate legislation necessary for the implementation and proper functioning of the Eurofed. For example, Community legislation will be necessary to create the obligation on the part of Member States to consult the ECB before adopting any national legislation within the System's field of competence. Further, because the Statute's statistical reporting requirements will impose obligations on third parties, Community legislation is needed that will define the natural and legal persons subject to these requirements, the confidentiality regime, and any related enforcement provisions. The EC will have to enact Community legislation to effect the transfer to the ECB of competence in the area of prudential supervision beyond the current Statute. Finally, the additional Community legislation must include provisions to permit transfers of foreign reserve assets to the ECB beyond the amounts specified in the Statute.

E. Harmonization of National Legislation

Member States must ensure that national legislation, including the statutes of all NCBs, are compatible with the Statute of the ECB and of the ESCB, as well as with the EEC Treaty and its amendments. The Member States' central bank statutes need not, however, be uniform.

Close examination of the Draft Statute reveals that in several areas harmonization of national legislation will be necessary. Current appointment procedures and minimum terms of office for NCB governors must conform to the Statute's requirements. In addition, some Member States will have to change national law in order to establish the independence of their NCBs vis-à-vis their respective governments.

The Draft Statute requests the ECB Council to establish rules that will guide the harmonization of both accounting and reporting by NCBs. In addition, the proposal authorizes the ECB to take measures relating to the harmonization of methods of collecting, compiling, and distributing statistics in the ECB's area of competence.

VII. EUROFED'S Role in EMU

By providing an institutional framework for the achievement of monetary union, and through its relationships with other EC institutions, Eurofed will play an integral role in the EC's move toward economic and monetary union (EMU).

A. Three Stages to EMU

At the summit meeting of the European Council in Hanover, Germany on June 27-28, 1988, the EC Heads of State and of Government gave to a committee chaired by the president of the Commission, Jacques Delors, the task of studying and proposing concrete plans for the multi-stage process of achieving EMU. The Delors Report, completed in Basel, Switzerland on April 12-13, 1989, set forth the political, economic, and institutional conditions necessary for EMU, proposed a three-stage plan for the realization of EMU, and developed the concept and framework for Eurofed.

The goals of the first stage are the achievement of a high degree of economic convergence among Member States, reinforcement of monetary policy coordination, and promotion of the European Currency Unit's (ECU) role. Further, the Treaty on EMU agreed upon at Maastricht requires that before moving to stage two, each Member State must abolish all restrictions on the movement of capital between Member States and between Member States and third countries. Moreover, each State must adopt, if necessary, multi-annual programs intended to ensure the lasting convergence necessary for the achievement of EMU, in particular with regard to price stability and sound public finances.

During stage [two], Member States "shall endeavor to avoid excessive government deficits" and begin the process leading to the independence of their national central banks. In addition, the Treaty requires that "the currency composition of the ECU bas-ket . . . not be changed" during the second stage. This stage also will involve intensive legal and technical preparation.

Eurofed was originally scheduled to be created during stage two. However, in late September 1991, the EC finance ministers, meeting in the Dutch town of Apeldoorn, decided to postpone the creation of Eurofed until stage three and to create a transitional monetary institution known as the European Monetary Institute (EMI).

The Treaty on EMU provides that the EMI will be established and take up its duties at stage two. Detailed work on the structure of the EMI by the EC's central bank governors began in January 1992. The Treaty on EMU contains general provisions concerning the EMI's functions and purposes.

The EMI—to be directed by a Council consisting of a President, Vice-President, and the Governors of the central banks of the Member States—will strengthen cooperation between the central banks of the Member States, strengthen the coordination of the monetary policies of the Member States with the objective of maintaining price stability, monitor the operation of the European Monetary System (EMS), hold consultations concerning issues falling within the competence of the central banks and affecting the stability of financial institutions and markets, facilitate the use of the ECU, and oversee the development of the ECU clearing system. Further, the EMI will prepare the instruments and procedures needed for implementing a single monetary policy in stage three of EMU; promote the harmonization of collection, compilation, and distribution of statistics; and prepare the rules for the operations that NCBs will carry out as part of the ESCB. Acting by qualified majority, the EMI also may formulate, and acting unanimously, then publish opinions or recommendations on monetary and exchange rate policy. These opinions and recommendations, however, will have no binding force.

The EMI has the power to hold and manage foreign exchange reserves as an agent for and at the request of NCBs. It is expected that the Banque de France and the Banca d'Italia will transfer a significant part of their currency reserves to the EMI, but that the German and Dutch central banks will refrain from doing so. Further, the EMI will take over the short-term gold and foreign exchange reserves that are presently pooled together as a part of the EMS. Under the Treaty on EMU, there will be two opportunities to move to the third stage of EMU. First, the European Council will meet no later than December 31, 1996 to determine whether at least a simple majority (seven) of the twelve Member States meet the strict convergence criteria set forth in the Treaty on EMU. These criteria include inflation, interest rates, budget deficits, and currency stability. According to the Treaty on EMU, the European Council's assessment will be based on reports by the Commission and the EMI. In the event of a determination to the affirmative, the European Council can vote to move to stage three, establishing a single currency and central bank on January 1, 1997.

If the convergence criteria are not met, or if the European Council does not vote to move to stage three in 1997, all States meeting the convergence criteria will automatically move to stage three on January 1, 1999, at which point the ECB will have been established, and shortly after which a single currency will be formed. In an "opt out" protocol to be attached to the Treaty on EMU, Britain has reserved the right to consult its Parliament after 1996 before deciding whether to join the move to stage three.

Those Members not immediately participating in the final stage would nevertheless be associated with Eurofed, but would not enjoy full voting rights. Indeed, the Draft Statute itself contemplates the possibility that one or more Member States might join EMU after the start of the third stage of the Delors plan, and calls for restricted rights and obligations of such a Member's central bank pending its full participation in the System.

B. Eurofed's Relationship with Other EC Institutions

When Eurofed begins operating, it not only will be responsible for the implementation of monetary union, but also will contribute to the achievement of EMU through its relationships with those Community institutions responsible for the implementation of economic union. The European Council will focus primarily on the coherence of Community economic and monetary policy, formally endorse multi-annual economic guidelines, and nominate the president of the System and the other members of the Executive Board. Further, Eurofed will report regularly to the European Council on monetary policy.

The Ecofin Council, composed of the Community members' economic and finance ministers, will issue recommendations and be responsible for the major decisions concerning the exchange-rate policy. Its president will participate, without the right to vote, in meetings of the Eurofed Council.

The Commission will monitor the consistency between monetary policy and general economic policy adopted at the Community level, while one of its members will participate in the Eurofed Council but will not have the right to vote.

The European Parliament (EP) will be consulted on the nomination of the Eurofed's president, and will regularly participate in debates concerning the Community's economic and monetary policy. Eurofed's president will report to the EP on monetary policy, regularly, and whenever necessary under exceptional circumstances. Other institutions also will consult Eurofed regarding matters within their respective fields of competence that relate to the System's objectives and tasks and will regularly report on monetary policy to the European Council and the EP.

VIII. The Practical Effects of Eurofed

The practical effects of the Eurofed's creation—irrevocably fixed exchange rates, nominal interest rate equalization, virtually perfect substitutability of national currencies, and a single monetary policy—will now be analyzed in terms of its costs and benefits to the Member States and its international ramifications.

A. Intra-Community Effects

1. Benefits

Benefits the System offers to the Member States include gains in terms of efficiency and growth, greater price stability, and gains in the public sector.

2. Microeconomic Efficiency Gains and Growth

The elimination of exchange rate related transaction costs and the suppression of exchange rate uncertainty will result in efficiency gains. This increased efficiency, coupled with increased certainty, will improve the risk-adjusted rate of return on capital and is thus likely to improve general business by encouraging increased investment, growth, and employment.

More specifically, the Draft Statute aims at ensuring full substitutability between national currencies even before a single currency is adopted by requiring notes to be exchanged by NCBs at par value and without any cost. While commercial banks would be allowed to charge commissions to cover their transaction costs, the Committee expects that competition would reduce these charges to a slightly higher level than that for single currency transactions.

3. Gains from Price Stability

The elimination of intra-Community exchange rates, and policy discipline in the monetary field based on Eurofed's statutory duty to pursue price stability as its primary objective, will result in macroeconomic stability in the form of very low average inflation and low price variability. The welfare losses associated with inflation will therefore be reduced.

4. Gains in Public Finance

Reduced inflation and exchange risk premiums will result in gains for national budgets through reductions in interest rates. These gains will probably be greater than any loss of seigniorage revenue that will be experienced by some countries. Competitive pressures on public expenditures and taxes on mobile factors also will encourage greater public sector efficiency.

5. Costs

Costs that the System imposes on Member States include the complete loss of national monetary and exchange rate policy, and constraints on national fiscal policy.

6. Loss of National Monetary and Exchange Rate Policy

The most significant cost resulting from the establishment of Eurofed will be the loss of monetary and exchange rate policy as an instrument of economic adjustment at the national level. Variability of output and inflation is considered welfare-reducing, particularly in the context of unexpected macroeconomic shocks of either domestic or foreign origin. The disappearance of exchange rates and interest rates as policy tools for economic adjustment at a national level, which otherwise could be used to reduce the harmful effect of economic shocks, might therefore decrease welfare.

On the other hand, exchange rates between the Community and the rest of the world could still be used as a policy tool for the EC as a whole. Further, the Member States have relinquished much of their control over exchange rates in the context of the EMS, and thus have already borne some of the costs associated with the loss of the exchange rate policy tool. Finally, in the context of EMU, country-specific shocks will be less likely, thereby reducing the need for national exchange rate adjustments and independent monetary policies.

7. Constraints on Fiscal Policy

Although the Draft Statutes do not vest Eurofed with control of national budgets, the Commission has suggested that limits would have to be placed on the fiscal policies of Member States in order to ensure the fiscal discipline necessary for successful EMU. Long-term consistency between the EC's single monetary policy and the fiscal policies of Member States is necessary to maintain monetary stability; yet the loss of national monetary and exchange rate instruments at the national level for short-term stabilization and medium-term adjustment purposes in the case of country-specific disturbances will make constraints on national fiscal policy particularly costly.

B. Regional Impact and National Differences

1. Less-Favored Regions

The costs and benefits offered by the System are not systematically biased against any particular region of the Community. Nevertheless, regions that are less favored in terms of per-capita gross domestic product, infrastructure, human capital, industrial structure, and financial structure may initially encounter greater difficulties, as Eurofed takes over monetary and exchange rate policy, than more favored regions. Less-favored countries generally argue that unless they are somehow compensated, Eurofed threatens to hinder their economic progress by taking away their ability to use currency devaluation as a means of encouraging national development. The Commission therefore has emphasized the importance of an effective Community policy to narrow regional and structural disparities and to promote balanced development in the interest of economic and social cohesion, as well as to foster the convergence necessary for successful achievement of EMU. Using structural funds as its primary tool, the EC's structural policy toward less-favored regions presently aims to improve infrastructures and human capital, convert industrial zones in decline, and promote rural development. In the final stage of EMU, further strengthening of the Community's structural policy might be necessary.

2. Convergence Within the EMS

Countries that are highly convergent within the EMS have already incurred the major costs of adjusting to the loss of monetary and exchange rate policy; the System will offer less convergent countries potentially greater gains, but will also impose on them greater transitional costs. In terms of price stability benefits, potential gains are the greatest for Italy, Spain, the United Kingdom, Portugal, and Greece, which have inflation rates above the 2-3% average for the rest of the EC. Of these five countries, Italy, Spain, and the United Kingdom have entered the exchange-rate mechanism (ERM) and thus already have incurred some of the adjustment costs that will be associated with the transfer of control over exchange-rate policy to Eurofed.

With respect to gains from lower real interest rates resulting from elimination of exchange rate variability, all countries except Germany and the Netherlands are likely to benefit. Current relatively low interest rates in Germany and the Netherlands are likely to increase. With respect to gains from the elimination of transaction costs, countries with poorly developed financial markets and traditionally weak currencies are likely to reap the greatest long-term benefits. These gains therefore would be less significant for Germany since much of its transactions are already carried out in deutsche marks. In contrast, the small open economies of Belgium, the Netherlands, and Luxembourg are likely to benefit the most from lowered transaction costs.

Luxembourg, because of its important financial sector, is a particularly interesting case. On the one hand, the liberalization of capital movements could favor that country's further development as a financial center. On the other hand, fixed exchange rates and the harmonization of banking legislation required by Eurofed's statutes will reduce the volume of banking activity generated by foreign exchange business and currency arbitrage.

3. International Ramifications and Implications for the United States

A common monetary policy under the control of Eurofed will put the Community in a stronger bargaining position in international monetary negotiations. International monetary coordination in general will be greatly facilitated once the voices of the twelve Member States are consolidated into the single voice of the ECB. This configuration may lead to the emergence of a tri-polar monetary regime comprised of the EC (represented by Eurofed), Japan, and the United States. Authorities at the Department of Commerce believe that an EC with a central monetary authority will benefit the United States. Because the establishment of Eurofed will strengthen the economies of the EC, European imports of U.S. goods are expected to increase. U.S. firms re-exporting goods in the EC and U.S. firms established in the EC will benefit from transaction cost reductions. In addition, firms already established in the EC will benefit from reduced interest rates and lower inflation within the Community.

Though the EC's potentially increased influence in global foreign exchange markets has led some analysts in the United States to believe that short run "intervention shocks" may result, U.S. policy responses might, in the long run, be facilitated by the greater predictability of Community policy once the exchange rate and monetary policies of the twelve Member States are taken over by Eurofed. Further, in the case of either a single currency or that of twelve different currencies with irrevocably fixed exchange rates, competition with the U.S. dollar for reserve currency status is likely to increase, thereby "accelerat[ing] the shift to a system of multiple reserve currencies, with power shared more evenly between them."

Finally, the creation of Eurofed could depress the U.S. dollar in two ways. First, with Eurofed managing a single currency, the dollar's dominance of financial markets could be eroded—the elimination of intra-EC foreign exchange transactions would make it less important for EC Members to hold reserves in dollars. Put simply, "Europe will need fewer dollars." Second, because Eurofed will be statutorily required to pursue price stability, Eurofed will probably be more anti-inflationary than the United States Federal Reserve. Consequently, to the extent that U.S. monetary policy is more inflationary than that of Eurofed, the value of the dollar vis-à-vis the ECU may be reduced.

IX. Conclusion

The creation of Eurofed not only required that the Treaty on EMU agreed to at Maastricht contain revisions to the EEC Treaty, but also requires that Community legislation be passed and national legislation be harmonized with Eurofed's statutes, as well as with the new treaty. In cooperation with other EC institutions, Eurofed will play a major role in the Community's movement toward economic and monetary union. Once the new central monetary authority begins operation, national central banks will become mere "branch offices" of Eurofed, as they will no longer have autonomous monetary powers. Without independent control of monetary policy and exchange rate policy, and with national fiscal policies constrained, Member States will be left with labor market and wage flexibility as their most important adjustment instruments.

With a single currency managed by a central monetary authority, the EC will surely play a much more important role in international financial fora. If the expected benefits of EMU actually materialize, Eurofed will lead the EC toward increasing competitiveness and prosperity. However, great challenges lie ahead for the Community's less-favored regions that will have to make considerable real adjustments to their economies before fully reaping the gains of EMU. While Eurofed will reduce relative U.S. influence on international financial markets, the United States and the rest of the world will be able to enjoy increased international financial stability and an economically stronger EC trading partner.

Despite the challenge of formulating profound institutional and legal changes, and despite the formidable economic and political challenges that had to be overcome, the creation of Eurofed can be expected as early as 1997. Eurofed will not only affect the EC, but will also profoundly affect the United States and the international financial community as a whole; EMI is due to appear in 1994; and Eurofed is scheduled to be in full operation before the end of the decade.